Tyne Cot Cemetery and Memorial

Tyne Cot Cemetery and Memorial

In Memory and In Mourning

Paul Chapman

Pen & Sword
MILITARY

First published in Great Britain in 2016 by
Pen & Sword Military
an imprint of
Pen & Sword Books Ltd
47 Church Street
Barnsley
South Yorkshire
S70 2AS

ISBN 978 1 47385 083 5

A CIP catalogue record for this book is available from the British Library

Typeset in Ehrhardt by
Mac Style Ltd, Bridlington, East Yorkshire
Printed and bound in the UK by CPI Group (UK) Ltd,
Croydon, CRO 4YY

Pen & Sword Books Ltd incorporates the imprints of Pen & Sword Archaeology, Atlas,
Aviation, Battleground, Discovery, Family History, History, Maritime, Military, Naval,
Politics, Railways, Select, Transport, True Crime, and Fiction, Frontline Books, Leo
Cooper, Praetorian Press, Seaforth Publishing and Wharncliffe.

For a complete list of Pen & Sword titles please contact
PEN & SWORD BOOKS LIMITED
47 Church Street, Barnsley, South Yorkshire, S70 2AS, England
E-mail: enquiries@pen-and-sword.co.uk
Website: www.pen-and-sword.co.uk

Contents

Author's Note

The role of the historian is to study, draw upon and interpret the narrative for the perception of the future.

Bishop, 1969

No matter how many times one visits the Western Front of France and Belgium, one cannot fail to be awed by the number of Commonwealth War Graves Commission cemeteries encountered at almost every turn. Some cemeteries are considerably larger than others but they all have one thing in common - the serried ranks of headstones, silently guarding the land in which they stand, paid for in the blood and self-sacrifice of those who lie beneath; their lives given that we might live in freedom. Every headstone and name on a memorial represents a personal tragedy; collectively they represent a lost generation of husbands, fathers, sons and brothers who answered their country's call to duty.

The visitor to these silent cities of the dead (all are easily accessible be it by foot or vehicle) usually falls into one of three categories - Personally related in some way to the casualty, historically minded, or casual. The relative, spurred by family connection, might be visiting for the first time, perhaps the very first time the casualty has received the comfort of a visit from home, or returning as part of annual pilgrimage; paying their respects to someone unknown to them personally yet ever remembered by the family. The historian, documenting his or her findings for personal interest or publication, might be researching a particular individual or action in which a certain division, brigade, regiment or battalion took part. The casual visitor is invariably someone passing through the vicinity, mildly curious, taking a brief break from his or her journey. But, for whatever reason the visit is made - and one can spend hours walking round - those who fail to be touched emotionally are few and far between.

Uniform in size and design the headstone informs the visitor of the casualty's name, rank, regiment, service number, date of death and (sometimes) age. Poignant epitaphs abound, but few give any insight into the man. The memorials to the thousands of missing record only regiment, rank and name. Examination of the appropriate cemetery or memorial register for further details will, with the exception of Victoria Cross recipients, rarely reveal more than next of kin. Whatever terminology one chooses, without additional information a list is just a list.

After over forty year's association with the Western Front, and, in particular the Ypres Salient, I have frequently asked myself the question - Who were these men, where did they come from, what happened? The answer to these questions can never be fully answered, the detail herein recorded began purely out of personal interest; researching a considerable number of casualties whose graves I had photographed. Initially drawing on the Marquis De Ruvigny's Rolls of Honour, published at the time and shortly thereafter in a series of parts, in time this expanded into page upon page of information bringing a personal aspect to the casualty - explaining and answering much more of the who, what, where and why than the norm.

Almost one hundred years after the Armistice the death toll of the First World War remains as a Roll of Honour, commanding as much respect today as it did at the time. Dubbed the Great War for Civilization it was the first total war in British history to affect every aspect of national life, and stands as the supreme icon of the horror and inhumanity of armed conflict. Our picture of the war is still vivid, the poems speak just as freshly to A-Level students today as they did to older generations, and the poignancy of the many photographs and newsreel footage touches us still.

Those smiling, young, unsuspecting faces marching into Flanders; those exhausted, shattered bodies struggling through the mud, the squalor and filth of the trenches where the ever present sense of death and the macabre were just another facet of everyday life - they could be our faces and bodies, or belong to those we know and love.

Throughout Great Britain and the Dominions there were few families who did not know of a husband, father, son, brother or uncle killed or wounded in the conflict. Behind the bald statistics of every account written at the time or years afterwards lie countless stories of individual tragedy. Drawn from a vast variety of sources, the accounts and casualty details (many at length) herein recorded, recount the gruesome horror of war in all its many facets. In an antidote to the adventure stories that pass for war in much of the literature of today mud, lice, rats, gas and death in every manner imaginable (and unimaginable). The biggest killer - shellfire - often buried men alive, or completely vaporised them, leaving no trace of their existence. Jagged chunks of red hot metal sliced through flesh in an obscene fashion, removing heads and limbs with ease. Snipers, grenades and the scything machine guns, skilfully used by well-trained specialists, all contributed to the horror; all get their due.

How soldiers endured all this is beyond comprehension, any part of the thin veneer of civilisation they had left behind was quickly eroded after a short time at the front. Men became dehumanised by the war, they brutalised and stripped the corpses of their enemies for souvenirs; snipers took special enjoyment in knocking off members of burial parties. But, it was a different matter when it came to their own dead. Under strict orders to ignore wounded comrades in an advance, soldiers repeatedly strove heroically to protect their own. Time and time again they risked their own lives to go out onto the bullet and shell swept battlefield to search for wounded and fallen comrades; bringing in the latter that they might be given 'the dignity of a decent burial' - rites that all too often proved short-lived. Some, hastily buried, re-emerged from the earth during the next rainstorm; countless numbers were exhumed or blown to pieces by bombardments. On reflection the question arises: 'Why bother at all?' In part the answer lies with those of the battalion who, after the fighting, answered the roll-call, heard the repeated silences that followed the reading of the names, only to be informed from higher up the attack had failed due to 'lack of pluck' on their part. When one takes all this into account one realises the importance of remembering the dead was often as much an act of tenderness by their comrades as it was in defiance.

Within the confines of the Ypres Salient are to be found one hundred and sixty nine Commonwealth War Grave Commission cemeteries and three memorials to the missing, honouring the memory of British and Commonwealth servicemen who gave their lives in the defence of this relatively small yet strategically important region of Belgium. Of the 210,000 casualties buried or commemorated in the Ypres Salient extended details relating to over 20,000 were drawn upon to compose these books. A small percentage of the total but who they were, where they came from, how they died are equally as important as the why. These men and the actions in which they gave their lives are a part of our history, our heritage; hopefully, by bringing something of the personal about them to the visitor, these books will ensure their memory never fades.

In Memory & In Mourning
Paul Chapman
March 2016

Acknowledgements

First and foremost to my long suffering wife Sandra, who, without complaint over the almost thirteen years this work has taken, has not only put up with my spending days on end with my head stuck in one book or another, making copious quantities of notes (and leaving papers all over the house), typing or searching the internet at all hours, but has also endured alone my long periods away from home spent trekking the salient.

Secondly to the staff of the Commonwealth War Graves Commission, Maidenhead and Ypres, the Imperial War Museum, London, and the National Archives, Kew; for their many kindnesses and willing assistance. Also to the Australian War Memorial, Canberra, the Auckland Cenotaph, New Zealand and the Canadian National War Memorial, Ottawa, whose archival material greatly assisted in providing additional detail, clarified numerous points and answered many queries.

Special thanks to Gladys Lunn, MBE, for her continued interest and encouragement, without whose personal influence I would never have made the acquaintance of so many regimental associations : Royal Army Medical Corps; Royal Tank Regt.; Machine Gun Corps; Royal Berkshire, Wiltshire & Gloucestershire Regiments. Major A.R. McKinnell, Black Watch; Capt. A.W. Hughes – Cheshire Regt.; Corpl. Bingley and the late Major Louch – Coldstream Guards; Major T.W. Stipling – Duke of Cornwall's Light Infantry; Major P.R. Walton – King's Liverpool Regt., Manchester Regt.; Major C.M.J. Deedes – King's Own Yorkshire Light Infantry; Lieut.Col. G. Bennett – Lancashire Fusiliers; David Ball and Harry 'Aitch' Hogan – Prince of Wales's Leinster Regt. Association; Capt. Richard 'Dick' Hennessy-Walsh – The Life Guards; Major J.C. Rogerson – Middlesex Regt., Queen's Own (Royal West Kent Regt.); The Buffs (East Kent Regt.); George, Bob and J.P. – Northamptonshire Regt.; Leslie Frater – Northumberland Fusiliers; Major S.A. Kennedy – Prince of Wales's Own (West & East Yorkshire) Regt.; Major R.J.R. Campbell – Queen's Own Cameron Highlanders, Seaforth Highlanders; Capt. W.G. 'Bill' Sutherland – Royal Scots; Major A.W. Russell – Queen's Royal West Surrey Regt.; Major G. Correa – Royal Artillery; Lieut.Col. P.A. Roffey, Royal Army Veterinary Corps; Major R.G. Mills – Royal Warwickshire Regt; Major A. Ellingham – Royal Welch Fusiliers : And, Major John Baines and John Howells – New South Wales Lancers Museum (Australian Light Horse); Capt. Gary 'Poppa Holdfast' Silliker, Royal Canadian Air Force (Engineers); and Alison Taylor, Auckland Museum.

Also a big thank you to the many people whose contributions to this work have in various degrees, enhanced the whole. In particular the members of the internet sites 'The Great War Forum,' 'World War 1 Remembered,' 'World War 1 Photographs' and 'The Aerodrome' whose knowledge (and resourcefulness) never ceased to amaze: My friend and work colleague Dick Atkins who, when my computer crashed at 1500 pages and all seemed lost, completely restored everything including my sanity: Linda 'Linny' Carrier, for distraction, constructive criticism and much inspiration (not necessarily in that order): Steve 'One Shot' Clews for photographic expertise and advice: Sue Cox, Richard 'Daggers' Daglish, Ian 'Scoop' Davies, Steve 'For Canada' Douglas, Derek 'Del' Doune, Pete Folwell, Frank 'The Oracle' Grande, Sandra Hanley, Bryan Harris, Tim Harrison and Anna Parker, Patricia Healey, John and Elizabeth Holbrook, Clive Hughes, Patricia Jackson (Jamaica), Carol Johnson, Ken Jones, the late Dr. John Laffin, Brian Little, Tony 'Squirrel' Nutkins, Dave Pain, Col. Graham Parker, Paul 'Nationwide' Smith, the late Ted Smith and the late Tony Spagnoly, Jennifer Spooner, Sandra Taylor, Colin and Geraldine Ward, Sylvia Watkins, my many colleagues 'in the job' who over the years have supplied copious quantities of notes and peripheral information gleaned from personal research and war memorials throughout the length and breadth of the British Isles, and – too numerous to mention – the many visitors I have had the pleasure to meet who kindly entrusted their stories to me in Flanders Fields.

In the years it took to compile and prepare this work, the like of which has never been attempted before, there were many times when it became necessary to call on local assistance – 'over there.' Particularly deserving of special mention Dries Chaerle and Jacques Ryckebosch whose combined knowledge of the region, the obscure and little known is second to none. Also 'Brother' Bart Engelen and An 'Girly' Van Der Smissen who, in response to many email (and postal) enquiries, always managed to find time out to visit (sometimes in atrocious weather) various sites, accurately recording and promptly supplying the information required. And, on my visits willingly continue to accompany me on my travels.

And finally, a special thank you to Laura Hirst and Jonathan Wright, Pen & Sword, for their support, interest, advice and attention throughout the seemingly unending days of editing, proof-reading, checking and cross-checking, embedding, the bits and pieces here and there that necessitated more than one delay: All this (and more) would have exhausted the patience of a saint. I thank you both.

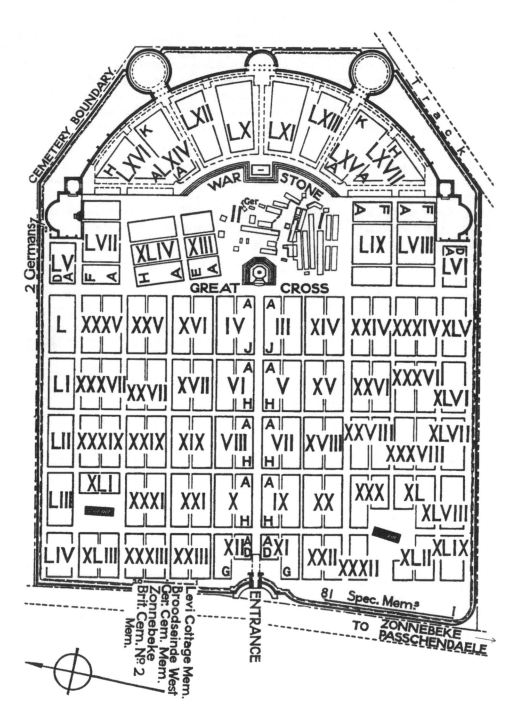

TYNE COT CEMETERY PASSCHENDAELE.

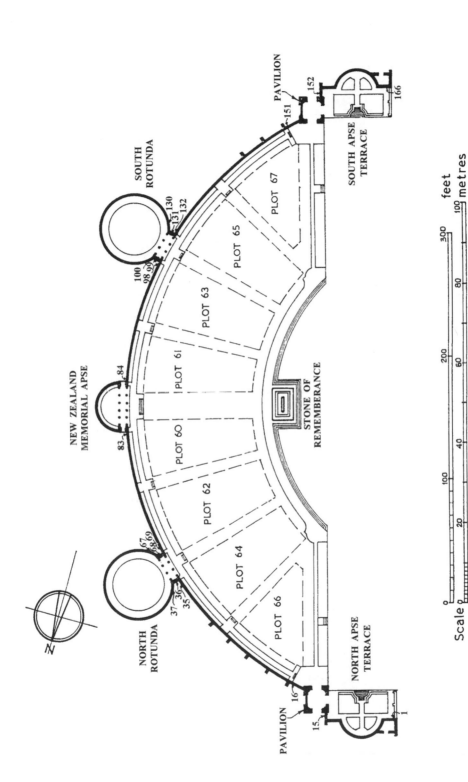

PAVILION

152

166

SOUTH APSE TERRACE

151

PAVILION

SOUTH ROTUNDA

PLOT 67

130
131
132

PLOT 65

100
98 99

PLOT 63

PLOT 61

84

NEW ZEALAND MEMORIAL APSE

83

PLOT 60

STONE OF REMEMBERANCE

PLOT 62

PLOT 64

67
68 69

37 36
35

N

NORTH ROTUNDA

PLOT 66

NORTH APSE TERRACE

16

15

1

PAVILION

LAYOUT OF THE TYNE COT MEMORIAL PANELS

feet

metres

300

200

100

80

60

40

100

20

Scale 0

0

Tyne Cot Cemetery (& Memorial), Passchendaele

'Tyne Cot' or 'Tyne Cottage' was the name given by British troops to a barn that stood 46 metres west of the level crossing on the Passchendaele – Broodseinde road. The barn had become the centre of five or six 'pill-boxes.' This formidable defensive position was the objective of 3rd Australian Division during the Battle of Broodseinde Ridge on 4 October 1917, as part of the advance on Passchendaele. In the half-light of morning, the Australians advanced towards Tyne Cot, overcoming several German strong-points along the way. As they neared what is now the cemetery, machine guns from five concrete pillboxes rained fire on them, causing heavy casualties. The two foremost pillboxes were so solidly constructed that they had been dubbed 'Irksome' and 'The Barnacle'. However, rushed by small parties of Australians, they were eventually overcome. The three other pillboxes in the immediate vicinity remained in enemy hands for several days. One of these latter 'pill-boxes' was unusually large and, after its capture, was utilised as an Advanced Dressing Station. From 6 October to the end of March, 343 graves were made on two sides of it, by 50th (Northumbrian) and 33rd Divisions, and two Canadian units. From its recapture on 13 April 1918 to 20 September it was in German hands, after which it was retaken, with Passchendaele, by the Belgian Army. Enlarged after the Armistice by the concentration of graves from the battlefields of Passchendaele, Langemarck, and a few smaller burial grounds, it is now the largest Commonwealth war cemetery in the world. There are nearly 12,000 1914-1918 war casualties commemorated on this site. Of these, over 8,300 are unidentified, and Special Memorials commemorate a further thirty-eight British, twenty-seven Canadian, fifteen Australian, and one New Zealand soldier, known or believed to be buried among them. Other Special Memorials record the names of sixteen British and four Canadian soldiers buried in other cemeteries whose graves were destroyed by shellfire. Also commemorated here are four German casualties. At the suggestion of King George V, the Cross of Sacrifice was constructed atop the original large pillbox, the memorial rotundas were built on top of two other pillboxes; 'Irksome' and 'The Barnacle' still stand as brooding sentinels either side of the main entrance. The eastern plots are laid out in the shape of a fan with paths radiating to the Cross, and a high flint wall, 152 metres in length, follows their outline. This wall carries the names of nearly 35,000 soldiers of the United Kingdom and New Zealand who fell in the Ypres salient 1917-1918, whose graves are not known.

Concentrated here:- *Iberian South Cemetery*, and *Iberian Trench Cemetery, Frezenberg*, close to a farm the Army named *'Iberian'*. These contained thirty British soldiers who fell August/September 1917 and March 1918: *Kink Corner Cemetery, Zonnebeke*, fourteen British, nine Canadian, and nine Australian soldiers who fell September/November 1917: *Levi Cottage Cemetery, Zonnebeke*, contained the graves of ten British, eight Canadian, and three Australian soldiers who fell September/November 1917: *Oostnieuwkerke German Cemetery*, contained the graves of two British soldiers: *Praet-Bosch German Cemetery, Vladslo*, six R.F.C./R.A.F. officers who fell 1917/1918: *Staden German Cemetery*, fourteen British and ten Canadian soldiers who fell 1915/1917: *Waterloo Farm Cemetery, Passchendaele*, seven British, ten Canadian and two New Zealand soldiers who fell 1917/1918: *Zonnebeke British Cemetery No.2*, contained the graves of eighteen men of 2nd Buffs, and twenty of 3rd Royal Fusiliers, buried by the Germans in April 1915.

After the capture of the large pill-box on which the cross of sacrifice now stands, it was utilised as one of a number of forward aid posts and gathering points for the stretcher-bearers toiling in the mud, fetching the wounded and dying back from the wastelands before Passchendaele. Years later, former New Zealand stretcher-bearer Stan Stanfield described the plight of the wounded lying out hereabouts: "We were picking them up from a gathering point, a regimental aid post. It was an old German concrete emplacement and you couldn't get them all inside, but the doctors were working inside. And they were just laying around where they'd been dumped by the stretcher bearers from off the field, and at one period I believe there were six hundred stretcher cases lying around the place in the wet and cold, just dying where they were dumped off. They weren't even lying on stretchers, just laying on the ground, with an oil sheet over them if anyone thought to do that, or if one of their mates could do it." The irregular layout of the burials immediately behind the Cross of Sacrifice (Plots I and II) bear witness to the many wounded and dying for whom the cold wet ground on which they lay became their permanent rest.

(I.AA.20) 2nd Lieut. Frederick Baldwin Ewen Falkiner, 17th (Service) Bn. The Royal Irish Rifles attd. Royal Flying Corps: *s.* of the late Henry Baldwin Falkiner, Solicitor, by his wife Euphemia ('Greenoge,' Terenure Road, Dublin), *dau.* of Thomas McEwen: and brother to 2nd Lieut. G. S. Falkiner, Royal Dublin Fusiliers, killed in action at Frezenberg, 16 August 1917: *b.* Dublin, 16 July 1885: *educ.* St. Stephen's Green School, there; St. Columba's College, Rathfarnham, co. Dublin, and Trinity College, Dublin: enlisted 7th Royal Dublin Fusiliers, 16 September 1914: underwent training Curragh Royal Barracks, Dublin, and in England: served with the Mediterranean Expeditionary Force at Gallipoli, acting as Corpl., Machine Gun Section: took part in the landing at Suvla Bay and, after an attack of dysentery, was sent to Salonika. He was specially commended for bringing away his guns in safety, and was awarded the Bronze Medal from the King of Italy for valour. He returned to Ireland and obtained a commission, 11 January 1917 before serving with the Expeditionary Force in France and Flanders. He took part in the Battle of Messines and was awarded the Military Cross ('*London Gazette*,' 18 Sept, 1917) for 'gallant conduct in taking a machine-gun position'. He subsequently joined R.F.C., and was killed in aerial action on 21 August 1917 when, while flying over the enemy lines nr. Ypres, he was shot down, aged 32. He was unmarried.

His brother George has no known grave; he is recorded on the Tyne Cot Memorial (Panel 144).

(I.B.1) Pte. 203846, James Willie Middleton, 2/5th Bn. The East Lancashire Regt. (T.F.): enlisted Burnley, co. Lancaster: *husb.* to Mary Jane (7, Nelson Street, Skipton, co. York): served with the Expeditionary Force from May 1917. Killed in action 3 December 1917: Age 34.

Christ Will Clasp The Broken Chain Closer When We Meet Again

(I.B.5) Sergt. 724051, Robert Percy Barr, D.C.M., 38th Bn. Canadian Infantry (Eastern Ontario Regt.), C.E.F.: *s.* of William Barr, of Oxford Mills, Ontario: *b.* South Mountain, Ontario, 6 March 1898: Religion – Presbyterian: Occupation – Farmer: 5'7½" tall, dark complexion, brown eyes, black hair: previously served one year, 56th Regt. (Militia), Kemptville: enlisted 109th Battn., C.E.F., Lindsay, Ontario, 6 March 1916: served with the Expeditionary Force in France and Flanders, transf'd. 38th Battn., from December 1916: one of 27 OR wounded during a raid on the German trenches at Vimy Ridge, 22 February 1917; rejoined his battn. 6 April following, and died of wounds 30 October 1917, received in action before Passchendaele the same day: Age 19. Recommended for a decoration for the part he played in the raid of 22 February He was awarded the Distinguished Conduct Medal, 'For conspicuous gallantry and devotion to duty when in charge of bombers. At a critical moment he established a block on an exposed flank, and with great gallantry and determination held in check superior numbers of the enemy until artillery support could be obtained. Throughout the entire action he encouraged his small party by his cheerfulness and personal example, undoubtedly giving the enemy the impression that the block was held in much greater strength than was actually the case.' The unit recommendation (3 July 1917) citied: 'During attack on Avion Trench June 27/17 this N.C.O. showed great judgement and courage in placing a block in the trench in our advanced position and holding our flank with only six bombers, against very great odds.'

May He Rest In Peace

(I.C.14) Pte. 76216, Walter Burnside, Piper, 29th Bn. (British Columbia Regt.) 6th Canadian Infantry Bde., C.E.F.: *s.* of Walter Burnside, of 'Eynesbury,' Sutherland Street, Sydney, New South Wales, Australia (formerly of Glasgow), by his wife Jane: *b*. Melbourne, Victoria, 16 October 1888: *educ*. Marrickville Public School, Sydney: went to the United States, 1913, and after the outbreak of war, August 1914, proceeded to Vancouver, Canada: enlisted Canadian Infantry, 4 May 1915: served with the Expeditionary Force in France and Flanders from 8 September following, and was killed in action during the engagement at Passchendaele, 6 November 1917, while acting as Stretcher Bearer. Buried at Ypres: Age 29, unmarried.

(I.C.28) Lieut. Percy Louis Barber, 21st Bn. Canadian Infantry (Eastern Ontario Regt.), C.E.F.: *s*. of Rev. F. Louis Barber, of The Rectory, Gananoque, Ontario: *b*. Southport, England, 13 April 1893: *educ*. Hill Croft School, Bobcaygeon; University of Toronto: Occupation – Schoolteacher; Hill Croft, Toronto and Edward County Schools: Cadet Corps member, 1914-15; attained rank of Major, and Colr. Sergt., C.O.T.C.: joined 2nd University Coy., Princess Patricia's Canadian Light Infantry, June 1915, from which he was transf'd. 38th Battn., later 59th Battn. with which he went overseas: joined 21st Battn. in France: twice wounded – Courcellette 1916 and Vimy 1917. Killed in action 3 November 1917, while leading his men against a severe counter-attack at Passchendaele, being shot in the chest by a sniper: Age 24. (*IWGC record age 21*)

(I.D.13) Pte. 427370, Raymond Tom Adams, M.M., 28th Bn. Canadian Infantry (Saskatchewan Regt.), C.E.F.: *s*. of William Tom (& Ellen Salt) Adams, of 'Inglewood,' Lambourn, co. Berks, England: *b*. Lambourn, 30 September 1890: Religion – Methodist: Occupation – Joiner: previously served six months Berkshire Yeomanry: joined C.E.F., Moose Jaw, 6 July 1915. Missing / killed in action, 6 November 1917, Passchendaele: Age 29.

In Sure And Certain Hope

(I.F.1) Lieut. Francis Geoffrey Danby, 'C' Coy., 5th Bn. Alexandra, Princess of Wales's Own (Yorkshire Regt), (The Green Howards), (T.F.): *s*. of Lovell Danby, of Brompton-by-Sawdon, co. York, by his wife Emma: *b*. Hutton Buscel, co. York, 8 August 1896: *educ*. St. Cuthbert's College, Sparken Hill, Worksop, co. Nottingham: a pre-war member of Yorkshire Hussars, Pte. 2906, volunteered for Active Service following the outbreak of war; applied for and obtained a commission 2nd Lieut. 5th Yorkshire Regt., 19 December 1915 (*London Gazette*, 29 December.). Killed in action 27 December 1917, at the same time as 2nd Lieut. W.H. Coles and Pte. 201822, J.W. Mudd; the result of a direct hit on 'C' Company's Headquarters: Age 21. Lieut. F. Green, wounded by the same explosion, died at Poperinghe the following day. (*IWGC record 28 December*)

Pte. Mudd is buried nearby (II.F.5). Lieut. Green lies in Lijssenthoek Military Cemetery (XXVII. CC.6).

(I.F.2) 2nd Lieut. William Henry Coles, 'C' Coy., 5th Bn. Alexandra, Princess of Wales's Own (Yorkshire Regt.) (The Green Howards), (T.F.): *s*. of William Coles, Stationmaster; of Station House, Skipton, by his wife Eliza: and brother to Corpl. R.J. Coles, 9th West Yorkshire Regt., killed in action 9 October 1917, at Passchendaele; and Spr. 386248, A.C. Coles, Royal Engineers, killed in action 15 June 1918, in Italy: a pre-war member of West Riding Territorial's, previous to which he served five years with Yorkshire Hussars; attained rank of Quartermaster Sergt.: offered (and accepted) a commission, Yorkshire Regt., November 1916. Killed in action, 27 December 1917, at the same time as Lieut. F.G. Danby and Pte. 201822, J.W. Mudd; the result of a direct hit on 'C' Company's Headquarters. Lieut. F. Green, wounded by the same explosion, died at Poperinghe the following day. One of three brothers who fell.

His brother Robert has no known grave, he is commemorated on the Tyne Cot Memorial (Panel 43); Arthur is buried in Cavalletto British Cemetery (I.F.11). Pte. Mudd is buried nearby (II.F.5), Lieut. Green lies in Lijssenthoek Military Cemetery (XXVII.CC.6).

(I.J.10) Pte. G/34908, William George Gough, 1st Bn. (57th Foot) The Duke of Cambridge's Own (Middlesex Regt.): only *s*. of William Edward Gough, of 4, Woodville Cottages, Woodville Road, South Tottenham, London, N., by his wife Frances Mary: *b*. Islington, London, N., 1895: *educ*. Woodlands Park, Tottenham: enlisted 23 November 1916: served with the Expeditionary Force in France and Flanders, and was killed in action 6 December 1917. Buried at Passchendaele. Sergt. A. Babbage wrote, "Your son was liked and respected by us all, and his death is deeply mourned. He was a splendid fellow, and a true friend to us all. Whilst he lived he did his duty as a soldier, and he did it nobly and well.": Age 22. *unm.*

His Memory Is As Dear To-Day As In The Hour He Passed Away

(II.A.3) Pte. 4574, Robert Samuel Davey, 45th Bn. Australian Infantry, A.I.F.: *s.* of Stephen C. Davey, of 11, Hale Road, Mosman, New South Wales, by his wife Agnes: *b.* Albury, New South Wales, 1893: Religion – Presbyterian: Occupation – Bricklayer: joined A.I.F., Cootamundra, 2 September 1915: served with the Expeditionary Force in France and Flanders from 8 June 1916: wounded (GSW facial) 6 August 1916, rejoined Battalion 29 March 1917: wounded (GSW Rt. leg) 7 June 1917; rejoined Battalion 7 October 1917. Wounded / reported killed in action 13 October 1917: Age 24. *unm.*

(II.A.3) Pte. 2376, Edward Michael Batten, 'D' Coy., 13th Platoon, 45th Bn. Australian Infantry, A.I.F.: *s.* of William Batten, by his late wife, Margaret: *b.* Rylestone, Phillip Co., New South Wales, 1877: Religion – Roman Catholic: Occupation – Glazier: previously served 2 years, 9 months Royal Garrison Artillery (Sydney): joined A.I.F., Bathurst, 15 April 1916; apptd. 5th Rfts, 45th Bn. 17 August: departed Sydney, 28 August 1916; joined the Expeditionary Force in France 14 March 1917: wounded (GSW neck), Messines, 7 June 1917; rejoined 45th Bn. 16 August 1917. Missing / reported killed in action 12 October 1917. A comrade, Pte. 3164, C. Moore, wrote, "On October 12 we were at Passchendaele and attacked the enemy during the morning. A number of our men including Batten and W. Lee were in a dug out which was blown up by an enemy shell. Many of them were buried in the debris. During the day the dug-out was cleared out and the bodies which could be recovered stacked up. Many of them were so badly damaged they were unrecognisable. There were 10 to 15 casualties in this dug out. At the time we were about 100 yards away and had our lines behind the enemy pill box. Most of our company were accounted for but Batten and Lee could not be traced, the conclusion being that they were buried in the debris. The same night the enemy took the dug-out;" and Pte. E. Peck wrote, "Re. 2376 Pte. E.M. Batten and 2447 Pte. W. Lee. They were killed on 12.10.17. We were at a certain position in the line, and that was the last that was seen of them. There were myself and two other men detailed off to bury a number of bodies at night about this position where they were last seen, and most of the bodies were unrecognisable.": Age 40.

Pte. William Lee has no known grave; he is commemorated on the Ypres (Menin Gate) Memorial (Panel 27).

(II.A.3) Pte. 5821, Clarence Cyril Brooks Galsworthy, 45th Bn. Australian Infantry, A.I.F.: *s.* of William Books Galsworthy, by his wife Rebecca West (Brockley, London): *b.* Southsea, Portsmouth, co. Hants, 1889: Religion – Church of England: Occupation – Station Hand: enlisted Sydney, New South Wales, 12 June 1916: proceeded overseas 7 October 1916; served with the Expeditionary Force in France from 26 June. Killed in action 10 October 1917: Age 28. Correspondence to be addressed to Margaret E. Galsworthy (38, Grafton Street, Woollahara, New South Wales), his widow.

Ever Remembered By His Loving Wife And Grace

(II.A.3) Pte. 32469, Robert Stokoe, 2/5th Bn. The East Lancashire Regt. (T.F.): *s.* of Thomas Stokoe, of 66, Shielfield Terrace, Tweedmouth, Berwick-on-Tweed: and younger brother to Pte. 33316, J. Stokoe, 8th York & Lancaster Regt., killed in action 28 August 1917: *b.* Tweedmouth, co. Northumberland, *c.*1896: enlisted Berwick. Killed in action 27 November 1917: Age 21. *unm.*

His brother James is buried in Railway Dugouts Burial Ground (Transport Farm) (IV.H.3).

(II.A.3) Pte. 242555, Edwin Wright, 2/5th Bn. The East Lancashire Regt. (T.F.): formerly no.6820, King's (Liverpool) Regt.: *s.* of Edward Wright, of 24, Green Lane, Middleton Junction, Manchester, by his wife Ellen: *b.* Lancaster, *c.*1898: enlisted Middleton. Killed in action 27 November 1917: Age 19.

(II.A.3) Pte. 30876, Peter Hulland, 2/5th Bn. The East Lancashire Regt. (T.F.): *b.* Forton, co. Lancaster, *c.*1894: enlisted Clitheroe. Killed in action 27 November 1917: Age 23. He leaves a widow Maggie Hulland (8, Union Street, Low Moor, Clitheroe)

(II.B.1) Sergt. 201353, William Ervine Lee, 5/6th Bn. The Cameronians (Scottish Rifles), (T.F.): *s.* of John Lee, of 26, Finnieston Street, Glasgow (Coachman) by his wife Margaret, *dau.* of the late Irwin

Thompson: *b*. Omagh, co. Tyrone, 7 September 1895: *educ*. Dundalk; Kent Road Higher Grade School, Glasgow: joined Scottish Rifles, Glasgow, 5 August 1915: served with the Expeditionary Force in France and Flanders from first week March 1916. Killed in action at Bailleul, 9 March 1918. Buried in Aid Post Cemetery: Age 22. His Commanding Officer, Capt. Kirkwood wrote, saying that he was a brave and gallant soldier, and had his entire confidence. He *m*. Cardonald; Jennie, *dau*. of Frederick Gardner, of Uddingston, Glasgow, and had two sons; John, *b*. 29 July 1913 and William Ervine, *b*. 17 February 1916.

(II.C.1) Rfn. R/34040, Lewis Ernest Orrow, 16th (Service) Bn. (Church Lad's Brigade) The King's Royal Rifle Corps: *s*. of Samuel Orrow, of Homerton, London, by his wife Elizabeth. Killed in action, 21 March 1918: Age 31. He leaves a widow, Sarah Elizabeth (9, Brooksby's Walk, Homerton), and children.

An Affectionate Husband And Father Dear, A Faithful Friend Has Left Us Here

(II.C.11) Pte. 45197, William Lawrence Muskett, 1/6th Bn. The Northumberland Fusiliers (T.F.): *s*. of John Muskett, of Urmston, co. Lancaster, by his wife Annie: enlisted Manchester. Killed in action, 30 January 1918: Age 24, unmarried.

To Memory Ever Dear

(II.C.17) L/Corpl. 27536, Alfred George Sore, 1/8th Bn. The Prince of Wales's Own (West Yorkshire Regt.), (T.F.): 5th *s*. of the late John Sore, by his wife Sarah (12, Reed's Buildings, Northgate Street, Bury St. Edmunds, co. Suffolk), *dau*. of Thomas Leathers, of Regent Street, Stowemarket: and brother to Signaller 240265, P. Sore, Suffolk Regt., killed in action nr. Gaza, Palestine, 4 November 1917: *b*. Bury St. Edmunds, 6 September 1894: *educ*. Guildhall Boys' School: Occupation – Baker; Messrs A. Cooper, Sheffield: enlisted 6th King's Own (Yorkshire Light Infantry) (no.11512), Sheffield, 24 August 1914: served with the Expeditionary Force in France and Flanders from 23 May 1915; wounded 27 July following (Hooge): on recovery proceeded to Malta with a West Yorkshire Garrison Battn.: returned to France, June 1917. Killed in action 26 December following. Buried at Keerselarhoek, nr. Zonnebeke: Age 23. *unm*.

Greater Love Hath No Man Than This

His brother Percy is buried in Gaza War Cemetery (VIII.F.2).

(II.F.5) Pte. 201822, John Waller Mudd, 5th Bn. Alexandra, Princess of Wales's Own (Yorkshire Regt.), (The Green Howards), (T.F.): *s*. of Michael Mudd, of West End, Stokesley, co. York, by his wife Annie. Killed in action, 27 December 1917, at the same time as Lieut. F.G. Danby and 2nd Lieut. W.H. Coles; the result of a direct hit on 'C' Company's Headquarters. Lieut. F. Green, wounded by the same explosion, died at Poperinghe the following day.

Though Gone From Sight To Memory Ever Dear

Lieut. Danby and 2nd Lieut. Coles are buried nearby (I.F.1 – I.F.2); Lieut. Green, Lijssenthoek Military Cemetery (XXVII.CC.6).

(III.D.2) Corpl. 421421, Albert Somers Bray, 2/8th Bn. The Worcestershire Regt. (T.F.): eldest *s*. of Albert Bray, Clerk, Malvern Council; of Willow Cottages, Lower Wyche, by his wife Valentine: *b*. Malvern, 14 November 1897: *educ*. Wyche School: enlisted 8th Worcestershire Regt., July 1915: served with the Expeditionary Force in France and Flanders; killed in action at the Third Battle of Ypres, 27 August 1917. A member of 1st Malvern Boy Scout Troop, a memorial service was held after Evensong, 9 September 1917, at All Saints Church, Wyche. His former Scoutmaster, a Captain in Pte. Bray's regiment, wrote, "Bertie was the pick of the Company and a great lad, always cheery and bright and always a smile on his face and ever to be relied on to do his job. His Company Commander thought a lot of him although he was so young. You know what I think of him, and I can't put it into words as my eyes become dim; but whether we live or die, anyone who has fought and died out here will surely rest in peace and what better rest could one have through knowing one has died to save others.": Age 19.

(III.D.22) L/Corpl. S/9050, Hugh Farquhar, 9th (Service) Bn. The Gordon Highlanders: *s.* of Henry Farquhar, Slater; of 15, Ogilvie Place, Arbroath, late of 11, Convent Street: *b.* Arbroath: sometime Plasterer; Frank Middleton, Lindsay Street; thereafter removed to Vancouver, Canada: returned to his native Scotland on the declaration of war; joined 9th Gordon Highlanders, Dundee: proceeded to France mid-1915. Killed in action on the night of 22 August 1917, being struck by a bullet. Death was instantaneous: Age 28. The Chaplain said, "He was a fine soldier and a good man; he did his duty nobly to the last." A Freemason, L/Corpl. Farquhar was a member of Lodge St. Thomas of Aberbrothock No.40, Arbroath. Remains exhumed, unmarked grave, 28.D.13.c.3.D.22, Tyne Cot Cemetery; identified – Disc. Reinterred, registered 21 August 1919. G.R.U. Cross erected.

(III.F.1) Pte. S/15370, Charles Clark, 9th (Service) Bn. The Gordon Highlanders: *youngest s.* of William Clark, of 9, Tarlair Street, Madcuff (former Farmer; Hill of Pitgair, Gamrie), by his wife Barbara Williamson, *dau.* of Margaret Norrie: *b.* Gamrie, 14 October 1885: *educ.* Clinterty Public School: enlisted 4 September 1916: served with the Expeditionary Force in France and Flanders; killed in action at Ypres, 26 August 1917: Age 31. Buried there. He *m.* Insch, co. Aberdeen, 18 May 1912; Jeannie Angus, *dau.* of William Philip.

(IV.G.21) 2nd Lieut. Arthur Conway Young, 4th (Extra Reserve) attd 7/8th (Service) Bn. The Princess Victoria's (Royal Irish Fusiliers): *s.* of Robert Young, Owner, 'The Japan Chronicle;' by his wife Annie, *née* Crockett: *b.* Kobe, Japan, 9 October 1890: sometimes worked on his father's newspaper; journeyed to England to enlist 1915; joined Inns of Court O.T.C., from whence he obtained a commission attd. Royal Irish Fusiliers. Killed in action 16 August 1917, at the Battle of Langemarck: Age 26. A pacifist and idealist, he had previously been a member of the South Place Ethical Society, London (his father was also a member). Two of his brothers also served. His epitaph is from a phrase spoken by H.G. Wells.

Sacrificed To The Fallacy That War Can End War

(V.C.19) Pte. 23724, Frederick 'Fred' Burrows, 9th (Service) Bn. (County Armagh) The Princess Victoria's (Royal Irish Fusiliers): *s.* of Joshua Burrows, of Gillis Road, Armagh: enlisted Lurgan, Co. Armagh. Killed in action 16 August 1917, aged 19.

Rest Where None Weep Till The Eternal Morrow

(VI.G.19) Pte. X.212, James Norman Munro, 'C' Coy., 1st South African Infantry Regt., S.A.E.F.: elder *s.* of James Munro, Engineering Works Manager, Torquil, Carmyle, co. Lanark; by his wife Annie ('Balmacron House,' Meigle, co. Perth), *dau.* of Thomas Hodgson: *gdson.* to Surgeon Dr. Munro, of Moffat, co. Dumfries: *b.* Seaforth, co. Lancaster, 2 March 1894: *educ.* Glasgow Academy: went to South Africa, 1912; engaged in Sheep Farming there: joined 8th Mounted Rifles, Midland Horse, January 1915: took part in the German West African Campaign of the same year: on his regiment being disbanded, he returned to England, where he joined the South African Contingent, proceeded to France and served with the Expeditionary Force there from October 1916: took part in the Battle of Arras, April 1917. Killed in action at Zonnebeke, 20 September following. Buried where he fell. His Commanding Officer wrote, "Your son was a general favourite, and we shall all miss his cheerful personality, which made him the excellent soldier he was.": Age 23. *unm.*

He Died That We Might Live

(VII.H.4) Pte. 21473, Alexander Asher, 8th (Service) Bn. The Seaforth Highlanders (Ross-shire Buffs, The Duke of Albany's): 2nd *s.* of William Asher, Farmer; of Bog O'Fern, Lhanbryde, co. Moray, by his wife Jane, *dau.* of Alexander Harrold: *b.* Lhanbryde, 4 February 1892: *educ.* Cranloch Public School, there: Occupation – Farmer: enlisted 2 April 1917: served with the Expeditionary Force in France and Flanders from 1 August following. Killed in action near Ypres on the 22nd of that month. Buried near Iberian, east-north-east of Ypres: Age 25. *unm.*

Ever Remembered

(VIII.E.9) Spr. 186640, Ernest Rogers, 247th Field Coy., Royal Engineers, 63rd (Royal Naval) Divn.: elder *s*. of John Rogers, of 8, Northfield Terrace, Ilfracombe, Carriage & Motor Body Builder; by his wife Sarah Ann, *dau*. of John (& Mary Jane) Cowler: *b*. Ilfracombe, co. Devon, 17 August 1894: *educ*. Ilfracombe School: Occupation – Assistant to his father: joined Royal Engineers 2 September 1916: served with the Expeditionary Force in France and Flanders from 11 April 1917. Killed in action near Ypres, 25 October following: Age 23. He *m*. Westdown, co. Devon, 25 November 1916; Ethel (9, Watermouth Road, Ilfracombe), *dau*. of Lewis (& Eliza Jane) Collins, and had a *dau*., Muriel, *b*. 2 November 1917, seven days after the death of her father.

The Path Of Duty Was The Way To Glory

(VIII.F.2) L/Corpl. 302459, Denis Frederic Church, 2/5th (City of London) Bn. (London Rifle Brigade) The London Regt. (T.F.): formerly no.4022: *youngest s*. of Frederic Church, of 25, Victoria Road, Oldfield Park, Bath, by his wife Clara Emma, *dau*. of James Gilson: *b*. Bath, co. Somerset, 26 November 1894: *educ*. King Edward's School: Occupation – Student: joined London Rifle Brigade, 10 January 1916: served with the Expeditionary Force in France from 25 January 1917; killed in action in the Ypres section, north-east of St. Julien, 20 September following. Buried east of the St. Julien – Poelcapelle Road. His Captain wrote "He was an excellent and reliable fellow, and I am very sorry to lose him.": Age 22. *unm*. Remains recovered unmarked grave 28.D.1.a.2.80; identified – Disc, 4022 5 C. of L.; reinterred 12 September 1919.

Until The Day Break And The Shadows Flee Away
R.I.P.

(VIII.H.9) Pte. 265817, Samuel Spilsbury, 1/6th Bn. The Cheshire Regt. (T.F.): *s*. of William Spilsbury, of 17, Bamford Street, Stockport, by his wife Mary Elizabeth: and brother to L/Corpl. 265400, W. Spilsbury, Cheshire Regt., who was killed in the same action, 31 July 1917.

His brother William has no known grave; he is commemorated on the Ypres (Menin Gate) Memorial (Panel 19).

(IX.B.4) Sergt. 305820, Hubert Horace Wheeldon, D.C.M., M.M., 1/8th Bn. The Royal Warwickshire Regt. (T.F.): *s*. of Horatio Wheeldon: *b*. West Bromwich, co. Stafford, 20 March 1886: *educ*. Burlington Street Board School: enlisted Royal Warwickshire Regt., 6 August 1914: served with the Expeditionary Force in France; killed in action 3½ miles north-north-east of Ypres on 27 August 1917. Buried where he fell. Awarded the D.C.M. for 'distinguished conduct in the field,' and the M.M. for 'bravery in the field.': Age 31. He *m*. Bishop Ryder's Church, Gem Street, Birmingham, 1904; Leah Lilian (75, Little King Street, Hockley, Birmingham, late of 44, Great Lister Street, Nechells), *dau*. of Howard Thomas Pearce, and had three children – Lily, *b*. 30 April 1908; Horace, *b*. 29 April 1914; Elsie, *b*. 11 May 1917. (*IWGC record age 29*)

(IX.C.24) Pte. 270208, Arthur James Grimes, 1st Bn. The Hertfordshire Regt. (T.F.): *s*. of Eliza Ward, *née* Grimes (Seaview Cottage, Alexandra Road, Great Wakering, co. Essex): employee to A. Kemsley, Esq.: enlisted Warley, 27 October 1916: served with the Expeditionary Force in France and Flanders from 1 January 1917. He was reported missing, presumed (since confirmed) killed, in action on 31 July 1917: Age 28. He leaves a wife, Martha E. Grimes (24, Beaufort Street, Southchurch, Southend-on-Sea).

We Loved Him In Life He Is Dear To Us Still

(IX.E.23) Capt. Henry Rawson Forde, M.C., 'D' Coy., 2nd Bn. (105th Foot) The King's Own (Yorkshire Light Infantry): only *s*. of Sir Henry J. Forde, of 'The Manor of St. John', Waterford, J.P., by his wife Lady Annie Catherine, *dau*. of Richard Rawson: *b*. Tramore, Co. Waterford, 24 June 1895: *educ*. Clifton College; Royal Military College, Sandhurst: gazetted 2nd Lieut., King's Own (Yorkshire Light Infantry), 12 January 1915; promoted Capt. 3 December 1916: served with the Expeditionary Force in France and Flanders from October following, took part in the fighting on the Somme where, after the attack on Munich and Frankfurt trenches (18 November 1916) only 2nd Lieut. Forde, the Adjutant, Intelligence

Officer, and 171 other ranks remained of the battalion; also took part in the advance to the Hindenburg Line, Spring 1917. He was killed in action near Passchendaele on 2 December 1917. Buried where he fell. A brother officer wrote, "It was an awful blow to us all...for he was looked upon by everyone as a true friend. He is a great loss to the battalion," and another, "A brave and gallant officer has been taken by God, but he did his work, and he was a man among men when danger lurked about." An officer of another regiment wrote, "All his company officers had been killed, and he was rallying his men when a German sniper hit him in the head, and, poor lad, he was killed at once." Awarded the Military Cross ('*London Gazette*,' 17 April 1917), the official record stating, "He led his men in the attack with great gallantry, and captured an enemy line of strong posts, together with 40 prisoners. He had previously done fine work.": Age 22. *unm.*

"Jesus Met Them Saying All Hail"
St. Matt. 28.9

(IX.F.1) 2nd Lieut. Alan Benjamin Buckworth, 3rd (Reserve) Bn. The Royal Inniskilling Fusiliers: *s.* of Ernest Benjamin Buckworth, of 47, Devonshire Road, Harrow-on-the-Hill, co. Middlesex, by his wife Bertha. Killed in action, 14 August 1917, aged 40. His nephews, Lieut. W. Buckworth, 10th Rifle Brigade, 2nd Lieut. W.A. Buckworth, 1st Royal Inniskilling Fusiliers, and Rfn, 592334, H.T. Buckworth, 18th (London Irish Rifles), London Regt., also fell.

Sleep On Beloved Till The Day Breaks And Shadows Flee Away

Lieut. William Buckworth, commemorated on the Ypres (Menin Gate) Memorial (Panel 46), is known to be buried in Oostaverne Wood Cemetery, Wytschaete (IV.A.3); 2nd Lieut. Wallace A. Buckworth has no known grave, he is commemorated on the Helles Memorial, Gallipoli; Rfn. Herbert T. Buckworth is buried in Bedford House Cemetery (I.C.5/Enc.No.4).

(IX.G.5) 2nd Lieut. Charles Darrell Heaton, 143rd Coy., Machine Gun Corps (Inf.): *s.* of William Lambert Heaton, by his wife Frances Christiana: and younger brother to Pte. 54800, W.L. Heaton, 11th Coy. Machine Gun Corps (Inf.), died 13 April 1917, aged 28. Killed in action, 26 August 1917: Age 21. *unm.*

His brother William is buried in Athies Communal Cemetery (B.2).

(IX.H.18) Lieut. 10275, Victor Richard Stanley Scott, 2nd Auckland Regt., N.Z.E.F.: *s.* of William Greer Scott, of Ngaroa, Waitoa, Thames Valley, by his wife Elizabeth: brother to Pte. 13/2369, R.H.V. Scott, 2nd Auckland Regt. Killed in action, 15 September 1916: *b.* Thames, Auckland: Occupation – Farmer: departed Wellington, 2nd Lieut., 12th Rfts., 6 May 1916: served in Egypt, and with the Expeditionary Force in France and Flanders (promoted Lieutenant). Killed in action, 4 October 1917: Age 30. He was married to Ruby Scott.

His brother Robert is buried in Caterpillar Valley Cemetery, Longueval (IX.H.29).

(X.A.32) Rfn. 302644, William Holliday, 5th (City of London) Bn. (London Rifle Brigade) The London Regt. (T.F.): only *s.* of William Henry Holliday, Farmer; of Stillers Farm, Ewshot, Farnham, co. Surrey, by his wife Julia, *dau.* of George (& Sarah) Cresswell: *b.* Charlwood, co. Surrey, 16 June 1881: *educ.* at Crookham: Occupation – Commercial Traveller: joined London Rifle Brigade, 29 March 1916: served with the Expeditionary Force in France and Flanders from 13 February 1917, and was killed in action on the Menin Road 20 September following. Buried at Triangle Farm, near St. Julien: Age 36. *unm.*

To Live In Hearts Of Those We Love Is Not To Die

(X.B.7) Pte. 40404, Joseph George Smith, 1/5th Bn. The Lancashire Fusiliers (T.F.): formerly no.39803, Bedfordshire and Hertfordshire Regt.: *s.* of Mrs S.C. Smith (Pantile Cottages, Barling, Southend-on-Sea): *b.* Wakering, co. Essex: enlisted Southend: served with the Expeditionary Force in France from June 1917. Killed in action, 6 September 1917: Age 25. Remembered on Barling (Parish Church) War Memorial.

Ever In Our Thoughts

(X.B.14) Pte. 306753, Thomas Eaves, 1/8th Bn. The Royal Warwickshire Regt. (T.F.): *s.* of the late William Eaves, by his marriage to Mary Elizabeth Keates, *née* Eaves (Kingsbury Road, Minworth, co. Warwick): brother to Pte. 7555, A. Eaves, 11th Hussars, killed in action 1 November 1914: enlisted Sutton Coldfield, co. Warwick: served with the Expeditionary Force. Killed in action, 26 August 1917. One of seven brothers who served.

His brother Albert has no known grave; he is commemorated on the Ypres (Menin Gate) Memorial (Panel 5).

(X.B.16) Sergt. 240447, Ronald McKelvie, 1/8th Bn. The Worcestershire Regt. (T.F.): *s.* of the late David McKelvie, by his wife Margaret (50, Sansome Walk, Worcester), *dau.* of David McBain: *b.* Worcester, 23 March 1890: *educ.* St. Martin's Boys' School; Secondary School; Victoria Institute (scholarship student): joined Worcestershire Territorials, August 1914: served with the Expeditionary Force in France and Flanders from 1 April 1915: took part in several engagements, being gassed in the Houthem sector at the end of 1915, and invalided to a convalescent camp: rejoined his regiment on recovery, and was killed in action at St. Julien, 27 August 1917, by a sniper, while leading in an advance. Buried at Springfields, nr. St. Julien: Age 27. *unm.*

In Loving Memory

(X.C.22) Pte. 6/4017, John Jennings Crompton, 1st Bn. Canterbury Regt., N.Z.E.F.: *s.* of the late Henry Jardine Crompton, of 3, Mount Pleasant Road, Mount Eden, Auckland, by his wife Louisa I.C. (Queen's Avenue, Dominion Road): *gdson.* to the late W.M. Crompton, First Editor of the 'Taranaki Herald,' and an initial member of the General Assembly on the Constitution Act (1853): elder brother to Corpl. 10/718, T.S. Crompton, 1st Bn. Wellington Regt., who fell on 5 March 1917: *b.* Omata, Taranaki, 1883. Killed in action, 1 October 1917, at Passchendaele: Age 34. Pte. Crompton's father saw service in the First Taranaki War, the armed conflict between the Maori and New Zealand Government regarding land ownership and sovereignty, March 1860 – March 1861.

His brother Thomas is buried in Tancrez Farm Cemetery (II.F.1).

(X.G.4) Pte. 266937, Charles Thomas Spicer, No.4 Coy., 1st Bn. The Hertfordshire Regt. (T.F.): *s.* of Samuel Spicer, of 2, Beecroft Cottages, Walkern, co. Hertford, by his wife Louisa: killed in action 31 July 1917, at St. Julien: Age 22. *unm.* See account, Ypres (Menin Gate) Memorial (Panel 54).

For Ever In Our Thoughts

(X.H.7) Pte. 201156, Hugh Davies, 1/5th Bn. The King's (Liverpool) Regt. (T.F.): only *s.* of the late Robert Davies, Platelayer Ganger, by his wife Annie (5, Elizabeth Villas, Llandudno), *dau.* of John Williams, of Bethesda: *b.* Dingle, Colwyn Bay, co. Denbigh, 17 October 1887: *educ.* Colwyn Bay: Occupation – Examiner; Carriage Dept. (Llandudno Station), London and North Western Railway: joined King's Liverpool Regt., 29 January 1915: served with the Expeditionary Force in France and Flanders, from 29 January 1916. Killed in action at Ypres, 20 September 1917. Buried there, by the side of Pommern Castle: Age 29. One of his officers wrote, "On the morning of 20 September your husband was killed by shell fire during the recent engagement. For five months I had the great pleasure of being his officer, and not a better man could I ever have desired to be the officer of." He *m.* Merthyr Tydfil; Annie (Flat No.3, York Mansions, 25, Vaughan Street, Llandudno, formerly of 32, King's Road, Llandudno), 2nd *dau.* of Daniel Hughes, of Llandudno, and had a *dau.*, Nancy, *b.* 8 May 1914.

(XI.B.14) L/Corpl. 200982, Alfred Atwell, 1st Bn. (26th Foot) The Cameronians (Scottish Rifles): *s.* of John William Atwell, of 7, Shaftesbury Cottages, Whiteinch, Glasgow, by his wife Ellen, *dau.* of James Lawther: *b.* Whiteinch, co. Lanark, 13 February 1895: *educ.* Scotstoun Public School, Glasgow: Occupation – Demurrage Clerk: enlisted 20 January 1915: served with the Expeditionary Force in France from June following. Killed in action at Passchendaele, Belgium, 8 January 1918. Buried there: Age 22. *unm.*

Ever In Our Thoughts

(XI.C.5) Pte. 242339, Albert Basford, 2/5th Bn. The Sherwood Foresters (Notts & Derbys Regt.), (T.F.): *s.* of James Basford, of 21, Liversage Street, Derby, by his wife Emma: and younger brother to Pte. 35451, J.A. Basford, 1st Sherwood Foresters, killed in action 15 July 1916: *b.* Derby: enlisted there: served with the Expeditionary Force in France and Flanders from February 1917. Killed in action 26 September 1917: Age 25.

His brother James has no known grave; he is commemorated on the Loos Memorial.

(XII.B.14) Lieut. Harvey Freeman, M.C., 11th Coy., Australian Machine Gun Corps attd. 11th Bde. 3rd Divn., A.I. F.: *s.* of Benjamin James Freeman, of 'Waverley,' 94, Western Beach, Geelong, Victoria, by his wife Emily: Killed in action 15 October 1917. Awarded the Military Cross for his actions on the morning of 4 October when, after following up to a key position behind 41st (Queensland) Battn., he rapidly and successfully deployed two of his machine gun crews to give a covering fire ahead of the advancing Queenslanders; the recommendation read, "During the advance over heavily shelled ground, his teams sustained casualties, but by rapid organisation he succeeded in getting the whole of his guns to the final objective. Under heavy enemy shell fire, he displayed skill in selection of gun positions and great courage and initiative in the handling of his guns, thus being able to inflict severe losses on the enemy."

(XII.C.15) Rfn. 391903, Harold Ivor Vincent Hartwright, 9th (County of London) Bn. (Queen Victoria's Rifles) The London Regt. (T.F.): *s.* of Frederick William Hartwright, of Salisbury, Queensland, Australia (formerly of North Ambersham, Fernhurst, co. West Sussex), by his first wife Kezia, *née* Slingo (dec'd.): and brother to Pte. 7574, F.G. Hartwright, Scots Guards, killed in action 11 November 1914; and father to Flying Officer, 44570, V.R. Hartwright, D.F.M., No.7 Sqdn., Royal Air Force, who died as a prisoner of war, 30 June 1941: *b.* Guildford, co. Surrey, 1890. Killed in action 27 September 1917: Age 27. He was married to Ada Blakeley, *née* Hartwright, *dau.* of Mr (& Mrs) Dobson.

His brother Frederick has no known grave, he is commemorated on the Menin Gate Memorial (Panel 11); his only son Valentine is buried in Becklingen War Cemetery, Germany (XIII.F.11-14).

(XII.C.17) Pte. 29874, Alfred Henry Mears, 6th Bn. The Royal Warwickshire Regt. (T.F.): late of City Cottages, Ditchling Common, Ditchling, nr. Lewes: 3rd *s.* of Alfred Mears, of The Old Cottage, Wivelsfield Green, nr. Lewes, co. East Sussex, by his wife Lucy E: and younger brother to L/Corpl. 13059, A.L. Mears, Coldstream Guards, killed in action 11 September 1917: *b.* Ditchling: *educ.* Ditchling (St. Margaret's) School: enlisted Hastings: served with the Expeditionary Force in France from 12 September 1917 (the day following his elder brother's death), and was killed in action, 4 October 1917. In response to enquiries made by Pte. Mears' parents, Lieut. W. J. Crump, wrote, "It is with the utmost regret that I have to pencil this letter to you in reply to your letter and telegram received yesterday. I realise what a great blow it must have been when I told you that your brave son was killed whilst gloriously fighting against the Germans on the 4 October. What a terrible war it is for your household, to think that you have given two sons in the past few weeks. The boy that I am writing about I knew personally, and I must say that he was a good and brave soldier. I assure you that he will be missed very much in the Company, since by his untiring efforts, whether conditions were good or bad, he made a great number of friends. My I offer you my very sincere sympathy in this your hour of trouble, and may God bless you and keep you, so that you may see that your sons have given their lives for the cause of right.": Age 19.

Not Dead But Sleeping
Matt. IX.24

His brother Arthur has no known grave; he is commemorated on the Tyne Cot Memorial (Panel 9).

(XII.F.7) Sergt. 20931, Colin John Alexander McLachlan, 1st Bn. Otago Regt., N.Z.E.F.: *s.* of Archie McLachlan, of Hazelburn, Dolyeston, Canterbury, by his wife Mary: Occupation – Engine Driver: departed Wellington, QM.Sergt. 19th Rfts., 'D' Coy., Otago Infantry, 15 November 1916: trained England, winter 1916 – 1917: proceeded to France. Killed in action, 12 October 1917, in the attack at Bellevue Spur: Age 26. *unm.* See account re. Major W.W. Turner, Tyne Cot (New Zealand) Memorial (Panel 3).

The weather on 31 July 1917 had begun slightly overcast, but by mid-afternoon torrential rain (heralding the wettest August in living memory) had begun to fall. The battlefield surrounding Ypres, which three years of continuous bombardment and fighting on both sides had turned into a scene of devastation even Dante's wildest nightmares could not match, had, by the end of the day, begun to resemble a swamp. After all day attacking the enemy in their heavily fortified positions and concrete pill-boxes, taking enormous numbers of casualties in the process, the exhausted survivors of the attacking British units found whatever shelter their objective afforded them (or where-ever fate had decreed they end up) and 'held on' as best they could. Throughout the night, with the sound of machine-gun bullets whipping and snapping all around them and shells hurtling through the night sky, men huddled in shell-holes, surrounded by the wounded, dying and dead, waiting for the light of dawn to assess their situation. In the vicinity of Iberian Farm at dawn, Pte. W. Morgan, dozing in a shell-hole, awoke with the rain still beating on his face. It was a large shell-hole, half-full of water...opposite Bill was an officer of the Cameron Highlanders who had crawled in during the night. He lay at an awkward angle, his mud-coated legs sticking out from beneath a bedraggled kilt. There wasn't a mark on his body, but his head lay under the water. Bill could see his face quite clearly. The eyes were closed. He had slipped in and drowned in his sleep."

It is believed the Cameron Highlander officer referred to was:

(XIII.C.35) Capt. James Hislop, M.C., attd. 6th (Service) Bn. The Queen's Own (Cameron Highlanders): eldest *s*. of William Hislop, of 776, Winnipeg Avenue, Winnipeg; formerly of Old Town, Peebles, Scotland: joined Cameron Highlanders, Inverness, 1900 (Boy soldier, age 15): served Malta, Cyprus, South Africa (with Mounted Infantry); thereafter Southern China, Northern China, and Poona, India: returned to England with his regiment November 1914: sent to Gailes as Sergt. Instructor to Glasgow Highlanders; thereafter invited by Lochiel to proceed to France as Regtl. Sergt. Major to 5th Battalion: served with the Expeditionary Force in France from early 1916; offered a commission and returned to England for training; returned to France July following: Awarded the Military Cross – 'For conspicuous gallantry and devotion to duty. The two companies, under the command of Second Lieutenants Hislop and Grindell, were ordered to take an enemy position. The operation was entirely successful, and it was solely due to the dash and skill of these two officers that a very difficult task was successfully accomplished.': killed in action 31 July 1917: Age 32. A fellow officer wrote, "It is my sad duty to have to inform you that your son, Capt. James Hislop, of this Battalion, was killed in action on 31st July. The Battalion took part in an attack on the enemy's lines on that day, and Capt. Hislop led his company with great skill and bravery. He was in the act of sending a message over the telephone when he was shot through the head by a sniper, death being instantaneous. Capt. Hislop was a most excellent officer, and his loss is a great blow to the Battalion, and is seriously regretted by the officers and men. We were all so grieved to hear of the death of your son in action. As I have served in the same Battalion with him all his service, I know only too well what a terrible loss it is to us. For years he worked for the regiment with energy and love which could not have been surpassed. Only the other day a brother officer, who was present at the time, related to me with much admiration your son's splendid conduct in France when he won the Military Cross." Another said, "I am very sorry to tell you that your son, Captain James Hislop, has been killed in action. It was in front of Ypres, where our last attack took place. We all miss him very much. Although a quiet chap, when you got to know him he was a most lovable man, with a dry sense of humour which called forth many a laugh. He was a fine soldier too – easily the best company officer in the Battalion. Our late Commanding Officer had a very high opinion of him. Unfortunately, the latter was also killed on the same day as your son. The officers who are left, his Company Sergeant-Major, and the men of his company asked me to convey their deep feeling of sympathy with you in your loss."

(XIII.E.36) Corpl. G/13706, William George Batchelor, M.M., 1st Bn. (2nd Foot) The Queen's (Royal West Surrey Regt.): *s*. of William Batchelor, of Stoke Bruerne Park, Towcester, co. Northampton, by his wife Rhoda, *dau*. of Richard Cockman: and brother to Pte. G/7953, R. Batchelor, 1st Queen's (Royal West Surrey Regt.), killed in action 25 September 1917: *b*. Rickmansworth, co. Hertford, 12 April 1886: *educ*. Harefield Elementary School: Occupation – Asst. Bailiff; Stoke Bruerne Estate: enlisted 9 November

1915: served with the Expeditionary Force in France and Flanders from 17 September following; killed in action in Belgium, 3 March 1918. Buried nr. Passchendaele, north-east of Ypres: Age 32. An officer wrote, "I have been his platoon commander since last November, and I cannot tell you how frightfully sorry I am that he has been taken. He was such a splendid fellow in every way," and another, "I have always had such a great opinion of him, and I know well how greatly he was liked by all who knew him." Corpl. Batchelor was awarded the Military Medal ('*London Gazette*,' 17 December 1917), 'for conspicuous bravery in the field in September 1917.' He *m.* Stoke Bruerne, Towcester, 21 April 1909; Edith Mary (Stoke Bruerne Park), *dau.* of the late Frederick Coy, and had three children – Frederick William, *b.* 17 January 1913; Edith Rhoda, *b.* 1 April 1910; Winifred Alice, *b.* 9 August 1911.

For God For King And For Country

His brother Richard is buried nearby (LVI.D.21).

(XIV.A.2) 2nd Lieut. Arthur Conrad, Michelsen, 'B' Bty., 64th Bde., Royal Field Artillery: *yst. s.* of the late Hugo Edward Michelsen, of 'Glenmead,' Glen Avenue, Herne Bay, co. Kent, by his wife Mary Walford (59, Earl's Court Road, Kensington, London, N.W.), *dau.* of W.L. Gomme: *b.* Harlesden, London, N.W., 25 June 1891: *educ.* Haberdashers' School, Cricklewood, London, N.W.: was a well-known Boy Scout Officer: joined Artists' Rifles, 1910, no.1581: served with the Expeditionary Force in France and Flanders from October 1914; present at the First Battle of Ypres: wounded, January 1916: gazetted 2nd Lieut., Royal Field Artillery, January 1917: wounded again, July 1917. Killed in action at Gravenstafel, 18 October following. Buried there. Letters from the Commanding Officer and comrades describe him as 'a great favourite with both men and officers, always cheerful and ready to take his part in everything, both military and social.': Age 26. He *m.* Camberwell, London, S.E., December 1916; Sarah (Nan), *dau.* of W.G. Hughes, of Blaengarw, co. Glamorgan: *s.p.*

"I Serve"

(XIV.B.14) 2nd Lieut. Ernest John Wilson Beynon, 4th (Hallamshire) Bn. The York & Lancaster Regt. (T.F.): *s.* of William John Beynon, of 14, Hawstead Road, Catford, London, S.E.6, by his wife Mary: killed in action south-west of Passchendaele, 9 October 1917. See 2nd Lieut. F. DeBell (XIV.F.19).

True And Loyal

(XIV.D.22) Pte. L/9065, Alec Henry Wood, 2nd Bn. (3rd Foot) The Buffs (East Kent Regt.): 3rd *s.* of Charles Wood, Farm Waggoner; late of Lower Ensigne Cottages, Chilham, co. Kent, by his wife Sarah Elizabeth: *b.* Chilham: served with the Expeditionary Force in France and Flanders from 17 January 1915. Reported missing believed killed in action following an enemy bombardment and attack on trench D.5, Verlorenhoek, on the afternoon of 3 May 1915: Age 24. *unm.*

Ever In Our Thoughts

(XIV.E.4) Sergt. 27959, William Machray, D.C.M., 12th (Service) Bn. The Royal Scots (Lothian Regt.): elder *s.* of William Machray, of Clyne, Newmachar, Farmer, by his wife Christina, *dau.* of George Anderson: *b.* Port Elphinstone, Inverurie, co. Aberdeen, 7 April 1895: *educ.* Gordon College, Aberdeen: Occupation – Accountant; Messrs Mitchell & Watt, Aberdeen: enlisted Royal Scots, 22 January 1916: served with the Expeditionary Force in France from June 1916: took part in the operations at Arras, April 1917. Killed in action at Ypres, nr. Strombeke, 12 October following. Awarded the D.C.M. for 'distinguished conduct in the field.' An officer wrote, "He was an N.C.O. we could depend on at all times for the fulfilment of his duties and orders, absolutely to the letter, in short. He was a fine specimen of a man and a good soldier. Men such as he can little be spared at such a time as the present.": Age 22. *unm.*

(XIV.F.19) 2nd Lieut. Francis DeBell, 'C' Coy., 4th (Hallamshire) Bn. The York & Lancaster Regt. (T.F.): *s.* of Francis De Bell, of 19, Rosedale Road, Sheffield, by his wife Emily: one of four Officers, and forty-two OR killed in the attack south-west of Passchendaele, 9 October 1917: Age 21. *unm.*

Of the four officers killed, two, Lieut. W.J.R.E. Poole and 2nd Lieut. R.W. Jackson, have no known grave. They are commemorated on the Tyne Cot Memorial (Panel 125); Lieut. E.J.W. Beynon is buried nearby (XIV.B.14).

(XIV.G.23) Pte. 33413, Maurice Smailes, 1/4th (Hallamshire) Bn. The York & Lancaster Regt. (T.F.): formerly no.45610, Yorkshire Regt.: *s.* of George Bean Smailes, of Rectory Street, Nunnington, co. York, by his wife Emma: and yr. brother to Pte. 202032, W. Smailes, 4th Yorkshire Regt., killed in action 20 September 1917: *b.* Nunnington, afsd.: enlisted Richmond. Killed in action, 9 October 1917: Age 19.

His brother has no known grave; he is commemorated on the Arras Memorial (Bay 5).

(XV.C.3) Sergt. 160075, David Donaldson, 31st Bn. Canadian Infantry (Alberta Regt.), C.E.F.: *s.* of James Melvin Donaldson, Works Manager (ret'd.); of 'Allandale', Seafield Street, Elgin, by his wife Mary Jane, *dau.* of John Lee: *husb.* to Henrietta Donaldson (7, Melville Gardens, Montrose, Scotland); and brother to Gnr. 316884, W.D. Donaldson, C.F.A. (late of 16, Spencer Street, Toronto), killed in action 22 August 1917, at Lens: *b.* Edinburgh, 5 September 1891: *educ.* George Heriot's School: removed to Oregon, U.S.A. with his brothers (March 1911); subsequently removed to Canada, settled in Alberta: found employ with Canadian Pacific Railway Service; became Deputy Buyer, Commissary Department: member of 103rd Rifles (Militia), volunteered and enlisted 82nd (Overseas) Bn. Canadian Infantry, Calgary, 16 September 1915; proceeded to England transf'd. 31st Battn., 1916: served with the Expeditionary Force in France and Flanders from October following and took part in much fighting: wounded at Vimy Ridge, May 1917, Sergt. Donaldson was killed in action at Passchendaele, 6 November following. Buried where he fell: Age 26.

His brother William is buried in Fosse No.10 Communal Cemetery Extension (II.C.34).

(XV.F.3) Pte. 43338, Albert Henry Clark, 9th (Service) Bn. The Princess Victoria's (Royal Irish Fusiliers): formerly no.353178, London Regt.: *s.* of Harriet Clark (57, Anthony Street, Commercial Road, London): enlisted Stepney, London: killed in action, 16 August 1917, before Langemarck: Age 20. *unm.*

What Nobler Offering Could He Give Than Yield His Life For Yours And Mine

(XVI.A.3) Pte. 133253, Frank Leslie, 85th Bn. (Nova Scotia Highlanders) Canadian Infantry, C.E.F.: late of Colvill Cottages, Dishland Street, Arbroath, Scotland: *s.* of James C. Leslie, of 24, Newton Avenue, Lynn, Massachusetts, and Isabella Buick, his wife: and brother to Lieut. G.B. Leslie, 73rd Canadian Infantry (surv'd.): *b.* Arbroath, co. Forfar, 6 August 1893: *educ.* Arbroath High School: formerly machinist, General Electric Co., Lynn; was, at enlistment, Hospital Attendant, Montreal: joined 73rd Royal Highlanders, Montreal, 3 January 1916; departed Canada, 1 April: trained Bramshott Camp, England (from 9 April): served with the Expeditionary Force in France from 13 August 1916; took part in several engagements, Ypres, Somme, and Vimy Ridge (9-13 April 1917) where 73rd Battn. suffered such heavy losses that the survivors were absorbed into other units (19 April). One of seven men transfd. 85th Bn. attd. 12th Inf. Bde., as Runner, Pte. Leslie was killed in action carrying out that work on 31 October 1917, before Passchendaele. His Officer said, "He performed his duties fearlessly and well, as became a soldier.": Age 24.

(XVI.B.2) Pte. 26874, Dafydd Griffith, 7th (Service) Bn. The King's (Shropshire Light Infantry): *s.* of David Griffith, of 2, Penybont, Rhydymain, Dolgelley, co. Merioneth, by his wife Elizabeth: and elder brother to Pte. 60263, R.W. Griffith, 9th Welsh Regt. Killed in action, 20 December 1917, aged 20 years: *b.* Dolgelley: enlisted Denbigh. Killed in action, 26 September 1917: Age 27.

Cu Iawn Fuost Gennym Ni

Translation: He Was Very Dear To Us

His brother Robert has no known grave; he is commemorated on the Thiepval Memorial.

(XVI.E.4) Pte. Charles Edward Raymond, 40th Bn. Australian Infantry, A.I.F.: *s.* of the late Anthony D. Raymond, of Burnie, Tasmania: *b.* Ulverstone, Tasmania, March 1894: religion – Presbyterian: Occupation – Motor Mechanic: volunteered Ulverstone, 27 September 1916; enlisted Hobart, 3 October: 5'9" tall, blue eyes, reddish hair: posted 22nd Rfts., 12th Battn., Claremount, 19 October: departed Melbourne (transf'd. 5th Rfts., 40th Battn.), A38 'Ulysses,' 25 October: served with the Expeditionary

Force in France from 4 May 1917: wounded 10 May (G.S.W. Foot); rejoined his unit on the 30th of that month: wounded 7 June (G.S.W. Shoulder, Chest, Face, Finger), returned to duty 26 August; reported missing believed killed in action, 5 October 1917: Age 23. GRU Report, Passchendaele 51.220E records remains exhumed and re-interred May 1921. He left a wife, Grace Beatrice Raymond (73, Cimetiere Street, Launceston, Tasmania), who although she has since (1922) re-married – now Mrs G.B. Turner, Longford, Tasmania – requests all correspondence continue to be addressed for her attention.

Edwin Grant and Bella Duncan had known each other virtually all their lives, long before they travelled to Canada and certainly long before they married. Their fathers had known each other years before Edwin and Bella were even thought about. An examination of the 1881 records of ships in port at Monkwearmouth, Sunderland reveals a Mate Seaman John Grant, of Aberdeen, age thirty-two, aboard the merchant ship 'Alexandra;' and nineteen year old Ordinary Seaman Alexander Duncan serving on the 'Olive Leaf.'

In Vancouver, British Columbia, Edwin found employment as a steelworker and the lives of Bella and his became intertwined with the Elligott family. John Elligott, a stonemason, and Edwin regularly crossed paths as neighbours and tradesmen and so it came as no surprise when, in February 1916, they joined up together. Their relationship was destined to take a surprising twist following Edwin's death at Passchendaele.

John Elligott first knew of Edwin's death on the battlefield near Ypres when, on moving up to the front, he met Edwin's brother James coming down from the battlefield and was told that Edwin had been killed. It would be another five weeks before Bella received official notification of his death from the Canadian Records Department.

After the war, the relationship between the Elligotts and the Grants remained as firm as before and, with skilled workmen being at a premium, men like John Elligott were ensured constant employment. He worked on some of Vancouver's landmark buildings, including the Hotel Vancouver and the Marine Building, and had a home there which, prior to the war, the Grants had briefly rented. Their daughter Lillian was born there. And, when the Elligotts returned, their son Joe – destined to become Lillian's future husband – was born there too.

In 1924 Bella married James Grant, Edwin's brother; they moved in with Bella's sisters on Dundas Street, North Vancouver; Joe Elligott married Lillian and they lived opposite (in a house built by Joe) and had two sons, called Alan and James.

Predeceased by her two husbands and son-in-law, Bella passed away in 1974, her daughter Lillian was admitted to a rest home in 2006. Her grandson James and his wife Marge are now the keepers of the story of the relationship between the Grants and the Elligotts. Indeed, relics of family history are evident in every corner of their North Vancouver home. Next to a portrait picture of Bella and Lillian (then a little girl, holding a doll that Edwin had sent her from Europe during his service) pride of place is given to a large oval-framed photograph of Edwin in his uniform. In a bedroom near the front room, full of family antiques and reminders of Lillian's eighty-one years in the family home on Dundas Street, stands an elegantly decorated mirror and hairbrush that belonged to Bella. And, in the kitchen, a handmade stained glass window glows with red poppies. It was made by Lillian's husband Joe.

(XVI.G.7) Pte. 703562, Edwin Grant, 'B' Coy., 47th Bn. Canadian Infantry (Western Ontario Regt.), C.E.F.: *s.* of John Grant, Harbour Commissioner, of Aberdeen, Scotland, by his wife Mary: *b.* 10 December 1884: religion – Presbyterian: sometime merchant sailor; lately steel worker: 5'5¼" tall, fair complexion, blue eyes, light brown hair: butterfly and bird tattoos on his left arm, butterfly and geisha girl on his right arm: enlisted Valcartier, 9 February 1916; posted 102nd Battn. Killed in action, 26–28 October 1917: Age 33. He *m.* First Presbyterian Church, Vancouver, 26 December 1914; Bella, *dau.* of Alexander Duncan, by his wife Isabella, *née* Proctor, and had a *dau.* Lillian, *b.* 16 August 1915.

Would Some Thoughtful Hand In This Distant Land Please Scatter Some Flowers For Me

Ruth Ross found the above inscription quite by chance, but the plea haunted her. The former college lecturer from Surrey, England, happened upon Pte. Grant's grave marker while conducting a war literature tour in Belgium (2000). "I could see there was something written on it and when I moved the shrub there was this lovely piece of verse and I could hear this woman's voice, surely his wife." Ms. Ross heeded the plea of the nameless woman, leaving a poppy cross on the grave each November for the past five years. But she always wondered who had spoken to her so powerfully; the words on his headstone "knocked me sideways…I thought: who is this woman who is saying to me, 'I'll never stand at my husband's grave where you are. But if you are there, would you please scatter some flowers for me?'"

In response to a letter to *The Vancouver Sun,* in the hope that Edwin Grant's family could be found, Ross discovered much of the above account and the identity of the woman's voice; Edwin's wife, Bella.

(XVI.J.7) Pte. 11062, Arthur Thomas Llewell, 2nd Bn. Canterbury Regt., N.Z.E.F.: *s.* of the late Robert Llewell, of Warkworth, Auckland: and brother to Tpr. 13/925, A.G. Llewell, Auckland Mounted Rifles (surv'd.); and Pte. 12/3083, J. Llewell, 1st Auckland Regt., killed in action 30 September 1916: Occupation – Labourer: departed Wellington, 1 May 1916. Killed in action 12 October 1917, at Broodseinde.

His brother James has no known grave; he is commemorated on the Caterpillar Valley (New Zealand) Memorial.

(XVII.A.12) Pte. 3/3027, Alexander Kerr, No.4 Field Ambulance, New Zealand Army Medical Corps, N.Z.E.F.: *s.* of William Laing Kerr, of 117, Venus Street, Georgetown, Invercargill, by his marriage to the late Susannah: and brother to Pte. 23564, G.J. Kerr, Otago Regt., killed in action 27 September 1916, aged 23. Killed in action, 12 October 1917.

His brother Gilbert has no known grave; he is commemorated on the Caterpillar Valley (New Zealand) Memorial, Somme.

(XVII.H.1) Pte. 278044, Walter Deeprose, 2nd Bn. (93rd Foot) The Princess Louise's (Argyll & Sutherland Highlanders): *s.* of William Deeprose, of 624, Duke Street, Dennistoun, Glasgow, co. Lanark, by his wife Elizabeth, *née* Scott: and brother to Pte. 1934, W. Deeprose, 15th Australian Infantry, killed in action 8 August 1915, at Gallipoli: *b.* Dennistoun, *c.*1898: enlisted Glasgow. Killed in action 20 November 1917: Age 19.

His brother William has no known grave; he is commemorated on the Lone Pine Memorial (46).

(XIX.D.1) Pte. 2917, John Nicholas Crowley, 34th Bn. Australian Infantry, A.I.F.: *s.* of Michael Crowley, of Temora, New South Wales, by his wife Bridget: *b.* Wollongong, New South Wales, 1865: Occupation – Editor; *The Wyalong Star,* West Wyalong: served with the Expeditionary Force. Killed in action by machine gun fire at Passchendaele, 12 October 1917: Age 52. During an emotional speech prior to his enlistment he informed a crowd of local people he would rather "sleep the eternal sleep in the cold earth of France" than shirk his responsibilities. Following his brother Matthew and his sons Ossie and John, who had already enlisted, he lied about his age and joined up. Shortly thereafter his youngest son, Reg, who was only sixteen years of age, also lied about his age and enlisted. All five Crowley men saw fierce fighting during their service in the war: Pte. 839, Matthew N. Crowley, 13th Bn., died of wounds at Gallipoli on 6 May 1915; Pte. 2626A, Reginald B. Crowley, 34th Bn., was killed in action at Villers Bretonneux, France, on 4-5 April 1918 ; Ossie and John (Jnr.) both survived. During the action in which John was killed, his officer, Capt. C.S. Jeffries, won the Victoria Cross (XL.E.1).

Though Wounded In The Morning He Fought Till Evening When He Fell

His brother Matthew and son Reginald have no known grave; they are commemorated on the Lone Pine Memorial (Panel 37), and Villers Bretonneux Memorial respectively.

(XX.B.8) 2nd Lieut. Arthur George Amies, 1/5th Bn. The York & Lancaster Regt. (T.F.): eldest *s.* of Thomas James Amies, of Spring Bank, Pontefract, co. York, Clerk to the Pontefract Board of Guardians; by his wife Alice Georgina, *dau.* of Arthur Bance Ebbutt: *b.* Dewsbury, co. York, 25 March 1894: *educ.* King's Grammar School, Pontefract, from whence (after matriculating First Class) he entered the offices of his uncle, Clerk to the Epsom Board of Guardians: apptd. Staff; Bedwelty Board of Guardians, two years later; subsequently obtained appointment on Staff; Tadcaster Union Offices: joined Bedfordshire Yeomanry, Pte., January 1915: served with the Expeditionary Force in France and Flanders from August following until July 1916 when, being injured by a horse, he returned to England; septicaemia (blood poisoning) being feared: returned to France, 21 August following: sent home February 1917, to train for a commission; gazetted 2nd Lieut., York and Lancaster Regt., 14 July: joined his battalion in France, 9 August 1917. Killed in action on the north-east of Ypres, 9 October following. Buried on the battlefield: Age 23. Lieut.Col. H.S. Kaye wrote, "He had not been with us very long, but we soon found out what a splendid fellow he was, a keen soldier and full of courage. His loss is deplored by all ranks." and Major-Gen. E.M. Perceval (then Commanding 49th Division), "It may be some comfort to you to know that your husband's fine qualities were appreciated, and that his death is much regretted. Although he had only recently joined his battalion, still he had gained a good reputation as a very gallant officer and a very promising one in every way. I feel that his death means a great loss to his battalion." He *m.* Tadcaster Parish Church, 2 August 1917; Annie (B.A.), *dau.* of the late Charles Tunningley, of Ouston Road, Tadcaster.

Ever Remembered With Boundless Love, Reverence And Regret

(XX.B.17) Pte. G/2357, William Leigh Bernard, 2nd Bn. (77th Foot) The Duke of Cambridge's Own (Middlesex Regt.): *s.* of Dr. Charles Bernard, of Harrington Gardens, Skegness, co. Lincoln, by his wife Annie Elizabeth, *dau.* of William Baines Rainey, M.R.C.S. and Physician: and brother to Pte. L/12835, H. Bernard, 2nd Middlesex Regt., killed in action 8 March 1918: and great-grandson to the late Thomas Bernard, M.P., and Lady Catherine Bernard, of Castle Bernard, Co. Carlow: enlisted Lambeth, co. Surrey: served with the Expeditionary Force in France and Flanders, and was killed in action at Ypres 16 August 1917.

His brother Hilton is buried in Hooge Crater Cemetery (XVII.J.5).

For nearly eighty years, the headstone of Sergt. Lewis McGee, 40th (Tasmanian) Battn., killed in action on 12 October 1917, incorrectly recorded he had died a day later. The Australian Official Historian, C.E.W. Bean recorded in his diary, "Sergt. McGee, B Company. During the advance, finding a machine-gun firing over a concrete structure and holding up the attack, walked straight up to the pillbox and shot the machine gunner through the head with his revolver. McGee was on every wiring party B Company ever put out at Armentieres from the very start. He was in every stunt. He went after and settled another machine-gun by organising a small bombing party and getting the gun. These machine-guns were holding up the advance. He was recommended for VC and commission. On October 12 he was with Lieut. Garrard, OC B Company, near Augustine Wood when machine-guns started firing at them, the whole of headquarters, all signallers and most of the runners, except Garrard, who was left alone. It was there that McGee, acting Company Sergeant Major, was shot through the head and killed."

In 1998 a relative of McGee, drawing on the account by Bean and others, brought the discrepancy to the notice of the C.W.G.C. The headstone was altered accordingly.

(XX.D.1) Sergt. 456, Lewis McGee, V.C., 'B' Coy., 40th Bn. Australian Infantry, A.I.F.: *yst.* s. of John McGee, of Avoca, Tasmania, by his late wife Mary, *née* Green (*d.*1895): *b.* Campbell Town, Tasmania, 13 May 1888: Occupation – Engine Driver, Tasmanian Railway Dept.: enlisted A.I.F., 1 March 1916: appointed L/Corpl. 22 May: departed Australia, HMAT 'Berrima,' 1 July 1916: served in the European War in France from 24 November 1916: promoted Corpl. 4 December 1916; Sergt. 12 January 1917: took part in a number of raids and small-scale operations: took part in the Battle of Messines, and was killed in action at Passchendaele, 12 October 1917: Age 29. In a letter to his widow, an officer said, "By his death we have lost a man we could ill afford to lose and one whom it will be most difficult to replace. It is with the greatest regret that I write and offer to you our deepest sympathy to the sad loss sustained by you in the death of your husband. He and I came to France together. I cannot too highly speak of him as a soldier and also of the excellent example he always set the men of cheerfulness, courage and devotion to duty. He was recognised throughout the battalion as one of the bravest men we had, being absolutely indifferent to danger." Posthumously awarded the Victoria Cross ('*London Gazette*,' 26 November 1917) "For most conspicuous bravery (Broodseinde, 4 October 1917). When in the advance to the final objective, Sergt. McGee led his platoon with great dash and bravery, though strongly opposed and under heavy shell fire.

His platoon was suffering severely and the advance of the company was stopped by machine-gun fire from a 'pill-box' post. Single-handed, Sergt. McGee rushed the post armed only with a revolver. He shot some of the crew, and captured the rest, and thus enabled the advance to proceed. He reorganized the remnants of his platoon, and was foremost in the remainder of the advance, and during consolidation of the position he did splendid work. This non-commissioned officer's coolness and bravery were conspicuous, and contributed largely to the success of the company's operations. Sergt. McGee was subsequently killed in action." He *m*. 15 November 1914; Eileen Rose Bailey, and had a *dau*. Natasha, *b*. 1915.

(XXI.G.23) Sergt. 35017, Stanley Wilberforce Davis, 11th (Service) Bn. The Border Regt.: *yst. s*. of James Bull Davis, of 134, Cowesley Street, Moss Side, Manchester, formerly resident at 138, Manley Road, by his wife Sarah Jane, *dau*. of F. Burcombe: *b*. Bradford-on-Avon, co. Wilts, 21 December 1889: *educ*. Princess Road School, Manchester: employee Messrs J.F. & H. Roberts: enlisted King's (Liverpool) Regt., 22 February 1916, being rapidly promoted Sergt.: served with the Expeditionary Force in France and Flanders from July 1917, and was killed in action at Passchendaele Ridge on the night of 25 November 1917 when, during a relief near Bellevue Spur, undue noise and commotion drew down a heavy German bombardment on the battalion resulting in the death of Sergt. Davis and eighteen other men. His Coy. Commander wrote, "He joined my company in July last, and was with us from then until his death in action. At all times he served most faithfully, and was liked by all in the company – officers, N.C.O's and men. As one of my senior non-commissioned officers, I had ample opportunity of observing his many good qualities, and these, combined with his capabilities, enabled me to trust him with many important things. I had recommended him to the Commanding Officer for a commission, and had he been spared I should have had the pleasure of addressing him as a brother officer.": Age 28. *unm*. See account re. L/Corpl. J. Nixon, Tyne Cot Cemetery (XXXVIII.H.6).

(XXII.G.14) Pte. 673, Arthur Wallace Turnour, 'B' Coy., 38th Bn. Australian Infantry, A.I.F.: *s*. of Keppel Arthur Turnour, of Black Rock, South Australia, by his wife Margaret A.: and brother to Lieut. J.E. Turnour, 59th Australian Infantry, died of wounds 28 September 1917, at Poperinghe; Pte. V/60176, D. Turnour (surv'd.) Pte. 5099, J.O. Turnour (severely wounded, lost leg, surv'd.); and Pte. 26626, K.E. Turnour (surv'd.): *b*. Toorak, Victoria: enlisted Bendigo. Killed in action, 13 October 1917, at Passchendaele. Pte. 513, Bridgman said, "... A.W. Turnour ... He went over at Passchendaele in October. I did not see him again after we started. We could not get onto the ridge and had to fall back. Three days later Turnour was found out in front by stretcher-bearers, half buried in a shell hole, and badly wounded by a shell in the stomach. The stretcher-bearers told me that it was probably because he was buried in mud that he had kept alive. He died before they got him to the dressing station, and I do not know if he was buried there or further back.".

Although his parents requested Arthur and his brother be buried together, the request was denied; John is buried in Lijssenthoek Military Cemetery (XXIV.B.8).

(XXIII.B.4) Pte. 878, James McMillan, 42nd Bn. Australian Infantry, 3rd Australian Division, 11th Infantry Bde., A.I.F.: eldest *s*. of Donald McMillan, Railway worker; formerly of 1, Acre Street Place, Nairn, now residing at 4, Portland Terrace, Nairn, by his wife Elspat, *dau*. of the late James Mackintosh Clune, of Letham: *b*. Caradale Kintyre, co. Argyle, 7 December 1887: *educ*. Public School, Nairn: some time member of the Volunteer Force, joined 4th Battn. Cameron Highlanders on the formation of that unit: went to Australia, January 1914, and settled at Inglewood, Queensland, where he worked in the Government Saw Mill: joined Australian Infantry, 6 January 1916: served with the Expeditionary Force in France and Flanders from 22 December following, and was killed in action at Ypres 4 October 1917. Buried at Zonnebeke. His Commanding Officer wrote, "Your son was a soldier of the finest type, on whom the greatest reliance was placed by officers and comrades. In the discharge of his duties he was alert and diligent, and in all ways his conduct was exemplary.": Age 29. *unm*.

Dearly Loved And Sadly Missed He Gave His Life For His Country

(XXIV.B.5) Sergt. 282802, Patrick Kearon, 2/7th Bn. The Lancashire Fusiliers (T.F.): 3rd *s*. of John Joseph Kearon, of Arklow, Co. Wicklow, by his wife Ellen, *dau*. of Thomas O'Brien: *b*. Dublin,

16 November 1878: enlisted 4th King's Own (Royal Lancaster Regt.) 31 May 1897: served in the South African War 1900-1902 (Queen's Medal with five clasps): subsequently employed by Manchester Ship Canal Coy. Shortly after the outbreak of the European War, he rejoined the Army as Pte., Lancashire Fusiliers (14 December 1914), and was apptd. Sergt. April 1915: served with the Expeditionary Force in France from February 1917, and was killed in action during the fighting on the Passchendaele Ridge, on or about 10 October, following. Capt. Turner, Commanding Officer of his Company, wrote, "He was magnificent, and died a noble death, I miss him very much, and so do all the company...He was a gallant soldier, and as such he died, leading his men in a great and glorious battle and serving his country.": Age 38. He *m.* 12 May 1903; Elizabeth Barry (*née* Kearon: since re-married, formerly of 25, St. James's Street, Trafford Road, Salford, co. Lancaster), *dau.* of Joseph Jones, and had six children – Elizabeth, *b.* 2 June 1905; Kathleen, *b.* 24 January 1908; Joseph Patrick, *b.* 10 August 1909; Ellen, *b.* 2 June 1911; Mary, *b.* 31 May 1913; Amy, *b.* 21 October 1915.

Oh Jesus Open Wide Thy Heart And Let Him Rest Therein

(XXV.F.24) Spr. 8593, Martin Flatley, 1st Field Coy., Australian Engineers, A.I.F.: brother to George Flatley, Esq., of Inverell, New South Wales: *b.* Batley, co. York, England, May 1890: was a Chainman: joined A.I.F. 1 February 1916, posted Dvr., 18th Rfts., 1st Field Coy., Engineers, Moore Park, 25 April: served with the Expeditionary Force in France from December 1916; apptd. Spr. 22 April 1917, and was killed in action at approximately 10 a.m., 4 October 1917, while taking shelter in a shell crater between first and second objectives: Age 27. *unm.* Memorial cross erected Belgian Battery Corner Cemetery. Correspondence to be directed c/o Messrs Millars Coffee Palace, Elizabeth Street, Sydney, New South Wales.

(XXVI.B.7) Pte. 44793, Charles Hebdon, 2/9th Bn. The Manchester Regt. (T.F.): formerly no.27333, Durham Light Infantry: *s.* of Thorpe Hebdon, of 41, Victoria Terrace, Catchgate, Annfield Plain, Co. Durham, by his wife Mary: and elder brother to Pte. 27023, N. Hebdon, 10th Durham Light Infantry, killed in action 16 September 1916, at the Somme: enlisted Stanley, Durham: killed in action 9 October 1917: Age 22. *unm.*

Rest In Peace

His brother Norman has no known grave; he is commemorated on the Thiepval Memorial.

(XXVI.H.23) Pte. 23885, George Albert Sharratt, 2nd Bn. (11th Foot) The Devonshire Regt.: *s.* of Annie Agnes Sharratt (8, Court Two House, New Buildings, Coventry): enlisted Coventry, co. Warwick: killed in action 31 July 1917: Age 22.

Till The Day Breaks And The Shadows Flee Away

(XXVIII.B.19) Lieut. Francis Leonard Hunter Jackson, R.N.V.R., Howe Bn., 63rd (Royal Naval) Divn.: eldest *s.* of the late Charles John Jackson, solicitor, by his wife Agnes Mary (Beaureper, Ilkeston), *dau.* of John Hunter: *b.* Ilkeston, co. Derby, 29 September 1891: *educ.* Worksop College: Occupation – Solicitor; having passed his Solicitor's examination with Honours, receiving the Nottingham Incorporated Law Society's prize: apptd. Sub.Lieut., R.N.V.R., May 1915: promoted Lieut., June 1917: served with the Mediterranean Expeditionary Force at Gallipoli, where he saw considerable service: subsequently sent to France; served there with the Expeditionary Force from May – September 1916 and from May – October 1917, and was killed in action at Passchendaele Ridge, 26 October 1917. Buried nr. St. Julien. The Chaplain wrote, "Wounded in the arm during the night of 25 October, he still carried on, and proceeded in front of his men to see how things were faring. Finding that his steel helmet was interfering with the working of his compass he discarded it altogether, and so fell a victim to a sniper, who shot him in the head...We can ill afford the loss of such a capable officer as your son, so quiet, so bright, so gentlemanly, so well-endowed mentally, and so courageous. He was beloved by officers and men alike.": Age 26. *unm.*

(XXVIII.D.13) Gnr. 168499, Wilfred Tetbutt, 'D' Bty., 23rd Bde., Royal Field Artillery: *yst. s.* of Silas Tetbutt, of Polebrook, nr. Oundle, builder, by his wife Emma, *dau.* of James Lox: *b.* Polebrook, co.

Northampton, 1 October 1888: *educ.* there: Occupation – Carter and Builder: enlisted 6 September 1916: served with the Expeditionary Force in France and Flanders from January 1917, and was killed in action 12 October following. Buried nr. Ypres: Age 29. His Commanding Officer wrote, "He was one of the finest gunners in the brigade, and always cheerful and willing." He *m.* Oundle, co. Northampton, 4 April 1912; Ada Maud ('Lyndhurst,' Polebrook), *dau.* of Edin Morlan, and had two children, Leslie, *b.* 21 March 1913 and Denis, *b.* 4 November 1914. (*IWGC record Tebbutt, 13 October, age 30*).

Jesus Touched Him And He Slept

(XXVII.H.24) L/Corpl. 30349, Sydney Edward Carley, 3rd Bn. Wellington Regt., N.Z.E.F.: *s.* of Charles Silver Carley, of Post Office, Cardiff, Stratford, Taranaki, by his wife Mary: and brother to Rfn. 26/91, C. Carley, N.Z. Rifle Brigade (surv'd.); Rfn. 30347, T. Carley, N.Z. Rifle Brigade (surv'd.); and Tpr. 11/451, H.J. Carley, Wellington Mounted Rifles, killed in action 27 August 1915, at Gallipoli: was a farmer: departed Wellington, HMNZT 71 'Port Lyttelton' 7 December 1916. Killed in action 4 October 1917: Age 21. *unm.*

His brother Henry has no known grave; he is commemorated on the Hill 60 (New Zealand) Memorial.

(XXVIII.G.17) Corpl. 24323, Norman Ashton, 16th (Waikato) Platoon, 2nd Auckland Infantry Bn., N.Z.E.F.: *s.* of Thomas Atherton Ashton, of Mount Albert, Auckland, New Zealand, by his wife Elizabeth Eleanor, *dau.* of Thomas Pearson, of Pendleton, Manchester: *b.* Pendleton, 12 June 1881: *educ.* Point Chevalier Public School, and Prince Albert College, Auckland: Occupation – Indent Agent: joined 17th Rfts., 4 April 1916: departed for England 23 September following: served with the Expeditionary Force in France and Flanders from 21 December 1916, and was killed in action at Passchendaele 4 October 1917. Buried at the foot of the ridge: Age 36. He *m.* Mount Albert Methodist Church, Auckland, 17 November 1915; Grace Florence Baker, *née* Ashton, since re-married, of Belmont Road, Mount Albert, Auckland, *dau.* of Samuel Edward Shrimpton, of Streatham, London, S.W., and had a son, Desmond Norman, *b.* 5 October 1916.

(XXIX.C.4) Corpl. 33173, James Frederick Bourhill, 2nd Bn. (11th Foot) The Devonshire Regt.: *s.* of David Bourhill, of 'Fairlight,' Sherwell Lane, Chelston, Torquay, co. Devon, by his wife Kate: and elder brother to Cook's Mate M/12064, A.G. Bourhill, H.M.S. 'Defence,' R.N., killed in action 31 May 1916, at the Battle of Jutland: *b.* Edmonton, London, N., 1895: killed in action, 31 July 1917: Age 21. *unm.* Remembered on Cockington (St. George & St. Mary's) Church Roll of Honour.

His brother Albert has no known grave but the sea; he is commemorated on the Plymouth Naval Memorial (17).

(XXIX.D.15) L/Corpl. 24/805, John Irving, 2nd Bn. 3rd New Zealand Rifle Brigade, N.Z.E.F.: *s.* of Edward Augustus, of 260, Remuera Rd., Remuera, Auckland, by his wife Jane: and elder brother to Rfn. 23388, A. Irving, 3rd Bn. 3rd New Zealand Rifle Brigade, who fell 7 June 1917: *b.* Ruapekapeka, *c.*1889: killed in action 12 October 1917: Age 28. *unm.*

His brother Augustus is buried in Messines Ridge British Cemetery (I.D.27).

(XXIX.D.20) Rfn. 45671, Percy Sylvester Davies, 'C' Coy., 2nd Bn. 3rd New Zealand Rifle Brigade, N.Z.E.F.: *s.* of George Davies, of 612, Queen Street, West Hastings, Hawkes Bay, by his wife Annie Jane: *b.* Christchurch, 16 May 1889: Occupation – Farmer: enlisted 17 January 1917, apptd. Corpl., 'H' Coy., 25th Rfts.: embarked Wellington, HMNZT. 84 'Turakina', 26 April 1917: disembarked Devonport, 20 July following, reverted to L/Corpl., posted 'D' Coy., 5th (Reserve) Bn., and proceeded to Sling Camp for training: reverted to Pte., 5 September 1917, and proceeded to France: served with the Expeditionary Force there and in Flanders, joining his battn. in the field on the 16th of that month, and was killed in action 12 October 1917. Reported buried D.3. Central 40.45, 10 yds. from Kronprinz Farm, by 2nd Corps Burial Officer. Body exhumed and re-interred; Tyne Cot Cemetery, G.R.U. Report 20 August 1920: Age 28. *unm.*

(XXIX.E.17) Pte. 690466, David Spencer Churches, 116th Bn. Canadian Infantry (Central Ontario Regt.), C.E.F.: *s.* of the late William Churches, of 86, Kincade Avenue, Hamilton, Ontario, by his wife Gertrude (172, Cannon Street East, Hamilton): *b.* St. Catherine's, Ontario, 18 December 1894:

Occupation – Saw Maker: enlisted Hamilton, 9 March 1916; posted 173rd Highlanders Battn., 12 April. Killed in action, 28 October 1917; Bellevue Spur: Age 22. *unm.* (*IWGC record age 21*)

(XXXI.B.19) Pte. 37784, Bernard Cantrell Davis, 1st Bn. Canterbury Regt., N.Z.E.F.: *s.* of Rev. Henry John Davis, of The Vicarage, Hampden, North Otago, New Zealand, and the late Sarah Harriett Davis, his wife: and half-brother to Sergt. 8/2513, E.N. Davis, 1st Otago Regt., killed in action 5 April 1918: Occupation – Clerk: departed Wellington, HMNZT 'Mokoia;' L/Sergt., 22nd Rfts., 'F' Coy., 13 February 1917. Killed in action, 2 October 1917: Age 35. Erected by the residents of Hampden Borough and Moeraki 'To The Sacred Memory Of The Soldiers Who Made The Supreme Sacrifice In The World's Great War 1914-1918;' B.C. and E.N. Davis are recorded on the Hampden War Memorial, Waitaki, Otago.

His half-brother Eric is buried in Auchonvillers Military Cemetery (II.L.27).

(XXXI.C.14) Pte. 26255, John Murray Eaglesome, 2nd Bn. Canterbury Regt., N.Z.E.F.: *s.* of William Eaglesome, of Simeon Street, Spreydon, Christchurch, by his wife Ellen: and brother to Rfn. 36434, C.A. Eaglesome, N.Z. Rifle Brigade (surv'd); and Dvr. 7/1549, R.J. Eaglesome, N.Z. Field Artillery, who died 27 May 1918 of disease: *b.* Prebbleton, Canterbury: religion – Presbyterian: Occupation – Engine Driver: enlisted 30 May 1916: 5'6" tall, pale complexioned, brown hair, blue eyes: embarked Wellington, 25 September following, HMNZT 65 'Pakeha;' 17th Rfts., 'C' Coy., Canterbury Regt.: disembarked Devonport, 18 November: trained Sling Camp, 18 November – 9 December, on which latter date he proceeded to France: joined 2nd Canterbury Regt. in the field 7 January 1917, posted 13 Coy.: hospitalised (sick) 9 March; discharged to duty after one week: killed in action 12 October 1917: Age 26. He leaves a wife, Grace May Eaglesome (20, Curletts Road, Riccarton, Christchurch), late of Church Street, Rangiora. Buried D.9.d.8.8., Bellevue Spur, Passchendaele, by Rev. J.A. Lush, attd. 2nd Canterbury Regt. Body exhumed by G.R.U. and re-interred Tyne Cot Cemetery, 13 November 1920.

His brother Robert is buried in Aldershot Military Cemetery (AA.NZ2)

(XXXI.D.19) Rfn. 26660, John McKechnie, 4th Bn. 3rd New Zealand Rifle Brigade, N.Z.E.F.: *s.* of James McKechnie, of Wellesley Bakery, Arthur Street, Wellesley, Invercargill, and Jean Hamilton, *née* Dawson, his wife: and brother to Pte. 8/1738, H. McKechnie, 1st Otago Regt., killed in action 15 August 1918: Occupation – Slaughter-Man: departed Wellington 23 September 1916. Killed in action, 12 October 1917: Age 44.

His brother Herbert has no known grave; he is commemorated on the Grevillers (New Zealand) Memorial.

(XXXI.E.4) Pte. 202965, George Morgan, 1/5th Bn. The Prince of Wales's Own (West Yorkshire Regt.), (T.F.): *yst. s.* of the late Charles Morgan, by his wife Hannah, *dau.* of Samuel Nichols: *b.* Hoyle Mill, co. York, 1885: *educ.* there: Occupation – Tradesman: enlisted 1 March 1916: served with the Expeditionary Force in France and Flanders from June following, and was killed in action at Passchendaele Ridge, 9 October 1917. *unm.*

(XXXI.E.15) Pte. 39279, Gordon Murray Stewart McDonald, 3rd Bn. Otago Regt., N.Z.E.F.: *s.* of the late Coll McDonald, of McMillan Street, Roslyn, by his wife Janet (Balmacewan Road, Maori Hill, Dunedin): and *yr.* brother to Tpr. 9/1196, J. McDonald, Otago Mounted Rifles, killed in action 11 January 1918: *b.* Kilmog, Otago, 10 October 1895: *educ.* Evansdales, Merton; and George Street School: Occupation – Labourer: served eight months with Coastal Defence: proceeded overseas 19 January 1917. Killed in action, 4 October 1917, at Bellevue: Age 21. *unm.*

His brother James is buried in Belgian Battery Corner Cemetery (II.G.14).

(XXXII.E.9) Lieut. Herbert Cheetham, 1/6th Bn. The Prince of Wales's Own (West Yorkshire Regt.), (T.F.) attd. 146th Trench Mortar Bty.: *s.* of Arthur Cheetham, of 20, Roundhay Grove, Harehills, Leeds, Schoolmaster, by his wife Margaret Alice, *dau.* of the late John Case, of Southport: *b.* Leeds, 15 April 1887: *educ.* Harehills Grammar School, where he obtained a 100 guineas' scholarship to Leeds Grammar School and was, for five years, a member of the O.T.C.: joined University O.T.C., August 1915: obtained a commission 2nd Lieut., 6 January 1916; promoted Lieut., 1 June following: served with the Expeditionary Force in France and Flanders from 2 September: took part in the operations at Thiepval: contracted trench fever 10 October 1916 but, on recovery, rejoined his regiment, and was killed in action at Calgary Grange, Passchendaele, 9 October 1917, while attending to a dying man of his own unit. Buried there. Major-General E.M. Percival, Comdg. 49th Divn., wrote, "He was a very good officer, and had gained the entire confidence of his men. He had done much excellent work, especially on patrol duty, when he displayed ability and initiative. His Battalion Commander reported very well on him, and considered him a keen and capable officer. He is much missed in his battalion," and his Captain, "It may be some consolation to think that he had displayed the greatest coolness throughout, and, as always, set a noble example of self-sacrifice and devotion to the men under him. He brought the unit up to a better state than I ever remember it to have been at any time. Not only was he energetic in his work, but deeply interested in the welfare of the men under him, an interest which brings its own reward. I do not remember the loss of an officer so keenly felt by his men." His servant also wrote, "It was early morning when the barrage started; there were no trenches, only shell-holes. The barrage was terrible, but Mr Cheetham did not allow this to prevent him from crawling from shell-hole to shell-hole with the rum ration. The men said he was a hero. This barrage continued more or less till about 4p.m., when it increased in intensity. He then ordered the Gun-Teams (Trench Mortar Battery) further back for safety, the guns having been previously lost. While the men were doing this, one of the men was hit by a large piece of shrapnel in the small of the back. Mr Cheetham and I did all we could for the poor fellow, but Mr C. would not leave until he was quite sure the man was dead. Just as we were leaving, your son was hit at the back of the head with a piece of shell. I did my best in bandaging, and then ran for help. Another officer prevented my return, as the barrage was still dreadful. Your lad was found the next morning lying dead on a stretcher.": Age 20. *unm.*

(XXXII.E.12) Corpl. 8/2956, Ralph Stanley Culling Jefferis, M.M., 2nd Bn. Wellington Regt. attd. 1st N.Z. Light Trench Mortar Bty., N.Z.E.F.: *s.* of Rowland Jefferis, of Torridge Street, Otiake, Oamaru, North Otago, by his wife Mary: and brother to Pte. 8/2957, R.G. Jefferis, Otago Regt.; died of typhoid 2 November 1915, en-route from New Zealand to Suez: *b.* Flag Swamp, North Otago, 2 February 1891: religion – Anglican: Occupation – Farmer: 5'8½" tall, dark hair and complexion, brown eyes: enlisted 12 June 1915: departed Wellington, 9 October 1915, Pte., 7th Rfts., Otago Regt.: served Suez, Egypt (from late November): subsequently proceeded to France, transf'd. Wellington Regt. Killed in action 4 October 1917, at Broodseinde: Age 26. *unm.* Awarded the Military Medal 'for acts of gallantry in the field.'

His brother Rowland has no known grave but the sea; he is commemorated on the Otago Provincial Memorial.

(XXXIII.A.9) Pte. 5147, James McLeod, 11th Bn. Australian Infantry, A.I.F.: *husb.* to Rebecca McLeod (Throssell Street, Collie, Western Australia); father to Margaret, Jean and James McLeod: *b.* Adelaide, June 1890: religion – Presbyterian: Occupation – Miner: joined A.I.F., Blackboy Hill, 10 February 1916; apptd. 16th Rfts., 11th Bn., Bunbury, 14 February: trained Egypt (from 24 April); proceeded to France, 29 May: joined 11th Bn. 29 July: invalided from Flers; hospitalised (coronary and sickness, mild) Rouen, 19 December, transf'd. England, 30 December; discharged to duty 29 January 1917: convalesced/retrained for three months in the south of England; returned to France with reinforcement draft, 9 May: rejoined 11th Bn. 20 May. Killed in action, 2 November 1917. Buried at Broodseinde: Age 37. Remains exhumed (GRU Report, Passchendaele 51/625.E), identified by identity disc, and reinterred September 1921.

(XXXIV.A.19) Pte. 32681, Thomas Lawson, 11th (Service) Bn. The Border Regt.: *s.* of James Lawson, of Carlisle, by his wife Martha: enlisted Carlisle: killed in action on the night of 25 November 1917 when, during a relief near Bellevue Spur, undue noise and commotion drew down a heavy German bombardment on the battalion resulting in the death of Pte. Lawson and eighteen other men. See account re. L/Corpl. J. Nixon (XXXVII.H.6).

Him That Cometh To Me I Will No Wise Cast Out

(XXXIV.B.7) Pte. 26784, Arthur Noel Brown, 2nd Bn. Auckland Regt., N.Z.E.F.: *s.* of Francis Hamilton Brown, of School House, Dawson Street, Takapuna, Hamilton, Waikato, by his wife Emily, *née* Beetham:

brother-in-law to Pte. 12/4142, J.T.M. Brewster, Auckland Regt. (surv'd.); and brother to Pte. 12/43, G.McP. Brown, Auckland Regt., killed in action 8 May 1915, at Gallipoli: *b.* 1897: *educ.* Auckland Grammar School: Occupation – Fruit Farmer: departed Wellington, 25 September 1916: killed in action 4 October 1917, at Broodseinde: Age 20. *unm.* His uncle, Gnr. 1814, G.A. Brewster, 4th N.Z.F.A., was killed in action 24 October 1942 (El Alamein War Cemetery, II.A.16).

His brother Geoffrey has no known grave; he is commemorated on the Twelve Tree Copse (New Zealand) Memorial.

(XXXIV.D.15) Sergt. 460881, George Matthew Pirie, 8th Bn. (Manitoba Regt.) Canadian Infantry, C.E.F.: *yst. s.* of the late George Pirie, of Fyvie, Mill Owner, by his wife Christina (Tirace, Waikato, New Zealand), *dau.* of James (& Ann) Matthew: *b.* Fyvie, co. Aberdeen, 18 September 1894: *educ.* Higher Grade School, there: went to Canada, March 1913, settled Winnipeg: Occupation – Engineer: volunteered for Foreign Service: joined Canadian Expeditionary Force, May 1915: served in France and Flanders from December following: wounded June 1916, and was killed in action at Passchendaele, 10 November 1917. Buried where he fell. The Chaplain wrote, "He was one of the best sergeants in the battalion, and esteemed by all," and comrades wrote saying that he was the life of the battalion, and did some valuable work, and showed a good example to all that were under him by the work he did the day he was killed: Age 23. *unm.* (*IWGC record XXXLV.D.15*)

(XXXIV.H.14) Brigadier-Gen. James Foster Riddell, Comdg. 1/1st Northumberland Infantry Bde.; late 2/5th Bn. Northumberland Fusiliers (T.F.): only *s.* of the late John Riddell (5th in descent from the Rev. Archibald Riddell, 3rd *s.* of Sir Walter Riddell, 2nd Bart. of Riddell, co. Roxburgh), by his first wife Jane, *dau.* of William Peppercorn: *b.* 17 October 1861: *educ.* Wellington College, Crowthorne, co. Berks, and R.M.C. Sandhurst: gazetted 2nd Lieut. 1 July 1881, Capt. 18 November 1899, Major 10 January 1900, Lieut.-Col. 10 February 1909, Brigadier commanding Northumberland Infantry Brigade, 3 July 1911, and Brig.Gen. 5 August 1914: served in the Hazara Campaign of 1888 (Mentioned in Despatches, Medal with clasp): the South African War, 1899 – 1900 and 1902, including the operations in Cape Colony, south of the Orange River, 1899-1900; in the Orange Free State, January – May 1902 (Queen's Medal, three clasps), and with the Expeditionary Force in France, 21 – 25 April 1915. During the South African War he raised the 3rd Battn. Northumberland Fusiliers (which he afterward commanded) and, on the battn. being disbanded after the war, was given the command of the 2nd Battn. with whom he finished his term of command in the regt. having served with it for about thirty years. His next command was in 1911 when he was made Brigade Commander of the Northumberland Infantry Brigade. On the outbreak of war in 1914 he was one of the first colonels to be gazetted Brigadier-General. Throughout the winter of 1914 – 15, Gen. Riddell guarded the important part of the north-east coast behind which lay the vast military resources of Newcastle-on-Tyne, and he further prepared his Brigade for service abroad. On the night of 20-21 April he crossed with his Brigade to France, and on 26 April – not a week later – was killed in the Second Battle of Ypres. As usual with all large units, it had been intended to quarter the Northumberland Brigade at a base in France. Billets were actually taken, but on the 22nd the Germans delivered their first gas attack and the Brigade was rushed up in all haste to help fill the great gap torn in our line. By Sunday, after a forced night march without food or rest, except the men's emergency rations, the Brigade was in touch with the enemy. All that day and the night before, Gen. Riddell was moving about among his men where the fire was hottest, inspiring the men with his extraordinary cheerfulness and absolute coolness. Men and officers alike speak of his example of absolute fearlessness. Next day, April 26, orders were received at Brigade Headquarters that the Brigade was to attack and retake at all costs the village of St. Julien – a frontal attack over open ground swept by fire of all kinds. At about three o'clock Gen. Riddell decided he must go forward into the firing line. His Brigade Major did all that he could to stop him, as in that officer's words, "There was a very murderous fire going on over the ground he had to cross. But he was much too brave a man to be deterred by anything I said." He reached his men, and wearing the marks of his rank exposed to every sniper, he stepped out before them, a stick in his hand. An eye-witness wrote, "It was only a question of time." The bullet entered the cap close to the fatally conspicuous gilt flap, and Gen. Riddell fell, killed apparently instantaneously. Field-Marshal Sir John French afterwards addressed the Brigade (depleted within a week from leaving England of more than half its officers and men), and speaking of Gen. Riddell said, "He fell at the head of his Brigade while leading you to attack the village of St. Julien. I deeply deplore the loss of one of the most gallant officers that ever lived and one of the best leaders." He *m.* St. Mary Abbotts, Kensington, 17 April 1912; Margaret Christabel (Lesbury House, Lesbury, R.S.O., Northumberland), *dau.* of the late Sir Henry Hall Scott, well known in Northumberland and of Eilanreach, co. Inverness. An old brother officer, who had known Gen. Riddell all his life, wrote in the Regimental Gazette, "Throughout his life he was a master soldier, no finer company officer ever lived or one who understood his men better...no truer hearted or more loyal comrade ever breathed. Always a fine horseman, and a very bold one, he was well known in the Cattistock country and in all the hunting fields of the Northumberland he knew and loved so well.": Age 53.

Killed Leading His Brigade But 5 Days Landed
Soldier And Great Gentleman

(XXXV.A.14) Pte. 1110, Raymond Crouch, 40th Bn. Australian Infantry, A.I.F.: *s.* of John Bird Crouch, of Ranelagh, Tasmania: and brother to Pte. 774, R.W. Crouch, 40th Battn., (drowned in an accident, 1935) *b.* Melbourne, Victoria, 1898: Occupation – Labourer: enlisted Claremont, 2 June 1916: departed Hobart aboard A.35 'Berrima,' 1 July 1916: served with the Expeditionary Force in France from 21 December following: recorded wounded and missing after the fighting, 13 October 1917 (confirmed killed in action 29 May 1918). A comrade said, "He was in 'D' Coy., on the same Machine Gun as me. On the morning of 12 October, at Passchendaele, he was carrying the magazines when he was hit by a bullet through the right arm above the wrist. It was not a bad wound and he was quite pleased and thought he would be sent to Blighty. He was sent back about 1½ miles to the First Aid Post, and has not been seen or heard of since.": Age 19. *The Hobart Mercury*, 20 October 1918, carried the following memoriam notice from his father and brothers:-

> Killed in action somewhere in France, 13/10/17
> Private Raymond Crouch of Ranelagh, Tasmania.
> On Tasmania's Roll of Honour,
> You will find his name.
>
> Midst the rearing of the battle
> And the roar of shot and shell,
> Fighting for King and Country,
> He, like a hero, fell.
>
> Somewhere in France he is lying,
> Sleeping the sleep of the brave
> He died an Australian hero –
> The noblest death of all.

(XXXV.B.11) Pte. 6068, Royal Ernest Henry Mitchell, 39th Bn. Australian Infantry, A.I.F.: *s.* of Ernest Henry Francis Mitchell, of Hopetoun West, Victoria, and Rosetta Mitchell: and elder brother to Pte. 7116, R.D. Mitchell, 23rd Australian Infantry, killed in action 3 October 1917, nr. Anzac, Broodseinde: *b.* Hopetoun, July 1895: Religion – Baptist: Occupation – Farm Labourer: 5'4" tall, dark complexion, brown eyes, brown hair: joined A.I.F., Ararat, Victoria, 20 April 1916; posted 19th Rfts., 8th Battn., Ballarat, 1 June: trained England (from 11 September); proceeded to join 39th Battn., France (24 November); reported missing (since confirmed) killed in action 4 October 1917, nr. Zonnebeke: Age 22. Buried near where he fell, Pte. Mitchell's remains were recovered (GRU Exhumation report Passchendaele, 51.405E) and re-interred, April 1921.

His brother Robert is buried in Perth Cemetery (China Wall) (V.C.16).

(XXXV.F.10) Pte. 44637, Harry Mountain, 147th Coy., Machine Gun Corps (Inf.): formerly no.17953, East Yorkshire Regt.: *s.* of Charles Mountain, of 14, Carlton Street, Bridlington, co. York, by his wife

Elizabeth: and younger brother to Gnr. 755358, C. Mountain, 251st Bde., Royal Field Artillery, killed in action 21 April 1917, aged 21 years: *b*. Brough, co. York: enlisted Bridlington: killed in action 8 October 1917: Age 19.

A Secret Thought, A Silent Tear, Keep Their Memory Ever Dear

His brother Charles is buried in Hibers Trench Cemetery, Wancourt (C.2).

(XXXV.G.18) Pte. 1643, Henry John De Voogd, 51st Bn. Australian Infantry, A.I.F.: *s*. of Henry De Voogd, of Franklin Street, Sailor's Gully, Eaglehawk, Victoria, and Mary Ann, his wife: *b*. Sailor's Gully, 11 July 1883: religion – Church of England: Occupation – Miner; Horseshoe Estates Gold Mine, Kalgoorlie, Western Australia: 5'10" tall, blue eyes, light brown hair: a member of Eaglehawk Rangers (Militia), joined A.I.F., Blackboy Hill, 28 January 1916: departed Alexandria, 5 May: trained England (from 16 June), proceeded to France, 17 July, with a draft of reinforcements to 51st Battn.: wounded in action (G.S.W. wrist, severe), 3 September 1916, and evacuated to England: returned to France 3 November; rejoined his battalion on the 17th: hospitalised England (mumps, inflamed lymphoma, abscesses, boils) 10 February –14 March 1917: rejoined his battalion 20 September. Killed in action, 12 October 1917: Age 34. Pte. De Voogd was a keen supporter and player of Rugby football, a talented musician and member of the Druids Lodge, Boulder, Western Australia. Tried by F.G.C.M., 12 December 1916, charged with 'Wilfully disobeying on Active Service a lawful command given by his superior officer;' Pte. De Voogd pleaded 'Not Guilty.' Found Guilty as charged, he was sentenced to two years 'Imprisonment with Hard Labour.' The sentence was later (18 January 1917) suspended and, posthumously 'remitted as soldier was killed, 12 October 1917.' Buried at Broodseinde Ridge his remains were recovered (GRU Report, Passchendaele, 51.418.E) in July 1920 and re-interred in Tyne Cot British Cemetery; next of kin notified 20 December 1920. His effects included a wallet, two photos, and a French note (damaged). They were received by his father on 8 October 1918 as were his British War and Victory medals, Memorial Plaque and Scroll (20 February 1922 – 10 April 1924). His original headstone recorded Denoogd.

(XXXV.H.6) Pte. 636923, John Chard, 21st Bn. Canadian Infantry (Eastern Ontario Regt.), C.E.F.: *s*. of John Chard, of Frankford, Ontario: and brother to Pte. 8536, E. Chard, 2nd Canadian Infantry, killed in action, 22 April 1915, at St. Julien: *b*. County Hastings, Canada, 8 March 1895: Religion – Methodist: Occupation – Miller: a serving member of 49th Regt. (Militia); enlisted Stirling, Ontario, 27 March 1916: killed in action 3-4 November 1917, at Passchendaele: Age 22. *unm*. (*IWGC record age 20*)

His brother Ezra has no known grave; he is commemorated on the Ypres (Menin Gate) Memorial (Panel 18).

(XXXV.J.20) Pte. 28929, George Davies, 11th (Service) Bn. The Border Regt.: formerly no.49913, Manchester Regt.: enlisted Manchester. Killed in action on the night of 25 November 1917 when, during a relief near Bellevue Spur, undue noise and commotion drew down a heavy German bombardment on the battalion resulting in the death of Pte. Davies and eighteen other men: Age 32. He leaves a wife, Mrs F.E. Davies (45, Stowell Street, West Gorton, Manchester). See account re. L/Corpl. J. Nixon, Tyne Cot Cemetery (XXXVII.H.6).

Duty Nobly Done

(XXXV.J.24) Pte. 42931, Albert Victor Collins, 2/5th Bn. The Manchester Regt. (T.F.): eldest *s*. of John Collins, Bootmaker, by his wife Eliza, *dau*. of William Bradshaw: *b*. Northampton, 22 July 1879: *educ*. Spring Lane Board School, there: Occupation – Bootmaker: joined Bedfordshire Regt. 5 March 1917: served with the Expeditionary Force in France and Flanders, from 29 May; transf'd. Manchester Regt., and was killed in action at Ypres 7 October following: Age 38. Buried nr. Ypres. His Commanding Officer wrote that he was a great loss to the company. He *m*. at Northampton, 5 May 1900, Annie (19, Lawrence Street, Northampton), *dau*. of William Brown, and had six children – Lily, *b*. 29 December 1901; Albert Victor, *b*. 27 March 1904; Ernest Charles, *b*. 23 February 1906; John, *b*. 26 November 1907; Annie, *b*. 18 March 1910 and William *b*. 13 June 1912.

(XXXVI.C.6) Lieut. 22525, Herbert Albert Edwin Milnes, 3rd Auckland Infantry Bn., N.Z.E.F.: *s.* of the late William Milnes, by his wife Mary Malvina, *dau.* of John Barton, by his wife Margaret: *b.* Beeston, Leeds, co. York, 29 March 1874: *educ.* Borough Road College, Isleworth, London; Royal College of Science, London, and London University (B.S.): Occupation – House Tutor; Borough Road Training College, London: removed to Auckland, 1905, to take up an appointment as Principal to the Training College there: enlisted Trentham Military Camp, 2nd Lieut., 7 March 1916: departed Wellington, HMNZT 75 'Waitemata,' 21 January 1917; Hdqrs Staff (Ship's Adjt.): disembarked Plymouth, 27 March following: served with the Expeditionary Force in France and Flanders from 28 May, and was killed in action 4 October 1917. Buried close to Otto Farm, Zonnebeke: Age 43. The Registrar, Auckland University College wrote, "Sincere and deep regret is felt throughout the educational circles in this city at the loss which has been sustained by us in the death of your esteemed brother, Mr H.A.E. Milnes, B.Sc. (London)." Well-known as an athlete, he distinguished himself in tennis, golf, basketball, Association and Rugby football. He was a personality of the Holbeck Club, and also played for Yorkshire (Rugby). He *m.* Ilkley, co. York, 19 December 1905; Louisa Heath (*d.* 19 October 1913), *dau.* of William Haler, His Majesty's Inspector of Schools. (*IWGC record 2nd Lieut.*)

To give as accurate an account as possible of the fighting and conditions under which the troops existed day after day, the official Australian War Photographer Charles Hurley and his assistant Lieut. Hubert Wilkins made regular visits to the battlefields; often in the thick of the fighting. On 12 October 1917, with the battle for Passchendaele raging all around, shells screaming through the air and exploding all about, the two men made their way north of Zonnebeke along the Ypres – Roulers railway cutting toward Tyne Cot; both men imagining they might at any moment be joining the ranks of the dead and mutilated bodies that lay everywhere. Hurley later noted in his diary "I noticed an awful sight: a party of, ten or so, telephone men all blown to bits. Under a questionably sheltered bank lay a group of dead men. Sitting by them in little scooped out recesses sat a few living, but so emaciated by fatigue and shell shock that it was hard to differentiate. Still the whole was just another of the many byways to hell one sees out here, and which are so strewn with ghastliness that the only comment is, 'Poor beggar copped it thick', or else nothing at all." Charles Macintosh copped it thick three days previously; Hurley might well have seen his body.

(XXXVI.C.15) Pte. 291, Charles Rae Macintosh, 5th Coy., Australian Machine Gun Corps: *s.* of Charles Anderson Macintosh, of Sydney, New South Wales, by his wife Sara: reported wounded and missing, later confirmed as killed in action, on 9 October 1917. Pte. 3855, J.M. McCulloch reported, "In the attack of 9.10.17 I found myself in company with Pte Macintosh and several other men of the section and the officer in charge, practically cut off by the enemy. The order was given for each man to look after himself, with the result that I found Pte. Macintosh and myself were taking cover in the same shell hole. We decided to make a dash for it and in doing so I saw Pte Macintosh wounded in the intestines and fall back into the shell hole we had just left. The Germans were almost upon us then so that I had no option but to keep going. There were only myself left of this party. The officer was killed...I am sorry I cannot say definitely what happened to him after being wounded, and I further regret the circumstances did not admit of my going back to find out." Believed buried Shands Cutting, Ypres – Roulers Railway, Passchendaele: Age 20. *unm.*

Only Child Of C & S Macintosh
For God & Country

(XXXVI.D.13) Lieut. George Kelman, 16th Bn. Canadian Infantry (Manitoba Regt.), C.E.F.: *b.* Pitlochrie, Scotland, 27 September 1884: *educ.* Pitlochrie Central School; thereafter employed by Commercial Bank of Scotland Ltd.: removed to Canada to take up an appointment as Manager; Bank of British North America; Wynard Street Branch: enlisted July 1915; apptd. Lieut. and, due to his previous experience and natural efficiency, promoted Capt. On arrival in England, the battalion was broken up into reinforcement drafts and, after reverting to Lieut. and a period of re-training, proceeded to France with a draft to 16th

Battn. with which unit he was serving when he was killed in action on 8 November 1917, while leading his men in the attack at Passchendaele: Age 31.

(XXXVI.E.24) Lieut. John William Hinckesman, 47th (British Columbia) Bn., Canadian Infantry, C.E.F.: *s.* of the late John William Hinckesman, of Charlcotte, Bridgnorth, co. Salop, by his wife Marion Margaret (Hadley, Droitwich, co. Worcester), *dau.* of the Rev. David Vaughan: *b.* Bridgnorth, afsd., 15 September 1891: Religion – Church of England: *educ.* Bridgnorth Grammar School: removed to Canada, 1907; settled Penticton, British Columbia: Occupation – Rancher: joined 2nd Canadian Mounted Rifles; Victoria, British Columbia, 8 December 1914, Pte. 2047; proceeded to England: served with the Expeditionary Force in France and Flanders from 22 September 1915: gazetted Lieut., 28 November 1916; killed in action at Passchendaele, 27 October 1917. Buried there. An officer wrote, "In his death the battalion has sustained a great loss, as he was looked upon as one of the most promising officers, and was actually due for immediate promotion for the good work he had done in this unit. By all he was looked upon as a thoroughly efficient, courageous and reliable officer, and the men of 'B' Coy., with whom he was more familiar, feel his loss particularly. During the whole of his connection with this battalion his relationship with all ranks was one of a most pleasant character. The operation in which the battalion was engaged at the time resulted very successfully, and the work done by Lieut. J.W. Hinckesman on the night of the 27th was most creditably performed, and the information he obtained was of great value, the situation being very precarious at the time." Lt. Hinckesman had three brothers on active service: Age 26. Remains 'Unknown Canadian Officer, Lt. 47 Cans.;' recovered unmarked grave 28.D.12.c.40.15; identified, reinterred Tyne Cot, 29 July 1921. (*IWGC records ...husband of Eva C. Hutchison (formerly Hinckesman), of 19, Ingleston Place, Greenock, Scotland, and age 27.*) Commemorated on the Ypres (Menin Gate) Memorial (Panel 28). IWGC:1926/MR.29,III,pg.122.

(XXXVI.F.3) Pte. 5918, Peter Callinan, M.M., 8th Bn. Australian Infantry, A.I.F.: *s.* of the late Edward Callinan, by his wife Ellen (24, Stanley Street, Richmond, Victoria): *b.* Carlton, Victoria, 1876: Religion – Roman Catholic: *educ.* Christian Brothers College, East Melbourne; thereafter undertook a four year apprenticeship with Victoria Land Department, finding employment as Assistant Surveyor: enlisted Richmond, 11 March 1916: 5'7½" tall, grey eyes, brown hair: posted 19th Rfts., 8th Battn., Broadmeadows, 6 June: departed Melbourne; Transport 'Themistocles,' 28 July: trained England, September – November, during which period he was hospitalised, (9 October – 7 November), Venereal Disease: proceeded to France 16 November: transf'd. 1st ANZAC Typo section, 15 February 1917: attd. Australian Artillery, 4 March: hospitalised, Etaples (11 March – 17 April), Venereal Disease, retd. 8th Battn., Etaples 17 April: rejoined his battn. in the field on 21 May; killed in action on 4 October 1917. Lieut. Hall recorded, "The Corporal and myself were walking round trying to identify the dead on 5 October and we came across Callinan. He had been hit on the head and his pay-book and identity disc were gone, but we recognized him by his face and two letters in his pocket. He was buried 6 hours later. We sent out a party to bury him. Shell-shot. Not shattered much. He was awarded the Military Medal, but did not know it before he died." Buried by Pte. 6220, A.J. Wood near a wood about 2 miles in front of Anzac Ridge; he said, "A rough wooden cross marked his resting place, but it would very likely be knocked down after as it was a lively place." Pte. Callinan was awarded the Military Medal for his actions during the attack at Polygon Wood, east of Ypres, 20 September 1917, "...when his Company Commander and Section Sergeant had been wounded on the way to the assembling position, Pte. Callinan guided his section and company on to the taped lines on which they were to form up, thereby being instrumental in having the Company formed up before zero hour.": Age 40.

To Memory Ever Dear
R.I.P.

(XXXVI.F.10) Pte. 39171, George Scott Cook, 1st Bn. Otago Regt., N.Z.E.F.: late of Awamangu, via Balclutha, Otago: *s.* of David Cook, of Hilderthorpe, Oamaru, by his wife Elizabeth: and elder brother to Pte. 26/535, J.S. Cook, 3rd Otago Regt., killed in action 4 October 1917: Occupation – Farm-Hand: embarked Wellington, HMNZT 76 'Aparima,' 16 February 1917, 22nd Rfts., 'D' Coy., Otago Regt.: after a period of training in England proceeded to France where he died of wounds 12 October 1917, received before Passchendaele: Age 27. *unm.*

His brother John has no known grave; he is commemorated nearby on the Tyne Cot (New Zealand) Memorial (Panel 3).

(XXXVII.F.20) Lieut. 222682, Norman Cahill Christie, 85th Bn. Canadian Infantry (Nova Scotia Regt.), C.E.F.: *husb.* to Ethel Christie (Amherst, Nova Scotia): *b.* Amherst, 24 April 1882: religion – Baptist: Occupation – Manufacturer: 5'7" tall, blue eyes, light brown hair: enlisted 85th Battn., as Pte., Halifax, Nova Scotia, 23 October 1915: served with the Expeditionary Force in France and Flanders from February 1917 and wounded in action at Passchendaele on the following 28 October; carried to the Regimental Aid Post, Lieut. Christie was killed by a shell shortly afterwards while awaiting treatment: Age 35. See account re. Lieuts. Anderson, Mackenzie and Martell, Ypres (Menin Gate) Memorial (Panel 30).

The moment when one unit relieved another on the Western Front, could be extremely difficult under the best of circumstances and was always dangerous. Both sides were well aware of the routine by which the other's relief took place but, the slightest noise out of the ordinary – and it was well-nigh impossible for large numbers of men, laden down like pack-mules with all the paraphernalia of war, to pass each other in the narrow confines of the trenches and make no noise at all – would draw down a salvo of shells or a burst of machine gun fire. The 11th Border Regt. found this out to their cost on the night of 25 November 1917 when, during a relief near the Bellevue Spur, undue noise and commotion drew down a savage bombardment resulting in the death of nineteen men:

(XXXVII.H.6) Corpl. 27994 Joseph Nixon, 11th (Service) Bn. The Border Regt.: *s.* of Richard Nixon, of Linstock, Carlisle, by his wife Jane: *b.* Scotby Ghyll, co. Cumberland, *c.*1896. Killed in action, 25 November 1917: Age 21. *unm.*

(XXXVIII.H.16/21) Pte. 34492, Henry Nevitt, 3rd Bn. Auckland Regt., N.Z.E.F.: *s.* of George Nevitt, of Rugeley, co. Stafford, by his wife Emmie: and brother to Sergt. Major 11/552, G. Nevitt, Wellington Mounted Rifles, died in Egypt, 2 June 1915, of wounds (GS abdomen) received in action at Gallipoli (buried 9 June): *b.* Stafford, 8 November 1880: Religion – Church of England: Occupation – Farmer: 5'7½" tall, brown-grey eyes, dark brown hair: enlisted Broadwood, N.Z., 24 April 1916: departed Wellington, Sergt., 11th Rfts., 'J'Coy., N.Z. Rifle Brigade, HMNZT 73 'Opawa,' 2 January 1917: killed in action, 28 December 1917: Age 37. *unm.* All correspondence regarding the deceased should be addressed c/o his brother, J.C. Nevitt, Esq., Liffey Street, Island Bay, Wellington.

His brother Gerald is buried in Alexandria (Chatby) Military And War Memorial Cemetery (M.102).

On the night of 26 December 1917, after a substantial and (under the circumstances) cheery Christmas dinner at St. Jean, 2nd Northamptons set off for a tour of duty in the left sub-sector of the Passchendaele front, one of the worst sectors in the whole of the Ypres salient; not a particularly cheerful prospect. With all of its approaches under close observation by the enemy on this night, matters were made worse by the ground being covered with snow and, with a full moon shining brightly, the dark uniforms of the Northamptons (winter white coveralls were few and far between) were certain to be seen and the unit suffer the direst of consequences as a result. Sure enough, exactly as anticipated, the enemy saw them coming from some considerable distance and opened up with a heavy barrage of artillery and machine-gun fire. Lieut. Martin, in the foremost platoon, tried to steady his men and lead them forward through the hail of shot and shell, but after scarcely a few steps he fell, severely wounded. Carried to the Tyne Cot Aid Post, he died shortly after arrival.

(XXXIX.H.3) 2nd Lieut. George Henry Martin, 3rd (Reserve) attd 2nd Bn. (58th Foot) The Northamptonshire Regt.: *s.* of Samuel Martin, by his wife Jane: Died of wounds, 26 December 1917: Age 37. (*IWGC record 27 December*)

In Loving Memory Of My Dear Brother
Peace Perfect Peace
Annie

(XL.A.23) Pte. 3842, Richard Murray Sharpe, 1st Bn. Australian Infantry, A.I.F.: *s.* of Ellen Hogan (61, Mount Vernon Street, Forest Lodge, Sydney): and brother to Pte. 3995, M.W. Sharpe, 1st Australian Infantry, who fell in the fighting at Pozieres, 22 – 25 July 1916: and Pte. 5197, S.M. Sharpe, Australian Corps. H.Qrs. (surv'd.): *b.* Sydney, 1890: Occupation – Carter: enlisted Holdsworthy, 18 August 1915: posted 12th Reinforcements, 1st Battn., Liverpool, 16 November: trained Egypt, from 14 February 1916: served with the Expeditionary Force in France and Flanders from 28 March: attd. A.P.M., Traffic Control, 14 May – 13 July, rejoining his battn. on the latter date: on leave (England) from 1 July 1917, rejoining his battn. on the 16th of that month, and was killed in action 3 October 1917: Age 27. *unm.* GRU Report Passchendaele, 51.723E, records remains exhumed and re-interred May 1921.

His brother Murray has no known grave; he is commemorated on the Villers-Bretonneux Memorial.

(XL.B.21) Pte. 5128, Arthur George Lee, 58th Bn. Australian Infantry, A.I.F.: *s.* of George Lee, of 89, Lennox Street, Moonee Ponds, Victoria, by his wife Sarah: *b.* Essendon, Victoria, December 1894: was a Labourer: enlisted Melbourne, 26 January 1916: trained Egypt, from 11 May 1916: served with the Expeditionary Force in France and Flanders from 30 June, joining his battn. in the field 30 September 1916, and was reported missing in action 25 September 1917: Age 22. A Court of Enquiry (assembled 'In the Field' 17 August 1918), drawing on information supplied by Pte. 3114, A. Brown who said that he had seen Pte. Lee blown to pieces by a shell while 'in the Reserves at Polygon Wood, adding his body was found but did not know whether it was buried, consequently confirmed Pte. Lee as having been killed in action on the aforementioned date and buried near where he fell. GRU Report Passchendaele, 51.735E, records remains exhumed and re-interred May 1921.

(XL.D.1) 2nd Lieut. Joseph Irvine (*a.k.a.* Joseph Denver Doak), 4th Bn. Australian Infantry, A.I.F.: *s.* of Margaret Irvine, c/o Y.M.C.A., 123, Murray Street, Perth: and younger brother to Dresser 716, C.C. Doak, South African Veterinary Corps, who died 16 April 1916: *b.* Buckland, New Zealand, 14 November 1886: religion – Church of England: *educ.* State School: Occupation – Brass Moulder and turner: 5'8½" tall, dark complexion, brown eyes, dark hair: enlisted Holdsworthy, New South Wales, 10 September 1915: posted 21st Rfts., 4th Battn., 3 October: applied for a commission 2 February 1916; gazetted 2nd Lieut., 16 March: departed Sydney, H.M.A.T. A.60 'Aeneas' 30 September: underwent training in England (inc. No.1 Officer's & N.C.O.'s School), November 1916 – July 1917: proceeded to France 12 July. After sixteen days awaiting trial, 2nd Lieut. Irvine was brought before a General Court Martial, Vieux Berquin, 10 September 1917, and Charged: (i) Striking a soldier in that he, on 25 August 1917, struck No.6763, Pte. C.J. McLean. Alternative Charge: Conduct to the prejudice of good order and military discipline in that he, on 25 August 1917, said to No.6763, Pte. C.J. McLean, "Will you have a punch?" or words to that effect. (ii) An act to the prejudice of good order and military discipline in that he, on 25 August 1917, shook No.6748, Pte. Lockhart by the shoulders. Pleading Not Guilty on all charges, he was found – Guilty on the first charge, Not Guilty on Alternate charge and second charge: and Sentenced (a) To be severely reprimanded. (b) To take rank and precedence in the army as if his appointment bore date 10 September 1917 (forfeiture of seniority). Reported missing believed killed by the enemy barrage, which immediately preceded zero-hour 4 October 1917: Age 30. Major G.S. Cook, Comd'g. 4th Battn., recorded 'Buried, Broodseinde Ridge, Square J.A. or B., Beclaere Map.' Exhumed May 1921 re. Graves Registration Unit report, Passchendaele, 51.736E, and re-interred Tyne Cot British Cemetery at the same time as Pte. 3842, R.M. Sharpe, 1st A.I.F. (XL.A.23), Pte. 5120, A.G. Lee, 58th A.I.F. (XL.B.21), Pte. 855, C.H. Neilen, 34th A.I.F. (XLI.A.4), Pte. 6562, H.A. Perry, 11th A.I.F. (XLI.A.5), and Pte. 2639, C.E. Raymond, 40th A.I.F. (XVI.E.4). Lieut. Irvine's effects, in a sealed valise – 'Leather Wallet, Wallet with Photos enclosed, Postcards, 1 Dictionary, 1 Badge, 1 Belt, 1 Small Spirit Level, 3 Ties, 3 Collars, 2 Handkerchiefs, 2 Singlets, 1 Suit Pyjamas, 1 Muffler, 1 Cap, 1 Sam Browne Belt, 1 Kit-bag, 1 Pr. Slacks, 1 S.D. Tunic, 1 Pr. Breeches' – a parcel – 'Book of Poems' – parcel – 'Note Book, Silver? Watch (damaged) and Strap, Diary, Photos, Cards' – cabin trunk – 'Books, Papers, Trench Coat, S.D. Tunic, Pr. Underpants, 2 Handkerchiefs, 2 Flannel Undershirts, White Linen Bag, Collars, Wall-Tidy, 4 Mufflers, Socks, Mittens, Gloves, 2 Prs. Woollen Knee Pads, 2 Balaclava Caps, Small Attache Case, Pr. Boots, Pr. Leggings, Playing Cards, 'Key of Heaven,' Shoulder Strap, Fountain Pen in Case, Postcards, Cooee

Writing Wallet, Photos, Banner, Bunch of Keys, Pr. Dividers, Badges, Silver Shield, Purse containing ore specimens, Button Stick' – were received by his widow, Agnes Jane Doak, *née* Irvine (255, Mandurah Road, South Fremantle, Western Australia), May – October 1918; she received his British War Medal (5 April 1921), Memorial Scroll (5 September 1921), Plaque (21 December 1922), and Victory Medal (26 April 1923). See account Re. Capt. J.R. Eddy; Reninghelst New Military Cemetery (IV.C.4).

Break Break Break On Thy Cold Grey Stones, O Sea

Recent enquiries revealed Dresser Christopher Doak to be buried in Johannesburg (Braamfontein) Cemetery (RCI Grave 2247); the CWGC is currently (2009) arranging for a headstone to mark his grave.

(XL.D.2) Lieut. Robert Burton Bennett, M.C., 4th Bn. Australian Infantry, A.I.F.: *s.* of the late William Christopher Bennett (*d.* September 1889), of Phillip Street, Neutral Bay, by his wife Sarah Jane (since died): *b.* Cumberland, Sydney, February 1887: Religion – Church of England: Occupation – Clerk; Wool Valuer: 6' tall, fair complexion, grey eyes, fair hair: joined Australian Imperial Force, Randwick, 27 August 1914; Pte. (No.563): appt'd. Dvr., No.2 Coy., Army Service Corps, 1 September: promoted L/Corpl., 16 October: departed Australia aboard A19 'Afric,' 18 October 1914: proceeded to Gallipoli, 5 April 1915: admitted to hospital, Mudros, 21 June (Dysentery): returned to Gallipoli, 25 June: admitted to hospital, Malta (Haemorrhoids), 21 August: rejoined his unit, Alexandria, Egypt, 6 October: proceeded to England, 8 December 1915: promoted Corpl., 30 March 1916; proceeded to France the following day: reverted to Pte. at his own request 1 August 1916: transf'd. 4th Battn. from No.2 Coy. 1st Divisional Train the following day, and commissioned 2nd Lieut. on the 5th of that month: wounded (G.S.W. back and neck), Mouquet Farm, 16 August 1916; admitted Kitchener Hospital, Brighton; discharged to duty 30 October: returned to France 13 November: promoted Lieut. 1 January 1917 (substantive 1 February): wounded (G.S.W. left chest, superficial), Demicourt, 15 April 1917; admitted 3rd London General Hospital, from whence after treatment, including the removal of a boil and recurrent bouts of pyrexia, he was discharged to Cobham (11 June) for further treatment and convalescence; returned to duty 7 July: returned to France on the 19th of that month and, after a period of training at Havre and one month at Central Army School, rejoined his battalion in the field 18 September. He was killed at the Battle of Broodseinde 4 October 1917, by shellfire: Age 30. Major G.S. Cook, Comd'g. 4th Battn., recorded 'Buried, Broodseinde Ridge, Square J.A. or B., Beclaere Map.' Remains of an Australian Officer exhumed 1922, 28.J.4.b.7.7, where the late Lieut. R.B. Bennett was recorded as having been buried, have been re-interred in Tyne Cot British Cemetery. With no possibility of connecting the remains with any other Australian Officer who was buried in the neighbourhood, the Imperial War Graves Commission consented to the erection of a Provisional Cross over the grave bearing his details with the inscription 'Believed To Be.' A Graves Registration Unit report (Zonnebeke, 117.144/C) recording a cross (No.15 in Memorial Row) erected in Buttes New British Cemetery, Polygon Wood: correspondence to his mother (June 1921) confirming his burial in the aforementioned cemetery was subsequently amended (April 1922). Lieut. Bennett was awarded the Military Cross, 10 May 1917 (*London Gazette*, No.30135, 15 June 1917) for 'conspicuous gallantry and devotion to duty. Although wounded he stuck to his post throughout the day, setting a fine example to his men, and inflicting heavy casualties on the enemy.' All correspondence regarding the deceased should be addressed to Miss Mary Keet Bennett, ('Douglas,' 14, Phillip Street, Neutral Bay, Sydney); and, if a casualty – W.R. Bennett Esq., c/o A.M.L. & F. Coy., 4, Bligh Street, Sydney – in preference to the Clergy. See account Reninghelst New Military Cemetery; Capt. J.R. Eddy (IV.C.4).

(XL.E.1) Capt. Clarence Smith Jeffries, V.C., 34th Bn. Australian Infantry, A.I.F.: *s.* of Joshua Jeffries, of Wallsend, New South Wales, by his wife Barbara: *b.* Wallsend, New South Wales, about 1894: *educ.* Newcastle High School: served in the Citizen Forces from the age of fourteen to the time of enlistment for Active Service, 8 August 1914: left Australia on 27 May 1916, as Provisional Lieut.: confirmed in this rank at Salisbury, July 1916: proceeded to France: was present at the Battle of Messines (where he was wounded, and promoted Capt.), and at Passchendaele where he was killed in action, 12 October 1917, aged 23. For his gallantry whilst serving in France, Capt. Jeffries was posthumously awarded the Victoria

Cross (*London Gazette*, 18 December 1917) "For most conspicuous bravery in attack, when his company was held up by enemy machine-gun fire from concrete emplacements. Organizing a party he rushed one emplacement, capturing four machine-guns and thirty-five prisoners. He then led his company forward under extremely heavy enemy artillery barrage and enfilade machine-gun fire to the objective. Later, he again organized a successful attack on a machine-gun emplacement, capturing two machine-guns and thirty more prisoners. This gallant officer was killed during the attack, but it was entirely due to his bravery and initiative that the centre of the attack was not held up for a lengthy period. His example had a most inspiring influence."

On Fame's Eternal Camping Ground Their Silent Tents Are Spread

'At about 11.00 p.m., December 28 1915, a small defensive patrol of one N.C.O. (Corpl. Aspin) and three men left the right company front. They had not been out very long and were near the north-west corner of Celtic Wood, when they saw a party about twenty strong, moving towards them along the northern edge of the wood. At first they believed this to be a New Zealand party from the battalion on the right, but soon they found it was a party of the enemy. All were clad in long white coats; most were armed with revolvers. The German party tried to surround the small British patrol, and succeeded in cutting off one man and capturing him. The other three broke through the cordon and made for their own line, with the enemy in pursuit. On reaching the wire there was a scuffle in which one man was killed. But Corporal Aspin and the other succeeded in forcing their way through the wire and gaining one of their own posts...'

1/4th Bn. Duke of Wellington's (West Riding Regt.) Regimental History

(XL.E.16) Pte. 268401, Harry Daley, 1/4th Bn. The Duke of Wellington's (West Riding) Regt., (T.F.): *s.* of John Daley, of 10, Roseberry Terrace, Stanningley, Leeds, co. York, by his wife Mary Jane. Killed when returning from a patrol he was shot on regaining the British wire, 28 December 1915: Age 20.

We Have Lost, Heaven Has Gained, One Of The Best Earth Sustained
J. & M.J.D.

(XLI.A.4) Pte. 855, Charles Henry Neilen, 34th Bn. Australian Infantry, A.I.F.: *s.* of Mary Eizabeth Neilen, O'Brien's Estate, Cessnock, New South Wales: *b.* Prospect, Sydney, *c.*1885: Religion – Roman Catholic: Occupation – Labourer: 5'5½" tall, grey eyes, brown hair: enlisted West Maitland, 22 January 1916: posted 'C' Coy., 34th Battn. Rutherford, 21 March: departed Australia, 2 May 1916: served with the Expeditionary Force in France from 22 November 1916, and was reported missing 12 October 1917. A Court of Enquiry held 13 June 1918, drawing on information supplied by Pte. Twomey, who was in a shellhole with Pte. Neilen when he was hit in the lungs by a shell fragment, confirmed Pte. Neilen as killed in action on the aforementioned date and buried near where he fell: Age 32. GRU Report, Passchendaele 51.738.E records remains exhumed and re-interred, May 1921.

(XLI.A.5) Pte. 6562, Harold Allan Perry, 'A' Coy., 11th Bn. Australian Infantry, A.I.F.: *s.* of Alfred A. Perry, of 'Corio,' Pennell Road, Claremont, Western Australia, by his wife Marion A.: *b.* Geelong, Victoria, February 1895: Religion – Methodist: Occupation – Warehouse Asst. / Salesman: 5'8" tall, blue eyes, fair hair: previously served 8 yrs. Senior Cadets, and, at the time of his enlistment (Fremantle, 10 April 1916), was a serving member of 86th Infantry Regt. (Militia): posted 21st Rfts., 11th Battn., Blackboy Hill Camp, 3 October: departed Fremantle, A23 'Suffolk,' 10 October: trained England, 3 December 1916 – 2 May 1917: served with the Expeditionary Force in France from 4 May: transf'd. and joined 11th Battn. in the field on the 10th of that month, and was severely wounded by the explosion of a shell on 2 November 1917; died within minutes: Age 22. *unm.* Buried where he fell. GRU Report, Passchendaele, 51.738.E records remains exhumed and reinterred May 1921.

In Memory Of The Dearly Loved Son Of Mr & Mrs Perry
Claremont W.A.

Pte. T.R. Cunningham, killed by the same shell, is buried nearby (XLII.C.5).

(XLI.B.6) Spr. 16515, Edmund George Brown, 1st Field Coy., Australian Engineers, A.I.F.: *s.* of Edmund Brown, of Gilbert Road, Wyalong, New South Wales, by his wife Mary Jane: *b.* Lachlan, Forbes, 1884: Occupation – Motor Mechanic: enlisted Sydney, 16 October 1916: served with the Expeditionary Force in France from 17 May 1917. Killed in action at approximately 10 a.m., 4 October 1917, when, while sheltering with comrades in a shell crater, a shell landed and exploded among them: Age 33. Memorial cross erected Belgian Battery Corner Cemetery. Remains recovered, unmarked collective grave (28NE, J.4.b.8.7), identified – Disc; reinterred 22 September 1920.

Have Mercy Upon Him Lord And Let Perpetual Light Shine Upon Him

(XLI.B.20) Corpl. 2410, Ernest William Serls, 'D' Coy., 44th Bn. Australian Infantry, A.I.F.: *s.* of Joseph Serls, of 'Hillside,' Armidale, Western Australia, by his wife Lydia: *b.* Freemantle, 1889: Occupation – Firewood Contractor: joined A.I.F. 5 April 1916, posted 4th Rfts., 44th Battn.: departed Australia 13 October following: served with the Expeditionary Force in France and Flanders from 4 February 1917, joining 44th Battn. in the field 8 August: promoted Corpl., 11 September, and was killed in action at Hill 40, Zonnebeke, 4 October 1917: Age 28. At the time of his death, Corpl. Serls, after being wounded while delivering a message to 'B' Coy., was making his way to the Regimental Aid Post when a shell burst nearby, killing him instantaneously. Buried in a shell hole beside Pte. 5746, F.D. McCann.

Only Goodnight Son, Till We Meet Again

After the war Pte. McCann's body could not be found; he is commemorated on the Ypres (Menin Gate) Memorial (Panel 27).

(XLII.D.14) 2nd Lieut. Cyril Raymond Crowley, 1st Bn. (11th Foot) The Devonshire Regt.: *s.* of Engr. Capt. Albert Edward Ernest Crowley, by his wife Susan Mary: one of seven officers of 1st Devons killed 4 October 1917, in the attack on Polderhoek Chateau: Age 19. See account, Tyne Cot Memorial (Panel 38).

In Thy Keeping
Beloved Son Of Engr. Capt. & Mrs E.A.E. Crowley
Plymouth

(XLII.E.22) Pte. 3558, Percy Andrew Goulburn Makepeace, 57th Bn. Australian Infantry, A.I.F.: *s.* of the late John William Makepeace, by his wife, Catherine K. Makepeace (Kirkwood Street, Eaglehawk, Victoria, Australia): *b.* Tarraville, 1896: Religion – Church of England: Occupation – Carpenter: 5'6" tall, dark complexion, green eyes, dark brown hair: enlisted Bendigo, 5 August 1915; apptd. 8th Rfts., 21st Bn., 17 December 1915: trained Tel-el-Kebir, Egypt, transf'd. 60th Bn. from 26 February 1916; transf'd. 57th Bn., 15 March: proceeded to France 17 June; disembarked Marseilles, 23 June 1916. Killed in action 24 September 1917: Age 21. A runner attd. Bde. HdQrs, he was carrying a message to 58th Bn. in the vicinity of Glencorse Wood when a shrapnel shell burst close overhead. A piece of shrapnel hit him, entering his head just above the eye; death was instantaneous. He was buried by the Comdg. Officer 58th Bn. Signallers, north-east corner Glencorse Wood. A cross with his name and number was put up. His brother, Spr. 14674, J. Makepeace, attempted to visit the grave the following day but, due to the intensity of the shelling at the time, was prevented from accomplishing this. Remains recovered (126 Labour Coy.) – unmarked grave (28.J.14.b.6.4); identified – Disc; reinterred October 1920.

The Beloved Son Of Mr. & Mrs. Makepeace And A Hero

(XLIII.C.8) Pte. 7944, Albert Evans, 1st Bn. (21st Foot) The Royal Scots Fusiliers: served with the Expeditionary Force from 14 August 1914. Killed in action at Ypres 11 November 1914. Remains recovered, unmarked grave, identified by disc; reinterred 12 October 1920.

(XLIII.C.10) Pte. 7708, Alexander Gibson, 1st Bn. (21st Foot) The Royal Scots Fusiliers: served with the Expeditionary Force from 14 August 1914. Killed in action at Ypres, 13 November 1914. *m.* Remains recovered, unmarked grave, identified by disc; reinterred 12 October 1920.

(XLIV.C.16) Sergt. 717, Edwin Ernest Schunke, 8th Bn. Australian Infantry, A.I.F.: *s.* of the late William Schunke, and his wife Anna Maria (Hopefield Post Office, Box 19, Natimuk, Victoria): and *yr.* brother to Pte. 1003, W.A. Schunke, 38th Bn. Australian Infantry, died of wounds 12 October 1917: *b.* Natimuk, 1893: religion – Lutheran: Occupation – Labourer: enlisted Broadmeadows, 14 August 1914; apptd. 8th Battn., 24 August: apptd. L/Corpl., 16 September 1916; promoted Corpl., 1 April 1917; Sergt., 5 September: served with the Expeditionary Force in Egypt, Gallipoli, France and Flanders (from 31 March 1916): twice wounded (25 July 1916, GSW Facial; 8 May 1917, SW Rt. Shldr.). Killed in action 25 October 1917: Age 24. Remains recovered, unmarked grave, identified – Correspondence; reinterred 1920.

His brother William is buried in Brandhoek New Military Cemetery No.3 (II.L.17).

(XLIV.D.20) Pte. 352590, Edward Taylor, 'D' Coy., 2/9th Bn. The Manchester Regt. (T.F.): *s.* of Benjamin Taylor, Newsagent; of 176, Manchester Road, Werneth, by his wife Martha Alice, *dau.* of Timothy Bentley: *b.* Hollinwood, co. Lancaster, 21 July 1897: *educ.* Freehold Board School, Werneth: Occupation – Clerk: joined Manchester Territorials 15 May 1916: served with the Expeditionary Force in France and Flanders from March 1917; killed in action at Passchendaele, 9 October following. Buried north-east of Ypres: Age 20. *unm.*

Time Passes But Memories Never Fade

(XLIV.D.27) L/Corpl. 3213, John Robert Wellman, 3rd (Reserve) Bn. (7th Foot) The Royal Fusiliers (City of London Regt.): *s.* of John Ambrose Wellman, of 17, Ray's Avenue, Montague Road, Upper Edmonton, London, N., by his wife Louisa Rebecca, *dau.* of Edward Gwyther: and brother to Pte. 22166, J.E. Wellman, Middlesex Regt., died No.57 Casualty Clearing Station, 25 April 1918: *b.* Clerkenwell, London, E.C., 1895: *educ.* Raynham Road School, Edmonton: employee Sparklets Mineral Works: enlisted 8 September 1914: served with the Expeditionary Force in France and Flanders from 11 February, and was killed in action at St. Jean 12 April 1915: Age 20. *unm.* (*IWGC record Pte., 14 April*)

His brother James is buried in Aubigny Communal Cemetery Extension (III.A.13).

(XLIV.D.38) Sergt. L/7098, Frank Murphy, 2nd Bn. (3rd Foot) The Buffs (East Kent Regt.): late of Newcastle-on-Tyne, Co. Durham: *s.* of Patrick Murphy, by his wife Mary: enlisted York: served with the Expeditionary Force in France and Flanders from 17 January 1915, and was killed by heavy trench mortar fire, his battalion's first experience of this weapon, 11 April 1915; Broodseinde Crossroads, Zonnebeke: Age 31. Four other men: Corpl. 8510, T. Dray, Ptes. B. Moss, G/5163, F. Setterfield and G/1921, H. Woodward, were also killed. Sergt. Murphy is the only one to have a known grave.

Rest In Peace

The other four men are commemorated on the Ypres (Menin Gate) Memorial: Corpl. Dray, Pte. Moss (Panel 14), Pte. Setterfield, Pte. Woodward (Panel 12).

(XLIV.F.7) Pte. 6830, Ernest William Werner, 3rd Bn. Australian Infantry, A.I.F.: *s.* of the late Henry Werner, by his marriage to Alice Mozzini, *née* Werner ('Tyrone Cottage,' Alfred Street, Mascot, New South Wales): and brother to Pte. 6831, N.H. Werner, 3rd Australian Infantry, killed about mid-night 24–25 June 1918, during a raid at Merris; aged 19 years: *b.* Nymagee, 1897: Occupation – Labourer: enlisted Cootamundra, 2 May 1916: departed Sydney, 8 November.: trained Larkhill Camp (from 10 January 1917): served with the Expeditionary Force in France (from 26 April); killed in action 20 September 1917; shellfire, nr. Halway House. Buried near where he fell, Sheet 28.N.W.: Age 21.

A Young Life Nobly Ended
Peace Perfect Peace

His brother Norman is buried in Outtersteene Communal Cemetery Extension, Bailleul (I.H.7).

(XLIV.G.37) Pte. G/17779, Albert Henry Bailey, 12th (Service) Bn. (2nd South Down) The Royal Sussex Regt.: only *s.* of Henry Bailey, of Croucham's Farm, Kirdford, near Billingshurst, co. Sussex, by his wife Charlotte, *dau.* of Henry Cheetham: *b.* Portsfield, Chichester, 6 June 1895: *educ.* South Bersted, and Tillington: Occupation – Carpenter: joined 4th (Territorial) Battn. Royal Sussex Regt., 21 September 1914: served with the Expeditionary Force in France and Flanders, from 12 July 1916, transf'd. 12th (Service) Battn, of the same regiment, and was killed in action at Tower Hamlets Ridge, 26 September 1917. Buried there: Age 22. *unm.*

Peace Perfect Peace

(XLV.A.12) Pte. 15042, Alfred Henry Saywell Tarrant, 2nd Bn. Canterbury Regt., N.Z.E.F.: *s.* of Alfred Tarrant, of 'Sunnymeade,' Tuamarina, Blenheim, by his wife Eleanor: and brother to Pte. 55562, L.A.B. Tarrant, N.Z. Infantry, died of pneumonia 15 December 1917; one week after arriving in England: Occupation – Farmer: proceeded overseas 26 June 1916: killed in action 12 October 1917, at Bellevue.

His brother Leonard is buried in Liverpool (Kirkdale) Cemetery (VII.N.C.925).

(XLV.E.2) Corpl. 27854, George Squires, 7th (Service) Bn. The Bedfordshire Regt.: late of Hemel Hempstead: *s.* of Herbert Squires, of 71, Park Street, Thame, co. Oxford, by his wife Amelia: and brother to Pte. 22664, B. Squires, 2nd Grenadier Guards, killed in action 28 March 1918, aged 21; and Pte. 14804, J. Squires, 20th Coy., Machine Gun Corps, died of wounds 27 October 1917, aged 25: *b.* Thame: enlisted Hemel Hempstead. Killed in action 16 August 1917.

His brother Benjamin has no known grave, he is commemorated on the Arras Memorial (Bay 1); Joseph is buried in Lijssenthoek Military Cemetery (XXI.G.4A).

On 4 October 1917, 12/13th Northumberland Fusiliers stood in their assembly positions, waiting for the signal to follow through right of the attack made earlier by 3/4th Queen's on the Broodseinde – Becelaere Ridge. When their time came to advance, at 8.10 a.m., the Fusiliers found that the 5th Division were held up at Polderhoek Chateau, with the result that 64 Brigade was being badly enfiladed by machine-gun fire from this region. This in turn affected the 12/13th who now found their right flank totally exposed, and at the same time being raked by machine-gun fire from the Chateau. 'Despite the fact that the situation must have been obscured by dust and smoke, the fire of the enemy's machine-guns from Cameron Covert and Polderhoek Chateau steadily increased in volume and caused great casualties in our ranks.' After advancing 150 yards the Northumberlands were forced to dig in and 'while reorganising, Lieut.-Col. Dix, commanding 12/13 Northumberland Fusiliers was shot as well as his four company commanders.'

(XLVI.B.1) Lieut.Col. Stephen Hamilton Dix, M.C., The Leinster Regt. (Prince of Wales's Royal Canadians) Comdg. 12/13th Bn. The Northumberland Fusiliers: *s.* of Stephen Dix, by his wife Annie, *née* Hamilton: *husb.* to Ida Mary (The Court House, Padstow, co. Cornwall): served in the South African Campaign, and in France and Flanders, and was killed in action 4 October 1917: Age 39.

Sacred Heart Of Jesus I Trust In Thee

(XLVI.F.14) Corpl. 34132, Donald Brown, 237th Coy., Machine Gun Corps (Inf.): only *s.* of Colin Brown, of 10, Craigpark Drive, Dennistoun, Glasgow, by his wife Jessie, *dau.* of Archibald McKay, late of Easdale: *b.* Glasgow, 11 September 1897: *educ.* Whitehill Higher Grade School, there: Occupation – Caledonian Railway Clerk: enlisted December 1914: served with the Expeditionary Force in France and Flanders from 14 July 1917, and was killed in action 4 October following. A comrade wrote, "Your son was the most honourable and straightforward chap I ever met, and this was thought by most of the fellows who came in contact with him...I could write and tell you thousands of things that would make your heart swell with pride, but it gives pain as well as esteem.": Age 20. *unm.*

Son Of Colin & Jessie Brown Dennistoun Glasgow
Looking Unto Jesus

(XLVI.H.1) L/Corpl. 551446, Edward 'Ted' Wilfred Hussey, 16th (County of London) Bn. (Queen's Westminster Rifles) The London Regt. (T.F.): *yst. s.* of Thomas Hussey, of 57, Gunterstone Road, West Kensington, London, W., Builder, late of Albert Hall Mansions, Westminster, by his wife Mary T., *dau.* of George Patrick Butler, by his wife Jane, *née* Lynch (32, St. Mary Abbot's Terrace, Kensington): and cousin to Rfn. 4794, P.J. Hussey, Queen's Westminster Rifles, who died in the British Army Hospital, Rouen, 15 September 1916, of gangrene poisoning from wounds received in action during the fighting on the Somme: *b*. Kensington, 1895: served with the Expeditionary Force in France and Flanders, and was killed in action 16 August 1917: Age 22. *unm*.

His cousin Philip is buried in St. Sever Cemetery, Le Grand Quevilly (B.19.3).

Leaving Chateau Segard on the evening of 19 September 1917, the first stage of 8th Australians approach to their assembly positions for the following day's fighting was completed without incident. On arrival at Zillebeke Bund however, due to the limited space available for sheltering troops, the battalion were forced to form up on mass on the banks of the lake and, to make matters worse, heavy rain fell until midnight. At 11.50 the battalion began to move off but, owing to the state of the terrain across which the battalion were to approach, a considerable amount of confusion was caused among the leading companies which resulted in the rear company leaving the Bund just before 3 a.m.

Taking over from 7th Battn. at Clapham Junction, intermittent shellfire to the right of the battalion made a further delay of two hours, waiting for the last companies to arrive, an extremely trying time. Almost immediately after the 7th had cleared Clapham Junction, the 8th moved forward, but had hardly begun their advance when the leading ranks of the 7th were deluged under a barrage of 77 mm fire. A combination of a certain number of the 8th not being in position at zero hour, the shellfire immediately before them and heavy casualties all around considerably delayed the 8th's advance, causing them to lose direction and touch with the battalion on their right. Miraculously, despite these setbacks, the battalion reached their first objective and, under heavy machine gun fire, captured a strongpoint and over fifty Germans and three machine guns on the way. Unfortunately, from here onwards the Australians were not destined to have it all their own way and for the most part their problem was not with the enemy.

After reaching the first objective the battalion were forced to fall back due to an artillery battery continually firing short of the intended barrage line. This battery, throughout the whole operation, caused as many casualties as the whole enemy fire. During the day's operations the battalion incurred casualties of four Officers killed, six wounded; 219 Other Ranks killed, missing or wounded. Among the dead officers was young Lieut. Horace Rintel who, without his parents knowledge, had secretly married on the eve of his departure from Australia, totally unaware that the average life expectancy of a young subaltern on the Western Front was less than three months. His young bride of less than twenty-four hours was destined to be a widow for considerably longer.

The Young Lieutenant

The young lieutenant's face was grey.
As came the day.
The watchers saw it lifting white
And ghostlike from the pool of night.
His eyes were wide and strangely lit.
Each thought in that unhallowed pit:
"I, too, may seem like one who dies
With wide, set eyes."

He stood so still we thought it death,
For through the breath
Of reeking shell we came, and fire,
To hell, unlit, of blood and mire.
Tranced in a chill delirium
We wondered, though our lips were dumb
What precious thing his fingers pressed
Against his breast.

His left hand clutched so lovingly
What none might see.
All bloodless were his lips beneath
The straight, white, rigid clip of teeth.
His eyes turned to the distance dim;
Our sleepless eyes were all on him.
He stirred; we aped a phantom cheer.
The hour was here!

The young lieutenant blew his call.
"God keep us all!"
He whispered softly. Out he led;
And over the vale of twisted dead,
Close holding that dear thing, he went.
On through the storm we followed, bent
To pelt of iron and the rain
Of flame and pain.

His wan face like a lodestar glowed
Down that black road,
And deep among the torn and slain
We drove, and twenty times again
He squared us to the charging hordes.
His word was like a hundred swords.
And still a hand the treasure pressed
Against his breast.

Our gain we held. Up flamed the sun.
"The ridge is won,"
He calmly said, and, with a sigh,
"Thank God, a man is free to die!"
He smiled at this, and so he passed.
His secret prize we knew at last,
For through his hand the jewel's red,
Fierce lustre bled.

Edward Dyson

(XLVII.D.4) Lieut. Horace Lisle Rintel, 8th Bn. Australian Infantry, A.I.F.: *s.* of Henri Rintel, of 'Coringa,' Warragul, Victoria, by his wife Jane ('Cheerio,' Victoria Street, Kerang): *b.* Clunes, Victoria, 26 August 1891: Religion – Church of England: *educ.* Melbourne University, graduated B.A., Diploma of Education, L.L.B. (3rd yr.): Occupation – Schoolteacher and Law Student: 5'11" tall, brown eyes, dark brown hair: prior to enlistment served 11 years Senior Cadets (qualified Lieut. 1909): joined A.I.F. Melbourne, 20 July 1915: trained Seymour (School Sergt., 5th Depot. Bn., from 20 July), Ballarat (14th Depot Bn., from 18 October), Broadmeadows (from 31 October), Castlemaine (12 May 1916), and Domain Camp (as 2nd Lieut. from 6 July, transf'd. Royal Park, 6 October): posted 23rd Reinforcements, 8th Battn. 3 November: departed Melbourne, H.M.A.T. A.20 'Hororata,' 18 November 1916: trained in England, 29 January – 20 April 1917: served with the Expeditionary Force in France from 22 April, joining 8th Battn., Biefvillers, 11 May following: promoted Lieut. 2 August, and was killed instantaneously by a shell in the advance, 20 September 1917, about 800 yards east of Clapham Junction. Buried J.14.d.3.7., Map 28, 2¼ miles south-south-west of Zonnebeke, nr. railway Ypres – Gheluvelt: Age 26. Remains exhumed re. GRU Report – Passchendaele, 51.825/E 51.558/C. Reinterred Tyne Cot British Cemetery, Plot 47, Row, D, Grave 4. He married on 17 November 1916; Gwendolyn ('Fairlight,' Girl's Grammar School,

Alma Road, East St. Kilda, Victoria), to whom his British War Medal (57114), Memorial Scroll (357135) and Brochure 'Where the Australians Rest' (24 August 1921) were duly forwarded; his father received his Victory Medal (56189) and Memorial Plaque (357135).

For Liberty

(XLVII.D.13) Lieut. William Edwin Jenkins, 'B' Flight, 60 Sqdn. Royal Flying Corps and East Surrey Regt.: *s.* of Edwin Jenkins, of Poplar Hall, Fen Ditton, co. Cambridge, by his wife Annie: *b.* Rushden, co. Northampton, 9 July 1898: enlisted in East Surrey Regt.: obtained Royal Aero Club Certificate (no.4414), 14 March 1917, joined 60 Sqdn. R.F.C. the following month. One of the most prestigious Scout Squadrons in the Corps, Jenkins' flight was commanded by the New Zealand 'Ace' Capt. K.L. 'Grid' Caldwell; another flight commander during his service was the famous (arguably infamous) Canadian, Capt. 'Billy' Bishop, V.C. Promoted Lieut. during the summer of 1917, by the time he was killed, Jenkins had been credited with ten victories, *viz.* – one balloon destroyed, three aircraft destroyed (two shared), and six aircraft downed out of control (four shared) – qualifying him as an 'Ace' in his own right. He was killed 23 November 1917, in a mid-air collision with another SE5A of his formation (2nd Lieut. M. West-Thompson), both aircraft crashing near Poperinghe: Age 19.

(XLVII.E.6) Pte. 28919, Ernest Bromley, 11th (Service) Bn. The Border Regt.: formerly no.49916, Manchester Regt.: enlisted Manchester: killed in action on the night of 25 November 1917 when, during a relief near Bellevue Spur, undue noise and commotion drew down a heavy German bombardment on the battalion, resulting in the death of Pte. Bromley and eighteen other men: Age 35. He leaves a wife, Sarah Bromley (37, Ollier Street, Cheetham Hill, Manchester). See account re. L/Corpl. J. Nixon (XXXVII.H.6).

(XLVII.H.13) Pte. 27752, Nicholas Palmer, 6th (Service) Bn. The Duke of Cornwall's Light Infantry: formerly no.22210, Somerset Light Infantry: *s.* of Nicholas Palmer; Tailor and Sub-Postmaster, of The Post Office, Bratton, Clovelly, co. Devon, by his wife Agnes: *b.* Bratton, 1887: Occupation – Postman: enlisted Okehampton. Killed in action 23 August 1917: Age 29. Dedicated 'In Honoured Memory Of The Men Of This Parish Who Gave Their Lives In Their Country's Service In The War 1914-1918;' Pte. Palmer is one of five men remembered on the War Memorial, Bratton.

(XLIX.B.13) 2nd Lieut. 1377, Eric Cecil Howard Ritchie, 'C' Coy., 3rd Bn. Australian Infantry, A.I.F.: *s.* of the late Evan Robert Evans Ritchie, by his wife Cecilia, *née* Crawford (Central Road, Miranda, New South Wales): *b.* Bega, Auckland, 8 January 1890: Occupation – Bank Clerk: enlisted Sydney, 19 August 1914, appointed Signlr. 'G' Coy., 3rd A.I.F., 12 September: departed Australia, 20 October: served at Gallipoli: thereafter proceeded to England: qualified fit to be Platoon Commander, Kandahar Barracks, Tidworth, November 1916 – January 1917, joined 3rd Battn., France, 6 June: promoted 2nd Lieut. 28 July: attended Small Arms Training, Camiers, from 23 August, rejoined Battn. 10 September, killed in action on the 20th; shellfire, Halfway House: Age 27 years, 1 month. Lieut. Allport said, "We were in support near Clapham Junction, which had been our old front line, but from which a recent advance had been made. We were just taking over the original front line when he was struck by pieces of a 5.9 shell, which killed him instantly. I saw him after he fell and examined his body. He was buried in the afternoon, just near where he was killed, and the usual cross erected…He was very well thought of in the battalion, and we were all sorry to lose him."

In Loving Memory
Born At Bega N.S.W. 8.1.1890
Greater Love Hath No Man Than This

(L.F.9) Pte. 24/1757, Henry Morris, 2nd Bn. Auckland Regt., N.Z.E.F.: *s.* of Charles (& Mrs) Morris, of Pah Road, Onehunga, late of Ararua, Matakohe, Kaipara: Occupation – Farmer: enlisted Matakohe, 18 October 1915: departed Wellington, 8 January 1916, 3rd Rfts., 2nd Bn. 'F' Coy., N.Z. Rifle Brigade: served in Egypt (from 8 February), and with the Expeditionary Force in France and Flanders: wounded (gun shot, chest), 15 September 1916, at the Somme: discharged to duty after convalescence and a second period of hospitalisation (mumps), April 1917: reported missing following the fighting at Passchendaele (4.10.1917). A later Court of Enquiry, held on 7 April 1918, finding no evidence of Private Morris having been admitted to hospital or captured as a Prisoner of War, adjudged him to have been killed in action on the aforementioned date: Age 24. *Auckland Weekly News*, 3 October 1918:-

In a hero's grave he sleepeth, somewhere in France he fell,
How little we thought when we parted, it was the last farewell.

(L.G.10) Coy.Sergt.Major 9499, James Hamilton, D.C.M., 2nd Bn. (59th Foot) The East Lancashire Regt.: *b.* Tottenham: enlisted London: served with the Expeditionary Force in France and Flanders from 6 November 1914, and died of wounds, 31 July 1917, received in action at Westhoek Ridge. See account re. Sergt. T.H. Briggs, M.M., 2nd East Lancashire Regt., Ypres (Menin Gate) Memorial (Panel 34).

(LI.C.11) 2nd Lieut. Thomas Tudor Thorp (Special Reserve) 'D' Bty., 83rd Bde., Royal Field Artillery: elder *s.* of Thomas Alder Thorp, of Pondgate Hall, by his wife Elizabeth Jane, *dau.* of Capt. Allen Peat: *b.* Alnwick, co. Northumberland, 5 June 1897: *educ.* Aysgarth School, and Charterhouse: gazetted 2nd Lieut. R.F.A., 16 June 1916: served with the Expeditionary Force in France and Flanders from the following month, taking part in the later battles of the Somme, September – November 1916; killed in action nr. Glencorse Wood, Ypres-Menin Road, 16 August 1917. His Commanding Officer wrote, "He was a most valuable officer, and one of the most fearless that I have ever known. During the last months, on several occasions, he had shown remarkable coolness and bravery under fire, and his conduct was an example to his section. When killed he was acting as Forward Observation Officer (F.O.O.), and had sent down some most valuable information during the morning, which enabled us to disperse an enemy counter-attack: Age 20. *unm.*

Beloved Elder Son Of T.A. Thorp And E. Thorp Pondgate Hall Alnwick

(LI.E.7) Pte. TF/201503, Sidney Herbert Jennings, 1/7th Bn. The Duke of Cambridge's Own (Middlesex Regt.), (T.F.): late of West Green, London, N.15: *s.* of the late Arthur Jennings, by his wife Mary Ann (23, Elm Grove, Dunmow Road, Bishop's Stortford, co Hertford): and elder brother to Pte. TF/4593, W.J. Jennings, Middlesex Regt., killed in action 30 November 1916: enlisted Hornsey, London, N.8. Killed in action 16 August 1917: Age 28. *unm.*

The Lord Gave The Lord Hath Taken Away

His brother William is buried in Pont-du-Hem Military Cemetery (II.C.18).

(LII.D.12) Pte. 241718, Richard Henry Albert Dymond, 5th (Service) Bn. The Queen's Own (Royal West Kent Regt.): *s.* of Richard Henry Dymond, of 37, Motley Street, Battersea, London, S.W., by his wife Louisa, *dau.* of J. Appel: *b.* London, 9 December 1897: *educ.* French Protestant School, London: enlisted 5 September 1916: served with the Expeditionary Force in France and Flanders from 12 September 1917, and was killed in action at Ypres three weeks later, on 4 October 1917: Age 19.

Rest In Peace

(LII.F.12) Pte. 410043, William Arthur Buckland, 38th Bn. Canadian Infantry (Eastern Ontario Regt.), C.E.F.: *s.* of Emily Maria Buckland (40, South Place, Oxford Road, Windsor, co. Berks): and brother to Pte. 788554, F.G. Buckland, 3rd Canadian Infantry, died 3 May 1917, aged 20 years: *b.* London, England, 26 September 1895: Occupation – Farmer: 5'6½" tall, grey eyes, brown hair: religion – Church of England: volunteered and enlisted Ottawa, 21 July 1915; posted 38th Battn.: served with the Expeditionary Force in France and Flanders from 14 August 1916. Killed in action 30 October 1917: Age 22. *unm.* Erected in 1931 by a local Women's Institute, the brothers Buckland are remembered on Vars (Ottawa) War Memorial.

Gone From Memory But Not Forgotten
Mother

His brother Frederick is buried in Orchard Dump Cemetery, Arleux-En-Gohelle (III.E.17).

(LIII.D.10) Pte. 12084, Charles Joseph Walshe, 9th Field Ambulance, Australian Army Medical Corps, A.I.F.: *s.* of George Henry Walshe, of 71, Vincent Street, Albert Park, Victoria, by his wife Esther Matilda: *b.* Rockdale, about 1888: enlisted Liverpool, New South Wales. Killed in action in the vicinity of Frost House, Zonnebeke, 12 October 1917: Age 29. *(IWGC record Walsh)* See Pte. E. Sullivan, Lijssenthoek Military Cemetery (XXII.B.2.A), and Pte. C.O.D. Edser, Ypres (Menin Gate) Memorial (Panel 31).

> *Greater Love Hath No Man Than This*
> *Brothers Reunited*
> *Perfect Peace*

(LIV.B.9) Pte. 26870, Arthur Hatton, 2nd Bn. (99th Foot) The Duke of Edinburgh's (Wiltshire Regt.): formerly no.55334, Sherwood Foresters, and no.32054, Lincolnshire Regt.; twice discharged under age: late of Eastwood, Nottingham: *b.* New Brinsley: Occupation – Miner; Pollington Colliery: enlisted Derby, June 1916 and, after a short period of home leave in September, went to France with 2nd Wiltshire Regt. later that month: took part in some of the severest fighting and was killed in action on 3 December 1917. In a letter to his parents, his Platoon Lieut. wrote, "I am very sorry indeed to write you the sad news of the death of Pte. A. Hatton, who was killed in action on December 3rd, 1917. He was very popular in the platoon, and we all feel his loss very greatly. It may be some consolation to you to know that he was killed instantaneously, and therefore suffered no pain. He was buried by his comrades near where he was killed, and I also was present and saw a cross erected over his grave. By his death I lose a valuable and plucky soldier." A well-known and popular figure in the Brinsley district, he was a member of the Brinsley Comic Band: Age 18.

(LV.A.19) Pte. 25946, Herbert Thomas Hill, 1st Bn. (11th Foot) The Devonshire Regt.: *s.* of Thomas Hill, of Long Street, Tetbury, co. Gloucester, and Emily, his wife: and brother to Pte. 12762, E.E. Hill, 1st Wiltshire Regt., died of wounds 9 June 1917: *b.* Tetbury: enlisted Newton Abbot, co. Devon. Killed in action 4 October 1917: Age 32. He leaves a wife, Grace Irene Hill (2, Rosedale, Westville, Kingsbridge, co. Devon), and family to whom the deepest condolences in their loss are sent. Remembered on Tetbury (St. Saviour's Churchyard) War Memorial.

> *In Memory Of My Beloved Husband*
> *God Touched Him And Took Him*

His brother Ernest is buried in Mendinghem Military Cemetery (II.D.18).

(LV.D.24) L/Corpl. 612489, William Harold 'Bill' Browne, 1st Canterbury Regt., N.Z.E.F.: *s.* of Gertrude (& S.W.) Browne (1, George Street, Rocky Nook, Auckland): and brother to Pte. 81637, A.G. Browne, Otago Regt., died 13 March 1919, of disease; Pte. 48440, A.H.M. Browne, Auckland Regt., died 14 September 1918, of wounds; Tpr. 13/2163, J. Browne, Auckland Mounted Rifles, killed in action 19 April 1917; and Pte. 12/1163, E. Browne, Auckland Regt. (surv'd.): *b.* 18 March 1890: Occupation – Driver: enlisted Auckland, 18 April 1915: departed Wellington, 13 June following: proceeded to Egypt, thence to Gallipoli (wounded 21 December 1915; discharged to duty 5 January 1916): after training in England, joined the Expeditionary Force in France and Flanders, and was killed in action 5 December 1917: Age 27. *unm.*

His brother Arthur is buried in Auckland (Waikumete) Cemetery (A.1.13); Archibald, Barastre Communal Cemetery (9); James has no known grave, he is commemorated on the Jerusalem Memorial (Panel 1).

(LVI.D.21) Pte. G/7953, Richard Batchelor, 1st Bn. (2nd Foot) The Queen's (Royal West Surrey Regt.): *s.* of William Batchelor, of Stoke Bruerne Park, Towcester, co. Northampton, by his wife Rhoda, *dau.* of Richard Cockman: and brother to Corpl. G/13706, W.G. Batchelor, M.M., 1st The Queen's, killed in action in Belgium 3 March 1918: *b.* Camberwell, co. Surrey: enlisted Guildford. Killed in action 25 September 1917. Remains recovered unmarked grave (28NE.J.21.b.48.30); refers GRU report Passchendaele 51 – 919/E; identified – Discs.

His brother William is buried nearby (XIII.E.36).

(LVII.B.20) Pte. 4282, Richard (*a.k.a.* Reuben) Richards, 'C' Coy., 11th Bn. Australian Infantry, A.I.F.: *s.* of the late Alfred (& Cecilia) Richards: *b.* Yarraville, Victoria, 1888: religion – Methodist: Occupation – Labourer: joined A.I.F., Blackboy Hill, 20 September 1915; apptd. 13th Rfts., 11th Bn., 20 November: joined the Expeditionary Force in France, 5 April 1916. Missing / killed in action on 2 November 1917. Buried Kink Cemetery (7 November): Age 29. Pte. Richardson said, "He was sent out of the line at Ypres, as he was more or less worn out. We came out of the line three days later and saw his dead body on the track out. He had apparently been killed by a shell. His body was carried back and buried, as far as I can remember, near Hell Fire Corner." (*IWGC record age 30*)

God Is Love

(LVII.F.11) 2nd Lieut. John Larkin, 41st Bn. Australian Infantry, A.I.F.: *s.* of James Larkin, of Foxton Street, Indooroopilly, Brisbane, Queensland, by his wife Sarah Ann: *b.* Brisbane, 1897: Religion – Church of England: Occupation -Schoolteacher: 5'10½" tall, hazel eyes, light brown hair: a serving Lieut., 'A' Coy. 6th Senior Cadets, enlisted as Pte. 13 January 1915: posted 41st Battn., Bells Paddock, 1 May 1916: promoted Sergt. 15 May and departed Australia the following day: proceeded to France 24 November 1916: returned to England for officer training, Trinity College, Cambridge, 3 January 1917: gazetted 2nd Lieut. 1 May following, posted General Infantry Rfts.: returned to France 15 May rejoining 41st Battn. on the 22nd of that month: attended Infantry School Training, 31 May – 27 June: hospitalised (Debility) 8 – 17 September, rejoined his battalion the following day and was killed in action 5 October 1917, at Zonnebeke: Age 20. Buried Zonnebeke, Sheet 28, NE1, D21.b.c.d., the same day by Rev. W.A. Moore, 43rd Battn. After eighteen months of hoping his son's resting place would be found, 2nd Lieut. Larkin's father wrote, "25 June 1919….Now that Peace Terms have apparently been definitely accepted and signed, and a renewal of hostilities appears remote, I am anxiously seeking information relative to the condition of the ground where my son was buried….I understand this area was, at a later date, under shell fire both from our own and the enemy's guns, and also in German occupation for some time afterwards; and I am afraid this last resting place of our dear dead boys may have been torn up and totally destroyed, leaving no trace of what remained of them. I shall be very grateful for any information you can afford me on the matter…" Following a note dated 21 December 1920 (Refers – Graves Registration Unit Report, Passchendaele, 51.222E) Mr Larkin received the following – "7 April 1921….the remains of your son…were exhumed on the 14 December last and reburied in Tyne Cot British Cemetery, Passchendaele. Identity was established by the inscription 'Jack Larkin from Mother and Father,' which appeared on a silver watch found on the remains…." This was returned to Mr and Mrs Larkin, 3 September 1921. See account Reninghelst New Military Cemetery; Capt. J.R. Eddy (IV.C.4).

(LVIII.A.28) 2nd Lieut. Charles Angelo Moody, No.1 Sqdn. Royal Flying Corps: *s.* of the Rev. Henry Moody, of Welshampton Vicarage, Ellesmere, co. Salop, by his wife Evelyn: and twin brother to Flt. Lieut. H. Moody, Royal Air Force, killed 28 April 1931, in a flying accident. At 6.20 a.m., 21 August 1917, after only ten days with the squadron in France, 2nd Lieut. Moody took off for a patrol over the Houthulst sector. Forty minutes later the patrol of six Nieuport Scouts attacked five enemy scouts, but were then in turn attacked themselves by about a dozen black and white painted Albatross Scouts. Last seen engaged in aerial combat with the larger enemy group, Moody was shot down somewhere over Westroosebeke by (it is believed) Leutnant Fritz Loerzer, of Jasta 26. Removed from the wreckage of his fallen craft, and given water by a German infantryman, 2nd Lieut. Moody succumbed to his wounds before medical assistance could be given. Buried in Hooglede German Cemetery: Age 17. (*IWGC record age 18*)

I Am The Resurrection And The Life Because I Live Ye Shall Also Live

(LVIII.B.16) Rfn. S/15496, John 'Jack' Corder, 9th (Service) Bn. The Prince Consort's Own (The Rifle Brigade): *s.* of the late Thomas Corder, by his wife Martha (The Bungalow, Barrow Hill, Southchurch): *b.* Great Wakering, co. Essex: enlisted Southend-on-Sea, February 1915: killed in action on 24 August

1917. His Company Officer wrote that he was "…a splendid soldier. His death is a severe loss to the company and to the battalion."

(LVIII.D.26) Pte. 552665, James Peter Robertson, V.C., 27th Bn. Canadian Infantry (Manitoba Regt.), C.E.F.: *s.* of Alexander Robertson, of Stellarton, Pictou, Nova Scotia, by his wife Janet: *b.* Stellarton, *afsd.*, 20 November 1883: *educ.* Springhill, Nova Scotia: enlisted 13th Canadian Mounted Rifles, April 1915. He was awarded the Victoria Cross (*London Gazette*, 11 January 1918), "For most conspicuous bravery and devotion to duty in attack. When his platoon was held up by uncut wire and a machine gun causing many casualties, Private Robertson dashed to an opening on the flank, rushed the machine gun, and after a desperate struggle with the crew, killed four and then turned the gun on the remainder, who, overcome by the fierceness of his onslaught, were running towards their own lines. His gallant work enabled the platoon to advance. He inflicted many more casualties among the enemy, and then, carrying the captured machine gun, he led his platoon to the final position, and got the gun into action, firing on the retreating enemy, who by this time were quite demoralised by the fire brought to bear on them. During the consolidation, Private Robertson's most determined use of the machine gun kept down the fire of the enemy's snipers. His courage and his coolness cheered his comrades and inspired them to the finest efforts. Later when two of our snipers were badly wounded in front of our trench, he went out and carried one of them in under very severe fire. He was killed just as he returned with the second man." From official Gazette: "'Singing Pete,' he was called in Alberta, where he was a railway engineer before the great call of the British Empire was heard across our land. Railroad men called him 'Singing Pete' because, day or night, in the cab or the road-house, his song could be heard. Every railroad man up and down the lines knew 'Singing Pete,' and many a time his sunny disposition cheered them and enlivened their hours of hard toil or recreation. In a great gathering of locomotive engineers in Cleveland, after Private Robertson's gallant deed and his fate became known, that gathering of 77,000 strong men from Canada and the United States rose and by a standing vote honoured the memory of the first Locomotive Engineer V.C. Every soldier who knew him and every friend bears testimony to the unfailing cheeriness of the disposition of Private Peter Robertson under every circumstance." One of 'Pete's' comrades wrote, "We all lost in Pete a good pal and friend. He was very popular with both officers and men. In fact, he refused promotion to be with the boys as plain 'Private,' instead of an N.C.O. He was a good soldier. On behalf of his chums and friends, I extend to you our deepest sympathy in your loss and bereavement and share with you in both." His Officer said, "A better soldier and truer comrade never stepped in uniform." Another officer, "He was a dandy soldier and so cheerful and optimistic at all times that he kept the boys in good spirits under even the most trying conditions." Private Robertson was killed in action at Passchendaele on 6 November 1917, aged 34, of perfect build, standing six feet three inches. He always had a song or a joke for everyone. In a letter from France he said, "I met a fine French girl when I was up the lines. She couldn't talk English and I couldn't talk French, but we got along fine, just looking at each other." The Victoria Cross was presented to his mother by Lieut.-Governor Brett, Alberta, at Medicine Hat, 25 April 1918. In the presentation address the Lieut.-Governor said, "This cross is only a small thing, its cost is very little, but it has engraved on it the words 'For Valour,' which means a great deal. Money can do much – with money titles can be bought, but money cannot buy the Victoria Cross. It must be won by valour and service."

Behold How Good And Pleasant It Is For Brethren To Dwell Together In Unity (Mother)

(LVIII.E.24) 2nd Lieut. Edward Lionel Haversham Whall, 18th (Service) Bn. The King's Royal Rifle Corps: only *s.* of the Rev. Edward Haversham Whall, Rector of North Barsham, near Walsingham, co. Norfolk, by his wife Elizabeth Mary, *dau.* of William Townley: *b.* Springfield, near Chelmsford, co. Essex, 6 March 1884: *educ.* Privately, and at Eversley School, Southwold, matriculating at the Dublin University: was a member of the firm of J.S. & C.A. Whall, Solicitors, Worksop: enlisted 3rd Battn. Norfolk Regt., as Private, 3 May 1916: obtained a commission, gazetted 2nd Lieut., King's Royal Rifle Corps, 26 April 1917: served with the Expeditionary Force in France and Flanders from 2 July following, and was killed in action at the Battle of the Menin Road, 20 September 1917, on the first day of his going into action. Buried where he fell. His Colonel wrote, "Although he had only been with us a short time, he had become a great favourite with all his brother officers, and I looked upon him as a most efficient and gallant soldier. He fell at the head of his platoon during the attack on the 20th. The attack was entirely successful, and the success on the particular part of the front on which he was engaged was in a large measure due to his leading and fearless self-sacrifice. We cannot grudge too hardly what he gave so willingly;" and his Commanding Officer, "He did splendidly. The company will miss him tremendously, always cheery, very unassuming and always ready to join in anything. I shall miss him very much; he had not been with me a great length of time, but still long enough for me to learn his worth. The regiment has lost a splendid officer.": Age 33. *unm.*

Thy Will Be Done

Rendezvous

I have a rendezvous with Death
At some disputed barricade,
When Spring comes back with rustling shade
And apple-blossoms fill the air –
I have a rendezvous with Death
When Spring brings back blue days and fair.

It may be he shall take my hand
And lead me into his dark land
And close my eyes and quench my breath –
It may be I shall pass him still.
I have a rendezvous with Death
On some scarred slope of battered hill,
When Spring comes round again this year
And the first meadow-flowers appear.

God knows 'twere better to be deep
Pillowed in silk and scented down,
Where love throbs out in blissful sleep,
Pulse nigh to pulse, and breath to breath,
Where hushed awakenings are dear …
But I've a rendezvous with Death
At midnight in some flaming town,
When Spring trips north again this year,
And I to my pledged word am true,
I shall not fail that rendezvous.

Alan Seeger

Major Tom Bourdillon, King's Royal Rifle Corps, had a rendezvous with death; in 1915 they just missed each other – two years later, under similar circumstances, in almost the same place:-

(LVIII.E.44) Major Thomas 'Tom' Louis Bourdillon, M.C., 8th (Service) Bn. The King's Royal Rifle Corps: only *s.* of Sir James Bourdillon, K.C.S.I., V.D., of Westlands, Liphook, co. Hants, by his wife Lady Bourdillon: *b.* India, 1887: *educ.* Marlborough College, and Corpus Christi, Oxford: passed for the Colonial Civil Service, 1911; left for a position of officialdom in Malay, November of the same year. In February 1915, the Malay Government having decided to release a number of officials, he returned to England: gazetted Lieut., King's Royal Rifle Corps, March 1915, posted 8th Battn.: served with the Expeditionary Force in France and Flanders from May following. On 30 July 1915 he was severely wounded during the counter-attack from Sanctuary Wood, near Hooge, and returned to England. After his recovery he served at home for some time with 14th (Reserve) Battn., until he rejoined the 8th Battn.

in July 1916, and was promoted Captain. In September he was slightly wounded on the Somme, and for his gallantry on that occasion (September15) was awarded the Military Cross. Capt. Bourdillon continued to serve with the 8th Battn. and, in April 1917, was promoted temporary Major and acted as Second-in-Command for several months. On the morning of 24 August 1917 he was slightly wounded by a German attack on the part of the line held by 41st Brigade, near Sanctuary Wood, and was carried into a dug-out; a shell subsequently entering by one of the ventilation holes killed all the unfortunate occupants. His Colonel wrote, "I feel his loss deeply, No one was more generally popular, always cheerful and unselfish… his influence was invariably for the good."

For That They Willingly Offered Themselves Bless The Lord

(LIX.B.11) L/Corpl. G/19275, George Cyril Stanley Mann, Machine Gun Section, 8th (Service) Bn. The East Surrey Regt.: *s.* of Samuel Edward Mann, of 23, Duppas Hill Road, Waddon, co. Surrey, by his wife Louisa, *dau.* of R. Sparrow: *b.* Clapham Common, London, S.W., 15 September 1897: *educ.* Whitgift Middle School, Croydon, where he was a Senior Prefect, and passed all his public examinations with honours: enlisted East Surrey Regt., 22 May 1916: served with the Expeditionary Force in France and Flanders from the following September, and was killed in action nr. Ypres, 9 August 1917. One of his officers wrote, "He had a keen sense of duty, and when any dangerous work was to be performed the boy was foremost in volunteering to do it. In addition to this quality he was a bright and charming lad." He was presented with a Parchment Certificate, signed by the Major General commanding his Division, for 'gallant conduct and devotion to duty in the field 3 May 1917, during operations against Cherisy, when, outnumbered by the enemy, who surrounded his party, he worked his Lewis gun with such effect that it enabled some of his men to escape. Finally, he brought his, the only gun, back to the lines.': Age 19.

His Noble Life Leaves A Glorious Memory

(LIX.B.24) Major Edward Cuthbert Norsworthy, 13th Bn. (Royal Highlanders of Canada) Canadian Infantry, 3rd Brigade, C.E.F.: eldest *s.* of James Counter Norsworthy, of Ingersoll, Ontario, Canada, by his wife Mary Jane, eldest *dau.* of Alexander Cuthbert, of Ingersoll, and *gdson.* of John Norsworthy, of the Parish of Widdicombe, co. Devon, England (who went to Canada in 1852): *b.* Ingersoll, *afsd.* 29 May 1879. Killed in action in the Battle of Langemarck, 22 May 1915: *educ.* Ingersoll, and St. Thomas' Public Schools, from which he passed to the Upper Canada College, and thence matriculated to McGill University, at which time he won the Governor-General's gold medal for mathematics. He subsequently became registered as a Student of the Institute of Actuaries of Great Britain along with his younger brother Stanley. At the examination held that year there were thirty-six candidates writing in the Dominion, of this number five were successful, including Major Norsworthy and his brother. In his student days he had been connected with the Cadet Corps at St. Thomas' Collegiate Institute, and the Upper Canada Rifle Corps. Deciding to adopt a career in the financial world, he obtained a position with Messrs. G.A. Stimson & Co., of Toronto, and in 1901 he opened an office in Montreal as Manager for the Dominion Securities Corporation. He joined the 5th Royal Highlanders as a subaltern, shortly after his arrival there, and after passing his examination at St. John's (Quebec) Military School, he became Capt. in 1905, and Adjutant three years later, and Major in 1909. On the outbreak of war, Major Norsworthy volunteered his services, and helped to organise the 13th Battn. for Active Service, and accompanied it to Europe as Senior Major and Second in Command. While in England he was offered an appointment with Sir Max Aitken, the Canadian 'Eye Witness,' but preferred to remain with his regt. On 22 April 1915, the Germans, using virulent and asphyxiating gases for the first time, were able to overcome a portion of the French troops adjoining our line. In the words of Sir John French's Despatch, 15 June 1915 – "The left flank of the Canadian Division was thus left dangerously exposed to serious attack in flank, and there appeared to be a prospect of their being overwhelmed, and of a successful attempt by the Germans to cut off the British troops occupying the salient to the east. In spite of the danger to which they were exposed, the Royal Highlanders of Canada held their ground with a magnificent display of tenacity and courage; and it is not too much to say that the bearing and conduct of these splendid troops averted a disaster which might have been attended with the most serious consequences." The 13th Battn. (5th Royal Highlanders) were the first Canadian troops to meet a charge of the Germans, and notwithstanding they were greatly outnumbered, and were being attacked in flank in their dug-outs, Major Norsworthy skilfully led his men out to the Ypres-Poelcappelle Road, manning the road ditches facing the advancing Germans, and heroically holding their position, and refusing to give one inch of ground, thereby setting the pace for the whole division. Major Norsworthy's part in the action was thus described by one of the privates present – "After having remained in the dug-outs for about one hour, with our throats parched and our eyes watering, caused by the gas, we could see that the Germans had broken our lines. It was reported to Major Norsworthy, and he gave the order to 'stand to' which we were waiting anxiously to do, and he led us out to the Ypres-Poelcappelle Road. It was not long before they began to pick our boys off. Major Norsworthy was hit in the neck by a bullet, but it did not stop him from walking up and down our line, encouraging our men to hold fast. It was not until he received the second bullet that he had to give in and lie down. We bound him up as well we could, but the second wound was serious, and he died about three-quarters of an hour after." Another Private who was with Major Norsworthy said, "As we advanced out of our dug-outs and trenches – that were being enfiladed – we met a perfect storm of shell and rifle bullets, when some inclinations of hesitancy and flinching were shown. Seeing this, Major Norsworthy sprang to the front and called out, 'Come on men, remember that we are Canadians and all the eyes of Canada are upon us.' His actions and words steadied those that were wavering, and we all followed him with a wild cheer, and advanced to the Ypres-Poelcappelle Road ditches – facing the advancing Germans – which gave us some little protection, and we stuck it there to the last man." The following are extracts spoken to the first Canadian Division after the twelve days and nights of fighting included in the period 22nd of April to the 4th of May, 1915 – "I tell you truly that my heart is so full I hardly know how to speak to you. It is full of sorrow for the loss of those comrades of ours who have gone, and pride in what the first Canadian Division has done. I think it is possible that you do not all of you quite realise that if we had retired in the evening of 22 April, when our allies fell back before the gas and left our left flank quite open, the whole of the 27th and 28th Division would probably have been cut off. This is what our Commander-in-Chief meant when he telegraphed as he did – 'The Canadians saved the situation.' My lads, if ever men have had a right to be praised in this work, you have." Mentioned in F.M. Sir John (now Lord) French's Despatch of 31 May 1915, for 'gallant and distinguished service in the field.': Age 35. *unm.*

Mentioned In Despatches For Gallant And Distinguished Conduct

(LIX.B.28) Lieut. Guy Melfort Drummond, 13th Bn. (Royal Highlanders of Canada) Canadian Infantry, C.E.F.: *s.* of the late Sir George Drummond, K.C.M.G., former President, Bank of Montreal, by his wife Lady Drummond (Montreal), Head of the Canadian Red Cross Information Bureau; Assistant Commissioner, Canadian Red Cross Society: *b.* 15 August 1887: *educ.* St. John's School, Montreal; Bradfield, England; L'Ecole Libre des Sciences Politiques, Paris (1909-1911): after leaving school returned to Canada, where he took a keen interest in military matters, and served with the Militia, attaining rank Capt.: on the outbreak of war with Germany, volunteered with the Active Service Battn. of his regiment, 13th Canadian Infantry, relinquishing his Captaincy that he might immediately proceed to France: commissioned Lieut. 22 September 1914: served with his regiment in Flanders, and was killed in action, 22 April 1915, on which date he was in charge of a support trench at Langemarck. That afternoon the Germans, using asphyxiating gas for the first time, broke in on the Canadian left flank, causing the French Algerians to fall back. Ordering his platoon to line the road, Capt. Drummond went out in front to rally the Turcos. Shot through the throat shortly afterwards, he died almost instantly; the first, it is said, of the Canadians to give his life in that long battle. A number of his men spoke of his wonderful coolness and bravery during all the awful confusion and the rain of bullets, and say that his example and heroism were a great factor in steadying the men in that first critical hour of the fight. His mother and his wife received innumerable tributes from fellow officers and men of his battalion regarding his worth as a soldier and a man, the most touching of these, adding precious detail to the story of his end, was written by his soldier servant, "I am writing these lines to you because Capt. Drummond asked me to write to you if anything happened to him, as he was going to do the same for me if anything happened to me. Well Madam, I don't know if you have heard the true story of your poor husband's death. It was on Thursday night, the 22nd, that the battle started. I was just getting ready to cook the supper for him when the French Turcos came running down towards us, as we were in the reserve trenches they came down, some with rifles and some without. As soon as they got to where we were, a terrific shelling started, so that we all had to get into our dug-outs and we could not move. Well, the Germans were approaching rather near, and we had to get out and look after them. I rushed out and put on your husband's equipment and see that his revolvers was all right, and then we lined the ditch on the road. In the meantime more of these French black fellows was still coming, and the shelling was something fierce, with poisonous gas and lyddite, it was awful; well, when we got into the road the rifle and machine-gun fire was very hot indeed. Major Norsworthy was injured and he sent me on a message. When I got back your poor husband was gone, the last thing I see him doing was trying to rally these Turcos, he was talking to them in French, he was trying to lead them on in battle, but they were too nervous. Your husband walked up and down the road, cheering and jollying us up and speaking to each one of us. Well, Mrs Drummond, your husband was shot through the throat, and him and Norsworthy both fell together; there was one thing I was glad for, your husband got a few Germans before he went under; and another, he did not suffer, his last words were to cheer the boys up. Madam, the Captain was one of the bravest men that I ever see, he use to love us boys and we all use to love him, and the boys miss him keenly, and of course they wish me to say that they wish to express their sympathies to you in your trouble, and I am sure that I do the same, and there are not many left now, there are only a dozen of us. We all hope you will bear up brave in your bereavement, and the boys wish you to convey to his mother a message of condolence, hoping you and his mother will bear up under such trying circumstances.": Age 27. He *m.*, April 1914, Mary Hendrie Stoker, *née* Drummond (692, Mountain Street, Montreal), *dau.* of A.D. Braithwaite, of Montreal, and left a son, Guy Melfort, *b.* posthumously, October 1915.

He Gave His Pure Soul To Unto His Captain Christ

(LIX.B.41) Pte. G/20033, Bertram Edward Worley, 7th (Service) Bn. The Buffs (East Kent Regt.): *s.* of Charles Worley, of 'Priory Mead,' Park Lane, Reigate, co. Surrey, by his wife Fanny: and elder brother to Pte. 10/2381, R.J. Worley, Wellington Regt., N.Z.E.F., died of wounds 28 August 1915, received in action at Gallipoli: *b.* Reigate: enlisted Guildford. Killed in action 6 August 1917: Age 34. Dedicated: "Sons Of This School Let This Of You Be Said That You Who Live Are Worthy Of Your Dead These Gave Their Lives That You Who Live May Reap A Richer Harvest Ere You Fall Asleep" – the brothers Worley are remembered on Reigate Grammar School War Memorial.

Dearly Loved

His brother Robin is buried in Pieta Military Cemetery, Malta (A.XII.5).

(LIX.C.14) Lieut. 82, James Norman Bennett, 1st Bn. Australian Infantry, A.I.F.: *s.* of P.C. (& Mrs A.J.) Bennett, of The Upper Baches, Upton Bishop, Ross, co. Hereford: missing in action 4 October 1917, since confirmed killed: Age 22. *unm.* Buried in a shell-hole by the village of Molenaarenshoek, 28.J.5.a.40.55. Lieut. J.N. Bennett's remains were identified by a damaged identity disc with the partial details '82. Benn.. 6th A.L.H.R.' found on an Australian Lieut. exhumed January 1921, 28.D.28.b.91.; less than ¼ mile north-west of the former referenced place of burial.

(LIX.C.35) Sergt. 8120, Robert Charles Courcoux, (Drmr.), 2nd Bn. (19th Foot) Alexandra Princess of Wales's Own (Yorkshire Regt.), (The Green Howards): *s.* of the late George Courcoux, by his wife Mary Annie (11, Lemperiere Street, St. Helier, Jersey, Channel Islands): and brother to Pte. 42342, J.H. Courcoux, 2nd Yorkshire Regt., 2 December 1917: *b.* St. Peter's, Jersey, 1890: enlisted there. Killed in action 2 August 1917: Age 27. He was married to Angelina Courcoux, *née* Beuchet (9, Francis Street, St. Helier, Jersey).

His brother John is buried in Poelcapelle British Cemetery (XX.C.18).

(LIX.E.33) Lieut. John Farquhar, 204th Sqdn. Royal Air Force: only *s.* of William Farquhar, of India Street, Alexandria, Engineer, by his wife Margaret, *dau.* of the late Frank Munro, of Portmahomack: *b.* Alexandria, co. Dumbarton, 16 September 1899: *educ.* Vale of Leven Academy: joined Royal Flying Corps, 17 September 1917: gazetted Flight Lieut. Royal Air Force, February 1918: graduated as Pilot, May following: proceeded to France, 15 June of the same year, and died, a prisoner of war, at Rosselare, near Roulers, 1 August 1918, of wounds received in aerial action on 31 July. Buried in De Russes Cemetery there. His Commanding Officer wrote, "…His flight got into combat with a flight of hostile machines, and when last seen he was following an enemy machine down… Your son was one of the most popular officers in the squadron, and certainly one of the best pilots. His loss is keenly felt by his brother officers.": Age 18.

Ever In The Memory Of Those Who Loved Him

(LIX.E.42) Corpl. 614181, Hugh William Rainbow, M.M., 2/1st (Warwicks) Bty., Royal Horse Artillery (T.F.): *s.* of the late Charles Rainbow, by his wife Harriett (5, Farley Street, Leamington Spa, co. Warwick): and brother to Pte. 692, F.G. Rainbow, 16th Royal Warwickshire Regt., killed in action 27 October 1917; and 2nd Lieut. A.E. Rainbow, 4th attd. 10th Royal Warwickshire Regt., killed in action 23 July 1916: *b.* Leamington Spa: enlisted there. Killed in action 4 October 1917.

His brothers have no known grave: Frank is recorded on the Tyne Cot Memorial (Panel 27), Albert, Thiepval Memorial, Somme.

(LIX.F.34) Pte. 32972, Albert William Whitwam, 13th (Service) Bn. The Durham Light Infantry: *s.* of Henry Whitwam, of 88, Swallow Lane, Golcar, Huddersfield, by his wife Lavinia: and brother to Pte. 40629, J.H. Whitwam, 8th Northumberland Fusiliers, killed in action 27 September 1918, during the fighting for the villages of Sauchy-Lestree and Epinoy: *b.* Golcar, co. York: enlisted Halifax. Killed in action 20 September 1917: Age 39. (*IWGC record 3rd Bn.*)

Ours In Thought Love And Memory

His brother John is buried in Chapel Corner Cemetery, Sauchy-Lestree (C.10).

(LX.F.19) Rfn. 371174, Herbert Ingham Armitage, 2/8th (City of London) Bn. (Post Office Rifles) The London Regt. (T.F.): *s.* of John Brooke Armitage, of 28, Water Lane, Dewsbury, co. York: *b.* Dewsbury: Occupation – Postman: enlisted London. Killed in action, 30 October 1917: Age 22. *unm.* Rfn. Armitage is one of eight staff members who sacrificed their lives in the Great War remembered on Dewsbury Post Office War Memorial.

Thoughts Of You Are Always Near
From Those Who Loved You Most Sincere

(LXI.B.9) 2nd Lieut. 1436, Percy Irvine Haylock Owen, 'B' Coy., 3rd Bn. Australian Infantry, A.I.F.: *s.* of Lieut. Col. Robert Haylock Owen, C.M.G., of Morton Grange, Tetbury, co. Gloucester, England, by his wife Hilda Grace: *b.* Gibraltar, Spain, 18 November 1890: *educ.* Felstead College: Occupation – Planter: joined A.I.F. 8 November 1915: apptd. Corpl., 'E' Coy., 30 November: obtained a commission, gazetted 2nd Lieut., 27 July 1916: departed Sydney, 7th Rfts., 58th Bn., 3 November 1916: served in France from 4 May 1917, transf'd. 3rd Battn. Killed in action 22 September 1917: Age 26. *unm.* Pte. H.L. Morris said, "We were holding the line on the Ypres – Menin road, and were in front of Polygon Wood. The German strong points, Tower Hamlets were on our right. Either a machine gun bullet or a sniper hit Lieut. Owen, killing him almost instantaneously. He lived about twenty minutes. He wanted to say something to Sergt. Arnold, but could not manage to articulate. Sergt. Arnold buried him at the back of the trenches. A sort of rough cross was put up, but there was little time…"

Dearly Loved Son Of Colonel R.H. And Hilda Grace Owen
He Died For England's Sake

(LXI.J.3) Sergt. 7727, William James Pearce, 2nd Bn. (99th Foot) The Duke of Edinburgh's (Wiltshire Regt.): late of Pembroke Dock, South Wales: *b.* Pewsey, co. Wilts: enlisted Devizes. Killed in action 4 November 1914. *Commemorated on the Ypres (Menin Gate) Memorial (Panel 53). IWGC:1926/MR.29, XXIX,pg.1135.*

(LXI.J.15) Pte. 204581, Malcolm Macphail Mackintosh, 1st Bn. (21st Foot) The Royal Scots Fusiliers: *s.* of James Dunbar Mackintosh, Solicitor; of 63, London Road, Kilmarnock, by his wife Janet, *dau.* of James Macalister: *b.* Kilmarnock, 24 January 1889: *educ.* Irvine Royal Academy; Glasgow High School, and Glasgow University, where he was preparing to sit for his final Law examination: enlisted King's Own Scottish Borderers, Hamilton, 1 September 1916; served in Ireland until January 1917: proceeded to France the following May: transf'd. Royal Scots Fusiliers, and was killed in action near Zonnebeke, 26 September 1917. An officer wrote, "He was a splendid soldier in every respect, and a faithful companion, and his loss is severely felt by the remaining officers and men in the company." An enthusiastic cricketer, Pte. Mackintosh was an exceptionally fine bowler: Age 28. *unm.*

(LXI.K.14) Pte. 8389, William James Barnfield, 1st Bn. (28th Foot) The Gloucestershire Regt.: *s.* of James (& Emma) Barnfield, of Upper Lode Locks, Tewkesbury, co. Gloucester. Killed in action 29 October 1914: Age 25. Remains recovered; Kruiseecke German Military Cemetery, 18 March 1921. *Commemorated on the Ypres (Menin Gate) Memorial (Panel 22). IWGC 1926/MR.29,XIII,pg.80.*

At Rest

(LXI.K.24) Pte. L/9300, Harry George Hambridge, 2nd Bn. (2nd Foot) The Queen's (Royal West Surrey Regt.: late of St. Johns, Knaphill, co. Surrey: employee Goldsworth Nursery: enlisted Guildford: brother to Mrs M.D. Field (2, Knaphill Cottages, Robin Hood Road, Knaphill, Woking): served with the Expeditionary Force in France: reported missing 29 October 1914; now assumed killed: Age 30.

(LXIII.C.3) Pte. 2731, John Middleton, 8th Bn. The Durham Light Infantry (T.F.): *s.* of Thomas Middleton, of 38, South Burns, Chester-le-Street, Co. Durham, by his wife Margaret: and yr. brother to Pte. 325091, J. Middleton, 1/8th Lancashire Fusiliers, killed in action 6 September 1917: *b.* Chester-le-Street, *c.*1896: enlisted Durham: served with the Expeditionary Force in France and Flanders from 17 April 1915; died of wounds 10 May following: Age 19.

Death Divides But Memory Clings

His brother James has no known grave; he is recorded on the Tyne Cot Memorial (Panel 58).

(LXIV.H.3) Pte. L/8915, Charles James Dennis, 2nd Bn. (2nd Foot) The Queen's (Royal West Surrey Regt.): *s.* of Charles Dennis, of 2, Layard Road, Thornton Heath, co. Surrey, late of Upper Norwood, London, S.E., by his wife Caroline: served with the Expeditionary Force from 6 October 1914; reported missing on the 21st of that month at Zonnebeke, nr. Ypres, and now (1916) assumed killed: 21 October 1914: Age 25. *unm.*

(LXV.G.5) Rfn. 38552, Hubert Theodore Langley, 'B' Coy., 4th Bn. 3rd New Zealand Rifle Brigade, N.Z.E.F.: *s.* of Arthur Edward Langley, of Titohi, Kawhia, Te Awamutu, by his wife Rewa Helen: and brother to Dvr. 13/826, R.F. Langley, N.Z. Field Artillery, died of wounds 31 October 1917: Occupation – Engineer; Messrs G. Gilbert, Huntly: enlisted 16 October 1916: departed Wellington, 16 February 1917: served with the Expeditionary Force in France from 26 April; joined 4th Bn. In the Field, 18 June; killed in action 16 November 1917, at Passchendaele: Age 23. *unm.*

His brother Robert is buried in Dozinghem Military Cemetery (XII.D.16).

(LXV.H.4) Pte. 14106, Robert Cameron, 2nd Bn. Grenadier Guards: *s.* of the late Robert Cameron, by his wife Jane (7, Somerset Avenue, Iver, Uxbridge): *b.* Paddington, London, W.2, 1892: enlisted Willesden, London, N.W.10. Killed in action 26 October 1914: Age 22. *unm. Commemorated on the Ypres (Menin Gate) Memorial (Panel 9) IWGC:1926/MR.29,XV,pg.227.*

(LXV.H.15) Pte. 8911, Thomas George Humm (served as Hunt), 1st Bn. (28th Foot) The Gloucestershire Regt.: *s.* of Robert Humm, of 37, Braintree Street, Devonshire Street, Mile End, London, and Mary Jane his spouse: and yr. brother to Pte. 14087, A.G. Humm, 1st Royal Fusiliers,

20 March 1916: *b.* Bethnal Green: enlisted Stratford: served with the Expeditionary Force in France and Flanders from 13 August 1914; killed in action on 30 October following: Age 24. *unm.*

His brother Alfred is commemorated in Sanctuary Wood Cemetery (Sp.Mem.).

(LXV.K.5) Pte. SR/687, George Henry Clark, 9th (Service) Bn. The Royal Sussex Regt.: *s.* of George Clark, of All Saints, co. Hants: *b.* All Saints, *c.*1880: enlisted Shepherd's Bush, London, W. Known to be one of six men reported as having been killed by shellfire on the afternoon of 13 February 1916, and believed to have been buried with Lieut. C.H. Tisdall in the trench they were defending at the time: Age 25. See Menin Road South Military Cemetery (I.G.3)

A Duty Nobly Done Rest In Peace

(LXVI.A.1) Pte. 204008, Cecil Charles Phillips, 5th Bn. The Bedfordshire Regt. (T.F.): *s.* of John Phillips, by his wife Emma: *educ.* Park School, Wellingborough, co. Northampton: Occupation – Foreman; Boot Trade: enlisted 19 January 1917: served with the Expeditionary Force in France and Flanders from 3 May, and was killed in action at Kemmel 25 September following. Buried on the outskirts of Shrewsbury Forest. He *m.* Wellingborough, 19 October 1912; Alice Jane (41, Glen Bank, Wellingborough), *dau.* of Robert Groom, and had a son, Raymond Cecil, *b.* 11 September 1913. (*IWGC record 6th Bn.*)

(LXVI.B.4) L/Corpl. S/8721, John Stanley Futter, 8th (Service) Bn. The Prince Consort's Own (The Rifle Brigade): *s.* of John Futter, of Bradfield, North Walsham, co. Norfolk, by his wife Eliza: and brother to Siglr. 13289, R.F.S. Futter, 10th Essex Regt., died 26 October 1915: *b.* Bradfield: enlisted Norwich: killed in action 16 October 1917.

His brother Robert is buried in Corbie Communal Cemetery (I.B.34).

(LXVI.D.11) Sergt. 24113, Francis Gilbert Curwen, No.1 Coy., 13th Bn. (Quebec Regt.) Canadian Infantry, C.E.F.: *yst. s.* of Robert Curwen, A.R.I.B.A., of 14, Buxton Road, Cricklewood, London, N., by his wife Ann Constance: *b.* Pinner, co. Middlesex, *c.*1886: served with the Expeditionary Force in France, and was killed in action there, 27 April 1915: Age 29.

(LXVII.A.1) Pte. 203141, David Gregory, 2nd Bn. (55th Foot) The Border Regt.: *s.* of the late David Gregory, of Barrow Bridge, Bolton, by his wife Jane, *dau.* of Thomas Booth: *b.* Barrow Bridge, Bolton, co. Lancaster, 15 May 1897: *educ.* Church Road Council School, there: Occupation – Cable Maker; Messrs Glovers, Trafford Park: enlisted Border Regt., 16 April 1917: served with the Expeditionary Force in France and Flanders from July of the same year, and was killed in action south of Zonnebeke, east-north-east of Ypres, 7 October 1917. Buried nr. Zonnebeke: Age 20. *unm.*

Duty Done

(LXVII.E.15) Pte. L/9057, Lionel Vernon Brown, 2nd Bn. (2nd Foot) The Queen's (Royal West Surrey Regt.): *s.* of Thomas Charles Brown, of Linden Wood Cottage, Fairseat, Wrotham, co. Kent, by his wife Emily: served with the Expeditionary Force from 6 October 1914; killed in action at Zonnebeke, 21 October 1914.

In Mem'ry's Hour Loved Ones Linger Near In Proud & Fond Remembrance

(LXVII.H.25) Pte. 5231, Archibald Sneddon, 8th Bn. Australian Infantry, A.I.F.: *s.* of William Sneddon, of 8, Boyle Street, Ballarat East, Victoria, by his wife Emily: *b.* Ballarat, 1878: *educ.* State School, Godden Point: Occupation – Blacksmith: 5'11" tall, blue eyes, dark hair: previously served five years, 7th Australian Infantry Regt.: enlisted Ballarat East, 29 January 1916: departed Melbourne, 1 April following: trained Suez, May 1916, and Perham Downs, June – August: served with the Expeditionary Force in France from 30 August 1916, joining 8th Battn. In the Field, 10 September following, and was killed in action at Polygon Wood, 20 September 1917: Age 39. Lieut. Hall, 8th Battn., recorded, "We were dug into a trench and cramped for room so he jumped into a shell hole alongside us, at Polygon Wood and half an hour after a German shell landed fairly in the hole, and he was badly wounded. He was carried away and died at the dressing station. We had gained the ground and were consolidating." And Pte. 5256, W. Whittington,

"There were a great number of casualties at the time and I am afraid there was no chance of his being taken out for burial and he must have been put under with a good many others on the spot."

Private F.Hodgson, 11th Canadian Field Ambulance:-

26 October 1917: "I was at a place called Tyne Cot. We had two pillboxes there. It was a group of pillboxes. The doctor and his helpers were in one (**R**) and we stretcher-bearers were in another (**L**) about a hundred feet away. It was half under the ground and the entrance was so low you had to wriggle through on your stomach.

The battalion bearers brought the wounded in from the line, which was about a thousand yards away or less. They had the worst job. The doctor dealt with those he could and then we took them down the line. There were three squads of us. Three squads of eight because it took six of us at a time to get one stretcher out through the mud. That day we drew lots to see who should go first. My squad drew the last carry. This was night-time by now, because it was that late before they could get the seriously wounded out, although the walking wounded had been coming in all day. It was a terrible job carrying in the dark – almost impossible. The first call came at about two o'clock in the morning. We wished them good luck, and off they went. They were a long time away. They hadn't come back when No.2 Squad were called out. After a long, long time they returned. Next, No.3 Squad went out. We were glad that it was daylight by then. Away we went with our wounded man, struggling down the track. After a few hundred yards we were caught in a barrage. We put the stretcher-case in a depression in the ground. He was very frightened, the wounded boy. He said to me, "Am I going to die mate?" I said, "Don't be stupid fella. You're going to be all right. As soon as Heinie stops this shelling we'll have you out of here, and they'll fix you up OK. You'll be back across the ocean before you know it." The shelling eased off and we picked him up and set off again. He died before we got him to the Dressing Station. On the way back we passed the remains of our No.1 Squad. There were nothing but limbs all over the place. We lost ten of our stretcher-bearers that day. Hell was never like that...."

Corporal H.C. Baker, 28th Bn. Canadian Infantry:-

7 November 1917: "We were relieved at nightfall on the seventh. We were told to pick up a wounded man, deliver him to the dump and proceed to Ypres. The mud had sucked me almost lifeless. When we got back to the support trench I tried to find a fresh man to help us as far as the dump. I went up to the trench and called down "Hi there!" There was no answer, but I could make out blurred figures below, so I slithered down in, thinking they were sleeping. I shall never forget what I found. Down that stretch of trench the boys were sitting in grotesque positions, and every one was dead. The trench was only shell holes joined up, and it was open to overhead shrapnel fire from both sides.

We took a brief rest and hurried on as best we could to the dump. Our wounded man was too near the Beyond even to know that we were handing him over. Then we set out across the mud and corruption for Ypres. By heading in a general direction, sometimes by blasted roadway, sometimes by duckwalk, sometimes through mud and swamp, we reached the precincts of Ypres. A sentry directed us to a covered-in stall, and here a comrade was ladling out hot soup. I will never forget that bowl of soup. When I've forgotten every sumptuous meal I've ever had, I'll still remember that bowl of good hot soup after seventy-two hours sleepless battle.

They guided us to bivouacs in the cemetery. At daybreak I took stock of my surroundings. I was looking for a not-too-rotten pool in which I could wash my face and hands, and get some water for a shave. I found myself in what had been No Man's Land in the First Battle of Ypres. Two years later all those churned-up remains were still lying there. Unless you walked blindfolded, you couldn't have avoided seeing them. They were French and Belgians. They must have been elite corps, for pretty well all that was left of them were high topped boots, bits of gold-braided uniforms and fancy-dress helmets.

A time was set for parade and roll–call. There weren't too many of us left to answer our names. If there was no response when a name was called, the sergeant would shout out, "Anybody know anything about him?" Sometimes someone replied. More often there was silence.My impression was that we had won the ridge and lost the battalion."

The Ridge and ruins of Passchendaele village were finally taken on 10 November.

Almost without exception, every tour party that visits the salient visits Tyne Cot Cemetery and regularly leave more than just a comment of sentiment in the Visitors Book. On a cold, wet, November afternoon (1997) a poem on a soggy piece of paper beneath a wreath at the Cross of Sacrifice:- *(q.v.)*

Death of Soldiers

Out of the muddy trenches they climb,
War-stricken they march to the front line,
Rat-a-tat-tat from the guns on the hills,
They fall one by one, bodies lying still,
As if they were mannequins on show,
Side by side, covered in blood, row by row,
They are thrusted in to the pit of forgotteness,
There corpses left to rot in loneliness,
And as we remember those men,
The fearful yet brave warriors of long ago,
They who fought for Queen and country,
They who the younger generation did not know,
Warriors who not only live in the memorics of the past,
May you forever more rest in peace at last.

Dedicated to the men and women who gave up their lives to give people like me and others a good future.

Peter D'Souza. 10.11.97.

Attempts to trace Mr D'Souza made at the time proved fruitless and one can only assume that, by his choice of words and grammar, English may not have been his native language; he was probably a member of a visiting local school group. In May 2001 a group from Richard Challoner School (UK) left a purpose made polished block of wood bearing a large poppy, school badge, dedication – *'In memory of all those who Lost their lives in the Great War. Dedicated: Battlefields Trip 2001. Richard Challoner School'* – and verse:-

Oh! Sleep in peace where poppies grow;
The torch your falling hands let go
Was caught by us, again held high,
A beacon light in Flanders sky
That dims the stars to those below.
You are our dead, you held the foe,
And ere the poppies cease to blow,
We'll prove our faith in you who lie
In Flanders Fields.
Oh! Rest in peace, we quickly go
To you who bravely died, and know
In other fields was heard the cry,
For freedom's cause, of you who lie,
So still asleep where poppies grow,
In Flanders Fields

As in rumbling sound, to and fro,
The lightning flashes, sky aglow,
The mighty hosts appear, and high
    above the din of battle cry.
Scarce heard amidst the guns below,
    are fearless hearts who fight the foe,
    and guard the place where poppies grow.
Oh! Sleep in peace, all you who lie
In Flanders Fields.
And still the poppies gently blow,
Between the crosses, row on row,
The larks, still bravely soaring high,
    are singing now their lullaby
    to you who sleep where poppies grow
In Flanders Fields.

(Zonnebeke British Cemetery No.2./Sp.Mem.7) Pte. G/8917, William Bennion, 3rd Bn. (7th Foot) The Royal Fusiliers (City of London Regt.): eldest *s.* of the late Robert Bennion, by his wife Mary (30, Brindley Street, Burslem, Staffordshire), *dau.* of Michael Sherlock: *b.* Burslem, co. Stafford, 14 September 1895: *educ.* Middleport Board School, there: volunteered and enlisted, Burslem, October 1914: served with the Expeditionary Force in France from 1 February 1915 and was killed in action at Zonnebeke, near Ypres, 14 April following. Buried in the cemetery there. He was a good shot, and won three prizes in training before going to the Front. While on duty in Dover one night, he captured a German spy, spying on the aeroplane shed: Age 19.

(Zonnebeke British Cemetery Sp.Mem.8) Pte. 2660, Frank Chilton, 3rd Bn. (7th Foot) The Royal Fusiliers (City of London Regt.): 3rd *s.* of John Chilton, of 8, New Cottages, Chenies, Rickmansworth, Labourer, by his wife Maria, *dau.* of James Chipps: *b.* Chenies, co. Hertford, 4 June 1890: *educ.* Chenies Parish Schools, there: Occupation – Gardener: enlisted Marylebone, 12 September 1914, after the outbreak of war: went to France, March 1915, and was killed in action 14 April following: Age 25. *unm.*

(Sp.Mem.38) Pte. 907426, Frank Dudley Forrester, 29th (Vancouver) Bn. Canadian Infantry (British Columbia Regt.), C.E.F.: *s.* of David A. Forrester, of Clinton, Ontario: *b.* Nokomis, Saskatchewan, 6 November 1889: Religion – Presbyterian: Occupation – Jeweller: serving member 33rd Huron County (Militia); volunteered and enlisted Regina, 20 March 1916. Killed in action 9 November 1917: Age 28. 'One of a burial party going to the forward area near Passchendaele; they were proceeding in groups of four, he being in the last group near to which an enemy shell dropped, exploding an ammunition dump. Death was instantaneous.' Buried Kink Corner Cemetery, 3¼ miles north-east of Ypres (Row B, Grave 4). Known To Be Buried In This Cemetery.

Their Glory Shall Not Be Blotted Out

(Sp.Mem.60) Piper 5173, Henry Barrie, 'D' Coy., 1st Bn. (79th Foot) The Queen's Own (Cameron Highlanders): *s.* of Mrs Mary Barrie: *husb.* to Mrs D Richards, *née* Barrie (13 Maxwell St. Morningside, Edinburgh): *b.* Leith, Midlothian: after enlistment at Edinburgh, 1900, he was posted to 2nd Bn. Cameron Highlanders, Gibraltar: appointed Piper, 1906, he served in Hong Kong and Tientsin, China, 1908 – 09: on the 2nd Battn's return to England, in 1909, transferred to 1st Battn.: was in England on the outbreak of war: volunteered for Service Overseas and went to the Front immediately: served with the Expeditionary Force in France and Flanders, and was killed in action by shellfire near Verbeek Farm, during the First Battle of Ypres, 5 November, 1914. Piper Barrie was a competitive dancer and piper: achieved 1st Place in Sword Dance at the Army Athletic Meeting 1910; also 1st Prize in Highland Fling and Reel, and 2nd Place in Pibroch, at the Annual Games, Murrayfield, 1913: Age 33.

Their Glory Shall Not Be Blotted Out

(Sp.Mem.67) Spr. 541643, Charles Forrest Patterson, 4th Canadian Divn. Signal Coy., Canadian Engineers, C.E.F.: late of 697, Dovercourt Road, Toronto: *s*. of Rev. J.R. Patterson, of 106, Peter Street North, Orillia, Ontario, by his wife Isabella: *b*. Nelles Corners, 4 August 1896: Religion – Methodist: *educ*. Thorold Public School; Brantford Public School and Collegiate; St. Catherine's Collegiate; Victoria College, Toronto, 1914-15, member C.O.T.C. (3 months): enlisted 4th Divn. Signal Coy., December 1915: promoted Corpl., but reverted to Pte. on proceeding to France attd. 11th Infantry Bde.: reached the front line 10 April 1917, the day after the attack at Vimy Ridge, and, from thereafter, served as a linesman through the engagements before Lens and Hill 70. On the day of his death at Passchendaele, 13 November 1917, he, with two others, was laying a line between the advanced Brigade Report Centre and 75th Battn. Headquarters, which was in support. The work had to be carried out under heavy shell fire across five hundred yards of open terrain, and as it was nearing completion a heavy barrage fire opened up preliminary to the German counter-attack. He persisted in carrying on to finish his task, and had almost reached the pill-box with which connection was being made when he was killed instantly by a shell. Of the thirteen signallers who were operating from this pill-box, twelve were killed or seriously wounded. Buried Tyne Cot Cemetery, Hill Crest Farm: Age 21. Known To Be Buried In This Cemetery.

I Thank My God Upon Every Remembrance Of You

UK – 8961, Aust – 1368, NZ – 520, Can – 1011, NF – 14, SAfr – 90, Guernsey – 6, BWI – 2, Ger – 4. Unnamed 8,366 (70% of total). Sp.Mem 101.

The cemetery was designed by Sir Herbert Baker.
The cemetery covers an area of 34, 941 square metres.

Tyne Cot Memorial to the Missing, a semi-circular flint wall, 4.25 metres high, 152 metres long, faced with Portland stone panels on which are carved the names of nearly 35,000 who have no known grave, forms the north-eastern boundary of Tyne Cot Cemetery. There are three apses and two rotundas. The central apse, with 1,179 names, forms the New Zealand Memorial to those who gave their lives in the Third Battle of Ypres and Broodseinde, October 1917. The other two apses, rotundas, and the wall itself, carry the names of 33,707 British, and one Newfoundland soldier who fell in Ypres Salient between 15 August 1917 and the Armistice; in the Third and Fourth Battles of Ypres. Two, domed, arched pavilions at either end of the wall are surmounted by a winged female figure, each bearing a wreath. Both pavilions were constructed atop of German 'pill-boxes'. The following inscription is carved on the frieze above the panels containing the names:- 1914 – HERE ARE RECORDED THE NAMES OF OFFICERS AND MEN OF THE ARMIES OF THE BRITISH EMPIRE WHO FELL IN YPRES SALIENT, BUT TO WHOM THE FORTUNES OF WAR DENIED THE KNOWN AND HONOURED BURIAL GIVEN TO THEIR COMRADES IN DEATH – 1918.

As the troops moved forward the classic drama of the Western Front, the scene that will forever haunt western civilization, was all too vividly, and graphically, re-enacted again. German machine-gunners began to play upon the advancing waves of men, their bullets lashing and spurting from pill-boxes and from behind parapets. In the flame and clamour British troops slogged forward deliberately, almost unhurriedly. They moved from crater to crater, but even in the craters they were not safe, for the German gunners streamed bullets against the edges of the holes and wounded many men lying near the rims. As the British advanced, some seemed to pause and bow their heads; they sank carefully to their knees, they rolled over without haste and then lay quietly in the soft, almost caressing, mud. Others yelled when they were hit, and grabbed frantically at limbs or torso. In their fear of drowning beneath the slime they tried to grip the legs of their comrades, who struggled to break free. The wounded in the muddy water-filled shell holes, shouting, sobbing, mostly drowned. Slowly, their feeble whispers and cries for help unheard by comrades passing by, they slipped down the muddy sides; too weak to hold themselves up, they slid beneath the water below. Thus as time passed by, the battlefield became converted into one vast limbo of dead and dying. Each shell hole, its water blood red, meant another corpse entombed below. A survivor described the scene "…a khaki-clad leg, three heads in a row, the rest of the bodies submerged, giving one the idea that they had used their last ounce of strength to keep their heads above the rising water. In another miniature pond, a hand still gripping a rifle is all that is visible, while its next-door neighbour is occupied by a steel helmet and half a head, the staring eyes glaring icily at the green slime which floats on the surface almost at their level."

Such was the battlefield before Passchendaele. Siegfried Sassoon said – "I died in Hell. They called it Passchendaele…Oh, Jesus make it stop!"

PANEL 1 BEGINS: CAPT. T. EDWARDS – ROYAL MARINES

(Panel 1) Sergt. PO/393 (S), Fred Parkin, 2nd Bn. Royal Marine Light Infantry, 63rd (Royal Naval) Divn.: *s.* of the late Francis Parkin, of North Molton, co. Devon, farmer, by his wife Eliza (North Molton): *b.* North Molton, 3 February 1893: *educ.* Council School, there: enlisted Royal Marine Light Infantry, 18 November 1914: served at the Persian Gulf, February – August 1915: the Expeditionary Force in France and Flanders from September 1916, and was killed in action at Ypres 26 October 1917. Buried there: Age 24. *unm.*

(Panel 1) Pte. PO/1987 (S), Alfred Richard John Anstey, 2nd Bn. Royal Marine Light Infantry, 63rd (Royal Naval) Divn.: eldest *s.* of Alfred Anstey, of 65, High Street, Upper Weston, Bath, by his wife Sarah, *dau.* of Richard Cumper, of Chepstow: *b.* Upper Weston, 13 July 1898: *educ.* C.E. School, there: enlisted 23 February 1917: served with the Expeditionary Force in France and Flanders from 16 July, and was killed in action at Passchendaele 26 October 1917: Age 19.

(Panel 1) Pte. PLY/1400 (S), Douglas Ronald Maurice Hannay, 2nd Bn. Royal Marine Light Infantry, 63rd (Royal Naval) Divn.: *s.* of John (& Mrs) Hannay, of Pouton, Garlieston, co. Wigtown: and *yr.* brother to Pte. 432300, J.D. Hannay, 49th Canadian Infantry, killed in action 4 October 1916: Killed in action 6 November 1917: Age 20. *unm.* Inscribed – "To The Glory Of God And In Memory Of Those Who Made The Supreme Sacrifice In The Great War" the Hannay brothers are among seventeen First World War and one Second World War men recorded on the Sorbie War Memorial situated between Whithorn and Wigtown..

His brother John also has no known grave; he is commemorated on the Canadian National Memorial, Vimy.

(Panel 1) Pte. PO/1677(S), Frank Hatherell, 2nd Bn. Royal Marine Light Infantry, 63rd (Royal Naval) Divn.: *s.* of Alfred Hatherell, of 17, Pembroke Road, Shirehampton, Bristol: and yr. brother to Pte. 3/8167, A.R. Hatherell, 1st Dorsetshire Regt., killed in action 3 May 1915, at the Second Battle of Ypres: Killed in action 26 October 1917, at Passchendaele: Age 20. *unm.*

His brother Alfred also has no known grave; he is commemorated on the Ypres (Menin Gate) Memorial (Panel 37).

PANEL 1 ENDS: PTE. T. ZEBEDEE – ROYAL MARINES

PANEL 2 BEGINS: SUB.LIEUT. W. DOUGLAS – ROYAL NAVAL VOLUNTEER RESERVE

One of the British soldier's great delights was to be able to talk to an officer in the dark and pretend not to know his rank. One black night in 1917, a party of the Artists' Rifles and other units were waiting for ration trucks to come up when the Germans started shelling the area. Quickly scattering, the men sought what available cover was to be had, and, when the shelling was over, the Artists' Rifles officer, in trying to collect his men together, mistakenly asked a member of the R.N.D., "Are you an Artist?" The sailor turned soldier quickly responded, "No, I'm a fucking comedian," and promptly disappeared into the darkness.

(Panel 2) AB. (Wales) Z/891, Henry 'Harry' Berry, Anson Bn., 63rd (Royal Naval) Divn., R.N.V.R.: *s.* of William Featherstone Berry, of 16, Bailey Street, Garndiffaith, co. Monmouth, Coal Miner, by his wife Mary Jane, *dau.* of Henry Cokeley: *b.* Garndiffaith, 31 March 1897: *educ.* Public School, there: Occupation – Miner: joined Royal Naval Division, 3 May 1915: served with the Mediterranean

Expeditionary Force at Gallipoli from the following August, where he remained until the evacuation: proceeded to France May 1916, and was killed in action at Passchendaele 26 October 1917. Buried there. His Commanding Officer spoke in the highest terms of his smartness and intelligence when on observation duty: Age 20. *unm.*

(Panel 2) AB. R/627, Bertie Burrows, Anson Bn., 63rd (Royal Naval) Divn., R.N.V.R.: *s.* of Harry Burrows, of Bardwell Green, Bury St. Edmunds, co. Suffolk, by his wife Sarah E.: *b.* Bardwell, 13 November 1898: *educ.* there: joined Navy 17 January 1917: served with the Expeditionary Force in France for ten months, and was killed in action there, 6 November 1917: Age 18 years, 11 months. (*IWGC record Age 20*)

(Panel 2) AB. (Clyde) Z/800, Joseph G. Forbes, Howe Bn., 63rd (Royal Naval) Divn., R.N.V.R.: *s.* of the late James Forbes, of Bleachfield House, Persleyden, Woodside, co. Aberdeen, by his wife Elizabeth ('Gownlea,' Fauldhouse, co. West Lothian): and brother to Pte. 109342, W.G. Forbes, 4th Canadian Mounted Rifles, killed in action 2 June 1916; and Pte. 1661, G. Forbes, 4th Gordon Highlanders, killed in action 25 September 1915. Killed in action 26 October 1917.

His brothers Walter and Gilbert also have no known graves; they are commemorated on the Ypres (Menin Gate) Memorial, Panels 32 & 38 respectively.

(Panel 2) AB. Z/4585, Walter Futter, Anson Bn. 63rd (Royal Naval) Divn., R.N.V.R.: *s.* of the late Frederick Futter, by his wife Elizabeth (Chapel Street, North Elmham, co. Norfolk): and brother to Pte. 59200, James Futter, N.Z.E.F., killed in action nr. Cambrai, 1 September 1918: *b.* 4 September 1892: *educ.* North Elmham National School: joined Royal Naval Division November 1915: served with the Expeditionary Force in France: reported wounded and missing after the fighting on 26 November 1917, and is now assumed to have been killed in action on or about that date: Age 26. *unm.*

His brother James is buried in Bancourt British Cemetery (I.G.11).

(Panel 2) AB. (London) Z/2502, Arthur William Raffe, Hood Bn., Royal Naval Volunteer Reserve, 63rd (Royal Naval) Divn.: *s.* of Mr (& Mrs) Raffe, of 20, Beatrice Road, Richmond: and brother to Pte. 22939, J.A. Raffe, Border Regt., who died at home, 7 September 1916, of wounds received on Active Service in France: *b.* Richmond. Killed in action in the vicinity of Varlet Farm, south of Poelcapelle, 26 October 1917.

His brother Joseph is buried in Richmond Cemetery (Z.5917).

(Panel 2) AB. (Bristol) Z/4016, Thomas Frederick Steeples, Anson Bn., Royal Naval Volunteer Reserve, 63rd R.N.Divn.: *s.* of George Steeples, of 11, Brandon Street, Leicester, by his wife Elizabeth: and elder brother to Pte. 53233, W.A. Steeples, 2/5th Lincolnshire Regt., killed in action 15 April 1918. Killed in action 26 October 1917: Age 21. *unm.*

His brother William also has no known grave; he is commemorated on the Ploegsteert Memorial (Panel 3).

PANEL 2 ENDS: AB. S. TURNER – ROYAL NAVAL VOLUNTEER RESERVE

PANEL 3 BEGINS: AB. R. TUSON – ROYAL NAVAL VOLUNTEER RESERVE

(Panel 3) AB.R/609, Sydney Rodney Cyril Vince, Anson Bn. 63rd (Royal Naval) Divn., R.N.V.R.: *s.* of R.S. (& Mrs) Vince, of The Post Office, Monks Eleigh, Ipswich: and brother to Corpl. 44510, S.G.G. Vince, Manchester Regt. (*d.*1969), and Pte. 17368, A.W. Vince, Suffolk Regt., who fell, 3 October 1915, at Loos. Killed in action 26 October 1917.

His brother Alfonso also has no known grave; he is commemorated on the Loos Memorial (Dud Corner).

(Panel 3) Corpl. (Actg) 878, Archie Reginald Silver, Household Battalion: formerly no.3986, 2nd Life Guards: *s.* of the late Henry Silver, by his wife Lucy (Chilton, Steventon): and yr. brother to Pte. 12846,

W.A. Silver, 6th Royal Berkshire Regt. attd. Royal Engineers, killed in action 31 March 1917: *b*. Chilton, co. Berks: enlisted Abingdon. Killed in action 12 October 1917: Age 25. *unm*.

His brother William is buried in Abbeville Communal Cemetery Extension (II.D.22).

(Panel 3) Tpr. 2145, Frederick William Barten Sergeant, Household Battalion: *s*. of Frederick John Sergeant, of 20 Park Street, Dover, co. Kent, by his wife Mary Ann, *née* Barten: and brother to Sergt. 1443, H.V. Sergeant, 1/15th London Regt., killed in action 15 October 1915, at Loos: enlisted Knightsbridge, London: served with the Expeditionary Force in France and Flanders from November 1916, took part in the Battle of Arras, April 1917, and was killed in action 11 October 1917, nr. Poelcapelle: Age 31. He was married to Bertha Agnes Sergeant (5, Salisbury Road, Dover).

His brother Harry is buried in Dud Corner Cemetery (V.G.10).

(Panel 3) Pte. 41191, Arthur Warner, The Leicestershire Yeomanry (T.F.): Trooper: *yst. s*. of Adam Warner, of Kibworth Beauchamp, by his wife Georgiana, *dau*. of Frederick Grainger: *b*. Kibworth Beauchamp, co. Leicester, 31 January 1889: *educ*. Grammar School, there: Occupation – Commercial Traveller: joined Leicestershire Yeomanry 13 December 1915: served with the Expeditionary Force in France and Flanders from March 1916, taking part in many engagements, and died at a Casualty Clearing Station, 18 April 1918, of wounds received in action while on patrol a few hours previously. Buried in a Military Cemetery. His Commanding Officer wrote, "He was in my squadron, and I always found him everything that an English soldier should be.": Age 29. *unm*.

PANEL 3 ENDS: WEST SOMERSET YEOMANRY

PANEL 4 BEGINS: HANTS CARIBINIERS YEOMANRY

(Panel 4) Lieut. Thomas Gair: 2nd West Lancashire Brigade, Royal Field Artillery (T.F.): only *survg. s*. of the late John Hamilton Gair, Solicitor, by his wife Martha Grace (Brunt How, Skelwith Bridge, Westmorland), *dau*. of James Thornely, of Liverpool, Solicitor: *b*. Prenton, co. Chester, 14 April 1889: *educ*. Malvern College, and New College, Oxford – graduated with Second Class Honours (History): subsequently articled to Sir Harcourt Clare; County Council Offices, Preston: obtained commission 2nd Lieut., R.F.A., 13 August 1914; promoted Lieut., September 1915: served with the Expeditionary Force in France and Flanders from January 1917, and was killed in action, nr. Ypres, 9 September following: Age 28. *unm*. (*IWGC record 'A' Bty., 276th Bde*.)

(Panel 4) Lieut. Alistair Hendry, 189th Bde., Royal Field Artillery: *s*. of the late William Hendry, by his wife Janet Morrison (The Bruce Hotel, Carnoustie, co. Forfar), *dau*. of the late John Anderson: *b*. Nairn, 31 July 1897: *educ*. High School, Dundee, co. Forfar: Occupation – Jute Apprentice / Clerk; Messrs James Smieton & Sons Ltd.: enlisted 4th Black Watch, August 1914: served with the Expeditionary Force in France and Flanders from 23 February 1915: returned home in September following and, after a period of training at Catterick, co. York, gazetted 2nd Lieut., R.F.A., 6 September 1916: promoted Lieut. July 1917: went back to France the same month, and was killed in action on Tower Hamlets Ridge 27 September following. Buried there: Age 20. He had gone out to find a company of Argyll & Sutherland Highlanders with whom his battery had lost touch for forty-eight hours. He succeeded in his mission, coming upon them when they had fired their last round and given up all hope. Afterwards he and six other infantry officers took cover in a German dugout where they were all killed by a single shell. For this act he was Mentioned in Despatches. His Commanding Officer wrote, "He was only with us a short time, but time to prove he was a gallant officer and out to do all that was possible for Britain. He was very keen to distinguish himself during the operation, so volunteered to go forward as 'Forward Observing Officer' for the Group. He was at the time forward trying to find out the situation, in order that he might inform our artillery as to where our infantry had got to. Had he succeeded, he would have undoubtedly given valuable information. The nation is at a loss of a most gallant officer. We have in our battery now some of his fellow-officers who have known him some time." Another officer wrote: "We, his brother officers in the battery, feel his loss immensely and will miss him tremendously. He was such a popular fellow, and, withal, a fine officer, and we got to hold him in very great esteem. The men, too, saw in him a good, kindly officer, and many were the regrets when they first heard of his decease," and again: "Alistair died nobly, doing a great duty and, had he lived, one which would doubtless have been suitably recognised.": *unm.*

(Panel 4) 2nd Lieut. Denis Godfrey Eagar, 160th Bde., Royal Field Artillery: *s.* of the late Capt. Edward Boaz Eagar (1st Northumberland Fusiliers, served on Nile Expedition, 1898; killed in action at Belmont, 23 November 1899), by his marriage to Ada Franks, *née* Eagar (The Priory, Bishops Cleeve, co. Gloucester): *gdson.* to Lieut.Col. Edward Hungerford Eagar, 40th Foot; and Elizabeth Kelly, of Castle Kelly, Co. Galway: and brother to 2nd Lieut. F.R. Eagar, Royal Field Artillery, killed in action 9 May 1915, aged 21 years: *educ.* Cheltenham College: Killed in action 28 September 1918: Age 19. Dedicated: 'To The Greater Glory Of God And In Loving Memory Of Those Men Who Laid Down Their Lives In The Great War;May They Rest In Peace' – the brothers Eagar are remembered on the Bishops Cleeve War Memorial. Their father (and Lieut. R.W.M. Brine) was killed 23 November 1899 at Belmont, South Africa; shot by a 'wounded' Boer brandishing a white flag.

His brother Francis is buried in Rue-Petillon Military Cemetery (I.A.6).

(Panel 4) Sergt. 36452, Alfred Elwell, 71st Bty., 36th Bde., 2nd Divn. Royal Field Artillery: *s.* of the late Thomas Elwell: *b.* Small Heath, Birmingham, co. Warwick: *educ.* Little Green Lane Council School, there: enlisted Royal Engineers, served 18 years with the Colours, and joined the Reserve: called up on mobilization: served with the Expeditionary Force in France and Flanders from August 1914, and was killed in action at Langemarck 24 October 1917. Buried south-east of Langemarck. His Officer wrote, "He was killed while giving orders to his men to take cover." He *m.* Phoebe (2B, 427, Bolton Road, Small Heath), *dau.* of Stephen Halloway, and had three children – Alfred, *b.* 18 November 1899, Eileen, *b.* 28 March 1913 and Hilda, *b.* 16 October 1914.

(Panel 4) Sergt. 59156, John Edwin Watson, 'D' Bty., 11th Bde., Royal Field Artillery: *s.* of John Thomas Watson, of 19, Baker Street, Doncaster, by his wife Miriam Edith: and brother to Pte. 18314, B.C. Watson, King's Own Yorkshire Light Infantry, killed in action 29 June 1915: *b.* Doncaster: enlisted there: Killed in action 13 April 1918.

His brother Bernard also has no known grave; he is commemorated on the Ypres (Menin Gate) Memorial (Panel 47).

(Panel 4) Corpl. 111981, Arthur Binks, 'D' Bty., 78th Bde., Royal Field Artillery: 2nd *s.* of the late John Hewitt Binks, by his wife Clara (20, Woodsley Road, Leeds), *dau.* of Elliot (& Mary) Moss: *b.* Leeds, 12 July 1898: *educ.* Bellevue Road Council School, and Central High School, there: enlisted 30 December 1915: served with the Expeditionary Force in France and Flanders, from 30 March 1916, and was killed in action near Langemarck 5 October 1917. Buried there.: Age 19.

PANEL 4 ENDS: GNR. A. BADHAM – ROYAL HORSE & ROYAL FIELD ARTILLERY

PANEL 5 BEGINS: GNR. W.H. BAILEY – ROYAL HORSE & ROYAL FIELD ARTILLERY

(Panel 5) Gnr. L/47138, James Beckley, 'A' Bty., 190th Bde., Royal Field Artillery: *s.* of William Beckley, by his wife Isabella: and brother to Pte. 43295, J. Beckley, Duke of Wellington's (West Riding) Regt., who fell, 28 September 1918, during the final advance across the old Somme battlefields: *b.* Beddington Corner, 1892: enlisted Wimbledon, London, S.W.: Killed 26 September 1917, at Passchendaele, Belgium: Age 25.

His brother John is buried in Vielle-Chapelle New Military Cemetery, La Couture (V.D.8).

(Panel 5) Gnr. 153753, Charles Bennett, 'A' Bty., 160th Bde., Royal Horse Artillery: *yst. s.* of the late Charles Bennett, of The Great House Farm, North Nibley, Dursley, co. Gloucester, by his wife Louisa, *dau.* of George Daw, of Nymphsfield: *b.* North Nibley, 11 October 1879: *educ.* Grammar School, Wotton-under-Edge: Occupation – Sole owner / Proprietor of a large dairy business, Islington, London, N.: enlisted 8 September 1916: served with the Expeditionary Force in France and Flanders from 9 May 1917, and was killed in action 22 October 1917. Buried between Boesinghe and Langemarck via Abri

Wood, north of Ypres. An officer wrote, "Gunner Bennett was killed whilst taking ammunition to the guns, under heavy shell fire. We all feel his loss very deeply, as he was very popular in the battery, and his name had been submitted for a commission; and Battery Sergt.Major Herbert Bealey, "His death was a great shock to all the non-commissioned officers and men in the Battery, and more so to myself, for he was one of those very rare men whom one could trust in every way.": Age 38. He *m*. North Nibley, Dursley, 14 April 1915; Ethel Maud (81, Oaklands Grove, Shepherd's Bush, London, W.), *dau*. of John Pollard Wilkins: *s.p.*

(Panel 5) Gnr. 915773, Harry Doe; Actg.Bmdr., 'D' Bty., 317th Bde., Royal Field Artillery: *s*. of George Doe, of 28, Epps Road, Sittingbourne, co. Kent, and Elizabeth, his wife: Killed by the direct hit of an aerial bomb dropped from a German aircraft 8 November 1917: Age 21.

(Panel 5) Gnr. 915697, Herbert Victor Gibson, 'D' Bty., 317th Bde., Royal Field Artillery: *s*. of William R. (& Mrs) Gibson, of 64, Burley Road, Sittingbourne, co. Kent: killed by an aerial bomb dropped from a German aircraft 8 November 1917: Age 20. In a letter to his father, his brother Gnr. William R. Gibson, serving in the same battery, wrote, "Dear Dad, It is not very often that I write you alone, but this time I must for I have some bad news for you. It concerns our Bert. He has met a glorious end and died bravely marking his gun. His death was instantaneous. I was very near him when he died. Do not grieve too much, for he felt no pain, and died like any soldier would wish to. I and another signaller were the only two men left alive on the position. I searched for two hours for his body, and a relief party searched all night, but the only trace we could find of him was a small piece of a letter written to him by grandma. This I am sending you, and also some of his small gear he used to use. Poor Harry Doe, from Epps Road also went, and many others. We have found no trace whatsoever of their bodies; so you see they could not have known anything about it. It gave me a knock, but whatever you do, bear up, and break the news gently, Dad. Believe me, it was a glorious death, and I'm convinced he felt no pain. They all were a splendid lot of heroes."

(Panel 5) Gnr. 931411, Hylton 'Hylt' Rodney Jolliffe, 'C' Bty., 291st Bde. Royal Field Artillery: c/o Mrs L. Jolliffe (c/o B. Ball Esq., Weelpram Chambers, Wolverhampton): *s*. of Rev. E. (& Mrs) Jolliffe, of 'Buena Vista,' Dial Hill, Clevedon, co. Somerset: *b*. Plympton, co. Devon, 1892: enlisted London, E.C.: served with the Expeditionary Force in France and Flanders: Awarded (23 April 1917) 7 Days Field Punishment No.2 – 'Dirty on parade while on active service': killed in action, 26 September 1917. Buried Track 'X' Cemetery: Age 25. Remembered on Compton Road (Trinity Methodist Chapel) War Memorial, Wolverhampton. Although his grave was lost in later fighting, the IWGC records regarding headstone placement and engraving record a memorial cross with Gnr. Jolliffe's details thereon being situated in Track 'X' Cemetery. The visitor's book for this cemetery 6 October 2013 records: 'Found after 96 years;' and 17 October 2013, 'A pleasure to have you back in the family.' A Royal British Legion cross with his name on had been placed there. See Track 'X' Cemetery (E.54).

(Panel 5) Gnr. 260745, Robert Foster Justice, 'D' Bty., 317th Bde., Royal Field Artillery: *s*. of Henry Justice, of Milnhay Road, Langley Mill; Flour-Mill Warehousman, Messrs Smith's, Cromford Road, by his wife Elizabeth: *b*. Milnhay Road, 1886: sometime Groom / Stable-Hand: enlisted Ripon, co. York, January 1917, posted Royal Field Artillery: served with the Expeditionary Force in France and Flanders from 20 April following, and was killed in action, 8 November 1917: Age 31. His widow (34, Station Road, Langley Mill) received the sad news in a letter from the Chaplain, who wrote, "I expect you will have heard by now officially of the death of your husband in action. I write on behalf of the Major, officers and men to offer you our deepest sympathy. Your husband was a brave soldier and died fighting." One of the best known athletes in Langley Mill, Gnr. Justice was a highly skilled football player, playing for both his home and the Eastwood Clubs, he was also a good cricketer, having a career dating back to the days of the Old Pottery Club in the Derbyshire Alliance and, in more recent times, assisted the United C.C. in the same combination. He was also a member of the Y.M.I. (*IWGC record 200745*)

(Panel 5) Gnr. 78060, Bert Pope, 55th Bty., 53rd Bde., Royal Field Artillery: *s*. of William Pope, Butcher, of Heathfield, co. Sussex, by his wife Emily: and brother to Pte. G/54988, W. Pope, Royal

Fusiliers, died of wounds, 9 October 1917, aged 18; and Pte. SD/3654, H.J. Pope, Royal Sussex Regt., died, 29 September 1916, of wounds, aged 27: *b*. Heathfield, *c*.1895: enlisted Woolwich: Killed in action 12 November 1917, nr. Ypres, Belgium: Age 22. *unm*.

His brother Wilfred also has no known grave; he is recorded on Panel 30. Harry is buried in Euston Road Cemetery, Colincamps (I.C.54).

(Panel 5) Gnr. 8231, Percy Albert Robbins, 41st Bty., 42nd Bdc., Royal Field Artillery: 3rd *s*. of the late Alfred John Robbins, by his wife Emily Sarah (1A, Sixth Avenue, Queen's Park, Paddington, London, W.), *dau*. of Lewis Boxall: *b*. Paddington, London, W., 23 December 1898: *educ*. London Orphan Schools, Watford: Occupation – Clerk; Messrs W.H. Smith & Sons, Publishers: enlisted R.F.A. 3 September 1914: served with the Expeditionary Force in France and Flanders from September 1915, and was killed in action at Ferme Vert-Gibet, Ploegsteert, 11 October 1917. His Commanding Officer wrote, "Gunner Robbins was killed instantaneously by a piece of shell at the back of the battery position. He was an excellent signaller and one of the best.": Age 20. *unm*.

PANEL 5 ENDS: GNR. T. RUDGE – ROYAL HORSE & ROYAL FIELD ARTILLERY

PANEL 6 BEGINS: GNR. F.N. SAUNDERS – ROYAL HORSE & ROYAL FIELD ARTILLERY

(Panel 6) Gnr. 198315, Walter Charles Taylor, 26th Bty., 17th Bde., Royal Field Artillery: 2nd *s*. of Albert Taylor, Carpenter, of 49, Sartoris Road, Rushden, co. Northampton, by his wife Sarah: and brother to Pte. 19650, H. Taylor, Northamptonshire Regt., died of wounds, 5 August 1917; and Pte. G/25264, P. Taylor, 1st Queen's, killed in action 13 April 1918: *b*. 1898: employee Messrs Duncan & Davison, Boot Manufacturers, Rushden: enlisted Irchester, co. Northampton: killed in action 12 September 1917: Age 29. A married man, his widow and two children are residing with her parents Mr & Mrs T. Cross, Pytchley Road, Rushden to which address his officer Lieut. Durrell wrote, "I am very sorry indeed to have the painful duty of telling you of your husband's death in action. If the sympathy of myself and of his friends – The NCOs and men of the battery – is any comfort to you in your grief, you have it in full. Though your husband had not been with us very long, he was well known and liked by us all, and his cheerful and willing nature under trying circumstances earned him the respect of officers and men. Nothing one can say can bring him back to you, but perhaps in time hereafter it may comfort you to know that he died a soldier's death. He was with me at the time, and three other gunners working on a new position for the guns. A German shell exploded not far away, and ended your husband's life. His death was absolutely instantaneous, and he felt no pain at all. Of that I can assure you. I took various papers from his pockets before we buried him, including a bible and several letters. These will be forwarded to you in due course, and also the location of his grave. I was present at his burial, and have made arrangements about erecting a cross. If there is any other information at all that I can give you, please let me know." A fourth brother, William, also served with the Royal Field Artillery (surv'd).

His brother Harold is buried in Mendinghem British Cemetery (IV.A.20); Percy has no known grave, he is commemorated on the Ploegsteert Memorial (Panel 2).

(Panel 6) Gnr. 227553, James George Thomson, 'A' Bty., 330th Bde., Royal Field Artillery: *s*. of James Thomson, of Fochabers, Cabinet Maker: *b*. Fochabers, 20 December 1893: *educ*. Milne's Institution, Fochabers, matriculated Arts (1913), and Aberdeen University, from whence, as a member of 'U' Coy., O.T.C., he was mobilised on the outbreak of war, August 1914, and went to France with 4th Gordon Highlanders, in which regiment he attained the rank of Sergt. and, after being wounded in 1915, transf'd. Royal Field Artillery, and was killed in action 19 October 1917. Remembered by his comrades in the University O.T.C. for his keen sense of humour; one was prompted to say, "Every experience, even in the dreary days of trench life, contributed something to the stock of good stories which he loved to tell.": Age 24. *unm*.

(Panel 6) Bmdr. 217889, Ernest Edward Francis, 85th Bty., 11th Army Bde., Royal Field Artillery: *s*. of Edward Francis, of 152, Wrexham Road, Whitchurch, by his wife Henrietta, *dau*. of James Beach:

b. Chelmarsh, Bridgnorth, co. Salop, 30 September 1896: *educ.* Arley King's School, Stourport-on-Severn; and Whitchurch School: Occupation – Apprentice Bootmaker: enlisted Army Veterinary Corps, 16 February 1916: subsequently transf'd. R.F.A.: served with the Expeditionary Force in France and Flanders from April 1917, and was killed in action nr. Mont Rouge, 25 April 1918. Buried where he fell: Age 21. *unm.* (*IWGC record Dvr.*)

(Panel 6) Bmdr. 23516, John David Limmex, 'D' Bty., 50th Bde., Royal Field Artillery: *s.* of the late John (& Sarah Ann) Limmex, of East Ham, London, E.: and brother to Pte. 18514, A.S. Limmex, 1st Essex Regt., died at sea 20 November 1915; Sergt. 17060, C.H. Limmex, 368th Bty., Royal Field Artillery, died 17 April 1915, also at sea; and Pte. 8712, W. Limmex, 1st Yorkshire Regt., died in India 6 February 1918, of sickness: *b.* London, E.: enlisted Stratford: Killed in action 18 October 1917. One of four brothers who fell.

His brothers Archibald and Charles have no known grave, they are commemorated on the Helles Memorial; Walter is buried in Peshawar (Right:B.C.XLIV.21), commemorated on the Delhi (India Gate) Memorial (Face 1).

(Panel 6) Bmdr. 22562, Sydney Henry Marshall, 'C' Bty., 82nd Bde. Royal Field Artillery: *s.* of Henry Marshall, of 10, Cunningham Road, South Tottenham, London, by his wife Ellen: Killed in action 27 October 1917, being 'blown to bits by a 15cm. shell' while returning to the battery with rations: Age 29. *unm.* See Gnr. J. Clarke, Dozinghem Military Cemetery (IX.A.20).

(Panel 6) Bmdr. 891295, John Edward Oakley, 'D' (Howitzer) Bty., 94th Bde., Royal Field Artillery: eldest *s.* of Henry Edward Oakley, Builder; of 162, Cromwell Road, Peterborough, by his wife Annie, *dau.* of John Bachelor: *b.* Peterborough, co. Northampton, 5 June 1898: *educ.* St. John's School: Occupation – Junior Clerk; Messrs Hall & Sons, Engineers: enlisted Royal Field Artillery, 28 August 1914, at the age of 16: was for some time employed as Signalling Instructor, High Wycombe, co. Buckingham: served with the Expeditionary Force in France and Flanders from 17 September 1917, and was killed in action at Inverness Copse, south of the Menin Road, 30 October following. Buried where he fell. His Commanding Officer, Major C.M. Taylor, wrote, "He was hit by a piece of shell and was killed instantly. He had only joined the battery a few weeks, but had done his work well while he was here," and the Chaplain, "He had time to win the respect and admiration of his comrades, and his death is a blow to all.": Age 18. (*IWGC record 'B' Bty.*)

(Panel 6) Bmdr. 845226, William Edwin Wells, 'B' Bty., 242nd Bde., Royal Field Artillery: *s.* of Joseph Wells, of 192, Balsall Heath Road, Birmingham, Engineer, by his wife Hannah, *dau.* of William Middleton: *b.* Birmingham, co. Warwick, 14 September 1893: *educ.* St. Paul's Schools, Vincent Street, Balsall Heath: Occupation – Tin Plate Worker; Randle & Smith's, Rea Street, Birmingham: joined 48th (South Midland) Bde. Royal Field Artillery Territorials, 8 June 1909: called up on mobilisation, 4 August 1914: served with the Expeditionary Force in France and Flanders from 31 March 1915: wounded in the fighting on the Somme, 16 May 1916: Killed in action nr. Zillebeke, 26 September 1917. Major H.P. Haynes, his Commanding Officer, wrote, "He was a very willing and reliable soldier, and will be missed by his comrades, who he had been with from first joining the Territorials.": Age 24. He *m.* St. Thomas-on-the-Moors, Birmingham, 29 November 1915; Edith Clara White, *née* Wells (202, Mary Street, Balsall Heath, Birmingham), *dau.* of Samuel Meddings: *s.p.*

(Panel 6) L/Bmdr. 97743, Thomas Fuller, 'A' Bty., 51st Bde. Royal Field Artillery: late of 67, Robert Street, West Gorton, nr. Longsight, Manchester: *s.* of the late William James Fuller, and his wife Agnes (Beaconsfield Place, Oliver Lane, Huddersfield): and brother to Pte. 82436, A.E. Fuller, 20th Durham Light Infantry, killed in action 14 October 1918: *b.* Swettenham, co. Chester: volunteered and enlisted Ashton-under-Lyne, co. Lancaster, August 1914: proceeded to France July 1916: took part in the Battle of the Somme, Messines, Third Ypres (Passchendaele), and was killed in action 19 July 1918, at Meteren: Age 22. In Remembrance: "*The Path Of Duty Was The Way To Glory*"

His brother Alfred also has no known grave; he is commemorated on Panel 129.

(Panel 6) Dvr. L/25333, Jonah Booth, 34th Divn. Ammunition Col., Royal Field Artillery: *s.* of George Booth, of 71, High Road, Short Heath, co. Stafford, by his wife Fanny: and brother to Pte. 14657,

C. Booth, 31st Machine Gun Corps (Inf.), killed in action 25 March 1918: *b*. Short Heath, 1896: Killed in action 20 October 1917: Age 21.

His brother Charles is buried in Bucquoy Road Cemetery, Ficheux (VI.D.2).

(Panel 6) Dvr. 831775, William Ness, M.M., 'A' Bty., 87th Bde., Royal Field Artillery: only *s*. of David Ness, of Loanhead Farm, Darvel, co. Ayr: *b*. West Kilbride, co. Ayr, 16 May 1895: *educ*. Riccarton, Kilmarnock: Occupation – Agriculturalist: enlisted December 1915: served with the Expeditionary Force in France and Flanders from May 1916, and was killed in action in the vicinity of Kemmel Hill, 14 April 1918. Buried south-east of Poperinghe. He was awarded the Military Medal for 'gallantry displayed in the field.': Age 22. *unm*.

(Panel 6) Dvr. 105999, Cecil Charles Gentle, 64th Bty., 5th Bde. Royal Field Artillery: *s*. of Albert Gentle, of Harpenden House, Hunstanton, co. Norfolk, by his wife Harriet Mary: and brother to Bmdr. 63835, A.T. Gentle, 86th Bty., 32nd Bde. Royal Field Artillery, died 23 April 1917, of wounds: *b*. Hunstanton: enlisted Norwich: Killed in action 16 September 1917: Age 23. *unm*.

His brother Albert is buried in Duisans British Cemetery (IV.A.6).

(Panel 6) Dvr. 70526, Harry Low Summers, 8th Divisional Ammunition Column, Royal Field Artillery: *s*. of the late James Summers, Sadler, by his wife Margaret (13, Glamis Road, Forfar), *dau*. of James Penny: *b*. Blairgowrie, co. Perth, 20 August 1897: *educ*. Burgh School, Forfar: Occupation – Grocer: enlisted 9 January 1915: served with the Expeditionary Force in France and Flanders from the following July, and was killed in action at Zonnebeke, 20 November 1917. Buried at Seine Corner, north of Zonnebeke. An officer wrote, "He will be greatly missed as he was a very reliable and plucky driver, and very cheery among his chums.": Age 20. *unm*.

(Panel 6) Siglr. 177485, Frederick Harry Spriggs, 'D' Bty., 38th Bde. Royal Field Artillery: *s*. of Harry Spriggs, of Royston Street, Potton, co. Bedford, by his wife Mary, *dau*. of John Jones: *b*. Sawston, co. Cambridge, 3 August 1888: *educ*. Potton Council School, co. Bedford: Occupation – Parchment Maker and Splitter: enlisted 1 October 1916: served with the Expeditionary Force in France and Flanders from 25 June 1917: was twice gassed, and was killed in action between Neuve Eglise and Dranoutre, 13 April 1918. Recommended by his Commanding Officer for the Military Medal, for taking important messages to Headquarters under heavy shell fire, 23 September 1917, and for laying a wire under shell fire, 150 yards from the German lines. Unfortunately his Colonel was killed: Age 29. He *m*. at the Wesleyan Church, Potton, co. Bedford, 18 March 1911; Louisa Ellen (Royston Street, Potton, Sandy, co. Bedford), since re-married, now Mrs Keeling (Bull Street, Potton), *dau*. of Charles Peck, of Everton Heath, Gamlingay, co. Cambridge, Market Gardener.

(Panel 6) Ftr.S/Sergt. 148869, David Drynan Forbes, 326th Siege Bty., Royal Garrison Artillery: 2nd *s*. of John Forbes, of 'Claremont', Bent Road, Hamilton, by his wife Jane, *dau*. of David Drynan: *b*. Hamilton, co. Lanark, 26 March 1892: *educ*. St. John's Grammar School, there: was an Engineer: enlisted in the 7th Battn. Seaforth Highlanders 22 October 1914, served with the Expeditionary Force in France and Flanders from 9 May 1915: was gassed at Loos the following September, and was twice wounded: transferred to the Royal Garrison Artillery in February 1917, and was killed in action 20 September following. His Commanding Officer wrote: "Your son's merits stood out conspicuously, and I am bringing his conduct to the notice of higher authority. He was a hard worker and skilful craftsman, and a fearless soldier. You may be very proud of him." He took a keen interest in football.: Age 25. *unm*.

PANEL 6 ENDS: BMDR. V. ZOLLER: ROYAL GARRISON ARTILLERY

PANEL 7 BEGINS: L/BMDR. T. BAILEY – ROYAL GARRISON ARTILLERY

(Panel 7) Gnr. 116326, Francis Edgar Giles, 280th Siege Bty., Royal Garrison Artillery: *s*. of the late J. Robert Giles, by his wife Martha (Stanton Fitzwarren, Highworth, co. Wilts): *b*. Stanton: enlisted Devizes: Killed in action 24 September 1917: Age 19. Dedicated: 'To The Brave Lads Of Stanton Fitzwarren Who Gave Themselves To God, King And Country In The Great War Beginning August

1914: On Whom & All Souls Jesu Mercy;' one of seven men remembered on the St. Leonard's (Parish Churchyard) War Memorial; five – Pte. F.H. Adams, Coldstream Guards; Gnr. F.E. Giles; Rfn. H. Giles, 21st London Regt.; Pte. W.J. Landfear, Wiltshire Regt. – are buried/commemorated within the confines of Ypres salient.

(Panel 7) Gnr. 56647, Wilfrid Walter Henbest, 24th Siege Bty., Royal Garrison Artillery: *s.* of William Murray Henbest, Farmer; of Ford Farm, Bisley, co. Surrey, by his wife Eliza, *dau.* of the late Daniel New, of Weybridge, co. Surrey: *b.* Bramshaw, co. Hants, 11 October 1892: *educ.* Elementary School, there: Occupation – Valet; Redhill, co. Surrey: enlisted R.G.A., 1 January 1915: served with the Expeditionary Force in France and Flanders from the following August, and was killed in action nr. Ypres, 26 September 1917. Buried at Verbranden-Molen, south-east of Ypres. His Commanding Officer wrote, "I came in touch with your son very much, and always found him cheerful, energetic and willing. He was, I am certain, a most popular man with all his comrades.": Age 24. *unm.* (*IWGC record age 25*)

(Panel 7) Gnr. 86540, Leonard Ellerm Jenkins, 250th Siege Bty., Royal Garrison Artillery: *s.* of the late George Jenkins, by his wife Harriet (38, Bell Road, Hounslow, co. Middlesex): and brother to Pte. 9247, George Jenkins, 2nd Honourable Artillery Coy., who was killed in action 15 May 1917: *b.* London, 24 May 1888: *educ.* Owen's School: Occupation – Hosier's Assistant: enlisted Royal Garrison Artillery, 25 May 1916: served with the Expeditionary Force in France and Flanders from the following August: was accidentally wounded while acting as a Despatch Rider for the Battery, and invalided home in April 1917: returned to France, March 1918; killed in action at Kemmel, nr. Ypres, 25 April following. Buried nr. La Clytte. He *m.* Nunhead, 1 September 1913; Edith Hilda (3, King's Avenue, Hounslow), *dau.* of Henry Morgan, and had a *dau.* Daphne Hilda, *b.* 1 October 1914. (*IWGC record age 29*)

His brother George also has no known grave; he is commemorated on the Arras (Faubourg d'Amiens) Memorial (Bay 1).

(Panel 7) Gnr. 135027, James Alfred Ward, 326th Siege Bty., Royal Garrison Artillery: *s.* of the late James Ward, of Morton Road, Lowestoft, by his wife Bessie (98, Norwich Road, Lowestoft), *dau.* of William Hall: *b.* Lowestoft, co. Suffolk, 28 April 1898: *educ.* Morton Road County Council School: employee Conservative Club, Lowestoft: enlisted Royal Garrison Artillery, 18 May 1916: served with the Expeditionary Force in France and Flanders from 20 September 1917, and was killed in action at Zillebeke Lake, nr. Ypres, 29 October following. Buried nr. Mount Sorrell: Age 19. (*IWGC record 31 October*)

(Panel 7) Gnr. 85898, Harry Stanley Wing, 70th Siege Bty., Royal Garrison Artillery: late of 33, West Street, Stratford-on-Avon: *s.* of the late Charles Wing, by his wife Lettitia Ann (11, Irchester Road, Rushden, co. Northampton): and elder brother to Sergt. 288, B. Wing, Queen's Westminster Rifles, killed in action 1 July 1916, at the Somme (*IWGC record 554820*): *b.* Bury St. Edmunds, co. Suffolk, 1883: Occupation – Butchery Manager: enlisted Stratford-on-Avon, co. Warwick, 8 December 1915: served with the Expeditionary Force in France from 26 May 1916, and was killed in action 29 April 1918, at duty as Dispatch Rider: Age 34.

His brother Bertie is buried in Gommecourt British Cemetery No.2, Hebuterne (III.J.18).

(Panel 7) Signlr. 87235, Thomas Rowe, 1/1st (Welsh) Heavy Bty., Royal Garrison Artillery (T.F.): *s.* of Thomas Rowe: *b.* St. Ives, co. Cornwall, about 1888: *educ.* there: employee Great Western Railway Co.: joined Royal Garrison Artillery, 23 May 1916: served with the Expeditionary Force in France and Flanders from 20 February 1917, and was killed in action at Zillebeke 25 April 1918. Buried there: Age 29. He *m.* New Connexion Chapel, St. Ives; Jane Wedge Collings, *née* Rowe (since re-married, 11, The Lawn, St. Blazey, co. Cornwall), *dau.* of Robert Welch, and had two children – Jane Wedge, *b.* 12 January 1908 and Thomas Stevens, *b.* 6 July 1911.

On the morning of 9 October 1917, 2nd Honourable Artillery Company moved up to head a limited attack by 7th Division on Reutel. Flanked on the left by 2nd Royal Warwicks, their objective was the Blue Line originally designated for 21st Division five days previously. At zero hour, 5.20 a.m., despite atrocious weather and the veritable bog across which they had to attack, thirty minutes after going over the top, green flares signalled the H.A.C. had reached their objective. But by the time this success had been relayed back to Battalion Headquarters, situated in the Buttes, the H.A.C. ".. had reached their final objective in the village of Reutel, shooting down many Germans as they retreated, and had established posts on the west and south east corners of the cemetery. These posts were reported to have no officers left, except Lieut. F.A. Kup, who was lying badly wounded…" After encountering considerable resistance from two pill-boxes in the vicinity of the cemetery, these were, after very stiff fighting during which most of 12 Platoon, C Company were killed, eventually overcome. "At 10.35 a.m. Capt. Murray, went forward to attempt to obtain more accurate information and to clear up the situation, which was then very obscure. Capt. Murray made towards the western edge of Reutel and Juniper Cottage, but apparently lost direction, passed unchallenged through a post of a battalion of Leicesters, and advanced beyond the British lines, when he was shot dead by a party of Germans. This gallant officer was observing the enemy's position from a shell hole when he was shot in the chest, but endeavoured to continue his observations and was shot through the head. By midday… no officer of those who took part in the assault remained unwounded."

(Panel 7) Capt. (Adjt.) Ernest Francis Hume Murray, M.C., D.C.M., 2nd Bn. Honourable Artillery Coy. (T.F.): *s.* of Francis Henry Murray, of 20, Conan Mansions, West Kensington, London, W., by his wife Mary Catherine: Killed in action 9 October 1917: Age 29. *unm.*

(Panel 7) 2nd Lieut. Raymond Cecil Devereux Moore, 2nd Bn. Honourable Artillery Company (T.F.): eldest *s.* of Reginald Devereux Moore, of Churchdown, co. Gloucester, Capt., Royal Army Medical Corps (T.F.)., by his wife Charlotte Mabel: *b.* Stoney Stanton, co. Leicester, 7 October 1897: *educ.* Glyngarth, Cheltenham; Cheltenham College; Oxford University (scholarship): joined Honourable Artillery Company, 8 May 1916: gazetted 2nd Lieut., 26 April 1917: served with the Expeditionary Force in France and Flanders from the following July, and was killed in action at Reutel, 9 October 1917. His Commanding Officer wrote, "He was leading his platoon, which came under heavy machine gun fire from the left flank, and he was unfortunately hit. From what I have been able to find out, he behaved most gallantly, urging his platoon forward, until he was hit a second time. He was a splendid boy, and everyone thought the world of him.": Age 20 years and 2 days. *unm.*

(Panel 7) Coy.Sergt.Maj. 2817, William Harry Thorne Worth, 2nd Bn. Honourable Artillery Company (T.F.): only *s.* of Harry Walter Worth, of The Feathers Hotel, High Street, Budleigh Salterton, co. Devon, by his wife Lucy A., *dau.* Charles Thorne: *b.* Broadclyst, nr. Exeter, co. Devon, 12 April 1891: *educ.* King's School, Ottery St. Mary; Pharmaceutical College, Bloomsbury Square, London, W.C.: Occupation – Chemist: volunteered for Active Service, August 1914: joined Honourable Artillery Coy., November following: served with the Expeditionary Force in France and Flanders from 1 October 1916, and was killed in action during the fighting at Polygon Wood, nr. Ypres, 10 October 1917. Buried where he fell. A comrade wrote, "I have lost a good pal in him, as well as an excellent colleague as Coy.Sergt.Major." He was a keen sportsman, and a valuable and prominent member of the Pharmaceutical Football Club: Age 26. *unm.*

(Panel 7) L/Corpl. 6700, Cyril John Dowley, 2nd Bn. Honourable Artillery Company (T.F.): *s.* of the late Pearse Walter Dowley, of 'Kenora,' Egmont Road, Sutton, co. Surrey, by his marriage to Kate Frost, *née* Dowley (87, Cranfield Road, Brockley, London, S.E.): and elder brother to Pte. 205361, H.F. Dowley, 2/4th York & Lancaster Regt., died 3 December 1918, at the Base, Etaples: enlisted Armoury House: Killed in action 28 October 1917: Age 28.

His brother Harold is buried in Etaples Military Cemetery (XLVII.A.3).

(Panel 7) Pte. 10570, Arthur Gwilliam Brown 2nd Bn. Honourable Artillery Company (T.F.): *s.* of the late Mr Brown, by his wife Florence Laverack: and *gdson.* to Dr. Brown, of Mortlake, London, S.W.: *b.* Dukinfield, co. Chester: 22 November 1880: *educ.* Urmston: Occupation – Sole proprietor of a Ladies Underskirt business, 27, Cannon Street, Manchester: joined H.A.C., 4 March 1917: served with the Expeditionary Force in France from 29 May following, and was killed in action at Reutel, Passchendaele, 9 October 1917, while dressing the wounds of a comrade: Age 36. He *m.* The Cathedral, Manchester, 4 February 1909; Jessie, *dau.* of William Henry Holt, of Ashton-under-Lyne, and had four children – Joan, *b.* 12 November, 1909, Nancy, *b.* 21 January 1913, David, *b.* 25 April 1915 and Gwilliam , *b.* 2 December 1917.

(Panel 7) Pte. 10494, Richard John Donovan, 2nd Bn. Honourable Artillery Company (T.F.): *s.* of the late Cornelius (& Mrs.) Donovan, who both died of typhoid fever: following the death of both parents he was raised by a maiden aunt, Theresa Donovan: *b.* Liverpool, 1883: *educ.* Ratcliffe College, co. Leicester, from eight years of age: in his last year he played for his school 1st XI football team and the cricket team. His School Obituary states – ".. His face, with its honest clear eyes, is one that stands out vividly from the multitude of faces that crowd in upon memories of the past, and where the lineaments of others grow dim as the years recede, his is not to be forgotten for its transparent goodness. His character was such as one associates with the ideal schoolboy, keen sportsman, straight-forward and to be relied upon, not wholly innocent of scrapes, unaffectedly good. 'He was of a type,' writes one who was at school with him, 'which it would be difficult to beat – quiet and kindhearted, but full of spirit and grit, the sort of fellow one liked to have in a football team for a tight corner and the clean sportsmanlike way he played games was the clue to the rest of his life.'" After enlisting at Armoury House, he was sent to France, 15 May 1917, with a draft sent out to bring the battalion up to strength following its losses at Bullecourt, and was killed in action either in Polygon Wood 'when one shell fell on the track between C and D Companies, killing and wounding half a dozen men', or when the battalion 'came under a heavy barrage on the way to Jolting Houses Trench and sustained further casualties.': Age 34. Pte. Donovan leaves a widow, Evelyn (6, Park Terrace, Waterloo Park, Liverpool), and two sons.

(Panel 7) Pte. 10557, Robert James Joint, 'D'Coy., 2nd Bn. Honourable Artillery Company (T.F.): eldest *s.* of the late William James Joint, Wholesale Game Dealer; by his wife Maud Mary (103, Boutport Street, Barnstaple), *dau.* of the late W.P. Janes: *b.* Barnstaple, co. Devon, 27 May 1896: *educ.* West Buckland School: prior to enlistment was (with his mother) in Wholesale Game Dealer business: joined Honourable Artillery Company, March 1917: served with the Expeditionary Force in France from the following May, and was killed in action at Passchendaele Ridge, 9 October 1917. Major Wright wrote, "Your son was reported as missing on the 9th, and there can be no doubt now that he was killed. I can only add that he died gallantly in an action in which the battalion was successful in obtaining its objective.": Age 21. *unm.*

(Panel 7) Pte. 10174, Felix Leopold Samuel, 2nd Bn. Honourable Artillery Company (T.F.): *yst. s.* of Jack Samuel, of 47, Goldhurst Terrace, Hampstead, London, N.W., Lithographic Printer, Nottingham, by his wife Frances 'Fanny' Alice Samuel, *dau.* of Julia Samuel: and gt.-nephew of Sir Marcus Samuel, Bart.: *b.* Clacton-on-Sea, co. Essex, 26 June 1897: *educ.* Haberdashers' School, Hampstead, London, N.W.: Occupation – Engineer: joined Honourable Artillery Company, 5 February 1917; served with the Expeditionary Force in France from 8 May following. Killed in action nr. Reutel, south of Zonnebeke, 8 October 1917. Buried where he fell.: Age 20. *unm.*

PANEL 7 ENDS: PTE. C.A. WOOD – HONOURABLE ARTILLERY COY.

PANEL 8 BEGINS: LIEUT. W.G. BRUCE – ROYAL ENGINEERS

(Panel 8) L/Corpl. 20022, Thomas Alexander Mathieson, 106th Field Coy., Royal Engineers: eldest *s.* of the late Robert Mathieson, by his wife Susan, *née* White: *b.* Waimangaroa, Buller, New Zealand, 24 February 1887: *educ.* there: came to England, March 1910; enlisted Royal Engineers: served three years with the Colours, and joined the Reserve: called up on mobilisation, 5 August 1914: served with the Expeditionary Force in France and Flanders from August 1915, and was killed in action near Neuve Eglise 17 April 1918. Buried where he fell: Age 31. He *m.* Ayr, 14 November 1913; Sarah (35A, Sandgate, Ayr), *dau.* of Robert Park, and had a *dau.* Edith, *b.* 23 April 1914.

(Panel 8) Spr. 414669, Alex Cain, 82nd Field Coy., Royal Engineers: *s.* of the late John Cain, by his wife Martha (Douglas House, Isle of Whithorn, co. Wigtown): and brother to Pte. 318322, D. Cain, Royal Army Medical Corps, who died 8 August 1918: enlisted Whithorn: Killed in action 11 April 1918.

His brother Daniel is buried in Hagle Dump Cemetery (II.F.2).

(Panel 8) Spr. 551124, Ernest Fletcher, 106th Field Coy., Royal Engineers: *s.* of the late Amos Fletcher, of Clevering Farm, Hacheston, Wickham Market, Suffolk, and Maria Fletcher, his wife: and brother to L/Corpl. 17823, H.C. Fletcher, 19th King's (Liverpool) Regt., died 1 May 1917: *b.* Easton: enlisted Wickham Market: Killed in action 9 April 1918: Age 30. He was married to Alice Louisa Lowick, *née* Fletcher (99, St. Helen's Street, Ipswich).

His brother Harry is buried in Hacheston (All Saints) Churchyard.

(Panel 8) Pnr. 203305, Arthur Cyril Jenkins, 209th Field Coy., Royal Engineers: *s.* of the late James Jenkins, of Pentre, co. Glamorgan, Surveyor, by his wife Margaret Ann, *dau.* of the late George (& Mary) Saunders: *b.* Ystradyfodwg, co. Glamorgan, 12 February 1890: *educ.* Board School, there; Porth County School, and Porth Pupil Teachers' Centre: was for some years Assistant Surveyor, Crawshay Bailey Estate, Pentre, and afterwards on the Engineers' Staff, Cardiff Railway Company: joined Royal Engineers, 17 October 1916: served with the Expeditionary Force in France and Flanders from 25 April 1917, and was killed in action between Langemarck and Poelcapelle 18 October following. Buried where he fell. His Commanding Officer wrote, "He had only been with this unit for about five months, but we all thought very highly of him, and I had noted his name for promotion. He did his work thoroughly well ... I miss him very much. He was always capable and always willing and cheerful.": Age 27. *unm.*

(Panel 8) Spr. 139542, George Polden Ledgley, 54th Field Coy., Royal Engineers: *s.* of James George Ledgley, of 40, Albany Road, Windsor, co. Berks, by his wife Harriet: and elder brother to Pte. TF/5514, E. Ledgley, 7th Middlesex Regt., who fell 26 August 1916, at the Somme: Killed in action 25 October 1917: Age 29. He leaves a wife, Mary Anne Ledgley (4, Jennings Street, Swindon, co. Wilts), by whom all correspondence from officers and comrades who knew her late husband would be most gratefully received.

His brother Ernest also has no known grave, he is commemorated on the Thiepval Memorial, Somme.

(Panel 8) Spr. 207254, William Lockley, 134th Army Transport Coy., Royal Engineers: formerly no.1747, Cheshire Regt.: *s.* of Thomas Lockley, of 26, Louise Street, Garden Lane, Chester, by his wife Ellen: and elder brother to Pte. 29550, J. Lockley, 2/8th Royal Warwickshire Regt., killed in action 4 September 1917, aged 26 yrs.; and Sergt. 1263, T. Lockley, D.C.M., 1/5th Cheshire Regt., killed in action 28 December 1915, aged 23 yrs.: *b.* Chester, *c.*1890: enlisted there: served with the Expeditionary Force in France, and was killed in action 26 October 1917: Age 27. *unm.* All correspondence regarding the deceased should be addressed c/o Spr. Lockley's parents.

His brother Joseph also has no known grave, he is recorded on Panel 26; Thomas is buried in Suzanne Communal Cemetery Extension (B.3).

PANEL 8 ENDS: PNR. S. WATSON – ROYAL ENGINEERS

PANEL 9 BEGINS: LIEUT. F.W.R. GREENHILL – GRENADIER GUARDS

(Panel 9) Lieut. Frederick William Ridge Greenhill, 3rd Bn. Grenadier Guards: *s.* of the late Henry Ridge Greehnhill, Solicitor, of 4, Cullum Street, London, E.C., and Stamford Hill, London, N.: *b.* 4 June 1892: *educ.* Merchant Taylors' School, and Lincoln College, Oxford: was articled to his father's partner in 1913, and had passed his intermediate examination when he joined the Artists' Rifles, February 1916: gazetted 2nd Lieut. Grenadier Guards, August 1916; promoted Lieut. the following December: served with the Expeditionary Force in France and Flanders from February 1917, and was killed in action at Poelcappelle 10 October following. Buried there. His Commanding Officer wrote, "It may be a comfort to you to know how highly we thought of our late comrade, and how deeply we deplore that a soul so bright and so useful should have been taken away from amongst us;" and another officer, "He had the satisfaction of knowing that we had been completely successful, and he had, as Intelligence Officer, materially contributed to that success. Thanks to his leading, the battalion avoided two barrages which would have caused serious casualties." Many other officers wrote in terms of warm admiration, both of his personal qualities as a man and a comrade, and of his capabilities as a soldier and an officer. He was a splendid athlete, captained the Merchant Taylors' cricket, football, and fives teams, and was a member of the Authentics Club, and played for his College and the Artists' Rifles O.T.C., as well as in the matches for public schools at the Oval in 1914: Age 25. *unm.*

(Panel 9) Pte. 22332, Thomas Anthony Brocklehurst, 3rd Bn. Grenadier Guards: *s.* of John Brocklehurst, of 'Ash Tree View,' Sheldon, Bakewell, co. Derby, by his wife Louisa: and brother to Pte. 8010, J. Brocklehurst, Northumberland Fusiliers, died of wounds 30 November 1916, at Rouen: *b.* Sheldon, *c.*1891: enlisted Buxton: Killed in action 9 October 1917: Age 26.

His brother John is buried in St. Sever Cemetery Extension (O.III.M.5).

(Panel 9) Capt. Claude Stewart Jackson, 3rd Bn. Coldstream Guards: 4th *s.* of the late Sir Thomas Jackson, by his wife Lady Amelia Lydia Jackson (8, Sussex Square, London, W.2, & Stanstead House, Stanstead, co. Essex), *dau.* of George Julius Dare: *b.* Chislehurst, co. Kent, 20 January 1892: *educ.* Harrow; Royal Military College, Sandhurst: gazetted 2nd Lieut., Coldstream Guards, 24 February 1912; promoted Lieut. 4 November 1914; Capt., 3 December 1915: served with the Expeditionary Force in France and Flanders from August 1914: took part in the Retreat from Mons, the Battles of the Marne and the Aisne, being severely wounded in the head in September and invalided home: held several staff appointments in France after convalescence: rejoined the battalion, September 1917, and was killed in action nr. Ypres, 9 October following. Buried where he fell: Age 25. His Colonel wrote, "He led his Company, as we all knew he would (until he was close to the final objective), with the utmost bravery and coolness under a heavy fire, both from artillery and machine guns; he never faltered or stopped, and his company, inspired by his example, showed the same spirit... Absolutely fearless and cool under fire, he served with distinction at Landrecies and again on the Marne. For these services he was Mentioned in Despatches... In him we had an ideal Company Commander, brave and resolute, beloved by his men. He is one of those we can ill afford to lose, and cannot replace." Mentioned in Despatches (*London Gazette*, 19 October 1914) by F.M. Sir John (now Lord) French, for 'gallant and distinguished service in the field.' He *m.* Brompton Parish Church, 6 May 1916; Laura Emily, *dau.* of the Hon. William Pearson, of Kilmany, Gippsland, Australia.

First published in the '*Westminster Gazette*,' and much admired in its day, '*A Plea for War*' was a poem 'poles apart from the agonised and bitter poetry of Wilfred Owen and Siegfried Sassoon.' A typical verse read:

> There were never such days as these to scan
> The God in man –
> And praised be war, if only that it brings
> Rest from the weary strife with little things.

One can be assured the strife of the author, Denis Buxton, was far from little, but one would hope that somewhere on the battlefield in front of Vee Bend Farm his God found the man in him and took him safely to His care.

(Panel 9) 2nd Lieut. the Hon. Denis Bertram Sydney Buxton, 2nd Bn. Coldstream Guards: *s.* of Sydney Charles Buxton, 1st Viscount, of Newtimber Place, co. Sussex, formerly Governor, South Africa; by his wife Viscountess Mildred Anne Buxton, *née* Smith (now Earl & Countess Buxton): *b.* 15, Eaton Place, London, 29 November 1897: *educ.* Eton College, Mr Well's House (September 1910) where he showed 'brilliant promise,' was House Capt., and 6th Form member: left Eton, summer 1915 and, prior to joining the Army, travelled to South Africa to visit his father: proceeded to France with a draft of reinforcements August 1917, killed in action 9 October 1917, being hit in the neck by a shell fragment while leading his company in an assault. Lieut. W.B. St. Leger, M.C., wrote, "I was told Denis was delighted at the prospect of going over the top. 'Won't St. Leger and Butler-Thwing – those two professional parapet poppers – be sick when they find what they have missed and we have gone over and they haven't." Corpl. Ronson informed that he found 2nd Lieut. Buxton lying in a shell hole, 'he had bled a tremendous lot and had slipped down into the bottom of the hole, up to his waist in water. He simply said, "I'm hit, Corporal Ronson" and told the men to go on. I pulled the piece of shell out of his neck, bandaged the wound, made him comfortable against the side of the hole where he could be seen, yet under cover, and went on. After the company reached its objective I sent a man back to look for Mr Buxton, but he could not find him. He had passed the first objective and gone altogether about a thousand yards when he was hit..." The *Eton Chronicle* recorded, "It is hardly possible to say how much he was loved by his friends and how deeply they will feel his loss. He combined the highest intellectual ability with a great personal charm and in the world of politics which he intended to enter after the war there was no distinction to which he might justly have aspired and the most brilliant future seemed to lie before him. His life, alas, has been cut short but it was full of happiness – a happiness which he unconsciously spread among all his friends who will never forget his high ideals and his noble character." Age 19.

Lieut. W.B. St. Leger was killed in action 27 April 1918; buried Ayette British Cemetery (A.4).

(Panel 9) 2nd Lieut. Eric Balfour Lundie, 3rd Bn. Coldstream Guards: late of Johannesburg, South Africa: *b.* Willowvale, Cape Province, 15 March 1888: Killed in action 12 September 1917: Age 29. Better known as Bill Lundie, he played cricket for South Africa. In the 1914 Test Match against England, at Crusaders Ground, Port Elizabeth, he bowled 46 overs into a strong wind, taking 4 for 106. He *m.* 1 November 1916; Susanna Elizabeth Hall (Queenstown).

(Panel 9) L/Corpl. 13059, Arthur Leslie Mears, 3rd Bn. Coldstream Guards: late of City Cottages, Ditchling Common, Ditchling, nr. Lewes: *s.* of Alfred Mears, of The Old Cottage, Wivelsfield Green, nr. Lewes, co. East Sussex, by his wife Lucy E.: and elder brother to Pte. 29874, A.H. Mears, Royal Warwickshire Regt., killed in action, 4 October 1917: *b.* Ditchling, 25 December 1893: *educ.* Ditchling (St. Margaret's) School: Occupation – Gardener, The Downs, Hassocks, and Preston, Brighton: enlisted Brighton, October 1914: served with the Expeditionary Force in France and Flanders, and was killed in action 11 September 1917, by a shell which killed several of his comrades also. He had only two weeks previously returned to his unit from a period of leave spent with his family. A Lieut. wrote, "Dear Mrs Mears...You are the mother of one of the best Englishmen that ever lived. In his death, too, he was an Englishman, and what better epitaph could be given to anyone?" A comrade stated that at the time of his death the battalion were under extremely heavy shellfire and L/Corpl. Mears inspired his men with his confidence. He added that not only was death instantaneous, but that he met it bravely with a smile on his face: Age 24. *unm.*

His brother Alfred is buried in Tyne Cot Cemetery (XII.C.17).

(Panel 9) Pte. 17519, Albert William Felgate, 1st Bn. Coldstream Guards: *s.* of John Felgate, of 5, Deben Road, Woodbridge, co. Suffolk, and Harriet, his wife: and elder brother to Pte. 1758, H.P. Felgate, 3/1st Suffolk Yeomanry, died 28 July 1916, at home: enlisted Colchester: Killed in action, 9 October 1917: Age 30. He was married to Lena Abbot, *née* Felgate (8, Church Lane Cottages, Ramsholt).

His brother Harry is buried in Woodbridge Cemetery (I.12.1).

(Panel 9) Pte. 17905, Thomas Grout, 3rd Bn. Coldstream Guards: *s.* of Egbert Grout, of Rose Bank, Bersted, Bognor, Gardener, by his wife Susan, *dau.* of Thomas Pay, of Felpham, co. Sussex: *b.* Bersted, afsd., 1893: *educ.* there: Occupation – Brickmaker: enlisted Coldstream Guards, 23 January 1916: served with the Expeditionary Force in France and Flanders from the following October, and was killed in action 9 October 1917. Buried in Houthulst Forest, nr. Ypres. His Commanding Officer, in a letter, stated that he had always been a bright and cheerful man, always ready to do his duty, and respected by all who knew him: Age 24. He *m.* Bersted Church; Lily (North View, Chichester Road, Bognor), *dau.* of William Clinch, formerly of Aldwick, co. Sussex: *s.p.*

PANEL 9 ENDS: PTE. T.G. HAINES – COLDSTREAM GUARDS

PANEL 10 BEGINS: PTE. W.F. HANCOCKS – COLDSTREAM GUARDS

(Panel 10) Pte. 18432, Harry Monnery, 3rd Bn. Coldstream Guards: 2nd *s.* of William Monnery, of Pullenbury Cottages, Grinstead Lane, Lancing, Market Gardener, by his wife Mary: and brother to Pte. 26156, W. Monnery, King's Shropshire Light Infantry, who fell, 22 August 1917: *b.* Sompting, co.

Sussex, 8 August 1882: *educ*. there: sometime salesman; Messrs. H. & A. Pullen-Burry, and Licensed Victualler; Ashurst: volunteered and enlisted Lord Derby Scheme, 10 December 1915: called up, apptd. Coldstream Guards Depot, Caterham, 7 June 1916: underwent basic training, and was sent to France, joining 3rd Battn. of his regiment in Flanders, where he was killed in action, 9 October 1917, during the battalion attack against German positions nr. Houthulst Forest: Age 35. He *m*. Lancing, 24 April 1908; Jessie Harriett Saunders, late of The Fountain Inn, Ashurst.

His brother William also has no known grave; he is recorded on Panel 112.

(Panel 10) Pte. 16239, Luis Harold Perez, No.1 Coy., 2nd Bn. Coldstream Guards: *s*. of Mario Atanasio Perez, of 11, Groby Road, Chorlton-cum-Hardy, Manchester, Buyer & Traveller, Manchester Export Trade; by his late wife Sarita, *dau*. of Thomas (& Sarah) Loudon, of Holliwood, Belfast: *b*. Chorlton-cum-Hardy, Manchester, co. Lancaster, 23 June 1897: *educ*. Manchester Grammar School: enlisted Scottish Borderers, September 1914, but was discharged as under military age: re-enlisted Coldstream Guards, 31 May 1915: served with the Expeditionary Force in France and Flanders from 8 June 1916: took part in the Battle of the Somme, and was killed in action by shell fire nr. Langemarck, 8 September 1917. Buried there. His Commanding Officer wrote, "He was a most excellent soldier in every way, and his death is a great loss to the company in which he had done invaluable service. He had lately been selected by his platoon officer, who was wounded by the same shell, as platoon orderly;" and his Chaplain, "You have the pride and joy of knowing that your son died a hero's death for his King and country. I know that his comrades will miss him now that he is gone." A comrade also wrote, "I shall always remember your son through an observation on his pay during my stay at Windsor. You can't take an interest in all if you have 1,066 men on your books. Perhaps I took greater notice of Luis than I do of others;" and another, "His loss will be keenly felt amongst us. He was a fine soldier, and knew no fear; rather an exception in that respect.": Age 20. *unm*.

(Panel 10) Pte. 11750, Robert Percival Teale, 2nd Bn. Coldstream Guards: 3rd *s*. of Robert Parker Teale, of 'Brownhill Cottage,' 149, Soothill Lane, Batley, by his wife Harriet Ann: and elder brother to Pte. 8518, E. Teale, 2nd Royal Scots, killed in action 24 November 1914: *b*. Batley, co. York, 1885: enlisted Dewsbury, September 1914: served with the Expeditionary Force in France and Flanders from 1915, and was killed in action on 10 October 1917, in the attack toward Houthulst Forest: Age 32. Prior to his death in action Pte. Teale had been four times previously wounded.

His brother Ernest also has no known grave; he is commemorated on the Ploegsteert Memorial (Panel 1).

(Panel 10) Pte. 15890, Harry Wardell, 2nd Bn. Coldstream Guards: *s*. of James Wardell, of 45, Mill Lane, Beverley, General Labourer, by his wife Hannah Mary, *dau*. of Hosdale Railton: *b*. Beverley, co. York, 28 July 1897: *educ*. Spencer Council School: Occupation – Brewer's Clerk: enlisted Coldstream Guards, 25 March 1915, at the age of 17: served with the Expeditionary Force In France and Flanders from the following December, being employed as Orderly Room Clerk for 15 months on account of his age, and died at Langemarck, 9 October 1917, from wounds received in action the same day. Buried near where he fell. His Commanding Officer wrote, "He had not been under my command very long, but he was in action with me on 31 July, when he behaved most gallantly, as he has always done in an attack, in holding his line. He was a fine example of a brave man. Coming out here to do his bit, he did it, and was always bright and cheerful. He died a Guardsman; I can say no more;" and a Corpl., "He was a good soldier, always so bright and cheerful.": Age 20. *unm*.

"My Company was given the job of throwing three pontoon bridges across a river, practically under the noses of the Bosches, and this was done without being spotted, thanks to a light yet moonless night. F Company, next door, were not so fortunate. Markham, in command of a party, was spotted relieving outposts across the same river in bright moonlight, and the Bosches killed two of his party of four and shot him through both knees – a strong party of them then came out, and our remaining two men had to run back. They tried to hold off the Bosches but their rifles were clogged with mud and they could not fire. Meanwhile poor Markham was lying propped against a tree between the two sides. A sergeant tried to bring him in, but he was in too great pain to be moved, so we had to leave him. Afterwards a Bosche was seen talking to him, but the following night when a patrol went out they could find no trace of him, so he is either killed or a prisoner....": *Wilfrid Ewart.*

(Panel 10) 2nd Lieut. Montagu Wilfred Markham, 2nd Bn. Scots Guards: *s.* of Lieut.Gen. Sir Edwin Markham, and his wife Emily Evelyn Lucy Markham, *née* Stopford: *b.* 20 November 1884: missing and wounded, believed killed in action on the night of 29 – 30 August 1917; before Langemarck: Age 32. He leaves a widow (*m.* 17 September 1914) Dorothy Markham, *dau.* of Rev. George Stopford Ram, and the Hon. Charlotte Ann O'Brien, and *dau.* Rosemary Anne, *b.* 17 July 1916.

(Panel 10) Pte. 15193, Alexander Rollo Adam, 1st Bn. Scots Guards: *s.* of James Adam, of 'The Laurels,' Perth Road, Blairgowrie, co. Perth, and his wife Jessie Ann, *dau.* of Alexander Rollo: *b.* Airlie, co. Forfar, 13 February 1896: *educ.* Clunie Public School; Blairgowrie High School, Perth: Occupation – Ironmonger: enlisted 27 January 1916: served with the Expeditionary Force in France from 2 May 1917; killed in action at Langemarck, Belgium, 9 October following. Buried where he fell: Age 21. His Commanding Officer wrote, "He was a splendid boy, and has been in my platoon for a long time, and I have always looked upon him as a very good soldier. He was very popular in the company, and will be missed by all." *unm.*

(Panel 10) Pte. 15799, George Quinton Angus, 2nd Bn. Scots Guards: 3rd *s.* of William Angus, of 7, Burns Road, Aberdeen, Merchant, by his wife Isabella, *dau.* of William Stephen: *b.* Aberdeen, 4 October 1891: *educ.* Gordon's College, there: subsequently joined his father in business: enlisted June 1916: served with the Expeditionary Force in France and Flanders, from August 1917, and was killed in action at Houthulst Forest, 13 October following. Buried where he fell: Age 26. *unm.*

(Panel 10) Pte. 15968, Thomas McKeddie Davie, 2nd Bn. Scots Guards: 3rd *s.* of James Johnston Davie, of South Auchray Farm, Strathmartin, nr. Dundee, by his wife Mary, *dau.* of David Bruce: *b.* Kirriemuir, 26 June 1889: *educ.* Airlie Public School: Occupation – Jute Stower; Dundee: enlisted 3 October 1916: served with the Expeditionary Force in France and Flanders from 6 August 1917; killed in action nr. Ney Wood, past Gautersgale Farm, nr. Langemarck, 12 October following: Buried there: His Commanding Officer wrote, "You will, ere this, have received the sad intimation of the death of Private T. Davie, No.15968. I saw him shortly before he was killed. He was at that time doing good and useful work in a brave and fearless manner. I have known him for some time, and early spotted him as a very good soldier. He was always cheerful and willing to undertake any duties which came his way, however difficult or dangerous they were. Everyone in his platoon grieves his loss. His confident and ready bearing inspired confidence in all ranks. I miss him much. It is difficult to offer you the usual regrets and consolation, but you can tell all his friends and relations that he died bravely doing his duty, and that they all have reason to be proud of him;" and the Chaplain, "I expect ere this reaches you, you will have had official notice of the death of your son, Private T. Davie. I have been away on leave, and so have been prevented from communicating with you earlier. Your boy was acting coy. orderly: the 12th inst. the orderly having been killed the night before. He was sent down with a water party to fetch rations for his comrades. He was caught in a shell burst and killed instantly. As far as I am aware none of his effects were recovered, owing to the heavy shelling. Officers and men unite with me in sending their deep sympathy in your great loss.": Age 28: *unm.*

(Panel 10) Pte. 15330, Harry Hardman, 1st Bn. Scots Guards: 2nd *s.* of Robert Hardman, Sheet Metal Worker; of 611, Halliwell Road, Bolton, by his wife Mary, *dau.* of William Keeley: *b.* Bolton, co. Lancaster, 3 January 1895: *educ.* Clarendon Street Board School, there: joined Lancashire Fusiliers at the age of 16: served with them in India, returning to England, 1912: joined Scots Guards, February 1916: served with the Expeditionary Force in France and Flanders from 9 August 1917, and was killed in action, 10 October following. Buried on the battlefield. His Commanding Officer wrote, "He has been in my company only a short while, but long enough to show what a sterling fellow he was and to become popular with all his comrades.": Age 22. *unm.*

(Panel 10) Pte. 16083, John Mitchell, 1st Bn. Scots Guards: 4th *s.* of the late Andrew Mitchell, Stonemason, by his wife Annie (*d. 18 February 1918*), *dau.* of the late Alexander Stephen: *b.* Haddock Cottages, Cairnie, 27 March 1898: *educ.* Rothiemay Public School, and on leaving there was apprenticed as a Stonemason: enlisted 19 October 1916: served with the Expeditionary Force in France and Flanders from 11 August 1917, and was killed in action at Poelcapelle 9 October 1917. Buried there. One of his officers wrote, "John was a great favourite with everyone in the platoon, always of a cheery nature and ready for anything that wanted doing, and we all miss him...He was a brave man.": Age 19.

(Panel 10) Pte. 12176, John Elliot Reid, 'C'Coy., 1st Bn. Scots Guards: eldest *s.* of Andrew Reid, Farmer; of 'Middlepark', Bridge of Cally, Blairgowrie, co. Perth, formerly Hailes Mill, Haddington, by his wife Jane Hubback, *dau.* of James Jackson: *b.* Haddington, co. North Berwick, 19 December 1893: *educ.* East Linton: prior to the outbreak of war, assisted his father in Farm and Contracting work: enlisted Scots Guards, 10 November 1914, after the outbreak of war: served with the Expeditionary Force in France and Flanders from 24 May 1915: took part in the Battle of Loos 25 September following: wounded nr. Hill 70, Lens; gassed 20 July 1917, after which he was invalided/repatriated to England: rejoined his regiment September 1917, and was killed in action at the attack at Poelcapelle, 9 October following. Buried on the banks of the Broenbeeke. His Commanding Officer, Lieut. the Hon. Arthur Kinnaird, wrote, "He was a very gallant soldier, and always did his work splendidly. He was very popular in his platoon, and we shall all miss him in the company.": Age 23. *unm.*

(Panel 10) Pte. 14226, Alec McIntosh Smith, Machine Gun Coy., 1st Bn. Scots Guards: only *s.* of Peter Smith, Business Manager (ret'd.); of Clachnastrone, Grantown-on-Spey, co. Moray, by his wife Emma Ethel, *dau.* of William Peart, of Fordham, co. Cambridge: *b.* East Finchley, London, N., 26 February 1889: *educ.* Leeds Grammar School: Occupation – Apprentice; Merchant Naval Service: enlisted August 1915: served with the Expeditionary Force in France and Flanders from September 1916, and was killed in action in the attack at Poelcapelle, Flanders, 9 October 1917. Buried half a mile in rear of Houthulst Forest: Age 28. *unm.*

(Panel 10) Capt. Raymond Juzio Paul Rodakowski, 1st Bn. Irish Guards: only *s.* of Major Ernest de Rodakowski-Rivers; 1st Austrian Lancers, and his wife Lady Dora Susan Carnegie, *dau.* of James Carnegie, 9th Earl of Southesk: *b.* 15 May 1885: *educ.* Charterhouse School, from whence he won a scholarship to Brasenose College, Oxford: obtained a commission 2nd Lieut., 1st Irish Guards, shortly after the declaration of war with Germany, and proceeded to France: killed in action 9 October 1917: Age 32. Mentioned in Despatches for his services in the Great War. A close friend of the author and war poet Robert Graves; Capt. Rodakowski is mentioned in his autobiography '*Goodbye To All That.*'

(Panel 10) 2nd Lieut. Thomas Samuel Vesey Stoney, 1st Bn. Irish Guards: elder *s.* of Robert Vesey Stoney, of Rosturk Castle, co. Mayo, by his wife Editha Phoebe, *dau.* of Robert Truell, of Clonmannon, co. Wicklow: *b.* 23 August 1898: *educ.* St. Clair, Walmer, and Harrow (Head of House; O.T.C. member): gazetted 2nd Lieut., Irish Guards, January 1917: served with the Expeditionary Force in France and Flanders from 20 September of the same year, and was killed in action in the attack on Passchendaele Ridge, east of Ypres, 9 October 1917. Buried where he fell. His Commanding Officer wrote, "He was a good, keen boy, and would have made a splendid soldier. I saw him just before he was killed and just before we reached our objective. He was full of keenness and excitement, and was doing splendidly. He was killed instantaneously leading his platoon, and died a very gallant death.": Age 19.

PANEL 10 ENDS: PTE. J. MCGUIRE – IRISH GUARDS

PANEL 11 BEGINS: PTE. J. MCKENNA – IRISH GUARDS

(Panel 11) Pte. 3145, Arthur Philip Johns, 1st Bn. Welsh Guards: *s*. of Alfred Johns, Poulterer; of 5, Melbourne Place, Swansea, by his wife Esther, *dau*. of Martha Griffiths, of Narbeth: *b*. Swansea, 24 April 1890: *educ*. National School, there: Occupation – Postman: enlisted 27 September 1916: served with the Expeditionary Force in France from 6 March 1917, and was killed in action at Ypres, 12 October following: Age 27. He *m*. Swansea, 5 October 1915; Rachel (44, Princess Street, Swansea), 3rd *dau*. of John Williams.

(Panel 11) Pte. 10877, Thomas O'Rorke, 1st Bn. Irish Guards: *s*. of James O'Rorke, of Carrowmore, Sligo, by his wife Anne: and brother to Gnr. 2321, P. O'Rorke, Royal Garrison Artillery, died 19 October 1917, at Ypres: *b*. Rainsborough, Co. Sligo, c.1892: enlisted Sligo: Killed in action, 19 October 1917: Age 25. *unm*. The official notifications of the brothers' deaths were received by their mother in the same week. (*IWGC record O'Rourke*)

His brother Patrick is buried in Ypres Reservoir Cemetery (I.C.57).

(Panel 11) Lieut. William Pollock Francis, 12th (Service) Bn. The Royal Scots (Lothian Regt.): only *s*. of the Rev. David Lawrence Francis, Minister of Raith Parish, Kirkcaldy, by his wife Katherine Ann, *dau*. of John Pollock: *b*. Raith Manse, Kirkcaldy, 30 August 1897: *educ*. High School, Kirkcaldy: Occupation – Apprentice Engineer: enlisted 8 February 1915: commissioned 2nd Lieut., 12th Royal Scots, 11 November following; promoted Lieut., 9 October 1917: served with the Expeditionary Force in France and Flanders, from 20 August 1916, and was killed in action at Poelcapelle 22 October 1917. Buried at Kronprinz Farm, near Ypres. His Commanding Officer wrote, "At the time of his death he was attached to the Trench Mortar Battery, and the guns he had charge of contributed very materially to the success of the attack that morning," and his Captain, "I share your grief in the death of a fine officer and a good man. He was always that, clean and enthusiastic. I wish to tell you that your son did exceptionally good work during the attack of 20 September, when I commanded 'D' Coy. Those of us who are left will remember him as a gentleman, a keen soldier, and one who loved and was loved by his men.": Age 20. *unm*.

(Panel 11) Lieut. Austin Theodore Long, 1/10th (Service) Bn. The Royal Scots (Lothian Regt.): 3rd *s*. of the late Eustace Earl Long, by his wife Sarah Wakeford (South View, Basingstoke, co. Hants), *dau*. of the late James Allen: *b*. Oakhill, co. Somerset: *educ*. Bishop Stortford Grammar School, and London University, where he graduated B.A. and B.Sc.: Occupation – Schoolteacher; Market Drayton Grammar School, thereafter Stramongate School, Kendal: enlisted December 1914: commissioned February 1915: served with the Expeditionary Force in France and Flanders, and was killed in action 22 August 1917, while leading his men. Buried there. Lieut.Col. Simpson wrote, "He was a grand fellow, and such a help. His work was splendidly done at all times – it was brilliant," and Lieut.Col. Hannay, "In him we lost an exceptionally valued officer." He was a keen sportsman, and only just before his death organised sports and games in camp behind the line. *unm*.

(Panel 11) Lieut. Charles John McLean, 9th Bn. (Highlanders) The Royal Scots (Lothian Regt.), (T.F.): eldest *s*. of Charles John McLean, of Hamstall Ridware, Rugeley, co. Stafford, by his wife Agnes, *dau*. of the late Rev. George Davies, Clergyman: *b*. Nether Peover, co. Chester, 7 February 1885: *educ*. Grammar School, Rugeley: Occupation – Staff; Deaf Mutes' School, Edinburgh: joined 2nd (Volunteer) Battn. King's (Liverpool Regt.), 1906; becoming L/Corpl.; joined the Reserve, 1913: volunteered for Foreign Service shortly after the outbreak of war; joined 9th Royal Scots, Pte., December 1914: received a commission, gazetted 2nd Lieut., 21 October 1915; promoted Lieut., July 1917: served with the Expeditionary Force in France and Flanders from 1 January 1917: wounded at Arras, 9 April, and was killed in action nr. Ypres 20 September 1917. Buried where he fell. His Commanding Officer wrote, "His behaviour was extraordinarily gallant on that morning, for though wounded twice he continued to lead and encourage his men till he was hit by a machine-gun bullet, while carrying forward a Lewis gun to support the battalion on our left." And a friend, "I learnt to know him intimately and well, and had a very high regard for him as an officer and a friend.": Age 22. He was a keen athlete, politician and Freemason. He *m*. Greenock, 4 April 1914; Mary (9, Hampton Terrace, Edinburgh), eldest *dau*. of Charles Robert Brodie, and *gd-dau*. of the late Provost Brodie, North Berwick, and had a *dau*. – Mary Dealia, *b*. 1 August 1916.

(Panel 11) 2nd Lieut. James Allison, 'D' Coy., 8th Bn. The Royal Scots (Lothian Regt.), (T.F.): *s*. of James Allison, of 8, Ventnor Terrace, Edinburgh, and Jane T. Young, his wife: and brother to L/S. Z/1005, F.C. Allison, Drake Bn. R.N.V.R., died of wounds 12 October 1917, received in action at Passchendaele: *b*. 1881: *educ*. George Watson College, 1887-97, and Edinburgh University (Law): Occupation – Solicitor: joined 8th Royal Scots after the outbreak of war, applied for a commission and trained Officer Cadet School, Gailes: gazetted 2nd Lieut., Royal Scots, 1916; he had served for only three months in France when he was killed in action nr. Ypres, 20 September 1917: Age 36.

His brother Frederick is buried in Dozinghem Military Cemetery (X.F.13).

Late in the afternoon, 22 October 1917, a communications breakdown between 16th Bn. Royal Scots attacking astride the Ypres-Staden railway at Poelcapelle and Battalion Headqurters, resulted in 2nd Lieut. Robert Johnston, acting Signal Officer, 16th Bn., being ordered forward to assess the situation. He wrote, "I went forward and came across Norman Honeyman who had been at Gailes with me and was the only one left with myself of the 12 officers who had joined the battalion in May 1917. He was commanding some 20 or 30 men – all who were left of Roger Owen's company. He...said he had been halted by the intensity of the barrages – both Bosche and British – which had fallen on our area. I continued my search to our left flank...and when dawn came I found myself with some 25 men on the original tape line to the left of the railway...We could see bodies all over the place. Most shell holes held a body – dead, wounded or unhurt. The wounded were hoping to pull out at darkness, but everyone remained out of a sense of duty and nothing else. All were soaking wet, cold, miserable, hungry and living for the minute. As soon as I located the area in which Norman Honeyman had his party I crawled and ran to him. He saw me and got up to meet me – and as he reached me he fell, shot through the head. Throughout the whole time there was a constant crackling of rifle fire and the noise of exploding shells...Norman's batman, who crawled over to us, helped me to cover his face with sandbags and placed the body in a shell hole. His personal effects in his pack, and his cigarette case which had a bullet hole through it, were left with his runner. We placed an upright rifle and bayonet in the shell hole and hung Norman's steel helmet on it, taking off one of his identity discs to give to the Padre after the battle..."

(Panel 11) 2nd Lieut. Norman Stark Honeyman, 8th Bn. The Royal Scots (Lothian Regt.), (T.F.): *s*. of the late Andrew Stark (& J.M.) Honeyman, of 158, Castle Road, Cathcart, Glasgow: Killed in action 22 October 1917: Age 25. *unm*.

(Panel 11) 2nd Lieut. David Chesney Kerr, 4th (Queen's Edinburgh Rifles) Bn. The Royal Scots (Lothian Regt.), (T.F.): *s*. of the late David (& Mrs) Kerr, of 36, Forbes Road, Edinburgh: *b*. Edinburgh: *educ*. George Watson's College: Occupation – Representative (East of Scotland); Messrs Suchard, London: joined Territorials, February 1916: commissioned 2nd Lieut., Royal Scots, 1 March 1917: served with the Expeditionary Force in France and Flanders from the end of April, being attached 12th Battn., and was killed in action 12 October following, while laying the tapes for the advance on the ridge at Ypres. Buried where he fell: *unm*.

(Panel 11) 2nd Lieut. Archibald Mitchell, 4th (Queen's Edinburgh Rifles) Bn. The Royal Scots (Lothian Regt.), (T.F.): *s*. of Archibald Mitchell, of 8, Melfort Avenue, Dumbreck, Glasgow, by his wife Jeannie: and elder brother to 2nd Lieut. F.K. Mitchell, 8th Cameronians (Sco.Rif.), who also fell: Killed in action 25 April 1918: Age 27. *unm*.

His brother Frank also has no known grave; he is recorded on Panel 68.

(Panel 11) Sergt. 350334, Alfred Ernest Shaw, 9th Bn. The Royal Scots (Lothian Regt.): late of 31, Broughton Place, Edinburgh: 5th *s*. of the late William Shaw, Plumber; of 48, Fergus Square, Arbroath, and Jessie Shaw, *née* Dorward: Occupation – Highland Ornament-Maker and Jeweller, Messrs Mackay and Chisholm, Princes Street, Edinburgh: a pre-war 'Dandy Ninth' Territorial, mobilised on the outbreak of war; proceeded to France with his battalion February 1915: saw a great deal of hard fighting; his battalion, owing to the extreme pressure of the enemy, occupying the same trenches for 31 days on one occasion: invalided home (1916), myalgia: returned to France later the same year; employed on hut construction, promoted Sergt.: took part in many engagements, appointed Platoon Sergt. in which capacity he was leading in an attack on enemy trenches when he was shot and killed, 20 September 1917: Age 24.

(Panel 11) L/Sergt. 21114, Gordon Black, 2nd Bn. (1st Foot) The Royal Scots (Lothian Regt.): *s.* of James (& Mrs) Black, of 20, Victoria Street, Forfar: enlisted Forfar: killed at the Battle of Polygon Wood, 26 September 1917, in the vicinity of Hill 40: Age 26.

(Panel 11) Corpl. 43318, William David Hardie Gray, 12th (Service) Bn. The Royal Scots (Lothian Regt.): *s.* of William L. (& Mrs) Gray, of 37, Arden Street, Edinburgh: *educ.* Boroughmuir School: enlisted Edinburgh, August 1915, aged 17 years, 6 months; posted 9th Royal Scots: proceeded to France July 1915, in charge of a draft of reinforcements: transf'd. 12th Battn. and served throughout the fighting at the Somme without injury: took part in the Battle of Arras and Vimy Ridge, at the latter taking command of his platoon, following practically all the officers becoming casualties: thereafter admitted to hospital suffering from shell shock; after treatment, rest and recuperation, rejoined his unit and took part in a number of trench raids: wounded 1 August 1917: returned to duty, and was killed in action 20 September; shot through the heart whilst attempting to capture a German blockhouse. His Capt., in writing to Mr Gray, said he was his most trustworthy Corporal, always cheery and encouraging, whether in danger or behind the line, popular with both officers and men, and looked up to by his platoon: Age 19.

PANEL 11 ENDS: CORPL. G. MARTIN – ROYAL SCOTS

PANEL 12 BEGINS: CORPL. J. MITCHELL – ROYAL SCOTS

(Panel 12) L/Corpl. Piper, 200737, Peter West, 12th (Service) Bn. The Royal Scots (Lothian Regt.): late of Falkirk, co. Stirling: enlisted Edinburgh: Killed in action, 25 April 1918. One of three pipers of 12th Battn. to make the supreme sacrifice. See L/Corpl. W. Fisher, Reninghelst New Military Cemetery (I.A.21).

PANEL 12 ENDS: PTE. A.G. EVEREST – ROYAL SCOTS

PANEL 13 BEGINS: PTE. A. FAGAN – ROYAL SCOTS

(Panel 13) Pte. 27688, Alexander Adam Flett, 2nd Bn. (1st Foot) The Royal Scots (Lothian Regt.): *s.* of Alexander Flett, of 2, Netherton Terrace, Findochty, co. Banff, Fisherman, by his wife Jane, *dau.* of Adam Davidson: *b.* Findochty, 26 December 1896: *educ.* Findochty Public School and Buckie Higher Grade School: entered the Aberdeen University as a Science Student: enlisted 29 November 1915: served with the Expeditionary Force in France and Flanders from 6 April 1916; wounded near Montauban, 22 July following, and admitted Base Hospital, Boulogne: rejoined his Regt. on recovery; transf'd. Sniper Section, and was killed in action 29 September 1917; Zonnebeke. Buried there: Age 20. *unm.*

(Panel 13) Pte. 59417, Harry Jack, 12th (Service) Bn. The Royal Scots (Lothian Regt.): formerly no.2/9662, 54th T.R. Bn.; formerly no. 38221, Cameronians (Sco.Rif.): 3rd *s.* of Henry Jack, of 605, Great Western Road, Glasgow, by his marriage to the late Margaret Coutts Jack: *b.* 1898: *educ.* Hillhead High School, Glasgow: Occupation – Clerk, Messrs Robert Ramsay & Co., Greendyke Street: registered Glasgow, 1915, aged 17 years; mobilised March 1917: trained Kirkcaldy and Nigg, with Cameronians (Sco.Rif.), proceeded to France with a draft of reinforcements attd. (subsequently transf'd.) 12th Royal Scots, March 1918: reported missing 25 April 1918; Kemmel, later confirmed killed in action: Age 19. At Hillhead, owing to weak eyesight, he did not take an active part in any games, but was interested in all activities, and held all his teachers in great regard. Returning to visit his old school, shortly before going to France, he had nothing but good to speak of his officers, comrades and Army life in general. Typically characteristic of him; he made the best of everything and never a grumble escaped him. Of a cheerful, contented, obliging disposition, and a great favourite with his comrades, 'on the day he died no more gallant, simple-minded soldier fell.'

(Panel 13) Pte. 27977, James Leslie, 'B' Coy., 16th Bn. The Royal Scots (Lothian Regt.): *s.* of the late Thomas Leslie, of Kirkstile, St. Vigeans, Arbroath, and Jane, *née* Hunter: Occupation – Ploughman; Mains, Letham: enlisted January 1916: wounded April 1917, Arras: Killed in action, 22 October 1917, at Passchendaele. He had but a few weeks previously rejoined his regiment from hospital: Age 24.

(Panel 13) Pte. 45935, Lewis McDonald, 3rd (Reserve) Bn. The Royal Scots (Lothian Regt.): *s.* of the late James McDonald, of Coltfield, Alves, Farm Manager, by his wife, Annie (3, Abbey Street, Elgin, co. Moray), *dau.* of Wiliam Whyte, Contractor Drainer, of Lossiemouth: and brother to Pte. 265840, J. McDonald, 6th Battn. Seaforth Highlanders, who was killed in action, 9 April 1917, at the Battle of Arras: *b.* Elgin, 1 November 1893: *educ.* Alves Public School: was employed as a Driver by the Glasgow Corporation: enlisted in the Royal Scots 1 March 1917: served with the Expeditionary Force in France and Flanders from 1 October following, and was killed in action at Ypres eight days later, on the 9th. Buried where he fell: Age 23. *unm.*

His brother John is buried in Highland Cemetery, Roclincourt (I.C.35).

(Panel 13) Pte. 59420, Andrew McNair, 12th (Service) Bn. The Royal Scots (Lothian Regt.): *s.* of Robert (& Mrs) McNair, of Gasworks House, Linlithgow, co. West Lothian: and yr. brother to Pte. 43212, A. McNair, 6/7th Royal Scots Fusiliers, who also fell: *b.* Linlithgow: enlisted Glencorse: killed in action, 25 April 1918: Age 19.

His brother Alexander also has no known grave, he is commemorated on Panel 60.

PANEL 13 ENDS: PTE. W. MILLIGAN – ROYAL SCOTS

PANEL 14 BEGINS PTE. G.W. MILLS – ROYAL SCOTS

(Panel 14) Pte. 39178, William Milne, 2nd Bn. (1st Foot) The Royal Scots (Lothian Regt.): formerly no.10800, Royal Highlanders: *s.* of William Milne, of Castle Street, Montrose, Flax Overseer, by his wife Margaret, *dau.* of John Lowden: *b.* Montrose, co. Forfar, 21 May 1888: *educ.* Public School, there: Occupation – Hairdresser: enlisted Royal Scots, Montrose, 29 February 1916: served with the Expeditionary Force in France and Flanders: was slightly wounded, and sent to hospital suffering from trench fever: reported missing after the fighting at Ypres, 26 September 1917, and is now assumed to have been killed in action on or about that date. He *m.* Montrose, 26 July 1916; Mary Carr (26, New Wynd, Montrose), *dau.* of John Carr: Age 29. *s.p.*

(Panel 14) Pte. 41801, Peter Mitchell, 'A' Coy., 15th (Service) Bn. The Royal Scots (Lothian Regt.): *s.* of the late Peter Mitchell, Shipmaster; by his wife Hester Kennedy (11, Park Road, Pollokshaws, Newlands, Glasgow), *dau.* of Dugald MacPherson: *b.* Milford, Co. Donegal, 9 June 1886: *educ.* there and Hughes' Academy, Londonderry: Occupation – Cashier employed by a firm of Ship Owners: enlisted 2/9th Highland Light Infantry (Glasgow Highlanders), no.1071, 26 August 1916: subsequently transf'd. Royal Scots: served with the Expeditionary Force in France and Flanders from 9 August 1917, and was killed in action at Houthulst Forest, 22 October following: Age 31. *unm.*

(Panel 14) Pte. 48465, William James Murray, 13th (Service) Bn. The Royal Scots (Lothian Regt.): elder *s.* of the late George Murray, by his wife Helen (8, Douglas Avenue, Carmyle, co. Lanark), *dau.* of James Murdoch: *b.* Colvend, Dalbeattie, 26 December 1885: *educ.* West Coats Public School, Cambuslang, co. Lanark: Occupation – Tailor/Clothier; Muirhead, Chryston: enlisted Army Pay Corps, Hamilton, co. Lanark, September 1916; transf'd. Royal Scots, May 1917; trained Montrose: served with the Expeditionary Force in France and Flanders from July following, and was killed in action at Frezenberg, nr. Ypres, 22 August 1917: Age 31. *unm.* (*IWGC record age 33*)

(Panel 14) Pte. 45969, David Norwood, 12th (Service) Bn. The Royal Scots (Lothian Regt.): *s.* of the late James Norwood, by his wife Agnes (141, New Street, Stevenston, co. Ayr): and brother to Corpl.

S/4790, J.A. Norwood, 9th Black Watch, killed in action 25 September 1915: *b*. Stevenston: enlisted Ardeer, co. Ayr: killed in action 20 September 1917: Age 22.

His brother James also has no known grave; he is commemorated on the Loos Memorial.

(Panel 14) Pte. 51549, Henry Patterson, 12th (Service) Bn. The Royal Scots (Lothian Regt.): formerly no.47832, Royal Scots Fusiliers: *s*. of John Patterson, of 3, Birtwhistle Street, Gatehouse of Fleet, Castle Douglas, co. Kirkcudbright, by his second wife Mary Patterson, *née* Carson; and, by first wife Elizabeth, *née* Hume, half-brother to Ptc. 266566, J.W. Patterson, King's (Liverpool) Regt., killed in action 15 August 1916; L/Corpl. S/4048, G. Patterson, 9th Black Watch, killed in action 25 September 1915; and cousin to Pte. 271207, J. Patterson, 17th Royal Scots, killed in action, 25 March 1918, and Gnr. 33393, G.A. Fisher, Royal Field Artillery, died 18 April 1916, of accidental injuries: *b*. Gatehouse, 1898: enlisted August 1917: Killed in action 25 April 1918: Age 19. A third half-brother Pte. T. Patterson, 7th Royal Scots Fusiliers, died in Kilmarnock 26 April 1920, consequent to wounds received at Cambrai, 1918.

Half-brothers John, George and cousin Jack also have no known grave; they are commemorated on the Thiepval, Loos and Pozieres Memorials respectively. Cousin George is buried in Bruay Communal Cemetery Extension (A.3).

(Panel 14) Pte. 33043, George Twiss, 13th (Service) Bn. The Royal Scots (Lothian Regt.): late of Liberton, co. Midlothian: brother to the late Pte. 33065, C. Twiss, 13th Royal Scots, killed in action, 15 September 1918: enlisted Bonnyrigg: Killed in action 22 August 1917.

His brother Charles is buried in St. Mary's A.D.S. Cemetery, Haisnes (IV.A.19).

(Panel 14) Pte. 41740, Victor Watmough, 15th (Service) Bn. The Royal Scots (Lothian Regt.): *s*. of John Watmough, and his late wife Helen Mary Watmough, formerly of Bramley, Leeds, co. York: and brother to 2nd Lieut. J.C. Watmough, 2nd Battn. Northumberland Fusiliers, killed in action 10 July 1915; and Bmdr. 750728, E. Watmough, 'A' Bty., 315th Bde., Royal Field Artillery, killed in action 31 August 1918: Killed in action 22 October 1917.

One Of Three Sons Who Gave Their All

His brother John is buried in Ridge Wood Cemetery (II.A.8); Edmund, Achiet-le-Grand Communal Cemetery (II.K.3).

On the 20 September 1917 1/9th Royal Scots formed the vanguard to the attack on the German positions at Poelcapelle. Launched at 5.40 a.m., in appalling conditions, the battlefield was a morass of interconnecting, flooded shell holes and mud which clung to everything and made progress extremely difficult. The battalion's objective – Pheasant Trench – was reached by "advancing with great skill and gallantry moving from shell hole to shell hole in twos and threes, pouring rifle grenades and rifle fire into the German defenders." The Scots carried the German position on the right of the attack and occupied it but, on the left of the attack, the assault by 'B' Company met with heavy fire, forcing them to retire to their start positions. There they were rallied by their officers and, together with men of the Argyll & Sutherland Highlanders, carried the day and completed the occupation of the enemy position. For an attack against such formidable positions the battalion's losses were surprisingly small, fifty-four men killed; among them 19 year old Arthur Webb, his body lost, sucked into the morass, never to be seen again.

(Panel 14) Pte. 302751, Arthur Webb, 9th Bn. The Royal Scots (Lothian Regt.): late of Edenbridge: *b*. Limpsfield: enlisted Red Hill: Killed in action 20 September 1917: Age 19.

On the night of 2 October 1917, 3/4 Queen's took over the front line trenches just east, and 'uncomfortably forward' of Polygon Wood. The following day (4 October) at 3 a.m., the battalion commenced assembling for 62 Brigade's assault on the enemy's defensive positions on the Broodseinde – Becelaere Ridge. At zero hour – 6 a.m. – the British barrage came down 150 yards in front of the attacking troops, who at once moved up to it, and almost immediately thereafter The Queen's encountered their first obstacle – a line of concertina and barbed wire right across the whole front – and heavy machine-gun fire from the right. The passage of the Polygon Beek and surrounding, almost impenetrable, morass 'presented some difficulties; time was lost and the men got too far behind the barrage, and there was a certain amount of confusion. Juniper Trench was then assailed, the wire in front of it offering no serious obstacle; many Germans emerged as The Queen's drew near, but in the darkness it was impossible to tell if they meant fighting or surrender, and they were all killed; and though an enemy concrete strong point made some resistance, this was overcome by a party of bombers under Lieut. Frost, the rest of this portion of the German line of defence being captured with no very great difficulty.' Throughout this action 'C' Company with two Lewis gun teams, were in close support, and as they came into the vicinity of Juniper Trench a German officer was seen to approach in surrender, but as Lieut. Cooper went forward to accept it, the German whipped out his pistol and shot him; the men who witnessed this gross act of treachery quickly riddled the German with bullets.

(Panel 14) Lieut. Augustus Herbert Cooper, 'C' Coy., 3/4th Bn. The Queen's (Royal West Surrey Regt.): Killed in action 4 October 1917.

PANEL 14 ENDS: LIEUT. A.H. COOPER – THE QUEENS (ROYAL WEST SURREY REGT.)

PANEL 15 BEGINS: LIEUT. T. DARLINGTON, M.M. – THE QUEEN'S (ROYAL WEST SURREY REGT.)

(Panel 15) Sergt. S/505, Albert Choney, M.M., 2nd Bn. (2nd Foot) The Queen's (Royal West Surrey Regt.): *s.* of William George Choney, of 15, Beaconsfield Cottages, East Street, Ewell, Epsom, co. Surrey, by his wife Alice Mary: and brother to Sergt. L/8977, W. Choney, 2nd Queen's (Royal West Surrey Regt., died 16 November 1914, of wounds: *b.* Bramley, co. Surrey: enlisted Kingston-on-Thames: served with the Expeditionary Force; killed in action, 26 October 1917, in the vicinity of Lewis House: Age 28. He leaves a wife, Elizabeth Annie Choney (10, Beaconsfield Cottages, East Street, Ewell, Epsom), to whom all correspondence should be forwarded.

His brother William is buried in Larch Wood (Railway Cutting) Cemetery (IV.D.14).

(Panel 15) L/Sergt. T/201574, Alfred George Tee, 3/4th Bn. The Queen's (Royal West Surrey Regt.), (T.F.): late of South Corydon, co. Surrey: *s.* of Frederick Tee, of 'Earnlea,' Buckingham Road, Worthing, co. Sussex, by his wife Emily: and brother to Pte. 200197, S.C. Tee, 1/4th Royal Sussex Regt., killed in action 6 November 1917, in Egypt; and Sergt. TF/201543, F.G Tee, 11th Royal Sussex Regt., killed in action 29 April 1918: *b.* Worthing, *c.*1897: enlisted Corydon: Killed in action 5 November 1917: Age 20. *unm.*

His brother Sidney also has no known grave, he is commemorated on the Jerusalem Memorial; Frederick is buried in Voormezeele Enclosure No.3 (XIV.C.13).

(Panel 15) L/Corpl. G/25759, John William Herd, 10th (Service) Bn. The Queen's (Royal West Surrey Regt.): Killed in action nr. Kemmel Hill, Flanders, 5 September 1918. See also Grootebeek British Cemetery.

(Panel 15) L/Corpl. T/201638, John William Stracey, 3/4th Bn. The Queen's (Royal West Surrey Regt.), (T.F.): *s.* of Frances Ellen Field (1, Rochester Road, Carshalton, co. Surrey): and elder brother to Pte. T/4787, T.H. Stracey, 1/5th Queen's (Royal West Surrey Regt.), died 26 June 1916, in Mesopotamia: *b.* Carshalton: enlisted Croydon: Killed in action 4 October 1917: Age 21. *unm.*

His brother Thomas also has no known grave; he is commemorated on the Basra Memorial (Panel 6).

Encamped at St. Jan-ter-Biezen, near Poperinghe, 4 October 1917, 7th Queen's, 55th Brigade, 'received news' that "a successful attack by Second and Fifth Armies on the Poelcapelle area and part of the Passchendaele Ridge from Broodseinde to the south" (the latest in the series of battles known collectively as Third Ypres) "had been a great success with 4,446 enemy prisoners and six guns captured, all objectives taken." Of course, the information issued to the troops neglected to mention the high number of casualties the 'great success' had exacted.

Six days later, 10 October, at Dirty Bucket Camp, the battalion were informed, "owing to the failure of 32 Brigade to achieve its objectives the preceding day, 55 Brigade will move forward to relieve that brigade and carry out the assault allotted to it." In briefing his officers, General Maxse, the Divisional

Commander, simply stated, "I have arranged a very nice battle for you, gentlemen, with lots of Huns to kill!"

The following day found the conditions in the front line areas absolutely appalling. Non-stop rain had made the approaches to the front assembly positions nigh-on impossible to reach owing to the all-cloying mud in which the guns sank and could not be got forward, while many of the men became stuck fast, helplessly trapped, falling victim to enemy snipers as they tried to extricate themselves, were killed by shellfire, or simply sucked down and drowned.

Not surprisingly, the attack went in on the 12th as planned and, not surprisingly – due to the losses incurred even before the battalion reached the front – the attack failed. After holding the front line throughout, the 13th the battalion returned to Dirty Bucket Camp where they counted the cost – one officer, fifteen other ranks killed; three officers, eighty-six other ranks wounded; thirty-six men missing. How many Huns the 'very nice battle' accounted for is unknown, similarly the fate of Charles Brown; he never reached the assembly positions on the 11th, one of eleven men killed on the approaches, he simply disappeared.

(Panel 15) Pte. L/10895, Charles Arthur Brown, 7th (Service) Bn. The Queen's (Royal West Surrey Regt.): *s.* of Charles Brown, of Argus Hill Lodge, Rotherfield, co. Sussex, by his wife Agnes: *b.* Limpsfield, co. Surrey, *c.*1897: enlisted Guildford, co. Surrey: served with the Expeditionary Force in France; reported missing 11 October 1917, now assumed killed: Age 20. *unm.*

(Panel 15) Pte. G/63494, Frederick Charles Chilvers, 10th (Service) Bn. The Queen's (Royal West Surrey Regt.): *s.* of the late Charles David Chilvers, by his wife Maggie Ann Bailey, *née* Chilvers (Tower End, Middleton, King's Lynn, co. Norfolk): *b.* Middleton, *c.*1899: Killed in action nr. Kemmel, 5 September 1918: Age 19. See also Grootebeek British Cemetery.

(Panel 15) Pte. G/68397, George William Cox, 10th (Service) The Queen's (Royal West Surrey Regt.): *s.* of George Cox, of Springfield Road, East Ham, London, E., by his wife Alice: *b.* East Ham, *c.*1899: Killed in action nr. Mount Kemmel, 5 September 1918: Age 19. See also Grootebeek British Cemetery.

(Panel 15) Pte. G/25895, Ernest Henry Duckett, 10th (Service) Bn. The Queen's (Royal West Surrey Regt.): *s.* of John W. Duckett, of 47, Bayes Street, Kettering, co. Northampton, by his wife Mary Violet: *b.* Stapleford, co. Nottingham: sometime employee Kettering Co-operative Clothing, Field Street: enlisted Kettering, May 1917: served with the Expeditionary Force in France and Flanders from March the following year, and was killed by a shell during the advance on the night of 29 – 30 September 1918: Age 19. His Company Officer, Lieut. F. E.B. Girling, said, "He was killed instantaneously by a shell, and did not suffer at all. He was a good soldier, and died whilst doing his duty with a cheerful heart. They were indeed sorry to lose him. His body was taken to the rear and properly buried." Prior to enlistment Pte. Duckett was a prominent member of the Salvation Army and played side-drum in the band.

(Panel 15) Pte. G/7094, George William Earl, 10th (Service) Bn. The Queen's (Royal West Surrey Regt.): *s.* of Edwin Earl, of 36, Charterhouse Road, Godalming, co. Surrey, by his wife Elizabeth: and yr. brother to Pte. 25868, T. Earl, 1st Somerset Light Infantry, died of wounds 11 August 1916, at Poperinghe: enlisted Godalming, 20 January 1916: Killed in action 20 September 1917: Age 22. *unm.*

His brother Thomas is buried in Lijssenthoek Military Cemetery (VIII.D.42).

(Panel 15) Pte. T/265338, Frederick Feston, 2nd Bn. (2nd Foot) The Queen's (Royal West Surrey Regt.): 2nd *s.* of the late William Henry Feston, of 48, Constance Road, Dulwich, Leather Striker/Dresser, by his wife Loretta (48, Green Hundred Road, Peckham, London, S.E.), *dau.* of George Pulling, by his wife Elizabeth, *née* Pritchard: *b.* 13 February 1891: Occupation – Carman: served with the Expeditionary Force in France and Flanders, and was killed in action 26 October 1917: Age 26. He *m.* Christ Church, Camberwell, co. Surrey, 24 March 1913; Ada Rosetta (51, Willow Walk, Bermondsey, London, S.E.), *dau.* of Alfred Hall, by his wife Ada Ruffeitt.

PANEL 15 ENDS: PTE. F. FESTON – THE QUEEN'S (ROYAL WEST SURREY REGT.)

PANEL 16 BEGINS: PTE. A. FINKELSTEIN – THE QUEEN'S (ROYAL WEST SURREY REGT.)

(Panel 16) Pte. T/242052, William Henry Franklin, 11th (Service) Bn. The Queen's (Royal West Surrey Regt.): formerly no.21900, Somerset Light Infantry: *s.* of Thomas Henry (& Eva S.) Franklin, of 16, Paultow Road, St. John's Lane, Bedminster, Bristol: and brother to Pte. 302639, S.C. Franklin, 2nd Royal Scots, died of wounds 29 March 1918, aged 19 yrs.: *b.* Bedminster: enlisted Bristol: Killed in action 20 July 1918: Age 24. *unm.* Commemorated Bedminster (St. Michael & All Angels) Church Memorial.

His brother Sidney is buried in Doullens Communal Cemetery Extension No.1 (V.C.19).

(Panel 16) Pte. T/202894, Arthur Frank Hall, No.1 Platoon, 'A' Coy., 3/4th Bn. The Queen's (Royal West Surrey Regt.), (T.F.): *s.* of John Hall, of Old Farm, Groombridge, co. Sussex, by his wife Mary, *dau.* of William Box, of Withyham: *b.* Groombridge, 28 January 1885: *educ.* National School, there: was for sixteen years in the employ of Messrs Hitchcock and Williams, St. Paul's Churchyard, London, E.C.: joined Queen's Royal West Surrey, 20 October 1916: served with the Expeditionary Force in France and Flanders from the following May, and was killed in action at Broodseinde Ridge, 4 October 1917. Buried where he fell: Age 32. He *m.* St. Peter's, Tunbridge Wells, 31 May 1909; Ada (2, Windmill Street, Tunbridge Wells, co. Kent), *dau.* of John Johnson, and had two *daus.*, Maisie Alice Gertrude, *b.* 8 March 1910 and Marjorie Mary, *b.* 10 December 1915.

(Panel 16) Pte. T/206826, Albert Handcock, 3/4th Bn. The Queen's (Royal West Surrey Regt.), (T.F.): formerly no.27683, Middlesex Reg.: *yst. s.* of William (& Annie) Handcock, of 'Pickersdane,' Brook, Ashford, co. Kent: and brother to Pte. 240560, F.J. Handcock, 1/5th Battn. The Buffs, died, 11 December 1918, in Mesopotamia, and Pte. T/2010, W.E. Handcock, died of wounds on the island of Malta, 31 May 1915, received in action at Gallipoli: *b.* Wye, 1898: enlisted Ashford: Killed in action at Broodseinde, 3 October 1917: Age 19. (*IWGC record age 20*)

His brother Frederick is buried in Baghdad (North Gate) War Cemetery (IV.C.2), William is buried in Pieta Military Cemetery, Malta (B.VII.1). All three brothers are commemorated on the village war memorial, Wye, Kent.

(Panel 16) Pte. G/25799, James Jonas, 10th (Service) Bn. The Queen's (Royal West Surrey Regt.): *s.* of Sarah Ann Jonas (39, Morrison Buildings, Aldgate, co. Middlesex): *b.* Spitalfields, London, *c.*1899: Killed in action nr. Kemmel, 5 September 1918. Age 19. See also Grootebeek British Cemetery.

(Panel 16) Pte. G/21091, Arthur Murfet, 7th (Service) Bn. The Queen's (Royal West Surrey Regt.): formerly no.26730, Suffolk Regt.: *s.* of Alfred (& Mrs) Murfet, of The Shade, Town End, Soham, co. Cambridge: and brother to Pte. 26674, F. Murfet, 14th Hampshire Regt., killed in action, 20 October 1916; and Pte. 17504, W. Murfet, 11th Suffolk Regt., fell, 1 July 1916: *b.* Fordham: enlisted Newmarket: Died of wounds 21 October 1917.

Twin brothers Frederick and Walter have no known grave; they are commemorated on the Thiepval Memorial, Somme.

(Panel 16) Pte. G/9746, George Edward Perry, 10th (Service) Bn. The Queen's (Royal West Surrey Regt.): *s.* of the late William Perry, by his wife Sarah (110, Bridge Road West, Battersea, London): and twin brother to Rfn. R/31615, J.R. Perry, King's Royal Rifle Corps, who fell one month previously: *b.* 1881: enlisted Battersea: Killed in action 22 September 1917: Age 36.

His brother John also has no known grave; he is recorded on Panel 118.

(Panel 16) Pte. G/39874, Ernest Robinson, 9th Platoon, 'C' Coy., 1st Bn. (2nd Foot) The Queen's (Royal West Surrey Regt.): *s.* of Mr (& Mrs) Robinson: *b.* Enfield, co. Middlesex: enlisted March 1917: served with the Expeditionary Force in France and Flanders, and was killed in action, 25 September 1917. His Capt. wrote, "I am writing to thank you in place of your husband for what he did for me – giving up his life in the attempt. As you have probably heard, the enemy attacked us just north-west of Ypres on the morning of 25 September After a very heavy bombardment they broke into our front position. C Coy. had to counter-attack and retake the line; I was attacked by a sniper, and your husband immediately came to my assistance, but was killed by the same sniper while he was lifting me up to carry me behind cover. As you can see, it was a very fine deed he attempted. I am sure you will feel proud of him... Your husband played the game all through, and never missed doing his duty under the most trying circumstances. He was liked by all." He *m.* Edmonton, London, N.; Eliza (217, Farrant Avenue, Wood Green, London, N.), *dau.* of George Emms, and had three children; Ernest Richard, Florence Hilda and Louisa Phillis.

PANEL 16 ENDS: PTE. J.P. TESTER – THE QUEEN'S (ROYAL WEST SURREY REGT.)

PANEL 17 BEGINS: PTE. S.J. THEOBALD: THE QUEEN'S (ROYAL WEST SURREY REGT.)

(Panel 17) Pte. G/23007, William Michael Thomas, 10th (Service) Bn. The Queen's (Royal West Surrey Regt.): formerly no.02106, Army Ordnance Corps: *s.* of David Thomas, of 'Areulfa,' Garnant, co. Carmarthen, and Elizabeth, his spouse: and brother to Pte. 129351, D. Thomas, 16th Canadian Infantry, killed in action 9 October 1916, at the Battle of Le Transloy: enlisted A.O.C., Ammanford, 1 September 1914, subsequently transf'd. Royal West Surrey Regt.: served with the Expeditionary Force in France and Flanders from May 1916: took part in the fighting at Flers-Courcelette, Somme later that year, and at Le Transloy: took part in the Battle of Messines (June 1917), and Pilckem, and was killed in action 20 September 1917, at the Battle of the Menin Road: Age 23.

His brother David also has no known grave; he is commemorated on the Canadian National Vimy Memorial, France.

(Panel 17) Pte. G/29709, Bertie Willey, 10th (Service) Bn. The Queen's (Royal West Surrey Regt.): *s.* of Charles Willey, of 39, Duncombe Road, Bengee, co. Hertford, by his wife Ellen: *b.* Bengee, *afsd., c.* 1899: Killed in action nr. Kemmel Hill, Belgium, 5 September 1918: Age 19. See also Grootebeek British Cemetery.

(Panel 17) 2nd Lieut. Herbert Thomas, 4th (T.F.) attd 7th (Service) Bn. The Buffs (East Kent Regt.): only *s.* of the late Rev. David Thomas, of Brynffynon, Dolgelly, Wesleyan Minister, by his wife Jane Elizabeth ('Ardre,' Dolgelly, co. Merioneth), *dau.* of J. Davies, of Oswestry, co. Chester: *b.* Aberystwyth, co. Cradigan, 20 May 1891: *educ.* Ruthin Grammar School: Occupation – Clerk; National Provincial Bank, London: joined 2/5th (Territorial) Battn. The Buffs, 8 May 1916: gazetted 2nd Lieut. 7th Battn., May 1917: served with the Expeditionary Force in France and Flanders from 19 June, and was killed in action at Poelcapelle 12 October following. His Commanding Officer wrote, "Since he had been under my command I had formed a high opinion of him. I regarded him as one of the most promising young officers I had. He took an immense interest in his work and in his men, and was never tired of learning his job. He will be a very great loss to his battalion;" and the Adjutant, "During the time he was with us he was universally popular with officers and men alike, always cheery and a thorough keen soldier, to whom the smallest job was as important as the biggest. His loss to us as an officer was keenly felt, and such an officer as he was is not replaced nowadays, and we cannot afford to lose such.": Age 26. *unm.*

(Panel 17) Corpl. G/2810, William Herbert Huckstep, M.M., 7th (Service) Bn. The Buffs (East Kent Regt.): *s.* of Stephen Huckstep, of Belmont House, Crow Hill Road, Garlinge, Westgate-on-Sea, co. Kent, by his wife Elizabeth: and elder brother to Pte. G/3067, A.F. Huckstep, 6th Bn. The Buffs, killed in action 31 August 1915: *b.* Garlinge: enlisted Margate: Killed in action 13 October 1917, nr. Poelcapelle: Age 22. *unm.*

His brother Arthur is buried in Calvaire (Essex) Military Cemetery (III.C.4).

(Panel 17) L/Corpl. G/8529, William Edward May, 7th (Service) Bn. The Buffs (East Kent Regt.): formerly Pte. 387, Australian Imperial Force: *s.* of Charles May, of 100, St. Vincent's Road, Dartford, co. Kent, by his wife Jane: and elder brother to Pte. 235067, J. May, 8th Lincolnshire Regt., who fell 4 November 1917: *b.* Dartford, 1890: religion – Church of England: 5'5" tall, brown eyes, brown hair: sometime went to Australia where he found employ as an Engineering Clerk, and, following the outbreak of war, joined A.I.F., 11 August 1914: posted 'C' Coy., 1st Tropical Force, 16 August: embarked Sydney, H.M.A.S. 'Berrima,' 19 August following: served at New Guinea until February 1915 (discharged from A.I.F. 11 March 'time expired'): subsequently returned to England, and enlisted The Buffs, Dartford:

served with the Expeditionary Force in France and Flanders, and was killed in action, 13 October 1917: Age 27. *unm.*

His brother Joseph also has no known grave; he is recorded on Panel 37.

(Panel 17) Pte. G/10270, William Ernest Buckland, 7th (Service) Bn. The Buffs (East Kent Regt.): *s.* of Richard Buckland, Lift Attendant; of 108, Glenwood Rd., Harringay, N., by his wife Jane *dau.* of Thomas Holloway: *b.* Barnsbury, London, N., 3 February 1887: *educ.* White Hart Lane School, N.: enlisted 20 June 1916: trained Dover: served with the Expeditionary Force in France and Flanders from 30 December following: wounded, Poelcapelle, 12 October 1917, and died the same day. Buried at Poelcapelle: His Commanding Officer wrote, "He had been a good soldier, and we always found him a sincere friend, who was liked by everyone who came in contact with him.": Age 30. He *m.* Christ Church, Harringay, N., 13 September 1914; Elizabeth Hannah Robson, *née* Buckland (Nunnington, co. York), *dau.* of Thomas Boneham, and had a son William Thomas, *b.* 18 September 1915. (*IWGC record L/Corpl.*)

(Panel 17) Pte. G/21080, Edward Tom Buswell, 7th (Service) Bn. The Buffs (East Kent Regt.): 4th *s.* of John Barber Buswell, by his wife Elizabeth, *dau.* of Shadrack Pettifer: *b.* Kettering, 22 August 1883: *educ.* St. Andrew's, Northampton: Occupation – Boot and Shoe Operative: enlisted 22 February 1917: served with the Expeditionary Force in France, and was killed in action at Poelcapelle, 12 October 1917. A comrade wrote, "We shall miss him very much as he was a keen soldier, and most popular with all the platoon.": Age 34. He *m.* St. Sepulchre's Church, Northampton, 1906; Ada (29, Compton Street, Northampton), eldest *dau.* of William Budworth, of Manchester, and had three children;William Arthur, *b.* 11 January 1907, Elsie Elizabeth, *b.* 14 October 1912 and Jack Chambers, *b.* 1 October 1917; little more than a week before the father he would never know was killed.

(Panel 17) Pte. G/13217, George Loftus Gallagher, 7th (Service) Bn. The Buffs (East Kent Regt.): *s.* of William Gallagher, of North Lodge, Straffan, co. Kildare, by his wife Mary, *dau.* of John McBrien: *b.* Deryherk, co. Leitrim, 7 October 1890: *educ.* Straffan Estate School: Occupation – Footman: enlisted 13 April 1916: served with the Expeditionary Force in France and Flanders, from 28 November 1916, and was killed in action at Poelcapelle 12 October 1917. His Commanding Officer wrote, "Your boy was immensely popular with everyone in the company. Always cheery, always ready to lend a hand to anyone in difficulties, you can imagine how well he got on with all. Personally, when the time comes for me to rejoin my battalion I shall miss him immensely;" and a comrade, "It is hardly necessary for us to speak to you of George's courage under all circumstances; his unfailing good humour and his splendid qualities of friendship, you must have known them better than we could hope to do, but we can assure you it is an honour to be called friend by such a man as George.": Age 27. *unm.*

(Panel 17) Pte. G/1422, Frank Albert Stannard, 7th (Service) Bn. The Buffs (East Kent Regt.): *s.* of Thomas Stannard, of Mount Pleasant, St. Augustine's, Canterbury, by his wife Alice: and *yr.* brother to Pte. 242181, N.J. Stannard, 2/5th Hampshire Regt. (T.F.), died, 20 March 1917, in India; and Pte. 38358, F.T. Stannard, 3rd Norfolk Regt., died, 10 July 1918, at home: *b.* Bekesbourne, co. Kent, 1892: enlisted Canterbury: Killed in action, 12 October 1917; Poelcapelle: Age 25. The Kingston (St. Giles Church) War Memorial, Kent records the names of six men of the parish who gave their lives in the Great War, three of them are the brothers Stannard.

His brother Norman has no known grave, he is commemorated on the Kirkee 1914-1918 Memorial (Face D); Frederick is buried in Canterbury Cemetery (B.503).

(Panel 17) Pte. T/202546, Stanley George Sutton, 7th (Service) Bn. The Buffs (East Kent Regt.): *s.* of James Albert Sutton, of Temple Cottages, Cressing, nr. Braintree, co. Essex, by his wife Esther, *dau.* of Philip (& Eliza) Palmer: *b.* Black Notley, co. Essex, 9 April 1898: *educ.* Cressing School: Occupation – Farm Labourer: enlisted The Buffs 22 January 1917: served with the Expeditionary Force in France and Flanders and was killed in action 12 October 1917. Buried where he fell: Age 19.

(Panel 17) Pte. G/20035, Francis Hugh Warwick, 'B' Coy., 7th (Service) Bn. The Buffs (East Kent Regt.): *yst. s.* of Edwin Warwick, of 94, Ferme Park Road, Stroud Green, London, N., Colliery Agent, by his wife Jane, *dau.* of the late Henry Brown, of Heanor, co. Derby: *b.* North Wingfield, co. Derby, 26 September 1888: *educ.* Owen's School, Islington, London, N.: employee London County and

Westminster Bank, Lombard Street, London, E.C.: enlisted 1 August 1916: served with the Expeditionary Force in France and Flanders from the following November: reported wounded and missing after the fighting at Poelcapelle 12 October 1917, and is now assumed to have been killed in action on that date. A Sergt. wrote, "He was as brave a man as ever put on the King's uniform. His contempt for death and danger was really remarkable, even amongst a crowd of men whose most marked trait is their reckless bravery.": Age 29. *unm.*

PANEL 17 ENDS: PTE. D.I. WORSTER – (THE BUFFS) EAST KENT REGT.

PANEL 18 BEGINS: CAPT. C.E. WITHEY – (KING'S OWN) ROYAL LANCASTER REGT.

(Panel 18) 2nd Lieut. Thomas Albert Hawling, 3rd (Reserve) Bn. The King's Own (Royal Lancaster Regt.) attd. 9th (Service) Bn. King's Own (Yorkshire Light Infantry): eldest *s.* of Thomas Hawling, of Grotton Hall, Grotton, Saddleworth, co. York, for twenty-eight years Dispenser of Medicines at the Royal Infirmary, Oldham, by his wife Mary Ann, *dau.* of William Timbs: *b.* Oldham, co. Lancaster, 27 December 1891: *educ.* Waterloo Higher Grade School, Oldham: Occupation – Secretary: joined Duke of Lancaster's Own Yeomanry at the age of sixteen; left after four years' training, rejoined as Trooper, 3 September 1914: served with the Egyptian Expeditionary Force in Egypt and Palestine from September 1914: promoted to the rank of Sergt.: returned home 9 October 1916, and after a period of training at Fleet, co. Hants, was gazetted 2nd Lieut., Royal Lancaster Regt., 31 August 1917: proceeded to France the following October, and was killed in action at Passchendaele, 4 November following. Buried where he fell, about half a mile in front of Polygon Mound: Age 26. *unm.*

(Panel 18) 2nd Lieut. (Temp.) Alan Scott Niven, The King's Own (Royal Lancaster Regt.) attd. 9th (Service) Bn. King's Own (Yorkshire Light Infantry): *yr. s.* of George Niven, of 'Shiantelle,' Aldrington Road, Streatham Park, London, S.W., Bank Director, by his wife Nellie, *dau.* of John Connell: *b.* Streatham Park, London, S.W., 9 April 1895: *educ.* New Beacon, Sevenoaks; and Tonbridge School, where he was a member of the O.T.C.: trained one year with a firm of Chartered Accountants, thereafter joined a firm of Brokers, where he developed great business aptitude: applied for admission to a Public Schools Battn. shortly after the outbreak of war, but was rejected owing to defective eyesight. After seeking and receiving remedial treatment was admitted Artists' Rifles O.T.C., no.764505, 2 January 1917; transf'd. Cadet Corps, Fleet, co. Hants, 5 May 1917: gazetted 2nd Lieut. (Temp.) King's Own (Royal Lancaster Regt.), 28 August following: served with the Expeditionary Force in France and Flanders from 23 October; attd. 9th King's Own (Yorkshire Light Infantry) 26 October; killed in action nr. Passchendaele, 4 November of the same year. Buried where he fell: Age 22. *unm.* His Commanding Officer wrote, "He was not long in my company, but during the short time he gained the admiration and respect of both officers and men alike; he was so keen and willing, and did much to encourage the men during a trying time in the line. Truly, his duty to King and Country has been well done!" A friend wrote, "Personally, we do not fear taking the plunge except for the sorrow it causes our dear ones. Alan held very strong views on this score, his only thought being for you at home in the event of what has happened taking place." His service in France, a mere thirteen days.

(Panel 18) Pte. 30399, Reginald Burton, 1st Bn. (4th Foot) The King's Own (Royal Lancaster Regt.): formerly no.204539, Middlesex Regt.: *s.* of E. Burton, of Ironbridge, co. Salop: and brother to 45259, H. Burton, Royal Defence Corps, died 4 July 1917, Military Hospital, Oswestry: enlisted Ironbridge. Killed in action 12 October 1917: Age 35.

His brother Harry is buried in Wenlock (Broseley) Cemetery (N.C.737).

(Panel 18) Pte. 23727, Robert Dickinson, Siglr., 1/4th Bn. The King's Own (Royal Lancaster Regt.), (T.F.): *husb.* to Mrs Dickinson (78, Oxford Road, Burnley, co. Lancaster); late of Milton Street: Occupation – Weaver; Messrs Proctor, Stonyholme: reported missing and wounded 20 September 1917; confirmed (October 1918) killed in action. A member of St. Aidan's Mission; he was father to one child.

(Panel 18) Pte. 242002, Edward Flood, 2/5th Bn. The King's Own (Royal Lancaster Regt.), (T.F.): *s.* of Patrick Flood, of 58, Bonsall Street, Blackburn, by his wife Ellen: and *yr.* brother to Pte. 241999, J. Flood, King's Own, who fell the same day; and Rfn. 48963, T. Flood, 6th King's (Liverpool) Regt., killed in action 9 April 1918: enlisted Blackburn, co. Lancaster. Missing / believed killed in action 26 October 1917; vicinity Poelcapelle – Schaap-Belle: Age 21. *unm.*

His brother James also has no known grave, he is recorded below; Thomas is buried in Brown's Road Military Cemetery, Festubert (IV.B.10).

(Panel 18) Pte. 241999, James Flood, 2/5th Bn. The King's Own (Royal Lancaster Regt.), (T.F.): *s.* of Patrick Flood, of 58, Bonsall Street, Blackburn, by his wife Ellen: and elder brother to Pte. 242002, E. Flood, King's Own, who fell the same day; and Rfn. 48963, T. Flood, 6th King's (Liverpool) Regt., killed in action 9 April 1918: enlisted Blackburn, co. Lancaster. Missing / believed killed in action 26 October 1917; vicinity Poelcapelle – Schaap-Belle: Age 26. *unm.*

His brother Edward also has no known grave, he is recorded above; Thomas is buried in Brown's Road Military Cemetery, Festubert (IV.B.10).

(Panel 18) Pte. 241971, Tom Jacques, 8th (Service) Bn. The King's Own (Royal Lancaster Regt.): eldest *s.* of William Jacques, of 36, Derby Street, Burnley, by his wife Mary Ann: *b.* Burnley, co Lancaster, 11 September 1895: *educ.* Sandygate School, there: was a Cloth Looker: enlisted 1 April 1916: served with the Expeditionary Force in France and Flanders from January 1917; invalided home in March, suffering from septic poisoning, but rejoined his regiment in May, and was killed in action at Polygon Wood, 26 September following, while waiting for the signal to attack: Age 22. One of his officers wrote, "Your husband was a staunch and brave man, and his loss is much regretted, both by officers and men." He *m.* St. John's Roman Catholic Church, Burnley, 12 September 1916; Mary Catherine Harker (formerly Jacques, 60, Hurtley Street, Burnley), eldest *dau.* of Richard Goodier: *s.p.*

PANEL 18 ENDS: PTE. E. ROBINSON – (KING'S OWN) ROYAL LANCASTER REGT.

PANEL 19 BEGINS: PTE. J. ROBINSON – (KING'S OWN) ROYAL LANCASTER REGT.

(Panel 19) Pte. 201821, George Titterington, 1/4th Bn. The King's Own (Royal Lancaster Regt.), (T.F.): *s.* of John Titterington, of 3, Broadacre, Caton, co. Lancaster, by his wife Margaret: and brother to Pte. 240579, H. Titterington, 5th King's Own, who died 31 August 1918, at home: *b.* Caton: enlisted Fleetwood. Killed in action 20 September 1917: Age 31. He leaves a wife, Margaret Agnes Titterington (47, Primrose Street, Lancaster), to whom all correspondence and effects regarding the late Pte. Titterington should be forwarded.

His brother Henry is buried in Caton (St. Paul's) Churchyard (nr. East Boundary).

(Panel 19) Lieut. John Halifax Fegetter, M.C., 12/13th (Service) Bn. The Northumberland Fusiliers.: *s.* of William Fegetter, Shipping Agent; of 9, Dilston Terrace, Gosforth, Newcastle, by his wife Amelia Stewart, *dau.* of William Young, of Dundee: *b.* Jesmond, Newcastle-on-Tyne, 16 June, 1895: *educ.* Rutherford College – matriculated to Armstrong College, 1914 (entered Honours School – English and Latin, 1915): a member of Durham University O.T.C.; obtained a commission, December 1915: served with the Expeditionary Force in France and Flanders from June 1916: took part in the operations on the Somme: was wounded at Mametz Wood, 13 July following, and invalided home: on recovery, rejoined his regiment, being made Signalling Officer, and was killed in action, 4 October 1917, at Broodseinde. Buried 100 yards north-west of the hamlet of Reutel. His Commanding Officer wrote, "On 4 October the battalion took part in the great victory then won, and paid a heavy price. Your son accompanied Lieut.Col. Dix as Intelligence Officer; the Colonel was killed whilst leading the battalion, and I greatly fear that your son fell at the same time. He will leave a splendid record of service with the battalion. Col. Dix thought most highly of him, as did all of us;" and his Chaplain, "Your son was one of the most cheerful, fearless and conscientious men I have ever met, and is sadly missed by the officers and men of the Fusiliers, and the 'Queen's' also, with whom he frequently came in contact." A brother officer wrote:

"On the morning of 4 October he went up in front of the battalion to mark out the jumping-off point, and later met the companies and put them in position... Always the most gallant of soldiers, he had no fear of death. His men thought the world of him, and would, and did, follow him anywhere. His coolness in danger and disregard of shellfire had become almost proverbial in the battalion, and was a constant inspiration to all who saw him." Awarded the Military Cross (*London Gazette*, 1 January 1918), the official record stating – "This officer has rendered most valuable service as Battalion Signalling Officer, and in the performance of duty has shown the greatest gallantry, thereby inspiring his men with the utmost confidence and determination. He did particularly well when, during a successful attack upon the enemy's trenches, he led his signallers through the hostile barrage across ground swept by machine-gun fire, and established telephonic communication between battalion headquarters and the captured second objective within a few minutes of the enemy's trench being cleared by our leading wave. This officer rendered splendid service in reorganizing men and inspiring all by his confidence and coolness under heavy shell and mortar-fire. After nightfall, on one occasion, Lieut. Fegetter, by order of the Commanding Officer, patrolled 'No Man's Land' in search of wounded, and was instrumental in bringing in a great number of wounded men from near the enemy's wire.": Age 22. *unm.*

(Panel 19) Licut. Philip Shaw, 6th attd. 5th Bn. The Northumberland Fusiliers: *s.* of the late Henry William Cross Shaw, of the firm Messrs Henry Shaw & Son, Birmingham, by his wife Katherine (Rosehill, Budleigh Salterton, co. Devon), *dau.* of the late Thomas Dickinson, of King's Lynn: and brother to 2nd Lieut. J.H. Shaw, 6th Northumberland Fusiliers, killed in action on the same date; Capt. H.L. Shaw, 10th Royal Warwickshire Regt., died of wounds 3 July 1916, and cousin to Nurse E.F. Shaw, First Aid Nursing Yeomanry, died 24 October 1918. Killed in action 26 October 1917: Age 41.

His brother John also has no known grave, he is recorded below; Henry is buried in Bapaume Post Military Cemetery, Albert (I.C.7), cousin Evelyn, Sezanne Communal Cemetery (A.40).

(Panel 19) 2nd Lieut. William Henry Lethbridge, 13th (Service) Bn. The Northumberland Fusiliers: only *s.* of Henry Lethbridge, of Walnut Cottage, Aveton Gifford, Kingsbridge, co. Devon, by his wife Elizabeth: *b.* Devonport, co. Devon, 19 November 1895: *educ.* Grammar School, Kingsbridge, co. Devon: enlisted 10th Devonshire Regt., 12 September 1914: served with the Salonika Army at Salonika from 22 September 1915: returned home December 1916, and after a period of training at Alston Hall, was gazetted 2nd Lieut., Northumberland Fusiliers, 26 April 1917: went to France, 13 June 1917, and was killed in action 4 October following. His Major wrote, "It was in the course of our victorious advance that morning that Lieut. Lethbridge was struck by a splinter, whilst leading his men with the utmost gallantry; his spine was injured and he felt no pain; he died where he fell on the battlefield shortly after he was hit. His loss is most keenly felt by officers and men alike, by all of whom he was regarded with respect and affection;" and his Captain, "He displayed great coolness and bravery up to the time of his death, encouraging and inspiring his men by his magnificent example; that he died so gloriously on the field of battle and by his courageous bearing throughout, helped in a very large degree towards the success which was finally gained.": Age 21. *unm.*

(Panel 19) 2nd Lieut. John Leslie Lowth, 12/13th (Service) Bn. The Northumberland Fusiliers: *s.* of Col. Francis R. Lowth, C.B., of Clarence House, 8, Granville Road, Eastbourne: and brother to Capt. F.R.L. Lowth, Lancashire Fusiliers, who fell 22 August 1915, at Gallipoli. Killed in action 4 October 1917: Age 27.

His brother Francis also has no known grave; he is commemorated on the Helles Memorial.

(Panel 19) 2nd Lieut. William Clarence May, attd. 1/5th Bn. The Northumberland Fusiliers (T.F.): *s.* of Thomas May, of Baynard's Green, Bicester, co. Oxford, by his wife Elizabet Hannah: and elder brother to Pte. H.S. May, Oxford & Buckinghamshire Light Infantry, who fell 22 August 1917, aged 21 years. Killed in action, 26 October 1917: Age 25. *unm.* Remembered on the St. Mary's Church, Ardley, and the Stoke Lyne War Memorials: '*God Proved Them And Found Them Worthy For Himself.*'

His brother Howard also has no known grave; he is recorded on Panel 97.

(Panel 19) 2nd Lieut. John Herbert Shaw, 6th Bn. The Northumberland Fusiliers (T.F.): 3rd *s.* of the late Henry William Cross Shaw, of the firm Messrs Henry Shaw and Son, Birmingham, by his wife

Katherine (Rosehill, Budleigh Salterton, co. Devon), *dau.* of the late Thomas Dickinson, of King's Lynn: and brother to Lieut. P. Shaw, 6th attd. 5th Northumberland Fusiliers, killed in action on the same date; Capt. H.L. Shaw, 10th Royal Warwickshire Regt., died of wounds 3 July 1916, and cousin to Nurse E.F. Shaw, First Aid Nursing Yeomanry, died 24 October 1918: *b.* Yardley, co. Worcester: *educ.* Solihull School: joined Worcestershire Yeomanry, 1899: took part in the South African War 1899-1902 (Queen's Medal, three clasps): subsequently engaged in farming in South Africa, being Manager to Thomas Fleming Esq., of Good Hope, Natal: joined Natal Carabiniers on the outbreak of the European War, saw service in German South-West Africa, 1914-1915: returned to England, January 1916; applied for a commission, gazetted 2nd Lieut., Northumberland Fusiliers, 28 May following: served with the Expeditionary Force in France and Flanders from May 1917, and was killed in action at Houthulst Wood 26 October following. Buried where he fell. He *m.* Glasgow Cathedral, 30 September 1916; Alice Jacqueline (34, Blythswood Drive, Glasgow), *dau.* of the late James Perry, of Galway, M.E., M.Inst.C.E.

His brother Philip also has no known grave, he is recorded above; Henry is buried in Bapaume Post Military Cemetery, Albert (I.C.7), cousin Evelyn, Sezanne Communal Cemetery (A.40).

(Panel 19) Sergt. 46152, Eddie Anderson, 8th (Service) Bn. The Northumberland Fusiliers: *yst. s.* of George Anderson, of 18, Church Street, Dunbar, East Lothian (formerly 85, High Street, Dunbar), by his wife Euphemia, *dau.* of the late George W. Wood, of Musselburgh, Midlothian: *b.* Musselburgh, Midlothian, 16 January 1896: *educ.* Grammar School, there, and Burgh School, Dunbar: was travelling on the Continent as a Valet: on the outbreak of war returned to England: enlisted Rifle Brigade, 4 September 1914: served with the Expeditionary Force in France and Flanders from July 1915: wounded in the leg 3 April 1916, and sent to the Canadian Red Cross Hospital, Taplow, co. Bucks.: on recovery acted as an Instructor at Seaford and Northampton: transf'd. Northumberland Fusiliers, 8 December; returned to France: slightly wounded twice at Messines: promoted Sergt. on the field, 3 April 1917, and was killed in action, 16 August following, while leading his platoon at Ypres. Capt. Angus wrote, "The company has lost in your son a good friend and a gallant gentleman;" and a comrade, "No man could wish for a braver son, and his name will always be remembered by his comrades. We knew him as a soldier and a gentleman. Now we know him as a hero who has made the supreme sacrifice for his country. You may well feel proud of him.": Age 21. *unm.*

(Panel 19) Sergt. 9544, Frederick Edwin Banks, 1st Bn. (5th Foot) The Northumberland Fusiliers: *s.* of Frederick Banks, Commercial Traveller; of 15A, Thorney Hedge Road, Chiswick, London, W.: *b.* Knightsbridge, London, S.W., 24 April 1879: served in the South African War, 1899-1902 (King's and Queen's Medals): on the conclusion of the war joined the Reserve: rejoined his old regiment October 1914: trained Scott's Camp, Newcastle: served with the Expeditionary Force in France and Flanders from 26 May 1917, and was killed in action 24 September following: Age 38. He *m.* Hammersmith, London, W.; Ada Alice (7, Dean's Road, Hanwell, London, W.), *dau.* of Henry Edward Bacon, and had a son Frederick, *b.* 15 September 1910.

(Panel 19) Sergt. 12801, Adam Tait, D.C.M., 12/13th (Service) Bn. The Northumberland Fusiliers: *s.* of James Tait, of Linton Colliery: *b.* Alnwick, co. Northumberland: enlisted Amble. Killed in action 27 April 1918. Awarded the Distinguished Conduct Medal (*London Gazette*, 26 June 1918) for 'conspicuous gallantry and devotion to duty. Before a raid he did valuable patrol work, and by his keenness and skill assisted greatly in the preparations for the operation. During the raid he took a prominent part in hand-to-hand fighting, in which all the enemy who offered resistance were put out of action. He showed courage and skill.'

PANEL 19 ENDS: L/CORPL. J.G. DOBSON – NORTHUMBERLAND FUSILIERS

PANEL 20 BEGINS: L/CORPL. T. DOBSON – NORTHUMBERLAND FUSILIERS

On 10 November 2003 a team of archaeologists excavating a length of trench-line in the vicinity of Track 'X' Cemetery uncovered six sets of human remains. One, of which very little was left, consisted of a few bones, some buttons and a pair of boots, lying in a crater gouged out by a shell which in all probability killed him. To identify these remains, like so many others recovered over the years, seemed highly unlikely but the remains of a fragment of uniform and an item of regimental insignia clinging to a shoulder bone provided the archaeologists with a possibility. The insignia in the form of a shoulder title 'T5 NF' led them to 5th Northumberland Fusiliers a detachment of which after going into action hereabouts on 26 October 1917 later recorded four men missing. Three were officers who wore no shoulder insignia, the fourth a young N.C.O., William Storey.

(Panel 20) L/Corpl. 243188, William Stephen Storey, 5th Bn. The Northumberland Fusiliers (T.F.): *s.* of Robert Storey, of 9, High Quay, Blyth, co. Northumberland, by his wife Elspet Ann: *b.* Blyth, afsd.: enlisted there. Missing / believed killed in action 26 October 1917: Age 21. *unm.* At the time of writing (July 2010) the remains recovered in November 2003 have not been positively identified as being those of L/Corpl. Storey.

(Panel 20) L/Corpl. 46884, Hugh Miller Templeton, 'A' Coy., 1/4th Bn. The Northumberland Fusiliers (T.F.): *s.* of the late James Templeton, of 543, Dalmarnock Road, Glasgow, by his wife Marion, *dau.* of Hugh Miller: *b.* Catrine, co. Ayr, 11 July 1884: *educ.* Glasgow: Occupation – Joiner and Cabinet Maker: enlisted Royal Engineers, 20 March 1916: transf'd. Northumberland Fusiliers, December following: served with the Expeditionary Force in France and Flanders from 1 January 1917: wounded at Arras, 3 May, and invalided home: returned to France, September, and was killed in action at Houthulst Wood 26 October 1917: Age 33. *unm.*

(Panel 20) Pte. 24457, Robert John Crisp, 23rd (Service) Bn. (4th Tyneside Scottish) Bn. The Northumberland Fusiliers: *s.* of Robert Crisp, of 'Fox Hemel', Thirston, Felton, co. Northumberland, by his wife Elizabeth: *b.* Broomhill, co. Northumberland, 26 May 1894: *educ.* Thirston School: enlisted Northumberland Fusiliers, 31 August 1914: served with the Expeditionary Force in France from 23 August 1915, and was killed in action at Rortebeek Farm, nr. Langemarck, 18 October 1917. Buried at Rortebeek Farm: Age 23. *unm.*

(Panel 20) Pte. 13746, George Cunnah, 10th (Service) Bn. The Northumberland Fusiliers: *s.* of John Cunnah, of 1, Chapel Row, North Wallbottle, Newburn-on-Tyne, co. Northumberland, by his wife Catherine 'Kate': and yr. brother to Pte. 28390, J.J. Cunnah, 4th South Wales Borderers, killed in action 15 January 1917, in Mesopotamia: *b.* Dublin, *c.*1895: enlisted Newburn. Died 11 October 1917, of wounds: Age 22. *unm.*

His brother John also has no known grave, he is commemorated on the Basra Memorial, Iraq.

(Panel 20) Pte. 22/264, George Curry, D.C.M., 22nd (Service) Bn. (3rd Tyneside Scottish) The Northumberland Fusiliers: *b.* Durham: enlisted South Shields. Killed in action 20 October 1917. Lieut. Col. S. Acklom, Comdg. 3rd Northumberland Fusiliers, in a letter to his widow, wrote, "I write to offer you my most sincere sympathy for the loss of your gallant husband. I wish I could adequately express to you the sense of personal grief which his death has caused me. He was killed instantaneously by a shell whilst on his way to visit our outpost with his Company Commander, who was dangerously wounded at the same time. I fear it will be a terrible blow to you, but there may be some consolation in the thought that he suffered no pain whatever, and he died doing his duty. I had an immense admiration for his soldierly qualities and the entire battalion will mourn him. I am only thankful that we succeeded in obtaining for him the D.C.M. before his death. No man has ever earned it better. It would be a pleasure for me to hear from you, if you care to write. I am wondering if you are left with any children who may be a consolation to you in your trouble. Again, assuring you of my profound sympathy, Yours Sincerely..." Pte. Curry was awarded the Distinguished Conduct Medal, 'For conspicuous gallantry and devotion to duty as a company runner carrying messages, each time successfully, through a hostile barrage. When a shell fell in a trench burying four men, he got on top of the parapet and under heavy machine gun fire dug them out.' (*IWGC record 221264*)

PANEL 20 ENDS: PTE. A.E. DAGLISH – NORTHUMBERLAND FUSILIERS

PANEL 21 BEGINS: PTE. T. DALE – NORTHUMBERLAND FUSILIERS

(Panel 21) Pte. 59056, Augustus Charles Eschbacher, 23rd (Tyneside Scottish) Bn. The Northumberland Fusiliers: and brother to Pte. 634185, V.C. Eschbacher, 2/20th London Regt., died of wounds 5 October 1918: *b*. Bermondsey, London, S.E.: enlisted Deptford. Died of wounds 17 October 1917. Two other brothers – Ptes. B.H. Eschbacher and F.S. Eschbacher – also served, both survived. 'Remembered with Honour and Pride – Holy Cross Roman Catholic Church, Catford.'

His brother Victor is buried in Grevillers British Cemetery (XV.D.12).

(Panel 21) Pte. 290781, John Keeney, 1/7th Bn. The Northumberland Fusiliers (T.F.): *s*. of the late Matthew (& Sarah) Keeney: and brother to Pte. 23/1411, J. Keeney, 23rd Northumberland Fusiliers, killed in action 1 July 1916, at the Somme: *b*. Ashington, co. Northumberland: enlisted Alnwick. Killed in action 26 October 1917, nr. Houthulst Forest, Belgium: Age 19.

His brother Joseph also has no known grave; he is commemorated on the Thiepval Memorial, Somme. (*IWGC record Jaspeth*)

PANEL 21 ENDS: PTE. C.F.G. KING – NORTHUMBERLAND FUSILIERS

PANEL 22 BEGINS: PTE. G.H. KING – NORTHUMBERLAND FUSILIERS

(Panel 22) Pte. 25/1135, John McAvoy, 8th (Service) Bn. The Northumberland Fusiliers: elder brother to Pte. 6320, T. McAvoy, 2nd Royal Munster Fusiliers, killed in action, 10 November 1917: *b*. Bishop Auckland, c.1873: enlisted Newcastle-on-Tyne: served with the Expeditionary Force in France and Flanders, and was killed in action 16 August 1917, at Langemarck: Age 44. All correspondence to be addressed c/o J. McAvoy, Esq., 13, South View, Chester-le-Street, Co. Durham.

His brother Thomas also has no known grave; he is recorded on Panel 143.

(Panel 22) Pte. 48346, Alexander MacGregor, 12/13th (Service) Bn. The Northumberland Fusiliers: formerly no.116521, Royal Garrison Artillery: *b*. Laggan, co. Inverness: enlisted Plymouth, co. Devon. Killed in action 13 April 1918. Known to all as 'Sandy Laggan' a son of the Isle of Lismore, Argyll, Scotland. Floral tribute September 2004 read: "*Sandy, until recently your departure for France was within living memory. These memories have passed to a new generation to keep, and pass on in their turn. We will not forget. Sleep well.*"

(Panel 22) Pte. 29688, John Robert McPherson, 8th (Service) Bn. The Northumberland Fusiliers: *s*. of the late Richard Esto McPherson, by his wife Elizabeth Ann (15, Elswick East Terrace, Newcastle-on-Tyne): and elder brother to Pte. 27946, M. McPherson, 10th Northumberland Fusiliers, killed five days later: enlisted Newcastle-on-Tyne. Killed in action 16 August 1917: Age 36. He leaves a wife Elizabeth McPherson (39, George Street, Newcastle-on-Tyne, co. Northumberland).

His brother Malcolm also has no known grave; he is recorded below.

(Panel 22) Pte. 27946, Malcolm McPherson, 10th (Service) Bn. The Northumberland Fusiliers: *s*. of the late Richard Esto McPherson, by his wife Elizabeth Ann (15, Elswick East Terrace, Newcastle-on-Tyne): and yr. brother to Pte. 29688, J.R. McPherson, 8th Northumberland Fusiliers, killed five days previously: enlisted Newcastle-on-Tyne. Killed in action 20 September 1917: Age 27. *unm*.

His brother John also has no known grave; he is recorded above.

(Panel 22) Pte. 21/290, John William Middleton, 21st (Service) Bn. (Tyneside Scottish) The Northumberland Fusiliers: *b*. Bedlington: enlisted there. Killed in action 17 October 1917.

(Panel 22) Pte. 242031, Charles 'Charlie' Ambrose Payne, 1/5th Bn. The Northumberland Fusiliers (T.F.): formerly no.27003, King's Royal Rifle Corps: *s*. of F. (& Mrs) Payne, of Haverhill, co. Suffolk: and brother to Pte. 33394, F. Payne, 6th Yorkshire Regt., killed in action, 27 September 1917; and Pte. TF/293037, A. Payne, 3/10th Middlesex Regt., killed in action 4 October 1917: *b*. Long Melford: enlisted Canning Town, London. Killed in action 26 October 1917.

His brothers Fred and Alf also have no known grave; they are recorded on Panels 53 & 114 respectively.

(Panel 22) Pte. 44906, Max Leopold Roscher, 1/5th Bn. The Northumberland Fusiliers (T.F.): only *s*. of the late Frederick Alfred Roscher, Tutor (University), by his wife Anna M. (Foden Road, Walsall), *dau*. of Edward Williams: *b*. Handsworth, co. Stafford, 7 July 1886: *educ*. Saffron Walden School, co. Essex: employee Lloyds Bank, Walsall: enlisted 20 June 1916: served with the Expeditionary Force in France and Belgium from the following December, and was killed in action at Poelcapelle 26 October 1917. Buried there: Age 31. *unm*.

PANEL 22 ENDS: PTE. S. SANDERSON – NORTHUMBERLAND FUSILIERS

PANEL 23 BEGINS: PTE. S.H. SANSOM – NORTHUMBERLAND FUSILIERS

(Panel 23) Capt. Cecil Llewellyn Norton Roberts, 2nd Bn. (6th Foot) The Royal Warwickshire Regt.: *s*. of the late Rev. Albert Pryor Roberts, Vicar of St. Margaret's, Birmingham, by his wife Constance C. Roberts (Ladywood Vicarage, Birmingham): and elder brother to A/B. Z/1285, L.G.H. Roberts, R.N.V.R., Hawke Bn., 63rd R.N. Divn., killed in action, 21 July 1915, at the Dardanelles. Killed in action, 9 October 1917, at Polygon Wood.

His brother Leonard is buried in Lancashire Landing Cemetery (F.101).

(Panel 23) 2nd Lieut. John Stanley Firth, 3rd attd. 2nd Bn. (6th Foot) The Royal Warwickshire Regt.: *s*. of Stanley Firth, of 28, Caledon Road, Sherwood, Engineer, by his wife Elizabeth May, *dau*. of the late William Mollart Harding: *b*. Hanley, 28 January 1898: *educ*. Tindal Board School, Birmingham, and High Pavement, Nottingham: was on the Staff of the National Provincial Bank, Nottingham: joined Nottingham University O.T.C., June 1916: obtained a commission 28 March 1917: served with the Expeditionary Force in France and Flanders; killed in action at Passchendaele, 9 October following. His Commanding Officer wrote, "Your son, 2nd Lieut. J.S. Firth, was beloved and admired by the men of his platoon, who were following his leadership when he fell and died during the attack on the 9th inst. His loss is keenly felt by his brother officers, with whom he was very popular, and by all ranks of the battalion. May the fact of knowing that he died the death of a gallant officer while fighting for his country help you to bear in a small way the sad blow which his end must cause you;" and one of his men, "He was greatly liked by all his company. He was very cool and brave in action, and always joined in all the sports with his platoon.": Age 18.

PANEL 23 ENDS: 2ND LIEUT. V.A. WRIGHT – ROYAL WARWICKSHIRE REGT.

PANEL 24 BEGINS: CSM. F. BILLINGTON, D.C.M. – ROYAL WARWICKSHIRE REGT.

(Panel 24) Sergt. 265740, Frederick George Bailey, 1/7th Bn. The Royal Warwickshire Regt. (T.F.): late of Leamington Spa, co. Warwick: *s*. of George H.P. Bailey, of High Street, Great Wakering, co. Essex, by his wife Helena M.: enlisted Coventry, September 1914. Severely wounded while leading a small working party in No Man's Land on the night of 8 October 1917. Later found and placed on a stretcher, Sergt. Bailey and his two bearers had almost reached the safety of the Warwicks trench when a shell burst overhead, killing Sergt. Bailey and one of the bearers instantly, badly wounding the other: Age 26.

(Panel 24) Sergt. 307359, Charles Redwood Dale, 2/8th Bn. The Royal Warwickshire Regt. (T.F.): formerly no.1309, Cheshire Regt.: *s*. of the late Charles J. Dale, by his wife Helena (45, Union Road, Macclesfield): and brother to Pte. 91828, F.J. Dale, 15th Durham Light Infantry, killed in action 9 September 1918, aged 19 years: *b*. Macclesfield. Killed in action 3 September 1917: Age 23. *unm*.

His brother Frederick also has no known grave; he is commemorated on the Vis-en-Artois Memorial (Panel 9).

(Panel 24) Sergt. 260365, William Henry Hannaford, 10th (Service) Bn. The Royal Warwickshire Regt.: formerly no.1965, Devonshire Regt.: *s*. of William Hannaford, of 3, Crescent Road, Ivybridge, co. Devon, by his wife Sibilla: and brother to Pte. 37275, A. Hannaford, 5th Duke of Cornwall's Light Infantry, who fell two days previously: enlisted Plymouth. Killed in action 19 April 1918: Age 25. He was married to Olive Hannaford (Filham, Ivybridge).

His brother Albert also has no known grave; he is commemorated on the Loos (Dud Corner) Memorial (Panel 68).

(Panel 24) Sergt. 200457, Albert Percy Summers, 'C' Coy., 1/5th Bn. The Royal Warwickshire Regt. (T.F.): *s.* of Peter Summers, of 24, Oliver Road, Cape Street, Smethwick, Confectioner, by his wife Eliza, *dau.* of Thomas Lawrence, of Langley, near Oldbury: *b.* Birmingham, co. Warwick, 22 June 1889: *educ.* Nelson Street Board School, there: Occupation – Clerk; Mitchells and Butlers' Brewery: joined the Warwickshire Regt. 6 September 1914: served with the Expeditionary Force in France and Flanders from April 1915, and was killed in action at St. Julien, 4 October 1917. Buried where he fell: Age 27. He *m.* at Handsworth Church, 27 January 1917, Beatrice (4, Queen's Avenue, Factory Road, Handsworth, co. Warwick), *dau.* of William Cooke: *s.p.* (*IWGC record age 24*)

(Panel 24) Sergt. 265374, William Joseph Wagstaffe, D.C.M., 1/7th Bn. The Royal Warwickshire Regt. (T.F.): *s.* of Joseph Wagstaffe, of 50, William Street, Attleborough, co. Warwick, formerly of Tunnell Cottage, Gadsby Street, Nuneaton, by his wife Annie, *dau.* of Charles Haynes, of Priors Marston, near Byfield: *b.* Priors Hardwicke, co. Warwick, 14 March 1893: *educ.* Weedon School: Occupation – Miner: joined the Warwickshire Territorials in May 1911: called up on mobilization 4 August 1914: served with the Expeditionary Force in France and Flanders from the same month: wounded 1 July 1916, and again on the Somme, and was killed in action at Terrier Farm, near Poelcappelle, 4 October 1917. Buried where he fell. His Commanding Officer, Capt. Mitford, wrote: "Sergt. Wagstaffe was a great friend of mine, and was most popular amongst his men. His courage and bravery knew no equal, and we were most sorry when he was killed. We have lost a very great friend." Awarded the D.C.M. ('*London Gazette*,' 6 April 1917) 'for conspicuous bravery and devotion to duty.': Age 24. *unm.*

(Panel 24) Sergt. 27272, Frederick Grange Wesselhoeft, 'B' Coy., 10th (Service) Bn. The Royal Warwickshire Regt.: only *s.* of Frederick Wesselhoeft, of 'Hillhead,' 13, Arlington Drive, Mapperley Park, Nottingham, by his wife Ellen, *dau.* of J.K. Grange, of Glasgow: *b.* Nottingham, 22 February 1897: *educ.* Waverley School, and Nottingham High School (O.T.C. member): joined 2/7th Battn. Sherwood Foresters, September 1914: proceeded to Ireland with his regiment, going through the Dublin Rebellion, April 1916: served with the Expeditionary Force in France and Flanders from the following September; transf'd. Royal Warwickshire Regt., and was killed in action at the Battle of the Menin Road 20 September 1917. Buried in the Military Cemetery near Ypres. His Commanding Officer wrote, "He had served faithfully and willingly all the time, and is greatly missed by all who knew him;" and a comrade, "He was the best pal I ever had, liked by all, and greatly missed by all his company.": Age 20. *unm.*

(Panel 24) Corpl. 2807, Albert Edward Pinchin, 1/5th Bn. The Royal Warwickshire Regt. (T.F.): *s.* of Mrs E. Pinchin (6, Council Houses, Pinvin, Pershore): and elder brother to Pte. 203963, S. Pinchin, Worcestershire Regt., who fell five days later, 9 October: *b.* Bricklehampton, co. Worcester, 1884: enlisted Warwick. Killed in action 4 October 1917: Age 33.

His brother Sydney also has no known grave; he is recorded on Panel 77.

(Panel 24) Corpl. 241420, Louis Henry Summerfield, 2/6th Bn. The Royal Warwickshire Regt. (T.F.): *s.* of the late Henry Summerfield, by his wife Clara Jane (4, Lime Tree Grove, Pugh Road, Aston, Birmingham), *dau.* of the late Alfred Hadley: *b.* Birmingham, co. Warwick, 7 March 1891: *educ.* St. Joseph's Roman Catholic School, Birmingham: employee Dunlop Rubber Co.: joined Royal Warwickshire Territorials, 17 November 1915: served with the Expeditionary Force in France and Flanders from 21 May 1916, and was killed at Ypres 2 September 1917: Age 26. *unm.*

PANEL 24 ENDS: L/CORPL. G. BAVERSTOCK – ROYAL WARWICKSHIRE REGT.

PANEL 25 BEGINS: L/CORPL. G. BAXTER – ROYAL WARWICKSHIRE REGT.

(Panel 25) L/Corpl. 5199, Robert Alexander Butler, M.M., 2nd Bn. (6th Foot) The Royal Warwickshire Regt.: *s.* of William Butler, of 19, Sydenham Grove, Sydenham Road, Sparkbrook, Birmingham, by his wife Mary Jane, *dau.* of Robert (& Jane) Chandler: *b.* Millwall, London, S.E., 28 September 1897: *educ.* Clarkson Street School, West Ham: enlisted September 1914: served with the Expeditionary Force in France and Flanders, from June 1915: wounded 2 March 1916 and invalided home: returned to France 31 August following, and was killed in action, 9 October 1917. His Commanding Officer wrote, "He was killed by a shell just as they entered the German trenches," and that "all the company thought a lot of him." He was awarded the Military Medal for carrying despatches through a heavy barrage fire: Age 20. *unm.*

(Panel 25) L/Corpl. 200605, Sydney Colloff, 1/5th Bn. The Royal Warwickshire Regt. (T.F.): *s.* of Charles Colloff, of 3, Seymour Place, Rosalie Street, Brookfields, Birmingham, by his wife Caroline, *dau.* of James Barker: *b.* Brookfields, Birmingham, co. Warwick, 7 December 1892: *educ.* Camden Street Council School: Occupation – Jeweller: enlisted 5 September 1914: served with the Expeditionary Force in France and Flanders from 3 March 1915, and was killed in action at Janet's Farm, St. Julien, 22 August 1917. Buried there. L/Corpl. Colloff was a student at the Birmingham School of Art; his work showed much promise, several of his paintings being hung in the Birmingham Art Gallery: Age 25. *unm.*

(Panel 25) Pte. 260081, Henry Atkinson, 1/6th Bn. The Royal Warwickshire Regt. (T.F.): *yst. s.* of Thomas Atkinson, of Tottenham, London, N.: *b.* London, 30 April 1886: *educ.* London: Occupation – Stock-Room Hand; H. Labus': enlisted Essex Regt., 10 June 1916: served with the Expeditionary Force in France and Flanders from June 1917; transf'd. Royal Warwickshire Regt., and was killed in action at Ypres, 27 August 1917. Buried in Small Cemetery, St. Julien, Ypres: Age 31. He *m.* Holy Trinity, Tottenham, London, N., 25 December 1911; Catherine Susan (162, High Cross, Tottenham, London, N.), *dau.* of Frank George Pratt, and had two sons,Robert Henry, *b.* 4 December 1913 and Charles Frank, *b.* 8 July 1915.

(Panel 25) Pte. 34697, Lawson Attwood, 16th (Service) Bn. The Royal Warwickshire Regt.: formerly no. 204568, Oxford & Bucks Light Infantry: *s.* of John Attwood, of 21, Park Lane, Netherend, Cradley Heath, co. Stafford, by his wife Clara: *b.* Cradley, 1898: enlisted Stourbridge, co. Worcester. Killed instantaneously when a shell exploded in the trench he was occupying, 11 November 1917: Age 19. Five other men were also killed.

(Panel 25) Pte. 1071, George Huband Ballard, 14th (Service) Bn. (Birmingham Pals) The Royal Warwickshire Regt.: stepson of the late Thomas Ballard, Builder's Labourer; of Church Row, Pershore, co. Worcester, by his marriage to Adelaide Ballard, *née* Huband (Hollow Meadows, Pinvin, Pershore): *b.* Pinvin, June 1887: enlisted Moseley, Birmingham. Killed in action, 5 October 1917: Age 29.

(Panel 25) Pte. 203377, Thomas Charles Brown, 1/5th Bn. The Royal Warwickshire Regt. (T.F.): formerly no.467, Huntingdonshire Cyclist Battn.: late of Godmanchester, co. Huntingdon: *s.* of Thomas (& Catherine) Brown, of Bank Cottage, Market Hill, Huntingdon; since removed to 8, Alms Houses, George Street, Huntingdon: and elder brother to Pte. S/43832, C.W. Brown, Gordon Highlanders (posted 1/14th London Regt.), killed in action 29 August 1918, aged 19 years: *b.* St. Ives: enlisted Huntingdon: killed in action, 22 August 1917: Age 25. *unm.*

His brother Charles is buried in H.A.C. Cemetery, Ecoust-St. Mein (V.J.9).

(Panel 25) Pte. 29236, Archie Callaway, 1/6th Bn. The Royal Warwickshire Regt. (T.F.): formerly no.21726, Somerset Light Infantry: late of Winsford, co. Somerset: yr. brother to Pte. 203369, F. Callaway, Somerset Light Infantry, who fell 4 October 1917: enlisted Taunton. Killed in action 17 August 1917: Age 27. All correspondence should be addressed c/o Miss Florence Callaway (2, Council Cottage, Winsford, nr. Taunton, co. Somerset).

His brother Frederick also has no known grave; he is recorded on Panel 41.

(Panel 25) Pte. 268478, James Dockerill, 1/7th Bn. The Royal Warwickshire Regt. (T.F.): *s.* of Emma Dockerill (Rectory Cottage, Popes Lane, Warboys, co. Huntingdon): and yr. brother to Pte. 30250, J.

Dockerill, 14th (1st Birmingham Pals) Battn. Royal Warwickshire Regt., killed 12 September 1916, in the fighting at the Somme: enlisted Huntingdon Cyclist's Battn., no.191, undertook Active Service obligations, transf'd. Royal Warwickshire Regt., and was killed in action 27 August 1917: Age 20. *unm.*

His brother John also has no known grave; he is commemorated on the Thiepval Memorial, Somme.

"My Dear Beloved, I am writing a few lines in the hope if anything should happen to me someone will be honest enough to send this on to you, as I know you would treasure a line from me. This I will carry about with me in case of accidents. I also enclose the few francs that I have saved since I have been out here. I have heard so much of the RAMC going through the wounded for what money they had, that I am sealing it up in the hope that a letter would be held sacred and you would get it. It is not much but it would come in useful; it is all I can do for you. My darling, if this should ever reach you it will be a sure sign that I am gone under and what will become of you and the chicks I don't know, but there is one above who will see to you and not let you starve. I don't fear for myself but for you at home. You have been the best of wives and I loved you deeply, and my children also. But my roving spirit would not let me rest, I must have inherited it from my forebears. Though I had a comfortable home I could not rest. I wanted to take part in the greatest war the world had ever known. I have been through hardships that even younger men would have gone under and could not stand. Still, I am as good as ever but my one trouble has been you, no doubt I should have thought about all that before I came here. This is where I wronged you, it is too late now, and I go to face what is before me like a man, and I hope I shall not flinch. Dear heart, do think of me sometimes in the future when your grief has worn a bit, and the older children I know won't forget me, and speak sometimes of me to the younger ones and the one it has been my lot never to see, and, when Bert is old enough to know, tell him his father tried to be a man and its my last wish that he will grow upright and honest and leave drink alone; that is my last words for him. And dearest if the chance should come your way, for you are young and good looking, and should a good man give you an offer, it would please me to think you would take it, not to grieve too much for me, for I did not know when I was well off, or I should not have left you thus bringing suffering and poverty on a loving wife and children for which in time I hope you will forgive me, and I also hope when my children grow up they will never marry a man of a roving disposition for it will only bring them misery. So, dear heart, I will bid you all farewell hoping to meet you in the time to come, if there is a hereafter. Know that my last thoughts were of you, in the dugout or on the firestep, my thoughts went out to you, the only one I ever loved, the one that made a man of me, hoping that the Lord will take care of you all. Goodbye my darling wife and children, your loving and faithful husband, Albert xxxxxx For my children xxxxxx"

(Panel 25) Pte. 21336, Albert James Ford, 'C' Coy, 14th (Service) Bn. The Royal Warwickshire Regt.: *s.* of the late William (& Caroline) Ford: *husb.* to Edith Alethea Ford (1, Avon Crescent, Cumberland Road, Bristol), and father to six children – five girls and a boy, Bert, who he was destined never to see as Edith was pregnant when he left for the Western Front. Killed in action, 26 October 1917: Age 40. Eighty-seven years after his death Pte. Ford is still remembered by his family, one of his great-grandchildren wrote:

> We never met,
> We weren't supposed to.
> You should have grown old before I was born,
> But you never grew old,
> You died young.
> I may carry your blood,
> But you helped give life to millions;
> Life that is free and safe,
> Together with you friends and comrades,
> The ultimate sacrifice.

We can never thank you,
We can never repay you,
But we must never forget.
Now, sleep well together
Safe from the horrors,
At peace.

(Panel 25) Pte. 265270, Ernest Alfred Frazer, 1/7th Bn. The Royal Warwickshire Regt. (T.F.): *s.* of the late Isaac Henry (& Mrs) Frazer, of Kenilworth, co. Warwick: brother to Miss Phyllis Frazer (13, Albion Street, Kenilworth); and Pte. G/21475, G.H. Frazer, 7th Queen's Own (Royal West Kent Regt.), killed in action, 21 September 1918: *b.* Kenilworth: enlisted there: killed in action, 27 August 1917; shot by a sniper: Age 21.

His brother George also has no known grave; he is commemorated on the Vis-en-Artois Memorial (Panel 7).

PANEL 25 ENDS: PTE. H.W.G. FUDGE – ROYAL WARWICKSHIRE REGT.

PANEL 26 BEGINS: PTE. T. FURBOROUGH – ROYAL WARWICKSHIRE REGT.

(Panel 26) Pte. 268265, Harold Garner, 1/7th Bn. The Royal Warwickshire Regt. (T.F.): *s.* of the late John Garner, by his wife Margaret (42, Traverse Street, St. Helens): and brother to L/Corpl. 20577, J. Garner, South Lancashire Regt., taken prisoner 23 March 1918: *b.* St. Helens, co. Lancaster, 2 July 1897: *educ.* Holy Trinity, Parr Mount, St. Helens: Occupation – Grocer's Assistant: joined East Lancashire Royal Engineers (T.F.) 3 May 1916: transf'd Royal Warwickshire Regt., November following: served with the Expeditionary Force in France and Flanders from 24 December, and was killed in action 21 August 1917. Buried north-east of Ypres: Age 20. *unm.*

His brother Joseph died at Westphalia, Germany, 10 July 1918; he is buried in Cologne Southern Cemetery (X.J.10)

(Panel 26) Pte. 10026, Albert Godson, 11th (Service) Bn. The Royal Warwickshire Regt.: late of Cherington, co. Warwick: brother to Pte. 10025, J. Godson, 11th Royal Warwickshire Regt., who fell the same day: *b.* Cherington: enlisted Stratford-on-Avon. Killed in action 9 October 1917. Remembered on the Cherington and Stourton War Memorial; brothers Harry, Charles and Percy also served.

(Panel 26) Pte. 10025, Joseph Godson, 11th (Service) Bn. The Royal Warwickshire Regt.: late of Cherington, co. Warwick: brother to Pte. 10026, A. Godson, 11th Royal Warwickshire Regt., who fell the same day: *b.* Snowshill, co. Gloucester: enlisted Stratford-on-Avon. Killed in action 9 October 1917. Remembered on the Cherington & Stourton War Memorial; brothers Harry, Charles and Percy also served.

(Panel 26) Pte. 18298, William Edward James Gunter, 14th (Service) Bn. The Royal Warwickshire Regt.: formerly no.22931, Prince Albert's (Somerset Light Infantry): stepson to Cornelius Samuel Hopkins, of 7, Court, 6, House, Denmark Street, Aston, Birmingham, by his marriage to the late Elizabeth Jane Hoskins, *née* Gunter: *b.* Birmingham, 1887. Killed in action 4 October 1917: Age 30.

(Panel 26) Pte. 8013, Richard Thomas Herbert, 14th (Service) Bn. The Royal Warwickshire Regt.: *b.* 1879: enlisted 1 October 1914: served with the Expeditionary Force in France and Flanders, and was killed in action 5 October 1917. His Captain wrote, "He had been in the company a long time, and by reason of his long service with me, I gave him a job at the Company's Headquarters which released him from such duties as sentry in the trenches. He always did very well, and there is not one of us in the company who does not miss him and realise a real loss in his death. He was much liked by the officers for his good ways and the thorough way in which he carried out his duties.": Age 38. He *m.* Aston, Birmingham; Gertrude (235, Herbert Road, Small Heath, Birmingham), and had four children, Rhoda, *b.* 17 July 1902, Thomas, *b.* 29 December 1906, William, *b.* 24 December 1908 and Leonard, *b.* 21 June 1911.

(Panel 26) Pte. 21613, Harry Hill, 2nd Bn. (6th Foot) The Royal Warwickshire Regt.: *s*. of Joseph Hill, of 60, Aston Lane, Aston, Birmingham, by his wife Mary: *b*. Aston, co. Warwick, 8 June 1898: *educ*. Aston Lane County School: enlisted Royal Warwickshire Regt., 11 December 1915: served with the Expeditionary Force in France, and was killed in action 9 October 1917.

(Panel 26) Pte. (Drmr.) 5064, Colin Charles Horton, 10th (Service) Bn. The Royal Warwickshire Regt.: *s*. of William Henry Horton, of 3, Poplar Avenue, Palmerston Road, Sparkbrook, Birmingham, by his wife Elizabeth Mary, *dau*. of Joseph Jones, of Bedford: and brother to Corpl. 79, Harold F. Horton, 15th Royal Warwickshire Regt., killed in action, Falfemont Farm, 3 September 1916: *b*. Birmingham, co. Warwick, 10 July 1896: *educ*. Stratford Road Council School, there: Occupation – Clerk; Messrs A.T. Becks and Co.: enlisted Royal Warwickshire Regt. September 1914: served with the Expeditionary Force in France and Flanders from February 1916: took part in the Battles of the Somme (1916) and many other engagements. He was killed in action at Zillebeke, 20 September 1917: Age 21. *unm*.

His brother Harold also has no known grave; he is commemorated on the Thiepval Memorial, Somme.

(Panel 26) Pte. 29254, John 'Jack' Robert Johnson, 1/7th Bn. The Royal Warwickshire Regt. (T.F.): Killed in action 8 October 1917, vicinity Water Street, Poelcapelle.

(Panel 26) Pte. 30215, Cyril Kisby, 14th (Service) Bn. The Royal Warwickshire Regt.: formerly no.1659, Hunts Cyclist Bn.: *s*. of the late Robert Kisby, of 51, North Street, Horncastle, co. Lincoln, by his wife Ruth (Upton House, Spilsby Road, Horncastle): and brother to Pte. 24430, A.W. Kisby, 2nd South Staffordshire Regt., killed in action 13 November 1916, at the Somme; and Pte. 3768, C.W. Kisby, 4th Lincolnshire Regt., died 3 July 1916, of wounds: *b*. Kexby, nr. Gainsborough: enlisted Huntingdon: killed in action, 24 October 1917, nr. Gheluvelt: Age 34.

His brother Arthur is buried in Serre Road Cemetery No.1 (I.G.41); Clarence, Doullens Communal Cemetery Extension No.1 (III.B.1).

(Panel 26) Pte. 29550, Joseph Lockley, 2/8th Bn. The Royal Warwickshire Regt. (T.F.): formerly no.61947, Cheshire Regt.: *s*. of Thomas Lockley, of 26, Louise Street, Garden Lane, Chester, by his wife Ellen: and brother to Spr. 207254, W. Lockley, 134th Army Transport Coy., Royal Engineers, killed in action, 26 October 1917, aged 27 years; and Sergt. 1263, T. Lockley, D.C.M., 1/5th Cheshire Regt., killed in action, 28 December 1915, aged 23 years: *b*. Chester, *c*.1891: enlisted there: served with the Expeditionary Force in France, and was killed in action, 4 September 1917, during the attack on Aisne Farm: Age 26. He leaves a wife, Caroline M. Lockley (3, St. John's Terrace, Louise Street, Chester), to whom correspondence regarding (and for the attention of) the deceased should be addressed.

His brother William also has no known grave, he is recorded on Panel 8; Thomas is buried in Suzanne Communal Cemetery Extension (B.3).

(Panel 26) Pte. 32788, Thomas Alexander McReynolds, 'B' Coy., 16th (Service) Bn. The Royal Warwickshire Regt.: eldest *s*. of Thomas Alexander McReynolds, Farmer; of King's Mills, Ardtrea, Stewartstown, co. Tyrone, member of Cookstown Rural District Council & Board of Guardians, by his wife Mary Eliza, *dau*. of James Stinson: *b*. Glasgow, 13 November 1892: *educ*. at home: Occupation – Farmer: enlisted 5th Dragoon Guards, September 1914: served with the Expeditionary Force in France and Flanders from the following November: transf'd. Royal Warwickshire Regt., August 1917: reported missing after the fighting, 9 October following, and is now assumed to have been killed in action on or since that date. An officer wrote, "He was a brave man and a good soldier.": Age 24. *unm*. (*IWGC record age 25*)

PANEL 26 ENDS: PTE. C.P.J. MILLER – ROYAL WARWICKSHIRE REGT.

PANEL 27 BEGINS: PTE. V. MILLER – ROYAL WARWICKSHIRE REGT.

(Panel 27) Pte. 22735, Wilfred Hiram Mills, 15th Bn. The Royal Warwickshire Regt.: *s*. of the late James Mills (*d*.27 October 1914, and his wife, Edith (115, Grosvenor Road, Aldershot): and brother to L/Sergt. 8071, F.H. Mills, 2nd Royal Scots Fusiliers, missing/believed killed in action 24 October 1914; and Pte.

B.J.H. Mills, 2nd Hampshire Regt., killed in action, 23 April 1917: killed in action, 28 October 1917: Age 23. His sister Ethel Annie passed away 30th November 1897; she was just twelve years of age. All four are remembered on their father's headstone (Aldershot Cemetery); the epitaph reads: "*We Loved Them In Life They Are Dear To Us Still, But In Grief We Must Bend As God's Holy Will. Our Sorrow Is Great The Loss Heavy To Bear, But Jesus Will Tend Our Loved Ones With Care.*" It closes with the penultimate verse from Charlotte Elliott's hymn '*My God And Father! While I Stray*' – "*Renew My Will From Day To Day, Blend It With Thine And Take Away. All Now That Makes It Hard To Say, Thy Will Be Done.*"

His brother Frederick also has no known grave, he is commemorated on the Ypres (Menin Gate) Memorial (Panel 33); Bertie is buried in Monchy British Cemetery, Monchy-Le-Preux (I.E.6).

(Panel 27) Pte. 32764, John 'Jack' Milton, 15th (Service) Bn. The Royal Warwickshire Regt.: formerly no.4346, 7th (Princess Royal's) Dragoon Guards: *s.* of James Milton, Steward, of The Ivel Club, Yeovil, by his wife Keziah: and brother to Spr. 251583, T. Milton, M.C., Royal Engineers, killed in action 30 October 1918: *b.* Landport, co. Hants: 21 years with the Colours; served in the South African Campaign, and with the Expeditionary Force in France and Flanders from August 1914; reported missing 26 October 1917, since confirmed killed in action: Age 39. He leaves a wife, Mrs L.E.M. Milton (5, Alpha Cottage, Broomhall, Sunningdale, co. Berks), and four children.

His brother Thomas is buried in Giavera British Cemetery, Arcade, Italy (2.H.1).

(Panel 27) Pte. 27241,Walter Charles Offord, 16th (Service) Bn. The Royal Warwickshire Regt.: formerly no.2802, Suffolk Regt.: *s.* of David Offord, of The Green, Great Waldingfield, Sudbury, co. Suffolk, by his wife Ellen: and yr. brother to Pte. 14917, A.A. Offord, 11th Suffolk Regt., killed in action 23 March 1918: *b.* Acton, 1897: enlisted Bury St. Edmunds: served with the Expeditionary Force in France and Flanders, and was killed in action 9 October 1917: Age 20.

His brother Arthur also has no known grave; he is commemorated on the Arras (Faubourg D'Amiens) Memorial (Bay 4).

(Panel 27) Pte. 33937, Walter Selves, 1/5th Bn. The Royal Warwickshire Regt. (T.F.): *s.* of Richard Walter Selves, Farm Labourer; of The Green, East Farleigh, co. Kent, by his wife Fanny, *née* Flint: and yr. brother to Pte. S/159, J. Selves, 1st Royal West Kent Regt., killed in action, 8 March 1915: *b.* Staplehurst: enlisted Maidstone. Killed in action 4 October 1917, at Pilckem: Age 30. He leaves a wife, Olive Annie Selves, *née* Cheeseman (Warnham's Cottage, West Farleigh, Maidstone).

His brother John is commemorated in Tuileries British Cemetery, Zillebeke (Sp.Mem.E.24).

(Panel 27) Pte. 692, Frank Grosvenor Rainbow, 16th (Service) Bn. The Royal Warwickshire Regt.: *s.* of the late Charles Rainbow, by his wife Harriett (5, Farley Street, Leamington Spa, co. Warwick): and brother to Corpl. 614181, H.W. Rainbow, M.M., Royal Horse Artillery, killed in action 4 October 1917; and 2nd Lieut. A.E. Rainbow, 4th attd. 10th Royal Warwickshire Regt., killed in action 23 July 1916: *b.* St. Paul's, Leamington, 1894: enlisted Leamington. Killed in action 27 October 1917: Age 23.

His brother Hugh is buried in Tyne Cot Cemetery (LIX.E.42); Albert has no known grave, he is commemorated on the Thiepval Memorial, Somme.

(Panel 27) Pte. 35441, Ernest Albert Sowden, 10th (Service) Bn. The Royal Warwickshire Regt.: formerly no.20964, Devonshire Regt.: late of Mill Barton, co. Devon: *s.* of James Sowden, of Coombe Cottages, Witheridge, Crediton, co. Devon, and Sarah Maria, his spouse: and brother to Pte. 203456, C. Sowden, 1st Devonshire Regt., killed in action 4 October 1917; and Coy.Sergt.Major, 62379, F.A. Sowden, Machine Gun Corps (Inf.), died 31 January 1920, consequent to wounds received in action on the Western Front: *b.* Thelbridge: enlisted Tiverton. Killed in action 19 April 1918: Age 24. Remembered on the Thelbridge (St. David's) Church War Memorial (*Sowdon*). Two other brothers also served; both survived.

His brother Charles also has no known grave, he is recorded on Panel 39; Frederick is buried in Washford Pyne (St. Peter) Churchyard.

PANEL 27 ENDS: PTE. PTE. J.W. TAYLOR – ROYAL WARWICKSHIRE REGT.

PANEL 28 BEGINS: PTE. W. TAYLOR – ROYAL WARWICKSHIRE REGT.

(Panel 28) Pte. 307840, David Weatherby, 1/8th Bn. The Royal Warwickshire Regt. (T.F.): late of 3, Station Road, Longford, Coventry: s. of David Weatherby, of Woodshires Green, Exhall, Coventry, by his wife Ellen: and yr. brother to Pte. 4182, S. Weatherby, 1/7th Royal Warwickshire Regt., who died 30 August 1921, consequent to wounds received in the Great War: enlisted Coventry. Killed in action 4 October 1917: Age 23.

His brother Samuel is buried in Exhall (St. Giles) Churchyard.

(Panel 28) Pte. 30013, Noah Whitehead, 1/7th Bn. The Royal Warwickshire Regt. (T.F.): s. of William Whitehead, of 26, Lawley Bank, Dawley, co. Shropshire, by his wife Sarah Ann: and brother to Pte. PLY/2446 (S), E. Whitehead, 2nd Bn. Royal Marine Light Infantry, 63rd (R.N.) Divn., died 4 April 1918, of wounds. Killed in action 27 August 1917. A well-known football player, Captain, Dawley Football Club.

His brother Ernest is buried in Etaples Military Cemetery (XXXIII.D.19).

(Panel 28) Pte. 267342, George Winwood, 10th (Service) Bn. The Royal Warwickshire Regt.: Signaller: s. of the late Frederick Winwood, by his wife Harriet: b. Birmingham, co. Warwick, 1 April 1890: educ. Stuart Street Board School, and Spring Hill School: Occupation – Newsagent: enlisted Royal Warwickshire Regt., 7 September 1916: served with the Expeditionary Force in France and Flanders from 16 May 1917, being employed as a Signaller, and was killed in action, 27 September following. Buried where he fell: Age 27. He m. Aston Parish Church, 8 August 1915; Maud Alice Bradley, née Winwood, since remarried (2, Manor Road, Witton, Birmingham), dau. of Annie Edwards: s.p.

(Panel 28) Capt. Hector Frederick Wood, M.C., 32nd (Service) Bn. (East Ham) The Royal Fusiliers (City of London Regt.): Occupation – Clerk; London Stock Exchange. Killed in action 20 September 1917, in the attack on Tower Hamlets spur, during which attack, after meeting little opposition for the first 200 yards, enemy fire from the left flank forced the battalion to take shelter in shell-holes whereupon the majority of the 32nd's officers became casualties, and the front assaulting company were virtually wiped out.

(Panel 28) Lieut. Eric Barrington Tristram, 13th (Service) Bn. The Royal Fusiliers (City of London Regt.) attd. 1/5th Bn. Lancashire Fusiliers: eldest s. of Charles Francis Tristram, of 146, Worple Road, Wimbledon, London, S.W., Assoc.M.inst.C.E., by his wife Mary, dau. of Horace Bronton Guarracino: b. Smyrna, Asia Minor, 3 July 1896: educ. St. George's College, Weybridge, and Wimbledon College, where he was captain of the school, and with a private tutor: joined the Civil Service Rifles May 1914: volunteered for Foreign Service on the outbreak of war: obtained a commission, being gazetted 2nd Lieut. Royal Fusiliers 25 February 1915: promoted Lieut. 1 July 1917: proceeded to Egypt January 1916, and took part in the Egyptian Campaign at El Arish, being attached to 1/5th Battn. Lancashire Fusiliers: left Egypt 3 February 1917: served with the Expeditionary Force in France and Flanders from that date, and was killed in action during the attack on Borry Farm, Frezenberg Ridge, east of Ypres, 6 September following. His Adjutant wrote, "Out in Egypt, when we trekked over the long stretch of desert, he was simply invaluable; his eye for the country always got us safe to camp, however far afield we were. .. He was a dear good fellow, and we loved him .. In a very real actual way he gave his life for his friend and commanding officer.": Age 21. unm.

(Panel 28) 2nd Lieut. Frederick John Snelling, 7th (Extra Reserve) Bn. The Royal Fusiliers (City of London Regt.).: only s. of Frederick Henry Snelling, of 13, Druce Road, Dulwich, London, S.E., by his wife Emily Mary Ann, dau. of John (& Emily) Savage: b. Dulwich, London, S.E., 9 October 1895: educ. Wilson's Grammar School, Camberwell, London, S.E.: Occupation – Staff Member; Northern Assurance Co. Ltd.: volunteered for Active Service on the outbreak of war, and enlisted in the 15th Battn. (Civil Service Rifles) The London Regt. (T.F.) 31 August 1914: served with the Expeditionary Force in France and Flanders from 17 March 1915: took part in the fighting at Festubert, Loos and Givenchy: was invalided home in November of the same year: applied for a commission, gazetted 2nd Lieut., Royal Fusiliers, March 1917: returned to France 12 April, and was killed in action at the attack on Passchendaele Ridge, 30 October following. Buried where he fell. His Commanding Officer, Lieut. Col. Charles Playfair, wrote, "Your boy met his death magnificently, nothing could be finer than his noble act; when wounded he disregarded his personal safety, exposed himself again to the enemy, and met his death assisting one of his non-commissioned officers. I was very fond of your boy; he took his profession seriously and spent much of his time looking after the welfare of his men, who, I hear, loved him so well;" and Capt. A. Ogle, "He was a great favourite with all ranks, especially the men of the company to which he was attached. He was privileged to command the company when they went into the line for the recent attack, and he just led the boys the whole way until they were stopped by a 'strong point.' He was shot through the wrist first, and then crawled out to pull in a wounded man, and was shot again, through the head and died instantaneously. He was a brave boy and died fearlessly, and everybody is proud to think that he belonged to our battalion." 2nd Lieut. G.H.Graves wrote, "Your son was – Yes, there is no other word to describe it – loved by every officer, N.C.O. and man he took with him into action, and by those whose duty it was to remain behind. They would follow him anywhere, and a great many have done so.": Age 22. *unm.*

(Panel 28) 2nd Lieut. George Piercey Spooner, M.M., 26th (Service) Bn. (Bankers) The Royal Fusiliers (City of London Regt.).: elder *s.* of the late George Fraser Spooner, House Furnisher, by his wife Eleanor (now wife of Harry Stott Oxley, of 70, Oakfield Road, Stroud Green, London, N.), *dau.* of William Piercey, Accountant: and brother to 2nd Lieut. R.W. Spooner, 53 Sqdn. Royal Flying Corps, killed in aerial action, 8 June 1917, whilst flying over the enemy;'s lines near Oostaverne Wood, engaged in aerial reconnaissance duty: *b.* Highbury, London, N., 26 May 1889: *educ.* Cowper Street Central Foundation School: enlisted 4 September 1914: immediately proceeded to Malta, where he was trained: served with the Expeditionary Force in France and Flanders from 4 January 1915: returned to England in April 1916, and after a period of training at Worcester College, Oxford, was gazetted 2nd Lieut. 5 August 1916: returned to France in September, and was wounded at Beaucourt 14 November, and invalided home: on recovery, in August 1917, again proceeded to France, and was killed in action at Tower Hamlets, on the Menin Road, 20 September following. His Commanding Officer wrote, "He was very highly thought of, both by all the officers and men of the battalion." Awarded the Military Medal ('*London Gazette,*' 3 June 1916), for 'having carried out several bombing expeditions successfully.' 2nd Lieut. Spooner was a keen sportsman, cricket and football being his favourite games.: Age 28. *unm.* (*IWGC record 20 – 23 September 1917*)

His brother Raymond has no known grave; he is commemorated on the Flying Services Memorial (Faubourg d'Amiens) Arras.

(Panel 28) Sergt. 2521, Moses Minor, 7th (Extra Reserve) Bn. The Royal Fusiliers (City of London Regt.): *s.* of the late Henry (& Charity) Moses, of 26, Festing Street, Hanley, Stoke-on-Trent: and elder brother to Pte. 45785, F. Minor, North Staffordshire Regt., killed 6 February 1918: *b.* Hanley, co. Stafford, *c.*1891: enlisted Stoke-on-Trent. Killed in action 30 October 1917: Age 26. *unm.*

His brother Frederick also has no known grave; he is recorded on Panel 125.

(Panel 28) L/Corpl. 8039, Alfred Bradshaw, 11th (Service) Bn. The Royal Fusiliers (City of London Regt.): formerly no.4174, Middlesex Regt.: *s.* of Simeon Bradshaw, of 122, Cross Lane, Radcliffe, Manchester, by his wife Sarah Alice: and brother to Pte. 16913, J. Bradshaw, 2nd King's Own, died 8 November 1916: *b.* Wellington Street, Radcliffe. Killed in action 10 January 1918: Age 33.

His brother James is buried in Radcliffe (St. Mary) Churchyard (25.174).

(Panel 28) L/Corpl. G/7660, Arthur James Peavot, 11th (Service) Bn. The Royal Fusiliers (City of London Regt.): *s.* of William George Peavot, of 21, Wyvenhoe Road, South Harrow, co. Middlesex: *b.* Willesden, London, N., 11 July 1894: *educ.* Harrow Council School: Occupation – Printer: enlisted August 1914: served with the Expeditionary Force in France and Flanders from early 1915: invalided home with frozen feet November following; volunteered again in 1917, and was killed in action near Ypres, 9 October 1917: Age 23. *unm.* (*IWGC record 2nd Bn.*)

PANEL 28 ENDS: PTE. E. ALLEN – ROYAL FUSILIERS

PANEL 29 BEGINS: PTE. F. ALLEN – ROYAL FUSILIERS

(Panel 29) Pte. G/47706, Alfred Heaton Brown, 2nd Bn. The Royal Fusiliers (City of London Regt.): formerly no.PS/8627, Royal Fusiliers: late of North Shore, Blackpool, co. Lancaster: *b*. Bury, 1896: enlisted Blackpool, September 1915: served with the Expeditionary Force in France and Flanders, took part in the fighting at the Battle of the Somme, summer 1916; wounded (shock) buried alive by the explosion of a shell; a second explosion freed him: evacuated to England from whence, after treatment, recuperation and a short period of home leave, he returned to France. One year later, on 9 October 1917, 2nd Royal Fusiliers were tasked with the capture of a number of German bunkers south of the Ypres-Staden railway line. Taking part in the same attack 1st Lancashire Fusiliers came under fire from the enemy and 2nd Royal Fusiliers came to their assistance. Advancing from one shell hole to the next, by 10 a.m., the two regiments had secured all the bunkers. Sadly, however, the success had not been without loss. Among those to lose their lives that day – twenty-one year old Alfred Brown. Informed of the tragic news of their son's death a couple of days later, his family had to wait until January 1918 before being made aware of the circumstances in the form of a letter written by a comrade, Pte. A. Spence., who had found Alfred's body in No Man's Land and buried him at Poelcapelle. He enclosed his wallet and discs which he had retrieved from the body.

(Panel 29) Pte. 48052, John Deacon, 1st Bn. (7th Foot) The Royal Fusiliers (City of London Regt.): *s*. of Thomas Deacon, of 5, Nicol Street, Desborough, nr. Market Harborough, by his wife Ellen, *née* Stratford: and yr. brother to Corpl. 20489, A. Deacon, 5th Northamptonshire Regt., killed in action 16 August 1918: *b*. Desborough, 24 June 1894: enlisted Northampton. Killed in action 23 August 1917: Age 23. *unm*.

His brother Arthur is buried in Ville-sur-Ancre Communal Cemetery Extension (C.1).

(Panel 29) Pte. 10765, Gwilym Tyndale Evans, 26th (Bankers) Bn. The Royal Fusiliers (City of London Regt.): *s*. of the late Rev. J.J. Evans, by his wife Charlotte ('Glan Rhydwilym,' Clynderwen, nr. Swansea, co. Carmarthen): *b*. Llandyssilio, Clynderwen, 1897: enlisted Haverfordwest, co. Pembroke: served with the Expeditionary Force in France and Flanders from May 1916: took part in the fighting at the battles of Flers and Le Transloy (Somme), Messines and Pilkem Ridge (Ypres), and was killed in action at the latter place during the Battle of the Menin Road, 23 September 1917: Age 20. *unm*. Under the heading 'To The Sacred Memory Of The Rhydwilym Boys Who Fell In The European War, 1914-1918' The Western Mail printed his photograph and those of four other men with the accompanying verse:

> Far away from their home and loved ones,
> Laid to rest in that far-away land;
> Never more shall our eyes behold them,
> Never more shall we clasp their hands.
>
> Their cheery ways, their smiling faces,
> Are a pleasure to recall;
> Though there's nothing left to answer
> But their photo on the wall.

PANEL 29 ENDS: PTE. H.J. KNIGHT – ROYAL FUSILIERS

PANEL 30 BEGINS: PTE. W. KNOWLES – ROYAL FUSILIERS

(Panel 30) Pte. 67247, Riley Lane, Royal Fusiliers, posted 2/2nd (City of London) Bn. (Royal Fusiliers) The London Regt. (T.F.): formerly no.18323, Territorial Reserve Battn.: *s*. of Mr R.W. Lane, of Hyde Cottages, Roade, co. Northampton. Killed in action 26 October 1917: Age 19.

(Panel 30) Pte. G/54988, Wilfred Pope, 2nd Bn. (7th Foot) The Royal Fusiliers (City of London Regt.): *s*. of William Pope, Butcher, of Heathfield, co. Sussex, by his wife Emily: and brother to Gnr.

78060, B. Pope, Royal Field Artillery, killed in action, 12 November 1917, aged 22; and Pte. SD/3654, H.J. Pope, Royal Sussex Regt., died of wounds, 29 September 1916, aged 27: *b.* Heathfield, *c.*1899: enlisted Eastbourne. Died of wounds 9 October 1917: Age 18.

His brother Bert also has no known grave, he is recorded on Panel 5; Harry is buried in Euston Road Cemetery, Colincamps (I.C.54).

(Panel 30) Pte. 57835, Geoffrey Trevor-Roper, 32nd (Service) Bn. (East Ham) The Royal Fusiliers (City of London Regt.): *yr. s.* of the late George Edward Trevor-Roper, of Rhual Isa, Mold, Solicitor, by his wife Henriette (Donnington Square, Newbury), *dau.* of Richard Trevor-Roper: and *yr.* brother to Capt. C.C. Trevor-Roper, Hampshire Regt., died of wounds 3 August 1917: *b.* Mold, co. Flint, 27 December 1885: *educ.* Bedford Modern School, and Dinglewood, Colwyn Bay. On the outbreak of war he volunteered for Foreign Service, and enlisted Royal Fusiliers, 4 September 1914: served with the Expeditionary Force in France and Flanders from November 1915, and was killed in action near Ypres, 20 September 1917. His Commanding Officer wrote, "His death was that of a soldier, having been sniped in the head whilst attacking an enemy dug-out. He showed the greatest gallantry and daring, and reached almost the furthest point reached in the action of the early morning of September 20.": Age 31. *unm.*

His brother Charles is buried in Duhallow A.D.S. Cemetery (I.A.30).

(Panel 30) Pte. 13849, John Elliot Yuill, 11th (Service) Bn. (Frontiersmen) The Royal Fusiliers (City of London Regt.): *yr. s.* of the late Daniel Yuill, by his wife Olivia (60, York Drive, Hyndland, Glasgow), *dau.* of John Elliot, Merchant, of Glasgow and Aberdeen: *b.* Partick, co. Renfrew, 18 August 1886: *educ.* Hamilton Crescent School, Partick, and Hutcheson's Grammar School, Glasgow; thereafter employed with the Niger Co. Ltd., West Africa: joined Royal Fusiliers, 15 March 1915: served with the West African Expeditionary Force from the following April to November 1916, when he was invalided to Cape Town: subsequently transf'd. 32nd Battn. (no.14865), and went to France, June 1917: served with the Expeditionary Force there and in Flanders, and was killed in action in the Menin Ridge attack 20 September following. Buried where he fell. His Commanding Officer wrote, "He met a soldier's death while gallantly going forward with his company to the attack of an enemy strong point.": Age 31. *unm.*

PANEL 30 ENDS: PTE. J.E. YUILL – ROYAL FUSILIERS

PANEL 31 BEGINS: CAPT. D. EASTWOOD – KING'S LIVERPOOL REGT.

(Panel 31) 2nd Lieut. Tom Harrop, 17th (Service) Bn. The King's (Liverpool) Regt.: *s.* of Joseph (& Mary E.) Harrop, of Daisy Hill House, Morley, Leeds. Killed in action 28 April 1918: Age 20. Making a reconnaissance at the time of his death, on failing to return to the safety of his company's trench his servant – Pte. C. Hankin – went out to look for him and in so doing was himself killed within moments.

Pte. Hankin also has no known grave; he is recorded on Panel 32.

(Panel 31) 2nd Lieut. Henry James Jephson Hepworth, 12th (Service) Bn The King's (Liverpool) Regt.: *s.* of the late Ambrose Hepworth, Butcher; by his wife Ellen, *née* Jephson (32, Outram Street, Sutton-in-Ashfield, Nottingham): *b.* 1882: Occupation – Manager, Gents Outfitters. Killed in action 12 August 1917: Age 32.

(Panel 31) 2nd Lieut. Herbert Prudent Oates, 5th Bn. The King's (Liverpool) Regt.: *s.* of the late Austin Oates, K.S.G., Private Secretary to Cardinal Vaughan; and Mrs Oates, *née* Plettinck, *dau.* of the late Dr. Prudent Plettinck, Burgomaster of Meulebeke, Belgium (*d.*1888), and his wife Isabelle (*d.*1882): *b.* 21 December 1887: religion – Roman Catholic: *educ.* St. Edmund's College, Ware, co. Hertford; St. Bede's College, Manchester: Occupation – Educational Assistant, L.C.C., voluntarily revoking this position on the outbreak of war: joined Officer's Training Corps; thereafter Artists' Rifles from whence he obtained his commission 5th King's Liverpool Regt. Killed in action 20 September 1917: Age 19. Shortly before going into what would prove to be his last action he attended Mass, Confession, and received Holy Communion. He won the praise of his commanding officers for his conscientiousness and devotion to duty. And to his fellow officers, as with all his friends and fellow students, he endeared himself by the charm of his sterling qualities, his unfailing kindness, his winning candour, and upright character.

(Panel 31) Corpl. 241019, Henry Edgar Dean, 1/6th Bn. (Rifles) The King's (Liverpool) Regt. (T.F.): eldest *s.* of John Henry Dean, of 36, Oxford Street, Mount Pleasant, Liverpool (formerly of 25, Buchanan Road, Egremont, co. Chester), by his wife Emma, *dau.* of David Seager: *b.* Fulham, London, S.W., 16 December 1895: *educ.* College School, Baldock, and at the Wallasey Grammar School: Occupation – Shipbroker's Clerk: joined King's (Liverpool) Regt., 11 November 1914: served with the Expeditionary Force in France and Flanders from 24 February 1915: reported missing after the fighting at Passchendaele Ridge, 20 September 1917; now assumed killed in action on that date: Age 21. *unm.* (*IWGC record age 22*)

(Panel 31) Corpl. 43489, William Thomas Hunt, 4th (Extra Reserve) Bn. The King's (Liverpool) Regt.: *s.* of Joseph Hunt, of 'Fairleigh,' King's Road, St. Albans, by his wife Mary Ann, *dau.* of William (& Sarah) Smith: *b.* St. Albans, co. Hertford, 8 March 1879: *educ.* St. Michael's School: sometime Coachman, was afterwards employed as Gamekeeper to the Marquis de Castiga: enlisted Liverpool Regt., 26 June 1916: served with the Expeditionary Force in France from 6 December following, and was killed in action, 25 September 1917: Age 38. Buried where he fell. Capt. Herbert Tripp wrote, "I cannot possibly tell you how much we all appreciate the fine soldierly qualities of Corpl. Hunt, who, though acting as cook at the officers' mess at the time, took his rifle and helped us, when we were being hard pressed by the enemy, to beat off the attack. It was whilst he was firing at the approaching enemy that he was shot through the head by a stray bullet. He died immediately....Your husband was undoubtedly one of the finest soldiers, and certainly the best-liked man in the battalion. He died as fine a death as any man has in this fearful war – a real hero's death." He *m.* Lydiate Church, 1 November 1911; Catherine (Haskayne, near Ormskirk, co. Lancaster), *dau.* of Robert Scarisbrick, and had a son, Robert, *b.* 11 September 1914. (*IWGC record L/Corpl.*)

(Panel 31) Corpl. 13381, Enrico James Walle, 13th (Service) Bn. The King's (Liverpool) Regt.: 3rd *s.* of the late Charles Walle, Stevedore, by his wife Jane, *dau.* of John Cooney: *b.* Seacombe, co. Chester, 12 November 1894: *educ.* St. Joseph's school, there: Occupation – Assistant; Liverpool Docks: enlisted 8 August 1914: served with the Expeditionary Force in France and Flanders from August 1915, and was killed in action at Ypres, 28 September 1917. An officer wrote, "His company was called upon to reinforce a hard-pressed front line, and your brother, with the rest of the company, worked and fought magnificently, with the result that the position was saved. It may comfort you to know that he suffered no pain, being killed instantly by a shell. He was a most capable N.C.O., respected by the officers and men of his company who deeply deplore his loss.": Age 22. *unm.*

(Panel 31) L/Corpl. 51744, Ernest Greenwood, 20th (Service) Bn. (4th City) The King's (Liverpool) Regt.: *s.* of John William Greenwood, of 23, Reynolds Street, Burnley, co. Lancaster, by his wife Susannah: and yr. brother to Pte. 5103, A. Greenwood, 4th Dragoon Guards, killed in action at the First Battle of Ypres exactly three years to the day previously: *b.* Burnley, c.1900: enlisted Liverpool. Killed in action 3 November 1917: Age 17.

His brother Albert also has no known grave; he is commemorated on the Ypres (Menin Gate) Memorial (Panel 5).

(Panel 31) L/Corpl. 306428, John Douglas Rivers Hayes, 2/8th Bn. (Irish) The King's (Liverpool) Regt. (T.F.): *s.* of William Hayes, of 8, Simpson Street, South Shore, Blackpool, by his wife Margaret Jane. Killed in action in the vicinity of Eagle Trench, north-east of Langemarck 26 October 1917: Age 21. *unm.* See account re. Pte. J. Entwisle, Cement House Cemetery (III.E.9).

(Panel 31) L/Corpl. 17371, Henry Ledsome Hughes, 19th (Service) Bn. The King's (Liverpool) Regt.: *s.* of Thomas Hughes, Furniture Salesman; of 60, Westbourne Road, Birkenhead, by his wife Winifred, *dau.* of Henry Ledsome: *b.* Rock Ferry, Birkenhead, co. Chester, 21 July 1893: *educ.* Wigan Grammar School: Occupation – Clerk; Messrs Joseph Bibby and Sons, Liverpool: enlisted Liverpool Regt. 30 August 1914: served with the Expeditionary Force in France from 1 November 1915, being employed first as a sniper; thereafter as signaller, and was killed in action nr. Ypres 16 October 1917. Buried behind the line there: Age 24. *unm.* (*IWGC record 18 October 1917*)

(Panel 31) L/Corpl. 48769, Lewis Swindell, 13th (Service) Bn. The King's (Liverpool) Regt.: formerly, no.49797, Sherwood Foresters: *s.* of the late John (& Mrs J.) Swindell, of 13, Dalesforth Street, Sutton-in-Ashfield: employee Great Northern Railway, Shirebrook, Kimberley; and later Hucknall Torkard: enlisted Hucknall, Nottingham, April 1916, posted Sherwood Foresters: proceeded to France transf'd. King's Liverpool Regt., and was killed in action 28 September 1917. In a letter to his widowed mother, Lieut. J.R. Ellis wrote, "He was an exceedingly capable N.C.O., greatly respected by the officers and men of his Company, all of whom deplore his loss. I have been in contact with your son on and off for nearly twelve months, and fully realise that his influence for good among his comrades was very great indeed. I can assure you that those amongst whom he lived were the better for, and profited by, his society, and that the King's Regiment is considerably the poorer by the loss of a truly gallant Englishman." An active member of the Reform Street Primitive Methodist Church, Sutton-in-Ashfield, and ardent supporter of the Sunday School Endeavour Society, and Band of Hope, Mr. Swindell showed great promise as a local preacher and, had not other commitments and the outbreak of war intervened, would in all likelihood have eventually entered the regular ministry of the church. *'The Notts Free Press'* 'In Memoriam,' 27 September 1918:-

> *Death doth hide, But not divide;*
> *Thou art but on Christ's other side.*

> Mother, Sister, Brothers, Ernest & Frank, in France.

> *'Twas hard we could not see his face, Or deck with flowers his resting place;*
> *Only those who have lost can tell, The pain at not saying a last farewell.*
> *The unknown grave is the bitterest blow, None but aching hearts can know.*

> Sorrowing fiancée, Ada Jackson, Hucknall.

(Panel 31) Pte. 135123, John Roland Baker, 13th (Service) Bn. The King's (Liverpool) Regt.: formerly no.203469, North Staffordshire Regt.: *s.* of Mary Ann Baker (8, Bank Street, Bradley, Bilston, co. Stafford): and elder brother to Pte. 60708, N. Baker, 15th West Yorkshire Regt., killed in action 20 October 1918: *b.* Bilston: enlisted there. Killed in action 27 September 1917: Age 31.

His brother Norman is buried in Nechin Communal Cemetery (S.W. Part).

(Panel 31) Pte. 50591, William Henry Birchall, 1/9th Bn. The King's (Liverpool) Regt. (T.F.): formerly T/3/029861, Royal Army Service Corps: *s.* of John Birchall, of Stanley Gate Farm, Bickerstaffe, co. Lancaster, by his wife Ellen: *b.* Wigan: Occupation – Horse Breeder: enlisted R.A.S.C., Warrington, 1914; posted Officer Horsemanship Instructor: proceeded to France July 1917, transf'd. King's (Liverpool) Regt.: reported missing and wounded 20 September 1917; since confirmed killed in action: Age 32. On the date of his death Pte. Birchall (and 24 other ranks) took part in a raid led by Capt. Laird; their objective – to capture two German blockhouses. Leaving their trench at 6am, the raiders were shortly thereafter observed by the enemy and came under heavy machine-gun fire from the blockhouses. Despite a determined attempt to carry their objective Capt. Laird and six other ranks were killed, and the raiders forced to retire. He *m.* 5 February 1907, Martha Rosbotham, Schoolteacher (348, Crow Lane West, Earlestown, Newton-le-Willows, St. Helen's), late of Ottershead Farm, Westhead; niece to Sir Samuel Thomas Rosbotham, M.P., of Bickerstaffe.

PANEL 31 ENDS: PTE. J. BLUNDELL – KING'S LIVERPOOL REGT.

PANEL 32 BEGINS: PTE. P. BOLLOM – KING'S LIVERPOOL REGT.

(Panel 32) Pte. 65467, Leo Clayton, 2/8th Bn. (Irish) The King's (Liverpool) Regt. (T.F.): late of Macclesfield: enlisted Chester. Killed in action north-east of Langemarck 27 October 1917. See account re. Pte. J. Entwisle, Cement House Cemetery (III.E.9).

(Panel 32) Pte. 305652, Leslie Coghlan, 2/8th Bn. (Irish) The King's (Liverpool) Regt. (T.F.): *s.* of Samuel Coghlan, of 4, Greenfield Street, Wallasey, co. Chester, by his wife Emma: *b.* Liscard, co. Chester: enlisted Liverpool. Killed in action in the vicinity of Eagle Trench, north-east of Langemarck 26 October 1917: Age 21. *unm.* See account re. Pte. J. Entwisle, Cement House Cemetery (III.E.9).

(Panel 32) Pte. 59569, Arthur Colville, 20th (Service) Bn. (4th City) The King's (Liverpool) Regt.: *s.* of the late Robert Colville, by his wife Sarah Ellen (47, Greenfield Lane, Litherland, Liverpool): and elder brother to Pte. 5144, R. Colville, 1/7th King's (Liverpool) Regt., killed in action 9 August 1916, at the Somme: *b.* Liverpool, *c.*1895: enlisted there. Killed in action 3 January 1918: Age 22. *unm.*

His brother Robert also has no known grave; he is commemorated on the Thiepval Memorial.

(Panel 32) Pte. 31303, Robert Edwards, M.M., 12th (Service) Bn. The King's (Liverpool) Regt.: late of Birkenhead, co. Chester: enlisted Liverpool. Killed in action, 16 August 1917. *Known to be buried in Sanctuary Wood Cemetery (V.B.19)*

(Panel 32) Pte. 56846, John Monkhouse Elliott, 2/8th Bn. (Irish) The King's (Liverpool) Regt. (T.F.): enlisted Liverpool. Killed in action north-east of Langemarck 27 October 1917. See account re Pte. J. Entwisle, Cement House Cemetery (III.E.9).

(Panel 32) Rfn. 50751, Robert Fairclough, 2/6th Bn. (Rifles) The King's (Liverpool) Regt. (T.F.): *s.* of Thomas Fairclough, of 14, Turncroft Road, Darwen, co. Lancaster, by his wife Alice: and yr. brother to Sergt. 34484, F. Fairclough, M.M., Royal Field Artillery, killed in action, 2 December 1917: *b.* Fenniscowles, co. Lancaster: enlisted Darwen. Killed in action 29 October 1917: Age 19.

His brother Fred is buried in Orival Wood Cemetery, Flesquieres (II.C.25).

(Panel 32) Rfn. 202580, Frank Alexander Gammons, 1/6th Bn. (Rifles) The King's (Liverpool) Regt. (T.F.): *s.* of Elizabeth Gammons (28, Greenacres Road, Oldham): and yr. brother to Pte. 12256, C. Gammons, Lancashire Fusiliers, who fell, 25 September 1918: *b.* Oldham, co. Lancaster, *c.*1896. Died of wounds 20 September 1917: Age 20. *unm.*

His brother Cecil also has no known grave; he is recorded on Panel 57.

(Panel 32) Pte. 50661, Charles Hankin, 17th (Service) Bn. The King's (Liverpool) Regt.: *s.* of Thomas Hankin, of 24, Torr Street, Liverpool, by his wife Annie Elizabeth, *dau.* of George Jones, Farmer: *b.* Liverpool, co. Lancaster, 15 December 1884: *educ.* Christ Church School, Everton: Occupation – Theatre Attendant: enlisted Liverpool Regt., June 1916: served with the Expeditionary Force in France and Flanders from May 1917, and was killed in action, 28 April 1918. Buried where he fell. At the time of his death he was Officer's Servant to 2nd Lieut. Harrop, and, on going out to search for his master, who had been killed while making a reconnaissance, was himself killed a few minutes later: Age 34. He *m.* West Derby, 11 February 1908; Harriet Martha (2, Atherton Grove, Torr Street, Liverpool), *dau.* of Richard Edwards, and had three children – James, *b.* 3 September 1911, Doris, *b.* 14 October 1913 and Patricia, *b.* 17 March 1916.

2nd Lieut. Tom Harrop has no known grave; he is recorded on Panel 31.

PANEL 32 ENDS: PTE. H.H. JONES – KING'S LIVERPOOL REGT.

PANEL 33 BEGINS: PTE. 10957, J. JONES – KING'S LIVERPOOL REGT.

(Panel 33) Pte. 356061, David Rankine, 2/10th (Scottish) Bn. The King's (Liverpool) Regt. (T.F.): *s.* of the late James Rankine, of 226, Poulton Road, Wallasey, co. Chester: and yr. brother to Pte. 430697, W.J. Rankine, 27th Canadian Infantry, died 4 October 1916, of wounds inflicted: enlisted Liverpool. Killed in action 5 November 1917: Age 26. *unm.*

His brother William is buried in Boulogne Eastern Cemetery (VIII.C.169).

(Panel 33) Pte. 306411, Robert Swarbrick, 2/8th Bn. (Irish) The King's (Liverpool) Regt. (T.F.): *s.* of the late Robert Swarbrick, by his wife Elizabeth (23, Thorburn Grove, St. John's Estate, Blackpool): *b.* St. Anne's, co. Lancaster, about 1880: enlisted Blackpool. Killed in action in the vicinity of Eagle Trench, north-east of Langemarck 26 October 1917: Age 37. See account re. Pte. J. Entwisle, Cement House Cemetery (III.E.9).

(Panel 33) Pte. 405662, Harry Toft, 4th (Extra Reserve) Bn. The King's (Liverpool) Regt.: *yst. s.* of the late William Toft, by his wife Margaret, *dau.* of John Davies: *b.* Bootle, Liverpool, 22 January 1889: *educ.* Council School: Occupation – nine years Saloon Steward; Western Ocean Service, White Star Line: enlisted 10 February 1916: served with the Expeditionary Force in France and Flanders from 14 June 1917, and was killed in action north-east of Ypres 25 September following. Buried at Inverness Copse, north-east of Ypres. An officer wrote, "Your husband was in my platoon ever since he joined the battalion, and I always found him to be a splendid and reliable worker in everything he ever did. We were to go over the top on September 26 and, while waiting in the trenches on September 25, the Germans began to shell very heavily, and your husband was with two more men in a shell hole forming part of the trench when a shell fell amongst them, killing the three instantly. We were unable to take anyone away, so they were buried quite close to where they were killed. Your husband was very well liked by all the men who came in contact with him, and they feel his loss very keenly indeed.": Age 28. He *m.* Liverpool, 27 November 1915; Bertha (10, Hale Road, Walton, Liverpool), *dau.* of the late Henry Frank Johnson.: *s.p.*

PANEL 33 ENDS: PTE. F.W. TOMLINSON – KING'S LIVERPOOL REGT.

PANEL 34 BEGINS: PTE. G.S. TOMLINSON – KING'S LIVERPOOL REGT.

(Panel 34) Pte. 266205, George Henry Winstanley, 1/7th Bn. The King's (Liverpool) Regt. (T.F.): Signaller: *s.* of the late George Henry Winstanley, by his wife Ellen Ann (now wife of Ernest Henry Altman, *s.* of the late Sir Albert Altman, of 18, Dean Street, South Shore, Blackpool), *dau.* of George Wellington Coldicutt: *b.* Blackpool, co. Lancaster, 16 August 1897: *educ.* High School, Blackpool: joined King's Liverpool Regt., 3 January 1915: served with the Expeditionary Force in France and Flanders from 16 August 1916, and was killed in action at Ypres 20 September 1917. Buried between Pommern Castle and Hill 35: Age 20. *unm.*

(Panel 34) 2nd Lieut. Frank Ablett Stone, 3rd (Reserve) Bn. The Norfolk Regt. attd. 1/8th Bn. (Irish) King's (Liverpool) Regt. (T.F.): *yst. s.* of the Rev. George Edward Stone, of 147, Earlham Road, Norwich, Methodist Minister, by his wife Florence Amelia, *dau.* of Capt. James Smith: *b.* Norwich, co. Norfolk, 20 December 1897: *educ.* City of Norwich Secondary School: Occupation – Trainee Accountant: joined 8th Norfolk Regt. 19 September 1914, Pte.: subsequently transf'd. 6th Battn. (Cycling Corps): served with the Expeditionary Force in France and Flanders from June 1915, taking part in operations on the Somme, 1916: recommended for a commission; gazetted 2nd Lieut., 3rd Norfolk Regt., July 1917; attd. 8th Liverpool Regt. the following month, and was killed in action south-east of St. Julien 20 September following. Buried where he fell. Capt. (Adjt.) J.F. Jones, wrote, "Your son met his death very early in the day, whilst gallantly leading his men. He had endeared himself to all ranks by his genial personality and his fearlessness in action," and 2nd Lieut. Allerton, "While fearlessly exposing himself in a counter-attack of the enemy, he was sniped. He could not have died more gallantly." His Batman also wrote: "His platoon led the way, and as an officer he behaved magnificently. His men have lost a good officer, and myself a kind and considerate master.": Age 19.

(Panel 34) Corpl. 14191, Harry Newson, 8th (Service) Bn. The Norfolk Regt.: *s.* of the late Charles Newson, by his wife Elizabeth (77, Peabody Avenue, Pimlico, London): and brother to Pte. 62597, F. Newson, 9th Royal Fusiliers, killed in action, 9 April 1917: *b.* Pimlico: enlisted Westminster. Killed in action 22 October 1917: Age 34.

His brother Frank is buried in Faubourg d'Amiens Cemetery (VII.G.25).

(Panel 34) Pte. 202153, Robert Harry Clow, 1st Bn. (9th Foot) The Norfolk Regt.: *s.* of the late Amos Clow, of 1, Newington Terrace, by his wife Emma: and *yr.* brother to Pte. 17816, B.T. Clow, 14th Royal Warwickshire Regt., killed in action, 30 July 1916, at the Somme: *b.* Newmarket, 1898: enlisted there. Killed in action 9 October 1917: Age 19.

His brother Bert also has no known grave; he is commemorated on the Thiepval Memorial.

(Panel 34) Pte. 14280, Leonard Gould, 1st Bn. (9th Foot) The Norfolk Regt.: *s.* of Mr (& Mrs) Gould, of Great Snoring, co. Norfolk: *b.* Fakenham. Killed in action 3 November 1917: Age 21. *unm.* November 2011: *"The cup was bitter, the sting severe, To part with one I loved so dear, There came a mist and a blinding rain, And the world was never the same again. His sister, who always loved him."*

PANEL 34 ENDS: PTE. C. HOWES – NORFOLK REGT.

PANEL 35 BEGINS PTE. J.H. HUNTER – NORFOLK REGT.

(Panel 35) Pte. 25987, Grantley Montague Leamon, 1st Bn. (9th Foot) The Norfolk Regt.: *s.* of Philip Augustus Leamon, of 195, Parkview Street, Headingley, Manitoba, by his late wife Lucy: and brother to Lieut. D.A. Leamon, 8th Norfolk Regt., killed in action, 14 August 1917, aged 22 years: *b.* Town Close, Norwich, 1884: enlisted Norwich. Killed in action 9 October 1917: Age 33. He leaves a wife Beatrice Grace Leamon (56, Connaught Road, Norwich, co. Norfolk), and children to mourn his loss.

His brother Douglas is buried in Lijssenthoek Military Cemetery (XV.A.15).

(Panel 35) Pte. 40089, Walter Mayes, 9th (Service) Bn. The Norfolk Regt.: *s.* of Mrs Mason Mayes (3,Baxter Row, East Dereham, co. Norfolk): and cousin to Pte. M2/021415, P. Mayes, Army Service Corps, died 10 May 1915, aged 25 years, Gnr. 101255, G. Mayes, 279th Siege Bty., Royal Garrison Artillery, killed in action, 29 November 1917, aged 29; and Pte. 40088, H. Mayes, 9th Norfolk Regt., killed in action, 18 October 1916, aged 20: *b.* East Dereham: enlisted Norwich. Killed in action 29 April 1918: Age 25. *unm.*

Cousin Percy is buried in Wimereux Communal Cemetery (I.G.10A), George in Vlamertinghe New Military Cemetery (XII.B.8) and Herbert in Bancourt British Cemetery (VIII.J.9).

(Panel 35) Capt. Roy Grote Cordiner, M.C., 8th (Service) Bn. The Lincolnshire Regt.: *s.* of the late Robert Charles Cordiner, M.A. (Oxford), by his wife Josephine Grote Burt (formerly Cordiner, 'Honiton,' Stein Road, Emsworth, co. Hants), *dau.* of the late Major J.W. Inglis, of Stockwell, London, S.W.: *b.* Great Malvern, co. Worcester, 9 February 1897: *educ.* Malvern Dames' School, and Lancing College: obtained a commission 2nd Lieut., 21 September 1914; promoted Lieut., January 1915; Capt. October following: served with the Expeditionary Force in France and Flanders from September 1915 (thrice wounded). Killed in action 4 October 1917. A brother officer wrote, "I should like to express to you my very great appreciation and admiration of Roy, who was not only my best friend in the regiment, but one of the most gallant officers I have ever known. Although so young he was an exceptionally capable officer, and the efficient, thoughtful and cool manner in which he commanded his company under all circumstances won for him the admiration of all his brother officers, and the almost idolized devotion of the men under his command. Although wounded at an early stage of the recent action in which the regiment took part, he refused to leave his men, and went on till he was shot through the head by a sniper. His winning personality made for him friends innumerable, and we all mourn his loss very deeply, and can only judge your sorrow by our own." Awarded the Military Cross (*London Gazette*, 22 September 1916) for continuing to lead his men when wounded: Age 20. *unm.*

(Panel 35) Capt. Douglas Llewellyn Jones, 'B' Coy., 6th (Service) Bn. The Lincolnshire Regt.: 2nd *s.* of the late Rev. John David Jones, Vicar of St. Mary-below-Hill, Lincoln, by his wife Ethel Lina Mary (6, Queensway, Lincoln), *dau.* of the late Rev. Frederick Carrol: *b.* Tallington Vicarage, Stamford, co. Lincoln, 28 March 1894: *educ.* Clevedon House School, Ben Rhydding; Haileybury College, and Hatfield Hall, Durham, where he was studying with a view to taking Holy Orders: joined the Universities and Public Schools Brigade in October 1914: gazetted 2nd Lieut., Lincolnshire Regt., January 1915: promoted Lieut.; and Capt., 20 July 1917: served with the Mediterranean Expeditionary Force at Gallipoli; thereafter proceeded to Egypt, thence to France (1917), and was killed in action at Langemarck, 22 August 1917. Buried between Langemarck and St. Julien. His Commanding Officer wrote, "He was one of the most popular officers in the battalion, both with his fellow-officers and with the men; I personally shall feel the loss terribly as he was one of my most promising officers.": Age 22. *unm.*

(Panel 35) Capt. Clement Neill Newsum, 2/5th Bn. The Lincolnshire Regt. (T.F.): *yr. s.* of Clement Henry Newsum, of Eastwood House, Lincoln, J.P., ex-Mayor of Lincoln, by his wife Alice Maude, *dau.* of George Neill, J.P.: *b.* Lincoln, 5 October 1895: *educ.* Gresham School, where he became Head of the School: gazetted 2nd Lieut. The Lincolnshire Regt. 1 February 1915: promoted Lieut. June 1916, and Capt. 1 January 1917: served with his regiment in Ireland during the Dublin Rebellion in 1916: proceeded to France, 26 February 1917: took part in several engagements, and was killed by shellfire near Zonnebeke, Flanders 26 September following. Buried where he fell. He was Mentioned in Despatches (*London Gazette*, 18 December 1917) by F.M. Sir Douglas Haig, for 'gallant and distinguished service in the field.' In the last Gresham's School *vs* Old Boys cricket match, 18 July 1914, Mr Newsum (No.8) was caught after 4 runs by his brother Henry: Age 21. *unm.*

(Panel 35) 2nd Lieut. Basil Walker Griffin, 2nd Bn. (10th Foot) The Lincolnshire Regt.: *s.* of the Rev. Horatio John Griffin, Rector of All Saints Church, Broxholme, co. Lincoln: and brother to Pte. 766202, R.N. Griffin, 19th Canadian Infantry, killed in action 9 May 1917; Fresnoy. Killed in action 2 December 1917; Passchendaele.

His brother Randle also has no known grave; he is commemorated on the Canadian National (Vimy) Memorial.

(Panel 35) 2nd Lieut. John Robertson Lish, 3rd (Reserve) Bn. The Lincolnshire Regt.: *s.* of Joseph John Lish, of Fencote, Fenham, Newcastle-on-Tyne, a Past President and Gold Medallist of the Society of Architects (London), by his wife Nancy, *dau.* of the late Edward McLeod, of Natal, South Africa: *b.* Newcastle-on-Tyne, 18 September 1879: *educ.* Singleton House School, Jesmond, Newcastle; Argyle House School, Sunderland, and at the De Aston School, Market Rasen, co. Lincoln: Occupation – Shipbroker and Coal Exporter, Newcastle: joined 9th Battn. Northumberland Fusiliers, 7 September 1914: served with the Expeditionary Force in France and Flanders from 15 July 1915: wounded nr. Ypres, 9 February 1916: rejoining his battalion after a month in hospital, and fought in safety throughout the heavy fighting on the Somme later that year: gazetted 2nd Lieut., 3rd Lincolnshire Regt., 30 May 1917, attd. 1st Battn., and was killed in action at Polygon Wood, 4 October following. Buried there. His Captain wrote, "He was in my Company for a few short months, but it was long enough for me and everyone else in his platoon to get to love him as a brother and a soldier. I was with him when he was hit, and the men in his platoon avenged his death tenfold. It may be a slight consolation to you to know that it was the most successful attack this battalion has ever done," and another Captain, "Your son was most popular with all in the battalion, a good leader of men, and one whose place will be difficult to replace. I am sure there was a great future for him as a soldier if only he could have been spared. It was a great price given during a great victory." Another officer also wrote, "As a fellow subaltern of his in the same company, I think I can say that no more popular officer, both with the men, particularly his own platoon who loved him, and with his brother officers, has ever come to this battalion. He had only been with us a short time, but in that time I had come to look upon him as a real friend, always ready to help and to stand by you in difficulties. Previous to the action in which he fell, he had done some fine reconnaissance work for the battalion, and had he lived was to have been recommended for the Military Cross. No finer death could his have been, and it may afford you some slight consolation to know that he died gallantly leading his platoon in one of the great successes of the war...The reconnaissance that your son carried out was as follows – Two days before the show he, with about three other officers, was sent to reconnoitre the ground the battalion was to occupy. They were stopped at Brigade Headquarters and told that it was impossible to go any further, as the shelling was so intense and the position of the front line very uncertain. Your son, however, after waiting there about an hour, got hold of his batman and slipped out on his own, and, absolutely regardless of shells or anything else, went on and thoroughly reconnoitred the ground. Thus, on the night we came up, he guided us the whole way, and got the whole battalion into position with very few casualties. I've been all over that ground, and I've experienced the shelling up in that sector, and it can only be described as 'hellish.' And to set out, as your son did, alone and against orders, was, I think you will agree, a very brave thing to do." He was an all-round sportsman, playing cricket, hockey, football, tennis and golf: Age 38. *unm.*

(Panel 35) 2nd Lieut. Ralph Lummis, The Lincolnshire Regt. attd. 12/13th (Service) Bn. Northumberland Fusiliers: *s.* of Louisa Lummis (Monk Villa, Coddenham, Ipswich), and her late husband, George Murrell Lummis: and yr. brother to Rfn. 1984, E.G.S. Lummis, 4th Rifle Brigade, killed in action 27 February 1915. Killed in action 4 October 1917: Age 26. *unm.*

His brother Eric is buried in Voormezeele Enclosure Nos. 1 & 2 (II.D.13).

On the night of 11 August 1917, after a week of rest, 2nd Lincolns were moved forward to the vicinity of Bellewaarde to support 74th Brigade, relieving 10th Cheshires on the Westhoek Ridge at 10 p.m. At 3.30 a.m., 14 August, the enemy launched a heavy barrage onto the ridge, followed thereafter by an infantry assault on the Lincolns positions, during the course of which 'A' and 'D' companies suffered numerous casualties. Throughout the night and the following day, the positions were subject to continuous artillery and machine gun fire and, at 6.30 a.m. on the morning of 16 August, the Lincolns were ordered to support the Brigade in an attack. But, shortly after achieving their first objectives, both flanks became exposed. In the face of mounting casualties from enfilade fire, a limited withdrawal to new positions was necessitated, and after consolidation these were counter-attacked in force by the enemy in the afternoon. Relieved at 11 p.m. that night, the sadly depleted Lincolns received little respite, being called upon to resume the fight the next day and, when they were finally withdrawn on the 18th, their casualty list recorded: 33 other ranks killed, 3 Officers, 104 other ranks wounded, 36 other ranks missing.

Of the 33 other ranks killed, 32 are recorded here; only one has a known grave, Pte. A. Holt, Bedford House Cemetery (III.E.9/Enc.No.4).

(Panel 35) Sergt. 13797, Herbert Ingall, 2nd Bn. (10th Foot) The Lincolnshire Regt.: *s.* of John Ingall, of Hallam's Lane, Timberland, Lincoln, by his wife Elizabeth. Killed in action on the Westhoek Ridge 16 August 1917: Age 25.

(Panel 35) Sergt. 15655, John Edward Walker, 1st Bn. (10th Foot) The Lincolnshire Regt.: eldest *s.* of the late John Edward Walker, Coachman; by his wife Hannah Eliza ('Ivy Cottage,' 3, Wood Street, Winthorpe, Newark), *dau.* of Thomas Parkinson: *b.* Winthorpe, co. Nottingham, 4 July 1883: *educ.* there: was a Valet: enlisted 5 March 1915: served with the Expeditionary Force in France and Flanders from the following October: returned shortly afterwards suffering from trench fever: on recovery, May 1916, returned to France. In May 1917 he was wounded and gassed, and promoted Corpl. and Sergt. on the field of battle, and was killed in action near Polygon Wood, 4 October 1917: Age 34. *unm.*

(Panel 35) Corpl. 40444, Frederick Lowe, 2nd Bn. (10th Foot) The Lincolnshire Regt.: formerly no.27698, Bedfordshire Regt.: *s.* of A. Lowe (2, Alexandra Road, King's Langley, co. Hertford): enlisted Hemel Hempstead. Killed in action on the Westhoek Ridge 16 August 1917: Age 22.

PANEL 35 ENDS: L/CPL. H. CLARK – LINCOLNSHIRE REGT.

PANEL 36 BEGINS: L/CORPL. G. CROSSLEY – LINCOLNSHIRE REGT.

(Panel 36) L/Corpl. 19340, Ernest Willoughby, 2nd Bn. (10th Foot) The Lincolnshire Regt. Killed in action during an attack on the Westhoek Ridge 16 August 1917.

(Panel 36) Pte. 38012, George Frederick Allsop, 2nd Bn. (10th Foot) The Lincolnshire Regt.: *s.* of the late Harold Arthur Allsop, Slaughterman, by his wife Eliza (52, Mason Street, Sutton-in-Ashfield, co. Nottingham): and cousin to Pte. G.W. Allsop, 2/5th Sherwood Foresters, who also fell: *b. c.*1899: enlisted Mansfield. Missing / believed killed in action 2 December 1917: Age 18.

His cousin George also has no known grave; he is commemorated on the Ploegsteert Memorial (Panel 7).

(Panel 36) Pte. 40053, George Ambrose, 2nd Bn. (10th Foot) The Lincolnshire Regt. Killed in action on the Westhoek Ridge 16 August 1917

(Panel 36) Pte. 41505, John William Barnett, 2nd Bn. (10th Foot) The Lincolnshire Regt.: formerly no. 34358, Leicestershire Regt.: *b.* Leverton, about 1890: enlisted Bourne, co. Lincoln: served with the

Expeditionary Force, and was killed in action 16 August 1917, during an attack near Bellewaarde Ridge: Age 26. He leaves a wife May Barnett (Butterwick, Boston, co. Lincoln).

(Panel 36) Pte. 24515, Frederick Wilson Boulton, 2/4th Bn. The Lincolnshire Regt. (T.F.): *s.* of Frederick Wilson Boulton, Farmer; of 29, Carter Gate, Bathley, Newark-on-Trent, co. Notts, by his wife Elizabeth, *dau.* of Richard Brunskill: *b.* Kirkby Stephen, co. Westmoreland, 4 August 1882: *educ.* Manchester and Newark: was engaged assisting his father in the milk trade: enlisted 10 April 1916: served with the Expeditionary Force in France and Flanders, from 10 March 1917, and was killed in action nr. Ypres 26 September following: Age 25. *unm.*

(Panel 36) Pte. 440195, Tom Burton, 2nd Bn. (10th Foot) The Lincolnshire Regt. Killed in action on the Westhoek Ridge 16 August 1917.

(Panel 36) Pte. 41451, James Billings, 2nd Bn. (10th Foot) The Lincolnshire Regt.: formerly no.35441, South Staffordshire Regt. Killed in action 16 August 1917.

(Panel 36) Pte. 41639, Charles Bircumshaw, 2nd Bn. (10th Foot) The Lincolnshire Regt.: formerly no.38227, Leicestershire Regt.: *s.* of Mrs Bircumshaw (47, Syston Street, Leicester). Killed in action on the Westhock Ridge 16 August 1917: Age 35. (*IWGC record 19 August*)

(Panel 36) Pte. 41701, Thomas Henry Bridge, 8th Bn. The Lincolnshire Regt.: *s.* of John George Bridge, of 14, High Street, Biggleswade, co. Bedford, by his wife Florence: and elder brother to L/Corpl. 14919, H.P. Bridge, 4th Bedfordshire Regt., killed in action, 30 October 1917: *b.* Codshall, co. Stafford: enlisted Bletchley, co. Buckingham. Killed in action 4 October 1917: Age 24. *unm.*

His brother Horace also has no known grave; he is recorded on Panel 49.

(Panel 36) Pte. 202823, Arthur Robert Clark, 2nd Bn. (10th Foot) The Lincolnshire Regt.: *husb.* to Eliza (283, Queen's Road, Plaistow, London, E.13). Killed in action on the Westhoek Ridge 16 August 1917: Age 39.

(Panel 36) Pte. 27302, Sydney Clarke, 2nd Bn. (10th Foot) The Lincolnshire Regt.: formerly no.31914, Leicestershire Regt.: *s.* of the late Joseph Clarke, of Leicester, by his wife Edith. Killed in action on the Westhoek Ridge 16 August 1917: Age 20. *unm.*

(Panel 36) Pte. 15559, Frederick William Dye, 2nd Bn. (10th Foot) The Lincolnshire Regt. Killed in action on the Westhoek Ridge 16 August 1917.

(Panel 36) Pte. 40220, George Eardley, 2nd Bn. (10th Foot) The Lincolnshire Regt. Killed in action on the Westhoek Ridge 16 August 1917.

(Panel 36) Pte. 26413, Giles Edwards, 2nd Bn. (10th Foot) The Lincolnshire Regt.: *husb.* to Lizzie (Manby, Louth, co. Lincoln). Killed in action on the Westhoek Ridge 16 August 1917.

(Panel 36) Pte. 26060, Robert James Fretter, 6th (Service) Bn. The Lincolnshire Regt.: formerly no.31456, Leicestershire Regt.: *s.* of George Fretter, of Broughton Astley, co. Leicester, by his wife Mary Ann: and brother to Pte. 67005, H.G. Fretter, 1st Sherwood Foresters, died 23 March 1917, of wounds: *b.* Broughton Astley, 1894. Killed in action 22 August 1917: Age 22. He was married to Sarah Jane Dann, *née* Fretter (Station Road, Broughton Astley).

His brother Horace is buried in St. Sever Cemetery Extension, Rouen (O.VIII.M.10).

(Panel 36) Pte. 10322, William Goodlad, 2nd Bn. (10th Foot) The Lincolnshire Regt. Killed in action on the Westhoek Ridge 16 August 1917.

(Panel 36) Pte. 240864, Edward Graham, 2nd Bn. (10th Foot) The Lincolnshire Regt.: *husb.* to Amelia (34, Burns Street, Gainsborough, co. Lincoln). Killed in action on the Westhoek Ridge 16 August 1917.

(Panel 36) Pte. 42348, Edwin Victor Harris, 1st Bn. (10th Foot) The Lincolnshire Regt.: *s.* of Edwin Harris, Joiner, of School Street, Great Glen, co. Leicester , by his wife Hannah Haycock, *née* Easom: *b.* Great Glen, 9 July 1898: enlisted 15th (Training Reserve) Battn. Leicestershire Regt., Great Glen, thereafter transf'd. Leicestershire Regt., no.38080: subsequently transf'd. Lincolnshire Regt. for Active Service in France and Flanders, and was killed by enemy artillery fire in the vicinity of Polygon Wood 4 October 1917: Age 19.

PANEL 36 ENDS: PTE. 40086, A HOLMES – LINCOLNSHIRE REGT.

PANEL 37 BEGINS: PTE. W. HORSFORD – LINCOLNSHIRE REGT.

(Panel 37) Pte. 18876, Harry Houlden, 2nd Bn. (10th Foot) The Lincolnshire Regt.: *s.* of Thomas Houlden, of Elder Tree Cottage, Kirkstead, Woodhall Spa, co. Lincoln, by his wife Susan: *b.* Wood Enderby, co. Lincoln, 1896: Occupation – Farm Labourer; Abbey Farm, Kirkstead: volunteered and enlisted Lincoln 6 September 1915: trained Weelsby Park, Grimsby: posted reinforcement draft to 2nd Battn. Lincolnshire Regt., and went to France, January 1917: wounded by shrapnel during first tour in the trenches, and evacuated Base Hospital, Boulogne: on recovery rejoined his unit August 1917, and was killed in action on the Westhoek Ridge during an enemy counter-attack 16 August 1917: Age 21. *unm.*

(Panel 37) Pte. 241909, William Henry Houlden, 7th (Service) Bn. The Lincolnshire Regt.: *s.* of Mrs C. Houlden (Little's Cottages, Cameron Street, Heckington): *husb.* to Mary Ellen Houlden (87, London Road, Spalding): and brother to Rfn. 5044, J.W. Houlden, 8th West Yorkshire Regt., killed in action, 3 September 1916: *b.* Heckington, co. Lincoln: enlisted Sleaford. Killed in action 25 November 1917: Age 35.

His brother James is buried in Tincourt New British Cemetery (IX.B.1).

(Panel 37) Pte. 41469, Thomas Johnson, 2nd Bn. (10th Foot) The Lincolnshire Regt.: formerly no.35307, South Staffordshire Regt. Killed in action on the Westhoek Ridge 16 August 1917.

(Panel 37) Pte. 235067, Joseph May, 8th (Service) Bn. The Lincolnshire Regt.: formerly no.10277, Suffolk Regt.: *s.* of Charles May, of 100, St. Vincent's Road, Dartford, co. Kent, by his wife Jane: and brother to L/Corpl. G/5829, W.E. May, 7th East Kent Regt., who fell 13 October 1917: *b.* 1897: enlisted Dartford. Killed in action 4 November 1917: Age 20. *unm.*

His brother William also has no known grave; he is recorded on Panel 17.

(Panel 37) Pte. 23624, James Edward Musson, 2nd Bn. (10th Foot) The Lincolnshire Regt.: Killed in action on the Westhoek Ridge 16 August 1917.

(Panel 37) Pte. 41547, William Henry Patchett, 'B' Coy., 2nd Bn. (10th Foot) The Lincolnshire Regt.: formerly no.57304, Leicestershire Regt.: *s.* of Edward Patchett, of 8, Smith Street, Otley Road, Shipley, co. York, by his wife Frances: enlisted Bradford. Killed in action during an attack on the Westhoek Ridge 16 August 1917: Age 20. He was married to Jessie Squires, *née* Patchett (1, Van Dockfield Road, Shipley).

(Panel 37) Pte. 241098, Arthur Rowland Payne, 2nd Bn. (10th Foot) The Lincolnshire Regt.: *s.* of the late Joseph Payne, by his wife Ellen (47, Barcroft Street, Cleethorpes, Grimsby, co. Lincoln). Killed in action on the Westhoek Ridge 16 August 1917: Age 25. *unm.*

(Panel 37) Pte. 41484, David Perkins, 2nd Bn. (10th Foot) The Lincolnshire Regt.: formerly no.35321, South Staffordshire Regt.: *s.* of Sarah Perkins (20, Duck Street, Upper Ettingshall, Bilston, co. Stafford): enlisted Tipton. Killed in action on Westhoek Ridge 16 August 1917: Age 21. *unm.*

(Panel 37) Pte. 6079, Anthony Piggott, 6th (Service) Bn. The Lincolnshire Regt.: *s.* of the late William Piggott, by his wife Hannah (Star Cross, Holbeach, co. Lincoln): and elder brother to Pte. 241720, H. Piggott, 2/5th Duke of Wellington's Regt., killed in action, 3 May 1917, aged 24 yrs.: *b.* Long Sutton, co. Lincoln: enlisted Holbeach. Killed in action 22 August 1917: Age 43. Remembered on Holbeach (St. Mark's) Parish War Memorial.

His brother Herbert also has no known grave; he is commemorated on the Arras (Faubourg d'Amiens) Memorial (Bay 6).

(Panel 37) Pte. 40368, Robert Plater, 2nd Bn. (10th Foot) The Lincolnshire Regt.: formerly no.32957, Suffolk Regt.: enlisted Wisbech, co. Cambridge. Killed in action on the Westhoek Ridge 16 August 1917.

(Panel 37) Pte. 40247, Fred Rainbird, 2nd Bn. (10th Foot) The Lincolnshire Regt.: *s.* of Benjamin Rainbird, of Church Lane, Great Holland, Clacton-on-Sea, co. Essex, by his wife Susan. Killed in action on the Westhoek Ridge 16 August 1917: Age 23. *unm.*

(Panel 37) Pte. 30992, Frank Robinson, 2nd Bn. (10th Foot) The Lincolnshire Regt. Killed in action on the Westhoek Ridge 16 August 1917.

(Panel 37) 26447, George Robinson, 2nd Bn. (10th Foot) The Lincolnshire Regt. Killed in action on the Westhoek Ridge 16 August 1917.

(Panel 37) Pte. 38250, Jesse Salvin, 'D' Coy., 8th (Service) Bn. The Lincolnshire Regt.: *s.* of the late Philip Salvin, of Curzon Street, Netherfield, co. Nottingham: and brother to Pte. 14905, R. Salvin, 1st Bedfordshire Regt., killed in action 30 June 1915: *b.* Nottingham: enlisted Hucknall. Killed in action 4 October 1917: Age 18.

His brother Ralph also has no known grave; he is commemorated on the Ypres (Menin Gate) Memorial (Panel 33).

(Panel 37) Pte. 41494, William Smith, 2nd Bn. (10th Foot) The Lincolnshire Regt.: formerly no.35711, South Staffordshire Regt. Killed in action 16 August 1917.

(Panel 37) Pte. 40359, Samuel Herbert Smithson, 2nd Bn. (10th Foot) The Lincolnshire Regt.: formerly no.32010, Suffolk Regt. Killed in action on the Westhoek Ridge 16 August 1917: Age 35. He leaves a wife Alice Louisa Smithson (Tolgate, Corpusty, Norwich), to mourn his loss.

(Panel 37) Pte. 241251, George William Steeley, 1st Bn. (10th Foot) The Lincolnshire Regt.: *s.* of the late George William Steeley, of Hull, by his wife Hannah 'Annie' Maria (8, Edwards Terrace, Garibaldi Street, Grimsby), *dau.* of Mr (& Mrs) Smith: *b.* North Kelsey, co. Lincoln, 27 January 1889: *educ.* Bean Street Council School, Hull: Occupation – Fisherman: enlisted July 1915: served with the Egyptian Expeditionary Force in Egypt and Palestine from the following November: proceeded to France the following January: wounded Arras, November 1917: returned to France, December following, and was killed in action at Ypres 26 April 1918. Buried in Ridge Wood, south-south-west of Ypres: Age 29. *unm.* (*IWGC record age 31*)

(Panel 37) Pte. 41561, Arthur Taylor, 2nd Bn. (10th Foot) The Lincolnshire Regt.: formerly no.34379, Leicestershire Regt. Killed in action on the Westhoek Ridge 16 August 1917.

(Panel 37) Pte. 41657, John William Tildesley, 2nd Bn. (10th Foot) The Lincolnshire Regt.: formerly no.38277, Leicestershire Regt. Killed in action on the Westhoek Ridge 16 August 1917.

(Panel 37) Pte. 40229, Albert Watson, 2nd Bn. (10th Foot) The Lincolnshire Regt. Killed in action on the Westhoek Ridge 16 August 1917.

(Panel 37) Pte. 41565, Randolphus Watson, 2nd Bn. (10th Foot) The Lincolnshire Regt.: formerly no.34322, Leicestershire Regt.: *s.* of Elsie E.A. Watson (16, Roydstone Terrace, Bradford Moor, Bradford, co. York): *b.* Doncaster, 1884. Killed in action during an attack on the Westhoek Ridge 16 August 1917: Age 33.

(Panel 37) Pte. 40438, George Richard Williams, 2nd Bn. (10th Foot) The Lincolnshire Regt.: formerly no.16243, Suffolk Regt.: enlisted Wisbech, co. Cambridge. Killed in action on the Westhoek Ridge 16 August 1917.

(Panel 37) Pte. 51500, Brooke Knowles Willis, 'C' Coy., 10th Bn. The Lincolnshire Regt.: formerly no.10356, Army Cyclist Corps: *s.* of William Joseph Willis, of 44, Henslowe Road, East Dulwich, London, by his wife Catherine Ellen: *educ.* Alleyn's School, Dulwich (Cribb's House): enlisted Whitehall and, after proceeding to France, was discovered to be underage and returned home for a period of six months: returned to France where, shortly after arriving at the front, he was shot and killed by a sniper; 17 April 1918: Age 19.

PANEL 37 ENDS: PTE. E. WYER – LINCOLNSHIRE REGT.

PANEL 38 BEGINS: LIEUT.COL. D.H. BLUNT, D.S.O. – DEVONSHIRE REGT.

(Panel 38) Lieut. Col. Duncan Hamilton Blunt, D.S.O., 1st Bn. (11th Foot) The Devonshire Regt.: *s.* of George Henry Blunt, of 152, Blaby Hill, Leicester: Twice Mentioned in Despatches. Killed in action 3 October 1917, east of Veldhoek. On the evening of 3 October, the battalion had advanced to their assembly position in readiness for their part in the attack on Polderhoek Chateau the following morning. "It was a memorable move: the tracks were slippery, the enemy was shelling vigorously and there were many casualties: as ill-luck would have it, one shell caught and killed both Col. Blunt and his Adjutant, Lieut. Sir B.R. Williams. A real leader and organiser, a soldier to his fingertips. Col. Blunt had done great things with the battalion, which put great trust in him: the officers were wont to say he could walk through any barrage. He was almost certain to have been given a brigade in the near future.": Age 39.

Lieut. Sir. B.R. Williams also has no known grave; he is recorded below.

(Panel 38) Major Harry Archer, D.S.O., 2nd Bn. (11th Foot) The Devonshire Regt.: 2nd *s.* of the late Henry 'Harry' James Archer, formerly of 'Rock House,' Halberton, and Mrs Archer (Alfoxton Park, Holford, Bridgwater): *b.* 1 September 1879: gazetted Lieut. 13 January 1915: promoted Capt. May 1916, and Major August 1917: served with the Expeditionary Force in France, from 12 May 1915, and was killed in action at Passchendaele 25 November 1917. Buried at Musselmarkt: Age 38. Awarded the D.S.O. (*London Gazette,* 26 September 1917) for 'conspicuous gallantry,' Major Archer was twice Mentioned in Despatches (*London Gazette,* 22 May 1917; 18 December 1917) by F.M. Sir Douglas Haig for 'gallant and distinguished service in the field.' He *m.* Tiverton, co. Devon, 27 July 1904; Mary, *née* Birmingham ('Salem House,' Uffculme, co. Devon), and had three *daus.*: Valentine Mary, *b.* 25 August 1906, Nancy Brice, *b.* 28 June 1909 and Diana Smeed, *b.* 24 August 1911.

(Panel 38) Lieut. Francis William Chick, 7th (Cyclist) Bn. (T.F.) attd. 1st Bn. (11th Foot) The Devonshire Regt.: *s.* of Frank Chick, of Park House, St. Thomas, Exeter, co. Devon, by his wife Emily. One of seven officers of 1st Devons killed 4 October 1917, in the attack on Polderhoek Chateau: Age 22. *unm.* See account below. (*Regimental History records 2nd Lieut.*)

(Panel 38) Lieut. William Southmead Langworthy, 7th (Cyclist) Bn. (T.F.) attd. 1st Bn. (11th Foot) The Devonshire Regt.: *s.* of William Southmead Langworthy, M.R.C.S., L.R.C.P., of Brock's Halt, Galmpton, Brixham, co.; Devon, by his wife Ethelind Marion. One of seven officers of 1st Devons killed 4 October 1917, in the attack on Polderhoek Chateau: Age 22. *unm.* See account below. (*Regimental History records 2nd Lieut.*)

(Panel 38) Lieut. Thomas Joseph Relf, 7th (Cyclist) Bn. (T.F.) attd. 1st Bn. (11th Foot) The Devonshire Regt.: *s.* of E.J. Relf, of Lloydminster, Saskatchewan, Canada. One of seven officers of 1st Devons killed 4 October 1917, in the attack on Polderhoek Chateau: Age 27. *unm.* See account below. (*Regimental History records 2nd Lieut.*)

(Panel 38) Lieut. Sir Burton Robert Williams, Adjt., 1st Bn. (11th Foot) The Devonshire Regt.: 6th Bart. 3rd and *yst. s.* of the late Sir William Robert Williams, 3rd Bart., of Tregullow, co. Cornwall, D.L. (*d.* 1903), by his wife Matilda Frances, Lady Williams (Widbrook House, Cookham, co. Berks), *dau.* of Edmund Beauchamp Beauchamp: *b.* 7 July 1889: gazetted Lieut. 3rd Devonshire Regt. Killed in action, 3 October 1917, east of Veldhoek; by the same shell that killed Lieut.Col. D.H. Hunt, D.S.O. An efficient and popular Adjutant, the double loss to the battalion was a severe blow: Age 28. *unm.* For his services in the Great War Lieut. Williams was twice Mentioned in Despatches. (*IWGC record 3 – 4 October, age 27*)

Lieut.Col. H.D. Blunt also has no known grave; he is recorded above.

(Panel 38) 2nd Lieut. John Morgan Blake, 1st Bn. (11th Foot) The Devonshire Regt. One of seven officers of 1st Devons killed 4 October 1917, in the attack on Polderhoek Chateau. See account below.

(Panel 38) 2nd Lieut. Charles Frederick King, 3rd (Reserve) Bn. The Devonshire Regt. attd. 6th (Rifles) Bn. The King's (Liverpool) Regt..: *s.* of James Frederick King, of 3, Longlands, Dawlish, co. Devon, by his wife Frances M., *dau.* of Joseph Nicholls, of Whitehall, Handsworth, Birmingham: *b.* Dawlish, aforesaid, 28 October 1883: *educ.* Gillingham Grammar School: joined Royal Navy, July 1900: served 14 years as Accountant Officer: joined 13th Gloucestershire Regt. (Capt.), August 1914: resigned (1916) and enlisted Coldstream Guards: served with the Expeditionary Force in France and Flanders from March 1916: promoted in the field 'for courage in the trenches': gazetted 2nd Lieut., Devonshire Regt., July 1917: subsequently attd. 6th (Territorial) Battn. King's (Liverpool) Regt., and was killed in action on the Menin Road, 20 September 1917. Buried there. The Colonel wrote, "He had not been with us long, but we all took to him at once, and I am certain he was a very fine soldier, and a great loss.": Age 33. *unm.* (*IWGC record 1/9 King's Liverpool, age 34*)

(Panel 38) 2nd Lieut. Francis Methuen Noel, 3rd (Reserve) attd. 9th (Service) Bn. The Devonshire Regt.: eldest. *s.* of Admiral Francis Charles Methuen Noel, of 33, Redcliffe Square, London, S.W., by his wife Wilmot Juliana, *dau.* of Thomas Maitland Snow, of Cleve House, Exeter: and *gdson.* to the late Colonel

Noel, of 'Clanna Falls,' co. Gloucester: *b*. Southsea, co. Hants, 28 December 1888: *educ*. Cheltenham College: was for some years on the staff of the Bank of England: soon after the outbreak of war he rejoined the Inns of Court O.T.C., obtained a commission – Devonshire Regt., gazetted 2nd Lieut., November 1916: served with the Expeditionary Force in France and Flanders from 13 January, showing conspicuous gallantry in several engagements, and was killed in action while leading his company, as Actg. Capt., at the attack on Gheluvelt, 26 October 1917: Age 28. *unm*. (*IWGC record 4th Bn.*)

(Panel 38) 2nd Lieut. William Garfield Port, 1st Bn. (11th Foot) The Devonshire Regt.: *s*. of William Henry Port, of Johannesburg, South Africa, by his wife Elizabeth Rowe: previously served with Witwatersrand Rifles, German South West African Campaign. One of seven officers of 1st Devons killed 4 October 1917, in the attack on Polderhoek Chateau: Age 26. *unm*. See account below.

(Panel 38) Sergt. 10492, Edmund 'Ned' Edmunds, D.C.M., 'B' Coy., 8th (Service) Bn. The Devonshire Regt.: 3rd *s*. of the late George Edmunds, Colliery Fireman (*d*. 22 May 1919), and his wife, Esther (*d*. Oakland, California, 12 December 1941), *dau*. of William Morgan, Stonemason, of Llanstephan, co. Carmarthen, by his wife Esther, *née* Thomas: *b*. 6, Dewinton Terrace, Ystradyfodwg, co. Glamorgan, 25 September 1880: served with the Expeditionary Force in France and Flanders, and was posted missing, possibly taken prisoner during the fighting, 26 October 1917; the first day of the Second Battle of Passchendaele. He was awarded the Distinguished Conduct Medal (posthumously) for 'gallantry on 4 October 1917 at Brodseinde, during the 3rd Battle of Ypres.' His Company Officer wrote, "9 November 1917: Dear Madam, You have probably heard by now the sad news that your son, No.10492, Sergt. E. Edmunds, is missing. He was acting as Sergt. Major to this Company in an attack on October 26 and the only information I have been able to obtain from those who have come back is that he was seen nearest the furthest limit of our advance, going forward well up with the front line with a party of men of this Company none of whom, I regret to say, have come back to us during the day the Germans counterattacked, and a number of prisoners were seen to be taken, but who they were I have been unable to find out. I sincerely trust that your son was among them. I have always had the greatest admiration for Sergt. Edmunds, and he will be the greatest loss to us out here. In action he has shown himself absolutely fearless, and as a fighting soldier simply splendid in every way. I was not with them on the 26th but in the attack on 4 October I was his Company Commander and so truly magnificent was his behaviour on that occasion that I recommended him for the D.C.M., which I now hear has been awarded. With the deepest sympathy for you and your suspense, I remain, yours truly, H. Raper, Capt., Comdg. 'B' Coy., 8th Devon." Later confirmed killed in action, 26 October 1917, Sergt. Edmunds body was never found: Age 37.

(Panel 38) Corpl. 24812, Harold Rupert Brinkworth, 9th (Service) Bn. The Devonshire Regt.: *s*. of the late Joseph Brinkworth, by his wife Ellen, *dau*. of James Woods: *b*. Stroud, co. Gloucester, 5 August 1880: Occupation – Sub-Postmaster; Loddiswell, afterwards on the Sorting Office Staff, General Post Office, Plymouth: enlisted Royal Field Artillery 14 November 1899: served eight years with the Colours: re-enlisted 21 June 1916: served with the Expeditionary Force in France and Flanders from 10 December following, and was killed in action at Hooge, 6 October 1917. Buried there. His Commanding Officer wrote, "It is with the very deepest sorrow that I have to tell you of the death of your husband, who has been with me for the last two or three months. I cannot tell you how great is my loss as the officer commanding of his platoon. He was always cheerful and helpful to his men, and under any circumstances I could always rely on him for a helping hand; never once did I hear him bullying the men; he always understood them and sympathized with them. He was one of the best N.C.O.'s and comrades I have ever met. All the officers of the battalion had the very highest esteem for him, and, personally, I would have trusted him with anything. He died without suffering the slightest pain, quite instantaneously. We buried him by men from his own platoon near where he fell at Hooge, 6 October": Age 37. He *m*. South Milton, co. Devon, 7 October 1908; Harriet Ellen (Bowhay, formerly Brinkworth, of Rock Villa, South Milton), *dau*. of James Ingram, and had two sons; Harold James Edwin, *b*. 20 December 1911 and William Ernest, *b*. 5 March 1913.

(Panel 38) Pte. 30276, Herbert Bale, 1st Bn. (11th Foot) The Devonshire Regt.: 3rd *s*. of Richard Bale, Farmer; of Damage Barton, Mortehoe, Ilfracombe, co. Devon, by his wife Jane, *dau*. of Thomas Down: *b*. Ilfracombe. 2 September 1892: *educ*. Mortehoe Council School: Occupation – Farming with his father:

enlisted Royal North Devon Hussars, 26 April 1916: served with the Expeditionary Force in France and Flanders from November following: transf'd. Machine Gun Section: took part in the operations at Vimy Ridge, and was killed in action at Polderhoek Chateau, north-east of Ypres, 4 October 1917, by a shell while carrying the Lewis gun under his arm. Buried there: Age 25. *unm.*

(Panel 38) Pte. 30716, William John Hargreaves Bartholomew, 1st Bn. (11th Foot) The Devonshire Regt.: *s.* of the late William Bartholomew, by his wife A. (43, Belgrave Road, Portswood, nr. Southampton), *dau.* of the late John Hargreaves, of Eastleigh: *b.* St. Denys, Southampton, co. Hants, 26 December 1894: *educ.* Portswood Council School: Occupation – Assistant Flour Mill Rollerman: enlisted, 3 January 1917: served with the Expeditionary Force in France from 19 March; killed in action nr. Hooge, 4 October following: Age 22. *unm.*

(Panel 38) Pte. 17551, Arthur Richard Brooking, 8th (Service) Bn. The Devonshire Regt.: *yst. s.* of the late William Henry Brooking, by his wife Sarah Jane (2, Vine Terrace, Loddisewell, co. Devon) *dau.* of Thomas Balershill: *b.* Loddiswell, South Devon, 7 September 1898: *educ.* Church Elementary School: joined local rifle club until he attained the required military age: enlisted April 1915: served with the Expeditionary Force in France and Flanders, and was killed in action, 7 October 1917. His Commanding Officer wrote, "Your son was an invaluable man, and in many ways irreplaceable. He has for some months been my Lewis Gun Storeman, and one of my best instructors," and a comrade:"We buried him outside the battle headquarters of the battalion in which he had served so long, and so nobly – just about where he fell. It is hard to realize he is gone." Another also wrote, "As his pal, I can assure you he died whilst doing his duty.": Age 19.

(Panel 38) Pte. 9317, Henry William Clapp, 1st Bn. (11th Foot) The Devonshire Regt.: *s.* of Henry Clapp, of Allen Cottage, Westleigh, Wellington, co. Somerset, by his wife Mary Ann: and brother to Stoker 2nd Class, K/20947, A. Clapp, H.M.S. 'Marlborough,' R.N., died 31 December 1914, aged 19 years: *b.* Burlescombe, 1893. Killed in action 4 October 1917: Age 24. *unm.* Remembered on Burlescombe (St. Mary's) Church War Memorial.

His brother Alfred is buried in Haslar Royal Naval Cemetery (E.23.3).

By late September 1917 the abnormal weather conditions, which had caused manifold problems and delays to previous attacks, had finally broken, and the ground had begun to dry, albeit slightly. 1st Devons, coming into the line just east of Veldhoek on the night of 1 – 2 October 1917 to their assembly positions for their part in the attack on the 4th, found the ground confronting them strewn with shattered trees, blocked ditches and streams full of debris. Torn and shell cratered by three years of almost constant artillery fire, the drainage system – which even under normal circumstances would not have been sufficient to handle the persistent rainfall of the preceding three months – had been totally destroyed. An observer commented the attack had as much if not more to fear from the ground than from the Germans. 1st Devons, attacking astride the Reutelbeek with three companies south of it were to fully realise and count the cost of this observation. To keep up with the barrage was difficult in the extreme and, with several morasses needing to be passed circuitously – in places men would literally have been swallowed if they had attempted to advance straight ahead – combined with the smoke and confusion of the attack, to keep direction was virtually impossible.

At zero hour, 6 a.m., 4 October 1917, the troops went over. 95th Brigade on the left had Cameron Covert as its objective, the Devons having to keep touch with 13th Brigade whose goal was Polderhoek Chateau. Any thought of dash was completely out of the question. Over the ground before them the Devons, despite the swamps, mud and German shelling, managed to keep up with the barrage. North of the Reutelbeek No.4 Company pushed on level with the D.C.L.I. on their flank; encountering stiff opposition from the enemy who had been expecting the attack and lying out in strength to meet it. A bog at the southern end of Cameron Covert proved impassable, and forced to consolidate west of it No.4 and the D.C.L.I. were later counter-attacked and forced back a short distance where, after being reinforced by two companies of East Surreys, they dug in on a line west of and through the Covert. By this time one officer and about twenty men were all that remained of No.4.

South of the impenetrable morass, 100 to 200 yards wide (which, in better times, may have been a stream), No.3 formed the leading wave, No.1 in support, No.2 reserve. Advancing in artillery formation, through thick mud which – if it provided any compensation – was soft, deep, and effectively smothered most shell bursts; made progress painfully slow, presenting a steady flow of easy targets to the German machine gunners.

A heavily fortified pill-box, checking the advance on the right, was dealt with by 2nd Lieut. Wheeler who, after bringing up two reserve platoons from No.2 (which only had three, and one of these was supporting No.4!) attacked and overwhelmed it. After this the leading wave had to swing right to avoid another morass, pushing forward to reinforce the leading lines and arriving just in time to help push back a counter-attack from the direction of Polderhoek Chateau. In swinging to the right to avoid the swamp a number of men had gone so far as to become mixed up with the K.O.S.B. with whom they helped to consolidate a position north-west of Polderhoek Chateau. Others, having managed to keep their direction, penetrated further and dug in north-north-west of the chateau.

A few actually managed to reach their objective north of the chateau, but their efforts were completely in vain. Cut-off, effectively trapped in a position where re-supply, reinforcement and retirement were not even remotely possible, the slightest movement meant certain death. The chateau, or the strongly fortified position constructed from the ruins, stood on a crest; the woods to the north-west, cut down by consistent shelling, provided clear fields of fire for its machine guns across the surrounding area and the only possible passage over the Reutelbeek. Several pill-boxes, held in considerable force, stood level with the chateau, and their garrisons soon dealt with the handful of attackers who had reached their objective.

After being forced to a virtual standstill by a combination of enemy action and the ground across which the attack had been forced to take, what remained of the attacking battalions dug in on a line west of the Polderhoek Woods where, despite their depleted ranks, under constant shelling, repeated counter-attacks, rifle, machine gun and sniper fire, they held on throughout the remainder of the day.

The main strength of the counter-attacks was directed against 13th Brigade, but the Devons took full advantage of any targets presented to them. On more than one occasion Germans, advancing in large numbers, were subjected to and heavily punished by an accurately placed artillery barrage. A German prisoner said that his battalion's losses had been colossal, especially from the British barrage in the morning.

Who suffered the greater losses? German? British? Who knows? Surely, the greatest loss would be felt by those they loved and had left at home. For these the hour was fast approaching when, by receipt of an envelope, their worst fear would become reality. For them the loss immeasurable.

(Panel 38) Pte. 25662, Edward Crook, 1st Bn. (11th Foot) The Devonshire Regt.: *s.* of Thomas Crook, late of The Stagg's Head, South Molton, by his wife Mary. Killed in action 4 October 1917, in the attack between Cameron Covert and Polderhoek Chateau: Age 31. He was married to Edith Lilian Crook (Vale Cottage, Charles' Bottom, Goodleigh, Barnstaple, co. Devon). See account above.

(Panel 38) Pte. 54508, Edwin Crook, 1st Bn. (11th Foot) The Devonshire Regt.: *s.* of John Crook, of The Village, Chittlehampton, co. Devon, by his wife Emily. Killed in action 4 October 1917 in the attack between Cameron Covert and Polderhoek Chateau, during which the battalion incurred casualties of 7 officers, 104 other ranks killed and missing: Age 19. See account above.

PANEL 38 ENDS: PTE. W.F. FORD – DEVONSHIRE REGT.

PANEL 39 BEGINS: PTE. A.W. FOSTER – DEVONSHIRE REGT.

(Panel 39) Pte. 30414, Richard Eastwood Jose, 8th (Service) Bn. The Devonshire Regt.: only *s.* of Frank Jose, of East End, Redruth, Cattle Dealer, by his wife Marion, *dau.* of John Dawe, Fruit Merchant: *b.* Redruth, co. Cornwall, 8 February 1894: *educ.* Redruth College: Occupation – Farmer and Cattle Dealer:

volunteered for Active Service, joined Devonshire Yeomanry, 11 November 1915: transf'd. Devonshire Regt., and served with the Expeditionary Force in France and Flanders from 19 November 1916: wounded at the Battle of Vimy Ridge, 9 April 1917, and invalided home: rejoined his regiment September following; killed in action south-east of Zonnebeke 6 October 1917. Buried where he fell: Age 23. He *m*. United Methodist Church, Redruth, 4 September 1917; Lillian, *dau*. of William Dunstan, of Redruth.

(Panel 39) Pte. 51365, Frederick Phillips, 1st Bn. (11th Foot) The Devonshire Regt.: *yst. s.* of William Henry Phillips, Boot and Shoe Manufacturer; of 153, High Street, Harborne, by his wife S., *dau*. of George Dixon: *b*. Birmingham, 12 March 1891: *educ*. Harborne School: enlisted Devonshire Regt., 23 January 1917: served with the Expeditionary Force in France from May of the same year, and was killed in action 4 October following, in the attack on Polderhoek Chateau: Age 26. Buried there. His officer wrote, "It was on 4 October that your son was killed instantaneously by a sniper, and his loss will be greatly felt by all his comrades." He *m*., Chatham, 27 December 1915; May (387, Dudley Road, Birmingham), *dau*. of Benjamin Stockdale Humphreys. *s.p.*

(Panel 39) Pte. 33842, Arthur Henry Sanders, 1st Bn. (11th Foot) The Devonshire Regt.: eldest *s*. of the late Arthur Sanders, of Birmingham, by his wife Elsie, *dau*. of Mr (& Mrs) Ellis: Occupation – Jeweller: enlisted 27 November 1916: served with the Expeditionary Force in France and Flanders from 1 September; killed in action 30 October 1917, nr. Ypres. Buried at a point north of Gheluvelt, east of Zillebeke. An officer wrote, "He was a very good fellow in the platoon, and was missed by them all." He *m*. 25 December 1910; Agnes (180, New John Street, West Hockley), *dau*. of Edward Clifford, and had two sons; Arthur William and Bert Henry.

(Panel 39) Pte. 203456, Charles Sowden, 1st Bn. (11th Foot) The Devonshire Regt.: late of Morchard Bishop, co. Devon: *s*. of James Sowden, of Coombe Cottages, Witheridge, Crediton, co. Devon, and Sarah Maria, his spouse: and brother to Pte. 35441, E.A. Sowden, 10th Royal Warwickshire Regt., killed in action 19 April 1918; and Coy.Sergt.Major, 62379, F.A. Sowden, Machine Gun Corps (Inf.), died 31 January 1920, consequent to wounds received in action on the Western Front: enlisted Exeter. Killed in action 4 October 1917: Age 24. Remembered on the Thelbridge (St. David's) Church War Memorial (*Sowdon*). One of five brothers who served, three of whom fell.

His brother Ernest also has no known grave; he is recorded on Panel 27, Frederick is buried in Washford Pyne (St. Peter) Churchyard.

(Panel 39) Pte. 9153, Frederick Street, 8th (Service) Bn. The Devonshire Regt.: *s*. of Henry Charles Moody Street, of 18, King William Terrace, Exeter, by his marriage to the late Ann Street: and yr. brother to L/Corpl. H. Street, 7th (Queen's Own) Hussars, who died at home, 2 February 1919, aged 30 years: *b*. Exeter, *c*.1890. Killed in action 2 October 1917: Age 27. *unm*.

His brother Harold is buried in Exeter Higher Cemetery (25).

(Panel 39) Pte. 290995, Samuel Trump, 9th (Service) Bn. The Devonshire Regt.: *s*. of the late George Trump, of Cockhill, Berrynarbour, and Sarah Jane Trump (1, Shambles, Castle Street, Combe Martin, co. Devon), his wife: and brother to Pte. 2375, A. Trump, 6th Devonshire Regt., died 30 November 1916, in Turkish hands, Mesopotamia: *b*. Morthoe, 1895. Killed in action 26 October 1917: Age 22. *unm*.

His brother Albert is buried in Baghdad (North Gate) War Cemetery (XXI.P.50).

PANEL 39 ENDS: PTE. A.G. WEBB – DEVONSHIRE REGT.

PANEL 40 BEGINS: PTE. J.R. WEBB – DEVONSHIRE REGT.

(Panel 40) Pte. 8159, Stanley John Williams, 1st Bn. (11th Foot) The Devonshire Regt.: *s*. of the late A.H. (& Mrs) Williams, of Plymouth. Killed in action between Polygon Wood and Polderhoek Chateau 4 October 1917, in the attack on Cameron Covert in which the battalion sustained 250 casualties; killed, missing and wounded: Age 34.

On the night of 17 November 1917, in advance of their relief the following night, a reconnoitring party from 8th Suffolks arrived at the pill-box headquarters of 102nd Bn. Canadian Infantry requesting permission to be sent up the line. After proceeding less than 200 yards, the flying splinters of a shell-burst some distance to their left caused the Suffolks seven casualties, two fatal.

(Panel 40) Sergt. 13923, Sidney Albert Painter, 8th (Service) Bn. The Suffolk Regt.: enlisted Lowestoft. Killed in action 17 November 1917. See also Pte. F. Prigg (Below).

(Panel 40) Corpl. 240650, William Robert Leathers, 2nd Bn. (12th Foot) The Suffolk Regt.: formerly no.2551, Suffolk Regt.: *s.* of Harriet Leathers (Alms Houses, Bridewell Lane, Bury St. Edmunds): and brother to Pte. 240337, J.C. Leathers, 1/5th Battn. Suffolk Regt., died in Egypt, 30 November 1917, of wounds: enlisted Bury St. Edmunds. Killed in action 27 September 1917: Age 34. He was married to Alice M. King, *née* Leathers (7, Church Walks, Bury St. Edmunds).

His brother James is buried in Kantara War Memorial Cemetery (F.180).

(Panel 40) L/Corpl. 201461, Ernest Catchpole, 1/4th Bn. The Suffolk Regt. (T.F.): *s.* of the late John Catchpole, of Elm Farm, Hessett, by his wife Isabella, *née* Groom: *b.* Hessett, 23 November 1878: *educ.* Hessett School: enlisted 1 April 1916: served with the Expeditionary Force in France and Flanders from 10 August, and was killed in action 26 September 1917. His Commanding Officer wrote, "He was killed by a shell as he was advancing to the attack with his Lewis gun team, and I shall miss him very much, for I have known him now for many months, and he has always done most gallant work in the company. He was previously one of my stretcher-bearers, and I have always found him working most gallantly under difficult circumstances. Personally, and on behalf of all my company, I offer you my sincere sympathy in your sad loss.": Age 38. *unm.*

(Panel 40) L/Corpl. 12164, Albert Fenn, 2nd Bn. (12th Foot) The Suffolk Regt.: *s.* of W. (& Annie) Fenn, King's Yard, York Terrace, Exning, Newmarket: and brother to Corpl. 9806, L. Fenn, 2nd Bedfordshire Regt., killed in action 8 November 1914, aged 21 years; and Sergt. 9668, F. Fenn, 71st Bde., Royal Field Artillery, died 7 August 1918, of wounds, aged 28 years: *b.* Parish of St. Martin, Exning, co. Suffolk: enlisted Newmarket. Killed in action 26 September 1917: Age 19. One of three brothers who fell.

His brother Leonard also has no known grave; he is commemorated on the Ploegsteert Memorial (Panel 4), Fred is buried in Aubigny Communal Cemetery Extension (IV.J.35).

(Panel 40) Pte. 290177, Frederick John Baldry, 11th (Service) Bn. (Cambridgeshire) The Suffolk Regt.: formerly no.3017, Suffolk Regt.: *s.* of Frederick J. Baldry, of 93, Stanley Street, Lowestoft, co. Suffolk, by his wife Hannah: and brother to L/Corpl. 20048, H.W. Baldry, 7th King's Shropshire Light Infantry, killed in action, 3 April 1916, and L/Corpl. 12490, T.E. Baldry, 9th Suffolk Regt., died of wounds, 14 September 1916: enlisted Bury St. Edmunds. Killed in action 25 October 1917: Age 33. Remembered with pride on Lowestoft (St. Margaret's) Church Roll of Honour. He leaves a wife Elizabeth Ann Baldry (3, Minden Road, Lowestoft). One of three brothers who fell.

His brother Henry also has no known grave, he is commemorated on the Ypres (Menin Gate) Memorial (Panel 47); Thomas is buried in La Neuville British Cemetery, Corbie (II.D.45).

(Panel 40) Pte. 9775, Alexander Dagless, 2nd Bn. (12th Foot) The Suffolk Regt.: *s.* of John Dagless, of Queen's Square, Attleborough, co. Norfolk, by his wife Florence: and brother to Pte. 242457, P. Dagless, 7th Duke of Wellington's Regt., died of wounds, 25 April 1918: *b.* Tottington, co. Norfolk: enlisted Norwich. Killed in action 27 September 1917: Age 19. Remembered on Attleborough War Memorial.

His brother Philip is buried in Grootebeek British Cemetery (A.10).

(Panel 40) Pte. 202505, James Edward Libretto, 4th Bn. The Suffolk Regt. (T.F.): *s.* of Luigi Libretto, of 14, Hawthorn Grove, Penge, London, S.E., by his wife Polly: and elder brother to Pte. L/6220, C.P. Libretto, 1st Queen's (Royal West Surrey Regt.), who fell at the First Battle of Ypres 31 October 1914: *b.* The Minories, London: enlisted Maidstone, co. Kent. Killed in action 26 September 1917, at the Third Battle of Ypres: Age 30. He was married to Alice Gertrude Libretto (65, Ridsdale Road, Anerley, London, S.E.). (*IWGC record 3 brothers fell*)

His brother Charles also has no known grave; he is commemorated on the Ypres (Menin Gate) Memorial (Panel 13).

(Panel 40) Pte. 32721, James Fulton Park, Signalling Section, 1/4th Bn. The Suffolk Regt. (T.F.): *yst. s.* of the late George Park, of Birbank Cottage, Mount Annan, Annan, co. Dumfries, by his wife Elizabeth (139, Westbrook Street, Bolton, co. Lancaster), *dau.* of James Fulton, of Eccles, nr. Manchester: *b.* Bolton, co. Lancaster, 5 October 1883: *educ.* Bolton Council School: Occupation – Male Nurse; attd. Male Nursing Association, 10, Thayer Street, Manchester Square, London, W.: member Royal Army Medical Corps, 1904-08: joined Suffolk Regt., 10 June 1916: served with the Expeditionary Force in France and Flanders from 31 May 1917, and was killed in action at Ypres, 26 September following. Buried in Polygon Wood Military Cemetery. Lieut. F.W. Woodcock wrote, "I understand he was close to his Commanding Officer when a shell burst nearby, and a piece struck him in the head, death being instantaneous. I am the Signalling Officer, and have known your husband for several months. He was a good signaller and a brave fellow, and I feel his loss keenly, as do all his friends in this section," and Lieut. K.H. Studdon, "He was a good soldier, and we shall miss him very much." The Secretary of the Male Nursing Association also wrote, "He was equally liked by one and all alike for his unassuming ways and manly character. I did my utmost to persuade him to stay with us when we still had unmarried men on the staff and no ties to prevent them going first, but he said he felt it his duty to go. He was one of those who put his country first in her hour of need.": Age 33. He *m.* West Ham, London, E., 1909; Esther Allen (22, Campsbourne Road, Hornsey, London, N.), *dau.* of William Chambers, and had two *daus.*; Elizabeth Helen, *b.* 1910 and Margaret Amy, *b.* 1911.

(Panel 40) Pte. 14109, Frederick Prigg, 'A' Coy., 8th (Service) Bn. The Suffolk Regt.: *s.* of William Prigg, of Moulton, Newmarket, co. Suffolk, by his wife Alice: enlisted Newmarket. Killed in action 17 November 1917: Age 28. See also Sergt. S.A. Painter (above).

(Panel 40) Pte. 200351, Harry Rumsey, 4th Bn. The Suffolk Regt. (T.F.): *s.* of the late George Rumsey, by his wife Sarah Ann (The Mill, Brundish, co. Sufolk): and elder brother to L/Corpl. 47386, A.G. Rumsey, 26th Royal Fusiliers, died of wounds, 28 September 1917; and Pte. 27932, F. Rumsey, 1st Essex Regt., killed in action, 9 December 1916: *b.* Brundish: enlisted Framlingham. Killed in action 27 September 1917: Age 26.

His brother Albert is buried in Godewaersvelde British Cemetery (I.J.15); Frederick has no known grave, he is commemorated on the Thiepval Memorial (Pier & Face 10D).

(Panel 40) Pte. 41824, Percy Edward Shelbourne, 'B' Coy., 4th Bn. The Suffolk Regt. (T.F.): *s.* of the late George Shelbourne, Land Surveyor; by his wife Selina, *dau.* of Edward Throsby, of Lincoln: *b.* Ipswich, co. Suffolk, 16 October 1882: *educ.* there: Occupation – Sub-Postmaster, Grocer and Draper: joined Suffolk Regt., 22 November 1916: served with the Expeditionary Force in France and Flanders from March 1917; killed in action at Passchendaele 20 November following: Buried there: Age 35. His Commanding Officer wrote, "He had not been very long in my company, but long enough to make himself very popular with his comrades. His loss is deeply felt both by me and the rest of the company." A member of the Livermere Voluntary Aid Detachment, co. Suffolk (No.9), he was a regular attendant at Ampton (Bury St. Edmunds) Hospital on the arrival of convoys of wounded. In the county Red Cross competitions held previous to the outbreak of war, he was always one of those selected to represent the detachment in the competing squads. He held the Proficiency Medal for First Aid. He *m.* Ixworth Parish Church, co. Suffolk, 21 November 1907; Florence (Post Office, Pakenham, Bury St. Edmunds), *dau.* of Alfred Taylor, and had three children; Brenda Vera, *b.* 21 November 1908, Edward Percy, *b.* 17 November 1912 and Freda Grace, *b.* 4 May 1914.

PANEL 40 ENDS: PTE. A.G.W. TAPLIN – SUFFOLK REGT.

PANEL 41 BEGINS: PTE. C. TAYLOR – SUFFOLK REGT.

(Panel 41) Capt. Frederick Charles Humphreys, M.C., 8th (Service) Bn. The Prince Albert's (Somerset Light Infantry): *s.* of Frederick L. Humphreys, of 13, Rotherfield Avenue, Hastings, co. Sussex; late of Monte Video, Uruguay, South America, and Mrs Humphreys (late of Longer House, Rye, co. Sussex):

and elder brother to Pte. 252124, G.H. Humphreys, 3rd London Regt. (Royal Fusiliers), killed in action, 8 March 1918: *educ.* Charterhouse. Killed in action 4 October 1917; Broodseinde: Age 37. One of two brothers who fell.

His brother Guy is buried in Roclincourt Military Cemetery (V.A.23).

(Panel 41) 2nd Lieut. Robert William Diggory Maddever, 4th Bn. The Prince Albert's (Somerset Light Infantry), (T.F.): only *s.* of the late William Maddever, by his wife Margaret (15, Duke Street, St. Stephen's-by-Launceston), *dau.* of the late Samuel Tonkin: *b.* Launceston, co. Cornwall, 25 September 1893: *educ.* Horwell Grammar School, and Camelford Grammar School: Occupation – School Teacher: volunteered for Active Service, joined Cornwall Territorials, 24 April 1915; gained rapid promotion, and was made Q.M.-Sergt., 16 December 1915: obtained a commission; gazetted 2nd Lieut., Somerset Light Infantry, 20 July 1917: served with the Expeditionary Force in France and Flanders from 10 September following, and died nr. Ypres 22 October 1917, of wounds received in action the same day. Buried in Sanctuary Wood. Col. Bellew wrote, "Your son had only been with the battalion a short time, but he shaped well, and would have made a good officer. He was a good athlete, popular with his brother officers, and respected by his men," and 2nd Lieut. V.C. Robinson, "He had come to be liked by all of us, and I can assure you that we feel his loss very severely. The fact, however, that your son did his duty so well under unusually trying and dangerous conditions will, I hope, afford you some small measure of consolation in your sorrow." 2nd Lieut. Maddever was a keen athlete, and associated with the Launceston Football, Cricket, Tennis and Bowling Clubs: Age 24. *unm.*

(Panel 41) 2nd Lieut. John Geoffrey Smerdon, 3rd (Reserve) Bn. The Prince Albert's (Somerset Light Infantry) attd. 2/5th Bn. Lancashire Fusiliers (T.F.): *yr. s.* of William Richard Smerdon, of Upcott, Bishop's Hull, Taunton, co. Somerset, Yeoman, by his wife Marian Edith, *dau.* of Thomas Slocombe Hall: *b.* Spriddlestone Barton, Plymstock, co. Devon, 14 April 1893: *educ.* Huish Grammar School, Taunton: joined West Somerset Yeomanry, May 1909; retired after four years' service: after the outbreak of war, rejoined as Sergt., September 1914; apptd. Instructor, Yeomanry Recruits: served with the Expeditionary Force in France and Flanders from 22 September 1916; transf'd. Somerset Light Infantry: took part in the Battle of the Somme: returned to England, 14 January 1917, and applied for a commission: gazetted 2nd Lieut., 3rd Somerset Light Infantry, June following: rejoined his regiment in France, August 1917: temporarily attd. 2/5th Lancashire Fusiliers, and was killed in action 20 September 1917, at the Battle of the Menin Road, while in temporary command of his company. Buried where he fell: Age 24. *unm.*

(Panel 41) 2nd Lieut. Henry James Smith, 8th (Service) Bn. The Prince Albert's (Somerset Light Infantry): *s.* of the late A.H.R. Smith, by his wife Hannah. Shot down and killed at the Battle of Broodseinde Ridge, 4 October 1917, while gallantly leading two Lewis-gun teams and a party of twenty men in a second attack on a strong-point in the vicinity of Jute Cotts: Age 20. *unm.*

(Panel 41) Sergt. 34888, George William Harding, 6th (Service) Bn. The Prince Albert's (Somerset Light Infantry): *yst. s.* of George Harding, Mason; of Pitway Hill, South Petherton, co. Somerset, by his wife Leah: *b.* South Petherton, 5 April 1892: *educ.* Boys' Council School, there: joined Territorial Force; mobilised on the outbreak of war, August 1914: served with the Indian Expeditionary Force (India): returned to England and, after a month's leave, proceeded to France; served with the Expeditionary Force there, and was killed in action 17 December 1917. An officer wrote, "Knowing Sergt. Harding so well, as he was my Platoon Sergt., his loss from a personal point of view alone has come as a great blow to me; moreover, ever since he joined the battalion he has been one of our most capable and trusted N.C.O.'s. He was always so well conducted, and his cheerful disposition stamped him as one of the best N.C.O.'s of his rank.": Age 25. *unm.* (*IWGC record 16 December, age 26*)

(Panel 41) Pte. 13773, Thomas George Bessant, 1st Bn. (13th Foot) The Prince Albert's (Somerset Light Infantry): *s.* of George Bessant, of 31, Brithweunydd Road, Trealaw, Dinas (Rhondda), co. Glamorgan, by his wife Ann: and *yr.* brother to Coy.Sergt.Major 15892, B. Bessant, 10th Battn. The Welch Regt., who fell two months previously to the day: *b.* Trealaw, 1898: enlisted Tonypandy. Killed in action 4 October 1917: Age 19.

His brother Benjamin also has no known grave; he is commemorated on the Ypres (Menin Gate) Memorial (Panel 37).

Under cover of darkness, 5 October 1917, the remnants of 8th Somerset Light Infantry, 63rd Brigade – after losing 3 officers killed, 3 wounded; 27 other ranks killed, 74 wounded and 12 missing (of whom all but one were later added to the number of killed) in the previous day's fighting before Broodseinde – were withdrawn from the line and transported by bus to Fermoy Farm for a few days well-earned rest from whence (after four days) the Somersets returned to the same sector and took over their old line of trenches, including No.4 Post; the most advanced of a number of posts previously dug by the battalion in front of the main line and less than thirty yards from the foremost German post, which was higher than No.4 but hidden from it by the bank of a cutting.

The positioning of No.4 was designed to deny the enemy the opportunity of launching a sudden attack on the front line or to come over at night into the British side of the ridge; its garrison of bombers and riflemen ordered to hold out at all costs until support came from the front line.

At 10.45pm, 14 October, the practicality of these orders were swept aside when, under cover of darkness, and assisted by a thick ground mist over the wet terrain and the smoke and confusion caused by a number of stick-grenades thrown into Post No.4, the enemy made a sudden attack on the British trenches. Further aided by the broken nature of the ground beyond No.4, the Germans rapidly advanced across the remaining twenty or so yards toward the British front line only to be halted in their tracks by concentrated Lewis-gun and rifle fire.

Wearing no greatcoats or equipment and armed only with bombs and revolvers, the attacking enemy troops, about fifty in number, had quickly surrounded the post. Inside all was confusion, thick mud clogged the feet of the garrison making rapid movement impossible; some had been wounded by the bombs, some killed, the remainder held their ground fighting gallantly to the last. When all the post had been put out of action, the Germans jumped in and, with their revolvers, killed all the wounded but one who, feigning death, managed afterwards to crawl back and give details of what had happened.

On the following afternoon (15th) the troops in the front line had the satisfaction of watching the havoc created by the 'Heavies' amongst the enemy's forward positions. The great shells blew posts and emplacements to pieces, and trench traverses, debris, and the bodies of mangled Germans shot up into the air to the delight of the Somerset men who had suffered at the hands of the enemy. It is admitted that all war is horrible, but it is necessary. The killing of the wounded in No.4 Post was the work of savages not soldiers.

(Panel 41) Pte. 203349, William Fern Stanley Branch, 8th (Service) Bn. The Prince Albert's (Somerset Light Infantry): *s.* of E.C. (& Mary J.) Branch, of Roseland Nursery, Swainswick, Bath: enlisted Bath. Killed in action on the night of 14-15 October 1917: Age 25.

(Panel 41) Pte. 203369, Frederick Callaway, 8th (Service) Bn. The Prince Albert's (Somerset Light Infantry): late of Winsford, co. Somerset: elder brother to Pte. 29236, A. Callaway, Royal Warwickshire Regt., who fell 17 August 1917: enlisted Taunton. Killed in action 4 October 1917: Age 32. All correspondence to be addressed c/o Miss Florence Callaway (2, Council Cottage, Winsford, nr. Taunton, co. Somerset).

His brother Archie also has no known grave; he is recorded on Panel 25.

PANEL 41 ENDS: PTE. W. LEWIS – SOMERSET LIGHT INFANTRY

PANEL 42 BEGINS: PTE. H. LITTLE – SOMERSET LIGHT INFANTRY

(Panel 42) Pte. 28283, Reginald Miles, 8th (Service) Bn. The Prince Albert's (Somerset Light Infantry): formerly no.2566, Bedfordshire Yeomanry: *b.* Wicken, co. Northampton: enlisted Leighton Buzzard, co. Bedford. Killed on the night of 14-15 October 1917. See Pte. W.F.S. Branch (Panel 41).

(Panel 42) Pte. 28465, Edwin Sanders, 8th (Service) Bn. The Prince Albert's (Somerset Light Infantry): *s*. of David Gillespie Sanders, of The Cottage, Bickleigh Court, Tiverton, co. Devon, by his wife Emily: *b*. West Worlington, co. Devon, *c*.1898: enlisted Tiverton. Killed on the night of 14-15 October 1917: Age 19. See Pte. W.F.S. Branch (Panel 41).

(Panel 42) Pte. 235056, Alan Tilbury, 8th (Service) Bn. The Prince Albert's (Somerset Light Infantry): formerly no.8096, London Regt.: *s*. of the late William Tilbury, of Chidbolton, co. Hants: and brother to Pte. 3575, L. Tilbury, 2/4th Dorsetshire Regt., died 16 December 1916, aged 38 years: *b*. Chidbolton: enlisted Purley, co. Surrey. Killed in action 4 October 1917: Age 36. He leaves a widow, Grace A. Tilbury (50, Willow Vale, Shepherd's Bush, London), and children.

Although buried at the time, his brother Lionel is commemorated on the Kirkee 1914-1918 Memorial (Face D), which stands within Kirkee War Cemetery (created to receive Second World War graves from parts of western and central India where their permanent maintenance could not be assured). The memorial commemorates over 1,800 servicemen who died in India during the First World War, buried in civil and cantonment cemeteries in India and Pakistan, whose graves can no longer be properly maintained. This total includes the names of 629 servicemen whose remains were brought from Bombay (Sewri) Cemetery for re-interment there in 1960. On the same memorial are commemorated almost 200 East and West African servicemen who died in non-operational zones in India in the Second World War, and whose graves either cannot be located or are so situated that maintenance is not possible.

(Panel 42) Pte. 28491, Albert Edward Webber, 8th (Service) Bn. The Prince Albert's (Somerset Light Infantry): *b*. Bath, *c*.1898. Killed on the night of 14-15 October 1917: Age 19. See Pte. W.F.S. Branch (Panel 41).

(Panel 42) Pte. 30117, Percy Edwin Wide, 1st Bn. (13th Foot) The Prince Albert's (Somerset Light Infantry): formerly no.27199, Duke of Cornwall's Light Infantry: *s*. of Mr (& Mrs) Wide, of Hemyock, co. Devon: and brother to Pte. G/17914, W.J. Wide, 6th Queen's Own (Royal West Kent Regt.), died of wounds, 5 December 1917: enlisted Tiverton. Killed in action 4 October 1917

His brother Wilfred also has no known grave; he is commemorated on the Cambrai Memorial (Panel 8).

(Panel 42) Pte. 28492, Frederick Richard Wilsher, 8th (Service) Bn. The Prince Albert's (Somerset Light Infantry): *s*. of Richard Wilsher, of 67, Aubrey Road, Chessells, Bedminster, Bristol, by his wife Elizabeth: *b*. Bedminster, *c*.1898: enlisted Bristol. Killed on the night of 14-15 October 1917: Age 19. See Pte. W.F.S. Branch (Panel 41).

(Panel 42) Pte. 28498, Arthur John Young, 8th (Service) Bn. The Prince Albert's (Somerset Light Infantry): *s*. of the late John Thomas Young, of Sturminster Marshall, Wimborne, co. Dorset: *b*. Sturminster Marshall, *c*.1898: enlisted Dorchester. Killed on the night of 14-15 October 1917: Age 19. See Pte. W.F.S. Branch (Panel 41).

(Panel 42) Major Ernest Walling, M.C., 7th Bn. (Leeds Rifles) The Prince of Wales's Own (West Yorkshire Regt.), (T.F.): eldest *s*. of George Walling, of 'Ferncliffe,' Ingleton, co. York, by his wife Margaret Ann: *educ*. Ingleton where, as a scholar of outstanding ability, he obtained a Minor County Scholarship to Giggleswick Grammar School where he passed his Matriculation (1st Division) and took a Major County Scholarship and Natural Science Exhibition at Magdalen College, Oxford: after graduating went as a Master to Dulwich, Oxford High School, Sheffield Grammar School, and Leeds Grammar School where he was Senior Science Master: a pre-war member of the Territorial Force (Leeds Rifles) in which he held a commission, he was at Scarborough Camp when war broke out: proceeded to France early 1915, and was killed in action 25 April 1918, at Mont Kemmel: Age 32. Awarded the Croix de Guerre (France), Major Walling was twice Mentioned in Despatches for his services. Whilst at Oxford, Mr Walling was a member of the Hockey and Football teams; a keen golfer, he was a member of the Leeds and Ingleton clubs.

Compiled and edited by E.B. Osborne, 'The Muse In Arms,' has been described as one of several "important anthologies in the canonization of poetic taste." Including works by Siegfried Sassoon and Rupert Brooke, while omitting other major war poets such as Wilfred Owen and Isaac Rosenberg, the collection is notable for the inclusion of poems by "servicemen who perished during wartime and whose literary output was strictly limited." Published at the point in the war where there was a shift from "patriotism and romanticism" to a more realistic verse, reflecting the "brutal reality of trench warfare," 'The Muse In Arms' answered "a public demand, particularly strong during the period of the great battles of 1915-17, for poetry from the trenches." The introduction by Osborne, described as articulating the "appallingly anachronistic concept of war as a game," has been criticised for using poetry to locate the war "within a spiritual landscape that makes mystical the English countryside by endowing it with heroic virtues."

One might easily write courageously of dying and play with fancies of what may happen after death if, writing as a distant onlooker and in no danger, one merely dramatised the thoughts and emotions of the men who were in the battle lines; but the strength and glory of these soldier poets is that they wrote in the heart of darkness, that the terrors they clothed in beauty were storming round about them, that they were fronting the bitter death they were doomed to die and welcomed in their songs, and justified in action the highest and proudest of their words. They could look forward without a tremor, and if they could not always glance back without regret it was because the sacrifice they were making was a very real one – they were all young, life was sweet to them and had been rich in promise; yet they had it in them to subdue themselves and trample their regrets unflinchingly underfoot, upheld by the faith that they gave their lives that the world might remain worth living in for the rest of us.

To My People Before The Great Offensive

If then, amidst some millions more, this heart
Should cease to beat,

Mourn not for me too sadly; I have been
For months of an exalted life, a King:
Peer for these months of those whose graves grow green
Where'er the borders of our Empire fling
Their mighty arms. And if the crown is death,
Death while I'm fighting for my home and king,
Thank God the son who drew from you his breath
To death could bring. .....

..... A wooden cross the clay that once was I
Has ta'en its ancient earthy form anew,
But listen to the wind that hurries by
To all the song of Life for tones you knew:
For in the voice of birds, the scent of flowers,
The evening silence and the falling dew,
Through every throbbing pulse of nature's power,
I'll speak to you.

Capt. E.F. Wilkinson, M.C.

(Panel 42) Capt. Eric Fitzwater Wilkinson, M.C., 'A' Coy., 8th Bn. (Leeds Rifles) The Prince of Wales's Own (West Yorkshire Regt.), (T.F.): *s.* of Herbert Ashburn Wilkinson, of Nethergrove, Portesham, Weymouth, co. Dorset, by his wife Mary E.: *educ.* Dorchester Grammar School; Ilkley Grammar School from whence he won a scholarship (Engineering) to Leeds University; member of the O.T.C.: intermediate to his studies was Junior Schoolmaster, Ilkley Grammar, and had just passed his qualifying examination with honours (B.A., London) when the outbreak of war put an end to his studies: obtained a commission, 2nd Lieut. (Leeds Rifles) and proceeded to France April 1915, where he took part in much hard fighting in the Ypres trenches: awarded the Military Cross for bringing in wounded under fire; was three times wounded (once gas); appointed Town Major, Varennes (1916), and promoted Capt. Killed in action, 9 October 1917, 'very gallantly leading his company in the attack on Passchendaele Ridge.'

In a letter written to his mother on the eve of his death he said that apart from "…a shrinking of the nerves, which I always have to conquer, I can honestly say that I have not the slightest fear of death in me, which makes it vastly easier." For his services in the Great War he was Mentioned in Despatches by F.M. Sir Douglas Haig: Age 26. One of the lesser known 'war poets' two of his poems were included in the anthology 'The Muse In Arms' (1917).

> *England Be Greater Because We Have Died;*
> *What End Can Be Finer Than This? E.F.W.*

(Panel 42) Lieut. Andrew John Hay Hobson, 8th Bn. (Leeds Rifles) The Prince of Wales's Own (West Yorkshire Regt.), (T.F.): eldest *survg. s.* of the late Rev. John Philip Hobson, M.A., of Legbourne Vicarage, Louth, co. Lincoln, by his wife Annie, *dau.* of the late Canon Miller, D.D.: *b.* Upper Holloway, London, N., 26 November 1891: *educ.* Bedford Grammar School, and Leeds Grammar School: went to Canada, March 1912, took employ on the staff of the Canadian Pacific Railway: enlisted 27th Battn. (Winnipeg Regt.), Canadian Expeditionary Force, August 1914: came to England, June 1915, with 2nd Canadian Contingent: gazetted 2nd Lieut., West York Regt., 31 August following; promoted Lieut., 1 June 1916: served with the Expeditionary Force in France and Flanders from 22 May 1916: gassed and wounded, 1 July 1916, at Thiepval; repatriated home: returned to France the following November, and was killed in action 9 October 1917. Buried on the Passchendaele Ridge. His Commanding Officer wrote, "He will be a great loss to the battalion, and I fear we shall not find anyone as good to take his place; always quiet and unassuming, he did his work in the most thorough manner possible. He was killed by an enemy sniper, while endeavouring to find the best way to get his men forward." Captain of his School Football XV; he won several races in the school sports, and was a qualified Wireless Operator: Age 25. *unm.*

(Panel 42) 2nd Lieut. Norman William Beech, D.C.M., 5th Bn. The Prince of Wales's Own (West Yorkshire Regt.), (T.F.): *s.* of William Beech, of 65, Louis Street, Leeds, Commercial Traveller, by his wife Eliza, *dau.* of James Nixon: *b.* Weaste, Manchester, 10 February 1895: *educ.* Harrogate: Occupation – Apprentice Outfitter; Messrs Allen and Sons, Harrogate: joined Territorials, September 1914, Pte.: served with the Expeditionary Force in France and Flanders from April 1915: given a commission In the Field, 8 October 1916, and was killed in action at Passchendaele, 9 October 1917. His Commanding Officer wrote, "I had a very great regard for your boy, and he had the confidence and affection of his men to a very marked degree, and that is everything. It was a sad day for the battalion, though it is some consolation to know that the battalion did splendidly, and gained a very great deal of praise for the way in which they fought against heavy odds. That your boy played his full share I know full well. He was full of pluck, and quiet courage, and we in the battalion will all feel his loss very keenly. I hope that the knowledge that his was a particularly fine career, in rising from the ranks, and winning his decoration so gallantly, and that he did his duty out there more than well for so many months, will prove some small consolation to you in your sorrow." And another officer, "I had a great admiration for his wonderful courage and cheerfulness in adverse times." Awarded the D.C.M. for bravery in the field: Age 22. *unm.*

(Panel 42) 2nd Lieut. John Granville Berry, M.C., 2nd Bn. (14th Foot) The Prince of Wales's Own (West Yorkshire Regt.): *s.* of W.N. (& E.A.) Berry, of 'Hawthorn House,' Earby, Colne, co. Lancaster: *educ.* Skipton Grammar School: reported missing 16 August 1917: Age 20. Lieut.Col. Jefferies, in a letter to Mr Berry, wrote, "He was one of my very best and trustworthy officers. He was commanding a company and would have been a Captain had he remained with the Bn. I always knew that when he undertook a job that it would be carried out to the letter, and this is one of the very highest recommendations it is possible to give to a soldier. The Regiment could ill afford to lose him, as officers of his type are far from being common." Awarded the Military Cross for "gallantry and devotion to duty in taking command of his Company when his Company Commander had become a casualty, and leading them for two days during which time he showed most remarkable initiative and determination. He attained all his objectives in the face of heavy fire, and was repeatedly in the fore in repelling counter-attacks. His personal gallantry won the admiration of all ranks."

(Panel 42) 2nd Lieut. Frank Hubert Gill, 2nd Bn. (14th Foot) The Prince of Wales's Own (West Yorkshire Regt.): *yst. s.* of John Gill, of 'Braeside,' Raikes Road, Skipton, co. York; formerly of Park Avenue, by his wife Jane: *educ.* Water Street Wesleyan Higher Grade School, and Ermysted's Grammar School. On the outbreak of war, August 1914, he relinquished a commission in the Skipton O.T.C. and joined 1/6th Duke of Wellington's Regt. as Private that he might proceed to the front without delay: subsequently earned a commission from the ranks and returned to England for training early 1917: returned to France attd. West Yorkshire Regt. (July), and was killed in action 16 August 1917: Age 23. He was married to Leah Adams, *née* Gill (Carleton Terrace, Skipton).

(Panel 42) 2nd Lieut. Ralf Leslie Mackridge, 4th (Reserve) attd. 1st Bn. (4th Foot) The Prince of Wales's Own (West Yorkshire Regt.): elder *s.* of Thomas Mackridge, of 'Charnwood,' Wombwell, co. York, by his wife Clara: *b.* Barnsley, 21 March 1898: *educ.* Ilkley Grammar School: was engaged in Farming: enlisted Cameron Highlanders, 19 May 1916: served with the Expeditionary Force in France and Flanders from 4 August following: saw much severe fighting on the Somme that year, and took part in the Battle of Arras, 9 April 1917: returned to England, August following, to train for a commission: gazetted 2nd Lieut., West Yorkshire Regt., 30 January 1918: joined his regiment in France, 4 April, and was killed in action during a counter-attack nr. Zillebeke, 26 April following. His Officer Commanding, Lieut.Col. D.L. Weir, wrote, "I can hardly let you know how much we all feel the loss of so gallant a young officer, whose military career has so suddenly been brought to a close," and his Commanding Officer, Capt. C.E. Peberdy, "I was very sorry to lose him. He was a very good officer, whom everyone admired, and showed an admirable example, both under fire and at all times.": Age 20. *unm.* Dedicated – "In Remembrance Of Those Who Enlisted From This Place, Most Of Whom Went Overseas To Fight For Their King And Country, 1914-1918" – 2nd Lieut. Mackridge is remembered on Hickleton War Memorial; also Wombwell (St. Mary's Church) Roll Of Honour.

(Panel 42) Sergt. 200847, George Herd, 1/5th Bn. The Prince of Wales's Own (West Yorkshire Regt.), (T.F.): *s.* of Peter Herd, of 'Dunira,' Otley Road, Harrogate, Manager of a Clothing Factory, by his wife Mary Russell, *dau.* of Edward Stokoe: *b.* Newcastle-on-Tyne, 2 October 1893: *educ.* Bilton Grange School, Harrogate: subsequently apprentice Draper, Messrs Shaw & Co., James' Street, Harrogate; thereafter employee to Messrs William Greensmith and Sons Ltd., Hosiers, 8, James Street, Harrogate: joined West Yorkshire Regt. 9 November 1914: served with the Expeditionary Force in France and Flanders from 15 April 1915. Reported missing after the fighting at Wytschaete, 25 April 1918, and is now assumed to have been killed in action on that date. Col. William Oddie wrote, "He was with his company in the front line on 25 April, and as not a man returned from the front line at the end of the day's fighting there is no information to work upon," and a letter written on behalf of the Earl of Lucan stated, "We have, I deeply regret to state, just received the following sad news regarding your son from a returned prisoner of war… He tells us he saw him killed by a machine gun bullet, and that death was instantaneous. The casualty occurred at Kemmel.": Age 24. *unm.*

PANEL 42 ENDS: SERGT. H. HULSE – WEST YORKSHIRE REGT.

PANEL 43 BEGINS: SERGT. H. JASPER – WEST YORKSHIRE REGT.

(Panel 43) Sergt. 240100, William Jenkins, 'D' Coy., 1/6th Bn. The Prince of Wales's Own (West Yorkshire Regt.), (T.F.): late of 27, Hallams Yard, Skipton, co. York: *s.* of A. (& Mrs) Jenkins, of 4, Horner Street, Finey Berth, Pengam, Cardiff: *b.* Gloucester, *c.*1895: a pre-war Territorial, undertook Imperial service obligations on the outbreak of war, and proceeded to France April 1916. Killed instantaneously by a shell 10 October 1917: Age 22. He leaves a wife, Frances Annie Jenkins (15, Tranter Road, Sutton Estate, Saltley, Birmingham), in a letter to whom Lieut. R. McLean wrote, "I have had a great deal to do with your husband for some time and had a great respect and liking for him. He was one of the most conscientious men I ever met. He was always cheerful and his men would have followed him anywhere. Since coming out of action I have heard expressions of great regret from all the men in the company. He was a soldier and a leader of men and we feel his loss very greatly." And Capt. W. G. Tetley: "...he was one of the best and bravest sergeants that I have ever known and all the officers, N.C.O.s and men mourn his loss more than words can tell. ..Your only consolation is that he died so he lived – a soldier to his finger tips. He was doing his duty nobly when he fell."

(Panel 43) Sergt. 265346, Joseph Thomas Mitchell, 1/7th Bn. (Leeds Rifles) The Prince of Wales's Own (West Yorkshire Regt.), (T.F.): formerly of 3, Belmont Terrace, Luddenfoot, co. York: a member of Luddenfoot Congregational Church and Sunday School. He had worked as a Police Constable in Leeds; an Attendant at Menston Asylum and, prior to enlistment in August 1914, was in the employ of R. Whitworth & Co., Cooper House Mill, where he worked as a Twister: enlisted Leeds: went to France 1915, and was reported missing, presumed killed, Peter Pan Sector, Passchendaele 9 October 1917: Age 31.

(Panel 43) Corpl. 236065, Robert John Coles, 9th (Service) Bn. The Prince of Wales's Own (West Yorkshire Regt.): formerly no.2007, 1st Yorkshire Hussars: *yst. s.* of William Coles, Stationmaster; of Station House, Skipton, by his wife Eliza: and brother to Lieut. W.H. Coles, 5th Yorkshire Regt., killed in action 27 December 1917; and Spr. 386248, A.C. Coles, Royal Engineers, killed in action 15 June 1918, in Italy: *b.* Skipton, co. York: enlisted Bradford. Killed in action 9 October 1917.

His brother William is buried in Tyne Cot Cemetery (I.F.2); Arthur, Cavalletto British Cemetery (I.F.11);

(Panel 43) L/Corpl. 241813, Howard Fletcher, 1/5th Bn. The Prince of Wales's Own (West Yorkshire Regt.), (T.F.): *b.* Hyde, co. Chester: enlisted Bradford. Died 25 April 1918. *Known to be buried in Sanctuary Wood Cemetery (III.D.21).*

On 27 August 1917, the initial stages of an advance by 9th West Yorks between Langemarck and St. Julien went well, but soon ran into difficulties coming under heavy machine-gun and rifle fire from German positions in Pheasant Trench, Vancouver and Vielles Maisons. Throughout the day the Yorkshiremen could make no headway and were forced to find shelter in shell holes and anywhere else they could as the enemy poured fire into anything that dared to move above ground. During the night, under-cover of darkness, the Germans withdrew to positions in rear of those occupied throughout the day, and an informal truce took place wherein both sides scoured no man's land with stretcher parties for their wounded and dead. During the course of the day the battalion lost 66 other ranks killed; some were buried, some were not.

(Panel 43) Pte. 33083, Ernest Adamson, 9th (Service) Bn. The Prince of Wales's Own (West Yorkshire Regt.): late of Elmwood Street, Harrogate: *b.* Ripon, co. York: prior to enlistment served 15 years employ with Harrogate Corporation: enlisted Harrogate: served with the Expeditionary Force in France and Flanders, and was killed in the advance, 27 August 1917.

PANEL 43 ENDS: PTE. P. ASQUITH – WEST YORKSHIRE REGT.

PANEL 44 BEGINS: PTE. F. ATKINSON – WEST YORKSHIRE REGT.

(Panel 44) Pte. 205092, Arthur Brook, 1/5th Bn. The Prince of Wales's Own (West Yorkshire Regt.), (T.F.): 2nd *s.* of the late Walter Brook, by his wife Elizabeth Ann (6, Prospect Street, Cudworth, near Barnsley): *b.* Cudworth, co. York, 26 February 1897: *educ.* Council School, there: Occupation – Miner: joined the West Yorkshire Regt., 30 March 1917: served with the Expeditionary Force in France and Flanders, from 9 July, and was killed in action at Passchendaele Ridge, 9 October following: Age 20. *unm.*

(Panel 44) Rfn. 307726, Percival Buckle, 1/8th Bn. The Prince of Wales' Own (West Yorkshire Regt.): *s.* of Edward (& Annie) Buckle, of Tockwith, co. York: and elder brother to L/Corpl. C/13036, T. Buckle, 16th King's Royal Rifle Corps, died of wounds 29 October 1918, aged 22; and L/Corpl. 2819, L. Buckle, 1/5th West Yorkshire Regt., killed in action, 3 September 1916, aged 23: enlisted York. Killed in action 9 October 1917: Age 27.

His brother Tom is buried in Awoingt British Cemetery (II.F.19); Leonard, Connaught Cemetery, Thiepval (IV.M.1).

(Panel 44) Rfn. 307712, John William Chadwick, 1/8th Bn. (Leeds Rifles) The Prince of Wales's Own (West Yorkshire Regt.), (T.F.): *s.* of John William Chadwick, of 10, Ashberry Road, Sheffield, Coach Wheeler, by his wife Mary, *dau.* of Thomas Piggott: *b.* Sheffield, 28 July 1889: *educ.* Upperthorpe Council School: Occupation – Coach Painter: enlisted 16 February 1916: served with the Expeditionary Force in France and Flanders: took part in the operations at Ypres, where he was gassed, 26-27 July 1917: rejoined his regiment on recovery, and was killed in action at Ypres, 9 October following, while moving up to a position during an advance. Buried there. His Commanding Officer wrote, "He was personally under my command for some time previous to his death, and was chosen by me for the very hazardous duty of Observer on account of his great attention to duty and cheerfulness under any conditions, and his great coolness in face of fire. He was a good comrade, and his loss is deeply regretted by me personally, and by all his old comrades.": Age 28. *unm.*

(Panel 44) Pte. 201021, Frederick Long 'Fred' Fairburn, 1/5th Bn. The Prince of Wales's Own (West Yorkshire Regt.), (T.F.): brother to Mrs Wrightson (46, Park Street, New Park, Harrogate, co. York): served with the Expeditionary Force in France and Flanders from April 1915: seriously wounded in the first day's fighting at Thiepval, Somme, 1 July 1916 and invalided home: after recovery, returned to France January 1917, and was killed in action 9 October following, during a major attack in the Peter Pan sector, Passchendaele, Belgium.

PANEL 44 ENDS: PTE. G.S. FRANKLAND – WEST YORKSHIRE REGT.

PANEL 45 BEGINS: PTE. W. FRANKLIN – WEST YORKSHIRE REGT.

(Panel 45) Pte. 202248, George Gawthorpe, 1/5th Bn. The Prince of Wales's Own (West Yorkshire Regt.), (T.F.): *s.* of Paul Gawthorpe, of 2, New Street, Ossett, co. York, by his wife Ada: and brother to Pte. 13143, W. Gawthorpe, 34th Machine Gun Corps Inf., killed in action 21 March 1918, nr. Arras: *b.* Darton, co York, *c.*1886: enlisted Ossett. Reported missing / believed killed in action following the attack toward Poelcapelle 9 October 1917: Age 31. Recorded among the 129 names listed in the programme for the Ossett War Memorial Service of Dedication (11 November 1928); George and his brother William are commemorated on Ossett (Holy Trinity Parish) Church War Memorial (dedicated All Saints Festival, 1921): 'Remember O Lord The Brave And True Who Have Died The Death Of Honour And Are Departed In The Hope Of Resurrection To Eternal Life.'

His brother William also has no known grave, he is commemorated on the Arras Memorial (Bay 10).

(Panel 45) Pte. 36668, Henry Kilding, 9th (Service) Bn. The Prince of Wales's Own (West Yorkshire Regt.): *s.* of James Kilding, of Preston-under-Sea, by his wife Mary: and brother to Rfn. C/12880, A.C. Kilding, 21st Baqttn. King's Royal Rifle Corps, who died 17 September 1916. Killed in action 27 August 1917: Age 33.

His brother Alfred is buried in Guards Cemetery, Lesboeufs (V.G.10).

(Panel 45) Pte. 202279, Edward Levi, 1/5th Bn. The Prince of Wales's Own (West Yorkshire Regt.), (T.F.): *s.* of the late Max Levi, by his wife Betsy (13, St. Peter's Square, Leeds): and elder brother to Pte. 25660, B. Levi, 10th West Yorkshire Regt., killed in action 30 October 1916, at the Somme: *b.* Leeds, *c.*1882: enlisted York. Killed in action 9 October 1917: Age 35.

His brother Barnet is buried in Serre Road Cemetery No.2 (XXIII.E.15).

(Panel 45) Pte. 202760, Lawrence Everett Marsden, 1/5th Bn. The Prince of Wales's Own (West Yorkshire Regt.), (T.F.): formerly of 10, New Laithe Place, Rastrick: *s.* of Edwin (& Mrs) Marsden, of 77, Highbury Place, Rastrick, Brighouse, co. York: a member of Rastrick Bowling Club: employee Ashbrow Mills, Huddersfield: enlisted March 1916: wounded once. Killed in action, Peter Pan sector, Ypres, 9 October 1917: Age 25.

PANEL 45 ENDS: PTE. S. MARSDEN, M.M. – WEST YORKSHIRE REGT.

PANEL 46 BEGINS: PTE. T. MARSDEN – WEST YORKSHIRE REGT.

(Panel 46) Pte. 205307, John Thomas Midgley, 1/6th Bn. The Prince of Wales's Own (West Yorkshire Regt.), (T.F.): *s.* of the late John Midgley, of 2, Woodbine Place, Hebden Bridge, co. York, and his wife, the late Elizabeth Anwell Midgley: and elder brother to Pte. 241625, E.R. Midgley, 9th Highland Light Infantry, who fell 27 September 1917: *b.* Hebden Bridge: enlisted Halifax. Killed in action 3 May 1918: Age 34. He leaves a wife, Florence Midgley (9, Cliffe Street, Hebden Bridge).

His brother Edward also has no known grave; he is recorded on Panel 132.

(Panel 46) Pte. 205377, Joseph Thomas Robins, 1/5th Bn. The Prince of Wales's Own (West Yorkshire Regt.), (T.F.): *s.* of George Robins, of Toll Bar, Haigh, nr. Barnsley, by his wife Elizabeth Ann, *dau.* of Thomas (& Martha) Allott, of Kexbrough: *b.* Haigh, co. York, 28 February 1892: *educ.* Bretton West: Occupation – Colliery Banksman: joined West Yorkshire Regt., 22 May 1917: served with the Expeditionary Force in France from August, and was killed in action there, 9 October 1917. Buried where he fell: Age 25. He *m.* Darton, 5 April 1915; Emma (Swithen Haigh), *dau.* of Fred Miller: *s.p.*

(Panel 46) Pte. 21122 Albert Rushworth, 1/5th Bn. The Prince of Wales's Own (West Yorkshire Regt.), (T.F.): formerly of 21, Hey Street, Brighouse: brother to Pte. 45890, W. Rushworth, 13th Northumberland Fusiliers, killed in action at Ypres, 30 October 1917: enlisted October 1915. Killed in action during an enemy attack at Wytschaete 25 April 1918.

His brother Wilfred is buried in Buttes New British Cemetery, Polygon Wood (XXIII.C.1).

(Panel 46) Pte. 235563, Thomas Linden-Struth, 11th (Service) Bn. The Prince of Wales's Own (West Yorkshire Regt.): formerly no.6185, 5th Bn. Northumberland Fusiliers: *b.* Sheffield, co. York, 18 December 1898: enlisted Sheffield: served with the Expeditionary Force in France and Flanders, and was killed on the Gravenstafel Road, 29 September 1917. '*Reunited with your brother, 89 years on. Never Forgotten. 16 November 2006.*'

PANEL 46 ENDS: PTE. J. TANNEY – WEST YORKSHIRE REGT.

PANEL 47 BEGINS: PTE. A. TAYLOR – WEST YORKSHIRE REGT.

(Panel 47) Rfn. 39646, Harry Whitney, 1/8th Bn. (Leeds Rifles) The Prince of Wales's Own (West Yorkshire Regt.), (T.F.): s. of Thomas Whitney, of Rectory Lane, Nunnington, Malton, co. York, by his wife Isabella: and elder brother to Stkr. 1st Class SS111525, F.W. Whitney, HMS 'Hampshire,' R.N., one of 643 crew (and Secretary of State for War, Earl Kitchener and his staff) lost at sea when that ship hit a mine and sank, 5 June 1916, between Brough of Birsay and Marwick Head: *b.* Nunnington: enlisted Barnsley. Killed in action 9 October 1917: Age 30. He leaves a wife Charlotte Emily Whitney (Grassthorpe, Newark, co. Nottingham).

His brother Frederick is commemorated on the Portsmouth Naval Memorial (20); Earl Kitchener is commemorated on the Hollybrook Memorial, Southampton.

(Panel 47) Pte. (Siglr.) 13557, Horace Alban Wood, 10th (Service) Bn. The Prince of Wales's Own (West Yorkshire Regt.): 3rd *s.* of Alban Wood, of 37, South Beech Avenue, Starbeck, Harrogate, co. York, by his wife Mary Lavinia: and brother to Pte. 243318, A. Wood, 5th Yorkshire Regt., died of wounds 28 July 1917, and Pte. 30763, W. Wood, 1st West Yorkshire Regt., died of wounds 3 May 1918: was employee Harrogate Hotel, Starbeck: volunteered and enlisted at the outbreak of war: served with the Expeditionary Force in France and Flanders from early 1915, and was killed in action by the explosion of a shell at the Battle of Passchendaele, 15 October 1917: Age 21. *unm.* A member of the Battn Signal Section, in writing to Pte. Wood's mother, said, "It is with very great regret that the necessity has arisen for writing to you. Doubtless by this time you will have heard from official sources that your son Horace has met his death in the field. I am writing to you on behalf of the lads in the section, whose comrade Horace was, to express to you our very deepest sympathy in the awful blow which has befallen you... We have lost one of the best comrades it was possible to have – cool in danger, resourceful at all times, helping to ease the hardships which always accompany this life; in fact proving himself every day one of the best of chums… I am glad to be able to tell you that he suffered no pain, for he was killed instantly by a shell which also grievously wounded many more of the section…We are only ordinary Tommies, but we still have feelings, and I can only tell you that we shall for ever cherish his memory as a true comrade and friend. On behalf of all the boys, believe me, yours in deepest sympathy, T.K. Winfield." One of three brothers who fell.

His brother Arthur is buried in Achiet-le-Grand Communal Cemetery Extension (I.O.29). William lies in Boulogne Eastern Cemetery (IX.B.32).

(Panel 47) Capt. John Leslie Derrick 7th (Service) Bn. The East Yorkshire Regt.: only *s*. of the late Rev. John George Derrick, Chaplain to Cheltenham Union, by his wife Edith (2, Royal Crescent, Cheltenham), *dau*. of H. Rée, of 11, Lansdown Crescent, Cheltenham: *b*. Cheltenham, 4 September 1890: *educ*, Cheltenham Grammar School; Pembroke College, Oxford, where he held the Townsend Scholarship, and took Honours in Mathematical Moderations and History Finals: was some time Assistant Master, Coatham Grammar School, Redcar: volunteered 4 September 1914, joined (Pte.) Old Public School & University Battn. Royal Fusiliers: gazetted 2nd Lieut., December 1914: served with the Egyptian Expeditionary Force (Egypt), January – July 1916, thereafter transf'd. to another battalion of his regiment: served with the Expeditionary Force in France and Flanders: promoted Capt., July 1917, and was killed in action at Langemarck, nr. Ypres, 27 August following. His Commanding Officer wrote, "He joined my battalion over 18 months ago, and during that time always showed himself to be as fine an officer as any Commanding Officer could wish to have. In action he was exceptionally cool. He would go, and be followed anywhere by his men who had implicit confidence in him. I can assure you that this battalion has suffered a very great loss, and both officers and men greatly feel his death." Age 26. *unm.* (*IWGC record Panel 52-54, 6th Bn., age 27*)

(Panel 47) 2nd Lieut. Heaton Foster, 1st Bn. (15th Foot) The East Yorkshire Regt.: *s*. of the late Charles Foster, by his wife Annie ('Wyton,' Elloughton Mount, Brough, co. York), *dau*. of the late John Taylor, Solicitor, Bedford Row, London, W.C.: *b*. London, 6 February 1899: *educ*. The Old College, Windermere; Shrewsbury, and Royal Military College, Sandhurst: gazetted 2nd Lieut., 13th East Yorkshire Regt., 27 September 1917: served with the Expeditionary Force in France and Flanders from 12 October 1917, being transf'd. 1st Battn., 8 February 1918. Reported missing after the fighting at Wytschaete, nr. Kemmel, 16 April of the same year; now known to have been killed on that date: Age 19.

(Panel 47) 2nd Lieut. Arthur Charles Vaughan Smith, The East Yorkshire Regt. attd. 8th (Service) Bn. The Duke of Wellington's (West Riding Regt.): 3rd *s*. of the Rev. Walter Edmund Smith, Vicar of Andover, by his wife Margaret Rose (The Vicarage, Andover, co. Hants), *dau*. of the late Rev. Canon Vaughan, Rector of Harpenden, co. Hertford: and nephew of the Rt.Hon. J. Parker Smith, and Sir. H. Babington Smith, K.C.B.: *b*. Corton, co. Suffolk, 4 January 1893: *educ*. Hymers' College, Hull, and Denstone College: Occupation – Corn Trader: volunteered for Active Service on the outbreak of war: enlisted as Private, East Yorkshire Regt.: served in Egypt, December – March 1916, and with the Expeditionary Force in France and Flanders, March 1916 – January 1917: took part in the Battle of the Somme: given a commission, gazetted 2nd Lieut. East Yorkshire Regt. 27 June 1917, being later attd. Duke of Wellington's (West Riding Regt.): returned to France September, and was killed in action during the attack on Poelcapelle, 9 October 1917. Buried where he fell. His Colonel wrote, "Our battalion was in action before Poelcapelle, and your son was leading his platoon in an attack upon one of the enemy's strongpoints. He was leading with great gallantry, and was calling out 'Come on, 13th' when he was shot through the head by a sniper and killed instantly. I desire to express the great regret and sympathy felt by all his brother officers. We have lost a splendid officer and an excellent fellow," and a brother officer, "Knowing him so well, it comes as a great blow to me to hear that so noble a fellow has paid the supreme sacrifice. I cannot express to you how brave a fellow he was.": Age 24. *unm.*

(Panel 47) Coy.Sergt.Major 12052, Fred Healey, 8th (Service) Bn. The East Yorkshire Regt.: *s*. of the late William Henry Healey, Railway Guard; by his wife Rachael: *b*. Hull, co. York, 23 June 1888: *educ*. Sir Henry Cooper's School: Occupation – Check Clerk: enlisted 8 September 1914: served with the

Expeditionary Force in France and Flanders from 13 July 1915. Killed in action at Ypres 26 September 1917. Buried there: Age 29. An officer wrote, "Your husband was an absolutely fearless soldier, and respected by everyone in the battalion, and his example did much to hold our boys together. He was an exceptionally brave man, and died doing his duty as he would have wished. He will always be remembered by all the N.C.O.'s, officers and men as one of the bravest." He *m.* at Hull, 6 May 1915, Lily Veal, *née* Healey (since re-married), formerly of 3, Wellesley Terrace, Hessle Road, Hull (now resident at 9, Brunswick Gardens, Brunswick Avenue, Beverley Road, Hull), *dau.* of Edwin Tute.

(Panel 47) Corpl. 1288, William Duncan Dymock, 10th (Service) Bn. The East Yorkshire Regt.: *s.* of William Dymock, of 46, King's Bench St., Hull, by his wife Sarah, *dau.* of W. Parker: *b.* Hull, 10 July 1891: *educ.* Day Street Board School: employee to Messrs. Holmes & Co. Ltd., Campbell St., Hull: enlisted 24 April 1915: served with the Egyptian Expeditionary Force (Egypt) from the following November; afterwards served in France and Flanders: wounded 24 June 1916 and invalided home: sent to Rugeley Camp on recovery, being subsequently transf'd. 1st East Yorkshire Regt. in France. Killed in action nr. Ypres 4 October 1917: His Commanding Officer wrote: "He was one of the best of a splendid set of N.C.O.'s. He died a true soldier, leading his comrades in the attack. He was respected by his officers and his comrades in the ranks, and I myself feel his loss keenly.": Age 26. He *m.* at Hull, 10 July 1915, Emily (205, Alliance Avenue, Hull), eldest *dau.* of John (& Mary Jane) Blackburn, of 9, Scarborough Terrace, Marmaduke St., Hull.

(Panel 47) L/Corpl. 201107, Samuel Chapman, 1/4th Bn. The East Yorkshire Regt. (T.F.): *yr. s.* of Samuel Chapman, by his wife Rachael (34, Walkergate, Beverley, co. York), *dau.* of the late Benjamin Banham: and brother to Dmr. 240402, J. Chapman, 5th Bn. Alexandra, Princess of Wales's Own (Yorkshire Regt.), died of wounds received in action at Passchendaele, 28 October 1917: *b.* Hull, 6 March 1898: *educ.* Beverley: Occupation – Assistant Steward; S.S. 'Romeo': enlisted March 1915: served with the Expeditionary Force in France and Flanders from the following August, and was killed in action at Passchendaele 14 December 1917. His Commanding Officer wrote, "Your son was a promising non-commissioned officer, and he will be a real loss to the company.": Age 19.

His brother John is buried in Dozinghem Military Cemetery (IX.B.23).

(Panel 47) L/Corpl. 28476, George Bernard Masterman, 8th (Service) Bn. The East Yorkshire Regt.: *s.* of John Masterman, Farm Worker, of Carthagena Farm, Menethorpe, Malton, by his wife Elizabeth: and brother to Pte. 76568, J.J. Masterman, 12th Manchester Regt., who also fell: *b.* Malton, co. York, 1889: enlisted Hull. Killed in action 26 September 1917, nr. Zevencote: Age 28.

His brother John is buried in Neuvilly Communal Cemetery Extension (B.18).

(Panel 47) Pte. 40416, Albert Adams, 6th (Service) Bn. The East Yorkshire Regt.: 3rd *s.* of William Adams, Mariner; of 138, Rochester Avenue, Rochester, by his wife Alice, *dau.* of John Adams: *b.* Rochester, co. Kent, 18 September 1876: *educ.* Troy Town School there: Occupation – Licensed Victualler; licensee "The Globe & Laurel", Gillingham: joined R.E., 26 February 1917: transf'd. East Yorkshire Regt., 9 September: served with the Expeditionary Force in France and Flanders from that month, and was killed in action on the Poelcapelle Road, 2 October following: Age 41. A Freemason, he was a Member of the Royal Lodge of Antiquity, No.20, and of the Livingstone Lodge of the Royal Ancient Order of Buffaloes. He *m.* St. Margaret's Church, Rochester, 24 November 1900; Ada Caroline (formerly 105, now 126, Britton Street, Gillingham), *dau.* of George Lower, of Rochester, and had a *s.*, Albert Edney, *b.* 24 December 1908.

PANEL 47 ENDS: PTE. T. BINGE – EAST YORKSHIRE REGT.

PANEL 48 BEGINS: PTE. I. BIRD – EAST YORKSHIRE REGT.

(Panel 48) Pte. 27917, William J. Brown, 8th (Service) Bn. The East Yorkshire Regt.: formerly No.4724, Northamptonshire Regt.: *s.* of Oliver Thomas Brown, of 27, Clinton Road, Far Cotton, Northampton, by his wife Emma: and brother to Pte. 1580, H.C. Brown, Northamptonshire Yeomanry, died of appendicitis,

Cambridge Hospital, 19 May 1915, while undergoing basic training: *b.* 1898: enlisted Northamptonshire Regt., Northampton, September 1915, subsequently transf'd. East Yorkshire Regt.: served with the Expeditionary Force in France and Flanders from September 1916: took part in the fighting on the Somme and was killed in action 27 September 1917, nr. Zonnebeke, at the Third Battle of Ypres: Age 19.

His brother Herbert is buried in Towcester Road Cemetery, Northampton (273.10648).

(Panel 48) Pte. 10/879, Harry Oakden Illingworth, 10th (Service) Bn. The East Yorkshire Regt.: Signaller: *s.* of Mary Anne Illingworth (6, Lily's Terrace, Finsbury Street, Hull): *b.* Hull, co. York, 19 February 1896: *educ.* Blundell Street School: Occupation – Pork Butcher's Assistant: enlisted 6 September 1914: served with the Expeditionary Force in France and Flanders from 15 April 1916, and was killed in action, near Ypres, 26 September 1917. His Comdg. Officer wrote, "He was a brave soldier and died gallantly whilst attacking a Hun blockhouse.": Age 21. *unm.*

(Panel 48) Pte. 30656, John Jackson, 1st Bn. (15th Foot) The East Yorkshire Regt.: formerly no.20537, Yorkshire Regt. (Green Howards): *s.* of Thomas Jackson, of Appersett, Hawes, co. York, by his wife Hannah: *b.* Hawes: enlisted Leyburn. Reported wounded and missing 16 April 1918: Age 23. *unm.*

(Panel 48) Pte. 42390, Tosti Langsford, 5th Bn. The East Yorkshire Regt. (T.F.): eldest *s.* of Roger Langsford, Farmer; of Cleave, St. Dominic, co. Cornwall, by his wife Polly, *dau.* of John Matthews, of Metherill: *b.* 29 January 1897: *educ.* St. Dominic: Occupation – Horseman on his father's farm: joined Royal Field Artillery, 2 August 1916: transf'd. East Yorkshire Regt. four months later: served with the Expeditionary Force in France and Flanders from 12 January 1917: wounded July following July, hospitalised for a short time; returned to his unit on recovery and was killed in action nr. Warneton, 28 October 1917. Buried there, north-east of Armentieres. His Captain wrote, "Your son had not been with us very long, but in that time had proved himself to be a keen and willing soldier, ready to do his duty anywhere, and was killed whilst in the foremost line.: Age 20. *unm.*

(Panel 48) Pte. 220461, George Thomas Wayman, 1st Bn. (15th Foot) The East Yorkshire Regt.: formerly no.1676, Cambridgeshire Regt.: *s.* of Betsy Wayman (6, Potters Lane, Ely, co. Cambridge): and elder brother to Pte. 325302, A.W. Wayman, D.C.M., Cambridgeshire Regt, who fell 31 July 1917: enlisted Ely. Killed in action 25 April 1918: Age 23. *unm.*

His brother Alfred also has no known grave; he is commemorated on the Ypres (Menin Gate) Memorial (Panel 50).

(Panel 48) Actg. Capt. John Hislop, M.C., 8th (Service) Bn. The Bedfordshire Regt.: eldest *s.* of Hon. Major & Q.M Archibald Hislop, Bedfordshire Regt. (1861-96, & 1900-02): *b.* Grave de Leq Barracks, Jersey, 1872: joined 1st Bn. (16th Foot), June 1888, aged 15 years, 11 months; apptd. L/Corpl.: posted to the Depot, from Malta, December 1890: promoted Corpl., August 1891, posted 2nd Battn, May 1892: returned 1st Battn., promoted Sergt., February 1896, and proceeded to the East Indies: promoted Col. Sergt., April 1900, and posted home to 2nd Battn., January 1906, reverting to Sergt. by personal request, August following: promoted Col. Sergt., July 1907, and went to Gibraltar: reverted to Sergt. a second time, January 1908, and, after serving 19 years, 8 months, discharged to a pension February Following: took up residence in Ealing, gained employ in the Prison Service: rejoined Bedfordshire Regt. (Pte.) on the outbreak of war with Germany; posted to the Depot, resuming rank Sergt, 21 September 1914, posted 8th Battn. 24 September; promoted Coy.Sergt.Major, 13 October 1914: proceeded to France with his battalion, August 1915: apptd. Actg. Regtl.Sergt.Major In the Field, October following; commissioned, Temp. 2nd Lieut. 8th Battn., December 1915; promoted Temp. Lieut., January 1916; Actg. Capt., 3 April 1917. Invalided home and hospitalised in the latter part of 1916 suffering from exposure contracted in the trenches, after two months convalescent leave joined 27th Training Reserve Battn., Bedfordshire Regt. Dovercourt: returned to France, Spring 1917, and was killed instantaneously by a shell in the late evening of 22 September 1917: Age 45. His Commanding Officer, in a letter to Capt. Hislop's widow, wrote, "He was killed at the head of his company, whilst leading it to the firing line, on the night of September 22. Fighting was very heavy, and, unfortunately, it was necessary to pass through a heavily shelled area. It was when doing this that your husband and several others lost their lives. We shall all miss him very much indeed. He died grandly, nobly doing his duty to the last as a British soldier, and is now resting from his labours with the many others who have made the supreme sacrifice for their country." Awarded the Military Cross (*London Gazette*) 'For distinguished service in the field. During a heavy gas attack, carrying ammunition up to the front line and digging out two machine gunners who had been buried by a shell, all under heavy fire.' He leaves a widow and six children.

(Panel 48) 2nd Lieut. Paul Norman Jones Christie, 'C' Coy., 1/2nd Bn. (16th Foot) The Bedfordshire Regt.: *s.* of Major Octavius Francis Christie, 19th Bn. London Regt. (T.F.), Barrister, of Culver, Much Hadham, co. Hertford, by his wife Christabel Frances: *b.* St. Dunstan's Road, Fulham, London, 18 April 1898: *educ.* Eton College (1912-15), member of the O.T.C.; Royal Military Academy, Sandhurst: gazetted 2nd Lieut., posted Bedfordshire Regt., April 1917: served with the Expeditionary Force in France from 25 June following, and was killed instantaneously in the late afternoon of 9 October 1917, during a heavy bombardment of his position while directing the fire of his platoon against German positions in Gheluvelt: Age 19. Buried near Battn. Headquarters, east of Veldhoek. His Comdg. Officer, Lieut. Col. P.R. Worral, wrote, "Dear Major Christie, Words are poor consolation in times like these, but I should like to send you a few words of sympathy in your heavy blow in the hope that He may enlighten it. He was such a nice boy, so full of promise, and I thought so much of him that it is a bitter blow to me. Quiet and trustworthy, I selected him only the day before for a particularly difficult job – marching by night with a compass. Both his pals, Reynolds and Fleming, were also killed, so there is a big blank left in the battalion at the loss of these cheery boys. I asked the battalion on parade today to never forget the example set us all by this trio, and to pray for you all that He may help you to bravely bear this cruel blow. Forgive a poorly expressed line of sympathy. P.S. He is buried in our cemetery hard by a famous road – famous since 1914. I went to Holy Communion yesterday and offered up a prayer for him and his relations." And one of his men, "...I saw your son just before he was hit by the shell on the 9th. He must have been killed somewhere between 4 and 6 o'clock on that evening as I received the news of his death at 7.25pm. I saw the Sergeant who was wounded by the same shell and, from what I could make out, Paul was giving orders to fire at the Boche in Gheluvelt. He is lying near other Officers who fell in the same stunt. I am sorry to lose such a friend and at his death the 1st Bedfords lost one of their bravest Officers..."

2nd Lieut. H.H. Reynolds (killed 4 October 1917) is buried in Hooge Crater Cemetery (XVIII.A.8). 2nd Lieut. H.W. Fleming (killed 5 October 1917) has no known grave; he is commemorated below.

(Panel 48) 2nd Lieut. Joseph Cotchin, 1st Bn. (16th Foot) The Bedfordshire Regt.: eldest *s.* of Joseph Cotchin, Farm Labourer; of 79, Station Road, Ridgmont, co. Bedford, by his wife Emma, *dau.* of Alfred White: *b.* Ridgmont, *afsd.*, 12 June 1886: *educ.* there: enlisted King's Royal Rifles, 1903: served three years with the Colours; thereafter joined the Reserve, and removed to Canada: returned from the colony; on recall to the Colours on the outbreak of war: served with the Expeditionary Force in France and Flanders from 12 August 1914: twice wounded and gassed (1914-15): promoted Sergt., 20 October 1916; gazetted 2nd Lieut., 30 May 1917, transf'd. Bedfordshire Regt., and was killed in action at Ypres, 9 October following. Buried in the little Bedford Cemetery. His Colonel wrote, "I thought no end of him. Only on the morning before he was killed we did an important reconnaissance together; he was so calm and cool, and such an excellent guide. I told him afterwards how pleased I was, and that I should recommend him for the Military Cross...I fear posthumous honours are not granted, but you will know that had he lived he would have gained a cross of silver. Only three weeks ago I introduced him to the Commander-in-Chief who congratulated him on his splendid rise.": Age 31. *unm.*

(Panel 48) 2nd Lieut. Harold Winning Fleming, 1st Bn. (16th Foot) The Bedfordshire Regt.: *s.* of the late Alexander John Fleming, M.D., by his wife Lily Huthart (147, Finchley Road, Hampstead, London, N.W., formerly of 22A, Frognal, Hampstead), *dau.* of the late F.L. Brown, of Bombay: *b.* Hampstead, N.W., 25 April 1898: *educ.* St. John's House, Hampstead; was a King's Scholar, Westminster; and Royal Military College, Sandhurst: enlisted August 1916: gazetted 2nd Lieut., 1 May 1917: served with the Expeditionary Force in France and Flanders and was killed in action by a sniper at Gheluvelt, on the Ypres-Menin Road, 5 October 1917. Buried in the Bedford Cemetery, Ypres-Menin Road. His Chaplain wrote, "I frequently saw him, both in and out of the trenches, and we all liked him for his bright and happy disposition, as well as for his keenness and great efficiency. It was no secret that he was considered one of the most promising of the junior officers in the battalion." A brother officer wrote, "I am certain that at his death the 1st Bedfords lost one of its bravest officers," and another: "The other officers of his company having become casualties early in the attack (Oppy Wood, nr. Arras), this officer, 2nd Lieut. H.W. Fleming, who was in the trenches for the first time, assumed command throughout the attack, and in the subsequent tour of duty he showed coolness, gallantry and ability, and his example afforded great encouragement to his men." Mentioned in Despatches by General (now F.M.) Sir Douglas Haig, for 'gallant and distinguished service in the field' as stated above: Age 19.

(Panel 48) 2nd Lieut. George Edward Inch, 1/2nd (16th Foot) attd. 6th (Service) Bn. The Bedfordshire Regt.: s. of George Edward Inch, of 2, Charlotte Street, Bolton, co. Lancaster, by his wife Alice. Killed in action, 22 September 1917, when, on approaching the front line to relieve 6th Cheshires, the battalion came under heavy artillery fire after being observed by the enemy and lost 1 officer and 4 other ranks killed, 29 wounded (1 died the following day): Age 27. He leaves a widow, Mary Inch. See also Ptes. P.W. Marks, Elzenwalle Brasserie Cemetery (II.B.5), and J. Bancroft, Perth Cemetery (China Wall), (II.J.36).

(Panel 48) Sergt. 14298, Leonard H. Bowsher, 7th (Service) Bn. The Bedfordshire Regt.: s. of Mary Jane Bowsher (Nash Mills, Hemel Hempstead): and yr. brother to Pte. 202268, W. Bowsher, 4th Royal Welch Fusiliers, killed 15 September 1916, at the Somme: b. Abbots Langley, 1894: employee to Messrs J. Dickinson & Co., Paper Makers, Apsley End, Hemel Hempstead: enlisted Hertford: served with the Expeditionary Force in France and Flanders, and was killed in action 17 August 1917: Age 23.

His brother William also has no known grave; he is commemorated on the Thiepval Memorial, Somme (Pier & Face, 4A).

(Panel 48) Sergt. 10190, Oswald Gentle, M.M., 'A' Coy., 1st Bn. (16th Foot) The Bedfordshire Regt.: s. of George Gentle, of 64, Icknield Way, Baldock, co. Hertford, by his wife Lizzie: and yr. brother to Spr. 87799, G. Gentle, Royal Engineers, died 3 July 1916: b. Baldock: enlisted Hertford. Killed in action 4 October 1917: Age 23. unm.

His brother George is buried in Salonika (Lembet Road) Military Cemetery (188).

PANEL 48 ENDS: L/SERGT. W. PECK, D.C.M. – BEDFORDSHIRE REGT.

PANEL 49 BEGINS: CORPL. L.T. GOODWIN – BEDFORDSHIRE REGT.

(Panel 49) L/Corpl. 14919, Horace Percy Bridge, 4th (Extra Reserve) Bn. The Bedfordshire Regt.: s. of John George Bridge, of 14, High Street, Biggleswade, co. Bedford, by his wife Florence: and yr. brother to Pte. 41701, T.H. Bridge, 8th Lincolnshire Regt., killed in action, 4 October 1917: b. Cottershill, co. Stafford: enlisted Biggleswade. Killed in action 30 October 1917: Age 22. unm.

His brother Thomas also has no known grave; he is recorded on Panel 36.

(Panel 49) L/Corpl. 17273, Harry Wagstaff, 4th (Extra Reserve) Bn. The Bedfordshire Regt.: s. of Sam Wagstaff, of Canal View, Biggleswade, co. Bedford: and brother to Rfn. 3406, G. Wagstaff, Post Office Rifles, died at home, 13 December 1916, consequent to wounds received in action: b. Huntingdon: enlisted Biggleswade. Killed in action 30 October 1917.

His brother George is buried in Campton and Shefford Cemetery (E.71).

(Panel 49) Pte. 204379, Percy Daniel Ayers, 'D' Coy., 4th (Extra Reserve) Bn. The Bedfordshire Regt.: s. of the late Frederick Ayers, by his wife Mary Ann (4, Priory Terrace, Northampton), dau. of the late George Mutton: b. Northampton, 13 August 1888: educ. British School, there: Occupation – Boot Operative: enlisted 8 January 1917: served with the Expeditionary Force in France from April following; killed in action at Passchendaele, 30 October 1917: Age 29. unm.

(Panel 49) Pte. 43185, Herbert Bright, 6th (Service) Bn. The Bedfordshire Regt.: formerly no.2206, Essex Regt.: s. of Joseph (& Mrs) Bright, of 3, Copous Place, Shenfield, Brentwood, co. Essex: enlisted Brentwood. Killed by shellfire on the evening of 22 September 1917: Age 24. unm. See 2nd Lieut. G.E. Inch (Panel 48).

(Panel 48) Pte. 19278, Herbert George Clements, 2nd Bn. (16th Foot) The Bedfordshire Regt.: s. of Noah Clements, of Damask Green, Weston, Stevenage, co. Hertford, by his wife Sarah Ann: and brother to Pte. 19761, N.J. Clements, 10th Hampshire Regt., killed in action, 7 December 1915: enlisted 17 January 1915. Killed in action 26 April 1918: Age 33. In a letter to his widow, Florence May Clements (Damask Green, Weston), the Duke of Bedford wrote, "Your husband served so long under me and was so well known to me, I hope I may be allowed to express to you my sincere sympathy in the loss you have sustained. Your husband died a gallant death, giving his life in the cause of the country," and Sergt. F. Wiles: "we were all so sorry to lose him as he was a good soldier and never seemed afraid. It is a terrible war, but God knows who to take and whom to leave. I hope you will find a little comfort in knowing that your husband died fighting for the cause of justice and for King and Country." Pte. Clements was a keen cricket and football player; he leaves two children, Robert and Thomas.

His brother Noah also has no known grave; he is commemorated on the Doiran Memorial.

(Panel 48) Pte. 40875, Wilfred Dibley, 6th (Service) Bn. The Bedfordshire Regt. attd. 1st Hertfordshire Regt. (T.F.): formerly no.39410, Northamptonshire Regt.: s. of George Dibley, of Westergate Street, Aldingbourne, nr. Chichester, by his wife Charlotte: and yr. brother to Pte. G/10763, H.G. Dibley, 1st Royal West Surrey Regt., died 21 December 1916, in the Base Hospital, Rouen: enlisted Chichester. Killed in action 24 September 1917; Shrewsbury Forest sector: Age 19. (*SDGW record Hertfordshire Regt.*)

His brother Herbert is buried in St. Sever Cemetery Extension (O.III.H.6).

(Panel 49) Pte. 31888, George Hornett, 6th (Service) Bn. The Bedfordshire Regt.: s. of Mr (& Mrs) Hornett, of 3, Newgate Cottages, Sandpit Lane, St. Albans: b. St. Albans, co. Hertford, 1893: enlisted Bedford. Killed by shellfire on the evening of 22 September 1917, whilst approaching the front line: Age 24. unm. See 2nd Lieut. G.E. Inch (Panel 48).

(Panel 49) Pte. 26786, Albert Lane, 6th (Service) Bn. The Bedfordshire Regt.: s. of John Lane, of Kirkham Cottages, Dunstable Road, Toddington, co. Bedford, by his wife Minnie: b. Toddington, c.1894: enlisted Ampthill. Killed in action 22 September 1917; shellfire: Age 23. unm. See 2nd Lieut. G.E. Inch (Panel 48).

(Panel 49) Pte. 23720, Edgar Massey, 4th (Extra Reserve) Bn. The Bedfordshire Regt.: s. of Fanny Massey (4, Aspley Hill, Woburn Sands): enlisted Ampthill. Missing / believed killed in action 30 October 1917, on which date, as the battalion began their advance, at 5.50 a.m., the enemy dropped a counter barrage on the attacking troops almost before they could begin to move, causing heavy casualties and those troops who were not caught by the barrage were effectively trapped and continually sniped at as they stuck thigh deep in the mud. At the close of day the Bedfords reported 54 killed, 155 wounded, 23 missing. After a brief leave, Pte. Massey had rejoined his battalion the previous evening: Age 23. unm.

(Panel 49) Pte. 204002, Alfred George Mayes, 6th (Service) Bn. Bedfordshire Regt.: eldest s. of J. (& E.) Mayes, of 45, George Street, Wellingborough: b. Wellingborough, co. Northampton, 7 August 1888: educ. there: Occupation – Shoe Hand: enlisted 19 January 1917: served with the Expeditionary Force in France and Flanders from 15 May, and was killed in action to the east of Ypres, 25 September following: Age 29. He m. Wellingborough Congregational Church, 1 August 1914; Ethel Frances (2, Holly Gardens, Wellingborough), yst. dau. of Mr (& Mrs) Eakey.

(Panel 49) Pte. 37590, Francis John Tidmarsh, 4th (Extra Reserve) Bn. The Bedfordshire Regt.: late of Aspley Hill, Woburn Sands: s. of the late George Tidmarsh, by his wife Mary (Sutton Lodge, Cookham, co. Buckingham): b. Tetworth, co. Oxford, 1891: enlisted Luton, co. Bedford, February 1917. Reported wounded and missing in action 30 October 1917, during the battalion's attack in the vicinity of the Paddebeek: Age 26. He leaves a wife, Gladys Winifred Tidmarsh, née Phipps (Studhampton, Wallingford, co. Berks), and one child; Francis Jerrold, b. 18 April 1917. See Pte. Massey, above.

PANEL 49 ENDS: PTE. H. TITMUS – BEDFORDSHIRE REGT.

PANEL 50 BEGINS: PTE. G.T. TRUSSELL – BEDFORDSHIRE REGT.

(Panel 50) Pte. 43487, Albert Edgar Weaver, 4th (Extra Reserve) Bn. The Bedfordshire Regt.: 3rd *s.* of the late Thomas Weaver, by his wife Mary (233, Slade Road, Gravelly Hill, Birmingham), *dau.* of Francis Brayne, of Wellington, co. Salop: *b.* Ashton, co. Warwick, 29 December 1890: *educ.* Higher Elementary School, there: was employed by a firm of Birmingham Stockbrokers: enlisted 30 September 1916: served with the Expeditionary Force in France and Flanders from September 1917, and was killed in action at Passchendaele 30 October following. A comrade wrote: "No better fellow ever trod the soil of France or Belgium.": Age 26. *unm.*

(Panel 50) Lieut.Col. Philip Eric Bent, V.C., D.S.O., 9th (Service) Bn. The Leicestershire Regt.: elder s. of Frank Pierce Bent, Superintendent, Railroad Mail Services; of Pugwash, Cumberland Co.: *b.* Halifax, Nova Scotia, 3 January 1891: *educ.* Ashby Boy's Grammar School, Ashby-de-la-Zouch, co. Leicester: joined Merchant Navy (aged 17); H.M.S. 'Conway': enlisted in the Army, as Pte., 15th Royal Scots, 2 October 1914; obtained a commission; gazetted 2nd Lieut. (Temp.), 30 November 1914: joined 7th Leicesters, April 1915; promoted Lieut., June; transf'd. 9th Battn., July: served with the Expeditionary Force in France and Flanders from 31 August 1915: created Companion of the Distinguished Service Order (*London Gazette*, 4 June 1917): subsequently apptd. Temp. Lieut.Col. Killed in action 1 October 1917. Twice Mentioned in Despatches (*London Gazette*, 15 June 1916, 22 May 1917). Awarded the Victoria Cross (*London Gazette*, no.30471, 11 January 1918) "For most conspicuous bravery when, during a heavy hostile attack (in the vicinity of Joist Farm), the right of his own command and the battalion on his right were forced back. The situation was critical owing to the confusion caused by the attack and the intense artillery fire. Lieut.Col. Bent personally collected a platoon that was in reserve, and together with men from other companies and various regimental details, he organized and led them forward to the counter-attack, after issuing orders to other officers as to the further defence of the line. The counter-attack was successful and the enemy were checked. The coolness and magnificent example shown to all ranks by Lieut.Col. Bent resulted in the securing of a portion of the line which was of essential importance for subsequent operations. This very gallant officer was killed whilst leading a charge, which he inspired with the call of, 'Come on, the Tigers.'" 'This gallant attempt was, for the moment, entirely successful, though Colonel Bent was shot through the temple while leading his men.' 'At an investiture held at Buckingham Palace, Mrs Sophia Bent, mother of Lieut.Col. Philip Bent, Leicestershire Regt., received both the D.S.O. and the Victoria Cross awarded to her son, who, though only a Second Lieutenant, was an Acting Lieutenant-Colonel.' Despite extensive searches of the battlefield, his body was never discovered.: Age 26. *unm.*

(Panel 50) Lieut. Cuthbert John Burn, 3rd (Reserve) attd 9th (Service) Bn. The Leicestershire Regt.: s. of the late Right Rev. William John Burn, of Qu-appelle, Canada, by his wife Mary Maud Frederica (26, Beaconsfield Road, Clifton, Bristol), *dau.* of the Rev. S. Banks, of Cottenham Rectory, Cambridge: *b.* Sydenham, London, S.E., 6 June 1893: *educ.* Clifton College; Gonville and Caius College, Cambridge: gazetted 2nd Lieut., Leicestershire Regt., September 1914; promoted Lieut., January 1915: served with the Expeditionary Force in France and Flanders from October 1914; wounded at Ypres 7 November following, and invalided home: on recovery returned to France, March 1915: wounded (2nd occasion) nr. Ypres, August 1915, on a bombing expedition: returned to France, June 1917; killed in action at Polygon Wood, Passchendaele, 1 October following. His Commanding Officer wrote, "He was held in the highest respect both by officers and men…he fell showing a great example of how an Englishman should die.": Age 24. *unm.*

(Panel 50) Lieut. Frank William Curtis, 'A' Coy., 6th (Service) Bn. The Leicestershire Regt. attd. King's Shropshire Light Infantry: eldest *s.* of the late James Curtis, of Colombo, Ceylon, by his wife Cecilia Beatrice (Longcroft, Harpenden, co. Hertford), *dau.* of the late Thomas Rowlinson, of Rugby: *b.* Leytonstone, co. Essex, 3 May 1894: *educ.* Bedford School: joined Universities and Public Schools Corps, September 1914: gazetted 2nd Lieut., Leicestershire Regt., 23 November 1914, promoted Lieut. 1 July 1917: trained Aldershot: went to Salonika, attd. King's Shropshire Light Infantry: stricken with malarial fever; admitted to hospital, Malta, later returned to England – sick leave: on recovery served with the Expeditionary Force in France and Flanders: wounded 28 April 1917 and again sent to England on sick leave: rejoined his regiment 2 September, and was killed in action at Polygon Wood, nr. Ypres, 4 November 1917, by a shell whilst waiting to go into action. Buried on the hill at Reutel, nr. Polygon Wood. His Comdg. Officer wrote, "He was a good boy, and although he had only been with us for a short time, we liked him very much for his quiet, unassuming ways," and a brother officer: "We were in front of Polygon Wood, near Reutel, and a shell landed right in the trench, and killed him and three of his men all instantaneously, and he was buried on the hill there.": Age 23. *unm.*

(Panel 50) 2nd Lieut. Ralph Archibald Bowie, 5th Bn. The Leicestershire Regt. (T.F.): *s.* of Alfred Henry Bowie, of 'Sarston,' Church Hill, Horsell, Woking, co. Surrey, and the late Elizabeth Bowie; his wife (9, Bernard Gardens, Wimbledon, London, S.W.19): *b.* Balham, London, 28 June 1890: religion – Church of England: *educ.* Upper Tooting High School: removed to Canada (1911) and entered the service of the Bank of Montreal: a serving member of the Militia; enlisted Vancouver, British Columbia, 17 February 1915, Pte. (no.75859) 29th Bn. Canadian Infantry, and arrived in France with his unit October following: took part in all the battles in which the Canadians were engaged until January 1917, in which month he was given his commission, 2nd Lieut. 5th Bn. Leicestershire Regt., B.E.F. Severely wounded in the hand while leading his platoon in an attack nr. Gravenstafel, in front of Ypres (Passchendaele sector), 26 September 1917, he remained at duty, and gallantly pressed forward at the head of his men, only to be killed a few minutes later by enemy fire: Age 27. *unm.*

(Panel 50) Sergt. 15307, Albert Edward Essery, M.M., 8th (Service) Bn. The Leicestershire Regt.: 3rd *s.* of John Essery, of Mill Green, Turvey, co. Bedford, by his wife Mary Ann, *dau.* of Thomas Collins: *b.* Turvey, *afsd.*, 23 January 1881: *educ.* there: Occupation – Butler: enlisted Melton Mowbray, September 1914: served with the Expeditionary Force in France and Flanders from 29 July 1915, and was killed in action 1 October 1917. Buried on the battlefield. Awarded the Military Medal for 'gallant and distinguished service in the field;' Mentioned in Battalion Orders, 4 February 1916: Age 36. *unm.* Remembered on Turvey War Memorial.

(Panel 50) Pte. 242277, Willie Booth, 'A' Coy., 2/5th Bn. The Leicestershire Regt. (T.F.): formerly no.1646, West Yorkshire Regt.: *s.* of Thomas J. Booth, of 2, Back, Queen Street, Greetland, Yorks, by his wife Annie: *b.* Huddersfield: attended Middle Dean Street United Methodist Church and Sunday School: Occupation – Woollen Piecer; Messrs J. Horsfall and Sons, West Vale: a pre-war member 1/4th (Territorial) Bn. Duke of Wellington's Regt., volunteered and enlisted West Yorkshire Regt., Elland, on the outbreak of war: went to the Western Front where he was wounded and subsequently repatriated to England; after treatment and convalescence proceeded to Dublin, Ireland, transf'd. Leicestershire Regt., Easter 1916: returned to Fovant, England, January 1917; proceeded to France, 24 February following; killed in action during the 3rd Battle of Ypres, 26 September 1917. He was a member (cornet player) of Elland Brass Band: Age 22.

(Panel 50) Pte. 33016, Walter J. Boultwood, 7th (Service) Bn. The Leicestershire Regt.: formerly no.6452, Bedfordshire Regt.: *s.* of Eliza Boultwood (50, Middle Row, Bishop's Stortford, co. Hertford): and elder brother to Pte. 25227, H.G. Boultwood, 8th Bedfordshire Regt., killed in action, 3 December 1917. Killed in action 28 October 1917: Age 28. *unm.*

His brother Herbert also has no known grave; he is commemorated on the Cambrai Memorial, Louverval (Panel 5).

(Panel 50) Pte. 33220, George Joseph Brown, 8th (Service) Bn. The Leicestershire Regt.: *s.* of Samuel Huntington Brown, of 2, Salisbury Street, Northampton, by his wife Catherine, *dau.* of William Page: *b.* Semilong, co. Northampton, 14 October 1898: *educ.* St. Paul's School, Northampton: Occupation – Shoe Clicker: enlisted April 1915: served with the Expeditionary Force in France from November 1916, and was killed in action 1 November 1917. Major Warner wrote, "He has always been a most cheerful, willing and reliable soldier.": Age 19.

(Panel 50) Pte. 43310, James Edwards, 1st Bn. (17th Foot) The Leicestershire Regt.: formerly no.14144, South Lancashire Regt.: *s.* of John Edwards, of Liverpool, co. Lancaster, by his wife Ellen: and *yr.* brother to Pte. 7201, W. Edwards, Lancashire Fusiliers, who fell, 29 October 1914: *b.* Liverpool. Killed in action 17 April 1918; Mount Kemmel. *(SDGW record 44310)*

His brother Walter also has no known grave; he is commemorated on the Ploegsteert Memorial (Panel 4).

PANEL 50 ENDS: PTE. F.A. FOWKES – LEICESTERSHIRE REGT.

PANEL 51 BEGINS: PTE. J. FREEMAN – LEICESTERSHIRE REGT.

(Panel 51) Pte. 24943, Leonard Gibson Hague, 8th (Service) Bn. The Leicestershire Regt.: *s.* of William Goodacre Hague, of 1, Forest Road, Loughborough, and his wife Emma: and brother to Pte. 2669, F.A.W. Hague, 7th Australian Infantry, killed in action 19 August 1916. Killed in action 21 October 1917: Age 24. Remembered on Holy Trinity Church War Memorial, Loughborough.

His brother Frederick is buried in Becourt Military Cemetery, Becordel-Becourt (I.T.6).

(Panel 51) Pte. 41516, Ernest Hall, 6th (Service) Bn. The Leicestershire Regt.: late of Dalesforth Street, Sutton-in-Ashfield, co. Nottingham: *b.* Skegby, *c.*1874: Occupation – Miner; Brierley Hill Colliery: enlisted Mansfield, December 1917: served with the Expeditionary Force in France from 3 April 1918, and was shot through the head and killed instantaneously by a sniper two weeks later, 17 April: Age 42. He leaves a wife and four children; one son currently (1918) serving in France.

(Panel 51) Pte. 41824, Walter Jaques, 8th (Service) Bn. The Leicestershire Regt.: formerly no.4001, 2/1st Yorkshire Hussars: *s.* of the late John Jaques, by his wife Sarah (24, James Street, Hull Road, York): and yr. brother to Corpl. 137, D. Jaques, 25th Battn. Australian Infantry, who died of wounds, 22 September 1917, at Rouen: *b.* Doncaster: enlisted York. Killed in action 29 April 1918: Age 20. *unm.* *(SDGW record Jacques)*

His brother Dan is buried in St. Sever Cemetery Extension (P.III.G.3A).

(Panel 51) Pte. 40852, George Hillard Ladds, 9th (Service) Bn. The Leicestershire Regt.: formerly no.25632, North Staffordshire Regt.: *s.* of Robert Ladds, of 'Brumby,' 324, Ashby Road, Scunthorpe, co. Lincoln, by his wife Mary Ladds: and elder brother to Pte. 51953, J. Ladds, 4th Notts & Derbys Regt., died 25 August 1916, consequent to wounds received at duty: served with the Expeditionary Force in France. Killed in action 1 October 1917: Age 23. *unm.*

His brother James is buried in Waddingham (Sts. Mary & Peter) Churchyard, Lincolnshire.

(Panel 51) Pte. 33124, Edward William Moore, 8th (Service) Bn. The Leicestershire Regt.: *s.* of William Moore, of Keeley Lane, Wootton, co. Bedford, by his wife Fanny: and brother to L/Corpl. 9597, F.J. Moore, Bedfordshire Regt., who fell 16 June 1915: enlisted 3/5th Bedfordshire Regt., March 1916: subsequently transf'd. 8th Leicestershire Regt.: served with the Expeditionary Force in France and Flanders: took part in the Battle of the Somme, 1916; Vimy Ridge, 1917, the fighting around Ypres and many other engagements, and died gloriously on the field of battle nr. Passchendaele, Belgium, 22 October 1917. '*He Passed Out Of The Sight Of Men By The Path Of Duty And Self Sacrifice*'.

His brother Frederick also has no known grave; he is commemorated on the Le Touret Memorial.

PANEL 51 ENDS: L/CORPL. J. BOARDMAN – ROYAL IRISH REGT.

PANEL 52 BEGINS: L/CORPL. T.W. CULVERHOUSE, M.M. – ROYAL IRISH REGT.

(Panel 52) Lieut. Noel William Groom, 'A' Coy., 9th (Service) Bn. Alexandra, Princess of Wales's Own (Yorkshire Regt.), (The Green Howards): *s.* of John Groom, Architect; of Sydenham, co. Kent, and Florence Browne, his second wife; *dau.* of David J. Evans, Journalist; of Rhayader, co. Radnor: and elder brother to L/Corpl. R/33455, P.L. Groom, 13th King's Royal Rifle Corps, died of wounds, 4 May 1917: *b.* Chelmsford, 1889. Killed in action 20 September 1917, in the advance toward Inverness Copse: Age 28. *unm.*

His brother Phillip is buried in Etaples Military Cemetery (XVIII.H.13A).

(Panel 52) 2nd Lieut. John William Brown, 7th (Service) Bn. Alexandra, Princess of Wales's Own (Yorkshire Regt.), (The Green Howards). Killed in action 16 October 1917; trenches, front-line, east of Langemarck. "The whole front was shelled heavily all day."

(Panel 52) 2nd Lieut. John Greenbank Campbell, 2nd Bn. (19th Foot) Alexandra, Princess of Wales's Own (Yorkshire Regt.), (The Green Howards): eldest *s.* of Thomas Campbell, of Town Head, Austwick, co. Lancaster, by his wife Agnes: Occupation – Clerk; Midland Railway Co.: enlisted 16th (Bradford Pals) Bn. West Yorkshire Regt., May 1915: served in Egypt from December 1915; France and Flanders from March 1916, where he joined the Cyclist Section: returned to England November following to train for his commission, and returned to France where, three weeks later, he was reported missing following an engagement 7 – 8 May 1918; since confirmed killed in action on the former date (7 May): Age 24. *unm.*

(Panel 52) 2nd Lieut. George Esmond Haggie, 'A' Coy., 9th (Service) Bn. Alexandra, Princess of Wales's Own (Yorkshire Regt.), (The Green Howards): *s.* of the late George Alfred Haggie, by his wife Ada ('Brumcombe,' Boar's Hill, Oxford), *dau.* of Capt. Rogers: *b.* Sunderland, co. Durham, 7 June 1890: *educ.* Radley College, Abingdon, co. Berks; Magdalen College, Oxford: subsequently articled to an Oxford firm of Solicitors: enlisted Durham Light Infantry, March 1916: served with the Expeditionary Force in France and Flanders from June 1917 – when he was gazetted 2nd Lieut., 9th Yorkshire Regt. – and was killed in action in Flanders, 2 October following. Buried on the battlefield. His Captain wrote, "Your son was liked and beloved by all the men, and was a universal favourite.": Age 27. *unm.* (*IWGC record Pte. 235467*)

(Panel 52) 2nd Lieut. Herbert Owen Roland Lewis, M.C., 1/2nd (19th Foot) attd. 9th (Service) Bn. Alexandra, Princess of Wales's Own (Yorkshire Regt.), (The Green Howards). With the assistance of a bombing party, this officer effected the retrieval of a captured Lewis gun, and removed a number of the enemy from the trench on his left, in the process of the latter he was shot by a sniper and killed, 1 October 1917.

(Panel 52) Coy.Sergt.Major 240710, Henry West, 2nd Bn. (19th Foot) Alexandra, Princess of Wales's Own (Yorkshire Regt.), (The Green Howards): *s.* of William West, of Waddingham Carr, Lincoln, by his wife Mary Jane, *dau.* of J. Rylatt: *b.* Thornton, nr. Lincoln, 19 September 1878: *educ.* Skirlaugh Church of England School: enlisted Yorkshire Regt., 28 September 1914: served seven years, nine months with the Colours; served in the South African War 1899-1902 (Queen's Medal), and joined the Reserve: joined National Reserve, August 1914; called up 28 September following: served with the Expeditionary Force in France and Flanders from 21 November 1917; killed in action at Ridge Wood, Ypres, 8 May 1918. Buried where he fell: Age 39. He *m.* Skirlaugh, 1 December 1908; Jane, *dau.* of Joseph Binnington, and had a son, Henry, *b.* 15 November 1909.

(Panel 52) Corpl. 43537, William Clamp, V.C., 6th (Service) Bn. Alexandra, Princess of Wales's Own (Yorkshire Regt.), (The Green Howards): formerly Cameronians (Sco.Rif.): *s.* of Charles Clamp, of 13C, Reid Terrace, Flemington, Motherwell, co. Lanark, by his wife Christina Dundas: *b.* 28 October 1891. Killed in action at Poelcapelle, 9 October 1917. Buried there: Age 25. Posthumously awarded the Victoria Cross (*London Gazette*, No.30433, 18 December 1917) "For most conspicuous bravery when an advance was being checked by intense machine-gun fire from concrete blockhouses and by snipers in ruined buildings. Corporal Clamp dashed forward with two men and attempted to rush the largest blockhouse. His first attempt failed owing to the two men with him being knocked out; but he at once collected some bombs, and, calling upon two men to follow him, again dashed forward. He was first to reach the blockhouse and hurled his bombs, killing many of the occupants. He then entered and brought out a machine gun and about twenty prisoners, whom he brought back under heavy fire from neighbouring snipers. This non-commissioned officer then again went forward encouraging and cheering the men, and succeeded in rushing several sniper's posts. He continued to display the greatest heroism until he was killed by a sniper. His magnificent courage and self-sacrifice was of the greatest value, and relieved what was undoubtedly a very critical situation."

On 11 October 1917, immediately prior to their taking part in the First Battle of Passchendaele, 7th Green Howards left their camp at Elverdinghe and proceeded through pouring rain to a 'camp' in the vicinity of the Yser Canal. On arrival they discovered the camp offered no shelter whatever, it was simply a bare area 'ankle deep in mud and water' and by evening, despite a few bivouacs having been procured, more than half the battalion were still exposed to the elements and remained so until the night of the 13/14 when the battalion moved up to relieve part of 51st Brigade in the front line. The relief was carried out in pitch darkness and torrential rain, the only tracks leading to the front were duck-boarded for miles and shelled at intervals all night long. Troops could only move in single file, and in the inky darkness it was little wonder the so-called guides lost their way more than once. It was an easy matter to miss the track altogether, turning and twisting as they did to avoid the enormous shell craters which covered the devastated battlefield. With the entire area under enemy observation, their machine-guns and snipers picked men off with ease. The shell-holes, either side of the duckboard track, filled with liquid mud, their sides continually slipping in, became the last resting place for many. The Green Howards, under continuous fire on their approach to (and at) the front, recorded Lieut. J.W. Brown and seven men killed along with a further fifteen missing (7 subsequently turned up). How many slipped from sight into one of the aforementioned shell-holes will never be known.

(Panel 52) Pte. 204474, Frank Adams, 7th (Service) Bn. Alexandra, Princess of Wales's Own (Yorkshire Regt.), (The Green Howards): *s.* of the late William Adams, by his wife Elizabeth (29, Harvey St., Byker, Newcastle-on-Tyne): *b.* Newcastle-on-Tyne, 1887. Missing / believed killed in action 15 October 1917: Age 30.

(Panel 52) Pte. 341610, John Clarke, 8th (Service) Bn. Alexandra, Princess of Wales's Own (Yorkshire Regt.), (The Green Howards): *s.* of the late John Edward Clarke, by his late wife Sarah: *b.* Leeds, co. York, 4 August 1895: *educ.* 'Indefatigable,' River Mersey: Occupation – Sailor: enlisted August 1915: served with the Expeditionary Force in France and Flanders from January 1916, and was killed in action 10 April 1918. He *m.* Birkenhead, 20 July 1915; Sarah Ann (102, Bridge Street, Birkenhead), *dau.* of Allan Makin: Age 23. *s.p.* (*IWGC record 34160*)

(Panel 52) Pte. 235232, Tom Clarke, 7th (Service) Bn. Alexandra, Princess of Wales's Own (Yorkshire Regt.), (The Green Howards): *s.* of George Clarke, of Buckden, by his wife Elizabeth: enlisted Huntingdon. Missing / believed killed in action 15 October 1917: Age 38. He leaves a widow, Alice Clarke (Silver St., Buckden, co. Huntingdon).

(Panel 52) Pte. 33536, Arthur Cockroft, 6th (Service) Bn. Alexandra, Princess of Wales's Own (Yorkshire Regt.), (The Green Howards): *s.* of John Cockroft, Joiner's Foreman; of 2, Fountain Street, Hebden Bridge, by his wife Jane, *dau.* of Wilson Calvert: *b.* Hebden Bridge, co. York, 25 July 1897: *educ.* Hebden Bridge Council School: Occupation – Joiner: enlisted 7 July 1916: served with the Expeditionary Force in France and Flanders from December following, and was killed in action by a sniper at Poelcapelle, nr. Ypres 9 October 1917. Buried there. His Commanding Officer wrote, "He died as he would have wished to, going forward, facing the enemy. He was a good soldier, and I never saw him flinch or hesitate at any job he was put to, although he was so young. He was always cheerful and merry, and had a lot of pals in the platoon; everybody liked him," and his Chaplain, "He was one of the bravest of British heroes, for he knew no fear in danger. He died (gallant soldier that he was) at the post of duty with his face to the foe. He is mourned deeply by all who knew him, for he was loved by his comrades and esteemed most highly by his officers.": Age 20. *unm.*

PANEL 52 ENDS: PTE. J. CRAIG – YORKSHIRE REGT.

PANEL 53 BEGINS: PTE. F. CROWN – YORKSHIRE REGT.

(Panel 53) Pte. 34086, Frederick Crown, 7th (Service) Bn. Alexandra, Princess of Wales's Own (Yorkshire Regt.), (The Green Howards): formerly no.83666, Durham Light Infantry: *b.* East Bilney, co. Norfolk:

enlisted Nottingham: missing / believed killed on the approach to the trenches on the night of 13 – 14 October 1917. No word having been heard since that time, death is now assumed.

(Panel 53) Pte. 27241, George Herbert Easton, 8th (Service) Bn. Alexandra, Princess of Wales's Own (Yorkshire Regt.), (The Green Howards): late of Scawton, co. York: *s.* of Thomas Easton, of Bagby, Thirsk, co. York, by his wife Clara: and yr. brother to Spr. 145281, R. Easton, 26th Field Coy., Royal Engineers, died 30 November 1918, at Bagby: *b.* Oldstead, Malton, 1896: enlisted Richmond. Killed in action 17 October 1917. He was awarded the Meritorious Service Medal: Age 21. *unm.* George and his brother Robert are commemorated on the Kilburn War Memorial, situated in St. Mary's Churchyard.

His brother Robert is buried in Kilburn (St. Mary) Churchyard.

(Panel 53) Pte. 235238, John Goodson, 7th (Service) Bn. Alexandra, Princess of Wales's Own (Yorkshire Regt), (The Green Howards): *s.* of W. (& Mrs.) Goodson, of Broadway, Farcet, co. Huntingdon: *b.* Bournemouth, 1880: enlisted Huntingdon. Missing / believed killed in action 14 October 1917: Age 37. He leaves a widow, Mrs E. A. Goodson (Derby Villa, Broadway, Yaxley, Peterborough).

(Panel 53) Pte. 33848, Percy James Harvey, 7th (Service) Bn. Alexandra, Princess of Wales's Own (Yorkshire Regt.), (The Green Howards): formerly no.G/32981, Middlesex Regt.: *b.* Saffron Walden, co. Essex: enlisted Enfield. Killed in action 16 October 1917.

(Panel 53) Pte. 39267, Nathan 'Nat' Burton Iveson, 10th (Service) Bn. Alexandra, Princess of Wales's Own (Yorkshire Regt.), (The Green Howards): 2nd *s.* of the late John (& Mrs) Iveson, of Gayle Lane, Hawes, co. York: *b.* Hawes: Occupation – Road Contractor; Aysgarth District Council: enlisted Leyburn, November 1916: served with the Expeditionary Force in France from May 1917, and was killed in action 4 October following: Age 29. In a letter to his sister his Comdg. Officer wrote, "I regret to inform you that your brother, Pte. Iveson, has been killed in action. Although he had only been with us a short time, we highly appreciated his services; all the officers and men of the Company join me in extending heartfelt sympathy in your sad bereavement. You have at least the satisfaction of knowing that he died doing his duty to King and Country." A devoted son, brother, true friend and loyal comrade, Pte. Iveson was ready at all times to do a good turn whenever such was needed and won the respect and liking of all with whom he came into contact.

(Panel 53) Pte. 201233, William Johnson, 4th Bn. Alexandra, Princess of Wales's Own (Yorkshire Regt.), (The Green Howards), (T.F.): *s.* of Thomas Johnson, of Long Street, Thirsk, co. York, by his wife Ada: and elder brother to Pte. 3888, F. Johnson, 4th Yorkshire Regt., who also fell: enlisted Thirsk. Died of wounds 29 October 1917: Age 23. *unm.* William and his brother Frederick are commemorated on a memorial tablet in Thirsk (St. Mary's) Church.

His brother Frederick is buried in Adanac Military Cemetery (VII.B.13).

(Panel 53) Pte. 15752, James Kelly, 'C' Coy., 8th (Service) Bn. Alexandra, Princess of Wales's Own (Yorkshire Regt.), (The Green Howards): *s.* of the late Patrick (& Mary) Kelly, of Argyle Street, Middlesbrough: and yr. brother to Pte. 8513, J. Kelly, 6th Yorkshire Regt., who fell the previous day: *b.* Grangetown, co. York, *c.*1892: enlisted Frensham, co. Surrey. Killed in action 28 September 1917: Age 25. *unm.*

His brother John also has no known grave; he is recorded below.

(Panel 53) Pte. 8513, John Kelly, 6th (Service) Bn. Alexandra, Princess of Wales's Own (Yorkshire Regt.), (The Green Howards): *s.* of the late Patrick (& Mary) Kelly, of Argyle Street, Middlesbrough: and elder brother to Pte. 15752, J. Kelly, 8th Yorkshire Regt., who fell the following day: *b.* Hartlepool, co. York, *c.*1879: enlisted Middlesbrough. Killed in action 27 September 1917: Age 38.

His brother James also has no known grave; he is recorded above.

(Panel 53) Pte. 33837, Harold Wiliam Leach, 7th (Service) Bn. Alexandra, Princess of Wales's Own (Yorkshire Regt.), (The Green Howards): formerly no.4913, Essex Regt.: *s.* of Alfred Leach, of Thistle Croft, Hersham, Walton-on-Thames, co. Surrey, by his wife Mary: *b.* Hersham, co. Surrey, 1887: enlisted Kingston-on-Thames. Missing / believed died of wounds 14 October 1917: Age 30.

(Panel 53) Pte. 23649, John Henry Long, 7th (Service) Bn. Alexandra, Princess of Wales's Own (Yorkshire Regt.), (The Green Howards): enlisted Doncaster, co. York. Killed in action 16 October 1917.

(Panel 53) Pte. 27468, Ernest Mellor, 'A' Coy., 7th (Service) Bn. Alexandra, Princess of Wales's Own (Yorkshire Regt.), (The Green Howards): *s.* of F.A. (& Mrs E.E.) Mellor, of 21, Nuttall Road, Bradford: enlisted Bradford. Killed in action 16 October 1917: Age 26. *unm.*

(Panel 53) Pte. 33394, Frederick 'Fred' Payne, 6th (Service) Bn. Alexandra, Princess of Wales' Own (Yorkshire Regt.), (The Green Howards): formerly no.2381, Suffolk Regt.: *s.* of F. (& Mrs) Payne, of Haverhill, co. Suffolk: and brother to Pte. 242031, C.A. Payne, Northumberland Fusiliers, killed in action 26 October 1917; and Pte. TF/293037, A. Payne, Middlesex Regt., killed in action, 4 October 1917: enlisted Haverhill. Killed in action 27 September 1917.

His brothers Charlie and Alf also have no known grave; they are commemorated on Panels 22 and 114 respectively.

(Panel 53) Pte. 36002, George Albert Riley, 7th (Service) Bn. Alexandra, Princess of Wales's Own (Yorkshire Regt.), (The Green Howards): *s.* of Thomas Henry Riley, of Hull, by his wife Ellen. Killed in action 16 October 1917: Age 43.

(Panel 53) Pte. 12371, William Idwal Roberts, 7th (Service) Bn. Alexandra, Princess of Wales's Own (Yorkshire Regt.), (The Green Howards): late of Brymbo, Wrexham, North Wales: enlisted Richmond, co. York. Missing / believed killed in action 14 October 1917.

PANEL 53 ENDS: PTE. E.M. SANDERS – YORKSHIRE REGT.

PANEL 54 BEGINS: PTE. G.H. SCOTT – YORKSHIRE REGT.

(Panel 54) Pte. 39114, Percy Scott, 7th (Service) Bn. Alexandra, Princess of Wales's Own (Yorkshire Regt.), (The Green Howards): enlisted Jarrow. Killed in action 16 October 1917.

(Panel 54) Pte. 235323, Tom Percy Singleton, 9th (Service) Bn. Alexandra, Princess of Wales's Own (Yorkshire Regt.), (The Green Howards): formerly no.8939, Northumberland Fusiliers: *s.* of the late Charles Singleton, Tailor; by his wife Mary, *dau.* of George Searby: *b.* Market Rasen, co. Lincoln, 23 November 1882: *educ.* Local School: Occupation – Printer: enlisted Scunthorpe, co. Lincoln, 7 September 1916: served with the Expeditionary Force in France and Flanders from 16 June 1917, transf'd. 9th Battn. Yorkshire Regt., and was killed in action at Menin Road, 20 September following. Buried at Gheluvelt, north-west of Ypres: Age 34. Capt. Thomson wrote, "He was held in high esteem by all who knew him." He was a keen footballer at one time, and well known in Scunthorpe, having served with the same firm for 13 years. He *m.* Scunthorpe Parish Church, 26 December 1912; Melissa Mary (13, Dale Street, Crosby), *dau.* of David Dixon, and had a son, David Raymond, *b.* 29 July 1915. Pte. Singleton's widow died shortly after his death. (*IWGC record age 35*)

(Panel 54) Pte. 38721, Isaac Smith, 7th (Service) Bn. Alexandra, Princess of Wales's Own (Yorkshire Regt.), (The Green Howards): enlisted Manchester. Missing / believed killed in action 14 October 1917; trenches, front line, east of Langemarck.

(Panel 54) Pte. 26640, Thomas Smith, 10th (Service) Bn. Alexandra, Princess of Wales' Own (Yorkshire Regt.), (The Green Howards): *s.* of Thomas Smith, of Snowdon Terrace, Brompton, Northallerton, co. York, and Hannah Smith, his spouse: and yr. brother to Pte. 200440, J.W. Smith, 4th Yorkshire Regt., killed at Potijze a few weeks later: *b.* Brompton: enlisted Northallerton. Died of wounds 6 November 1917. Buried nearby: Age 29.

His brother James is buried in Potijze Chateau Grounds Cemetery (I.E.9).

From the German positions on the Passchendaele ridge the advantages this provided in the way of observation necessitated virtually all movements by the British army to be carried out under cover of darkness. Every night ration parties, after making their way back to supply dumps on the fringe of the battlefield, made their way back with food for the men at the front; every step was fraught with danger from the German artillery batteries who knew exactly the routes these men had to follow and shelled them randomly throughout the night. Whether a ration party got caught by this shellfire was simply a matter of luck. On the night of 31 August 1917 a party led by Lieut. G. Horridge, Lancashire Fusiliers, ran out of luck; he later recorded:

"The ration party consisted of two parties and we'd arrived at this trench. At the side of the trench was a steel plate, about nine feet long by three feet wide, which someone had put up. The first party were dumping the rations against this steel plate. I was on one end of it, another officer was in the middle and another on the left. I happened to look up to the right and could see shadowy forms approaching. I said, 'Hello, here's the second ration party, I'll just give them a shout, tell them where we are.' I took two steps, not more, when a big shell fell on the plate I had just been leaning against. A tremendous flash and I was blown down against the side of the trench. I picked myself up, realising that as far as I knew nothing had hit me. There was dead silence. I enquired of the two officers who had been with me, 'Are Mr Mashiter and Mr Hudson here?' There was no reply. Then a sort of commotion broke out. Not only had this shell killed the two officers, it had killed five of the ration party, one of whom had both his legs blown off, and wounded about eight others. The whole thing was a dreadful shock. We had to get the wounded away in the dark, and we knew the gun was pointing at the same place and might fire another shell at any moment."

(Panel 54) Capt. Austin Patrick Hudson, 1/5th Bn. The Lancashire Fusiliers (T.F.): *s.* of Rev. Richard Hudson, of St. John's Vicarage, Bury, co. Lancaster, by his wife Violet Ellen. Killed in action on the night of 31 August – 1 September 1917: Age 24. *unm.*

Lieut. T.A.G. Mashiter, 10th York and Lancaster Regt. attd. 1/5th Lancashire Fusiliers, also has no known grave; he is commemorated on Panel 125.

(Panel 54) Lieut. John Elliott Mottram, 2/7th Bn. The Lancashire Fusiliers (T.F.): eldest *s.* of the late Sir Richard Mottram, of Beech House, Pendleton, by his wife Margaret Edith, *dau.* of William Aikman Morton, of Horwich, nr. Bolton: *b.* Pendleton, co. Lancaster, 20 November 1896: *educ.* Rossall School, Fleetwood; and Salford Royal Technical Institute: was training to be an Electrical Engineer: volunteered for Active Service on the outbreak of war; enlisted Manchester Regt., August 1914: obtained a commission; gazetted 2nd Lieut., Lancashire Fusiliers, 14 May 1915: promoted Lieut. July 1917, being Signalling Officer to his battalion: served with the Expeditionary Force in France and Flanders from March 1917; killed in action at Passchendaele Ridge, nr. Ypres, 9 October following. Buried where he fell. Lieut.Col. Hobbins wrote, "He was taking part in a great battle that was fought here the other day. He was advancing with his usual dash and gallantry, when a shell exploded close to him. His death was instantaneous. I must tell you frankly how much we all miss him. He had, by his cheerfulness, unselfishness and devotion to duty, endeared himself to us all, and his death has taken from us one of my most popular and promising officers. He died a very gallant gentleman. As one of my officers said to me today, 'It was a sunny life cut short.' One never saw him without a smile and his brightness impressed everyone" and the Chaplain, "Dicky, as we called him, was a great favourite. He was always so full of life and fun, and never allowed us to feel dull. His men, too, were very fond of him, and would do anything for him and follow him anywhere.": Age 20. *unm.*

(Panel 54) 2nd Lieut. Ernest Reginald Rushmore, 4th (T.F.) attd. 11th (Service) Bn. The Lancashire Fusiliers: *s.* of Ernest (& Caroline) Rushmore of, Victoria House, Esplanade, Lowestoft. Killed in action in the vicinity of Railway Dump, 6 September 1917; buried the following day (ref. 'Zillebeke Sheet: 28 N.E.5., J.7.d.9.9') with Pte. 34098, H. Nugent of the same battn. The burial of both men was performed and recorded by Padre Canon M.S. Evers attd. 74th Bde., 25th Divn.

(Panel 54) 2nd Lieut. John Sydney Scrivener, 8th (T.F.) attd. 15th (Service) Bn. The Lancashire Fusiliers: *s.* of George Henry Scrivener, of Greenfield, Upholland, Wigan, co. Lancaster, Secretary of the Upholland Agricultural Society by his wife Elizabeth, *dau.* of the late James Thompson, of Digmoor Hall, Upholland: *b.* Upholland, 7 January 1897: *educ.* Upholland Grammar School: Occupation – Bank Clerk: enlisted Kings Own (Royal Lancaster Regt.), October 1914, and after a period of training with the O.T.C. at Lincoln's Inn, gazetted 2nd Lieut., Lancashire Fusiliers: served with the Expeditionary Force in France and Flanders from January 1917, and was killed in action at Passchendaele 2 December following. His Commanding Officer wrote, "We all feel that we have lost an officer who cannot easily be replaced; he was so keen on his work and so brave in action;" and the Chaplain, "He was so keen and enthusiastic, and as brave as any man can hope to be; we played games together, so I saw quite a lot of him, and grew to love him for his straight, upright, fearless character. I have lost a good friend." Another officer wrote, "He died the death of a gallant officer, nobly defending the traditions peculiar to our race. He died winning. His death was an example of sacrifice and devotion to duty.": Age 20. *unm.*

(Panel 54) 2nd Lieut. Geoffrey Owen Thomas, 19th (Service) Bn. (Pioneers) The Lancashire Fusiliers: *s.* of the late Samuel James (& Mrs) Thomas, of Barnet, London: *b.* 1884: was a Member (1910), London Stock Exchange: volunteered and enlisted as Pte., Royal Fusiliers, October 1914, after the outbreak of war: went to France as Corpl., November following, and served with the Expeditionary Force there and in Flanders: sometime served attd. Trench Mortar Bty., and believed to have been recommended for gallantry on at least one occasion: offered a commission and returned to England from where, after undergoing several weeks officer training at a cadet school, he returned to France, as 2nd Lieut. attd. 19th Lancashire Fusiliers, June 1917. 2nd Lieut. Thomas was reported missing in action at Kemmel, 25 April 1918. At the time of his death he was acting as Assistant Adjutant to his battalion and after volunteering to carry a message forward from battalion headquarters, there being no runner available to perform this duty, he duly completed the task and is believed to have been killed on the return journey. He leaves a wife, Ethel Mabel ('Evanston,' Churchfields, Woodford, co. Essex), in a letter to whom his Colonel said, "Your husband died like a soldier. He gave the last ounce for the battalion. He was always perfectly cool and collected under fire, and always most energetic in all his duties," and one of his men: "He undoubtedly was one of the most popular officers in the Battalion. He always inspired one with confidence by his great unconcern under the worst of conditions." Another wrote: "He was a real fine man and as straight as a die. When he was in command of his platoon his men almost worshipped him. A real true British gentleman and one whom everyone misses.": Age 34.

(Panel 54) 2nd Lieut. Alfred Warrell, 5th (T.F.) attd. 2nd (20th Foot) Bn. The Lancashire Fusiliers: *yst. s.* of the late William Warrell, of 36, Herbert Street, and formerly of Glen Avenue, Brackley, Manchester, by his wife Ellen, *dau.* of John Hugh Worrill: *b.* Hull, co. York, 30 January 1895: *educ.* Moston Lane School: enlisted 6th (Territorial) Battn. Manchester Regt. 9 February 1915, in which he acted as Machine Gun Instructor: given a commission, gazetted 2nd Lieut., 5th Lancashire Fusiliers, 5 August 1916: subsequently attd. 2nd Battn., and served with the Expeditionary Force in France and Flanders from January 1917: took part in the fighting at Rouen, 3 May following, and in many other engagements, and was killed in action on the Passchendaele front 9 October of the same year, being shot by a sniper as he was leading his men into action. Buried where he fell. His Officer Commanding, Col. H.W. Glinn, wrote, "Your son was a very keen and cheery officer, and loved by all, and his death is keenly felt by us," and his Commanding Officer, "I soon recognised his sterling qualities, and early came to consider him my most reliable and capable officer. He was very efficient, always cheerful and willing to undertake any job that had to be done." Capt. Hunstable also wrote, "He was brave and reliable in the line beyond average, and when we had a dangerous piece of work to do, he always went through with it where others failed, as at Ypres. In the attack on the chemical works at Rouen on May 3 he was the only officer left in the front line, and alone he collected what was left of the battalion under his command. He had, too, the great gift of understanding how to treat his men.": Age 22. *unm.*

PANEL 54 ENDS: L/SERGT. W. BLEARS – LANCASHIRE FUSILIERS

PANEL 55 BEGINS: L/SERGT. H. BROADHURST – LANCASHIRE FUSILIERS

With the welfare and well-being of the fighting men foremost in their intentions, groups from all manner of societies (and society) individuals and groups devoted much of their spare time to raising funds and obtaining comforts for the troops. One, 12 year old, Miss H. Bisby composed a poem 'The Lads of Todmorden' the proceeds from the sale of which were allocated to 'Wounded Soldiers and British Friendless Prisoners of War in Germany.'

> *"We are the proud lads of Todmorden*
> *Who at the bugle call;*
> *Put on the Country's armour*
> *And rushed to duty's call...*
>
> *...Their names shall live in history*
> *Their names we will adore,*
> *And Todmorden shall be proud of them*
> *When they return once more."*

Seventy members of Todmorden's Patmos Congregationalist Church answered the bugle's call; fifteen never returned.

(Panel 55) Sergt. 241322, Albert Seal, 1/6th Bn. The Lancashire Fusiliers (T.F.): *s.* of George Seal, of Hey's Buildings, Rochdale: religion – Congregationalist: served with the Expeditionary Force in France from February 1917. Killed in action 6 September 1917: Age 26. He was married to Ellen Seal (48, Sackville Street, Todmorden).

(Panel 55) L/Corpl. 39068, Harold Llewellyn Phillips, M.M., 2/8th Bn. The Lancashire Fusiliers (T.F.): eldest *s.* of Thomas Edward Phillips, of Penrhwceiber, Colliery Manager, by his wife Alice, *dau.* of T. Llewellyn, of Beechfield, Hengoed: and *gdson.* of Alderman N. Phillips, of New Tredegar, J.P.: *b.* Mountain Ash, co. Glamorgan, 1 March 1898: *educ.* Tutorial College, Penarth, and Taunton School: Occupation – Assistant Surveyor; Penrikyber Navigation Colliery Company, Penrhwceiber, co. Glamorgan: enlisted Royal Engineers, 5 February 1917: subsequently transf'd. Duke of Wellington's (West Riding) Regt.: proceeded to France, there again transf'd. Lancashire Fusiliers: served with the Expeditionary Force there from June of the same year, and was killed in action between Passchendaele and Zonnebeke, 20 November following. Buried where he fell. An officer wrote, "Your son met his death in the early morning of the 20th. We had been relieved, and were on our way back to billets when Harold, with others, was struck by a shell. He suffered no pain – in fact, I was unable to find a mark on his body; his face looked quite peaceful. He was a Corpl. in charge of a Lewis Gun Section. We were only waiting for his papers to come through to send him home on commission. For one so young he was a noble boy, and is sadly missed by all his officers and men in this company. Up to this time he was the only one in the company to wear a decoration, and we were all so proud of him." He was awarded the Military Medal for swimming across the River Yser to gain important information about the enemy: Age 19. (*IWGC records Pte., 2/18th Bn.*)

(Panel 55) L/Corpl. 22749, Cecil Wood, 18th (Service) Bn. The Lancashire Fusiliers: formerly no.165931, Royal Field Artillery: *s.* of John Henry Wood, of 70, Lawrence Street, York, by his wife Eliza: and *yr.* brother to Gnr. 66565, J.H. Wood, Royal Field Artillery, killed in action, 13 September 1918: enlisted York. Killed in action 22 October 1917: Age 22. *unm.*

His brother John is buried in Peronne Communal Cemetery Extension (IV.D.6).

(Panel 55) L/Corpl. 38162, John Henry Wood, M.M., 15th (Service) Bn. The Lancashire Fusiliers: *yst. s.* of the late George Henry Wood, Farmer, by his wife Ellen (59, Roydhouse, Linthwaite, co. York): *b.* Linthwaite, 12 February 1893: *educ.* there: Occupation – Crane Driver: enlisted South Staffordshire Regt., 11 November 1916: served with the Expeditionary Force in France and Flanders from January 1917: subsequently transf'd. Lancashire Fusiliers, and was killed in action, 20 March 1918. An officer wrote, "Your son was a gallant soldier, and very fond of his work; he was a good lad, and we shall miss him in the battalion very much." Awarded the Military Medal for bravery in the field in February 1918: Age 25. *unm.*

PANEL 55 ENDS: PTE. L. BRADY – LANCASHIRE FUSILIERS

PANEL 56 BEGINS: PTE. H.W.T.C. BRAITHWAITE – LANCASHIRE FUSILIERS

PANEL 56 ENDS: PTE. J.W. FURBES – LANCASHIRE FUSILIERS

PANEL 57 BEGINS: PTE. A. GAFFIN – LANCASHIRE FUSILIERS

(Panel 57) Pte. 12256, Cecil Gammons, 1st Bn. (20th Foot) The Lancashire Fusiliers: *s.* of Elizabeth Gammons (28, Greenacres Road, Oldham): and elder brother to Rfn. 202580, F.A. Gammons, King's Liverpool Regt., who died 20 September 1917, of wounds: *b.* Oldham, co. Lancaster, *c.*1898: enlisted Manchester. Killed in action 25 September 1918: Age 22. *unm.*

His brother Frank also has no known grave; he is recorded on Panel 32.

(Panel 57) Pte. 202836, Cecil Rowland Gibbons, 1/5th Bn. The Lancashire Fusiliers (T.F.): *s.* of John Gibbons, of 60, Wilton Street, Whitefield, Manchester, by his wife Mary: and brother to Pte. SP/3987, A. Gibbons, Royal Fusiliers, who fell 29 July 1916: *b.* Hillock Lane, Whitefield: enlisted Bury. Killed in action 6 September 1917: Age 20.

His brother Albert also has no known grave; he is commemorated on the Thiepval Memorial, Somme.

(Panel 57) Pte. 39022, Fred Swaine Harrison, 2/8th Bn. The Lancashire Fusiliers (T.F.): 2nd *s.* of the late Samuel Holdsworth Harrison, Master Draper, of Leeds, by his wife Sarah Ann, *dau.* of Joseph Heywood: *b.* Leeds, co. York, 25 February 1890: *educ.* Cockburn High School: Occupation – Master Draper; Stanningley Road, Armley: joined Army Service Corps, 31 July 1916: served with the Expeditionary Force in France and Flanders from June 1917: transf'd. Lancashire Fusiliers, and was killed in action at Passchendaele, 16 January 1918. Buried where he fell: Age 27. His Sergt.Major wrote, "He was a good chum and exceedingly well liked, and his loss will be deeply felt;" and the Corpl. wrote of him, "One of the best in my gun team." He *m.* St. Bartholomew's Church, Leeds, 20 September 1916; Elsie Gertrude (16A, Harehills Road, Harehills, Leeds) formerly of 47, Aviary Mount, Armley, *dau.* of Robert Neal, and had a son Robert Neal, *b.* 10 December 1917.

(Panel 57) S/Smith, 40567, Reginald Herbert, 2nd King Edward's Horse and 2nd Bn. (20th Foot) The Lancashire Fusiliers: 2nd *s.* of Thomas Herbert, of Denton Lodge, Stilton, Peterborough, co. Northampton, Farmer, by his wife Martha, *dau.* of Thomas Wilson: and brother to Pte. 6071, C. Herbert, 23rd Battn. A.I.F., killed in action at Passchendaele; and Pte. 13092, A. Herbert, 2nd Northamptonshire Regt., killed in action at Aubers Ridge, 26 April 1915: *b.* Little Gidding, co. Huntingdon, 26 December 1888: *educ.* Denton and Stilton schools: was a Butcher in England and the U.S.A.: enlisted 19 April 1915: served with the Expeditionary Force in France from July following, and was killed in action at Passchendaele Ridge, 9 October 1917. Buried there. A comrade wrote, "…The best chum I ever had, no man could have a better;" and an officer, "He was one of a draft of the finest men we ever had.": Age 28. *unm.* His brother Charles was killed the same day.

His brother Charles is buried in Aeroplane Cemetery (VII.B.38); Albert, Rue Petillon Military Cemetery (I.C.31).

(Panel 57) Pte. 5037, Frederick Samuel Howis, 2/7th Bn. The Lancashire Fusiliers (T.F.): 3rd *s.* of George Howis, Wool Packer; of Barnstaple Cottage, North St., Ashburton, by his wife Emma, *dau.* of Joseph Jeffery, of Chagford: *b.* Ashburton, co. Devon, 19 December 1894: *educ.* Board School there: was for a time engaged at the Racing Stables, Malvern Wells, and then became a Miner; subsequently served on board a Mail Boat: joined Lancashire Fusiliers, 27 July 1916: served with the Expeditionary Force in France and Flanders from February 1917, and was killed in action at Ypres, 9 October following. His Platoon Officer wrote, "Private Howis played his part as nobly as any. He was shot by a sniper and wounded, and hit again, by shrapnel, before he could be conveyed to the dressing station. I have known him about six months as the best in platoon work. He was at all times, and in all places, a soldier and a gentleman; a nicer man I have never met. The best sniper in the battalion and everybody loved him. His loss is a great blow to all of us.": Age 21. He *m.* Colchester, 30 September 1916; Elsie May (Sycamore Cottage, Malvern Wells), *dau.* of Ernest Smith, of Malvern: *s.p.* (*IWGC record No.282127*)

At 7.15 am., 6 September 1917, following a heavy artillery bombardment, three companies of 1/6th Territorial Battalion of the Lancashire Fusiliers left their trenches on the Frezenberg Ridge to capture the German positions at Beck House and Iberian Farm, with their sister battalion 1/5th attacking Borry Farm. Crossing ground already strewn with the dead of previous attacks, the Lancashires achieved early success but with heavy casualties and, after coming under heavy German machine gun fire and counterattacks, the remnants of the companies were forced to retire to their original positions. Eleven of the dead were from the village of Littleborough; among them Pte. Parker 1/5th Bn. and Pte. Jackson, 1/6th Bn.

(Panel 57) Pte. 241457, Stanley Jackson, 1/6th Bn. The Lancashire Fusiliers (T.F.): *s.* of Thomas Jackson, of 85, Todmorden Road, Littleborough, co. Lancaster, by his wife Emma: *b.* Littleborough, afsd.: enlisted Rochdale. Killed in action 6 September 1917: Age 24. Inscribed "To The Glory Of God And In Memory Of Twelve Brave Men Who Gave Their Lives For Us ... For They Are Worthy," Pte. Jackson is one of the twelve recorded on the Rochdale (Victoria Street) Wesleyan Methodist Chapel War Memorial.

PANEL 57 ENDS: PTE. S. KENDRICK – LANCASHIRE FUSILIERS

PANEL 58 BEGINS: PTE. T. KENT – LANCASHIRE FUSILIERS

(Panel 58) Pte. 40373, George Frederick Mapley, 'C' Coy., 1/5th Bn. The Lancashire Fusiliers (T.F.): formerly no.26170, Bedford & Hertfordshire Regt. (T.F.): *s.* of George Mapley, of 14, Beaconsfield Place, Newport Pagnell, co. Buckingham, by his wife Clara M.: and brother to Pte. 14712, T.M. Mapley, 7th Bedfordshire Regt., killed in action, 7 July 1916; Somme: *b.* Newport Pagnell, 14 April 1889: was a Painter: enlisted St. Neots, co. Huntingdon. Killed in action 6 September 1917: Age 28. He leaves a wife, Alice Mapley (7, St. Paul's Road, Queen's Park, Bedford).

His brother Thomas also has no known grave, he is commemorated on the Thiepval Memorial (Pier & Face 2C).

(Panel 58) Pte. 235496, John James Maughan, 1/5th Bn. The Lancashire Fusiliers (T.F.): *s.* of Edward Maughan, of 30, Sheraton Street, Spital Tongues, Newcastle-on-Tyne, by his marriage to the late Annie Maugham: *husb.* to Emily Robson Maugham (112, Morpeth Street, Spital Tongues). Killed in action on the night of 31 August – 1 September 1917, while at duty on a ration party: Age 27. Buried where he fell. See account re. Capt. A.P. Hudson (Panel 54).

(Panel 58) Pte. 325091, James Middleton, 1/8th Bn. The Lancashire Fusiliers (T.F.): formerly no.2102, Northumberland Cyclist Bn.: *s.* of Thomas Middleton, of 38, South Burns, Chester-le-Street, Co. Durham, by his wife Margaret: and brother to Pte. 2731, J. Middleton, 8th Durham Light Infantry, who also fell: *b.* 1893: enlisted Newcastle-on-Tyne. Killed in action 6 September 1917: Age 24. *unm.*

His brother John is buried in Tyne Cot Cemetery (LXIII.C.3).

(Panel 58) Pte. 34098, Harry Nugent, 11th (Service) Bn. The Lancashire Fusiliers: *s.* of Thomas and Eliza Nugent, of 5, Heaton St., Rhodes, Manchester. Killed in action in the vicinity of Railway Dump, 6 September 1917, and buried the following day (ref. Zillebeke Sheet: 28 N.E.5., J.7.d.9.9) with 2nd Lieut. E.R. Rushmore of the same battn. The burial of both men was performed and recorded by Padre Canon M.S. Evers attd. 74th Bde., 25th Divn.

(Panel 58) Pte. 203419, Tom Parker, 1/5th Bn. The Lancashire Fusiliers (T.F.): *s.* of Henry Parker, of 78, Victoria Street, Littleborough, co. Lancaster, by his wife Lizzie: enlisted Rochdale. Killed in action 6 September 1917: Age 22. See account re. Pte. S. Jackson (Panel 57).

PANEL 58 ENDS: PTE. J. RAFFERTY – LANCASHIRE FUSILIERS

PANEL 59 BEGINS: PTE. J. RAMSBOTTOM – LANCASHIRE FUSILIERS

(Panel 59) Pte. 201647, Richard Smethurst, 1/5th Bn. The Lancashire Fusiliers (T.F.): *s.* of Richard Smethurst, of Heywood, co. Lancaster, by his wife Hannah: *husb.* to Annie Smethurst (34, Marlborough Street, Hopwood, Heywood). Killed in action on the night of 31 August – 1 September 1917, by shellfire. Buried where he fell: Age 34. See account re. Capt. A.P. Hudson (Panel 54).

PANEL 59 ENDS: PTE. J. WELCH – LANCASHIRE FUSILIERS

PANEL 60 BEGINS: PTE. A. WELSBY – LANCASHIRE FUSILIERS

(Panel 60) Pte. 241232, Thomas Wild, 2/6th Bn. The Lancashire Fusiliers (T.F.): *s.* of Robert Wild, Cotton Weaver; of 26, Peel Street, Littleborough, Manchester, and Emma Frances Wild, his spouse: *b.* Taylor Street, Littleborough, c.1899: enlisted Rochdale. Killed in action 9 October 1917, on which date, shortly before 5.15 a.m., (immediately prior to their taking part in an attack toward Poelcapelle) the battalion's position was heavily bombarded by high-explosive and gas shells: Age 19. 'With kindest regards, His sorrowing Mother' chose the following words of sentiment for his Memorial Card:

> Not now as once we fondly hoped
> Each others face to see
> But in a better brighter world
> There let our meeting be.

(Panel 60) 2nd Lieut. Robert Smith, 2nd Bn. (21st Foot) The Royal Scots Fusiliers: *yst. s.* of John Smith, of Bankhead, Springside, co. Ayr, Joiner, by his wife Mary, *dau.* of James Campbell: *b.* Springside, aforesaid, 30 July 1897: *educ.* Irvine Royal Academy: Occupation – Medical Student: enlisted 4 July 1916: gazetted 2nd Lieut. Royal Scots Fusiliers April 1917: served with the Expeditionary Force in France from 2 August, and was killed in action at Polderhoek Chateau 15 December 1917. His Commanding Officer wrote, "He was a fine example to all that morning. He was beloved by officers and men alike. He died a splendid death. He cannot be replaced," and another officer, "He died fighting against great odds, and had he been spared he would in all probability have been decorated." The Chaplain wrote: "He was a lad of excellent parts, and was a special friend to me.": Age 20. *unm.*

(Panel 60) Pte. 47513, Robert Parker Love, 6/7th (Service) Bn. The Royal Scots Fusiliers: *s.* of Gavin Love, of 19, Harvey Terrace, Lochwinnoch, by his wife Jane: *b.* Lochwinnoch, 6 June 1898: *educ.* Public School, there: Occupation – Apprentice; Messrs Hamilton and Crawford, Chair Makers: joined Territorial Force, 10 March 1914: called up for service on the outbreak of war, but was discharged until he reached the military age, when he re-enlisted 10 April 1917: served with the Expeditionary Force in France and Flanders from 18 June, and was killed in action 22 August following while going into the trenches.: Age 19.

(Panel 60) Corpl. 204671, Duncan Downie, 9th Bn. (Glasgow Highlanders) The Highland Light Infantry (T.F.) attd. 2nd Bn. (21st Foot) Royal Scots Fusiliers: eldest *s.* of Neil Downie, of 36, Woodend Drive, Jordanhill, Glasgow, by his wife Janet, *dau.* of George Cunningham: *b.* Glasgow, 8 January 1887: *educ.* Hermitage Higher Grade School, Helensburgh, co. Dumbarton: Occupation – Partner; Messrs Downie and Co., Confectioners, Glasgow: joined Argyll & Sutherland Highlanders, 1904, transf'd. Lanarkshire Yeomanry, 1908; 9th (Territorial) Bn. Glasgow Highlanders, September 1914: served with the Expeditionary Force in France from August 1917, there attd. Royal Scots Fusiliers, and was killed in action at Zonnebeke, 14 December 1917: Buried at Poldsbeck Chateau, Zillebeke, 600 yards rear of Zonnebeke. His Commanding Officer wrote, "Corpl. Downie was being recommended for a commission. He won the esteem of both officers and men, and died a gallant soldier at his post.": Age 31. *unm.*

(Panel 60) Pte. 40818, Gilbert Gray, 1st Bn. (21st Foot) The Royal Scots Fusiliers: late of Lerwick, Shetland Islands: *s.* of William (& Catherine B.) Gray, of 88, Coburg Street, Leith: *b.* Grangemouth, co. Stirling, 1896: enlisted Edinburgh. Killed in action 26 September 1917, at Zonnebeke, nr. Ypres: Age 21.

(Panel 60) Pte. 33509, Thomas Mands, 1st Bn. (21st Foot) The Royal Scots Fusiliers: *s.* of the late James Mands, by his wife Jean, *dau.* of Thomas Blackie: *b.* Oathlaw, co. Forfar, 28 December 1880: *educ.* Oathlaw Public School: Occupation – Ploughman: enlisted 11th Black Watch (Royal Highlanders), 1 August 1916: transf'd. Royal Scots Fusiliers, November; served with the Expeditionary Force in France and Flanders from that month, where he acted as Stretcher-bearer, and was killed in action east of Ypres, 26 September 1917: Age 36. He *m.* Incheoch, 8 December 1905; Jemima (New Alyth, Alyth, Blairgowrie, co. Perth), *dau.* of John Nicoll, and had four children; James, *b.* 27 September 1906, John, *b.* 11 November 1908, William, *b.* 12 April 1911 and Betty, *b.* 2 April 1916.

(Panel 60) Pte. 43212, Alexander McNair, 6/7th (Service) Bn. The Royal Scots Fusiliers: *s.* of Robert (& Mrs) McNair, of Gasworks House, Linlithgow, co. West Lothian: and elder brother to Pte. 59420, A. McNair, 12th Royal Scots, who also fell: *b.* Linlithgow: enlisted there. Killed in action 22 August 1917: Age 20. *unm.*

His brother Andrew also has no known grave, he is recorded on Panel 13.

PANEL 60 ENDS: PTE. T. ORR – ROYAL SCOTS FUSILIERS

PANEL 61 BEGINS: PTE. F. PALING – ROYAL SCOTS FUSILIERS

(Panel 61) Pte. 14182, George Shirley, 1st Bn. (21st Foot) The Royal Scots Fusiliers: late of Dalmuir, co. Dumbarton: *s.* of the late Robert John Shirley, by his wife Elizabeth (4, James Street, Coleraine, Co. Londonderry): and brother to Pte. 23824, R.J. Shirley, 11th Royal Inniskilling Fusiliers, killed in action, 1 July 1916: *b.* Coleraine: enlisted Cumnock, co. Ayr. Killed in action 26 September 1917: Age 25. *unm.*

His brother Robert also has no known grave, he is commemorated on the Thiepval Memorial.

(Panel 61) 2nd Lieut. Hubert Pumphrey, 10th (Service) Bn. The Cheshire Regt.: *s.* of Thomas Edwin Pumphrey, of Mayfield, Sunderland, co. Durham, J.P., by his wife Mary Anna, *dau.* of the late Joshua Wilson: and elder brother to Capt. A. Pumphrey, D.S.O., Durham Light Infantry, killed in action at Tower Hamlets, 21 September 1917: *b.* Sunderland, 9 January 1881: *educ.* Quaker School, Bootham, York, and Durham College of Science: Occupation – Chartered Patent Agent; Manager of the Bradford branch of Messrs W.P. Thompson and Co., Patent Agents, Liverpool: joined Inns of Court O.T.C., 6 December 1915: gazetted 2nd Lieut., Cheshire Regt., 22 November 1916: served with the Expeditionary Force in France from 25 January 1917: wounded at Ypres the following July: on recovery returned to France, 13 April 1918, and was killed in action at Kemmel Hill, 26 April following. An officer wrote, "He was very gallantly leading his men. While running ahead of them to charge a machine-gun position, he was shot and killed instantly. He was a keen soldier and a fearless leader." 2nd Lieut. Pumphrey was a keen sportsman, fishing and climbing being his favourite pastimes: Age 37. He *m.* Little Broughton, co. Cumberland, 11 December 1907; Daisy (since died, late of South Bank, Oxton, co. Chester), *dau.* of the late Charles Hodgson Bigland, of Birkenhead, and had a *dau.* Anstice Mary, *b.* 4 December 1908.

His brother Arnold also has no known grave, he is recorded on Panel 128.

(Panel 61) Corpl. 39980, Herbert Hobson, 15th (Service) Bn. The Cheshire Regt.: *s.* of Benjamin (& Mrs) Hobson: *b.* Barnsley, co. York, August 1889: *educ.* there: Occupation – Miner:enlisted in the Cheshire Regt. 1 December 1914: served with the Expeditionary Force in France and Flanders, and was killed in action 24 October 1917. Buried where he fell: Age 28. Capt. R. Frost wrote, "He was on his way back to report the situation when a shell struck him, killing him instantly. I shall feel his loss most keenly myself, as he was a most reliable N.C.O., and very brave." He *m.* St. George's Church, Barnsley; Annie (late of 11, George Street, Barnsley, now Mrs Stead, 9, George Street), and had two children.

(Panel 61) Corpl. 244940, Harold Edward Liles, 10th (Service) Bn. The Cheshire Regt.: of 75/77, High Street, Cheadle, co. Chester: *b.* Cheadle, about 1884: Occupation – Butcher's Assistant; Frank Liles, High Street, Cheadle: served with Cheshire Yeomanry Territorials, no.1536: enlisted from the Territorials, Chester, prior to May 1916: transferred 10th Battn. Cheshire Regt. After a few days spent behind the lines in late April 1918, the Cheshires returned to the trenches at Kemmel on the evening of 1 May. On 3 May (1918), in what was believed at the time to be preparation for an attack, the enemy subjected the Cheshires position to continual heavy shelling throughout the day; the attack did not materialise but four soldiers, including Harold, were killed.

(Panel 61) L/Corpl. 9655, William Robert Hughes, M.M., 10th (Service) Bn. The Cheshire Regt.: *s.* of William Robert Hughes, of 31, St. Albans Road, Liscard, Wallasey, by his wife Jane: *b.* Rock Ferry, 1896: enlisted Birkenhead, co. Chester. Killed by shellfire 3 May 1918: Age 21. See Corpl. H.E. Liles, above.

(Panel 61) Pte. 50425, William Austin, 'A' Coy., 16th (Service) Bn. (2nd Birkenhead) The Cheshire Regt.: *s.* of Charles Austin, of 55, Church Lane, Marple, co. Chester: and elder brother to Pte. 21939, L. Austin, 7th King's Own Scottish Borderers, killed in action 11 May 1916: enlisted 1915: served with the Expeditionary Force in France and Flanders from early 1916, and was killed in action 22 October 1917: Age 28.

His brother Leonard is buried in Arras Road Cemetery, Roclincourt (II.G.3).

(Panel 61) Pte. 18002, Fred Blackhurst, 1st Bn. (22nd Foot) The Cheshire Regt.: *s.* of Isaac Blackhurst, of Woodheath Farm, Lower Withington, Chelford, co. Chester, by his wife Ellen, *dau.* of John Leighton: *b.* Chelford, aforesaid, 10 December 1894: *educ.* there: Occupation – Teamsman: enlisted 9 November 1914: served with the Expeditionary Force in France and Flanders from 25 September 1915, and was killed in action at Century (Sanctuary) Wood 4 October 1917. Buried there: Age 22. *unm.*

(Panel 61) Pte. 72262, Archibald Blank, 10th (Service) Bn. The Cheshire Regt.: formerly no.3964, Devon Yeomanry: *b.* Stoke Gabriel, co. Devon: enlisted Newton Abbot. Killed by shellfire 3 May 1918. See Corpl. H.E. Liles, above.

PANEL 61 ENDS: PTE. S. BURGESS – CHESHIRE REGT.

PANEL 62 BEGINS: PTE. A. BUSCALL – CHESHIRE REGT.

(Panel 62) Pte. 72232, Alfred Buscall, 1/6th Bn. The Cheshire Regt. (T.F.): formerly no.8376, Devonshire Yeomanry: *s* of John Buscall, of Moorlands, Bournemouth, co. Hants, by his wife Hannah: and yr. brother to L/Corpl. 25008, J. Buscall, Middlesex Regt., killed in action, 25 August 1917: *b.* Forest Gate, London: enlisted Bournemouth. Killed in action 21 September 1918: Age 19.

His brother John is buried in Zandvoorde British Cemetery (IV.G.12).

(Panel 62) Pte. 7268, Fred Gidman, (Signaller) 9th (Service) Bn. The Cheshire Regt.: *s.* of the late John Gidman, by his wife Emily, (44, Fence St., Macclesfield), *dau.* of William Simms: *b.* Hurdsfield, co. Chester, 14 February 1885: *educ.* Townley St. School, Macclesfield: Occupation – Weaver: enlisted in the Cheshire Regt., 2 November 1903: served three years with the Colours, and joined the Reserve: called up on mobilization, 5 August 1914: served with the Expeditionary Force in France and Flanders from that month, taking part in the retreat from Mons and in many engagements: was accidentally injured at the Battle of the Marne through the collapse of a building, and invalided home in November 1914: on recovery proceeded to Mesopotamia in September 1915: invalided home suffering from heat-stroke in April 1917: returned to France, 7 September following, and was killed in action at the Battle of Vimy Ridge (*q.v.*), 3 May 1918. Buried at Voormezeele: Age 33. His Commanding Officer, 2nd Lieut. A.B. Inchboard wrote, "He was a noble fellow, one whom we all loved and esteemed....and all the men of my command join me in sympathizing with you in your sad bereavement, when you lost so honoured and trusted a man." He *m.* Hurdsfield Church, 24 August 1911; Sarah Elizabeth (37, Waterloo St., Macclesfield), *dau.* of Walter Clark, and had three children; Selina, *b.* 29 January 1918, James, *b.* 22 December 1915 and Edward, *b.* 29 May 1913.

(Panel 62) Pte. W/272, John Hindley, (No.1 Lewis Gun Section), 15th (Service) Bn. The Cheshire Regt.: 4th *s.* of John Hindley, of 13, Violet Street, Widnes, Foreman Platelayer, by his wife Elizabeth: *b.* Widnes, co. Chester, 30 November 1884: *educ.* there: Occupation – Captain of the 'Starlight' (Sunlight

Boats): enlisted September 1914: served with the Expeditionary Force in France and Flanders: invalided home in September 1916, with trench feet: rejoined his regiment on recovery. Killed in action 24 October 1917 at Ypres, where he was buried: Age 32. He *m.* New Ferry, 8 February 1905; Sarah Jane Rimmer, *née* Hindley (23, Western Avenue, Port Causeway, New Ferry, Birkenhead), *dau.* of George Ball, of Widnes, and had three children; John George, *b.* 8 August 1906, Edwin, *b.* 21 January 1910 and Ivy, *b.* 20 December 1912. (*IWGC record age 33*)

(Panel 62) Pte. 9611, William King, 10th (Service) Bn. The Cheshire Regt.: *s.* of Marie King (85, Egerton Street, Sale, co. Chester): *b.* St. Joseph's, Sale, 1893: enlisted Chester. Killed in action 3 May 1918, by enemy shellfire: Age 24. *unm.* See Corpl. H.E. Liles (Panel 61)

(Panel 62) Pte. 266419, Harry Marshall, 1/6th Bn. The Cheshire Regt. (T.F.): *s.* of George Marshall, of 20, Carr Cottages, Carrbrook, Stalybridge, co. Chester, by his wife Ann: and brother to Pte. 2567, H. Marshall, 1/7th Duke of Wellington's Regt., died of wounds 11 December 1915; and Pte. 242470, G. Marshall, 1/5th South Lancashire Regt., killed in action, 13 May 1917: *b.* Barnsley, co. York: enlisted Stalybridge. Killed in action 29 October 1917: Age 25. *unm.*

His brother Harry is buried in Lijssenthoek Military Cemetery (IV.C.25A); George, Vlamertinghe Military Cemetery (V.M.11).

PANEL 62 ENDS: PTE. W.C. MUGGERIDGE – CHESHIRE REGT.

PANEL 63 BEGINS: PTE. E.G. MUNGEHAM – CHESHIRE REGT.

(Panel 63) Pte. 211447, Griffith Thomas, Trench Mortar Bty., 9th (Service) Bn. The Cheshire Regt.: eldest *s.* of William Thomas, Carpenter; of Curzon Road, Craig-y-don, Llandudno: *b.* Wesley Terrace, Penygroes, Llanllyfni, co. Carmarthen, 6 March 1880: Occupation – Bricklayer: enlisted Cheshire Regt., 1 September 1914: served with the Expeditionary Force in France and Flanders from the following June, and was killed in action at Ypres, 20 September 1917, being shot by an enemy sniper whilst trying to save a badly wounded comrade. Buried in a wood near the firing line. Lieut. H.T Horsfall wrote, "Words cannot express my appreciation of your husband's gallant conduct on that morning: cool, calm, collected under deadly fire; helping me invaluably with the guns which he took over the top. He was a hero of heroes, and what more can be said of any man? He gave his life for another, while performing an act of mercy. He was a man to be proud of, a heart of gold, and a worthy comrade of any officer or man. His loss will be felt throughout the whole battery.": Age 37. He *m.* Christ Church, Ormskirk, 18 April 1903; Elizabeth, since died, late of 22, Myrtle Street, Birkenhead, co. Chester, *dau.* of the late James Mealor, and had three children; William, *b.* 24 January 1904, Winifred, *b.* 1 February 1907 and Ernest, *b.* 16 October 1908. (*IWGC record age 36*)

(Panel 63) Pte. 49581, Herbert Topping, M.M., 13th (Service) Bn. The Cheshire Regt.: *s.* of the late Edward Wilson Topping, by his wife Martha (87, Oliver Street, Birkenhead), *dau.* of Thomas Croft: *b.* Manchester, co. Lancaster, 15 September 1895: *educ.* St. John's Schools, Birkenhead: employee Laird's Shipbuilding Yard: enlisted Cheshire Regt., 14 July 1915: served with the Expeditionary Force in France and Flanders from July 1916; wounded in action on the Somme, October following, and invalided home: returned to France 24 May 1917; killed in action 4 October following. Buried where he fell: Age 22. *unm.*

(Panel 63) Pte. 44264, George Alfred Woods, 9th (Service) Bn. The Cheshire Regt.: *s.* of George Woods, of 75, Paterson Street, Birkenhead, by his wife Sarah: *b.* Birkenhead, co. Chester, 10 March 1885: *educ.* Woodlands School: Occupation – Baker's Manager: enlisted May 1916: served with the Expeditionary Force in France and Flanders from the following November, and was killed in action at Zillebeke, south-east of Ypres, 20 September 1917: Age 32. He *m.* Birkenhead, 1 August 1910; Margaret (33, Maybank Road, Birkenhead), *dau.* of George Jones, and had a son Alfred, *b.* 7 April 1913.

On 25 September 1917, 2nd Bn. Royal Welsh Fusiliers were allotted the task of covering the right flank of the 5th Australian Division in an attack scheduled for the following day, as part of the Australians continued advance through Polygon Wood. Supposed to move forward from their support positions just south of the Menin Road, near Clapham Junction, at 10 a.m., a hurried conference between the company commanders and Major R.A. Poore, commanding the battalion, brought to light the fact that there were not enough maps for the company officers, and a certain amount of confusion arose as to which heading each company would advance towards. B and D were to advance to Polderhoek Chateau, A in reserve, or C in support, would follow, but towards Jut Farm to link with 15 Australian Brigade. Major Poore was then advised by the C.O. 11 Field Coy., Royal Engineers, of a more circuitous route through 4th Australian Division's sector. 'Crossing the Menin Road east of Clapham Junction, on the fringe of the barrage, one man was hit. Behind Inverness Copse half a dozen tanks lay foundered in bog. The bog, over which the battalion had to pass, extended a great part of the way behind Glencorse Wood, where the spongy ground and the soft places that had to be jumped caused delay. Soon the track was lined with Lewis gun magazines and rifle grenades cast aside by the carriers. However, by utilising this route, even when passing through the barrage between Glencorse Wood and Nonne Boschen, less than half a dozen casualties were sustained.' Forming up east to west, with their left on Black Watch Corner, D Company were the first to arrive; B Company arrived in time to advance at zero, their Adjutant, Capt. J.C. Mann, being shot through the throat after seeing the last platoons jump off; Capt. E. Coster, D Company, was killed, shot through the head as he entered a scraggy orchard north of Jerk Farm. B Company, after clearing a crescent shaped line of pill-boxes enclosing Carlisle and Jerk Farms, lost 2nd Lieuts. E.F.C. Colquhoun and I. Williams (both wounded). Major Poore, seeing B and D lose contact, ordered elements of A Company in to the gap thus created, gaining contact with B. D Company, after rapidly getting through Jerk Farm, had changed front and advanced eastward where they found some 31st Australians in shell-holes; advancing with these to a trench between Carlisle and Jerk Farms in rear, and Jut Farm and Cameron House in front. There the mixed force remained, firing to their front and right into the wooded slope of Polderhoek Chateau. At about 1.30 p.m. Lieut. W.H. Radford's, C Company, were sent to a less exposed position in rear of the line of deployment. At about 2.30 a signaller informed Capt. J.C. Dunn (Medical Officer) that "Major Poore was dead. While he and Casson and Colquhoun, who had joined them, were sitting in a shell-hole talking, a shell fell on them, killing all three."

(Panel 63) Capt. Ernest Coster, M.C., 'D' Coy., 2nd Bn. (23rd Foot) The Royal Welsh Fusiliers. Shot through the head, north of Jerk Farm, 26 September 1917.

Major Poore, 2nd Lieuts. Casson and Colquhoun are buried in Poelcappelle British Cemetery (LV.F.11, 12, and 13 respectively).

(Panel 63) Capt. John Charles Mann, M.C., (Adjt.) 'B' Coy., 2nd Bn. (23rd Foot) The Royal Welsh Fusiliers: *s.* of Mr (& Mrs) Charles W. Mann, of 'Kenton,' Sutton, co. Surrey. Shot through the throat, in the vicinity of Black Watch Corner, 26 September 1917. Age 23.

(Panel 63) 2nd Lieut. Hywel Llewellyn Evans, attd. 'A' Coy., 2nd Bn. (23rd Foot) The Royal Welsh Fusiliers. Died of wounds, 26 September 1917, received in action a few hours previously, between Jerk Farm and Lone Farm, during his battalion's part in the attack made by 5th Australian Division.

PANEL 63 ENDS: CORPL. R.O. DAVIES, D.C.M. – ROYAL WELSH FUSILIERS

PANEL 64 BEGINS: CORPL. J. EVANS, M.M. – ROYAL WELSH FUSILIERS

(Panel 64) Corpl. 21151, Samuel Soar, M.M. (Siglr.), 14th (Service) Bn. The Royal Welsh Fusiliers: *s.* of Edward Soar, of Forest Villa, Mansfield Road, Sutton-in-Ashfield, by his wife Susannah: *b.* Stoneyford Lane, 31 March 1895: Occupation – Painter and Decorator; Messrs Robinson, Mansfield: enlisted Mansfield, January 1915. Killed in action 2 September 1917, while at duty in his capacity as Signaller: Age 22. *unm.* The Chaplain, D. Morris wrote, "Please accept my sincerest sympathy with you in your sad bereavement, caused by the death of your dear son. I knew your son very well, and knew the officer who until lately was in charge of the signallers. This officer gave your son a high character and paid great tribute to his intelligence and devotion to duty. I assure you that Corpl. Soar was a splendid soldier and a good friend. His place is sadly missed in the battalion. It will be some comfort for you to know that a burial service was held over his grave, and portions of Psalm 90 and I. Cor. 15 were read. Turn to these passages and I am sure you will find comfort in them. Also remember that death came instantaneously, so that there was no pain to be suffered. A shell hit the place where he was, with the result that it collapsed. Do not mourn as one without hope, for we have a hope of reunion again with our dear ones. May God bless his sacrifice that peace may come soon and bless you abundantly with His grace to enable you to bear your hard time." Sergt. F. Morgan wrote, "Just a few lines on behalf of the Signal Section to send you our greatest sympathy in this your great trouble and sad bereavement, as I dare say the War Office has already informed you of the sad end of poor Sam. He was killed on the 31 August (*q.v.*) by a dugout being blown in on him in company with seven of his mates. I would have written before, but could not bring myself to start on such an awful task, because he was always such a pal of all of us. I can only say that he did not suffer at all as death was instantaneous. I am proud to say, as a friend, that he died doing his duty, in fact more than his duty, work that no man would need to be ashamed to have shirked. I know that it does not do any good to praise him now. All I can say is that none mourns him more than myself and the remainder of the old boys of our Signal Section who have known him so long. I will not say any more at present as I am an awful letter writer, and hope you will forgive me for any brusqueness in this." And, in a letter to his brother Charlie, Pte. 20874, A. Burton, "A few lines in deepest sympathy in connection with the sad news of your brother Sam's death. He was killed in action on the morning of the 1/9/1917 (*q.v.*) by a shell exploding in the dugout. I can assure you he felt no pain as his death was instantaneous. It is impossible for me to describe how we felt over the sad affair, as you can imagine. Sam was well liked by the section and battalion, as he was everything desired as a N.C.O. and a friend. He was popular throughout. May you and your people bear up at this time of sorrow in the best possible manner. On behalf of the Signal Section I hope you will accept these few lines as a small token of the esteem with which we regarded him, and as a message of condolence." Awarded the Military Medal, May 1916, for 'keeping up communication with headquarters during an exceedingly heavy bombardment, when all wires had been broken and everything all around blown to pieces.' Connected with St. Michael's Church and Sunday School for the greater part of his life, he was well-known and respected. '*The Notts Free Press*' 'In Memoriam,' 6 September 1918:-

Not our will, But thine, O Lord, be done

Father, Mother, Jennie, Charlie and Meg.

(Panel 64) L/Corpl. 73010, William Hughes, 24th (Dismounted Denbighshire Yeomanry) Bn. The Royal Welsh Fusiliers (T.F.): *yst. s.* of the late Peter Hughes, by his 2nd wife Mary Jane (Church Cottages, nr. The Red Lion Hotel, Northop, co. Flint): *b.* Northop, 1888: enlisted there: served with the Expeditionary Force in Palestine (from late 1915); France and Flanders from 7 May 1918, and was killed in action 30 October 1918, nr. Menin: Age 30.

(Panel 64) Pte. 201813, William Bailey, 2nd Bn. (23rd Foot) The Royal Welsh Fusiliers: *s.* of John Bailey, of 61, Thursby Road, Burnley, co. Lancaster, by his wife Elizabeth: and *yr.* brother to Pte. 235213, J. Bailey, King's (Liverpool) Regt., killed 24 July 1917. Killed in action 26 September 1917; Polygon Wood: Age 34.

His brother Joseph also has no known grave, he is commemorated on the Ypres (Menin Gate) Memorial (Panel 6).

(Panel 64) Pte. 73207, Walter James Griffiths, 2nd Bn. (23rd Foot) The Royal Welsh Fusiliers: *s.* of Joseph Griffiths, of Haroldstone Hill, Broad Haven, Haverfordwest, co. Pembroke, by his wife Frances: *b.* Broad Haven, 1898: enlisted Carmarthen, 1916: served with the Expeditionary Force in France and Flanders: took part in the fighting at Bullecourt. Killed in action at Ypres 28 November 1917: Age 19. The Broadhaven War Memorial records the names of 9 local men who made the supreme sacrifice; Pte. Griffiths is not among them. (*IWGC record 73267, 26 November 1917*)

(Panel 64) Pte. 25341, Albert Higginson, 'A' Coy., 17th (Service) Bn. The Royal Welsh Fusiliers: *s.* of Geoffrey Higginson, of 204, Blackburn Road, Great Harwood, co. Lancaster, by his wife Ann Ellen: and brother to Pte. 44822, T. Higginson, 18th Gloucester Regt. attd. 2nd Employment Base Depot, died of sickness, 24 October 1918, aged 19 years: *b*. Bamber Bridge, co. Lancaster: enlisted Blackburn. Killed in action 25 August 1917: Age 23. *unm*.

His brother Tom is buried in St. Sever Cemetery Extension, Rouen (S.II.DD.10).

PANEL 64 ENDS: PTE. E. MORRIS – ROYAL WELSH FUSILIERS

PANEL 65 BEGINS: PTE. J. MORRIS – ROYAL WELSH FUSILIERS

(Panel 65) Pte. 40262, John Richard Thomas, 2nd Bn. (23rd Foot) The Royal Welsh Fusiliers: eldest *s*. of John Thomas, of 'Groes Bach,' Abergele Road, Colwyn Bay, by his wife Maria, *dau*. of Richard Jones: *b*. Bodfari, co. Denbigh, 24 January 1892: *educ*. Llanelian, co. Denbigh: Occupation – Gardener to Lord Aberconway: enlisted 11 February 1915: served with the Expeditionary Force in France and Flanders from the following July. Reported missing after the fighting at Polygon Wood 26 September 1917; now assumed killed in action on that date: Age 25. *unm*.

(Panel 65) Lieut. Ivor Dryhurst Jones, 'D' Coy., 5th (Service) Bn. (Pioneers) The South Wales Borderers: *s*. of the late Rev. William Jones, Vicar of Prestatyn, co. Flint, and Mrs M.E. Jones ('Gorphwysfa,' Victoria Road, Prestatyn): and twin brother to Lieut. A.S. Jones, 108th Sqdn. Royal Air Force, killed in action 27 September 1918. Killed in action 10 April 1918; Messines: Age 18.

His twin Arthur is buried in Sanctuary Wood Cemetery (V.T.8).

(Panel 65) Corpl. 22300, James Henry James, 11th (Service) Bn. (2nd Gwent) The South Wales Borderers: *s*. of William James, of 101, Henry Street, Newport, co. Monmouth, by his wife Alice: *husb*. to Florence May James (19, Castle Street, Newport): and brother to Pte. 49716, A.T. James, 2nd Royal Inniskilling Fusiliers, killed in action 1 September 1918: enlisted Newport. Killed in action 27 August 1917.

His brother Albert is buried in Bailleul Communal Cemetery Extension (III.G.130).

(Panel 65) Corpl. 39614, John Trevor Williams, 2nd Bn. (24th Foot) The South Wales Borderers: *s*. of John Jenkin Williams, Provision Merchant; of Aberdare House, Ogmore Vale, co. Glamorgan, by his wife Kate, *dau*. of Samuel Adams, of Caldicot, co. Monmouth: *b*. Ogmore Vale, 16 December 1896: *educ*. there, and Bridgend: Occupation – Engineer's Apprentice: enlisted 16 December 1915: served in Ireland during the Irish Rebellion, April 1916: proceeded to France, September following, and was killed in action near the Bronbeke Stream, 27 August 1917. His Commanding Officer wrote: "Corpl. Williams volunteered for the duty... It was one of those bits of bad luck we have to contend with... He was a fine lad, and had tons of pluck," and another officer: "We were in many scraps together, but Trevor always turned up with a smiling face." Another also wrote: "He was a capable soldier, popular with his men, and a brave man," and a comrade: "I never knew a non-commissioned officer like him; he will be greatly missed." In 1815 his great-great-grandfather, a Breconshire farmer, joined up, was sent to Brecon, and drafted into the South Wales Borderers. Whilst in training, Waterloo was fought, and they were disbanded. Exactly 100 years and five generations later, his descendant, Corpl. J.T. Williams, joined up in the winter of 1915, in the Yeomanry, was sent to Brecon, and transferred to the same regiment: Age 20. *unm*. (*IWGC record 28 August*)

(Panel 65) Pte. 40777, Albert Baldwin, 2nd Bn. (24th Foot) The South Wales Borderers: formerly no.22949, Oxford and Bucks Light Infantry: *s*. of Edward Baldwin, of 151, Gordon Road, High Wycombe, co. Buckingham, by his wife Ellen: and elder brother to Pte. 12989, L.G. Baldwin, 6th O.B.L.I., killed in action, 3 September 1916, at the Somme: *b*. High Wycombe, afsd: Occupation – Chair Polisher: enlisted High Wycombe. Killed in action 16 August 1917: Age 31.

His brother Leonard also has no known grave; he is commemorated on the Thiepval Memorial.

PANEL 65 ENDS: PTE. E.W. DYER – SOUTH WALES BORDERERS

PANEL 66 BEGINS: PTE. J.W. EDMONDS – SOUTH WALES BORDERERS

(Panel 66) Pte. 28283, John Wynne Evans, 'B' Coy., 2nd Bn. (24th Foot) The South Wales Borderers: *s.* of the late David Evans, of Caegwyn, Llangeitho, Farmer, by his wife Elizabeth, *dau.* of the late John Edwards: *b.* Caegwyn, Llangeitho, co. Cardigan, 29 April 1879: *educ.* Council School, Llangeitho; County School, Aberystwyth, and University College of Wales, Aberystwyth: went to Canada, June 1913; settled at Ontario: returned to England December 1915: enlisted 11 July 1916: served with the Expeditionary Force in France and Flanders from the following November, and was killed in action at Langemarck, 16 August 1917. Buried near the ruins of Montemial Farm, over the Steenbeke River. The Chaplain wrote, "In the company the loss is very keenly felt of a thoroughly good soldier, and a well-liked and trustworthy comrade.": Age 36. *unm.*

(Panel 66) Pte. 40296, William John Holmes, 10th (Service) Bn. The South Wales Borderers: 2nd *s.* of George Edward Holmes, of Lodsworth, Petworth, co. Sussex, Gamekeeper to Col. W. Kenyon Mitford, by his wife Kate, *dau.* of John William Inglefield, of High Cliff, Winchester, co. Hants: *b.* Crendall, near Farnham, co. Surrey, 31 March 1898: *educ.* Lurgashall Schools, near Petworth: Occupation – Assistant Gamekeeper on the estate of Col. Barkley, Midhurst, co. Sussex: enlisted Royal Sussex Regt., 9 November 1914, subsequently transf'd. South Wales Borderers: served with the Expeditionary Force in France and Flanders, and was killed in action during the Battle of Langemarck, 24 August 1917. Buried at the north-eastern ridge of the village of Langemarck. The Rev. W.T. Havard, Chaplain, wrote, "He went into action with his battalion, and, taking shelter for a moment under cover of a house, during the intense hostile bombardment, he was instantly killed by shell fire; the shell striking and exploding, bringing down most of the ruined house. We recovered his body next day;" and Lieut. C.A. Lundy, "Every officer and man in D Coy. loved and respected him, and all feel his loss keenly. I do especially, as he was in my platoon." Sergt. G. Parsons also wrote, "Your son was one of the very best boys in my platoon; a strong, fearless and gallant lad was he, and respected by all. I am sure it will be a great loss to his platoon and to the company." And Corpl. J. Mathews, "I lost a good little chum in him...He was a good boy, always ready to do any one of us a good turn. I may say Sergt. Parsons would never allow a man to speak rough of him, as he thought so much of him." He won a Silver Medal in a competition for bayonet fighting while on service in France, which he sent home to his parents only a few days before his death.: Age 19.

(Panel 66) Pte. 44629, Walter Kissack Looney, 1st Bn. (24th Foot) The South Wales Borderers: only *s.* of James Looney, of 22, Cleveland Street, Birkenhead, Dock Board Employee, by his wife Annie S., *dau.* of Walter Hughes: *b.* Ramsey, Isle of Man, 26 November 1883: *educ.* Ramsey Grammar School: Occupation – Bank Clerk; Liverpool: enlisted Lancashire Fortress Royal Engineers, March 1916: afterwards transf'd. South Wales Borderers: served with the Expeditionary Force in France from January 1917. Reported missing after the fighting at Passchendaele on 9 November following; now assumed killed in action on or about that date. Age 33. *unm.*

(Panel 66) Pte. 40800, Joseph Middleton, 2nd Bn. (24th Foot) The South Wales Borderers: formerly no.51072, Welch Regt.: *b.* Paddington, London. Killed in action 16 August 1917.

(Panel 66) Pte. 40258, Arthur Potter, 10th (Service) Bn. (1st Gwent) The South Wales Borderers: formerly no.30142, East Surrey Regt.: late of New Malden, co. Surrey: *s.* of Emma Potter (58, Dennis Road, Eastbourne, co. Sussex): and elder brother to Pte. TF/201212, E. Potter, 4th Royal Sussex Regt., died of wounds 28 March 1917, in Egypt; aged 18 years: *b.* Eastbourne, c.1883: Occupation – Marine Dealer: enlisted Kingston-on-Thames. Killed in action 25 August 1917: Age 34.

His brother Ernest is buried in Deir El Belah War Cemetery (A.30).

(Panel 66) Pte. 39816, George Montague Price, 5th (Service) Bn. (Pioneers) The South Wales Borderers: *s.* of the late Andrew Price, of Orleton, Builder, by his wife Alice (21, Daisy Bank, Macclesfield), *dau.* of Thomas Pritchard: *b.* Orleton, co. Hereford, 5 February 1878: *educ.* Orleton School, and Lucton School, Hereford: Occupation – Stonemason: enlisted South Wales Borderers, 1 May 1916: served with the Expeditionary Force in France from the following August, and was killed in action nr. Hill 60, 2 October

1917. Buried there. Captain L. Rose wrote, "He was a good soldier, performed his work well, and will be greatly missed by myself and the men of the company.": Age 39. *unm.*

(Panel 66) Pte. 13735, Joseph Yemm, 1st Bn. (24th Foot) The South Wales Borderers: *s.* of Llewellyn Yemm, of 9, John Street, Pontypool, co. Monmouth, and Agnes Yemm, his wife: and elder brother to Pte. 36078, W.H. Yemm, 1st Welsh Regt. died of wounds 7 October 1915: *b.* Pontypool: enlisted Newport. Killed in action 10 November 1917: Age 29. Dedicated 'They Died That We Might Live In Peace And Liberty,' the brothers Yemm are remembered on the Ross-on-Wye War Memorial (Face 4, Col.2).

His brother William is buried in St. Sever Cemetery, Rouen (A.12.10).

(Panel 66) Capt. James Ernest Ford, 1st Bn. (25th Foot) The King's Own Scottish Borderers: eldest *s.* of James Henry William Ford, Hon. Lieut. in Army, of 13, Appleton Gate, Newark, co. Nottingham, by his wife Sarah, *dau.* of the late T. Barratt: *b.* Newark-on-Trent, June 1893: *educ.* Magnus Grammar School, Newark, and Wandsworth College: entered the offices of Messrs Tallent and Co., Solicitors, Newark: was afterwards articled to Mr T. Harrison, Borough Accountant: joined Motor Cyclists, Notts Sherwood Rangers Yeomanry, June 1911: on the outbreak of war, was called up for Service: went to Egypt, April 1915: obtained a commission October following: served with the Mediterranean Expeditionary Force at Gallipoli: contracted dysentery, and was invalided to Egypt and thence to England: on his recovery became attd. East Lancashire Regt., Colchester: later rejoined his regiment at Edinburgh: proceeded to France and was killed in action, 4 October 1917, while leading his company at Polderhoek Chateau.: Age 24. *unm.*

(Panel 66) 2nd Lieut. William Millar Douglas, 5th (Dumfries & Galloway) Bn. (T.F.) attd. 7/8th (Service) Bn. The King's Own Scottish Borderers. Killed by shellfire 19 August 1917, between Zonnebeke Road and Frost Farm. At the time of his death 2nd Lieut. Douglas was commanding 'B' Coy., 7/8th Battn.

Mortally wounded by the same shell, 2nd Lieut. J. Black died later the same day; he is buried in Brandhoek New Military Cemetery No.3 (II.G.26).

PANEL 66 ENDS: L/CORPL. A. FORTUNE – KING'S OWN SCOTTISH BORDERERS

PANEL 67 BEGINS: L/CORPL. J. GARDNER – KINGS OWN SCOTTISH BORDERERS

(Panel 67) L/Corpl. 20028, John Hughes, 1st Bn. (25th Foot) The King's Own Scottish Borderers: eldest *s.* of the late Peter Hughes, by his wife Catherine Ann (18, Close Street, Hemsworth, nr. Wakefield): *b.* Barnsley, co. York, August 1895: *educ.* Holy Road School: Occupation – Miner: enlisted 29 May 1915: served with the Expeditionary Force in France and Flanders, and was killed in action 16 August 1917. His Commanding Officer wrote: "Your son was a good soldier. He was one of my best junior N.C.O.'s. He was working hard in his part of the trench when he met his fate. You will always know that he died at his post doing his duty." Age 22. *unm.*

(Panel 67) Pte. 40471, Walter Mellish Campbell, 2nd Bn. (25th Foot) The King's Own Scottish Borderers: eldest *s.* of Duncan Campbell, of The Lodge, Soonhope, Peebles, by his wife Annie, *dau.* of the late Walter Mellish, of Ormsary, Argyle: *b.* Ardrishaig, co. Argyle, 27 June 1897: *educ.* Peebles Burgh, and County High School: enlisted 20 January 1915: attd. 2/9th Royal Scots, January 1916: served with the Expeditionary Force in France and Flanders, from 1 September following: took part in the operations on the Somme: invalided home, December 1916, suffering from trench feet: on recovery returned to France; joined 2nd King's Own Scottish Borderers, and was killed in action 27 October 1917, while returning from the attack on Polderhoek Chateau, Passchendaele. Buried south-south-west of Zonnebeke, north-east of Ypres. A comrade wrote, "He was a good and brave lad, and many are the little incidents I could name to show the true quality of so brave and faithful a soldier when in the firing line. I am sure he will be missed by all the boys who knew him, for he was esteemed by all.": Age 21. *unm.*

(Panel 67) Pte. 40655, Harry Cutt, 6th (Service) Bn. The King's Own Scottish Borderers: formerly no.21696, Northumberland Fusiliers: *s.* of Mary Cutt (Bell Lane Terrace, Ackworth Moor Top, Pontefract): and elder brother to Pte. 203643, W. Cutt, 2/4th Leicestershire Regt., died of wounds 22 October 1917: *b.* Upton, 1882: enlisted Hemsworth, co. York. Killed in action 22 October 1917: Age 35.

His brother Wilfred is buried in Nouex-les-Mines Communal Cemetery Extension (II.C.21).

(Panel 68) Pte. 21505, George Firth, 1st Bn. (25th Foot) The King's Own Scottish Borderers: s. of Silvester Firth, of 11, Granny Avenue, Churlwell, Leeds, by his wife Elizabeth Ann: and brother to Pte. 40977, William Firth, 1st Cameronians (Sco.Rif.), killed in action, 19 December 1916: *b.* Churlwell: enlisted Leeds. Killed in action 27 August 1917.

His brother William is buried in Hem Farm Military Cemetery, Hem-Monacu (I.D.4).

(Panel 67) Pte. 27639, George Macnab, 2nd Bn. (25th Foot) The King's Own Scottish Borderers: eldest *s.* of the late Richard Macnab, by his wife Mary (Briar Bank, Innellan), *dau.* of Peter Maclean, of Colintraive: *b.* Innellan, co. Argyle, 30 September 1886: *educ.* there: Occupation – Master Plumber: enlisted Scottish Borderers, October 1916 served with the Expeditionary Force in France and Flanders from 1 May 1917; killed in action nr. Gheluvelt, 4 October following. Buried where he fell. The Chaplain wrote, "Your brother did his duty to the last. He was a splendid fellow, and I saw quite a lot of him. He set a fine example to his comrades in every way.": Age 31. *unm.*

(Panel 67) Pte. 13099, Stephen Ramage, 'C' Coy. 6th (Service) Bn. The King's Own Scottish Borderers: *s.* of Janet B. Ramage (87, Bonnington Road, Leith): and yr. brother to Sergt. S/2962, II. Ramage, 8th Black Watch, killed in action, 12 October 1917; and Pte. 10139, J. Ramage, Highland Light Infantry, killed in action, 11 January 1917, in Mesopotamia. Killed in action 30 September 1918: Age 23. He leaves a widow, Cecilia B. Ramage (59, Bonnington Road, Leith).

His brothers Hugh and James also have no known grave; they are recorded on Panel 94 and the Basra Memorial, Iraq respectively.

PANEL 67 ENDS: PTE. J. ROONEY (FOLLOWED BY PTE. W. WILLIAMSON [INSERTED]) – K.O.S.B.

PANEL 68 BEGINS: PTE. A. ROSS – KING'S OWN SCOTTISH BORDERERS

(Panel 68) Pte. 41241, John Davidson Smith, 2nd Bn. (25th Foot) The King's Own Scottish Borderers: *s.* of Charles Smith, of 61, South Drumlanrig Street, Thornhill, co. Dumfries, by his wife Elizabeth: and brother to Corpl. 18917, H. Smith, 11th Royal Scots, killed in action, 1 July 1916, at the Somme. Killed in action 26 October 1917: Age 28.

His brother Henry also has no known grave; he is commemorated on the Thiepval Memorial, Somme.

(Panel 68) 2nd Lieut. Albert Shepherd Collins, 5th Bn. The Cameronians (Scottish Rifles), (T.F.): *s.* of John T. Collins, of 45, Clifford Street, Ibrox, Glasgow, by his wife the late Martha Ann, *dau.* of the late Thomas Shepherd: *b.* Hollinwood, near Manchester, 9 January 1895: *educ.* Bellahouston Academy: Occupation – Staff; Messrs MacLehose and Co., Printers, Anniesland: Territorial Force member: called up on the outbreak of war: served with the Expeditionary Force in France and Flanders from November 1914: wounded, February 1915, repatriated to England for treatment and recuperation: obtained a commission, January 1916: returned to France, and took part in the operations on the Somme: wounded (second occasion) May 1917, and was killed in action at Ypres, 25 September 1917. Buried nr. Ypres. His Commanding Officer wrote, "His work was always good, he was quite fearless, and an example of cheerfulness to us all. All the time the shells were falling, he was smiling as ever.": Age 22. *unm.* (*IWGC record 10th Bn.*)

(Panel 68) 2nd Lieut. Alexander Currie Goudie, 9th (Service) Bn. The Cameronians (Scottish Rifles): *s.* of the late George Goudie, by his wife Jane Selanders ('Dunard,' 14, Leslie Road, Pollokshields, Glasgow), *dau.* of Alexander Currie: *b.* Glasgow, 7 September 1895: *educ.* Glasgow High School: Occupation – Staff Employee; Messrs Donaldson Brothers, Shippers, Glasgow: joined Scottish Horse, 1914: obtained a commission Cameronians (Sco.Rif.), March 1917: served with the Expeditionary Force in France and Flanders from the following month, and was killed in action 20 September 1917: Age 22. *unm.*

(Panel 68) 2nd Lieut. Frank Kinniburgh Mitchell, 8th Bn. The Cameronians (Scottish Rifles), (T.F.): *s.* of Archibald Mitchell, of 8, Melfort Avenue, Dumbreck, Glasgow, by his wife Jeannie: and yr. brother to 2nd Lieut. A. Mitchell, 4th Royal Scots, who also fell. Killed in action 8 May 1918: Age 24. He leaves a wife, Maisie Laird Mitchell ('Kelvinbank,' Kelvinside, Glasgow).

His brother Archibald also has no known grave; he is recorded on Panel 11.

(Panel 68) Sergt. 202134, William Gardiner, M.M., 5/6th Bn. The Cameronians (Scottish Rifles), (T.F.): *s.* of Harry Gardiner, of 54, Dalziel Street, Hamilton, co. Lanark, by his wife Jeannie: and elder brother to Pte. 42447, H. Gardiner, 16th Highland Light Infantry, killed in action 28 November 1917: *b.* Bolton, co. Lancaster: enlisted Hamilton. Killed in action 8 May 1918: Age 26. *unm.*

His brother Harry also has no known grave; he is recorded on Panel 132.

(Panel 68) Sergt. 11344, Gerald William Walker, 9th (Service) Bn. The Cameronians (Scottish Rifles): eldest *s.* of Gerald Thomas Walker, Under Manager, Glengowan Print Works; of Hillend House, Caldercruix, nr. Airdrie, by his wife Ella, *yst. dau.* of the late William Mackintosh, of Invergordon: *b.* Barrhead, nr. Glasgow, co. Renfrew, 10 May 1893: *educ.* Public School, there, and Allen Glen's School, Glasgow: Occupation – Apprentice Calico Printer: enlisted Scottish Rifles, 14 August 1914: served with the Expeditionary Force in France and Flanders from 15 May 1915, and was killed in action near the Bremen Redoubt, 20 September 1917. Buried where he fell. His Commanding Officer wrote, "I am certain there was never a platoon sergeant who was higher in his officer's estimation than your son; in fact, we were more like chums to one another. He died like a true soldier, immediately after doing great work in capturing 80 German prisoners, for which he was to be recommended for the Military Medal...You may well be proud of your son, for he died a hero's death, and what more can be said of him?" He was a keen footballer, and extremely fond of music.: Age 24. *unm.*

(Panel 68) Corpl. 43704, Ferguson Connon, 'D' Coy., 9th (Service) Bn. The Cameronians (Scottish Rifles): *s.* of Ferguson Anderson Connon, of 58, Watson Street, Aberdeen, by his wife Helen, *dau.* of Peter Copland: *b.* Aberdeen, 5 October 1898: *educ.* Mile End School, and Robert Gordon's College, there: left college and enlisted Highland Light Infantry, November 1916: went to France at the beginning of April 1918, transf'd. Cameronians; and was killed in action nr. Ypres on the 25th of that month. Buried at Poperinghe (*q.v.*).: 25 April 1918: Age 19.

(Panel 68) L/Corpl. 200588, Allan Bell Sievewright, M.M., 5/6th Bn. The Cameronians (Scottish Rifles), (T.F.): 3rd *s.* of William Sievewright, Master Plumber; of Hill Road, Stonehouse, co. Lanark, by his wife Helen, *dau.*, of Allan Bell: *b.* Glasgow, co. Lanark, 5 October 1893: *educ.* Stonehouse: employee Messrs Andrew Cochrane and Sons, Provision Merchants: joined Scottish Rifles, Glasgow, October 1914: served with the Expeditionary Force in France and Flanders from 14 January 1915, and was killed in action at the Menin Road, nr. Ypres, 26 September 1917. Buried where he fell. Capt. Lyon R.M. Malloch, M.C. (since killed), wrote, "He was a brave man and always cool, even when under the heaviest shell fire. His bravery was rightfully rewarded last year by the Military Medal," and a comrade, Pte. 39505, W. White (since killed), "I have had the pleasure of knowing him during the last two years, and among the many fine men we have had and lost he stands out as one of the best and most gallant soldiers we have known. When in the line he was always the same cool and collected chap, and no matter how difficult or dangerous the work, he always did it well." He was awarded the Military Medal for bravery in the field.: Age 23. *unm.*

Capt. L.R.M. Malloch, M.C., killed in action 18 November 1917, is buried in Menin Road South Military Cemetery (III.M.32); Pte. W. White, killed in action 16 April 1918, has no known grave; he is commemorated on the Ploegsteert Memorial (Panel 5).

(Panel 68) Pte. 31743, William Ballantine Boyd, 1st Bn. (26th Foot) The Cameronians (Scottish Rifles): eldest *s.* of William Boyd, of 5, Church Road, Bellahouston, Glasgow, by his wife Janet Dalrymple, *dau.* of John Ballantine: *b.* Glasgow, 4 April 1892: *educ.* Bellahouston Academy, Glasgow: employee Grand Trunk Railway System, Glasgow and Liverpool: enlisted 1 January 1917: served with the Expeditionary Force in France and Flanders from 10 November following, and was killed in action at Passchendaele on the 25th of that month. Buried behind the line: 25 November 1917: Age 25. *unm.*

(Panel 68) Pte. 43119, Arthur Duroe, 9th (Service) Bn. The Cameronians (Scottish Rifles): formerly no.18562, King' Own Scottish Borderers: *s.* of William Duroe, of 34, Matthew Street, Wolverhampton, by his wife Emma: and brother to Pte. 40542, J. Duroe, 12th (Norfolk Yeomanry) Battn. Norfolk Regt., who died 9 November 1918: *b.* Moseley Village, co. Stafford. Killed in action 20 September 1917.

His brother John is buried in Kezelberg Military Cemetery (I.D.16).

(Panel 68) Pte. 18408, Charles Gascoigne, 5/6th Bn. The Cameronians (Scottish Rifles), (T.F.): late of 30, Brookdale Road, Sutton-in-Ashfield, co. Nottingham: enlisted Chesterfield, August 1914 – shortly after the outbreak of war – and, although discharged in March 1915, he re-enlisted the following month: served with the Expeditionary Force in France and Flanders and in Salonika, returning to the Western Front early 1917, and was killed in action, 8 May 1918: Age 40. He leaves a wife and four children. In a letter to Mrs Gascoigne Lieut. S.L. Brand-Crombie wrote, "I regret to have to inform you that your husband was killed in action on the 8th inst. His death was instantaneous being hit by a piece of shell as he was advancing with his platoon. I may say that Rifleman Gascoigne was brave and reliable, and it was with deep regret that I learned of his death. He was buried by his comrades where he fell as it was impossible to get his body away. As his Platoon Officer I beg to tender the deepest sympathy of his comrades and myself in your bereavement." And the Chaplain, R. Honise, "You probably have already heard the sad news that your husband has been killed in action on the evening of May 8th. Others who were with him when he fell will, I am sure, be writing to you and giving you all the particulars that can be given. This is just a little note of sympathy from myself as Chaplain to the battalion. Your husband was a fine fellow in every way, and a brave and faithful soldier. He was greatly esteemed and liked by us all, and will be greatly missed. You, however, and all at home to whom he was dear will miss him most, but it will always be a comfort to you to remember that he died nobly, fighting for a good cause. I know that in sending you this message of sympathy I speak not only for myself, but also for all who knew your husband here. Our earnest prayer is that God might comfort you in your great sorrow."

(Panel 68) Pte. 52425, James Hastie, 3rd (Reserve) Bn. The Highland Light Infantry attd. 9th (Service) Bn. The Cameronians (Scottish Rifles): *s.* of William Hastie, of Smith's Road, Darnick, Melrose, Dardener, by his wife Helen Goodfellow, *dau.* of John Lunn: *b.* Darnick, Melrose, co. Roxburgh, 23 June 1899: *educ.* Public School, there: Occupation – Assistant Gardener: enlisted Highland Light Infantry, 27 November 1917: attd. (no.42356) Scottish Rifles: served with the Expeditionary Force in France and Flanders from 27 March 1918; killed in action nr. Dickebusch, 28 April following. Buried where he fell: Age 18. (*IWGC record The Cameronians*)

PANEL 68 ENDS: PTE. J.W. CRINAGE – CAMERONIANS (SCOTTISH RIFLES)

PANEL 69 BEGINS: PTE. W. CROLY – CAMERONIANS (SCOTTISH RIFLES)

(Panel 69) Pte. 41128, William Paterson, 10th (Service) Bn. The Cameronians (Scottish Rifles): formerly no.1354, Lanarkshire Yeomanry (T.F.): *s.* of the late William Paterson, by his wife Agnes ('Birchgrove,' 8, Buchanan Drive, Rutherglen): and brother to Spr. 209617, I. Paterson, 2nd Spec. Coy., Royal Engineers, killed in action, 19 April 1917: *b.* Barony, co. Lanark, 1888: enlisted Glasgow. Killed in action at Ypres 23 August 1917: Age 29. *unm.*

His brother Irvine is buried in Philosophe British Cemetery, Mazingarbe (II.O.4).

PANEL 69 ENDS: PTE. R.G. TEASDALE – CAMERONIANS (SCOTTISH RIFLES)

PANEL 70 BEGINS: PTE. G. TEDDS – CAMERONIANS (SCOTTISH RIFLES)

(Panel 70) Pte. 202183, Robert Templeton, 5/6th Bn. The Cameronians (Scottish Rifles), (T.F.): eldest *s.* of William Templeton, Farmer; of Broadfield, Wigtown, by his wife Margaret, *dau.* of John Steele, of Shaw Farm, Kilmaurs, co. Ayr: *b.* Riccarton, co. Ayr, 26 January 1891: *educ.* Kirkinner, co. Wigtown, and the Kilmarnock Academy, co. Ayr: subsequently managed his father's farm, being a first-class ploughman: enlisted 26 July 1916: served with the Expeditionary Force in France and Flanders from 14 November following, and was killed in action at Polygon Wood, 26 September 1917: Age 26 years, 8 months precisely. *unm.*

(Panel 70) L/Corpl. 29180, William Bayliss, 9th (Service) Bn. The Royal Inniskilling Fusiliers: elder *s.* of James Bayliss, of Belvedere, Mullingar, by his wife Jane: *b.* Mullingar, Co. Westmeath, 24 April 1882: *educ.* there: enlisted March 1916: served with the Expeditionary Force in France, and was killed in action nr. Ypres, 16 August 1917. The Chaplain wrote, "He was a brave soldier, reliable in the presence of great danger. I have heard officers speak of him in the highest terms, and he is much missed both by the officers and men of his company.": Age 30. *unm.*

(Panel 70) L/Corpl. 42364, Ernest Seaman, V.C., 2nd Bn. (108th Foot) The Royal Inniskilling Fusiliers: *s.* of the late Henry Seaman, of 9, Derby Street, Heigham, Norwich, and Mrs Palmer, *née* Seaman ('The King's Inn,' Bungay Road, Scole, co. Norfolk), *dau.* of William March, of Horsford, co. Norfolk: *b.* Heigham, *afsd.*, 16 August 1883: *educ.* Council School, Scole: joined Regular Army, December 1915, as Pte.; Expeditionary Force Canteens: served with the Expeditionary Force in France and Flanders from 24 December 1915: saw considerable service in the Ypres sector, where he was killed in action during the attack of 29 September 1917, and also around Passchendaele Ridge: promoted L/Corpl. about 14 days before he was killed. Posthumously awarded the Victoria Cross (*London Gazette*, 15 November 1918), "For most conspicuous bravery and devotion to duty. When the right flank of his company was held up by a nest of enemy machine guns, he, with great courage and initiative, rushed forward under heavy fire with his Lewis gun, and engaged the position single-handed, capturing two machine guns and twelve prisoners, and killing one officer and two men. Later in the day he again rushed another enemy machine-gun post, capturing the gun under heavy fire. He was killed immediately after. His courage and dash were beyond all praise, and it was entirely due to the very gallant conduct of L/Corpl. Seaman that his company was able to push forward to its objective and capture many prisoners." Capt. V.E.S. Mattocks, Officer Commanding 'A' Company, wrote, "He was one of the best soldiers whom I had ever met, an excellent soldier in every sense of the word, and very keen in his duties. He always volunteered to help in any extra work that had to be done, no matter how dangerous and difficult, and for his constant devotion to duty and gallantry in voluntarily attending his wounded comrades under heavy fire, I recommended his being awarded the Military Medal.": Age 34. *(IWGC record Corpl.)*

(Panel 70) Pte. 40867, Thomas Blunt, 8th (Service) Bn. The Royal Inniskilling Fusiliers: formerly no.28057, Essex Regt.: *s.* of Thomas (& Mrs A.) Blunt, of Adderley House, Walsoken, Wisbech: and brother to Tpr. 1884, S.J. Blunt, Household Battalion, who died 20 April 1917, of wounds: *b.* Walsoken, co. Norfolk: enlisted Norwich. Killed in action 16 August 1917.

His brother Samuel is buried in Aubigny Communal Cemetery Extension (II.B.39).

PANEL 70 ENDS: PTE. A. CRAWSHAW – ROYAL INNISKILLING FUSILIERS

PANEL 71 BEGINS: PTE. L.W. CREASE – ROYAL INNISKILLING FUSILIERS

PANEL 71 ENDS: PTE. A.H. SANDERS – ROYAL INNISKILLING FUSILIERS

PANEL 72 BEGINS: PTE. G.L. SAVAGER – ROYAL INNISKILLING FUSILIERS

(Panel 72) Sergt. 200495, Victor Charles Binding, 4th (City of Bristol) Bn. The Gloucestershire Regt. (T.F.): *yst. s.* of Thomas Binding, of 40, Kenn Road, Clevedon, late of 1st Somerset Volunteer Regt.: volunteered and enlisted Clevedon, 1914: served with the Expeditionary Force in France and Flanders: a regular correspondent with those at home, some of his letters were reproduced in the '*Clevedon Mercury & Courier.*' During the 4th Battalion's attack on Poelcapelle, in the early morning of 9 October 1917, 2nd Lieut. Alex Taylor reported seeing Sergt. Binding wounded. After the fighting, despite extensive searches of the fought over ground, no trace of Sergt. Binding could be found and he is now assumed to have been killed in action on this date: Age 21. *unm.* Four of his brothers also served.

(Panel 72) L/Sergt. 265559, Albert Paver, 1/6th Bn. The Gloucestershire Regt. (T.F.): *s.* of the late William (& Julia) Paver, of Bristol: and *yr.* brother to Pte. 3752, W. Paver, 2/4th Gloucestershire Regt., killed in action 19 July 1916: *b.* St. Jude's, Bristol, 1896. Killed in action 9 October 1917: Age 21. *unm.*

His brother William also has no known grave; he is commemorated on the Loos Memorial (Dud Corner).

(Panel 72) Corpl. 20783, Ralph Edwin Crowley, 14th (Service) Bn. The Gloucestershire Regt.: 2nd *s.* of Thomas Crowley, of Priory Cottages, Lapworth, co. Warwick, retired Postman, by his wife Hannah, *yst. dau.* of Thomas Walton, of King's Norton: *b.* Hockley, Birmingham, co. Warwick, 21 June 1881: *educ.* Foundry Road Council School, Winson Green: Occupation – Millwright; Birmingham Metal and Munitions Ltd.: enlisted May 1915: served with the Expeditionary Force in France and Flanders from January 1916, and was killed in action in the Poelcappelle region, 21 October 1917. Buried there. His Captain wrote, "He was one of the best and most reliable N.C.O's, and I feel his loss very much, and in some little way can realize what it must mean to you. Your son was a great favourite with officers and men alike. He had a great fund of dry humour, and many a good laugh has he given us with his quaint sayings. He was a great help in the company, and I shall miss him very badly indeed, for he always helped to keep the men in a cheery mood, be the conditions good or bad. I have not heard how he was killed, but I know it would be doing his duty fearlessly;" and another officer, "I cannot speak too highly of him, as his courage and endurance was a splendid example to us all. He was greatly esteemed by everyone, and was ready to do more than his share of duty.": Age 36. *unm.* (*IWGC record 20793*)

Reliefs were always a time when tensions ran high, both sides being all too aware of the pattern by which these were carried out, and casualties were almost a certainty. On the night of 1/2 November 1917, after four days and nights holding the line between Reutelbeek and Polderhoek, the enemy shelled 12th Gloucesters as they were being relieved, and a number of men were hit. Lieut.Col. H.A. Colt, D.S.O., M.C., wrote, "Coming out we had many casualties, not in the least among them being Corpl. Parry, a stout-hearted original member of the battalion. Lying with his back broken, by the side of Jerk Track, he flatly refused to be moved, saying he was dying, and cheered his comrades as they reluctantly passed by…"

(Panel 72) Corpl. 14375, Claude Cecil Parry, 12th (Service) Bn. (Bristol) The Gloucestershire Regt.: late of South Parade, Fishponds Road, Bristol: *s.* of William John Parry, of Homefield, Saltford, Bristol, by his wife Emily: *b.* 1895: *educ.* Fairfield Grammar School: enlisted Eastville, Bristol. Died of wounds 2 November 1917. Buried on the field of battle: Age 22. *unm.*

(Panel 72) L/Corpl. 267227, Bede Guthrie, 1/5th Bn. The Gloucestershire Regt. (T.F.): *s.* of William Guthrie, of Southwoods, Brancaster Staithe, King's Lynn, co. Norfolk, by his wife Ellen: and brother to Sergt. 2363, H.N.D. Guthrie, 7th Royal Fusiliers, killed in action 16 April 1917: *b.* King's Lynn: enlisted North Walsham. Killed in action 16 August 1917: Age 21.

His brother Harold is buried in Bailleul Road East Cemetery, St. Laurent-Blangy (I.O.17).

(Panel 72) L/Corpl. 266788, John Burke Houghton, 1/6th Bn. The Gloucestershire Regt. (T.F.): *s.* of Frederick Burke (& Bridget) Houghton, of 7, King Street, Queen Square, Bristol: and *yr.* brother to Corpl. 2055, C.D. Houghton, 1/4th Gloucestershire Regt., killed in action, 18 February 1916, aged 26 yrs.: *educ.* St. Mary's (R.C.) School, Bristol: enlisted Bristol. Killed in action 9 October 1917: Age 23. Remembered on St. Mary's-on-the-Quay Roll of Honour.

His brother Charles is buried in Bienvillers Military Cemetery (XVI.A.I).

PANEL 72 ENDS: L/CORPL. S. MORRISH – GLOUCESTERSHIRE REGT.

PANEL 73 BEGINS: L/CORPL. R. MUSTOE – GLOUCESTERSHIRE REGT.

(Panel 73) Pte. 265915, Wilfrid Gordon Anson, 14th (Service) Bn. The Gloucestershire Regt.: eldest *s.* of the Rev. Harcourt Suft Anson, of 'The Gables,' The Close, Salisbury, co. Wilts, Clerk in Holy Order, by his wife Edith, *dau.* of Edward Thomas Busk: *b.* Littleover Vicarage, Derby, 14 September 1890: *educ.* Eastfield House, Ditching, and Technical College, Brighton: employee Bristol Aeroplane Works: enlisted 3 October 1914; served with the Expeditionary Force in France and Flanders, from April 1915, and was killed in action at Houthulst Wood, 22 October 1917. Col. Walker Nott, D.S.O., wrote, "Your son was in my company when we came out two years ago, and so I knew him pretty well. He was an extremely plucky boy, and his spirit was always willing, though his flesh was weak. I used to admire him very much for the grit which he showed by sticking it out even on the worst march, and also for his absence of fear under fire," and Capt. Coates, in a letter dated 22 April 1915, "Your boy has already proved himself a real good lad, plucky and a splendid worker.": Age 27. *unm.*

(Panel 73) Pte. 203703, Frederick James Brown, 14th (Service) Bn. (West of England) The Gloucestershire Regt.: *s.* of William Brown, of 15, Granville Street, Cheltenham, by his wife Eliza: and brother to Pte. 21541, F.W. Brown, 1st Coldstream Guards, who also fell: *b.* Cheltenham: *educ.* Parish Boy's School: enlisted Gloucester. Killed in action 22 October 1917.

His brother Francis also has no known grave; he is commemorated on the Cambrai Memorial, Louverval (Panel 2).

(Panel 73) Pte. 202633, Harold Wookey Clark, 2/4th Bn. The Gloucestershire Regt. (T.F.): 2nd *s.* of Thomas Clark, of Rose Cottage, Langford, by his wife Alice, *dau.* of the late Henry Wookey: and brother to Percy Arthur Clark: *b.* Yatton, co. Somerset, 30 December 1886: *educ.* Abbot's Leigh, and Wrington, co. Somerset: Occupation – Gardener; employed by Mr R. Todd, of Clifton: enlisted 29 May 1916: served with the Expeditionary Force in France from 8 October following; killed in action, 27 August 1917: Age 32. He *m.* Stoke Bishop, co. Gloucester, 30 October 1910; Virtue Mary (1, Stoke Cottages, Stoke Bishop, Bristol), *dau.* of the late Thomas Gray, and had a daughter, Kathleen Mary, *b.* 8 January 1912. (*IWGC record 202640*)

(Panel 73) Pte. 260433, Merton Duckham, 12th (Service) Bn. The Gloucestershire Regt.: *s.* of the late James Duckham, Cattle Salesman, by his wife Theresa ('Mayfield,' Clytha Square, Newport), *dau.* of James Shiel: *b.* Newport, co. Monmouth, 7 November 1894: *educ.* privately: enlisted April 1915: served with the Expeditionary Force in France and Flanders, and was killed in action, 8 October 1917. A comrade wrote, "During a night attack their platoon got lost, and in trying to get back to their battalion Merton was killed, and was buried at a place named 'Clapham Junction.'": Age 22. *unm.*

(Panel 73) Pte. 21205, Arthur John Fowles, 10th (Service) Bn. The Gloucestershire Regt. attd. 9th Bn. The Rifle Brigade: *s.* of William J. Fowles, of 5, Brandon Place, Cheltenham, by his wife Hannah: *b.* Norbiton, co. Surrey, 1892. Died 19 April 1918: Age 26. *unm. Known to be buried in Villers-Bretonneux Military Cemetery, Fouilloy (IV.D.4).*

PANEL 73 ENDS: PTE. W.J. HILLMAN – GLOUCESTERSHIRE REGT.

PANEL 74 BEGINS: PTE. D.G. HINE – GLOUCESTERSHIRE REGT.

(Panel 74) Pte. 30260, Evan Henry Price, 8th (Service) Bn. The Gloucestershire Regt.: only *s.* of the late Henry Price, by his wife Elizabeth (28, Woodland Street, Mountain Ash), *dau.* of the late Evan Duggan, of Hereford: *b.* Mountain Ash, co. Glamorgan, 27 June 1877: *educ.* Duffryn Schools: Occupation – Collier; Cwmpennar Colliery, Mountain Ash: served some time with Cardigan (Royal Artillery) Militia: joined Royal Field Artillery, and transf'd. Gloucestershire Regt., 26 April 1915: served with the Expeditionary Force in France and Flanders from November 1916, and was killed in action at Ypres, 20 September 1917: Age 40. Buried there. He *m.* St. Margaret's Church, Mountain Ash, 22 May 1899; Mary Josepha (28A, Woodland Street, Mountain Ash), *dau.* of William Richards, and had five children; Doris Rosemary, *b.* 1 September 1899, William Henry, *b.* 9 December 1900, George Harold, *b.* 17 November 1903, Gertrude Anna, *b.* 9 July 1906, and Gwyneth Elizabeth, *b.* 27 August 1910.

The Oxfordshire village of Adderbury has been known for its association with Morris dancing since the 17th century. After a decline in the tradition during the Victorian era, Adderbury village school revived the practice at the turn of the twentieth century and within a few years the village, like many of those in the surrounding Cotswolds, had its own team of dancers. By the end of the First World War five members of the Adderbury Morris Men had enlisted and gone off to fight on the Western Front, only one, Charlie Coleman, returned alive; none of the four that died has a known grave. Percy Pargeter, 6th Oxford & Bucks Light Infantry, was the first to die, two years later his brother Ronald, 2nd Royal Berkshire Regt., was killed on the same sector of the front; they are commemorated on the Thiepval and Pozieres Memorials respectively. Harry Wallin, 1st Border Regt., killed at the Battle of Arras in May 1917, is recorded on the Arras Memorial. The fourth member, George Robins, 6th Gloucester Regt., is recorded here.

(Panel 74) Pte. 267404, George Robins, 1/6th Bn. The Gloucestershire Regt. (T.F.): *b.* Twyford: enlisted Banbury. Died of wounds 9 October 1917. Remembered on St. Mary's Parish Church Memorial, Adderbury. In 2008, marking the 90th Anniversary of the Armistice, the present day Adderbury Morris Men made a pilgrimage of remembrance and danced at all three memorials.

> I danced on a Friday when the sky turned black
> It's hard to dance with the devil on your back
> They buried my body and they thought I'd gone
> But I am the Dance and I still go on.

(Panel 74) Pte. 202873, Frederick Thomas Taylor, 2/4th Bn. The Gloucestershire Regt. (T.F.): 3rd *s.* of John Taylor, of 30, Carlton Road, Gloucester, by his wife Ellen: *b.* Gloucester, 30 December 1892: *educ.* Carlton Road School, there: was employee at Glevum Works, Gloucester: joined Territorial Force, 24 April 1911: called up on mobilisation, 4 August 1914; served with the Expeditionary Force in France and Flanders from 29 March 1915: discharged time-expired 5 May 1916; recalled to the Colours, 5 July following; returned to France, 19 September. Reported wounded and missing after the fighting at Ypres, 27 August 1917; assumed killed in action on or about that date.: Age 24. *unm.*

PANEL 74 ENDS: PTE. G. THOMAS – GLOUCESTERSHIRE REGT.

PANEL 75 BEGINS: PTE. H. THOMAS – GLOUCESTERSHIRE REGT.

(Panel 75) Pte. 266852, Thomas Henry Toghill, 1/5th Bn. The Gloucestershire Regt. (T.F.): *s.* of Thomas Toghill, of Tower Road, Warmley, Bristol, by his wife Emily: *husb.* to May L. Toghill (New Cheltenham, Kingswood, Bristol): and brother to L/Corpl. 201247, H.J. Toghill, 2/4th Gloucestershire Regt., died of wounds, 29 September 1917; and Pte. 16067, J. Toghill, 11th Worcestershire Regt., killed in action 12 February 1917, in Salonika: *b.* Siston, co. Gloucester: enlisted Bristol. Killed in action 16 August 1917: Age 23. Inscribed – 'To The Memory Of The Brave Lads Of This Ecclesiastical Parish Who Gave Their Lives For Their Country 1914-1918,' the Toghill brothers are commemorated on the Warmley War Memorial.

His brother Herbert is buried in Duisans British Cemetery (V.B.34); Joseph, Karasouli Military Cemetery (E.1171).

(Panel 75) Pte. 15529, David Westacott, 2/6th Bn. The Gloucestershire Regt. (T.F.): 3rd *s.* of John Sullivan Westacott: *b.* 10 October 1882: *educ.* St. Paul's Council School, Cardiff: Occupation – Seaman: enlisted Gloucestershire Regt., 15 November 1914: served with the Expeditionary Force in France and Flanders from 5 February 1915; killed in action, 28 August 1917. Buried where he fell. His Commanding Officer, Capt. C.M. Hughes, wrote, "He was a fine man, and one of the mainstays of the platoon. I had heard of his athletic fame, and he died as he lived, a true sportsman." He was a Cardiff and Welsh International Rugby Football player, and a man of enormous strength, a very fast forward and a great runner. For a forward, he was a prolific scorer, and had once secured five tries in a county match for Glamorgan against Somerset: Age 34. *unm.*

Worcestershire Regt.

(Panel 75) Lieut. Ralph Longhurst Hancock, 2/8th Bn. The Worcestershire Regt. (T.F.): *s.* of Sardius Hancock, of 'The Pastures,' Tan House Lane, Upper Housell, Malvern Link, Lecturer, by his wife Mary Jane, *dau.* of Joseph Green Longhurst: and brother to Pte. R/17405, W.J. Hancock, 11th Battn. King's Royal Rifle Corps, reported missing and wounded after the fighting on the Somme, 3 September 1916, now believed to have died on that date: *educ.* Hollingbourne, and Harrietsham, co. Kent; St. John's, Worcester: apprenticed as Painter on china, Royal Worcester Porcelain Works; afterwards became a Journalist; *'Worcestershire Echo'*: enlisted Royal Sussex Regt. (Cyclist Corps), 15 June 1915: obtained a commission, 2nd Lieut., 31 December following; promoted Lieut. 25 July 1917: served with the Expeditionary Force in France and Flanders, where he suffered wounds to his face and a broken leg at the Battle of the Somme, July 1916; invalided home, and after recovery spent some time at a training camp in Yorkshire: subsequently returned to France, and was killed in action at the Steenbeek, Belgium, 27 August 1917. His Commanding Officer wrote, "In the action in which he was killed he was leading his platoon in a splendid manner against a very strong position, amidst very heavy fire. All his work, and especially his conduct, during his last action proved him to be a very brave and gallant soldier.": Age 24. He *m.* Worcester, 10 June 1915; Ada Dorothy, *dau.* of Samuel Smith, and had a *dau.* Joan Dorothy, *b.* 17 November 1916.

His brother Wilfred also has no known grave; he is commemorated on the Thiepval Memorial, Somme.

(Panel 75) Lieut. William Hancocks, 1/7th Bn. The Worcestershire Regt. (T.F.): only *s.* of the late William Hancocks, of Blakeshall, Wolverley, nr. Kidderminster, by his wife Edith (Church House, Severn-Stoke, co. Worcester): *b.* Blakeshall, Wolverley, *afsd.*, 12 January 1890: *educ.* Rugby, and Oriel College, Oxford: obtained a commission 2nd Lieut., Worcestershire Regt., September 1914: served with the Expeditionary Force in France and Flanders, and was killed in action at Poelcapelle, 9 October 1917. Buried on the battlefield: Age 25. *unm.* (*IWGC record Capt.*)

(Panel 75) 2nd Lieut. Hugh Chignell, 3rd Bn. The Worcestershire Regt.: elder *s.* of George Street Chignell, of Hill House, St. John's, Worcester, by his wife Emma Mary, *dau.* of B. Chignell, of Romsey, co. Hants: *b.* St. John's, Worcester, 30 June 1898: *educ.* Tredennyke, Worcester; Hereford Cathedral School; King's School, Worcester; Royal Military College, Sandhurst: gazetted 2nd Lieut., 1 May 1917: served with the Expeditionary Force in France and Flanders from July following, and was killed in action at Kemmel, while acting as Adjutant, 26 April 1918. His Colonel wrote of him that he was one of the best subalterns, clever, well-informed, a capital companion, understanding men well, and possessing many gifts which would have led to great success in his profession: and his Commanding Officer in the action at Kemmel, records that he had behaved so gallantly that had he lived he would have recommended him for the M.C.: Age 19.

(Panel 75) 2nd Lieut. John Guilding, 1/8th Bn. The Worcestershire Regt. (T.F.): prior to enlistment was employee at London City and Midland Bank, Malvern: joined Worcestershire Yeomanry on the outbreak of war, August 1914: applied for and obtained a commission, 2nd Lieut., 8th Worcestershire Regt.: served with the Expeditionary Force in France and Flanders, and was killed in action near the Steenbeek, by the explosion of an artillery shell in company with his Servant (Pte. H.J. Harris) on the evening of 17/18 August 1917.

Pte. Harris also has no known grave; he is recorded on Panel 76.

(Panel 75) Sergt. 11184, Arthur Thomas Matthews, 2nd Bn. (36th Foot) The Worcestershire Regt.: *s.* of Thomas Matthews, of Quinton, Birmingham, by his wife Mary Healey: *b.* Bromsgrove, co. Worcester, 19 April 1884: *educ.* there: enlisted Worcestershire Regt., 1907: served seven years in India, and was still serving when war broke out: served with the Expeditionary Force in France and Flanders from August 1914, taking part in the Retreat from Mons on the 26th of the same month: wounded at the Battle of the Marne, 8 September following: invalided home: rejoined his regiment, 17 May 1915: badly gassed at the battle of the Somme, 23 July 1916, and again invalided to England: returned to his unit 18 December following, and was killed in action at the Battle of Ypres, 25 September 1917. Buried at Gheluvelt: Age 33.

He *m.* Devonport, 14 December 1916; Emily (268, Victoria Road, Aston, Birmingham), *dau.* of Auguste Huber.: *s.p.* (*IWGC record 26 September*)

(Panel 75) L/Corpl. 203360, William Henry Cash, 2/7th Bn. The Worcestershire Regt. (T.F.): *b.* Leamington, 8 February 1886: *educ.* there: was an Infirmary Assistant at Selly Oak Infirmary: enlisted 7 June 1916: served with the Expeditionary Force in France and Flanders, and was killed in action at Ypres, 19 August 1917, while conveying water to his comrades in the front line. Buried there. An officer, writing to his wife, said: "He was a good N.C.O., popular with officers and men, and had been recommended for further promotion." He *m.* at Selly Oak, 6 June 1914, Lillian Adelaide, *dau.* of the late Thomas Daniel Parker, and had a *dau.*, Margaret Maisie, *b.* 16 November 1917.

(Panel 75) L/Corpl. 40076, James Lees, 10th (Service) Bn. The Worcestershire Regt.: 11th child of Jonas Lees, of The Green, Cannock Road, Burntwood, co. Stafford, and his wife, Susannah Lucy, *née* Thompson: and brother to Spr. 626, J. Lees, Australian Mining Coy. (surv'd.); and Pte. 13144, A. Lees, 7th South Staffordshire Regt., killed in action 27 July 1917: *b.* Chase Terrace, 11 November 1890: *educ.* Church Road School, Burntwood: was a Miner; Fair Lady Colliery, Heath Hayes: enlisted South Staffordshire Regt., Lichfield, 12 February 1915: subsequently transf'd. Worcestershire Regt. Killed in action 20 September 1917: Age 26.

His brother Albert is buried in No Man's Cot Cemetery (A.29).

(Panel 75) Pte. 235223, Frank Ernest Austin, 2/7th Bn. Worcestershire Regt. (T.F.): Stretcher-bearer: *yr. s.* of the late William Alabaster Austin; Draper, by his wife Charlotte (Ardingly, nr. Haywards Heath, co. Sussex), *dau.* of Albert Sayers, of Ardingly: and brother to Rfn. 24/339, E.M. Austin, 2nd Bn. 3rd N.Z. Rifle Brigade, killed in action at Flers, 15 September 1916: *b.* Brockley, London, S.E., 8 October 1895: *educ.* Russell Hill School, Purley, and on leaving there was employed with a firm of Land Agents and Surveyors, being stationed at the head office for about five years, when, his health not being good, he was appointed by the firm Resident Sub-Agent on Lieut.Col. J. Innes' Roffey Park Estate, and later acted in a similar capacity, but with more personal responsibility, on the Sussex Estate, Parham Park, Pulborough: volunteered for the Royal Engineers, May 1915, but was rejected as medically unfit: attested under the Derby Scheme, and, after being again twice rejected, was finally passed for garrison duty at home: called up, September 1916, posted 2/6th (Cyclists) Suffolk Regt., and stationed on the East Coast, being passed as an A1 man, March 1917: served with the Expeditionary Force in France and Flanders from June, then, being drafted into the Worcestershire Regt., acted as stretcher-bearer to the battalion, and died 28 August as a result of wounds received in action nr. Ypres, while bringing in wounded under heavy bombardment. Buried nr. Ypres: Age 21. *unm.*

His brother Eric also has no known grave, he is commemorated on the Caterpillar Valley (New Zealand) Memorial.

PANEL 75 ENDS: PTE. F.E. AUSTIN – WORCESTERSHIRE REGT.

PANEL 76 BEGINS: PTE. W. AYRE – WORCESTERSHIRE REGT.

(Panel 76) Pte. 242019, Oswald Adams Bere, 'B' Coy., 2/8th Bn. The Worcestershire Regt. (T.F.): *s.* of Edwin Bere, of 'Lynwood,' Copplestone, co. Devon, and Elizabeth Tremlett, his wife: and *yr.* brother to Pte. B/19502, S.E. Bere, Royal Fusiliers, died 11 June 1916, aged 26 years: enlisted Exeter. Killed in action 28 August 1917: Age 23. *unm.* Dedicated – To The Glory Of God And In Grateful Memory Of The Men Of This Parish Who Gave Their Lives For Their Country In The Great War 1914-1918 – the brothers Bere are remembered on Down St. Mary (St. Mary The Virgin) Church War Memorial.

His brother Stanley is buried in Etaples Military Cemetery (V.E.16).

(Panel 76) Pte, 204188, Harry Bruton, 1/8th Bn. The Worcestershire Regt. (T.F.): *s.* of the late Henry 'Harry' Bruton, of Dudley, co. Worcester, and Margaret Bruton, his spouse: and elder brother to 2nd Lieut. T. Bruton, 6th attd. 4th Worcestershire Regt., killed in action, 1 September 1918: *b.* Dudley:

enlisted Worcester. Killed in action 9 October 1917, at Ypres: Age 38. He leaves a wife, Lily Maud Bruton (9, Tinchbourne Street, Dudley).

His brother Thomas is buried in Baileul Communal Cemetery Extension (III.H.1).

(Panel 76) Pte. 235142, Alfred Fossard, 2/7th Bn. The Worcestershire Regt. (T.F.): *m.* formerly of 5, Ainley Grove, Elland, Yorkshire: enlisted (no.3653) 2/4th Bn. Duke of Wellington's Regt., subsequently transfd. Worcestershire Regt. On the evening of 24 August 1917, a platoon of 2/7th Worcesters, in the face of enemy machine gun fire, attempted unsuccessfully to outflank Aisne Farm north of Frezenberg. At 11p.m the following evening, another unsuccessful assault was made; it is highly likely, given the lateness of the hour, that Alfred Fossard was killed in this attack: 26 August 1917. On notification of his death, his widow, overwrought with grief, committed suicide in the Salterhebble canal.

(Panel 76) Pte. 242410, Harold James Harris, 1/8th Bn. The Worcestershire Regt. (T.F.): *s.* of James Silus Harris, of 'Yew Tree Cottage,' The Rampings, Longdon, by his wife Eileen Ann: employee Messrs Tipping and Morris; Lyttleton House, Malvern: volunteered and enlisted Worcestershire Yeomanry at the outbreak of war: transf'd. Worcestershire Regt. for Active Service: served with the Expeditionary Force in France and Flanders, and was killed in action by an artillery shell near the Steenbeek on the evening of 17 August 1917, in company with his officer (2nd Lieut. J. Guilding) to whom he acted as Servant: Age 24. *unm.*

2nd Lieut. Guilding also has no known grave; his name is recorded on Panel 75.

(Panel 76) Pte. 207278, Frederick Rowland Hutt, 3rd Bn. The Worcestershire Regt.: formerly Queen's Own Oxfordshire Hussars: late of Henley-in-Arden: *s.* of John William Hutt, of Deddington, co. Oxford; late of Claverdon, co. Warwick, by his wife Mary Frances: and yr. brother to Sergt. Major 204649, A.W. Hutt, 5th O.B.L.I., killed in action one month previously (21 March 1918), at St. Quentin: was sometimes a Domestic Groom, Deddington: enlisted Oxford. Killed in action 26 April 1918: Age 28.

His brother Archie is buried in Montescourt-Lizerolles Communal Cemetery (141).

(Panel 76) Pte. 30884, Arthur George Jeynes, 2nd Bn. (36th Foot) The Worcestershire Regt.: of Mill Cottage, Castlemorton, co. Worcester: *b.* Castlemorton, *afsd.*: enlisted Upton-on-Severn: served with the Expeditionary Force in France and Flanders, and was killed in action on the Menin Road, Ypres, 25 September 1917: Age 33. Married to Florence E. Hicks, *née* Jeynes (1, Glen Cottage, Lower Quest Hills Road, Castlemorton); an officer wrote stating her husband had been killed by a bullet while his platoon were reinforcing the front line, adding, "..he did excellent work and was in every way a good soldier. We shall all miss him. His death was a noble sacrifice, and I say this in earnestness, because had your husband not been where he was the bullet would inevitably have hit me. He saved my life by giving his. My sympathy is very sincere and my regret is very deep."

(Panel 76) Pte. 241569, Arthur (*a.k.a* 'Tiny') Balfour Lavers, 2nd Bn. (36th Foot) The Worcestershire Regt.: *yst. s.* of William Lavers, of 36, Bristol Street, Newport, co. Monmouth, by his wife Matilda: Occupation – Postman; Cwmbran; Tenby: served with the Expeditionary Force in France: wounded November 1916. Killed in action 26 September 1917: Age 22. *unm.*

PANEL 76 ENDS: PTE. T.H. LLOYD – WORCESTERSHIRE REGT.

PANEL 77 BEGINS: PTE. H.S. LOCKE – WORCESTERSHIRE REGT.

(Panel 77) Pte. 203963, Sydney Pinchin, 1/7th Bn. The Worcestershire Regt. (T.F.): *s.* of Mrs E. Pinchin (6, Council Houses, Pinvin, Pershore): and *yr.* brother to Corpl. 2807, A.E. Pinchin, 1/5th Royal Warwickshire Regt., who fell five days previously, on 4 October: *b.* Bricklehampton, co. Worcester, 1896: enlisted Pershore. Killed in action 9 October 1917: Age 21. *unm.*

His brother Albert also has no known grave; he is recorded on Panel 24.

(Panel 77) Pte. 37331, Charles Edward Squires, 4th Bn. The Worcestershire Regt: *s.* of John Squires, of Portsmouth, by his wife Ellen: and brother to L/Corpl. 34163, H.R. Squires, M.M., 2nd Hampshire Regt., died of wounds, 24 August 1917, and Rfn. 331545, A.T. Squires, 1/8th Hampshire Regt., killed in

Palestine, 19 April 1917: served with the Expeditionary Force in France and Flanders, and was killed in action, 9 October 1917.

His brother Harry is buried in Dozinghem Military Cemetery (III.H.4); Albert has no known grave, he is commemorated on the Jerusalem Memorial.

PANEL 77 ENDS: SERGT. P. KELLY – EAST LANCASHIRE REGT.

PANEL 78 BEGINS: SERGT. B. LEAVER – EAST LANCASHIRE REGT.

(Panel 78) Pte. 203806, James Ashworth, 2/4th Bn. The East Lancashire Regt. (T.F.): *s.* of James Henry Ashworth, of 4, Clegg Street, Haslingden, co. Lancaster, by his wife Elizabeth Ann: and brother to Pte. 244901, H.R. Ashworth, 4/5th Loyal North Lancashire Regt., killed in action 26 October 1917; and Pte. Deal/3915(S), H. Ashworth, Royal Marine Medical Unit, 63rd (R.N.) Divn., killed in action 26 August 1918: *b.* Haslingden: enlisted there. Killed in action 10 October 1917: Age 28. He leaves a wife, Mrs H.E. Ashworth (5, Cornmill Terrace, Barnoldswick, Colne, co. Lancaster).

His brother Harry has no known grave, he is recorded on Panel 103; Harold is buried in Bucquoy Communal Cemetery Extension (B.7).

(Panel 78) Pte. 240607, James Hartley Astin, 2/5th Bn. The East Lancashire Regt. (T.F.): *husb.* to the late Nora Astin, of Burnley, co. Lancaster: *s.* of David Astin, of 1A, Waterbarn Street, Burnley, by his wife Grace Hannah: Occupation – Weaver; Messrs Burrows, Britannia Mill: enlisted 1915: served with the Expeditionary Force in France and Flanders from March 1916, and was killed in action, 9 October 1917, at Frezenberg. One of his officers wrote, "He was one of the best soldiers I had, and could have been a Non Commissioned Officer had he so desired. He will be sorely missed both by his comrades and his Officers.": Age 31.

(Panel 78) Pte. 38661 (formerly no.37412), Tom Taylor Fitton, 8th (Service) Bn. The East Lancashire Regt.: eldest *s.* of the late Albert Fitton, by his wife Emily (25, Hollin's Vale, Whitefield, Manchester): and brother to Pte. 26622, A.E. Fitton, 18th Lancashire Fusiliers, killed in action 26 March 1918: *b.* Heywood, co. Lancaster: enlisted Whitefield. Killed in action 6 October 1917: Age 26. Remembered on the Unsworth Pole War Memorial, Lancashire.

His brother Albert also has no known grave; he is commemorated on the Pozieres Memorial.

(Panel 78) Pte. 30264, Alfred Victor Gardner, 2/4th Bn. The East Lancashire Regt. (T.F.): *s.* of John Gardner, of 13, Bowerham Terrace, Lancaster, by his wife Annie: and elder brother to L/Corpl. 23202, R. Gardner, 8th King's Own, killed 9 April 1917, at the Battle of Arras, aged 20 yrs.; and Pte. TR/3/6649, J. Gardner, 49th Training Reserve Battn., died 2 November 1917, at home, aged 26 yrs.: *b.* Lancaster *c.*1887. Killed in action 10 October 1917: Age 30.

His brother Reginald also has no known grave; he is commemorated on the Arras Memorial (Bay 2); James is buried in Lancaster Cemetery (A.CE.453).

(Panel 78) Pte. 34186, Richard Hoyles, 8th (Service) Bn. The East Lancashire Regt.: *s.* of George Hoyles, of 14, Montgomery Street, Skipton, by his wife Alice, *dau.* of Richard Birch, of Grassington, co. York: and brother to Sergt. 47870, E. Hoyles, 48th Canadian Highlanders, killed in action at Ypres, 3 June 1916; and Corpl. 266968, G. Hoyles, 1/6th Duke of Wellington's Regt., died of wounds, 23 March 1917: *b.* Hebden, co. York, 24 January 1881: *educ.* Skipton: Occupation – Weaver: enlisted East Lancashire Regt. 21 August 1916: served with the Expeditionary Force in France and Flanders from 12 December following, and was killed in action 5 October 1917. Buried where he fell: Age 37. He *m.* Baptist Church, Skipton, 27 March 1909; Mary Alice (10/12, Dorset Street, Skipton), *dau.* of James Haithwaite, of Clitheroe Street, Skipton, and had a son Frederick, *b.* 21 June 1916.

His brother George is buried in Merville Communal Cemetery Extension (III.A.1); Ernest has no known grave, he is commemorated on the Ypres (Menin Gate) Memorial (Panel 24).

(Panel 78) Pte. 28788, Rowland Moulding, 2nd Bn. (59th Foot) The East Lancashire Regt.: *b*. Blackburn, co. Lancaster, 1887. Killed in action 20 November 1917: Age 30. He leaves a wife Harriet (3, Progress Street, Blackburn), and *dau*. May, b. 1914.

PANEL 78 ENDS: PTE. T. NUTTER – EAST LANCASHIRE REGT.

PANEL 79 BEGINS: PTE. P. OGDEN – EAST LANCASHIRE REGT.

(Panel 79) Pte. 241447, John Shears, 2/5th Bn. The East Lancashire Regt. (T.F.): *s*. of the late John Shears, by his marriage to Isabella Slater, *née* Shears (7, Villiers Street, Burnley, co. Lancaster): and elder brother to Pte. 4897, E. Shears, 2nd East Lancashire Regt. attd. Royal Engineers, killed in action 9 July 1916, at the Somme; Pte. 16533, V. Shears (served as Slater), 10th Cameronians (Sco.Rif.), killed in action 25 September 1915, at Loos; and brother-in-law to Pte. 25386, J.S. Hargreaves, 1st Loyal North Lancashire Regt., killed in action 18 September 1918: *b*. Burnley: enlisted there. Killed in action 9 October 1917: Age 33. A third brother, Philip, who had previously served twelve years with the Colours, died at home after a long and lingering illness; William, the only surviving son, is currently (1918) serving with the Lancashire Fusiliers somewhere in France.

His brothers Edwin and Victor are buried in Hersin Communal Cemetery Extension (I.F.3) and Dud Corner Cemetery (VII.C.8) respectively; James Hargreaves has no known grave, he is commemorated on the Vis-en-Artois Memorial (Panel 7).

(Panel 79) L/Corpl. 33922, Clifford James Ford, 8th (Service) Bn. The East Surrey Regt.: *s*. of Frederick William Blight Ford, by his wife Alice (Victoria Square, Holsworthy, co. Devon): and brother to L/Corpl. 36855, C.E. Ford, 1st Wiltshire Regt., killed in action 18 September 1918; and Pte. 72216, E. Ford, 7th Cheshire Regt., died 21 May 1919: *b*. Holsworthy, 1891: enlisted Kingston-on-Thames. Killed in action 26 November 1917: Age 26.

His brother Charles is buried in Targelle Ravine British Cemetery, Villers-Guislain (G.23); Edwin, Teignmouth Cemetery (EE.87).

PANEL 79 ENDS: PTE. F.L. COLLINS – EAST SURREY REGT.

PANEL 80 BEGINS: PTE. C.G.E. COPPICK – EAST SURREY REGT.

(Panel 80) Pte. 25924, William Cross, 'C' Coy., 8th (Service) Bn. The East Surrey Regt.: *s*. of the late Harry Cross, by his wife Betsy (104A, Rochdale Road, Brittania, Bacup), *dau*. of Jonas Horsfall: *b*. Bacup, co. Lancaster, 9 October 1885: *educ*. Brittania Council School: Occupation – Steam Wagon Driver: enlisted Army Service Corps (Mechanical Transport), 28 August 1916: served with the Expeditionary Force in France and Flanders from May 1917, being transf'd. East Surrey Regt., 30 July, and was killed in action at Polygon Wood, nr. Ypres, 12 October 1917. Buried where he fell: Age 32. He *m*. St. Saviour's, Bacup, 27 October 1908; Mary (9, Nelson Street, Britannia), *dau*. of Ashworth Brearley, and had a son, Ashworth, *b*. 5 April 1913.

(Panel 80) Pte. 30744, William Daysh, 9th (Service) Bn. The East Surrey Regt.: *s*. of the late Joseph Daysh, by his wife Caroline: *b*. Tottenham, London, N.: *educ*. Seven Sisters Road School: enlisted 16 June 1916: served with the Expeditionary Force in France and Flanders, and was killed in action at Ypres, 18 August 1917. Buried there. He *m*. Tottenham, London, N.; Lydia (8, Woodville Grove, South Tottenham), *dau*. of the late Henry Bartlett, and had five children; William, Joseph, Robert, Edward and Lydia.

(Panel 80) Pte 34742, John Ginn, 8th (Service) Bn. The East Surrey Regt.: *s*. of the late James Ginn, of Cowlinge, by his wife Elizabeth: *b*. Cowlinge, Newmarket, co. Cambridge, 20 April 1880: *educ*. Cowlinge Village School: Occupation – Labourer: enlisted East Surrey Regt. 14 December 1916: served with the Expeditionary Force in France, from 1 August 1917, and was killed in action at Poelcappelle, 12 October following. Buried on the battlefield. 2nd Lieut. Fred W. Lovell wrote, "He was a great favourite with his comrades, who sadly miss him, and on more than one occasion has done his duty under most difficult and trying circumstances, and set a good example to the younger soldiers.": Age 37. He *m.* Cowlinge Church; Sarah (Park Road, Cowlinge, co. Suffolk), *dau.* of Charles Bowyer, and had three sons; Leslie Charles, *b.* 12 June 1907, Harry John, *b.* 20 March 1910 and Hugh Joseph, *b.* 14 April 1912.

(Panel 80) Pte. 22801, Alexander Griffiths, 8th (Service) Bn. The East Surrey Regt.: only *s.* of the late Alfred Griffiths, by his wife Clara (85, Rosebank Road, Hanwell, London, W.), *dau.* of John Price: *b.* Hanwell, 22 July 1897: *educ.* Oaklands Road, and St. Mark's Schools: Occupation – Printer's Apprentice: enlisted 18 May 1916: served with the Expeditionary Force in France and Flanders, from 27 August following, and was killed in action at Ypres, 12 October 1917. His Commanding Officer wrote, "His loss is greatly felt by all, as he was very popular with his comrades; your son was a fine soldier and he died doing his duty nobly on the field of honour." And his employer, "He always showed great interest in his work, and, had he been spared, would have become a good workman." Age 20. *unm.*

(Panel 80) 2nd Lieut. Hubert Claud Cater Yeo, 6th (Service) Bn. The Duke of Cornwall's Light Infantry: *s.* of Harry Treble Yeo, of 5, Princes St., Bude, by his wife Annie Marie, *née* Cater: *b.* Bude, co. Cornwall, 31 August 1895: *educ.* County School: enlisted January 1916: received a commission; gazetted 2nd Lieut., Duke of Cornwall's Light Infantry, March 1917: served with the Expeditionary Force in France and Flanders, and was killed in action at Inverness Copse, 24 August 1917, one week short of his 20th birthday. Buried where he fell: Age 19.

(Panel 80) 2nd Lieut. Edward Byrne, 6th (Service) Bn. The Duke of Cornwall's Light Infantry: eldest *s.* of the late Henry Byrne, of Dunlavin, co. Wicklow, by his wife Mary, *dau.* of Andrew Halpin: and nephew to Patrick Byrne, ex-Superintendent of the Dublin Metropolitan Police: *b.* Dunlavin, 8 December 1886: *educ.* De La Salle College, Waterford; Leeds University, and London University: Occupation – Teacher; London County Council: gazetted 2nd Lieut., Duke of Cornwall's Light Infantry, from London University O.T.C., 9 October 1915: trained Weymouth and Wareham: served with the Expeditionary Force in France and Flanders, from 9 September 1916: took part in the fighting on the Somme, the Battle of Arras, and the fighting round Ypres, and was killed in action at Inverness Copse, 23 August 1917, while leading his platoon into action. His Colonel wrote, "He was killed instantaneously by a rifle bullet through the head whilst leading his platoon very gallantly. His loss is mourned by all ranks, by whom he was universally liked and admired.": Age 30. *unm.*

PANEL 80 ENDS: 2ND LIEUT. E.M. GRAHAM – DUKE OF CORNWALL'S LIGHT INFANTRY

PANEL 81 BEGINS: 2ND LIEUT. W.S. HAMLYN – DUKE OF CORNWALL'S LIGHT INFANTRY

(Panel 81) 2nd Lieut. Wilfred Stephen Hamlyn, 6th (Service) Bn. The Duke of Cornwall's Light Infantry: *s.* of Tom Parker Hamlyn, lately of Craig Moor, Okehampton, co. Devon, former Head Postmaster – Okehampton & District, presently of 'Leybourne,' Grove Avenue, Yeovil, by his wife Anna Maria, *dau.* of Stephen Wellington, of Okehampton: *b.* Exeter, 19 June 1892: *educ.* Moorside School, Okehampton: Occupation – Clerk; National Bank of England, Southsea Branch; afterwards at Newcastle: enlisted 21st (4th Public Schools) Battn. Royal Fusiliers (City of London Regt.), 17 July 1915: trained Epsom and Salisbury Plain: served with the Expeditionary Force in France and Flanders from November 1915: recommended for Cadetship, March 1916; returned to England, underwent Cadet Training Course, Gailes Camp, co. Ayr; gazetted 2nd Lieut., 26 September 1916, and after a few months at Freshwater, Isle of Wight, returned to France: took part in the operations at Arras, and was killed in action, 24 August 1917, whilst leading his platoon at Inverness Copse. Buried there. His Commanding Officer wrote, "He was killed instantaneously, and died a very gallant death leading his platoon in the attack. His loss is deeply mourned by all ranks of the battalion, amongst whom he was most deservedly popular.": Age 25. *unm.*

(Panel 81) 2nd Lieut. Richard Henry Kelynack, 1st Bn. (32nd Foot) The Duke of Cornwall's Light Infantry: only *s.* of Capt. Richard Henry Kelynack, of Loch Broom, Newlyn, Penzance, Harbour Master, by his wife Edith, *dau.* of Walter Semmens: *b.* Poplar, London, E., 29 January 1897: *educ.* Thomas Street School, Limehouse, London, E.: entered Civil Service, 1912: joined Honourable Artillery Company, 12 July 1915: gazetted 2nd Lieut., Duke of Cornwall's Light Infantry, 22 May 1917; served with the Expeditionary Force in France from June following. Reported wounded and missing after the Battle of Ypres, 4 October 1917; now known to have been killed in action on that date.: Age 20. *unm.*

(Panel 81) 2nd Lieut. Wymond Nicholas Richard Pole-Carew, 'D' Coy., 1st Bn. (32nd Foot) The Duke of Cornwall's Light Infantry: *yst. s.* of Charles Edward Pole-Carew, of Parkhill, Totnes, co. Devon, by his wife Ellen Henrietta, *dau.* of William Ayshford Sanford, of Nynehead Court, Wellington, co. Somerset: and nephew of General Sir Reginald Pole-Carew: *b.* Hatton, Ceylon, 3 October 1896: *educ.* Marlborough; Wye Agricultural College; Royal Military College, Sandhurst: gazetted 2nd Lieut., Wiltshire Regt., October 1914, with which he went to India (1915); acted as A.D.C. to Lord Willingdon, Governor of Bombay, for six months: transf'd. to enter Sandhurst, where he was under-officer for a great portion of the time and, on leaving, received the King's Gold Medal, and the Anson Memorial Sword on passing out of the Royal Military College first: gazetted 2nd Lieut., Duke of Cornwall's Light Infantry, October 1916: served with the Expeditionary Force in France from 23 March 1917, and was killed in action at Polderhoek, when in command of 'D' Coy., 6 November following. He had been in command of 'D' Coy. for six weeks. His Commanding Officer wrote, "He was killed in an attack on a strong hostile position on 6 November. He was commanding 'D' Coy., and led them to the assault in the early morning. He had gained a reputation for gallantry in previous actions, and he had been recommended for the Military Cross after the operations on 4 October." Mentioned in General Sir Douglas Haig's Despatch (7 November 1917), for 'gallantry and distinguished service in the field.' He was a keen sportsman, and had shown his prowess in big game hunting: Age 21. *unm.*

(Panel 81) Corpl. 7815, Charles William Foskett, 1st Bn. (32nd Foot) The Duke of Cornwall's Light Infantry: *s.* of Joseph M. Foskett, Carpenter, of Harris, Saskatchewan, late of 18, Raunds Road, Stanwick, nr. Wellingborough, co. Northampton, by his wife Mary: and elder brother to Corpl. 628614, G.E. Foskett, 47th Canadian Infantry, who fell four days previously: *b.* Stanwick, *c.*1886: emigrated with his parents to Canada, 1907: a member of the Reserve, was called up on mobilisation, returned to England and re-enlisted Northampton, September 1914: served with the Expeditionary Force in France and Flanders from 1915: took part in much heavy fighting; particularly on the Somme, 1916; Broodseinde Ridge, 4 October 1917, and was reported missing believed killed in action on the 30th of that month on which date his battalion (in reserve at Tor Top and Stirling Castle) was engaged in carrying supplies to the front line battalions under heavy artillery fire: Age 31. A talented musician, formerly a member of the Stanwick Church Choir, he was a member of the regimental band. Corpl. Foskett, like his brother George, partook of his leave from France in England, staying with his aunt, Mrs Clarke, 'Rose Cottage,' Grange Road, Stanwick. He leaves a wife, Annie Elizabeth Foskett (Prince Albert, Saskatchewan), and three children. His eldest son Pilot Officer J/9523, C.R. Foskett, 407 Sqdn. Royal Canadian Air Force, was killed in action, 6 September 1942.

His brother George also has no known grave, he is commemorated on the Ypres (Menin Gate) Memorial (Panel 30); similarly, like his father and uncle, Charles R. Foskett also has no known grave, he is commemorated on the Runnymede Memorial (Panel 100).

(Panel 81) L/Corpl. 28869, William Henry Lovell, 7th (Service) Bn. The Duke of Cornwall's Light Infantry: eldest *s.* of the late Robert Lovell, of Bawcombe, Bradstone, Lifton, co. Devon, Farmer, by his wife Patience (Old School House, Milton Abbot, Tavistock, co. Devon), *dau.* of Henry Baskerville: *b.* Titchington, co. Devon, 21 October 1891: enlisted 30 November 1914: served with the Expeditionary Force in France and Flanders from September 1916, and was killed in action 16 August 1917. A comrade wrote, "He was a real good chum, and he possessed a splendid Christian spirit.": Age 25. *unm.*

(Panel 81) L/Corpl. 6042, William Whitehouse, 2nd Bn. (46th Foot) The Duke of Cornwall's Light Infantry: *s.* of John Whitehouse, by his wife Sarah: *b.* Oldbury, 1881: *educ.* Spon Lane Board Schools:

Occupation – Labourer; Messrs Taylor and Farley, West Bromwich, co. Stafford: served 18 years with the Colours: fought during the South African War 1899-1902 (Queen's and King's Medal – two clasps): thereafter joined the Reserve: called up on mobilisation at the outbreak of war, August 1914: served with the Expeditionary Force in France and Flanders from June 1915, and was killed in action at Passchendaele, 4 October 1917: Age 38. He *m.* Holy Trinity Church, West Bromwich, Florence (21, Neal Street, Spon Lane, West Bromwich), *dau.* of Charles Probyn, and had two *daus.*; Florence, *b.* 5 April 1909 and Mercy, *b.* 7 January 1914.

(Panel 81) Pte. 202766, Alfred John Badcock, 7th (Service) Bn. The Duke of Cornwall's Light Infantry: *s.* of William Henry Badcock, of Barton House, Buckland Filliegh, Beaworthy, co. Devon, and Jane Badcock, his wife: and yr. brother to Pte. 2353, F. Badcock, 1/6th Devonshire Regt., killed in action 8 March 1916: *b.* Buckland Filleigh: enlisted Barnstaple. Killed in action 27 September 1917: Age 19.

His brother Frank also has no known grave; he is commemorated on the Basra Memorial, Iraq (Panel 11).

(Panel 81) Pte. 35252, Cecil John Philip Oke, 7th (Service) Bn. The Duke of Cornwall's Light Infantry: *s.* of Thomas Oke, of 24, Victoria Road, Bude, co. Cornwall, by his wife Elizabeth Annie: and yr. brother to Pte. 201234, A.T.W. Oke, 2/4th D.C.L.I., died 22 October 1918, in India: *b.* Gloucester, 1899: enlisted Bude. Killed in action 9 February 1918: Age 19.

His brother Arthur is buried in Delhi War Cemetery (8.B.19).

PANEL 81 ENDS: PTE. M. PARKIN – DUKE OF CORNWALL'S LIGHT INFANTRY

PANEL 82 BEGINS: PTE. F.T. PARSONS – DUKE OF CORNWALL'S LIGHT INFANTRY

(Panel 82) Pte. 24542, Fernley Sexon Smith, 1st Bn. (32nd Foot) The Duke of Cornwall's Light Infantry: *b.* Penzance, co. Cornwall, 26 December 1889: *educ.* there: enlisted 10 February 1916: served with the Expeditionary Force in France and Flanders from 10 June following: wounded 4 September 1916, and invalided home: returned to France on recovery, and was killed in action at Ypres 4 October 1917: Age 27. *unm.*

(Panel 82) Pte. 34850, Freddie Waters, 6th (Service) Bn. The Duke of Cornwall's Light Infantry: *s.* of George Waters, of Chapel Place, Mousehole, Penzance, and Elizabeth, his spouse: enlisted Penzance, aged 18 yrs., 4 months; posted 3rd (T.R.) Battn., Freshwater, Isle of Wight, where he underwent 16 weeks training: thereafter posted 6th D.C.L.I.: proceeded to France, January 1916: took part in the fighting at the Somme (the battalion being relieved in the front line nr. Arras, 28 July 1916 to proceed south): entered into the fighting for Delville (Devil's) Wood, 16 August where, over the four days the battalion spent in the line, it incurred casualties of 366 all ranks. Pte. Waters was killed by shrapnel on 11 December 1917, Meetchaele – Passchendaele sector, Ypres salient: Age 19. At the time of his death, although the Battalion were not involved in any action, life in the salient was – particularly in winter when the weather and swamp-like conditions dictated men should never be dry – uniquely miserable. And constantly dangerous with an attrition rate to match. Formerly a chorister at United Methodist Church, Mousehole, he is remembered on the Mousehole Methodist Church War Memorial, and on his parent's headstone in Paul Parish Churchyard.

(Panel 82) Lieut. Joseph Cyril Walton, 1/4th Bn. The Duke of Wellington's (West Riding) Regt. (T.F.): 2nd *s.* of the Rev. John Maxton Walton, Vicar of Southowram, Halifax, by his wife Catherine, *dau.* of the late Charles E. Graham, of Wakefield: *b.* Alversthorpe, Wakefield, co. York: *educ.* Rishworth Grammar School, Sowerby Bridge, co. York, leaving there in 1903: Occupation – Journalist; 15 years employee to the *Yorkshire Post* (commenced aged 12 yrs.): enlisted Duke of Wellington's Regt.: obtained a commission, gazetted 2nd Lieut., West Riding Regt., 24 July 1915: promoted Lieut. July 1916: served with the Expeditionary Force in France and Flanders from September 1915, as Battalion Intelligence Officer: wounded (1917), and was killed by the explosion of an enemy shell at Kemmel Hill, Ypres, on the last day of the German Spring Offensive, 29 April 1918. The General Commanding the Division wrote, "He was a very capable and gallant officer, and we miss him badly. I thought it might be some small consolation to you to know that we, his comrades out here, appreciated his worth;" and his Commanding Officer, "He was, as you know, my Intelligence Officer, and his death is a very great loss to me and to the battalion. He was quick and very efficient, and most popular with us all." In a letter home the Adjutant said, "Lieut. Walton had gone out to ascertain what the situation was, and was struck by a shell which killed him instantaneously. We shall miss him very much. Ever since he came to the battalion he has taken the greatest interest in everything connected with it, and during the many engagements of the past three weeks has rendered valuable services both to the battalion as Intelligence Officer and to us individually in the Mess.": Age 30. He *m.* St. Cuthbert's, Bradford, 20 May 1916; Mary Winifred, *dau.* of the late Edwin Wood, of Darlington. *s.p.*

(Panel 82) Corpl. 305643, Charles Escott, 1/7th Bn. The Duke of Wellington's (West Riding Regt.), (T.F.): late of Mossley, Ashton-under-Lyne, co. Lancaster: *s.* of former L/Corpl. Richard Escott (surv'd.): and brother to Pte. 305151, R. Escott, 1/7th Duke of Wellington's Regt., killed the same day; and Pte. 300053, W.H. Escott, 2/6th Duke of Wellington's Regt., killed in action 3 May 1917: *b.* Uppermill, Saddleworth, co. York: enlisted Milnsbridge: served with the Expeditionary Force in France and Flanders from 15 April 1915, and was killed in action 14 April 1918.

His brothers also have no known grave; Richard is recorded on Panel 83; William, the Arras Memorial (Bay 6).

PANEL 82 ENDS: L/CORPL. J. LINDLEY – DUKE OF WELLINGTON'S (WEST RIDING) REGT.

PANEL 83 BEGINS: L/CORPL. C.R. MELLOR – DUKE OF WELLINGTON'S (WEST RIDING) REGT.

(Panel 83) Pte. 16995, John Adamthwaite, 1/6th Bn. The Duke of Wellington's (West Riding) Regt. (T.F.): *s.* of I. (& Mrs) Adamthwaite, of Stone Gate, Low Bentham. Killed in action 11 April 1918: Age 22. *unm.*

(Panel 83) Pte. 24612, Edward Butler, 1/7th Bn. The Duke of Wellington's (West Riding) Regt. (T.F.): brother to Pte. 242657, H. Butler, King's Own Yorkshire Light Infantry, who fell 4 October 1917: enlisted Bradford, co. York. Killed in action 13 April 1918. All correspondence should be addressed to Mr F. Butler, 55, Sydenham Place, Bradford.

His brother Herbert also has no known grave; he is recorded on Panel 109.

(Panel 83) Pte. 205274, William Bewsher, 8th (Service) Bn. The Duke of Wellington's (West Riding) Regt.: *husb.* to Kate Bewsher (33, Stewart Road, Sharrow Vale, Sheffield, co. York): *s.* of Benjamin Denton Bewsher, of 41, Cecil Road, Sheffield, and Susannah, his wife: and elder brother to Pte. 21806, J. Bewsher, 7th Canadian Infantry, killed in action, 24 April 1915. Killed in action 9 October 1917: Age 37.

His brother John also has no known grave; he is commemorated on the Ypres (Menin Gate) Memorial (Panel 24).

(Panel 83) Pte. 305151, Richard Escott, 1/7th Bn. The Duke of Wellington's (West Riding Regt.), (T.F.): late of Mossley, Ashton-under-Lyne, co. Lancaster: *s.* of former L/Corpl. Richard Escott (surv'd.): and brother to Corpl. 305643, C. Escott, 1/7th Duke of Wellington's Regt., killed the same day; and Pte. 300053, W.H. Escott, 2/6th Duke of Wellington's Regt., killed in action, 3 May 1917: *b.* Uppermill, Saddleworth, co. York: enlisted Uppermill: served with the Expeditionary Force in France and Flanders from 15 April 1915, and was killed in action, 14 April 1918.

His brothers also have no known grave; Charles is recorded on Panel 82; William, the Arras Memorial (Bay 6).

(Panel 83) Pte. 201739, Henry Garside, 2nd Bn. (76th Foot) The Duke of Wellington's (West Riding) Regt.: formerly of Stainland: *husb.* to Lillian Garside (14, Rogerson Square, Bonegate Road, Brighouse, co. York): attendee St. Martin's Church, Brighouse: Occupation – Corporation Gasworker: enlisted May 1915: twice wounded previously. Killed by a sniper at the 3rd Battle of Ypres, 10 October 1917: Age 27.

(Panel 83) Pte. 18955, John Thomas Gray, 1/7th Bn. The Duke of Wellington's (West Riding) Regt. (T.F.): *s.* of Thomas Gray, of 19, Albert Street, Brigg, co. Lincoln, by his wife Elizabeth (15, Wrawby Street, Brigg): and elder brother to Dvr. 21358, G.W. Gray, 46th Bde. Royal Field Artillery, died of wounds 28 November 1917: native to Holton Holgate, Spilsby, co. Lincoln: enlisted Bradford, co. York. Killed in action 13 April 1918: Age 25.

His brother George is buried in Dozinghem Military Cemetery (XIV.E.12).

(Panel 83) Pte. 266726, John William Hilton, 1/6th Bn. The Duke of Wellington's (West Riding) Regt. (T.F.): late of Pendleton, co. Lancaster: *gdson.* of Mrs Hilton (Langcliffe, co. York): previously employed at Langcliffe Mills: enlisted, Skipton, co. York, May 1916: served with the Expeditionary Force in France and Flanders from Christmas Day 1916: took part in the fighting at Ypres, Broodseinde, Poelcapelle and Passchendaele, and was killed by shell fire while carrying ammunition 19 April 1918. (*IWGC record 14 April*)

PANEL 83 ENDS: PTE. J. IBBERSON – DUKE OF WELLINGTON'S (WEST RIDING) REGT.

New Zealand Memorial to the Missing, Tyne Cot

PANEL 84 BEGINS: PTE. P. INGHAM – DUKE OF WELLINGTON'S (WEST RIDING) REGT.

(Panel 84) Pte. 17676, William Walker Jackson, (Siglr.) 'D' Coy., 10th (Service) Bn. The Duke of Wellington's (West Riding) Regt.: late of Dub Cote, Horton-in-Robertsdale: eldest *s.* of William Jackson, of Ivy Cottage, Horton-in-Ribbersdale, Settle, co. York, by his wife Harriet: *b.* 31 May 1895: *educ.* Horton School: Occupation – Farm Worker: enlisted 16 November 1915: served with the Expeditionary Force in France from February 1917, and was reported wounded and missing, since confirmed killed in action, 20 September following: Age 22. *unm.* In a letter to his mother, a comrade wrote, "I am writing to let you know that Willie was rather badly wounded when we were in another roughish corner, and although I have made enquiries I cannot get any definite information respecting him. So far he is reported wounded and missing, as they have not got any word as to his passing through any of the dressing stations. It happened on the morning of the 20th. Although we had a rough time of it we had quite a victory. The night before we went up I had a talk with Willie, who was quite up with it. We realised that some would be sorted out and would not come back. The Colonel made a touching speech yesterday when we got back and congratulated us on the splendid manner in which we did the task allotted to us. Tears of pride came into our eyes as we stood listening to him, mingled with tears of sorrow as we thought of those who had paid the price. It is only in moments such as these that you would think we have any feeling at all. Our Commanding Officer is a rare sort, and I don't think there is a man who would not give his life for him."

He left his home at duty's call,
He gave his life for one and all.

(Panel 84) Pte. 203108, Wilfred Isaac Johnson, 1/4th Bn. The Duke of Wellington's (West Riding) Regt. (T.F.): late of 9, Crossley Street, Todmorden, co. York: *b.* Cross Stone, *c.*1886: prior to enlistment (Todmorden, May 1916) was employee Messrs Barker Clegg Ltd.: served with the Expeditionary Force in France and Flanders from December 1916, and was killed in action, 19 November 1917: Age 31. In a letter to his widow, Emily Summerton, *née* Johnson (since remarried; 4A, Anchor Street, Todmorden), Lieut. Hirst wrote, "I regret to inform you that your husband was killed on November 19th by shellfire. I am sure his loss will be a great blow to you. We shall miss him very much, as he was of a most cheerful disposition and was the life of his platoon. You will no doubt be a little satisfied in your mind to know that everything possible was done for him at the time, and he was buried by his comrades, and his grave is now marked by a neat white wooden cross. I trust God will give you strength to bear your sorrow, and hope that you will accept the deepest sympathy of the officers and men in the company."

(Panel 84) Pte. 200445, John Patrick Kelly, 1/4th Bn. The Duke of Wellington's (West Riding) Regt. (T.F.): *s.* of the late Joseph Kelly, of 2, Delph Hill Lane, Midgley, by his wife Ann: a member of Luddenden Mechanic's Institute, and employee Messrs R.T. Riley & Sons, Peel House Mills: enlisted 14 August 1914: went to France, April 1915, and was killed in action at the Battle of Passchendaele, 9 October 1917, while moving forward with a machine gun team in support of attacking infantry: Age 25. *unm.*

(Panel 84) Pte. 269073, Harold Oliver, 10th (Service) Bn. The Duke of Wellington's (West Riding) Regt.: *s.* of John Oliver, of Wold View, Spittle, Wilberfoss, co. York, by his wife Martha: and yr. brother to Pte. 8792, R.A. Oliver, 2nd Scots Guards, killed in action, 19 April 1916: *b.* Fangfoss, York: enlisted York. Killed in action 20 September 1917: Age 19. Fangfoss Parish War Memorial – "...Erected By The Parishioners...To The Glory Of God And To Record The Names Of The Men Of This Parish Who Fell In The Great War A.D. 1914–1919. R.I.P" – records three names; the Oliver brothers and Pte. F.F. Pearson, East Yorkshire Regt., who died September 1919.

His brother Robert also has no known grave; he is commemorated on the Ypres (Menin Gate) Memorial (Panel 11).

(Panel 84) Pte. 307333, William Taylor, 1/7th Bn. The Duke of Wellington's (West Riding) Regt. (T.F.): formerly no.26912, King's Own Yorkshire Light Infantry: *s.* of George Taylor, of 7, Cromwell Avenue, Filey, co. York, by his wife Ellen: and brother to Pte. 24422, S. Taylor, 2nd King's Own Yorkshire Light Infantry, killed in action 3 February 1917; and Pte. 37763, F. Taylor, 16th Highland Light Infantry, killed in action, 14 April 1917: *b.* Filey, afsd.:enlisted Dewsbury. Killed in action, 13 April 1918: Age 25. *unm.*

His brother Silas is buried in Auchonvillers Military Cemetery (II.K.25); Fred lies in Chapelle British Cemetery, Holnon (I.I.11).

(Panel 84) Pte. 204184, Frank Helliwell Thorpe, 1/4th Bn. The Duke of Wellington's (West Riding) Regt. (T.F.): late of 17, Bank Buildings, Luddenfoot: *s.* of Thomas Thorpe, of 9, Lane Side, Luddenfoot, co. York, by his wife Mary: attended United Methodist Church: employed by J. Clay & Son: enlisted September 1916; proceeded to France, January 1917. Reported missing during the fighting in the Peter Pan sector, Passchendaele 10 October 1917; now presumed killed: Age 32.

(Panel 84) Pte. 202225, Fred Woodhead, 1/4th Bn. The Duke of Wellington's (West Riding) Regt. (T.F.): *s.* of Abner Woodhead, Warp Dresser; of 64, Fair Road, Wibsey, Bradford, co. York, by his wife Ann: and elder brother to Pte. 267484, H. Woodhead, 2nd West Yorkshire Regt., died of wounds, 25 April 1918: *b.* Wibsey, 1879: Occupation – Factory worker; Messrs E. Ripley & Sons, Bowling Dye Works: enlisted Bradford, 7 March 1916: wounded 3 May 1917. Killed in action 9 October 1917: Age 28. *unm.* Dedicated 'In Grateful Remembrance Of The Young Men Of This School Who Gave Their Lives In The European War, 1914–1919,' the brothers Woodhead are remembered on the Wibsey (Wesleyan Church) Sunday School War Memorial.

His brother Herbert is buried in Crouy British Cemetery, Crouy-sur-Somme (I.B.11).

PANEL 84 ENDS: PTE. F.P. YOUNG – DUKE OF WELLINGTON'S (WEST RIDING REGT.)

PANEL 85 BEGINS: CAPT. R. ABRAM – BORDER REGT.

(Panel 85) Capt. Peter McEwan Martin, 11th (Service) Bn. The Border Regt.: formerly Pte. S/43260; formerly 3164, Royal Highlanders: *s.* of Joseph Rundle Martin, of Fowlis Wester, Crieff (late Scots Guards), Schoolmaster Registrar, and Inspector of the Poor, by his wife Jane, *dau.* of the late John McEwan: and brother to Pte. S/43893, H.S. Martin, 6th Gordon Highlanders, killed in action 23 July 1918: *b.* The Schoolhouse, Fowlis Wester, co. Perth, 18 October 1896: *educ.* Public School, there, and Perth Academy: Occupation – Apprentice; Clydesdale Bank, Crieff: joined Black Watch, 14 March 1915: served with the Expeditionary Force in France and Flanders from 3 September 1916: took part in the fighting on the Somme in that year, being wounded three times: gazetted 2nd Lieut., Border Regt., 15 February 1917; promoted Lieut., 6 April; Capt. (for bravery on the field) 11 August 1917, and was killed in action at

Passchendaele Ridge, nr. Ypres, 2 December following. Buried where he fell. His Commanding Officer wrote, "Your son was a real good fellow, and most popular with all ranks. He was one of the bravest boys it has been my good fortune to meet, and he died like the good soldier and fearless leader he always proved himself to be. He leaves behind him a splendid memory of duty well and gallantly done, which will remain with us as a cherished example for all time.": Age 21. *unm.*

His brother Henry is buried in Marfaux British Cemetery (V.D.5).

(Panel 85) Capt. John Ebenezer Stewart, M.C., 8th (Service) Bn. The Border Regt. attd. South Staffordshire Regt.: *s.* of William A. Stewart, of 37, Kildovan Street, Coatbridge, and Isabella Shaw Stewart, his late wife. Killed in action 26 April 1918, nr Messines: Age 29. *unm.* Author of the poem '*The Messines Road.*'

> The road that runs up to Messines
> Is double-locked with gates of fire,
> Barred with high ramparts, and between
> The unbridged river, and the wire.
>
> None ever goes up to Messines,
> For Death lurks all about the town,
> Death holds the vale as his demesne,
> And only Death moves up and down.
>
> Choked with wild weeds, and overgrown
> With rank grass, all torn and rent
> By war's opposing engines, strewn
> With debris from each day's event!
>
> And in the dark the broken trees,
> Whose arching boughs were once its shade
> Grim and distorted, ghostly ease
> In groans their souls vexed and afraid.
>
> Yet here the farmer drove his cart,
> Here friendly folk would meet and pass,
> Here bore the good wife eggs to mart
> And old and young walked up to Mass.
>
> Here schoolboys lingered in the way,
> Here the bent packman laboured by,
> And lovers at the end o' the day
> Whispered their secret blushingly.
>
> A goodly road for simple needs,
> An avenue to praise and paint,
> Kept by fair use from wreck and weeds,
> Blessed by the shrine of its own saint.
>
> The road that runs up to Messines!
> Ah, how we guard it day and night!
> And how they guard it, who o'erween
> A stricken people, with their might!
>
> But we shall go up to Messines
> Even thro' that fire-defended gate.
> Over and thro' all else between
> And give the highway back its state.

(Panel 85) Sergt. 35028, Thomas Arthur Garrett, 11th (Service) Bn. The Border Regt.: formerly no.189633, South Lancashire Regt.: late of Salford, co. Lancaster: *s.* of Joseph Garrett, of 401, Grafton Street, Dingle, Liverpool: enlisted Liverpool. Killed in action on the night of 25 November 1917, when, during a relief near Bellevue Spur, undue noise and commotion drew down a heavy German bombardment on the battalion resulting in the death of Sergt. Garrett and eighteen other men: Age 24. *unm.* See account re. L/Corpl. J. Nixon, Tyne Cot Cemetery (XXXVII.H.6).

(Panel 85) L/Sergt. 28278, George Wainman, M.M., 11th (Service) Bn. The Border Regt.: formerly no.32925, Essex Regt.: *s.* of Alfred (& Mrs) Wainman, of 44, Blenheim Road, Stratford, London: *b.* Bow, London, E., *c.*1886: enlisted Warley, co. Essex. Killed in action on the night of 25 November 1917 when, during a relief near Bellevue Spur, undue noise and commotion drew down a heavy German bombardment on the battalion resulting in the death of L/Sergt. Wainman and eighteen other men: Age 31. He leaves a widow, Florence Mabel Wainman (57, Pembroke Road, Seven Kings, co. Essex), and family. See account re. Corpl. J. Nixon, Tyne Cot Cemetery (XXXVII.H.6).

(Panel 85) Corpl. 201612, John Youdale, 2nd Bn. (55th Foot) The Border Regt.: *s.* of Richard Youdale, of 14, Southey Street, Keswick, co. Cumberland, by his wife Sarah Jane: *b.* Keswick, 1888: *educ.* Keswick School, 1902–04: Occupation – Clerk; Keswick Railway Station: volunteered and enlisted, April 1915: served with the Expeditionary Force in France and Flanders from 1917, and was reported missing after the action at Gheluvelt, 20 October 1917. With no accurate information as to the circumstances of his death being obtainable, an extract from a letter from one of his comrades gives partial explanation, "There were very few of us left out of that 'stunt,' and I remember being told that your son had given his life with many others. During that awful time we found the mud so thick that once you got stuck in it, it was almost impossible to get out, and many poor chaps lost their lives on that account." Corpl. Youdale (Sergt.) is recorded in the Keswick School Book of Remembrance with 22 other Old Boys of that school in ".. a small tribute of admiration and gratitude from the School to those gallant sons who went forth on the Great Adventure, and by sacrifice of their lives helped to save the world. May it long keep green our memory of these splendid boys who loved honour more than they feared death.": Age 29.

(Panel 85) L/Corpl. 32085, William James Crick, 11th (Service) Bn. The Border Regt.: *s.* of Henry George Crick, of 5, Sultan Road, Wanstead, co. Essex, by his wife Elizabeth Ann: enlisted Leyton. Killed in action on the night of 25 November 1917 when, during a relief nr. Bellevue Spur, undue noise and commotion drew down a heavy German bombardment on the battalion resulting in the death of L/Corpl. Crick and eighteen other men: Age 25. *unm.* See account re. L/Corpl. J. Nixon, Tyne Cot Cemetery (XXXVII.H.6).

(Panel 85) L/Corpl. 27250, Francis Eli Hammond, 11th (Service) Bn. The Border Regt.: formerly no.32807, Manchester Regt.: *s.* of William Henry Hamond, of Levenshulme, Manchester, by his wife Florence May. Killed in action on the night of 25 November 1917 when, during a relief nr. Bellevue Spur, undue noise and commotion drew down a heavy German bombardment on the battalion resulting in the death of L/Corpl. Hammond and eighteen other men: Age 21. *unm.* See account re. L/Corpl. J. Nixon, Tyne Cot Cemetery (XXXVII.H.6).

(Panel 85) Pte. 16854, William Eglin Armer, 7th (Service) Bn. (Westmorland & Cumberland Yeomanry) The Border Regt.: *s.* of Greenwood Armer, of Sedbergh, co. York, by his wife Agnes: *b.* Sedbergh, 1894: prior to the outbreak of war was employee of Messrs Williamson and Sons, Manchester: enlisted Manchester, October 1914: served with the Expeditionary Force at Gallipoli, July 1915, and in France and Flanders: returned home on leave late August 1917: returned to France, and was killed in action six weeks later, 12 October 1917. His parents received notification of their son's death on what would have been his 23rd birthday. An officer wrote, "It is my painful duty to inform you of the death of your son, Pte. W.E. Armer. He was an excellent fellow and did very good work the last time up the line. He was wounded in the head and died at an Advanced Dressing Station shortly afterwards. I shall miss him very much, and although my sympathy may be of small consolation to you in your great loss, I hope that you will find some comfort in the knowledge that your son suffered no pain and passed away peacefully without regaining consciousness.": Age 23. *unm.*

(Panel 85) Pte. 20208, Charles Bintcliffe, 'B' Coy., 2nd Bn. (55th Foot) The Border Regt.: formerly of Brighouse: his father of 4, Cross Street, Brighouse, was a Sergeant with the Territorials: prior to enlistment (April 1915) sometime employee Messrs Helliwells Patent Glazing Co., later employed by Messrs Brough Nicholson & Hall, Silk Spinners: served with Mediterranean Expeditionary Force in the Dardenelles where he was wounded; repatriated to England: returned to his regt. on the Somme, 1916, and was wounded again. Killed in action during the Battle of Passchendaele, 4 October 1917: Age 24. He was married to Gladys May Pickering, *née* Bintcliffe (9, Cromwell Terrace, Leek, co. Stafford).

(Panel 85) Pte. 28824, Arthur James Bishop, 11th (Service) Bn. The Border Regt.: formerly no.2692, Kent Cyclists Bn.: late of Hanwell, nr. Banbury: *b.* Caterham, co. Surrey: enlisted Ealing, co. Middlesex. Killed in action on the night of 25 November 1917 when, during a relief near Bellevue Spur, undue noise and commotion drew down a heavy German bombardment on the battalion resulting in the death of Pte. Bishop and eighteen other men. See account re. L/Corpl. J. Nixon, Tyne Cot Cemetery (XXXVII.H.6).

(Panel 85) Pte. 260209, Thomas Henry Cannon, 11th (Service) Bn. The Border Regt.: enlisted Liverpool. Killed in action on the night of 25 November 1917 when, during a relief near Bellevue Spur, undue noise and commotion drew down a heavy German bombardment on the battalion resulting in the death of Pte. Cannon and eighteen other men. See account re. L/Corpl. J. Nixon, Tyne Cot Cemetery (XXXVII.H.6).

(Panel 85) Pte. 28828, John Jack Clark, 11th (Service) Bn. The Border Regt.: formerly no.G/86931, Middlesex Regt.: *s.* of Frederick Clark, of 4, Russell Place, Dover, by his wife Rachel: enlisted Dover, co. Kent. Killed in action on the night of 25 November 1917 when, during a relief near Bellevue Spur, undue noise and commotion drew down a heavy German bombardment on the battalion resulting in the death of Pte. Clark and eighteen other men: Age 20. See account re. L/Corpl. J. Nixon, Tyne Cot Cemetery (XXXVII.H.6).

(Panel 85) Pte. 263108, Reginald Walls Crayston, 6th (Service) Bn. The Border Regt.: formerly no.3642, King's Own (Royal Lancaster Regt.): *s.* of Richard R. Crayston, of 9, Cromwell Road, Lancaster, by his wife Fanny: and yr. brother to L/Corpl. L/4403, R.A.N. Crayston, XIIth Royal Lancers, died of wounds 31 October 1914, aged 20 years: *b.* Kirby Lonsdale: enlisted Lancaster. Killed in action 22 August 1917: Age 19. Remembered on Lancaster War Memorial.

His brother Richard is buried in Kemmel Churchyard (B.3).

(Panel 85) Pte. 260213, John William Clegg, 11th (Service) Bn. The Border Regt.: formerly no.203203, King's (Liverpool) Regt.: *s.* of Mary Jane Clegg (150, Vauxhall Road, Liverpool): *b.* Liverpool, *c.*1898. Killed in action on the night of 25 November 1917 when, during a relief near Bellevue Spur, undue noise and commotion drew down a heavy German bombardment on the battalion resulting in the death of Pte. Clegg and eighteen other men: Age 19. See account re. L/Corpl. J. Nixon, Tyne Cot Cemetery (XXXVII.H.6).

(Panel 85) Pte. 260216, Joseph James Demellweek, 11th (Service) Bn. The Border Regt.: *s.* of John Henry Demellweek, of 71, Thomaston Street, Everton: *b.* Everton, Liverpool, co. Lancaster, 19 November 1892: *educ.* St. Peter's Church School, there: Occupation – Carter: enlisted in the Border Regt. 7 March 1917: served with the Expeditionary Force in France and Flanders from 24 June, and was officially reported to have been killed in action or died of wounds, 2 December 1917. Buried at Passchendaele, Flanders. He *m.* Everton; Louisa (178, Great Homer Street, Liverpool), *dau.* of William Howard, and had a son, Joseph James, *b.* 2 September 1916: Age 24.

(Panel 85) Pte. 260223, William Henry Fox, 11th (Service) Bn. The Border Regt.: formerly no.203155, King's (Liverpool) Regt.: enlisted Seaforth, Liverpool. Killed in action on the night of 25 November 1917 when, during a relief near Bellevue Spur, undue noise and commotion drew down a heavy German bombardment on the battalion resulting in the death of Pte. Fox and eighteen other men. See account re. L/Corpl. J. Nixon, Tyne Cot Cemetery (XXXVII.H.6).

PANEL 85 ENDS: PTE. C. HARRIS – BORDER REGT.

PANEL 86 BEGINS: PTE. T. HARROLD – BORDER REGT.

(Panel 86) Pte. 260234, William Robert Logan, 11th (Service) Bn. The Border Regt.: formerly no.203118, King's (Liverpool) Regt.:enlisted Liverpool. Killed in action on the night of 25 November 1917 when, during a relief near Bellevue Spur, undue noise and commotion drew down a heavy German bombardment on the battalion resulting in the death of Pte. Logan and eighteen other men. See account re. L/Corpl. J. Nixon, Tyne Cot Cemetery (XXXVII.H.6).

(Panel 86) Pte. 29095, Redcar George Matthews, 2nd Bn. (55th Foot) The Border Regt.: formerly no.344151, Royal Army Service Corps: *s.* of Walter Matthews, of Coltishall Road, Buxton, co. Norfolk, by his wife Ellen: and brother to Wkr. 47814, M.M. Matthews, Queen Mary's Auxiliary Army Corps, died 17 February 1919, of sickness (influenza): *b.* Buxton Lammas, co. Norfolk: enlisted Fulham, London, S.W. Killed in action 26 October 1917. Remembered on the Buxton (St. Andrew's) War Memorial.

His sister Mary is buried in Etaples Military Cemetery (LXXII.B.36).

(Panel 86) Pte. 260641, Horace Pearson-Parker, 7th (Service) Bn. The Border Regt.: formerly no.315149, Westmorland & Cumberland Yeomanry: *s.* of the late Pte. 15348, D. Pearson-Parker, Royal Defence Corps, died 23 June 1917; and his wife Janet Pearson-Parker (11, Market Place, Cockermouth, co. Cumberland): *gdson.* to the late Joseph (& Betsy) Pearson-Parker: *b.* Cockermouth, *c.*1893: enlisted there. Killed in action 12 October 1917: Age 24. *unm.* Dedicated – 'Our Glorious Dead Who Died In The Great War 1914-1919. Let Those Who Come After See To It That These Names Be Not Forgotten...They Found Death In The Path Of Duty' – Father and son are remembered on the Cockermouth War Memorial.

His father Daniel is buried in Cockermouth Cemetery (O.CE.01).

(Panel 86) Pte. 260253, Henry Pedder, 11th (Service) Bn. The Border Regt.: late of New Hey, nr. Rochdale, co. Lancaster: *b.* Burscough, Ormskirk: enlisted Liverpool. Killed in action on the night of 25 November 1917 when, during a relief near Bellevue Spur, undue noise and commotion drew down a heavy German bombardment on the battalion resulting in the death of Pte. Pedder and eighteen other men. See account re. L/Corpl. J. Nixon, Tyne Cot Cemetery (XXXVII.H.6).

(Panel 86) Pte. 18812, William Smith, 11th (Service) Bn. The Border Regt.: *s.* of Mary Jane Smith (17, Baber Street, Bolton, co. Lancaster): enlisted Bolton. Killed in action on the night of 25 November 1917 when, during a relief near Bellevue Spur, undue noise and commotion drew down a heavy German bombardment on the battalion resulting in the death of Pte. Smith and eighteen other men: Age 27. He leaves a widow, Mary Louisa Smith (20, Back, Haydock Street, Bolton). See account re. L/Corpl. J. Nixon, Tyne Cot Cemetery (XXXVII.H.6).

(Panel 86) Pte. 28970, Thomas Robert Steele, 11th (Service) Bn. The Border Regt.: formerly no.50036, Manchester Regt.: enlisted Manchester. Killed in action on the night of 25 November 1917 when, during a relief near Bellevue Spur, undue noise and commotion drew down a heavy German bombardment on the battalion resulting in the death of Pte. Steele and eighteen other men. See account re. L/Corpl. J. Nixon, Tyne Cot Cemetery (XXXVII.H.6).

(Panel 86) Pte. 32579, Patrick Woods, 11th (Service) Bn. The Border Regt.: *b.* Mullingar, Co. Westmeath: enlisted Longtown, co. Cumberland. Killed in action on the night of 25 November 1917 when, during a relief near Bellevue Spur, undue noise and commotion drew down a heavy German bombardment on the battalion resulting in the death of Pte. Woods and eighteen other men. See account re. L/Corpl. J. Nixon, Tyne Cot Cemetery (XXXVII.H.6).

> Hills that heed not Time or weather, Sussex down and Kentish lane,
> Roads that wind through marsh and heather feel the mail shod feet again;
> Chalk and flint their dead are giving – spectres grim and spectres bold –
> Marching on to cheer the living with their battle-chant of old –
> Chant of knight and chant of bowman,
> Chant of squire and chant of yeoman;
> Witness Norman! Witness Roman!
> Kent and Sussex feared no foeman
> In the Valiant days of old!

(Panel 86) 2nd Lieut. William Rolph Botting, 'B' Coy., 3rd (Reserve) attd. 11th (Service) Bn. (1st South Down) The Royal Sussex Regt.: *s.* of the late Dr. Herbert William Botting, F.R.C.O., L.R.A.M., of 81, Stanford Avenue, Brighton, by his wife Florence Mary, F.R.C.O., *dau.* of Farmer Rolph: *b.* Brighton, co. Sussex, 29 July 1895: *educ.* Brighton College: Assistant Organist; St. Augustine's Church, Preston, and Fellow of the Royal College of Organists: joined Inns of Court O.T.C., January 1915; gazetted 2nd Lieut., March 1917: served with the Expeditionary Force in France and Flanders, and was killed in action on the Menin Road, 25 September 1917. Buried there. The Chaplain wrote, "I have never met anyone of a more beautiful character, nor has any officer in my experience given me such loyal support in the work of the Church amongst the men. It was a very hard task the division was called on to take last week, and they achieved it with complete and magnificent success; but the cost was many of our bravest and best. Your son, amongst others, fell in the forefront of the Empire's great battle-line, a gallant and splendid fellow in the day of trial." Lieut.Col. Cohey Millwood wrote: "He was a most brave officer and always showed utter contempt of danger, and was much admired by his brother officers and men. I assure you that I have lost a splendid officer, and I much regret his loss.": Age 22. *unm.*

(Panel 86) 2nd Lieut. Edmund Davison, 3rd (Reserve) attd. 11th (Service) Bn. (1st South Down) The Royal Sussex Regt.: *yst. s.* of the late George Henry Davison, by his wife Edith (16, Gordon Square, London, W.C.), *dau.* of Edmund Richardson: *b.* London, 27 December 1895: *educ.* Westminster, where he was Coy.Sergt.Major of the school O.T.C.: gazetted 2nd Lieut., December 1915: served with the Expeditionary Force in France and Flanders from June following, and acted as Intelligence Officer/Assistant Adjutant: after four months' service, was admitted to hospital suffering from shell-shock and a slight wound: returned to France, July 1917, and was killed in action 24 September following. The Lieut. Colonel wrote, "Your son had not been with me very long, but in that short time he proved himself a very brave man, and a good and hard-working officer. The men were very fond of him, and I regret his loss very much. He was the kind of officer that all battalions like to have, and I shall miss him;" and another officer, "Although he was not long with the 11th Battn. he had endeared himself to all of us, and both officers and men feel his loss deeply.": Age 21. *unm.*

(Panel 86) 2nd Lieut. Charles William McKinley Knifton, 2nd Bn. (107th Foot) The Royal Sussex Regt.: *s.* of John Knifton, of 7, Vicarage Park, Plumstead, Woolwich, London, by his wife Agnes Mary: and brother to 2nd Lieut. J.M. Knifton, 3rd attd. 2nd Royal Sussex Regt., who fell 21 July 1918: previously served with London Scottish, October 1915 – August 1916, thereafter entered Royal Military College, Sandhurst, from whence he was commissioned 2nd Lieut. 2nd Royal Sussex Regt., April 1917. Killed in action 23 November 1917: Age 20. *unm.* (*IWGC record McKinlay*)

His brother James also has no known grave; he is commemorated on the Loos Memorial.

(Panel 86) 2nd Lieut. Richard Stephen Oxley, M.C., 13th (Service) Bn. (3rd South Down) The Royal Sussex Regt.: *s.* of Percy Hunter Oxley, Architect & Surveyor; of 51, Carisbrooke Road, St. Leonards-on-Sea, by his wife Bertha L., *dau.* Stephen Watling: *b.* St. Leonards-on-Sea, co. Sussex, 30 December 1895: *educ.* Collegiate School, there: Occupation – Clerk; London County and Westminster Bank, Arundel: joined 25th (Cyclists) Battn., London Regt. (T.F.), 25 February 1913: called up on the outbreak of war, August 1914, and served on the East Coast until discharged as medically unfit, March 1915: re-enlisted (after an operation) Honourable Artillery Company, 14 June following: served with the Expeditionary Force in France and Flanders from November of the same year: obtained a commission, gazetted 2nd Lieut., Royal Sussex Regt., 7 February 1918. Killed in action nr. Wytschaete, 18 April following. Capt. Howard J. Rose wrote, "Your boy was commanding a company at the time of his death, and had done exceptionally well through the previous two days' operations. On the evening of the 19th *ulto* he was making a reconnaissance with a sergeant, and was shot by a sniper a little in front of our lines. If he had come through safely he would certainly have been recommended for a decoration for the excellent work he had done. I cannot tell you how deeply we feel the loss of your son, one of the most promising of our young officers, and how deeply we sympathise with you in your terrible bereavement." He was awarded the Military Cross (*London Gazette*, 6 July 1917), and the Italian Bronze Medal (*London Gazette*, 26 May 1917), for 'gallantry in the field.': Age 22. *unm.*

PANEL 86 ENDS: COY.SERGT.MAJOR A.W. LINFORD, M.M. – ROYAL SUSSEX REGT.

PANEL 87 BEGINS: COY.SERGT.MAJOR G.W. SWAIN – ROYAL SUSSEX REGT.

(Panel 87) Corpl. SD/1145, Charles 'Charley' Alfred Page, 11th (Service) Bn. (1st South Down) The Royal Sussex Regt.: *s.* of Alfred Page, Labourer; of 2, Brougham Road, Worthing, by his wife Harriett: *b.* Lancing, co. Sussex, 19 February 1877: Occupation – General Labourer: volunteered and enlisted after the outbreak of war: joined 11th Royal Sussex Regt.; one of three battalions raised locally by Lieut.Col. Claude Lowther, known as 'The South Downs' or 'Lowther's Lambs': served with his battalion in France and Flanders, where, between December 1916 and January 1918, the battalion suffered continuous casualties in the trenches around Ypres. By March 1918, what remained of the 11th was moved south to the Somme, only to be virtually annihilated in the German spring offensive in that region. By early April the few survivors had been brought back to the Ypres Salient where, after moving up to the front line at Elzenwalle Chateau, on the night of 19 April 1918, another two men were killed by enemy shellfire on the 23rd of that month: Age 31.

(Panel 87) Corpl. SD/2020, Percy Turville, 11th (Service) Bn. (1st South Down) The Royal Sussex Regt.: *s.* of William Turville, of Warninglid, Hayward's Heath, co. Sussex, by his wife Elizabeth: and brother to Pte. 16526, G. Turville, Hampshire Regt., killed in action 7 December 1915, in Macedonia: *b.* Hayward's Heath: enlisted Brighton. Killed in action 25 September 1917. Two of 49 local men who made the supreme sacrifice recorded on Slaugham (Parish Church) War Memorial, Sussex.

His brother George also has no known grave; he is commemorated on the Doiran Memorial.

(Panel 87) L/Corpl. G/21157, William Archibald Dutnall, 'B' Coy., 13th (Service) Bn. (3rd South Down) The Royal Sussex Regt.: *s.* of Frederick Dutnall, of Swanton Street, Bredgar, Sittingbourne, by his wife Clara: and brother to Gnr. 123574, E.J. Dutnall, Royal Field Artillery, killed in action, 29 May 1917: enlisted Sittingbourne, co. Kent. Killed in action, 16 April 1918, by heavy machine gun fire while attacking an enemy position: Age 20. *unm.*

His brother Edgar is buried in Locre Churchyard (I.C.7).

(Panel 87) L/Corpl. G/12932, Leonard Jarvis, 13th (Service) Bn. (3rd South Down) The Royal Sussex Regt.: *s.* of Albert Jarvis, of Spring Bank, Waldron, co. Sussex, by his wife Philadelphia: and yr. brother to Pte. G/1431, O. Jarvis, 2nd Royal Sussex Regt., died of wounds, 30 April 1915, in the Base Hospital nr. Calais: enlisted Warley, co. Essex. Killed in action 6 November 1917: Age 20. *unm.*

His brother Owen is buried in Wimereux Communal Cemetery (I.F.12A).

(Panel 87) L/Corpl. G/15929, Edward John Harris, 11th (Service) Bn. (1st South Down) The Royal Sussex Regt. Killed in action 26 April 1918. See Pte. C. Newick, below.

(Panel 87) L/Corpl. L/10381, Edgar Veness, 12th (Service) Bn. (2nd South Down) The Royal Sussex Regt.: *s.* of the late William Veness, by his wife Ellen (Pound Street, Pitworth, co. Sussex): *b.* Tunbridge Wells: enlisted Brighton. Killed in action 18 October 1917: Age 25. *unm.* Buried by the Rev. Maurice Murray attd. 12th Royal Sussex; with the words, "Lord, we thank Thee for the example of this brave man who gave his life for his country. Grant him eternal rest and so teach us to number our days that we apply our hearts unto wisdom. Amen."

(Panel 87) Pte. 21240, Francis John Bailey, 2nd Bn. (107th Foot) The Royal Sussex Regt.: *s.* of Francis John Bailey, Shoemaker; of 102, East Street, Epsom, co. Surrey, by his wife Sarah, *dau.* of James Nicholls: *b.* Epsom, 29 August 1887: *educ.* Boys' School, there: Occupation – Tram Driver; Croydon Corporation: enlisted 23 February 1917: served with the Expeditionary Force in France and Flanders, from 21 May, and was killed in action, 22 November following, by a shell, while going into the trenches at Poelcapelle. Buried south-east of Poelcapelle. His Commanding Officer wrote, "We all miss so fine a soldier, as he was always so cheerful under the most trying conditions.": Age 30. He *m.* Cobham; Christina Daisy (The Island, Downside, Cobham, co. Surrey), *dau.* of the late William Edward Sawyer, and had a *dau.* Megan Gwen Daisy, *b.* 1 September 1916.

(Panel 87) Pte. G/17304, Leslie Henry Beeley, 11th (Service) Bn. (1st South Down) The Royal Sussex Regt.: *s.* of John Henry Beeley, of 120, Courthill Road, Lewisham, London, S.E., by his wife Rose Christina: and brother to Pte. G/10060, J.E. Beeley, 11th Royal West Kent Regt., killed in action

15 September 1916, aged 19 years: *b*. Lewisham: enlisted there. Killed in action 24 September 1917: Age 19.

His brother John also has no known grave; he is commemorated on the Thiepval Memorial, Somme.

(Panel 87) Pte. G/16405, Frederick Charles Blackman, 13th (Service) Bn. (3rd South Down) The Royal Sussex Regt.: eldest *s*. of Thomas Charles Blackman, of 30, Mount Street, Battle, co. Sussex, Coal Merchant (66, High Street, Battle), by his wife Harriett, *dau*. of Amos Collins: *b*. Battle, 3 May 1890: *educ*. National School, there: joined Territorial Force, 1907: served six years, joined the Reserve; called up on the outbreak of war, August 1914: served with the Expeditionary Force in France and Flanders from February 1915, and was killed in action near Canadian Tunnels, 19 October 1917. Buried at Voormezeele. An officer wrote, "Your son was my servant for some time, and a more efficient and reliable soldier it would be impossible to find.": Age 27. *unm*.

(Panel 87) Pte. G/5798, Frederick Boden, 11th (Service) Bn. (1st South Down) The Royal Sussex Regt.: *s*. of Frederick Boden, Labourer; of 38, Minniver Street, Blackfriars, London, S.E., by his wife Jane, *dau*. of Richard Hunter: *b*. Walworth, London, S.E., 27 January 1882: *educ*. Friar's Street School: Occupation – Carman; Messrs Cooper, Fruiterers: enlisted Royal Sussex Regt., 13 May 1915: served with the Expeditionary Force in France and Flanders from 1 October 1915, and was killed in action on the Menin Road, 27 September 1917. Buried where he fell: Age 35. His Commanding Officer wrote, "With sympathy and regret at losing a good soldier and comrade, who always had a good character." He *m*. Catherine (20, Minniver Street, Friars Street, Blackfriars, London, S.E.), *dau*. of the late Thomas Alexander Turner, and had five children, Catherine Turner, *b*. 1 July 1902, Clara Jane, *b*. 19 May 1904, Frederick, *b*. 19 January 1909, Sarah Jessie, *b*. 16 January 1913 and John, *b*. 29 November 1915. (*IWGC record 26 September 1917, age 34*)

> That gentle rolling country turned to Hell;
> He'd known another sharper Downland; loved it well
> Sussex gone,
> Life is done.

(Panel 87) Pte. G/1331, George Thomas Coleman, 'B' Coy., 2nd Bn. (107th Foot) The Royal Sussex Regt.: 3rd *s*. of the late George Coleman, Gardener, by his wife Annie Maria (35, Parklands Road, Hassocks, co. Sussex), *dau*. of the late Thomas Chatfield: *b*. Brighton, co. Sussex, 1 April 1889: *educ*. Hassocks Council School: Occupation – Telegraph Messenger; afterwards Market Gardener, Sompting: enlisted 28 August 1914: served with the Expeditionary Force in France and Flanders from 1 January 1915: took part in the operations at La Bassée: invalided home, returned to France, April: took part in the Battle of Loos, September following, being wounded and again repatriated to England: rejoined his regiment, February 1916: took part in the Battle of the Somme, was again wounded. Killed in action at the Third Battle of Ypres, 23 November 1917. Buried at Passchendaele Ridge. His Commanding Officer wrote, "He had been bringing a message up to me, and on his way back got caught in a barrage at a place called Vine Cottage. He was killed at once...He had been a battalion runner for some time; as a runner he could always be relied on to take his messages through the heaviest fire.": Age 28. *unm*.

(Panel 87) Pte. G/17817, Walter George Figg, 12th (Service) Bn. (2nd South Down) The Royal Sussex Regt.: *s*. of Albert Edward Figg, of 28, Western Road, Haywards Heath, co. Sussex, by his wife Emily Ann, *dau*. of William Bishop: *b*. Brighton, 24 October 1897: *educ*. Haywards Heath Council School: enlisted 27 October 1915: served with the Expeditionary Force in France and Flanders from 12 July 1916, and was killed in action at Ypres, 22 October 1917: Age 19.

(Panel 87) Pte. G/17132, Alfred Charles Langford, 13th (Service) Bn. (3rd South Down) The Royal Sussex Regt.: *s*. of Alfred Langford, Gardner; of The Lodge, Watcombe Park, Torquay, co. Devon, late of Thames Field Farm, Henley-on-Thames, by his wife Edith, *dau*. of Charles Gulliver: *b*. Banstead, co. Surrey, 24 August 1898: *educ*. Little Heath, Potters Bar: Occupation – Gardener; Thamesfield Gardens: enlisted 33rd Training Reserve, 19 February 1917: served with the Expeditionary Force in France and Flanders from early September 1917, transf'd. Royal Sussex Regt., and was killed in action on the 26th of the same month. His Commanding Officer wrote, "It might console you to know that your son died the death of a brave soldier, and that a more capable and competent soldier one could never wish to have by the side of him.": 26 September 1917: Age 19.

(Panel 87) Pte. TF/202342, George Arnold Lark, 2nd Bn. (107th Foot) The Royal Sussex Regt.: *s.* of Robert John Lark, of Gresham, Roughton, co. Norfolk, by his wife Pamela: *b.* Metton, Norwich, co. Norfolk, 31 May 1898: *educ.* Aylmerton County Council School: enlisted 16 February 1917: served with the Expeditionary Force in France and Flanders from July, and was killed in action at Passchendaele Ridge, 13 November 1917. His Commanding Officer wrote, "It is with feelings of deepest regret that I have to inform you of the death of your son, Private G. Lark. He was killed on the 13th by a shell which landed in the trench he was in. It is a slight comfort to know that he suffered no pain, as it must have been instantaneous. He had not been with us very long, but I know he will be greatly missed by all in B Coy. I should like you to know that he has been buried close by, and his grave has been marked, so as to be identified later.": Age 19.

Founded in 1885 and financed by public subscription (at the express wish of Queen Victoria) the Gordon Boy's Home was intended as a national memorial to General Gordon who had been killed at Khartoum in January of that year. Gordon had personally organised and performed a large amount of charitable work with the underprivileged boys of Gravesend, Kent, often welcoming into his lodgings there '... direct from the town streets such lads as had been running wild nearly all their life with little restraint beyond the fear of the police.' (we need to make it clear where these quotes have come from) On entering the Home, boys exchanged their everyday clothes, often little more than rags, for a uniform consisting of a glengarry cap, dark blue tunic and Gordon tartan trews. In a world where accommodation was barrack-style and good healthy outdoor exercise, cleanliness and orderliness were the rule, after four months of military-style training (generously leavened with a respect for all that was Christian) such was the success in encouraging the better nature of these boys that nine out of ten received character references of 'good' and 'very good.' Not surprisingly (given the military lifestyle they had followed whilst at the Home) on leaving, a substantial number of boys entered directly into the armed forces; among them:

(Panel 87) Pte. G/17101, William Male, 13th (Service) Bn. (3rd South Down) The Royal Sussex Regt: *s.* of William Male, of High Street, Stoke-under-Ham, co. Somerset, by his wife Bessie: *b.* Bridgwater: *educ.* Gordon Boy's Home, West End, Woking, co. Surrey: enlisted Yeovil. Killed in action 26 September 1917: Age 19.

(Panel 87) Pte. G/19861, Charles Newick, 11th (Service) Bn. (1st South Down) The Royal Sussex Regt.: *s.* of Henry Newick, Farm Labourer; of 1, Darby's Cottages, Wadhurst, co. Sussex, by his wife Emily, *née* Duplock: *b.* Gold's, Mayfield, co. Sussex, 16 April 1886: Occupation – Carter; employee Major Courthope, M.P.: enlisted Chichester: served with the Expeditionary Force in France and Flanders. From December 1916 to January 1918 the battalion suffered continuous heavy casualties rotating in and out of the trenches around Ypres. By March 1918, what remained of the 11th and 13th battalions were moved to Hem, south of the Somme, where both battalions were practically wiped out in attempting to stem the German offensive in that sector. In early April 1918, those who had survived were transferred back to the salient, and put into the front line trenches at Elzenwalle Chateau. On 26 April, amidst heavy enemy attacks and artillery shelling, a further two men, L/Corpl. Harris, and Pte. Newick were killed. Pte. Newick leaves a widow, Emily, *née* Baker. Prior to enlistment he was a member of Wadhurst Band, and a willing assistant to the bands of neighbouring parishes at their Hospital Parades: Age 22.

L/Corpl. E.J. Harris also has no known grave; his name is recorded above.

(Panel 87) Pte. (Siglr) TF/260025, Ira Paling, 1/5th (Cinque Ports) Bn. (Pioneers) The Royal Sussex Regt. (T.F.): *s.* of George Thomas Paling, of Alfreton Road, Sutton-in-Ashfield, by his wife Elizabeth: *b.* Marehay, Derby, 1895: *educ.* Higher Standard School, and Hucknall Teacher's Centre, from whence he was subsequently engaged on the staff of Mansfield Road School, before going up to Nottingham University to commence a three year course and, being of a studious inclination Mr Paling showed every promise of a successful future in his chosen profession but, after barely ten months he was called to the

Colours and sent with a draft to France, January 1917, where he was killed in action, 26 September 1917: Age 22. *unm*. Much beloved by his friends, reference was made to Pte. Paling at a Memorial Service conducted by the Rev. J.W. Neild held at the Huthwaite Free Church, October 1918. *The Notts Free Press* 'In Memoriam,' 27 September 1918:

> *Still we think of him, and keep unbroken the bond which nature gives,*
> *Thinking that our remembrance, though unspoken, May reach him whereso'er he lives.*

Mother, Father, Sisters and Brothers.

(Panel 87) Pte. G/17107, George James Hunnerkin Pearce, 13th (Service) Bn. (3rd South Down) The Royal Sussex Regt.: *s*. of John James Ridson Pearce, of 7, Quarry Park Road, Peverell, Plymouth, formerly 19, Edgcombe Park Road, Plymouth: *b*. Plymouth, 15 August 1898: *educ*. there: Occupation – Clerk; Messrs Brown, Wills and Nicholson, Plymouth: enlisted 17 February 1917: served with the Expeditionary Force in France and Flanders from 7 September, and was killed in action, 24 September 1917. One of his officers wrote, "Your son was always a good fellow, being willing and ready to obey his officers…We shall all miss him, especially his intimate comrades.": Age 19.

One of the least written about, yet not unimportant, branches of the services is the Royal Army Chaplain's Department. During the Great War numerous members of the R.A.Ch.D. distinguished themselves greatly, both behind the lines and in the front line trenches. Christopher Chavasse, brother of Capt. Noel Chavasse, V.C. and Bar, M.C., was awarded the M.C., for bringing in wounded under fire at Bullecourt in 1916; Father William Doyle, was awarded the M.C. at Ginchy in 1916. The Rev. Noel E. Mellish was awarded the R.A.Ch.D.'s only V.C. for repeatedly going backwards and forwards over three consecutive days under continuous heavy shell and machine gun fire in order to tend and rescue wounded men, bringing in no less than thirty men from the fire swept battlefield around St. Eloi. Other padres such as Philip 'Tubby' Clayton, M.C. and Geoffrey Ankctell Studdert Kennedy, M.C., both became household names. Clayton for running the soldier's house in Poperinghe and founding the post-war TocH movement; Kennedy, better known as 'Woodbine Willy,' for his prose and always having a ready supply of Woodbine cigarettes to hand out to the troops wherever he encountered them.

The Rev. Maurice Murray, attd. 12th and 13th Royal Sussex Regt., never received any official recognition for his work, yet like many of his colleagues, he too regularly exposed himself to danger. On 25 September 1917, as the Sussex battled toward Pilckem Ridge, the Rev. Murray was in the thick of the action attempting to supply succour and comfort to the wounded and dying. He wrote: "Poor old Piper was hit at 3 p.m. A liaison officer told me where he was. He had taken shelter from the shelling with some others under the lee of a sort of low roofed shed. I told Gatchell and he did him up as soon as I had found him. He used the pointed stick which I had given Piper at Poperinghe as a splint, and I kicked away another piece from the trench for another. I sat with him in a dip on the side of the shed which was 12th Battalion Headquarters til 8 p.m. when at last stretcher-bearers came for him. He asked me to sing Hymns; 'Abide with Me' and 'Sun of my Soul.' He had lost a lot of blood before I found him and was very white. His foot was nearly blown off and he was in great pain, and I put his head on my knees."

(Panel 87) Pte. G/17891, George Piper, 12th (Service) Bn. (2nd South Down) The Royal Sussex Regt.: *s*. of William Piper, of Hoskins Cottage, East Grinstead, co. Sussex, by his wife Ellen Mary: killed 25 September 1917: Age 20. *unm*.

PANEL 87 ENDS: PTE. PTE. G. PIPER – ROYAL SUSSEX REGT.

PANEL 88 BEGINS: PTE. W.H. PLUMMER – ROYAL SUSSEX REGT.

(Panel 88) Pte. G/16063, Arthur Potter, 13th (Service) Bn. (3rd South Down) The Royal Sussex Regt.: *s*. of George Potter, of Worthing, by his wife Caroline: *b*. Lancing, 30 April 1885: *educ*. Sompting: enlisted 1 March 1916: served with the Expeditionary Force in France and Flanders from 7 September following, and was killed in action near Ypres, 27 September 1917: Age 32. *unm*. (*IWGC record age 31*)

(Panel 88) Pte. G/14864, Ernest Rodell, 13th (Service) Bn. (3rd South Down) The Royal Sussex Regt.: *s.* of Ernest Rodell, Dye-yard Labourer; of 3, Surrey Street, Luton, by his wife Mary Ann, *dau.* of John Wakefield, of Berkhampstead: *b.* Luton, co. Bedford, 11 June 1894: *educ.* Surrey Street Boys' School: Occupation – Iron Moulder: joined 5th Bedfordshire Regt., May 1914: called up on mobilisation, 4 August 1914, transf'd. Royal Sussex Regt.: served with the Expeditionary Force in France from August 1916; died at Gheluvelt, Ypres, 18 October 1917, of wounds received in action the same day. Buried where he fell: Age 23. *unm.* His Commanding Officer wrote, "Your son was killed while with a carrying party… almost instantaneously. He had been carrying out most useful work with his comrades in performing this duty;" and a comrade, "He was such a brave boy…We all miss him in the company, as he was always willing to lend a hand in need. He was respected by every one of us."

(Panel 88) Pte. G/15535, Arthur Scales, 11th (Service) Bn. (1st South Down) The Royal Sussex Regt.: *s.* of the late Joseph Scales, by his wife Ann (Essendon, co. Hertford): and brother to Pte. TF/201029, D.J. Scales, 7th Middlesex Regt., killed in action, 20 May 1917: *b.* Hatfield, 1891: Occupation – Labourer; Messrs. Norton and Sons, Builders: enlisted Hertford. Killed in action 24 September 1917: Age 26. *unm.*

His brother David also has no known grave; he is commemorated on the Arras Memorial (Bay 7).

(Panel 88) Pte. G/9591, 'George' Spencer Maryon Smith, 13th (Service) Bn. (3rd South Down) The Royal Sussex Regt.: 3rd *s.* of James Smith, Agricultural Labourer; of Yew Tree Cottage, Colonels Bank, Newick, nr. Lewes, co. Sussex, by his wife Margaret Emma 'Emily,' *née* Diplock: and elder brother to Pte. 126, S.S. Smith, 14th Australian Infantry, killed in action 19 August 1915, Gallipoli; Pte. 200583, F.J. Smith, 4th Suffolk Regt., killed in action, 17 April 1917, at the Battle of Arras; and Pte. 3469, E.G. Smith, 5th Royal Sussex Regt., killed in action 26 July 1916, at the Somme: *b.* Barcombe, c.1886: *educ.* Newick: Occupation – Gardener: enlisted Chichester. Killed in action 26 April 1918: Age 32. One of four brothers who made the supreme sacrifice.

His brothers Septimus and Frederick also have no known grave, they are commemorated on the Lone Pine Memorial (42) and Arras Memorial (Bay 4) respectively; Edward is buried in Puchevillers British Cemetery (II.A.56).

(Panel 88) Pte. SD/3220, James Stepney, 13th (Service) Bn. (3rd South Down) The Royal Sussex Regt.: *s.* of Marchant Stepney, of Royal George Road, Burgess Hill, co. Sussex, by his wife Mary Ann: and elder brother to Gnr. 82524, J. Stepney, 86th Bde. Royal Field Artillery, killed in action 1 August 1917: *b.* Pulborough: enlisted Haywards Heath. Killed in action 24 September 1917: Age 37.

His brother Jack is buried in Dickebusch New Military Cemetery Extension (I.C.9).

(Panel 88) Pte. TF/241506, Sydney Thomas George Welling, 11th (Service) Bn. (1st South Down) The Royal Sussex Regt.: eldest *s.* of the late William Sydney Welling, Chiropodist; of 30, Lansdowne Street, Hove: *b.* Brighton, co. Sussex, 25 March 1885: *educ.* Christ Church Schools, East Hove: Occupation – Manager; Norfolk Toilet Saloon, Brighton: enlisted Royal Sussex Regt., 1 June 1916: served with the Expeditionary Force in France and Flanders from 20 September 1917, and was killed in action at the Menin Road Battle five days later. Buried north-north-west of Gheluvelt, south of Veldhoek: 25 September 1917: Age 32. He *m.* St. Patrick's Church, Hove, 27 September, 1908; Evelyn Mary (Bungalow West, Burgess, co. Sussex), *dau.* of John Thomas Emery, the well-known angler: *s.p.*

(Panel 88) Major Frank Goldsmith, M.C. & Bar, 14th (Service) Bn. The Hampshire Regt.: *yst. s.* of James Goldsmith, of Old Blendworth, Horndean, Cosham, by his wife Jeannette, *dau.* of Henry Giles Gale, of Blendworth, Horndean: *b.* Blendworth, 27 December 1893: *educ.* Lancing College, Shoreham, co. Sussex: gazetted 2nd Lieut. The Hampshire Regt. October 1914: promoted Lieut., May 1915, Capt. about October 1916; Major about May 1917: served with the Expeditionary Force in France and Flanders from 1916, and was killed in action on the Menin Road, 26 September 1917. Buried there. Col. Isherwood wrote, "He was as brave as a lion and beloved by his men. There can be no greater tribute than that paid to any soldier, and I looked forward to his having a great career in the service;" and Col. Hickie, "I quickly recognised he was the best officer in the battalion… He was one of the bravest I have ever met." Awarded the Military Cross for conspicuous gallantry and devotion to duty, 3 September 1916, and a Bar to his Cross, 1 February 1917: "Major Goldsmith led his men forward to the front line under heavy gun fire in readiness to deliver a counter-attack. Later, he organised a patrol which he personally led into 'No Man's Land' in pursuit of the enemy raiders. On this occasion Major Goldsmith had to lead his men through mud up to their waists in very cold wind and rain. Passing a senior officer, who was wounded and unable to move, he took off his own tunic to cover him up, and then went on with a few men into a German trench. Arriving in the latter, he found he had discarded his revolver with his tunic, but picked up a German one which was empty and which his cartridges would not fit. However, he went on down the trench and 'held up' eight Germans with the empty pistol, bringing them back with him, and rescuing the Colonel on his way. The exposure to inclement weather without a tunic for several hours gave him a severe chill, seriously threatening pneumonia. A typical instance of his character." Major Goldsmith was a keen sportsman, and a fearless horseman in the hunting field and show ring. He rode when in his teens in the International Horse Show: Age 23. *unm.* (*IWGC record 27 September 1917*)

(Panel 88) Capt. Thomas Rocliffe Nicholls, 14th (Service) Bn. The Hampshire Regt.: eldest *s.* of the late Thomas Henry Nicholls, of Newcastle, co. Stafford, by his wife Annie Elizabeth ('Craiglands,' Craig-y-Don, Llandudno): *b.* Guisborough, co. York, 24 August 1876: *educ.* Newcastle High School, near Stafford: gazetted 2nd Lieut., North Staffordshire Regt., 1894: resigned his commission 1896: rejoined as Lieut., Hampshire Regt., November 1913: served with the Expeditionary Force in France and Flanders from June 1917, and was killed in action near Polygon Wood, at the Battle of Gheluvelt, 26 September 1917. Buried where he fell. His Commanding Officer wrote, "I had a very great regard and esteem for him, and we all felt the value of his friendship, and miss in him a good officer and comrade. He had been doing very strenuous and dangerous work in the three days before he fell, as he was in charge of the important work connected with a large attack;" and another officer, "We undertook a good many difficult tasks together, and I was with him just before he was killed on the evening of the 26th, when after four days of hard work, under exceptional difficulties, he was still keen and cheerfully carrying on. If anyone worked hard for the success which our recent operations achieved, it was he, for he faced his work with the courage of a true British soldier, and died nobly for the great cause we all have at heart.": Age 41. He *m.* St. Mary's, Charlcombe, Bath; Hilda, *dau.* of the late John Culverhouse, of Burcott House, Brondesbury, and had four sons; Thomas Henry Lee, *b.* 10 December 1908, Cecil George, *b.* 3 May 1911, Richard Aubrey, *b.* 1 March 1913 and John Gervase, *b.* 9 October 1915.

(Panel 88) Lieut. John Stuart Bainbridge, 14th (Service) Bn. The Hampshire Regt.: 2nd *s.* of John William Bainbridge, Merchant; of Westoe, Lewisham, London, S.E., by his wife Elizabeth, *dau.* of Thomas Glass: and brother to 2nd Lieut. C. Bainbridge, The Buffs, killed in action nr. Hulluch, Loos, 13 October 1915: *b.* Lewisham, 3 February 1897: *educ.* Collegiate School, Catford, London, S.E.; Elstow School, Bedford: Occupation – Shipowner's Clerk: enlisted December 1914: obtained a commission 2nd Lieut., April 1915; promoted Lieut. 1916: served with the Expeditionary Force in France and Flanders from March 1916: took part in several engagements, including the operations at Thiepval: invalided home October 1916, suffering from shell-shock and trench fever: on recovery, rejoined his regiment in France, March 1917, and was killed in action at Tower Hamlets 27 September following. Buried there. His Colonel wrote, "He was a good officer and leader, always cheerful under heavy fire and in the most trying conditions. It will be a little satisfaction to you to know that the attack in which your son was engaged was a magnificent success, and that his death was not in vain;" and his Chaplain, "To myself it is a great personal sorrow, for I have known him so well now for nearly two years, and a straighter, better-living young man I have never known, and so cool and level-headed at all times. He was one of the best.": Age 20. *unm.* (*IWGC record 26 September*).

His brother Carlyle is buried in Vermelles British Cemetery (I.E.13)

(Panel 88) Sergt. 204669, Harry Noakes, 15th (Service) Bn. (Hampshire Yeomanry) The Hampshire Regt.: *b.* Hadlow Down, co. Sussex, 1890: from employ as Groom, to L. Chattas, Esq, Highams, he joined Surrey Constabulary, Guildford, 16 September 1912, appt. no.1630, P.C. 214: 5'10" tall, pale complexion, dark brown hair, hazel eyes: enlisted Hampshire Yeomanry, Winchester, 1915: served with the Expeditionary Force in France and Flanders, and was killed in action, 9 August 1918: Age 28. He leaves a widow, Alice Annie (2, Woodside Cottages, Ewhurst Road, Cranleigh, co. Surrey).

PANEL 88 ENDS: PTE. C.J. CLARKE – HAMPSHIRE REGT.

PANEL 89 BEGINS: PTE. A. COBDEN – HAMPSHIRE REGT.

(Panel 89) Pte. 13042, Ralph Stuchfield, 1st Bn. (37th Foot) The Hampshire Regt.: *s.* of the late Ralph Stuchfield, by his wife Anne Maria (195, Aston Lane, Aston, Birmingham): *b.* Vauxhall, Birmingham, co. Warwick, September 1883: *educ.* Loxton Street County Council School: enlisted Hampshire Regt., August 1914: served with the Expeditionary Force in Salonika from 1915: proceeded to France, served with the Expeditionary Force there from August 1917, and was killed in action, 4 October following: Age 34. *unm.* (*IWGC record age 35*)

PANEL 89 ENDS: PTE. G.T. TIMBRELL – HAMPSHIRE REGT.

PANEL 90 BEGINS: PTE. F. TOWNSEND – HAMPSHIRE REGT.

(Panel 90) Capt. William Horace Curry, D.S.O., 3rd (Reserve) attd. 1st Bn. (38th Foot) The South Staffordshire Regt.: 2nd *s.* of William John Curry, of 43, Leinster Avenue, East Sheen, and his late wife Florence Ellen, *dau.* of the late Horatio Bethune Leggatt, of Brownwich, co. Hants: *b.* Crouch End, London, N., 14 August 1894: *educ.* Rothbury, St. Leonard's-on-Sea; Merchant Taylor's School: removed to Canada, 1912: returned to England on the outbreak of war, 1914: joined 18th (Service) Battn. (University and Public Schools Battn.) Royal Fusiliers (City of London Regt.), November 1914, with which he went to France, November 1915: returned home, April 1916, and after a period of training at the O.T.C., Denham, nr. Uxbridge, was gazetted 2nd Lieut., South Staffordshire Regt., 5 August 1916; promoted Capt., May 1917, and was killed in action at Tower Hamlets Ridge, 25 October following. Buried there. Mentioned in Despatches ('*London Gazette,*' 18 December 1917) by F.M. Sir Douglas Haig, for 'gallant and distinguished service in the field,' and was awarded the D.S.O. (*London Gazette*, 26 May 1917), "He collected men from three different companies and led them forward as far as it was possible to advance, and later, although nearly surrounded by the enemy, he succeeded in consolidating and maintaining his position. On another occasion he took command of two companies and handled them in a most able manner.": Age 23. *unm.*

(Panel 90) L/Corpl. 43047, James Ball, 8th (Service) Bn. The South Staffordshire Regt.: *s.* of Arthur Ball, of 61, High Street, Warsop, co. Nottingham, by his wife Mary Booth, *dau.* of James Wells: *b.* Warsop, 1 October 1888: *educ.* Church of England Schools: Occupation – Bricklayer: enlisted Notts and Derbys Regt., 9 November 1914: served with the Mediterranean Expeditionary Force in Gallipoli and Egypt: proceeded to France, July 1916, transf'd. South Staffordshire Regt., and was killed in action nr. Passchendaele, 12 October 1917: Age 29. *unm.*

(Panel 90) L/Corpl. 12516, John Charles Clarke, 8th (Service) Bn. The South Staffordshire Regt.: stepson of Henry Cooper, of 99, Steward Street, Spring Hill, Birmingham, by his marriage to the widow Mrs. E.L. Clarke, *dau.* of Mr (& Mrs) Dudley: *b.* Ladywood, Birmingham, 14 May 1888: *educ.* Aston Council School: enlisted South Staffordshire Regt. 16 September 1915: served with the Expeditionary Force in France and Flanders from 1916: wounded three times, and was killed in action 10 April 1918. Buried where he fell: Age 29. *unm.* (*CWGC record North Staffordshire Regt., Panel 124*)

(Panel 90) L/Corpl. 242164, Harry Jenkins, 2/5th Bn. The South Staffordshire Regt. (T.F.): formerly no.30088, Leicestershire Regt.: *s.* of George Jenkins, Gardener; of Burton Overy, by his wife Ada (School Street, Great Glen, co. Leicester): *b.* Great Glen, *c.*1898. Killed in action 26 September 1917, when, after an advance the previous day (25th) and after digging in on a line running north east from Primrose Cottage (thereafter moving to captured positions nr. Pommern Castle), at 6pm on the following day (26th), the battalion were subjected to a heavy enemy bombardment, followed by a counter-attack to recapture the positions held by the South Staffs. Repulsed by 7 p.m., the day's action cost the battalion the loss of 1 Officer (Capt. C.V.T. Hawkins) and 36 Other Ranks killed: Age 19.

Capt. Clarence Hawkins, M.I.D., also has no known grave; he is incorrectly commemorated on the Loos Memorial.

(Panel 90) Pte. 45313, James Russell Aitken, 7th (Service) Bn. The South Staffordshire Regt.: *s.* of Peter Aitken, of Ballencrieff Nursery, Bathgate, Nurseryman; by his wife Jessie Lawrie, *dau.* of George Russell: and brother to Pte. 40895, J. Aitken, 17th Royal Scots, died of wounds, 14 September 1917; and Actg./Corpl. 43276, P. Aitken, Royal Scots Fusiliers, killed in action, 22 March 1918: *b.* Torphichen, Bathgate, West Lothian, 19 July 1886: *educ.* Bathgate Academy: Occupation – Nurseryman: joined Army Service Corps, April 1917; transf'd. South Staffordshire Regt. the following month: served with the Expeditionary Force in France and Flanders from August 1917; reported wounded and missing 4 October following, after the fighting at Poelcapelle, and is now assumed to have been killed in action on that date. Age 31. *s.p.* He *m.* Edinburgh, December 1914; his cousin Margaret (Bughtknowes Farm, Bathgate, West Lothian), *yst. dau.* of James (& Elizabeth) Porter.

His brother John is buried in Villers Faucon Communal Cemetery Extension (I.F.16). Peter has no known grave, he is recorded on the Arras Memorial, Faubourg, d'Amiens (Bay 5).

(Panel 90) Pte. 15410, John Charles Bagnall, 8th (Service) Bn. The South Staffordshire Regt.: *s.* of Charles Bagnall, of 22, Oxford Street, Pleck, Walsall, by his wife Louisa Matilda, *dau.* of Peter Powell: *b.* Walsall, co. Stafford, 29 October 1891: *educ.* Wisemoor Schools, Walsall: Occupation – Caster: enlisted South Staffordshire Regt., 2 November 1914: served with the Mediterranean Expeditionary Force in Gallipoli from April 1915; invalided home December following: rejoined his regiment on recovery; served with the Expeditionary Force in France and Flanders from March 1916, and was killed in action 12 October 1917. Buried where he fell: Age 25. He *m.* Pleck Parish Church, Walsall, 13 August 1913; Lydia, *dau.* of Edward (& Mrs) Walters, and had a son, Charles Edward, *b.* 19 December 1914.

(Panel 90) Pte. 40121, Arthur Cartlidge, 1st Bn. (38th Foot) The South Staffordshire Regt.: *s.* of Mary Ann Cartlidge (57, Stoke Old Road, Hartshill, co. Stafford): and brother to Pte. 8284, T. Cartlidge, 'A' Coy., 1st North Staffordshire Regt., killed in action 21 March 1918: *b.* Hartshill, *c.*1884: enlisted Stoke-on-Trent: served with the Expeditionary Force and was killed in action, 26 October 1917: Age 33. He was married to Mary Ann Gibson, *née* Cartlidge (Hartshill).

His brother Thomas also has no known grave; he is commemorated on the Pozieres Memorial.

(Panel 90) Pte. 41697, Arthur Claude Clark, 1st Bn. (38th Foot) The South Staffordshire Regt.: *s.* of Henry 'Harry' Clark, Soap Boiler, of 22, Plough Lane, Sudbury, co. Suffolk, by his wife Annie: and brother to Pte. 16736, H.W. Clark, 7th Royal Berkshire Regt., killed in Salonica, 27 August 1916, aged 22 yrs: *b.* Sudbury, 1888: enlisted there. Killed in action 26 October 1917: Age 19.

His brother Harry is buried in Karasouli Military Cemetery (F.1352).

(Panel 90) Pte. 9244, Harold Wilfred Coxsell, 1st Bn. (38th Foot) The South Staffordshire Regt.: *s.* of William Coxsell, of 83, Carter Road, Wolverhampton, by his wife Annie Miriam: and brother to Pte. 11456, W.A. Coxsell, 11th Royal Fusiliers, killed in action, 26 September 1915, at Loos: *b.* Wolverhampton, 1896. Killed in action 26 October 1917: Age 21.

His brother William also has no known grave; he is commemorated on the Loos Memorial, Dud Corner.

PANEL 90 ENDS: PTE. M. DAVISON – SOUTH STAFFORDSHIRE REGT.

PANEL 91 BEGINS: PTE. J.H. DAWSON, SOUTH STAFFORDSHIRE REGT.

(Panel 91) Pte. 40887, Samuel Joseph Hodges, 1st Bn. (38th Foot) The South Staffordshire Regt.: *s.* of George Walter Hodges, Labourer; of St. John's Common, Crowborough, by his wife Mary, *dau.* of James Goldsmith: and brother to Pte. 5/2810, J.E. Hodges, 5th Royal Sussex Regt., killed in action at Hebuterne 13 April 1916, and L/Corpl. G/L/7454, G.W. Hodges, 2nd Royal Sussex Regt., reported wounded and missing, 9 May 1915, after the fighting at Richebourg l'Avoué: *b.* Crowborough, co. Sussex, 2 August 1898: *educ.* St. John's School, Wittingham: employee of Messrs Peerless and Dennis, Government Contractors: enlisted South Staffordshire Regt. 2 March 1917: served with the Expeditionary Force in France from 5 August, and was killed in action 2 October following. Buried where he fell: Age 19 years, 2 months.

His brother James is buried in Hebuterne Military Cemetery (I.Q.13). George has no known grave, he is commemorated on the Le Touret Memorial.

(Panel 91) Pte. 32333, Elijah Hollister, 8th (Service) Bn. The South Staffordshire Regt.: *s*. of Emma Hollister (63, Bold Street, Northwood, Hanley, Stoke-on-Trent): late *husb*. to Esther Hollister (43, Bold Street): and elder brother to Pte. 16679, R.J. Hollister, 7th North Staffordshire Regt., killed in action 7 January 1916: *b*. Hanley: enlisted Stoke-on-Trent. Killed in action 12 October 1917: Age 26.

His brother Robert also has no known grave; he is commemorated on the Helles Memorial.

(Panel 91) Pte. 45088, Robert Major, 2/5th Bn. The South Staffordshire Regt. (T.F.): *s*. of Robert Major, of Waddingham, Kirton-in-Lindsey, co. Lincoln, by his wife Ellen: *b*. North Kelsey, 1895: enlisted Scunthorpe. Killed in action 23 September 1917: Age 22. *unm*. The Bishop's Norton War Memorial takes the form of a lych-gate to St. Peter's Parish Church; inside the lych-gate two stone tablets record the names of six local men who made the supreme sacrifice. Three have known graves, three do not; one is within the confines of the Ypres salient: *Death Is The Gate To Heaven.*

(Panel 91) Pte. 23411, Harry Toplis Smith, 7th (Service) Bn. The South Staffordshire Regt.: *s*. of William Toplis Smith, of 9, Rose Cottages, Newton Street, Burton-on-Trent, by his wife Annie, *dau*. of the late George Yates: and brother to Pte. 145012, A.E. Smith, 34th Machine Gun Corps (Inf.), died in a French Hospital, 26 July 1918, from wounds received in action; and L/Corpl. 9765, J.G. Smith, 7th North Staffordshire Regt., killed in action at Mesopotamia, 25 February 1917: *b*. Burton-on-Trent, co. Stafford, *c*. 1884: *educ*. Christ Church School: enlisted 3rd South Staffordshire Regt., 25 March 1916: served with the Expeditionary Force in France and Flanders, and was killed in action 4 October 1917. Buried where he fell: Age 33. *unm*. (*IWGC record Topliss*)

His brother Arthur is buried in Verberie French National Cemetery (D.85). John has no known grave, he is commemorated on the Basra Memorial (Panel 34).

PANEL 91 ENDS: PTE. R.W. WILSON, SOUTH STAFFORDSHIRE REGT.

PANEL 92 BEGINS: PTE. T.D. WINTER, SOUTH STAFFORDSHIRE REGT.

Raised in Schleswig-Holstein, a Danish province forcibly incorporated into Germany during the 19th Century, Hans Hansen detested anything and everything even remotely associated with Germany. Feigning acceptance of *kultur* his family remained staunchly Danish, defying the regulations the Prussian regime imposed and – on more than one occasion – suffered in consequence. More inclined to burn the German flag than kiss it, the Hansens had been forced to kneel on the flag and do this. Not surprisingly, when Hans was old enough, he escaped across the border and found work aboard a ship. By August 1914 he had travelled around the globe and was employed as a harbour worker in Singapore. Enlisting instantly with one of the British units in the colony, he eventually found his way into 6th Dorsets under the alias 'Anderson.' Blending into his new battalion well, his unusual command of the English language almost lead to his downfall when, on completing the bible (he was an avid reader) he informed his company commander he had "read the whole bleedin' lot, and it was full of damn good stories!" Sometime later, when he decided to get married, he was forced to reveal his true identity and, in a display characteristic of British xenophobia and farce, his commanding officer promptly had him placed under arrest and almost shot as a spy! Fortunately for Hans, reason prevailed, and after being released he rejoined his battalion wherein he was a respected bomber and scout. In this capacity, on the night of 5 December 1917, he volunteered to go out into no man's land to deal with a troublesome enemy machine gun post: He never returned. The Regimental History simply records,'Killed by the enemy he detested.'

(Panel 92) Sergt. 12708, Hans Yessen Hansen, 6th (Service) Bn. The Dorsetshire Regt.: late of Singapore, Malay Peninsula: *b*. Campbellton, New Brunswick, Canada: employee Singapore Harbour Board: enlisted London. Missing / believed killed in action 5 December 1917; confirmed killed (January 1918).

(Panel 92) L/Corpl. 25488, Thomas Kelly, 8th (Service) Bn. The Dorsetshire Regt.: eldest *s*. of Thomas Kelly, of Deptford, London, S.E., by his wife Mary: *b*. Peckham, London, S.E., 16 August 1883:

Occupation – Marine: enlisted Wiltshire Regt., August 1914: discharged, and re-enlisted Dorsetshire Regt., 28 June 1915: served with the Expeditionary Force in France and Flanders, and was killed in action 16 Aug 1917; his 34th birthday. An officer wrote, "Your husband was an exceedingly reliable N.C.O. I was with him myself during most of the advance, and his coolness and courage were an example to all. He met his death fearlessly, and I have lost an N.C.O. I could ill afford to lose.": Age 34. He *m.* Walworth, London, S.E., 24 November 1907; Sarah Ellen (27, Acorn Place, Meeting House Lane, Peckham), and had five children.

(Panel 92) Sergt. 240434, Edmund Gill, 1/5th Bn. The Prince of Wales's Volunteers (South Lancashire Regt.), (T.F.): *yst. s.* of John Gill, Glass Blower (ret'd.); of 25, Spray Street, St. Helens, by his wife Mary Ellen, *dau.* of Peter (& Mary Ellen) Tickle: *b.* St. Helens, co. Lancaster, 9 May 1891: *educ.* St. Thomas' National School: Occupation – Glass Blower; Messrs Pilkington Brothers Ltd., Glass Works: enlisted South Lancashire Regt., 6 August 1914, served with the Expeditionary Force in France and Flanders from August 1916, having been employed for two years on Home Service as Instructor, and was killed in action nr. Ypres, 20 September 1917. Buried where he fell. Coy.Sergt.Major T. Burbridge wrote, "We shall always remember Edmund for he was ever esteemed by the officers, and popular amongst the men.": Age 26. *unm.*

PANEL 92 ENDS: PTE. T. HOPKINS, SOUTH LANCASHIRE REGT.:

PANEL 93 BEGINS: PTE. J. HOWARTH, SOUTH LANCASHIRE REGT.:

(Panel 93) Pte. 37409, John Morcom, 2nd Bn. (82nd Foot) The Prince of Wales's Volunteers (South Lancashire Regt.): *s.* of the late Richard Morcom, Fisherman, by his wife Jane, *dau.* of Edward Polard: *b.* Crantock, co. Cornwall, 25 July 1880: *educ.* Council School: Occupation – Mason: enlisted in the South Lancashire Regt. 5 June 1916: served with the Expeditionary Force in France and Flanders from 30 December following, and was killed in action on the Reserve Lines, behind La Clytte, 29 April 1918. Buried there: Age 37. He *m.* Parish Church, Crantock; Mina Lily (Crantock, Newquay, co. Cornwall), *dau.* of William Crabb, of Crabb Loders, Bridport, co. Dorset, and had four children; Lottie Irene, *b.* 11 April 1908, Winifred Edna, *b.* 17 December 1909, Edward John, *b.* 29 November 1911 and Wilfred, *b.* 12 April 1913.

(Panel 93) Pte. 32108, James William Phipps, 2nd Bn. (82nd Foot) The Prince of Wales's Volunteers (South Lancashire Regt.): *s.* of James W. (& Mrs) Phipps, of Military Road, Dover: and elder brother to Pte. 32107, E.A. Phipps, 7th South Lancashire Regt., killed in action, 3 August 1917; Pte. G/5360, C. Phipps, 7th East Kent Regt., killed in action, 1 July 1916, at the Somme; and L/Corpl. 8713, F.E. Phipps, 2nd East Kent Regt., died of wounds, 5 April 1915, in the Base Hospital, Rouen. Killed in action 21 August 1918: Age 35. A fifth brother also served.

His brothers Edward and Charles also have no known grave, they are commemorated on the Ypres (Menin Gate) Memorial (Panel 37) and Thiepval Memorial (Pier & Face 5D) respectively. Frederick is buried in St. Sever Cemetery (A.7.10).

(Panel 93) Pte. 201218, Plato Postlethwaite (served as Ward, Arthur), 2/4th Bn. The Prince of Wales's Voluteers (South Lancashire Regt.), (T.F.): *s.* of Robert Postlethwaite, of 20, Barnes Green, Blackley, Manchester, by his wife Hannah: and brother to Pte. 241821, R.W. Postlethwaite, 1/4th Cheshire Regt., who fell 25 October 1918: *b.* Salford, 1897: enlisted Warrington. Killed in action 1 January 1918: Age 20. *unm.*

His brother Robert is buried in Outrijve Churchyard (close to the east end of the church).

(Panel 93) Lieut. Percy Hier Davies, 17th attd. 15th (Service) Bn. (Carmarthenshire) The Welch Regt.: eldest *s.* of the late Percy Llewellyn Davies, by his wife Mary (75, Claude Road, Cardiff): and nephew of Sir Reginald Brade, K.C.B.: *b.* Chepstow, co. Somerset, 14 June 1893: *educ.* Intermediate School, Swansea: Occupation – Architect: gazetted 2nd Lieut. 5 June 1915: served with the Expeditionary Force in France and Flanders, and was killed in action at Ypres, 16 August 1917. Buried at St. Julien. Col.

Parkinson wrote, "He was always a most cheery little man, and always had a smile ready, no matter what was going on. Your son will always be to me, and to all of us, an example of the most cheerful and unselfish devotion to duty at all times and in all places.": Age 23. *unm.*

(Panel 93) Pte. 56359, Hugh Byrne, 9th (Service) Bn. The Welch Regt.: *s.* of Patrick Byrne, of 14, Windsor Street, Rhyl, co. Flint, by his wife Catherine: and brother to Pte. 9115, F.P. Byrne, 17th Bn. Manchester Regt., who fell on the first day of the Somme Battle, 1 July 1916: *b.* Rhyl, afsd.,1899: enlisted Wrexham. Killed in action 17 April 1918: Age 19.

His brother, known as Patrick, also has no known grave. He is commemorated on the Thiepval Memorial, Somme.

PANEL 93 ENDS: PTE. W. EVANS, 55357, WELCH REGT.

PANEL 94 BEGINS: PTE. W.B. EVANS, WELCH REGT.

(Panel 94) Pte. 59380, William Duthie Grassick, 15th (Service) Bn. The Welch Regt.: *s.* of Alexander Grassick, of Wanton Wells, Dunecht, F.E.I.S., late Head Master of Craigievar School, by his wife Margaret, *dau.* of John Donald, of Cluny, Farmer: *b.* Leochel-Cushnie, co. Aberdeen, 8 September 1897: *educ.* Craigievar Public School, and Kemnay High Grade School: Occupation – Clerk; Accountants' Department, Royal Insurance Company, Aberdeen: enlisted 9 October 1916: served with the Expeditionary Force in France and Flanders, from 19 May 1917, and was killed in action at Langemarck, 22 August 1917. His Commanding Officer wrote, "He fell in action on the 22nd inst., during the advance. Although he had not been with us long, yet he proved to be a brave and excellent soldier. He was always cheerful, and did his duty willingly and well.": Age 19.

(Panel 94) Pte. 56215, John Holden, 9th (Service) Bn. The Welch Regt.: *s.* of Benjamin Holden, of 64, Fountain Street, Accrington, co. Lancaster, by his wife Elizabeth: and brother to Pte. 201925, S.G. Holden, King's Own (Royal Lancaster Regt.), died of wounds, 21 October 1917, at Oswaldtwistle: *b.* Accrington: enlisted there Killed in action 17 April 1918: Age 19.

His brother Sam is buried in Oswaldtwistle (Immanuel) Churchyard (29.6).

(Panel 94) Pte. 24152, William Thomas Hugglestone, 16th (Service) Bn. The Welch Regt.: *s.* of Alfred Hugglestone, of 103, Wyeverne Road, Cardiff, by his wife Amelia Henrietta, *dau.* of Robert Brown: and brother to Corpl. 20452, A.H. Hugglestone, 6th Bn. York & Lancaster Regt., killed in action 29 September 1916, Pozieres: *b.* Cardiff, 17 August 1895: *educ.* Crwys Road Council School: employed Park Hotel, Cardiff: enlisted 16 January 1915: served with the Expeditionary Force in France and Flanders from 18 November following; killed in action at the Battle of Langemarck, 27 August 1917. Buried there. His officer wrote, "He was a good and faithful soldier, and officers, N.C.O.'s and men, wish me to express their great sorrow at the loss you have sustained." He was a prominent member of the Miskin Street Chapel, Cardiff: Age 22. *unm.*

His brother Alfred also has no known grave; he is commemorated on the Thiepval Memorial, Somme.

(Panel 94) Pte. 20301, Edward Pollard, 9th (Service) Bn. The Welch Regt.: *s.* of the late John Pollard, by his wife Margaret Ann (37, Castle Street, Brierfield, Burnley, co. Lancaster): and elder brother to Pte. G/21334, T. Pollard, 3/4th Queen's (Royal West Kent Regt.), killed in action, 22 November 1917: *b.* Brierfield: enlisted Nelson: killed in action 17 April 1918; Kemmel: Age 34. *unm.*

His brother Thomas is buried in Welsh Cemetery (Caesar's Nose), (I.C.2).

(Panel 94) Lieut. Alexander Simpson Harper, 'D' Coy., 8th (Service) Bn. The Black Watch (Royal Highlanders): 2nd *s.* of the late William Harper, by his wife Margaret (Rosebank Cottage, Abbey Road, Scone, co. Perth; late of The Gardens, Tulliebelton, Bankfoot), *dau.* of the late Alexander Simpson, of Urquhart, Elgin, Farmer: and brother to Piper 265290, J.R. Harper, 6th Black Watch, died of wounds, 25 December 1917: *b.* Tulliebelton, Bankfoot, co. Perth, 5 November 1891: *educ.* Urquhart Public School; Elgin Academy; Aberdeen and Edinburgh Universities (specialising in the science of Astronomy): joined Territorial Force, 1908: re-enlisted 5 August 1914: served with the Expeditionary Force in France and

Flanders from 1 May 1915, and, after a period of training at General Headquarters Cadet School, France, was gazetted 2nd Lieut., 8th Black Watch, 14 August 1916; apptd. Temp. Lieut. July 1917: killed in action, 12 October following; Passchendaele. Buried there. His Officer Commanding wrote, "I cannot say how deeply I and all the other officers of the battalion regret his loss, which is a very great one to the battalion. His death was as gallant as was to be expected...He was leading his men to capture a German strongpoint, which they did – as usual he was among the first; he was regarded as an example of a Platoon and Company Officer. He gave his life in a fight which was one of the bitterest and hardest this battalion has taken part in, and by his leadership helped to maintain the high tradition which the battalion has earned;" and the Chaplain, "Through his sterling worth he had completely won the admiration and trust of his men, and I know how much his fellow officers relied on him." At school and college he was a distinguished student. He graduated M.A. at Aberdeen University with Honours in Mathematical Science, and gained the Neil Arnott Prize in Natural Philosophy. The Rector of Elgin academy said of him, "In mathematics he displayed an outstanding ability." Professor Niven, of Aberdeen University, gives the following testimonial: "At the examination for the Arnott Prize his work was so good that the examiners could hardly find a flaw in it, and had no hesitation in handing him the prize. His written papers showed a faculty of lucid exposition which I have never in all my experience as a professor seen surpassed." Age 26. *unm.*

His brother John is buried in Grevillers British Cemetery (X.A.12).

(Panel 94) Sergt. S/2962, Hugh Ramage, 'B' Coy., 8th (Service) Bn. The Black Watch (Royal Highlanders): *s.* of Janet B. Ramage (87, Bonnington Road, Leith): and yr. brother to Pte. 13099, S. Ramage, 6th King's Own Scottish Borderers, killed in action 30 September 1918, at Ypres; and Pte. 10139, J. Ramage, Highland Light Infantry, who fell 11 January 1917, in Mesopotamia: *b.* Leith, c.1892: enlisted Kirkcaldy, co. Fife. Killed in action 12 October 1917: Age 25.

His brothers Stephen and James also have no known grave, they are recorded on Panel 67 and the Basra Memorial, Iraq respectively.

PANEL 94 ENDS: CORPL. C. THOMSON, THE BLACK WATCH

PANEL 95 BEGINS: L/CORPL. G. ALLAN, THE BLACK WATCH

(Panel 95) Pte. 240765, Frederick Anderson, 4/5th Bn. The Black Watch (Royal Highlanders), (T.F.): *s.* of David Anderson, of 70, Howard Street, Arbroath, by his wife Elizabeth, née Baxter: Occupation – Farm Servant; Auchterforfar: enlisted January 1915; proceeded to France, November following: twice wounded (September 1916; August 1917); killed in action 29 October 1917: Age 21.

(Panel 95) Pte. S/16991, James Myles Cowie, 8th (Service) Bn. The Black Watch (Royal Highlanders): eldest *s.* of David Cowie, of Muiredge, Carmyllie, by his wife Janet, *née* Myles: *b.* Blackmuir, 9 June 1889: Occupation – Insurance Representative (Prudential); Forfar Branch: enlisted Perth, September 1915. Killed in action, 28 September 1917, in company with seven other stretcher bearers when the pill-box they were sheltering in (nr. Railway Wood) took a direct hit from a shell: Age 28. His Captain wrote, "The eight stretcher-bearers of the company were all sheltering in a concrete shelter known as a 'pill-box' when it was smashed by a direct hit from a heavy shell. Five men, of whom Pte. Cowie was one, were killed instantaneously. All five were buried together and the stones of the 'pill-box' built into a cairn by their comrades. A cross was erected on the spot in view of the historic city of Ypres. Pte. Cowie was a cheery companion in days of rest and a loyal comrade in action." He *m.* December 1910; Sarah, *née* Smith, and leaves a son and two daughters.

(Panel 95) Pte. S/16520, Alexander Cowper, 8th (Service) Bn. The Black Watch (Royal Highlanders): *s.* of James Cowper, of Newlands, Errol, co. Perth, by his wife Mary Ann, *dau.* of James Imrie, of New Scone: *b.* Errol, 13 April 1892: *educ.* there: employee at Stanley Cotton Mills: enlisted 13 July 1916: served with the Expeditionary Force in France, from 16 November following, and was killed in action at Ypres, 12 October 1917: Age 29. *unm.*

(Panel 95) Pte. 18877, William Robertson Crighton, 8th (Service) Bn. The Black Watch (Royal Highlanders): 3rd *s.* of William Crighton, Head Gardener; Dalhousie Castle, Bonnyrigg, Midlothian; of Mortonhall Gardens, Liberton, Edinburgh, by his wife Sarah, *dau.* of Donald Leitch: *b.* Portobello, Edinburgh, 27 May 1898: *educ.* Oathlaw Public School, and Forfar Academy: Occupation – Gardener; Brechin Castle, co. Forfar: enlisted 6 February 1917: served with the Expeditionary Force in France and Flanders from 28 June, and was killed in action at Zonnebeke, Ypres, 28 September following. Buried there: Age 19.

(Panel 95) Pte. 202830, Charles Duncan, 8th (Service) Bn. The Black Watch (Royal Highlanders): *s.* of William Duncan, Ploughman; of Morrone Cottage, Ballater, co. Aberdeen, by his wife Anne, *née* Young: and brother to L/Corpl. S/11944, L.G. Duncan, Gordon Highlanders, killed in action, 31 July 1917; and Pte. 290652, M. Duncan, Gordon Highlanders, died of wounds, 7 October 1918: *b.* Glenmuick: enlisted Aberdeen. Killed in action 12 October 1917.

His brother Lewis also has no known grave; he is commemorated on the Ypres (Menin Gate) Memorial (Panel 38). Murray is buried in Bucquoy Road Cemetery, Ficheux (IV.E.20).

(Panel 95) Pte. S/40724, James McBay, 6th Bn. (Perthshire) The Black Watch (Royal Highlanders), (T.F.): *s.* of Jane McBay (68, Brechin Road, Arbroath, co. Forfar): Occupation – Ploughman; Mr. Binnie, Fauldie Hill, Arbirlot: joined Black Watch, March 1916: served with the Expeditionary Force in France and Flanders from July following: wounded, September, invalided to England: returned to France, May 1917: posted missing after the fighting, 16 September 1917; since reported killed in action: Age 25. His brother William served with the Royal Field Artillery; and Alex, Canadian Infantry.

(Panel 95) Pte. S/19968, George Adam Murray, 8th (Service) Bn. The Black Watch (Royal Highlanders): *gdson.* to George Murray, Farm Servant; of Distillery Cottages, Fettercairn: *b.* Fettercairn, co. Kincardine, 21 December 1895: *educ.* Public School, there: Occupation – Farm Servant; Steelsrath: enlisted Black Watch, 22 December 1916: served with the Expeditionary Force in France and Flanders from March 1917, and was killed in action nr. Railway Wood, Ypres, 28 September following. Buried where he fell. His Commanding Officer, Capt. Alexander, wrote, "He was a fine soldier who had volunteered for the noble and arduous duties of a stretcher-bearer. In billets he was a kind and merry companion, in action a loyal and gallant comrade.": Age 21.

PANEL 95 ENDS: PTE. H. STEWART, THE BLACK WATCH

PANEL 96 BEGINS: PTE. S. STEWART, THE BLACK WATCH

(Panel 96) Pte. 241251, Robert Wallace Turner, 5th (T.F) attd. 8th (Service) Bn. The Black Watch (Royal Highlanders): *yst. s.* of George Turner, of Newtown Hotel, Kirriemuir, by his wife Helen, *dau.* of William Wilson: *b.* Kirriemuir, co. Forfar, 30 April 1896: *educ.* Webster Seminary: Occupation – Butcher: joined 1st Fife and Forfar Yeomanry, 10 November 1915: transf'd. 5th Black Watch, August 1916: served with the Expeditionary Force in France and Flanders from April 1917, attd. 8th Battn., and was killed in action at Passchendaele, 12 October 1917. Buried where he fell. His Platoon Commanding Officer wrote, "Your boy was one of the best men in my platoon. Always so cheery, and willing to do any job that came our way, he was liked by all who came in contact with him.": Age 21. *unm.*

(Panel 96) 2nd Lieut. Felix Ernest Jones, M.C., 4th Bn. The Oxford & Bucks Light Infantry (T.F.): *s.* of William Jones, Solicitor; of 24, Sunnyside Road, Hornsey Lane, London, N., by his wife Madeline Mary, *dau.* of Felix Weiss: *b.* Stroud Green, Hornsey, co. Middlesex, 27 May 1888: *educ.* Highgate School: Occupation – Solicitor: joined Inns of Court O.T.C., June 1915: obtained a commission, Oxford and Bucks Light Infantry, December 1915: served with the Expeditionary Force in France and Flanders from March 1916; killed in action nr. Ypres 16 August 1917. Awarded the Military Cross (*London Gazette*, 22 September 1916), for "conspicuous gallantry in action; though wounded in the leg he led his platoon in a charge into the enemy's trench, which was successfully captured before he would go back and have his wound dressed.": Age 29. *unm.*

(Panel 96) 2nd Lieut. John Gardiner Smith, 6th (Service) Bn. The Oxford & Bucks Light Infantry: eldest *s.* of William Howard Smith, Butcher and Grazier; of 'The Nook,' Market Street, Lewes, by his wife Annie J. Margaret, *dau.* of John Gardiner, of Faversham: and brother to 2nd Lieut. D.G. Smith, 42 Sqdn. Royal Flying Corps, shot down and killed, 10 April 1918: *b.* Lewes, co. Sussex, 5 May 1890: *educ.* Brighton Grammar School: joined 1st City of London Royal Army Medical Corps (T.F.)., Pte., 6 August 1914: went to Malta: acted as Nursing Orderly, Imtarfa Hospital, engaged on X-Ray work, subsequently apptd. St. Julien's Hospital: thereafter went to Salonika, and was again employed as a Radiographer in a hospital: on his return to England, wishing for more active service, he volunteered for the fighting line, and joined the O.T.C.: received a commission: gazetted 2nd Lieut. Oxford & Bucks Light Infantry, August 1917: served with the Expeditionary Force in France, and was killed in action on the Menin Road, 20 September following. Buried where he fell. His Commanding Officer, Lieut.Col. Boyle wrote, "He died a true soldier's death at the head of his men in battle. Though he had only been with us a short time, he had made himself universally liked and respected by the officers and the men," and 2nd Lieut. Winter Taylor, "He met his death not long after going 'over the top,' being killed instantaneously by machine gun fire. One who says he saw the actual occurrence states that his company was held up by machine gun fire and were distributed in shell holes. An advance was again made, and he saw your son going forward, revolver in hand, leading his men around him, when he fell dead, shot through the head. You must seek comfort in the fact that he died at the head of his men, as we all hope to do if the time comes." His servant, Pte. Jerrams, also wrote, "Your son set a splendid example by his fearless and gallant conduct, which undoubtedly led to his end, for after being wounded and I had bandaged him up, we got to a shell hole for cover, as the machine gun was giving raking fire. But your son was not content with this, he wanted to push forward, which in the ordinary way would have been safest, and we had both of us got up to go when he got his fatal wound in the head with a bullet, and died instantly.": Age 27. *unm.*

His brother Donald also has no known grave; he is commemorated on the Arras Flying Services Memorial.

(Panel 96) Sergt. 202972, Gerald Lansom, 5th (Service) Bn. The Oxford & Bucks Light Infantry: *s.* of Thomas Lansom, Railway Signaller; of 'Melrose,' Church Street, Burton Latimer, nr. Kettering, co. Northampton, by his wife Lizzie, *dau.* of the late Thomas Perkins, of Bedford: and brother to Pte. L. Lansom, 5th East Surrey Regt., reported wounded and missing after the fighting at Cherisy, 3 May 1917: *b.* Raunds, co. Northampton, 26 September 1895: *educ.* Kettering Secondary School, and St. John's College, Battersea, London, S.W.: preparing to be an Elementary School Teacher; joined Oxford & Bucks Light Infantry, July 1915: served with the Expeditionary Force in France and Flanders from March 1917, and was killed in action nr. Ypres, 23 October following. Buried in the Menin Road Cemetery. 2nd Lieut. Stace wrote, "His loss will be most deeply felt by everyone in the company. He was one of the best N.C.O.'s we had, absolutely reliable, and always cheerful under the most trying circumstances. Recently he had been acting as my platoon sergeant, and I had absolute confidence in him and so had the men. Had he been spared, I am perfectly certain he would have made an excellent officer.": Age 21. *unm.* (*IWGC record age 22*)

(Panel 96) L/Corpl. 201270, Eric George Cheasley, 2/4th Bn. The Oxford & Bucks Light Infantry (T.F.): *s.* of George Henry Cheasley, of Station House, Shiplake, co. Oxford, by his wife Charlotte Maria. Killed in action 22 August 1917: Age 20. "*Remembered by the Staff and Boys of Shiplake College, 16 November 2006.*"

(Panel 96) L/Corpl. 200937, Edwin George Pipe, 2/4th Bn. The Oxford & Bucks Light Infantry (T.F.): *s.* of William Dalby Pipe, of 9, Queen's Road, Beccles, co. Suffolk, by his wife Emma: and brother to Sergt. 200939, R.H. Pipe, Oxford & Bucks Light Infantry, died of wounds, 29 March 1918, the same day as brother, Pte. 200938, P.D. Pipe, Oxford and Bucks Light Infantry, was killed in action; a fourth brother, Pte. 9764, W.J. Pipe, 2nd Honourable Artillery Coy., also fell: *b.* Beccles, 1896: enlisted Oxford. Killed in action 10 September 1917: Age 21. *unm.* One of four brothers who fell.

His brother Robert is buried in Etratat Churchyard Extension (II.B.11), both Percy and William have no known grave; they are commemorated on the Pozieres Memorial and Arras Memorial (Bay 1) respectively.

(Panel 96) Pte. 8655, Harold Carter, 'B' Coy., 6th (Service) Bn. The Oxford & Bucks Light Infantry: *s*. of Leonard Carter, Chairmaker; of 47, Green Street, High Wycombe, co. Buckingham, by his wife Emma 'Emily' Ellen: and elder brother to Pte. 4229, R. Carter, 2/1st (Bucks) Battn. O.B.L.I., killed in action, 19 July 1916: *b*. High Wycombe, 26 September 1893: enlisted there. Killed in action 20 September 1917: Age 23. *unm*. (*IWGC record age 24*)

His brother Roland also has no known grave; he is commemorated on the Loos (Dud Corner) Memorial.

PANEL 96 ENDS: PTE. S. CLARKE, OXFORDSHIRE AND BUCKINGHAMSHIRE LIGHT INFANTRY.

PANEL 97 BEGINS: PTE. W.C. CLARKE, OXFORDSHIRE AND BUCKINGHAMSHIRE LIGHT INFANTRY.

(Panel 97) Pte. 265204, Sydney Davis, 6th (Service) Bn. The Oxford & Bucks Light Infantry: late of Stoney Stratford, co. Buckingham: *s*. of William Davis, of Cattle End, Silverstone, nr. Towcester, by his wife Caroline: and brother to Pte. 17393, E.G. Davis, 7th Northamptonshire Regt., killed in action, 31 July 1917: *b*. Ditchley, co. Oxford: enlisted Wolverton, co. Buckingham. Killed in action, 20 September 1917: Age 22. *unm*. The brothers Davis are recorded on the Silverstone village War Memorial – erected to the Glory of God and in memory of 25 young men of Silverstone who fought bravely and died nobly during the Great War 1914 -1918, and in appreciation of the splendid service of those who, having taken part in the great struggle, returned to their homes and friends – It bears the inscription "Pass Not This Stone In Sorrow But In Pride And May We Live As Nobly As Those That Died." (*IWGC record Sidney*)

His brother Edward also has no known grave; he is commemorated on the Ypres (Menin Gate) Memorial (Panel 43).

(Panel 97) Pte. 24184, Francis Harold Duckenfield, 6th (Service) Bn. The Oxford & Bucks Light Infantry: only *s*. of the late Albert Duckenfield, by his wife Louisa (41, Abbey Street, Hockley, Birmingham), *dau*. of James Beach, of Birmingham: *b*. Birmingham, co. Warwick, 30 August 1896: *educ*. St. Mark's Church of England School: Occupation – Diamond Mounter's apprentice: enlisted Oxford and Bucks Light Infantry, 15 June 1916: served with the Expeditionary Force in France and Flanders from 5 December following. Reported wounded and missing after the fighting at Langemarck, 20 September 1917; now assumed to have been killed on or since that date: Age 21. *unm*. (*IWGC record H.F. Duckenfield*)

(Panel 97) Pte. 266328, Christopher Gillions, 1/1st (Buckinghamshire) Bn. (43rd Foot) The Oxford & Bucks Light Infantry: *s*. of the late Harry Gillions, Butcher; by his wife Minnie (47, Queen Street, Aylesbury): and elder brother to Pte. 35630, V.J. Gillions, 4th Yorkshire Regt., killed in action, 27 May 1918: *b*. Islington, London, 1894: enlisted Aylesbury, co. Buckingham. Killed in action 16 August 1917; St. Julien, Ypres: Age 23.

His brother Victor also has no known grave; he is commemorated on the Soissons Memorial.

(Panel 97) Pte. 285172, Archibald Richard Hayman, 1/1st (Buckingham) Bn. (43rd Foot) The Oxford & Bucks Light Infantry: *s*. of the late Richard Hayman, of Dinworthy, Bradworthy, co. Devon, by his wife Bessie: and elder brother to Pte. 345728, J. Hayman, 16th Devonshire Regt., killed in action, 3 December 1917: *b*. West Putford, nr. Holsworthy, 1895: enlisted Holsworthy. Killed in action 16 August 1917: Age 22.

His brother Josiah is buried in Jerusalem War Cemetery (A.71).

(Panel 97) Pte. 240742, George William Haynes, 2/1st (Buckingham) Bn. (43rd Foot) The Oxford & Bucks Light Infantry: formerly no.3678, Royal Berkshire Regt.: *s*. of Mark (& Mrs) Haynes, of Southampton Street, Faringdon, co. Berks: and brother to Pte. 7365, O.M. Haynes, 1st Royal Berkshire Regt., killed in action, 16 May 1915. Killed in action 22 August 1917: Age 42. He leaves a wife, Fanny Haynes (Elm Tree Cottages, London Street, Faringdon).

His brother Oliver also has no known grave; he is commemorated on the Le Touret Memorial (Panel 30).

(Panel 97) Pte. 200931, Howard Stanley May, 2/4th Bn. The Oxford & Bucks Light Infantry (T.F.): *s.* of Thomas May, of Baynard's Green, Bicester, co. Oxford, by his wife Elizabeth: and yr. brother to 2nd Lieut. W.C. May, attd. 1/5th Northumberland Fusiliers, who fell 26 October 1917: *b.* 1896: *educ.* Bicester: enlisted Oxford. Killed in action 22 August 1917: Age 21. *unm.* Remembered on the St. Mary's Church, Ardley, and the Stoke Lyne War Memorials: '*God Proved Them And Found Them Worthy For Himself.*'

His brother William also has no known grave; he is recorded on Panel 19.

PANEL 97 ENDS. PTE. G. PAYNE, OXFORDSHIRE AND BUCKINGHAMSHIRE LIGHT INFANTRY.

PANEL 98 BEGINS: PTE. R.H. PAYNE, OXFORDSHIRE AND BUCKINGHAMSHIRE LIGHT INFANTRY.

(Panel 98) Pte. 266396, John Todd, 2/1st (Buckingham) Bn. (43rd Foot) The Oxford & Bucks Light Infantry: *s.* of Henry William Todd, of 9, St. John's Street, Aylesbury, by his wife Fanny: and brother to Pte. 9132, H. Todd, 1st O.B.L.I., died of sickness, 6 April 1916, Mesopotamia: *b.* 8 March 1888. Killed in action 22 August 1917: Age 29. *unm.* (*IWGC record age 28*)

His brother Henry also has no known grave, he is commemorated on the Basra Memorial (Panel 26).

(Panel 98) Pte. 285192, Philip Andrew Watts, 1/1st (Buckingham) Bn. (43rd Foot) The Oxford & Bucks Light Infantry: eldest *s.* of Philip Watts, of Manor Farm, Ilkerton, late of South Stock Farm, Lynton, by his wife Alice, *dau.* of George Delbridge, Carpenter: *b.* Barbrook, nr. Lynton, co. Devon, 30 November 1895: *educ.* there: Occupation – Ploughman; South Stock Farm: joined 4th Battn. Devonshire Regt., 17 January 1917: served with the Expeditionary Force in France and Flanders from 26 June following: subsequently transf'd. Oxford and Bucks Light Infantry, and was killed in action at Ypres 4 October 1917. Buried where he fell: Age 21. *unm.*

Following the armistice a significant percentage of those who had experienced life in the trenches of the First World War chose not to speak of their experiences; that which they had endured and witnessed was beyond comprehension to all but those who had shared the same. Some wrote of their experiences and had them published, but no literary work would or ever could truly do justice. For the survivors the sights, sounds, smells, rats, lice, blood, mud, death in all forms imaginable (and unimaginable) and a myriad of other memories would haunt them throughout the remainder of their lives.

Pte. 41946, Charles Colman, 1st Essex Regt., 1916-1919, wrote, "I have seen sights which no man should ever see; sights which stay firmly in your mind for the rest of your life. Vivid images of my mates and comrades-in-arms, lying face down in the trenches with scores of rats scavenging their exposed flesh. I can see it as if it were yesterday, men clambering over the bodies to get out of the line of fire, limbs and torsos entwined. Shell-shocked men wallowing in the blood-soaked mire they called home." His comrade Robert Batterbee witnessed the same but never got to write about it; he joined the ranks of the dead who would haunt Colman and other survivors until their reunion.

(Panel 98) Pte. 41940, Robert Batterbee, 1st Bn. (44th Foot) The Essex Regt.: formerly no.26754, Norfolk Regt.: *s.* of John Batterbee, of The Lodge, Hill House, Dersingham, co. Norfolk, by his wife Caroline: enlisted King's Lynn, 1916. Killed in action 16 August 1917: Age 20.

PANEL 98 ENDS: PTE. H. BRUCKMAN, ESSEX REGT.

PANEL 99 BEGINS: PTE. H.G. BRUNTON, ESSEX REGT.

(Panel 99) Pte. 203055, George William Bunn, 7/10th (Service) Bn. The Essex Regt.: 3rd *s.* of George William Bunn, Farm Steward; of Park Farm, Saham Toney, Watton, nr. Thetford, by his wife Sarah Ann:

b. Old Buckingham, co. Norfolk, 6 April 1891: *educ.* Kennighall: Occupation – Farm Labourer: enlisted Essex Regt., 28 February 1917: served with the Expeditionary Force in France and Flanders from the following May. Reported wounded and missing after the fighting at Passchendaele Ridge, 22 October 1917, now assumed to have been killed in action on or about that date: Age 26. *unm.*

(Panel 99) Pte. 26888, William John Burrells, 2nd Bn. (56th Foot) The Essex Regt.: *s.* of Eliza Burrells (May Cottages, Shoebury Road, Great Wakering, co. Essex): *b.* North Benfleet, 1891: enlisted Southend-on-Sea: served with the Expeditionary Force in France and Flanders, from whence he was invalided home suffering from shell shock, returning to the Front in the summer of 1917 and reported wounded and missing following the fighting 10 October 1917, since confirmed killed in action on or about that date: Age 26. *unm.*

(Panel 99) Pte. 10363, Frederick Charles Deeks, 2nd Bn. (56th Foot) The Essex Regt.: late of Stapleford Tawney: *s.* of Charles Deeks, of Kingston Hall Cottage, Potter Street, Harlow, co. Essex, by his wife Louisa: and brother to Pte. CH/17839, W. Deeks, Royal Marine Light Infantry, died 27 April 1916, when his ship, H.M.S. 'Russell,' was sunk by mines laid by a German submarine about three miles off Malta: *b.* Brentwood: enlisted Stratford, London, E.15. Killed in action 10 October 1917: Age 26. *(SDGW record F.C. Decks)*

His brother William has no known grave but the Mediterranean; he is commemorated on the Chatham Naval Memorial (18).

(Panel 99) Pte. 203026, Frederick George Patman, 2nd Bn. (56th Foot) The Essex Regt.: formerly no.330958, Cambridgeshire Regt.: *husb.* to Eliza Patman (2, Arthur Street, Cambridge): and father to Pte. 225122, J.G. Patman, 1/4th Northamptonshire Regt., died 19 October 1918, in Egypt, aged 21 years: *b.* Chesterton, 1876: Occupation – Grocer's Warehouseman: enlisted Cambridge. Killed in action 10 October 1917: Age 41. Remembered on Cambridge (St. Luke's) Parish War Memorial.

His son John is buried in Alexandria (Hadra) War Memorial Cemetery (A.206).

(Panel 99) Pte. 203011, Levi Smith, 2nd Bn. (56th Foot) The Essex Regt.: formerly no.271647, Hertfordshire Regt.: *s.* of Robert Smith, of Apethorpe Road, King's Cliffe, Peterborough, co. Northampton, by his wife Selena: and brother to L/Corpl. G/14578, J.W. Smith, 6th Queen's Own (Royal West Kent Regt.), died 3 April 1918, of wounds: *b.* King's Cliffe, afsd.: enlisted Peterborough. Killed in action 10 October 1917: Age 18.

His brother John is buried in Warloy-Baillon Communal Cemetery Extension (VIII.E.25).

(Panel 99) Lieut. Percy Dorrington, 10th (Service) Bn. The Sherwood Foresters (Notts & Derbys Regt.): *s.* of the late John William Dorrington, by his wife Edith ('Rowan House,' Carmen Sylva Road, Llandudno): and yr. brother to Pte. 3/28396, W. Dorrington, 4th South Wales Borderers, died 13 May 1917, in Mesopotamia. Killed in action 12 October 1917: Age 22. *unm.*

His brother Walter is buried in Basra War Cemetery (IV.N.12).

(Panel 99) 2nd Lieut. Hugh Stirling Moore, 7th Bn. (Robin Hood) The Sherwood Foresters (Notts & Derbys Regt.), attd. 9th (Service) Bn. Leicestershire Regt.: *s.* of the Rev. John Moore, of 2G, Dean Street, Blackpool, co. Lancaster, late of 30, Coppice Road, Nottingham, Home Mission Secretary of the United Methodist Church, by his wife Mary Jane, *dau.* of William Witham, of Burnley: *b.* Brighouse, co. York, 14 August 1891: *educ.* High School, Nottingham; Grammar School, Burnley, and Ashville College, Harrogate: Occupation – Solicitor: enlisted University and Public Schools Battn. Royal Fusiliers, November 1914: obtained a commission 2nd Lieut., Sherwood Foresters, 5 August 1916, being subsequently attd. Leicestershire Regt.: served with the Expeditionary Force in France and Flanders from the following November and died, 1 October 1917, of wounds received in action at Polygon Wood, nr. Ypres. Buried there. His Chaplain wrote, "Your son, by his fearlessness, and coolness and leadership, helped to save a tremendously important position during a heavy counter-attack. In fact he helped to save Polygon Wood – which the Germans had strict orders to recapture at all costs. Your son proved absolutely on 1 October what we had often heard, and all knew before, that his men would follow him anywhere. Everyone loved him – he was always so cheerful and good natured, and he proved himself a first-rate officer." And a brother officer, "His passing is a loss to me in a personal sense. To all of us who remain he left a splendid example of devotion to duty. He had more than the respect of his men; he had their affection.": Age 26. *unm.*

(Panel 99) L/Sergt. 305489, Charles Edward Barnes, 2/5th Bn. The Sherwood Foresters (Notts and Derbys Regt.), (T.F.): late of Bishop Street, Sutton-in Ashfield: *s.* of John Barnes, Coal Hewer; of Spring Street, Sutton-in-Ashfield, by his wife Hannah: *b.* Huthwaite, co. Nottingham, *c.*1893: Occupation – Miner; Summit Colliery: enlisted 8th Sherwood Foresters, Mansfield, 7 September 1914: served with the Expeditionary Force in France transf'd. 2/5th Battn. (February 1917), and was killed in action 26 September 1917. He leaves a wife and son, Charlie. In a letter to his widow, 2nd Lieut. R. Stone, wrote, "It is with the deepest regret that I have to acquaint you of the death in action of your husband, with whom I was associated as his Platoon Officer. He was killed in action on 26 September, and it may be some consolation to you to know that he suffered no pain, his death being caused instantaneously by several bullets from a machine gun. Your husband had not been with us long, although, as you know, he had been in the army some years, but he had been with us long enough for us to know that he was an efficient and keen non-commissioned officer. I am grieved to have to write you with such bad news, but please accept my sincere sympathy in your trouble. His loss is greatly felt by his comrades here.": Age 25. The '*Notts Free Press,*' 27 September 1918, carried the following memoriam notice from his family:

> *We never thought when he said "Good-Bye,"*
> *He had gone to a far off land to die;*
> *His heart was true, his spirit brave,*
> *His resting place a soldier's grave.*

(Panel 99) Sergt. 265740, Joseph Frank Booth, 2/7th Bn. (Robin Hood) The Sherwood Foresters (Notts and Derbys Regt.), (T.F.): only *s.* of the late Frank Charles Booth, by his wife Edith (formerly of 'Beechurst,' Knighton Road, Leicester, now resident at 39, Waldeck Road, Nottingham), *dau.* of Joseph Benjamin Fields Clow: *b.* Leicester, 12 February 1899: *educ.* Elm Bank School, Nottingham: enlisted 29 September 1914, aged 15 years and 7 months: served in Ireland during the Rebellion: promoted Corpl. by the King, for 'bravery under fire and special services in the field;' Sergt., August 1916, being apptd. Regimental Grenade Instructor; Mentioned in Despatches, by General Maxwell, Commander-in-Chief, Forces in Ireland (*London Gazette*, 25 January 1917): served with the Expeditionary Force in France, from February 1917, and was killed in action, north-east of Ypres, 26 September following. Sergt. Booth was recommended for the D.C.M., and brought to the notice of the Secretary of State for War, for his distinguished services in connection with the war: Age 18.

(Panel 99) Sergt. 306791, Charlie Evans, 2/8th Bn. The Sherwood Foresters (Notts and Derbys Regt.), (T.F.): 5th *s.* of Thomas G. Evans, of Sampson's Buildings, Huthwaite: *b.* Huthwaite, co. Nottingham, 5 September 1892: *educ.* Board School, there: joined Sherwood Foresters, 5 February 1916: took part in the suppression of the Dublin Rebellion, April following: thereafter proceeded to France, served with the Expeditionary Force there and in Flanders, and was killed in action, 26 September 1917: Age 25. Capt. C. Pynsent Elliott wrote, "He had been in my company for some time, and he will be a great loss to us. He was a good soldier, and was very keen, and had been a great help to me on several previous occasions, and had done some valuable work with the company." He *m.* 15 November 1915, Sarah Elisabeth, *dau.* of John Wood, of Sutton-in-Ashfield.: *s.p.*

(Panel 99) Sergt. 32407, Edward Gascoigne, 17th (Service) Bn. (Welbeck Rangers) The Sherwood Foresters (Notts and Derbys Regt.): *s.* of Thomas Gascoigne of North Muskham, Newark, Nottingham: by his wife Ann. Missing / believed killed in action 20 September 1917: Age 26. *unm.* See L/Corpl. H. Shooter, Hooge Crater Cemetery (VII.G.5).

(Panel 99) L/Corpl. 201011, Harold John Burton, 2/5th Bn. The Sherwood Foresters (Notts and Derbys Regt.), (T.F.): *s.* of Henry Burton, of 'Charnwood,' 88, Nottingham Road, Long Eaton, co. Derby, and Frances Taylor Burton, his wife: and elder brother to Pte. 13925, F.W. Burton, 2nd Northamptonshire Regt., killed in action 9 May 1915: enlisted Long Eaton: served with the Expeditionary Force in France from 26 February 1917; killed in action there seven months later 26 September 1917: Age 29.

His brother Francis is buried in Merville Communal Cemetery (II.T.4).

PANEL 99 ENDS: L/CORPL. G. NEWTON, NOTTS & DERBYS REGT.

PANEL 100 BEGINS: L/CORPL. H. PENDLETON, NOTTS & DERBYS REGT.

(Panel 100) L/Corpl. 72741, William Rowland Roberts, 7th Platoon, 'B' Coy., 2nd Bn. (95th Foot) The Sherwood Foresters (Notts and Derbys Regt.): *s.* of William Roberts, of The Post Office, Dwrbach, co. Pembroke, by his wife Ann, *dau.* of William Rowlands, of Cufferne: *b.* Scleddy, co. Pembroke, 17 March 1891: *educ.* Tredavid National School, and County Intermediate School, Fishguard: was a Draper's Assistant: joined the Army Service Corps 27 January 1915: served with the Expeditionary Force in France and Flanders from June 1915: transf'd. Sherwood Foresters, November 1917, and was killed in action at Mount Kemmel, 19 April 1918. A comrade wrote: "He was so highly liked and respected by all his comrades.": Age 27. *unm.*

(Panel 100) Pte. 72498, Sydney Baxter, 16th (Service) Bn. (Chatsworth Rifles) The Sherwood Foresters (Notts and Derbys Regt.): formerly no.34436, Royal Flying Corps: *s.* of William Baxter, of 'Erpingham,' 88, King's Road, Richmond, co. Surrey, by his wife Elizabeth Ann: and elder brother to twins – Corpl. 2099, A.G. Baxter, 2/18th Bn. London Regt.; and Corpl. TF/590566, W.J. Baxter, 2/18th Bn. London Regt., both of whom were killed in action, 9 October 1916, on the Somme. Killed in action at Ypres 24 October 1917: Age 40. He leaves a wife, Mrs Edith Baxter (13, Jocelyn Road, Richmond), to whom all effects and correspondence should be addressed. One of three brothers who fell, two of whom were twins.

His brother Albert is buried in Ecoivres Military Cemetery (III.G.23); William has no known grave, he is commemorated on the Arras (Faubourg d'Amiens) Memorial (Bay 10).

(Panel 100) Pte. 32623, Joseph Bell, 2/8th Bn. The Sherwood Foresters (Notts and Derbys Regt.), (T.F.): 2nd *s.* of Matthew Bell, of 8, Victoria Terrace, June Street, Barnsley, co. York, by his wife Lilly, *dau.* of Isaac Sykes: and brother to Spr. T.F. Bell, Royal Engineers, killed in action at Ypres 19 December 1915: *b.* St. Helens, co. Lancaster, 22 May 1898: *educ.* Hoyle Mill School, nr. Barnsley, and on leaving there gained employ Monks Bretton Colliery: enlisted 24 November 1915: served with the Expeditionary Force in France, from January 1916, and was killed in action (or died of wounds) on or about 26 September 1917: Age 19.

His brother Thomas also has no known grave; he is commemorated on the Menin Gate Memorial, Ypres (Panel 9).

(Panel 100) Pte. 11582, Frank Ernest Edney, 'C' Coy., 1st Bn. (45th Foot) The Sherwood Foresters (Notts and Derbys Regt.): *s.* of Joseph Edney, of 9, Eckington Terrace, Clapton Road, Nottingham, by his wife Jane: *b. c.*1893: enlisted Nottingham. Killed by a 'drop-short' shell which landed in his trench, 23 November 1917; Ptes. J.W. Roper and H.L. Powell were also killed: Age 24. *unm.*

Ptes. Powell and Roper also have no known grave; they are recorded on Panel 101.

(Panel 100) Pte. 306669, Samuel Fowler, 2/8th Bn. The Sherwood Foresters (Notts and Derbys Regt.), (T.F.): *s.* of the late Edwin Fowler, Bricklayer's Labourer; by his wife Elizabeth, *née* Hunt (4, Phoenix Street, Sutton-in-Ashfield): *b.* Forest Side, Sutton-in-Ashfield, 11 December 1894: employee Mansfield and Sutton Co-Operative Society, Outram Street: enlisted 19 January 1916. Pte Fowler went to Ireland, April following, to take part in the suppression of the rebellion there and was in the thick of the fighting in the streets of Dublin. Afterwards remained in Ireland for some time before returning with a draft to Salisbury Plain and thence onward to France where he took part in some heavy fighting, February 1917: slightly wounded, 27 April following, andwas killed in action 26 September 1917: Age 22. *unm.* The *Notts Free Press,* 'In Memoriam,' 27 September 1918:

> *Not now, but in the coming years, It may be in that better land,*
> *We shall read the meaning of our tears, And there sometime we will understand.*

> From his sorrowing Mother, Father, Brothers & Sisters.

PANEL 100 ENDS: PTE. W. HALLAM, 203165, NOTTS AND DERBYS REGT.

PANEL 101 BEGINS: PTE. W. HALLAM, 241086, NOTTS AND DERBYS REGT.

(Panel 101) Pte. 14487, Edward Haynes, 10th (Service) Bn. The Sherwood Foresters (Notts and Derbys Regt.): *s.* of William Alsop Haynes, of Beeley, Rowsley, co. Derby, by his wife Rebecca: and brother to Pte. M2/034995, S. Haynes, Royal Army Service Corps, died 30 November 1918: *b.* Beeley, 1893: enlisted Derby. Killed in action 12 October 1917: Age 24. *unm.* Remembered on Beeley (St. Anne's) Parish War Memorial.
  His brother Stanley is buried in Tourcoing (Pont-Neuville) Communal Cemetery (G.1).
  (Panel 101) Pte. 70359, Horace Leonard Powell (Siglr.), H.Q. Coy., 1st Bn. (45th Foot) The Sherwood Foresters (Notts and Derbys Regt.): formerly no.4978, Leicestershire Regt.: *s.* of Corpl. Charles Powell, Leicestershire Regt., by his wife Elizabeth Ann (58, Dover Street, Leicester): *b. c.*1897: enlisted Leicester. Killed 23 November 1917, in company with Ptes. F.E. Edney and J.W. Roper by a shell which dropped short and exploded in their trench: Age 20. *unm.*
  Ptes. Edney and Roper also have no known grave; they are recorded on Panel 100 and below respectively.
  (Panel 101) Pte. 21690, John William Roper, 'C' Coy., 1st Bn. (45th Foot) The Sherwood Foresters (Notts and Derbys Regt.): eldest *s.* of the late John Roper, by his wife Elizabeth Ann, *née* Naylor (23, Lime Street, Sutton-in-Ashfield): *b.* Forest Side, 22 May 1894: was a Miner, Bentinck Colliery: enlisted Sutton-in-Ashfield, Nottingham, January 1915. Killed in action 23 November 1917: Age 23. *unm.* Capt. A.S. Giles, O.C., 'C' Coy., wrote: "It is with very great regret that I have to write and tell you that your son was instantly killed by shellfire on November 23rd. A Large shell landed in the trench just where your son was sitting. Your son was a stretcher bearer in my Company, and it is only the best men who are stretcher bearers. He was buried along with two other men (Ptes. Edney and Powell), who were killed at the same time, and a cross was erected. Should there be any other particulars that you may require please let me know, and I will do all I can. Please accept the sympathy of the whole Company and especially from myself in your great loss." And a comrade, Pte. F. Townsend, 'B'Coy., 1st Battn.: "Just a line to you with extreme regret to say your son Johnny has been killed. It was one of our own shells that dropped short and killed him and three others. He was found with his hands in his pockets, so he had no pain. He was very much liked by everyone that came into contact with him. It is such a very painful task to write and send you such bad tidings, but I expect that by this time you will have received official news about him. I have made enquiries about where he was buried, and I have found out that he was decently laid away, and a white cross denotes his resting place. I did not know he was killed till after we got relieved, and it was a very severe blow to me when they told me about him. May God bless you and help you bear this burden that has suddenly been put upon you." The *Notts Free Press,* 'In Memoriam,' 22 November 1918:

> *With aching hearts we shook his hands, Tears glistening in our eyes;*
> *We wished him luck but never thought it was his last "Good-bye."*
> *Too dearly loved to be forgotten.*

Mother, Father, Brother and Sisters.

I loved him in life, He is dear to me still; But I must bend to God's holy will.

Sweetheart, Hilda.

Ptes. F.E. Edney and H.L. Powell also have no known grave, they are recorded above and on Panel 100 respectively. The third man mentioned by Pte. Townsend, Pte. A.V. Potter, died of wounds the following day; he is buried in Nine Elms British Cemetery, Poperinghe (IX.C.6).
  (Panel 101) Pte. 306701, Herbert Slater, 8th Bn. The Sherwood Foresters (Notts and Derbys Regt.), (T.F.): *s.* of the late Sam Slater, by his wife Elizabeth Annie, *dau.* of the late William (& Sarah) Radford: *b.* Mansfield, co. Nottingham, 4 September 1894: *educ.* Rosemary, and Catholic Schools, Mansfield, aforesaid: Occupation – Miner: enlisted 31 January 1916: served in Ireland during the Rebellion, April: proceeded to France 27 February 1917; killed in action nr. Ypres, 26 September following. Buried at

Schuter Farm, Ypres. A comrade wrote, "He was a jolly fellow, and we shall miss him very much.": Age 23 years, 22 days. *unm.*

(Panel 101) Pte. 16164, Frederick Smith, 2/5th Bn. The Sherwood Foresters (Notts and Derbys Regt.), (T.F.): *s.* of Harriet Nixon (135, Sherwood Street, Mansfield Woodhouse): and *yr.* brother to Pte. 18478, J.W. Smith, 1st Sherwood Foresters, killed in action, 9 May 1915: *b.* Ilkeston, co. Derby, 1898: enlisted Mansfield, September 1914. Killed in action 26 September 1917: Age 19.

His brother James also has no known grave, he is commemorated on the Ploegsteert Memorial (Panel 7).

PANEL 101 ENDS: PTE. J.A. SMITH, NOTTS AND DERBYS REGT.

PANEL 102 BEGINS: PTE. P. SMITH, NOTTS AND DERBYS REGT.

(Panel 102) Pte. 306137, George Brown Southerington, 2/8th Bn. The Sherwood Foresters (Notts and Derbys Regt.), (T.F.): *s.* of William Southerington, of 9, North Gate, Newark, by his wife Susan, *dau.* of George Brown: and brother to Pte. 47409, A.E. Southerington, Royal Scots, who died of wounds 14 October 1917: *b.* Newark-on-Trent, co. Nottingham, 4 August 1880: *educ.* Council School, there: was a Stoker in the employ of the Trent Navigation Company, and latterly a Stoker in the Gas Works: joined the Sherwood Foresters, 8 April 1915: served in Ireland during the Dublin Rebellion, April 1916: sent to France and served with the Expeditionary Force there from February 1917; killed in action during the taking of Passchendaele Ridge, at Wieltje, north-east of Ypres, 26 September following. Buried where he fell. An officer wrote, "As Medical Officer I have seen a good deal of him and his death will be a great loss to the Sanitary Squad, as well as to numerous personal friends," and his Company Sergt., "George had been attached to my squad for a considerable time, and was always ready and willing to do anything that was asked of him. I am deeply grieved at the loss of so dear a comrade.": Age 37. He *m.* St. Leonard's Church, Newark, 29 December 1904; Mary Ann (11, Northgate, Newark), *dau.* of Mr (& Mrs) Clark, and had a son, Herbert, *b.* 3 August 1908.

His brother Alfred is buried in Dozinghem Military Cemetery (X.F.20).

(Panel 102) Pte. 16287, George Sperry, 2/5th Bn. The Sherwood Foresters (Notts and Derbys Regt.), (T.F.): *s.* of Thomas Sperry, of Cromford Road, Langley Mill, by his wife Elizabeth: *b.* 1880: prior to enlistment, Ripley, September 1914, was an Iron Striker, Messrs G.R. Turner and Co. Ltd.: served with the Expeditionary Force in France and Flanders from 1915: wounded (head) during the fighting at Delville Wood, July 1916, and returned to England: after a period of convalescence, during which he obtained leave to visit his parents, returned to France and was killed in action at the Battle of Ypres, 26 September 1917: Age 36. His officer, in a letter to Pte. Sperry's parents, said that their son was killed in the big push the battalion took part in that day, stating the attack was entirely successful. At the time of his death Pte. Sperry was but a few days short of his thirty-seventh birthday.

(Panel 102) Pte. 55881, George Henry Udall, 'D' Coy., 1st Bn. (45th Foot) The Sherwood Foresters (Notts and Derbys Regt.): *b.* Mansfield, co. Nottingham: employee Co-operative Banking Society Ltd., Dixie Street, Jacksdale: enlisted Sherwood Foresters, Eastwood: served with the Expeditionary Force in France and Flanders from 12 February 1916, wounded during the fighting at Messines 10 June 1917, returned to duty 20 August following and was killed by shellfire in the trenches nr. Bellevue Spur, 21 November 1917. Buried there.

(Panel 102) Pte. 21341, Joseph Walter Wilkinson, 16th (Service) Bn. (Chatsworth Rifles) The Sherwood Foresters (Notts & Derbys Regt.): *s.* of William Wilkinson, of Mill Ash, Whitwell, Mansfield, by his wife Fanny: and *yr.* brother to Pte. 31009, A. Wilkinson, 17th Sherwood Foresters, who fell 3 September 1916, at the Somme: *b.* Ollerton, co. Nottingham: enlisted Worksop. Killed in action 20 September 1917: Age 23. *unm.* Remembered on Whitwell (Parish) War Memorial.

His brother Albert is buried in Ancre British Cemetery, Beaumont Hamel (II.F.24).

A Grave In Flanders

Here in the marshland, past the battered bridge,
One of a hundred grains untimely sown,
Here, with his comrades of the hard won ridge,
He rests unknown.

His horoscope had seemed so plainly drawn –
School triumphs, earned apace in work and play;
Friendships at will; then love's delightful dawn
And mellowing day.

Home fostering hope; some service to the State;
Benignant age; then the long tryst to keep
Where in the yew-tree shadow congregate
His fathers sleep.

Was here the one thing needful to distil
From life's alembic, through his holier fate,
The man's essential soul, the hero will?
We ask; and wait.

Lord Crewe
The Harrovian

(Panel 102) Capt. Allen Brodie Hoare, 'A' Coy., 1/5th Bn. The Loyal North Lancashire Regt. (T.F.): *yst. s.* of the late Edward Brodie (& Mrs) Hoare, M.P., Banker;of 'Tenchleys,' Limpsfield, co. Surrey: and brother to 2nd Lieut. M.B. Hoare, 1/5th Loyal North Lancashire Regt. (gazetted 7 December 1914; *surv'd.*): *b.* Caterham, 1882: *educ.* Hazelwood School, Limpsfield; Harrow (Boarder) 1896-1901, and Pembroke College, Cambridge: employee Bleachers' Association, Firwood, Bolton: gazetted 2nd Lieut., 1/5th Loyal North Lancashire Regt., 19 October 1914: subsequently promoted Lieut. and Capt.: served with the Expeditionary Force in France from February 1917; wounded during the Battle of Messines, June following, at which time his battalion were in support on the right flank of Ploegsteert Wood. Capt. Brodie-Hoare was killed in action, 26 October 1917, while leading his platoon to the attack at Poelcapelle: Age 35. He *m.* 1916; Audrey Lois, *née* Collier (64, Napier Court, Hurlingham, London).

(Panel 102) Lieut. Allen Aquila Baldwin, 2/5th Bn. The Loyal North Lancashire Regt. (T.F.): eldest *s.* of the late Dr. Aquila Baldwin, of Birmingham, by his wife Amanda Mary, *dau.* of George E. Allen, of Birmingham, Jeweller: *b.* Birmingham, co. Warwick, 7 January 1887: *educ.* High School, there, and Malvern College: trained at the Inns of Court, London, and Berkhampstead 1915: gazetted 2nd Lieut., Loyal North Lancashire Regt., 1 January 1916: served with the Expeditionary Force in France and Flanders from February 1917, and was killed in action at Kemmel Hill 26 April 1918. Buried where he fell: Age 31 years, 8 days. He *m.* London, 15 January 1918; Artye, *dau.* of Charles William Crouch, of Hastings, and had a *dau.*

(Panel 102) 2nd Lieut. Alan Bellingham, 4th Bn. The Loyal North Lancashire Regt. (T.F.): *s.* of Arthur Allen (& Annie) Bellingham, of 'Lyndhurst,' Rose Hill Road, Burnley, co. Lancaster: kinsman to 2nd Lieut. W.O. Lancaster, 21st Manchester Regt., killed in action the same day (26 October): served with the Expeditionary Force in France and Flanders with Public Schools Bn. Royal Fusiliers; wounded at the Somme: repatriated to England, obtained a commission, 2nd Lieut., Loyal North Lancs: returned to France and was killed in action, 26 October 1917, at Poelcapelle: Age 23.

2nd Lieut. William Lancaster also has no known grave; he is recorded on Panel 120.

(Panel 102) 2nd Lieut. William Rimmer, 4/5th Bn. The Loyal North Lancashire Regt. (T.F.): *s.* of Alderman William Rimmer, of 'Wyndene,' New Hall Lane, Bolton, Outfitter, by his wife Rebecca Stanley, *dau.* of Thomas Gibbs: *b.* Bolton, co. Lancaster, 31 July 1894: *educ.* Denstone College, co. Stafford: was in business with his father: joined East Lancashire Field Ambulance, 1 September 1914: went to Egypt on the 9th: proceeded to Gallipoli, 1915; present at the landing at Suvla Bay: contracted enteric fever, and invalided home: on recovery returned to Egypt, thence to England, December 1916, where, after a period of training at Oxford, he was gazetted 2nd Lieut., Loyal North Lancashire Regt., 13 May 1917: served with the Expeditionary Force in France and Flanders from 22 July, and was killed in action at Langemarck 26 October 1917. He was a good all-round sportsman: Age 23. *unm.*

(Panel 102) L/Corpl. 40284, Herbert Ingram, 2nd Bn. (47th Foot) The Loyal North Lancashire Regt.: formerly no.7021, Sherwood Foresters: *s.* of the late John Ingram, by his wife Mary (44, Colville Street, Derby): *husb.* to Elizabeth (74, Cobden Street, Derby). Killed in action 28 September 1918: Age 36. "*God Bless Grandad Ingram, It is a privilege to pay our respects. With love from your grandson Dennis and his wife Barbara. 16 November 2006*"

PANEL 102 ENDS: PTE. W. ALLEN, LOYAL NORTH LANCASHIRE REGT.

PANEL 103 BEGINS: PTE. R. ALTY, LOYAL NORTH LANCASHIRE REGT.

(Panel 103) Pte. 244901, Harry Robert Ashworth, 4/5th Bn. The Loyal North Lancashire Regt. (T.F.): *s.* of James Henry Ashworth, of 4, Clegg Street, Haslingden, co. Lancaster, by his wife Elizabeth Ann: and brother to Pte. 203806, J. Ashworth, 2/4th East Lancashire Regt., killed in action, 10 October 1917, and Pte. Deal/3915(S), H. Ashworth, Royal Marine Medical Unit, 63rd (R.N.) Divn., killed in action 26 August 1918: *b.* Haslingden: enlisted there. Killed in action 26 October 1917: Age 19.

His brother James also has no known grave, he is recorded on Panel 78; Harold is buried in Bucquoy Communal Cemetery Extension (B.7).

(Panel 103) Pte. 241007, William Henry Beckett, 4th Bn. The Loyal North Lancashire Regt. (T.F.): *s.* of Harry Beckett, of 173, Bolton Road, Edgworth, co. Lancaster, by his wife Anna, *dau.* of William Gregory, Miner: *b.* Edgworth, nr. Bolton, 25 January 1897: *educ.* St. Anne's School, Turton, Bolton: Occupation – Joiner: enlisted 17 October 1914: served with the Expeditionary Force in France and Flanders, from 12 February 1915, and was killed in action at Passchendaele 26 October 1917. Buried at Elverdinghe. An officer wrote, "He was a most reliable, capable, and invariably cheerful soldier; in his duties as scout were these qualities, together with intelligence above the average, and so much nerve. With his capabilities he would certainly have been an N.C.O. if he had stayed with his company, he preferred, however, to remain in the Scout Section, and his work as a scout was invariably excellent.": Age 20. *unm.*

(Panel 103) Signlr. 242290, John Clayton, M.M., 5th Bn. The Loyal North Lancashire Regt. (T.F.): *s.* of Henry Clayton, of 63, John Brown Street, Bolton, co. Lancaster, by his wife Margaret, *dau.* of John (& Sarah) McLaughlin: *b.* Bolton, 19 September 1897: *educ.* there: employee Park Mill Spinning Company: enlisted South Lancashire Regt., 9 April 1915; discharged 21 May and rejoined (Loyal North Lancashire Regt.) the same day: served with the Expeditionary Force in France from February 1917, and was killed in action at Passchendaele Ridge, 26 October following. A Sergt. wrote, "There was something about him different to others of his age, which caused him to make many friends. His companions speak of him as most cheerful and most willing to assist anyone he could." Signaller Clayton was awarded the Military Medal "For conspicuous gallantry on 4 May 1917; at 11.45a.m; at Petillon, France, the enemy began to shell the front line heavily with high explosive and shrapnel. One of the first shells made a direct hit on the S.O.S. line. Without a moment's hesitation Signaller Clayton, together with another man of the signal section, ran down the line, being under heavy shell fire all the time, collected the ends of the broken wire out of the shell crater and joined them. This work took eight to ten minutes under continuous shell fire. It was owing to this man's resource, devotion to duty, and disregard of personal danger, that communication on the S.O.S. line was re-established." Mentioned in Despatches by F.M. Sir Douglas Haig, for general and distinguished service in the field, and was awarded a certificate for devotion to duty and gallantry on the field the day before he was killed, which certificate was forwarded to his parents. When training he won three medals for cross-country running: Age 20. *unm.*

(Panel 103) Pte. Pte. 235265, Richard Charles Myers, 4/5th Bn. The Loyal North Lancashire Regt. (T.F.): *s.* of Francis John Myers, House Decorator; of 39, Upper Richmond Road, Mortlake, London, S.W., by his wife Alice C.: *b.* Highgate, London, N., 28 June 1896: *educ.* Hargrave Park L.C.C. School, Upper Holloway, London, N.: joined 6th Battn. East Surrey Regt. 1913; subsequently transf'd. Loyal North Lancashire Regt.: served with the Expeditionary Force in France and Flanders, and was killed in action, 26 October 1917. Buried where he fell. Second Lieut. Roy E. Ray wrote, "The same blow that deprived you of your dear son also deprived his regiment and myself, his platoon officer, of a courageous and splendidly efficient soldier. .. We shall all miss him greatly .. He died, as I would have expected of him, fighting bravely to the last.": Age 21. *unm.*

PANEL 103 ENDS: PTE. F. PLATT, LOYAL NORTH LANCASHIRE REGT.

PANEL 104 BEGINS: PTE. H. POWELL, LOYAL NORTH LANCASHIRE REGT.

(Panel 104) Pte. (Signlr.) 242811, John Wood, 4/5th Bn. The Loyal North Lancashire Regt. (T.F.): *s.* of the late John Wood, by his wife Sarah (66, Shaw Street, Bolton), *dau.* of William Barnes: *b.* Bolton, co. Lancaster, 13 April 1898: *educ.* Council School, there: Occupation – Side-Piecer: enlisted 3 August 1915: served with the Expeditionary Force in France and Flanders from 7 February 1917, and was killed in action on the Passchendaele Ridge, 26 October following. An officer wrote, "He was originally reported missing, but I heard yesterday that he had been found and buried. I did not know your son very well, but Lieut. Dixon tells me he has lost a valuable signaller, and I know his comrades have lost a good friend.": Age 19.

(Panel 104) Sergt. 3/7136, Joseph Henry Bond, 2nd Bn. (58th Foot) The Northamptonshire Regt.: *s.* of the late William Bond, by his wife Annie Maria: a pre-war Reservist, enlisted Landguard, co. Essex, was recalled to the Colours on the outbreak of war August 1914: served with the Expeditionary Force in France and Flanders from March 1915; took part in the fighting at Festubert, Loos, the Somme, Bellewaarde Ridge, and was killed in action at Passchendaele, 23 November 1917: Age 32. He leaves a wife, Ellen Bond (9, Maycock's Row, Bridge Street, Northampton), and four children.

(Panel 104) L/Corpl. 19030, William Arthur Balaam, 2nd Bn. (58th Foot) The Northamptonshire Regt.: *husb.* to Susan Annie Balaam (Buckhurst Hill, co. Essex): and father to Corpl. 5728403, D.A. Balaam, 1st Dorsetshire Regt., killed in action 31 July 1943, in Sicily. Killed in action, Boxing Day, 26 December 1917.

His son Dudley is buried in Catania War Cemetery, Sicily (III.K.23).

(Panel 104) Pte. 40746, Alfred Charles Elgood (served as Totterdill, A.), 1st Bn. (48th Foot) The Northamptonshire Regt.: formerly no.RTS/513, Royal Army Service Corps: 3rd *s.* of the late William John Elgood, by his wife Emily Edith, *née* Edmonds (7, Briscoe Road, Collinswood, Merton, London): and brother to Pte. 9520, A.E. Elgood, 1st Bn. Lincolnshire Regt., who fell at Le Cateau 26 August 1914: and Pte. 9060, R.W. Elgood, 2nd Bn. Lincolnshire Regt., who fell during the fighting nr. Neuve-Chapelle 10 March 1915: *b.* Balham, London, 1896. Killed in action 10 November 1917: Age 21. *unm.* One of three brothers who fell.

His brother Archibald also has no known grave, he is recorded on the La Ferte-Sous-Jarre Memorial; Robert is buried in Neuve-Chapelle Farm cemetery (A.1).

(Panel 104) Pte. 40367, Sydney Bridgeford Roe, 2nd Bn. (58th Foot) The Northamptonshire Regt.: *s.* of Robert Roe, of Farcet Fen, co. Cambridge, by his wife Wilhelmina, *née* Ruff: and *yr.* brother to Pte. 11852, I.H. Roe, Lincolnshire Regt., killed in action at Arras, 3 June 1917, aged 22 years: *b.* 1898: enlisted Peterborough. Killed in action, Boxing Day, 26 December 1917: Age 19.

His brother Isaac is buried in Croisilles British Cemetery (I.C.3).

(Panel 104) Pte. 14403, Robert Sears, 2nd Bn. (58th Foot) The Northamptonshire Regt.: *s.* of William Sears, of 82, Wellingborough Road, Rushden, co. Northampton, by his wife Elizabeth: and yr. brother to L/Bmdr. 110585, E.E. Sears, 112th Bde., Royal Field Artillery, killed in action, 8 October 1918, by a bomb dropped from an enemy aircraft: *b*. Rushden, 23 October 1896: employee Messrs Nurrish and Pallett; Boot and Shoe Manufacturers: enlisted Northampton, 1 September 1914, aged 16 years: served with the Expeditionary Force in France and Flanders from early 1915: wounded in the advance at Aubers Ridge, 9 May 1915; invalided to England 9 June: following treatment and convalescence returned to France February 1916: took part in the Battle of the Somme where (9 July 1916) he was buried alive when the detonation of a shell collapsed the portion of trench he was in and, after being rescued, was hospitalised (in France) suffering from shell-shock: allocated home leave to commence 23 August 1917, he was killed in action, 16 August 1917: Age 19. His brother-in-law, Pte. J.H. Shipman, Northamptonshire Regt., is currently a prisoner of war in Germany.

His brother Ernest is buried in Bellicourt British Cemetery (VII.L.10).

(Panel 104) Pte. 20162, John William Upex, 6th (Service) Bn. The Northamptonshire Regt.: *s*. of John Upex, Farm Labourer; of 17, Robinson's Yard, Warmington, nr. Oundle, co. Northampton, by his wife Louisa Jane: and brother to Pte. 20163, H. Upex, 6th Northamptonshire Regt., died 26 November 1918, whilst a Prisoner of War; and Pte. 276208, J.A.E. Upex, 6th Essex Regt., died 13 September 1917, in Mesopotamia: *b*. Warmington, afsd., *c*.1893: Occupation – Farm Labourer: enlisted Coventry, co. Warwick: served with the Expeditionary Force in France and Flanders from 20 October 1915; killed in action 20 October 1917, nr. Poelcapelle: Age 25. *unm*. One of three brothers who fell.

His brother Harry is buried in Spy Communal Cemetery, Namur. James is buried in Baghdad (North Gate) War Cemetery (XXI.G.38).

PANEL 104 ENDS: PTE. F. WALKER, NORTHAMPTONSHIRE REGT.

PANEL 105 BEGINS: PTE. A. WEBSTER, NORTHAMPTONSHIRE REGT.

(Panel 105) Capt. Walter Ronald Wacher, 2nd (66th Foot) attd. 6th (Service) Bn. Princess Charlotte of Wales's (Royal Berkshire Regt.): 2nd *s*. of the late Alfred Wacher, of the Anchor Brewery, Bermondsey, London, S.E., and Herne Bay; by his wife Lucy Durant, *dau*. of Henry Gibbings, of North Tawton, co. Devon: and elder brother to Sergt. 517, G.G. Wacher, Queen's Westminster Rifles, killed in action 9 August 1915, at Hooge. Killed in action 12 October 1917.

His brother Geoffrey is commemorated in Maple Copse Cemetery (Sp.Mem.F.17).

(Panel 105) 2nd Lieut. Geoffrey Herbert Tigar, 6th (Service) Bn. Princess Charlotte of Wales's Own (Royal Berkshire Regt.): *s*. of Walter Tigar, of 112, Nibthwaite Road, Harrow, co. Middlesex, by his wife Mary Agnes: and yr brother to Lieut. H.W. Tigar, 3rd Middlesex Regt., killed in action, 9 May 1915, aged 22 years: religion – Roman Catholic. Killed in action 13 October 1917: Age 21. *unm*.

His brother Harold also has no known grave; he is commemorated on the Ypres (Menin Gate) Memorial (Panel 49).

(Panel 105) Lieut. Herbert Alfred Vincent Wait, 'D' Coy., 2nd Bn. (66th Foot) Princess Charlotte of Wales's (Royal Berkshire Regt.): only child of George Vincent Wait, of 45, Eastern Avenue, Reading, by his wife Mary, *dau*. of the late Stephen Hill, of Penzance, co. Cornwall: *b*. Reading, co. Berks, 19 April 1898: *educ*. Oakham School; and Royal Military College, Sandhurst: gazetted 2nd Lieut., Royal Berkshire Regt. 7 April 1916: promoted Lieut. 7 October 1917: served with the Expeditionary Force in France and Flanders from 26 April 1917: wounded August 1917; reported missing at Passchendaele, 2 December 1917; presumed killed in action on that date: Age 19.

(Panel 105) Corpl. 200506, Alexander John Gregory, 1/4th Bn. Princess Charlotte of Wales's (Royal Berkshire Regt.), (T.F.): *s*. of the late John B. Gregory, by his marriage to Sarah Jane Gates, *née* Gregory ('The Moorhen Inn,' Hitchin Hill, co. Hertford): and brother to Pte. 253026, F. Gregory, 10th Canadian Infantry, reported missing, 2 September 1918; since confirmed killed: *b*. Aston End, Stevenage, 1885: enlisted Reading, co. Berks. Killed by shellfire 10 October 1917, east of Passchendaele: Age 32.

His brother Frank is buried in Upton Wood Cemetery, Hendecourt-les-Cagnicourt (F.15).

(Panel 105) Pte. 36275, Alfred Campkin, 6th (Service) Bn. Princess Charlotte of Wales (Royal Berkshire Regt.): formerly no.5871, Hertfordshire Regt.: *s.* of John Campkin, of 19, Kibes Lane, Ware, co. Hertford, by his wife Charlotte: and brother to Pte. 268093, A.J. Campkin, Hertfordshire Regt., died of wounds, 18 April 1918; and Pte. 266739, E.R. Campkin, 1st Hertfordshire Regt., killed in action 23 August 1918: enlisted Hertford. Killed in action 12 October 1917: Age 30. One of three brothers who fell.

His brother Albert is buried in Lijssenthoek Military Cemetery (XXVII.G.6); Edward, Bucquoy Communal Cemetery Extension (B.15).

PANEL 105 ENDS: PTE. J. JACKMAN, ROYAL BERKSHIRE REGT.

PANEL 106 BEGINS: PTE. C. JACKSON, ROYAL BERKSHIRE REGT.

(Panel 106) Pte. 200916, Henry Kinchin, 1/4th Bn. Princess Charlotte of Wales's (Royal Berkshire Regt.), (T.F.): *s.* of William Kinchin, of 50, Filey Road, Reading, co. Berks, by his wife Sarah: and yr. brother to Pte. 9905, W.J. Kinchin, 1st Royal Berkshire Regt., who fell 14 September 1914: *b.* 1897: enlisted Reading. Killed in action 9 October 1917: Age 20. *unm.*

His brother William is buried in Chauny Communal Cemetery British Extension (5.K.1).

(Panel 106) Pte. 202147, Edwin Little, Lewis Gun Section, 6th (Service) Bn. Princess Charlotte of Wales's (Royal Berkshire Regt.): only *s.* of the late Richard Edwin Little, Farmer; of Treworgie Vean, Ruan High Lanes, Grampound Road, co. Cornwall, by his wife Eliza Ann ('Tresemple', St. Clement, Truro, co. Cornwall), *dau.* of John Davey: *b.* Treworgie, *afsd.*, 15 July 1896: *educ.* Veryan, and Truro College: Occupation – Farmer: enlisted 3 May 1916: served with the Expeditionary Force in France and Flanders from the following September, and was killed in action, 12 October 1917: Age 21. *unm.*

(Panel 106) Pte. 35600, Leo Horton Summerfield, 6th (Service) Bn. Princess Charlotte of Wales's (Royal Berkshire Regt.): *husb.* to Annie C. (28, Moorpool Avenue, Harborne, co. Warwick): enlisted Birmingham. Killed in action 12 October 1917: Age 37.

(Panel 106) Lieut. John Bentley Freeman, 3rd attd. 11th (Service) Bn. The Queen's Own (Royal West Kent Regt.): *s.* of the Rev. Herbert Bentley Freeman, Vicar of Burton-on-Trent, by his wife Ida Gertrude, *dau.* of Prebendary Cardwell, of St. Pauls Cathedral, London: *b.* London, 20 January 1897: *educ.* Waveney House, Burton-on-Trent; Merton House, Southwick, and Marlborough College: commissioned 2nd Lieut., Special Reserve, August 1916, temporarily attd. the Guards, Chelsea: served with the Expeditionary Force in France and Flanders, from 23 October following; apptd. Battalion Bombing Officer: killed in action by a German sniper while leading his men in front of Tower Hamlets, at the Battle of Menin Road, 20 September 1917. Buried there. His Commanding Officer wrote, "I had not intended that he should go into action on the 20th inst., but at the very last moment, as all the officers of one company had been wounded, and he was up helping me, I had to order him to go with his company. I can see his face now, when I gave him the order. I think he was glad to have the chance to be in it. I saw him once more on the early morning of the 20th, gallantly leading his men in the attack, and am told he was shot in the head by a sniper. He was a very great favourite with us all, and I was much interested to watch him developing from a schoolboy into a fine manly soldier...It may be some small consolation to you and his father in your great sorrow to know your son always did his duty, and never complained from the day he joined me to the day of his death," and his Adjutant: "Your son was so popular with us all, that each one has hesitated to send you details of his death. We went up the line into tunnels on 19 September, preparatory to making an attack on the following day. Just as the battalion was moving out on the night of the 19th, one company lost all its officers by shellfire, and your son was detailed to lead this company. When on their final objective, near Tower Hamlets, he was shot by a sniper through the head. I was very friendly indeed with your son. I have lived in the same mess with him since he was made Bombing Officer, and although I have seen many officers come and go in the battalion, I can honestly say I never felt the loss of anyone so much as of him. In the Headquarters mess we all used to chaff of your son, he was so young and boyish, but we all had a very deep affection for him. He was the best type of public schoolboy. The Colonel will be very upset, as your son was, if I may say so, his favourite in the battalion. The other officer in the company your son was with when he was killed says he was magnificent right through the attack until he was shot, and if he had lived he would have had the Military Cross.": Age 20. *unm.*

(Panel 106) 2nd Lieut. Reginald Walter Coles, attd. 7th (Service) Bn. The Queen's Own (Royal West Kent Regt.). Killed in action 12 October 1917; Poelcapelle. See 2nd Lieut. A. Michell, below.

(Panel 106) 2nd Lieut. Sydney Richard Hickmott, 4th (T.F.) attd. 10th (Service) Bn. The Queen's Own (Royal West Kent Regt.): *s.* of the late Edward Richard Hickmott (*d.*1927), Builder; by his wife Fanny Flora, *née* Foreman (41, Victoria Road, Tunbridge Wells): *gdson.* to the late Timothy Joseph Hickmott (*d.*1902), Builder, Carpenter and Undertaker; of Tunbridge Wells, and Amphilla Harriet Hickmott, *née* Edgson (*d.*1902): *husb.* to Ellen Margaret Hickmott, *née* Oaten (55, Forest Road, Tunbridge Wells); by whom he had a son, the late Sergt. Pilot. 1162408, R.S.K. Hickmott, Royal Air Force Volunteer Reserve, killed in action, May 1941: and yr. brother to Pte. S/10770, E.A. Hickmott, 2nd The Buffs (East Kent Regt.), killed in action, 14 April 1915: *b.* 1885. Died 1 October 1918, of wounds: Age 33.

His brother Edward also has no known grave; he is commemorated on the Ypres (Menin Gate) Memorial (Panel 14). His son Richard is buried in Tunbridge Wells Cemetery (Cons.Sec.7A, Grave 125).

After taking part in several tactical exercises over a model of the ground they were to assault in the attack on Passchendaele Ridge, 7th Queen's Own, with less than 24 hours notice, were switched to 53rd Brigade's attack to secure the northern sector of Poelcapelle village. Moving up to the relief of 11th Division on the night of 10/11 October, in pitch darkness, pouring rain, and mud that surpassed all previous experience, the Queen's Own barely arrived in position in time for the attack. Because the front line ran diagonal to the objectives, the plan of attack involved the companies in the front line withdrawing to an assembly position some distance behind, leaving detachments at intervals in the front line with orders to rejoin their companies as they came up in the second wave of the attack. The flaw with the plan, as in so many other plans, was that the withdrawal increased the distance to be covered in the attack. If the distance to be covered was not problem enough, the mud made it all the more serious. It was so bad in places men stuck fast in it and, being unable to move, were killed where they stood. Even those who were lightly equipped could hardly move in such conditions, and for men encumbered with equipment, weapons and ammunition, their progress amounted to little more than a crawl. Even though the mud negated the effect of the enemy's barrage to a certain extent, the battalion lost heavily from rifle and machine gun fire before it had cleared its own front line.

'B' Company, on the right, initially made good progress but, after being held up by fire from strongpoints on their right and east of the Staden road, they were forced to a standstill and could do no more than hold their ground. On the left a platoon of 'C' Company, after a reasonable start, got held up by machine-gun fire from an enemy strongpoint; Pte. C.R. Ives rushed it with a Lewis gun, knocked the machine-gun out, and thus enabled the platoon to continue (awarded M.M.). Led by Sergt. C. Hamblin, who took over after 2nd Lieut. Michell fell, the platoon not only reached their objective, capturing a strongpoint, a couple of machine-guns and 52 prisoners along the way (awarded D.C.M.) but, after being reduced to just 16 men and getting mixed up with the Household Battalion, continued onward with 4th Division. The remainder of 'C' Company were less fortunate. Brought to a standstill by a strongpoint at the northern end of Poelcapelle and, even though reinforcements from 'A' managed to reach them, they were denied any further advance and forced to dig in a short distance from their starting line.

In proportioning the blame for the failure of the attack a large part was laid on the ineffectiveness of the British barrage – largely due to the guns which should have provided it being stuck fast in the mud and therefore unable to get into action: The difficulties of getting forward over terrain which rain and shellfire had reduced to a veritable sea of mud: And there being no opportunity to familiarise with the plan of attack or to (even cursorily) reconnoitre the area.

Despite the difficult conditions and its failure to accomplish more, the battalion hung on tenaciously, maintaining its positions throughout the following day, until relieved by 8th Suffolks that evening (13 October).

Of the 600 men who went 'over the top' on October 12 a little under half of them had become casualties. 14 Officers had been killed, wounded or died of wounds, among them Capts. F.H. Lewin and H.T. Gregory, 2nd Lieuts. G.J. Allen, R.W. Coles and A. Michell, added to this Capts. Anstruther and F.H. F. Smith were wounded; of all the officers who took part, only Col. Cinnamond and Lieut. Duffield escaped unscathed.

(Panel 106) 2nd Lieut. Arthur Michell, 7th (Service) Bn. The Queen's Own (Royal West Kent Regt.). Killed in action, 12 October 1917; Poelcapelle.

2nd Lieut. R.W. Coles also has no known grave, he is commemorated above. Capt. F.H. Lewin is buried in Bard Cottage Cemetery (V.A.40); Capt. H.T. Gregory, Minty Farm Cemetery (I.D.21); and 2nd Lieut. G.J. Allen, Mendinghem British Cemetery (VI.E.20).

(Panel 106) Sergt. L/10229, Robert George Godfrey Falkner, 1st Bn. (50th Foot) The Queen's Own (Royal West Kent Regt.): *s.* of the late Q.M.S. Falkner: and brother to Pte. L/10230, J.L.H. Falkner, 7th Queen's Own, died, 4 August 1918, of wounds: *educ.* Duke of York's Military School, Dover. Missing / believed killed in action 26 October 1917: Age 31. He was married to Beatrice Lily Falkner (18, Albert Street, Maidstone).

His brother Louis is buried in St. Sever Cemetery Extension, Rouen (Q.IV.J.4).

(Panel 106) Sergt. G/10684, George Jones, 10th (Service) Bn. (Kent County) The Queen's Own (Royal West Kent Regt.): *b.* Liverpool, co. Lancaster: enlisted Maidstone, co. Kent. Missing / believed killed 27 April 1918, at Brandhoek. See account Hagle Dump Cemetery (Plot I, Rows C & D); also Red Farm Military Cemetery.

'Lance Corporal Henry John Martin, I was mobilised from the reserve in August 1914 and fought at St. Ghislain, Mons, retreated to the Marne, raced toward the sea via the Aisne, and survived Neuve Chapelle, despite being almost surrounded. With C Company I helped to take Hill 60 on 17th April 1915. Fought through 2nd Ypres, and was wounded at High Wood on 22nd July 1916; I spent 14 months convalescing in Blighty only to return to Passchendaele and be blown to pieces at Poelcappelle on 27th November 1917. I have no known grave, only my name on this panel, and a plaque dedicated to me at St. George's Memorial Church, Ieper. I did my best. Please remember me.'

The above account – found in a glass frame beneath Panel 106 – refers to:

(Panel 106) L/Corpl. 242077, Henry John Martin, 3/4th Bn. The Queen's Own (Royal West Kent Regt.), (T.F.): *b.* Islington, 14 October 1880. Killed in action 27 November 1917. Age 37.

(Panel 106) L/Corpl. G/18490, Walter Frederick Ransom, 11th (Service) Bn. The Queen's Own (Royal West Kent Regt.): eldest *s.* of Walter Ransom, of New Cottages, Sittingbourne, co. Kent, by his wife Ellen C., *dau.* of A. Smith: *b.* Wormshill, co. Kent, 14 May 1896: *educ.* Rodmersham Green School: enlisted in the East Kent Mounted Rifles, October 1914: served with the Expeditionary Force in France and Flanders from September 1916: transf'd. Royal West Kent Regt., and was killed in action, 20 September 1917: Age 21. *unm.*

(Panel 106) L/Corpl. 240864, Frederick William George Sleath, 10th (Service) Bn. The Queen's Own (Royal West Kent Regt.): Actg.Corpl.: 2nd *s.* of Westley Edward Sleath, of 13, Barmeston Road, Catford, London, S.E., who was for three years a Special Constable, by his wife Marian Kate, *née* Filmer: *b.* Walworth, London, S.E., 2 February 1898: *educ.* Plassy Road London County Council School, Catford: was employed as a Clerk in the City: enlisted 2/5th (Territorial) Battn. Royal West Kent Regt. 1 March 1915: served with the Expeditionary Force in France and Flanders from 13 September 1917: subsequently transf'd. 10th Battn. of his regiment, with whom he proceeded to Italy in November: returned to France, March 1918, and was killed in action nr. Ypres, 29 September following. Buried at Comines Canal. His Sergt. wrote, "He and his men were caught by machine-gun fire while advancing over open ground. The men were scattered, and, seeing a shell hole nearby, Corpl. Sleath tried to get his men into it. It was while he was thus engaged that he was sniped through the brain." Corpl. Sleath was recommended for a commission for services rendered in the field. He was for nearly three years the leading chorister at St. John's Chapel, Catford, and later was organ blower and bell-ringer: Age 20. *unm.*

PANEL 106 ENDS: L/CORPL. H. SOUTH, ROYAL WEST KENT REGT.

PANEL 107 BEGINS: L/CORPL. C.H. WOOLF, ROYAL WEST KENT REGT.

(Panel 107) Pte. G/16618, Albert Baily, 1st Bn. (50th Foot) The Queen's Own (Royal West Kent Regt.): *s.* of Edwin Baily, of Maidstone, by his wife Anne: *b.* Maidstone, 1886: *educ.* St. Paul's School, there: was employed as Cowman: enlisted 20 July 1916: served with the Expeditionary Force in France and Flanders, from 15 October following, and was killed in action, 4 October 1917. His Commanding Officer wrote, "It is with regret I have to inform you of the death of your husband. He was killed in action on the morning of the 4th. I have known him quite a long time and had a great respect for him, and feel his loss greatly, as does the whole platoon, for he was a splendid soldier. In your sad loss I hope you will find consolation in the fact that he died a true soldier's death in the front and thick of a terrific battle.": Age 31. He *m.* Maidstone, 17 February 1912; Rachel (1, Rose Cottages, Sandling Lane, Maidstone), *dau.* of John Springall, and had a *dau.* Clara, *b.* 5 July 1914. (*IWGC record Bailey*)

(Panel 107) Pte. G/19495, George Duffill, 7th (Service) Bn. The Queen's Own (Royal West Kent Regt.): formerly no.82152, Sherwood Foresters: *s.* of Fred Dufffill, of White House, Worlaby, Brigg, co. Lincoln, by his wife Fanny: and elder brother to Pte. 42217, D. Duffill, 6th Leicestershire Regt., who fell 18 September 1918, aged 18 years: *b.* Tipperary, Co. Cork, *c.*1895: enlisted Lincoln. Killed in action 12 October 1917, at Poelcapelle: Age 22. *unm.*

His brother Dick is buried in Villers Hill British Cemetery, Villers-Ghislain (II.B.6).

(Panel 107) Pte. 202755, Harris Filar, 10th (Service) Bn. The Queen's Own (Royal West Kent Regt.): formerly no.5162, Oxford and Bucks Light Infantry: *s.* of Barnett Filar, of 8, Challis Court, Cannon Street, Commercial Road, London, E.1: and neighbour to Pte. 253940, A. Kohle, 2/4th London Regt., killed in action 26 October 1917, nr. Cameron House, and Pte. 92323, W. Kohle, 3rd Bn. London Regt., died of wounds 11 September 1918, in the Base Hospital, Rouen: enlisted Stepney. Killed in action 29 September 1918: Age 19.

The Kohle brothers were residents of 1, Challis Court: Albert has no known grave, he is recorded on Panel 149; William is buried in St. Sever Cemetery Extension, Rouen (R.III.H.7).

(Panel 107) Pte. G/9605, Alfred John Thomas Growns, 18th (Service) Bn. The Queen's Own (Royal West Kent Regt.): *s.* of the late George Growns, by his wife Fanny Emily (4, Mill Croft Road, Cliffe-at-Hoo, co. Kent): *b.* Maidstone, co. Kent, 25 September 1896: *educ.* Cliffe Council School, nr. Rochester: enlisted August 1914: trained Maidstone and Aldershot: served with the Expeditionary Force in France and Flanders, and was killed in action, 21 September 1917. His Commanding Officer wrote, "He died like a gentleman, and they buried him on the ridge he was helping to fight for.": Age 21. *unm.*

(Panel 107) Pte. G/5001, Sidney Charles Hammond, 'D' Coy., 1st Bn. (50th Foot) The Queen's Own (Royal West Kent Regt.): *s.* of the late John Rouse Hammond, Captain, Cross-Channel boats; by his wife Mary Anne (4, Richmond Street, Folkestone), *dau.* of Stephen Standing: *b.* Folkestone, co. Kent, 24 June 1881: *educ.* St. Mary's Higher Grade School, there: Occupation – Assistant Steward; Cross-Channel boats: enlisted October 1914: served with the Expeditionary Force in France and Flanders, from April 1915, and was killed in action at Passchendaele 4 October 1917. His Commanding Officer wrote, "We shall all miss him; it is a great loss to us. He was invariably cheerful under all circumstances and was extremely reliable. He has done some excellent work, especially of late, which would certainly have received some recognition had he lived. I was quite near him when he was killed. He was shot through the heart and died almost at once.": Age 36. *unm.*

(Panel 107) Pte. G/19510, Frederick Charles Hobson, 7th Bn. The Queen's Own (Royal West Kent Regt.): formerly no.82831, Sherwood Foresters: late of South Moor Road, Brimington, Chesterfield, co. Derby: enlisted Sheffield, March 1917: proceeded to France, transf'd. Queen's Own with a draft of reinforcements, June 1917: killed in action, 12 October 1917: Age 23. Shortly after his death his widow, to whom he married five days before enlisting, was informed her husband had been wounded but, after a considerable period wherein she received no word from him, a letter to his commanding officer elicited the reply that he had been killed at Passchendaele. His close friend Pte. Hurst, with whom he had enlisted at the same time, was killed at his side.

(Panel 107) Pte. G/23598, Francis William Hooper, 'A' Coy., 7th (Service) Bn. The Queen's Own (Royal West Kent Regt.): *s.* of Francis Robert Hooper, of 110, Knithton Road, Plymouth, Sergt. Major, Army Ordnance Corps, by his wife Jessie Maud (1, Vicarage Park, Plumstead, London): *b.* Mauritius, 10 November 1897: *educ.* Mr Hann's Dockyard Preparation School, Devonport, Plymouth: Occupation – Shipwright's Apprentice; H.M. Dockyard, Plymouth: enlisted October 1915: trained Shoreham; became Musketry Instructor: served with the Expeditionary Force in France and Flanders from 16 November 1916: underwent a course on Lewis Gunnery, and was killed in action 12 October 1917. He was presented with a parchment and scroll by the General Commanding his Division for 'gallant conduct and devotion to duty during operations at Cherisy on 3 May 1917,' and was also commended again for the handling of a Lewis Gun on the field: Age 19. (*IWGC record L/Sergt., age 20*)

(Panel 107) Pte. G/19517, Charles William Hurst, 7th Bn. The Queen's Own (Royal West Kent Regt.): formerly no.83186, Sherwood Foresters: *s.* of Arthur Hurst, of 18, Queen Street, Brimington, by his wife Annie: *b.* Oakley, co. Bedford: employee, Midland Railway Co.: enlisted Chesterfield, March 1917: proceeded to France, transf'd. Queen's Own with a draft of reinforcements, June 1917. Killed in action, 12 October 1917: Age 22. His close friend Pte. Hobson, with whom he had enlisted at the same time, was killed at his side.

(Panel 107) Pte. G/12672, John William Kemp, 1st Bn. (50th Foot) The Queen's Own (Royal West Kent Regt.): *s.* of Benjamin Kemp, of 32, Upper Street, Rusthall, Tunbridge Wells: *b.* Rusthall, Tunbridge Wells, co. Kent, 10 April 1893: *educ.* St John's School, there: was a Gardener: enlisted in the Royal West Kent Regt. 18 March 1916: served with the Expeditionary Force in France and Flanders from the following July, and was killed in action, 4 October 1917. Buried there. Second Lieut. Frank Cook wrote, "I have known him for quite a time, and had a great respect for him, and feel his loss greatly, as does the whole platoon, for he was a splendid soldier.": Age 24. *unm.* (*IWGC record 3 October 1917, age 25*)

(Panel 107) Pte. G/18842, George Henry Locke, 11th (Service) Bn. The Queen's Own (Royal West Kent Regt.): *s.* of Albert Locke, Farm Labourer; of Moat Cottage, Rougham, nr. Bury St. Edmunds, by his wife Alice: *b.* Rougham, co. Suffolk, 12 September 1893: *educ.* there: enlisted 10 June 1916: served with the Expeditionary Force in France, and was killed in action at Polygon Wood 20 September 1917: Age 24. *unm.*

(Panel 107) Pte. G/18472, Horace John Norton, M.M., 11th (Service) Bn. The Queen's Own (Royal West Kent Regt.): *s.* of Charles C. Norton, of 2, Barrow Hill Cottages, Ashford, co. Kent, Farm Labourer, by his wife Alma 'Annie,' *dau.* of Henry Bannister: *b.* East Guildford, nr. Rye, co. Sussex, 14 September 1897: *educ.* Council Schools, Ashford: employee Messrs J.W. Buglers Ltd., Ashford: enlisted May 1915: served with the Expeditionary Force in France and Flanders from 20 September 1916, and was killed in action 20 September 1917. His Commanding Officer wrote, "He was killed by shellfire on his way back from Battalion Headquarters, and we were all sorry, for he was invincible, cheerful and brave beyond words." He was awarded the Military Medal (*London Gazette*, 31 July 1917) for 'conspicuous gallantry in the attack on Hollebeke.': Age 20. *unm.*

(Panel 107) Pte. G/19744, William Thayer Percival, 7th (Service) Bn. The Queen's Own (Royal West Kent Regt.): *s.* of the late William Percival, by his wife Ada Mary (11, Hawkins Crescent, Harrow-on-the-Hill, late of 75, Vaughan Road, Harrow), *dau.* of Frederick Joseph Hobson: *b.* London, 22 March 1884: Occupation – Traveller; Messrs Johns, Son and Watts, London: enlisted Royal Fusiliers, 17 July 1916; transf'd. Royal West Kent Regt., 9 September: served with the Expeditionary Force in France and Flanders from 14 August 1917; killed in action at Poelcapelle 12 October following. His Commanding Officer wrote, "He was greatly missed by the whole battalion, as he was the friend of all.": Age 33. *unm.*

PANEL 107 ENDS: PTE. J.A. POTTER, ROYAL WEST KENT REGT.

PANEL 108 BEGINS: PTE. C.F. POWLES, ROYAL WEST KENT REGT.

(Panel 108) Pte. G/30838, Martin Richardson Toyne, 10th (Service) Bn. The Queen's Own (Royal West Kent Regt.): formerly no.29580, Royal West Surrey Regt.: *s.* of Joseph M.R. Toyne, of Edlington, Horncastle, co. Lincoln, by his wife Elizabeth: and brother to Pte. G/15317, G.H. Toyne, 13th Royal Sussex Regt., killed in action, 19 October 1916: *b.* Ashby, co. Lincoln, 1899: enlisted Brighton, co. Sussex: served with the Expeditionary Force in France and Flanders, and was killed in action 23 October 1918: Age 19.

His brother George also has no known grave; he is recorded on the Thiepval Memorial, Somme (Pier & Face 7.C.)

(Panel 108) Pte. 242446, Alfred Horace Woodall, 2/5th Bn. The Queen's Own (Royal West Kent Regt.), (T.F.): *s.* of James Woodall, by his wife Sarah, *dau.* of John Box: *b.* St. James's, London, S.W., 18 June 1876: served with the Expeditionary Force in France and Flanders from 12 September 1917, and was killed in action at Menin Road, Ypres, three weeks later, 3 October 1917. Buried where he fell: Age 41. He *m.* St. Peter's Church, Paddington, London, W., 10 September 1916; Emily Louisa (26, Shirland Road, Maida Hill, London, W.), *dau.* of Thomas Frederick Pratt: *s.p.* (*IWGC record age 43*)

(Panel 108) Pte. 19763, John Woods, 11th (Service) Bn. The Queen's Own (Royal West Kent Regt.): *s.* of Robert Woods, of Walkden Cottages, Sinacre Lane, Bickerstaffe, nr. Ormskirk, co. Lancaster, by his wife Mary: *b.* Bickerstaffe, co. Lancaster, 23 July 1898: *educ.* Church School, there: Occupation – Labourer; Walkden Farm: contrary to his parents consent, enlisted 21st King's (Liverpool) Regt., 24 May 1915, aged 16 years: subsequently transf'd. 11th Royal West Kent Regt.: served with the Expeditionary Force in France and Flanders from 25 August 1917, and was killed in action at Passchendaele Ridge 22 September following. Buried where he fell. Corpl. White wrote, "Your son was killed on the morning of 22 September, during the execution of the most tedious of duties, namely bringing rations to his comrades in the front line, who had been without food or drink for nearly two days. I was not present at his death, but from information I have received, he was shot by a sniper, and killed instantly.": Age 19. Commemorated on his parents headstone, Holy Trinity Churchyard, Bickerstaffe; Pte. Woods was killed exactly ten years to the day that his brother William died in infancy.

On 9 October 1917 1/4th King's Own Yorkshire Light Infantry were in support to 4th and 5th York and Lancaster Regt., and their sister battalion (1/5th K.O.Y.L.I.) at Passchendaele. Leaving their positions 800 yards forward of the ridge 'Abraham Heights' the 4th went forward in two waves, advancing down the forward slope of the ridge suffering numerous casualties from a strong-point on the Belle Vue spur, and forced to close on the Meetcheele – Gravenstafel road on account of the impassable condition of the ground (due to the overflowing of the Ravebeek stream whose banks had been destroyed by shellfire). In the front line the companies on the left were being steadily depleted by heavy rifle and machine gun fire, on the right men were temporarily losing direction in the heavy glutinous mud and, in response to both shouting desperately for reinforcements, two companies were sent forward.

The advance up the long slope, under continuous rifle and machine gun fire, progressed as far as possible by sections; the fire from Belle Vue at the top and Wolf Copse on the left devastating and while leading his men forward to the latter Capt. R.W. Moorhouse was mortally wounded.

Taken back to battalion headquarters at Abraham Heights his father Lieut.Col. H. Moorhouse – despite the efforts of those with him and his son (fully aware that any assistance he might receive would not save him) begging him not to go due to the nature of the machine gun and rifle fire at that time – left the dugout to find a doctor and almost immediately thereafter was shot and killed. The regimental history states father and son died within 30 minutes of each other.

(Panel 108) Lieut.Col. Harry Moorhouse, D.S.O., T.D., 4th Bn. The King's Own (Yorkshire Light Infantry): Chevalier de Legion D'Honneur: served in the South African Campaign (Queen's Medal, 4 clasps): father to Capt. R.W. Moorhouse, 4th K.O.Y.L.I., killed in action at the Battle of Poelcapelle the same day: 9 October 1917. Mentioned in Despatches for his services in the Great War, he was awarded the D.S.O. (*London Gazette*, 14 January 1916).

(Panel 108) Capt. Ronald Wilkinson Moorhouse, M.C., 4th Bn. The King's Own (Yorkshire Light Infantry), (T.F.): *s.* of the late Lieut.Col. H. Moorhouse, D.S.O., 4th K.O.Y.L.I., killed in action at the Battle of Poelcapelle the same day: 9 October 1917. Awarded the Military Cross (*London Gazette*, 18 June 1917, 'For conspicuous gallantry and devotion to duty when in command of a raiding party. In spite of heavy hostile fire and the most difficult conditions, he succeeded in gaining his objective and successfully carrying out his task.'

(Panel 108) Capt. Reginald Cuthbert Welsford Smithers: 3rd (Reserve) attd. 7th (Service) Bn. The King's Own (Yorkshire Light Infantry), (T.F.): *yr. s.* of the late Herbert Welsford Smithers, of Hove, co. Sussex, by his wife Elizabeth Lilian (now the wife of Capt. A.J. Hollick, of 9, Eaton Gardens, Hove): *b.* Brighton, co. Sussex, 24 September 1897: *educ.* Belvedere School, Brighton; The Lodge, Uppingham (joined the Army class; was a member of the O.T.C.); Royal Military College, Sandhurst: gazetted 2nd Lieut. King's Own Yorkshire Light Infantry, 15 July 1915; promoted Lieut., 1 July 1916; Capt. 16 July 1917 (apptd. Adjt. Same day): served with the Expeditionary Force in France and Flanders from September 1916, and was killed in action at Langemarck, nr. Ypres, 16 August 1917: Age 19.

PANEL 108 ENDS: L/CORPL. J. BROWN, KING'S OWN YORKSHIRE LIGHT INFANTRY.

PANEL 109 BEGINS: L/CORPL. F.M. BRUCE, KING'S OWN YORKSHIRE LIGHT INFANTRY.

(Panel 109) L/Corpl. 203237, Sydney Stephen Jepson, 1/4th Bn. The King's Own (Yorkshire Light Infantry), (T.F.): *s.* of John Jepson, of 27, Mayfield Grove, Harrogate, by his wife Susannah: *b.* Harrogate, co. York, 7 September 1892: *educ.* Grove Road Board School: joined Yorkshire Dragoons Yeomanry (T.F.), 20 August 1914: transf'd. King's Own Yorkshire Light Infantry, October 1916: served with the Expeditionary Force in France and Flanders from that month: gassed nr. Ypres (1917), and was killed in action by a shell while endeavouring to save the wounded, after the engagement at Dickebusch, 27 April 1918: Age 25. A comrade wrote, "He died a hero's death." He *m.* at Sunderland, in April 1916, Eleanor Marion, *dau.* of Mr and Mrs Messenger, and had a *dau.*, Kathleen, *b.* 22 March 1917.

(Panel 109) Pte. 36078, Walter Adams, 1/4th Bn. The King's Own (Yorkshire Light Infantry), (T.F.): formerly 5/15163, 4th (T.R.) Battn.: *s.* of Jonathan Adams, of Starnhill, Ecclesfield, Sheffield, by his wife Fanny: and yr. brother to Pte. 23865, H. Adams, Duke of Wellington's Regt., killed in action 1 November 1918: enlisted Sheffield. Killed in action 9 October 1917: Age 19.

His brother Henry is buried in Auberchicourt British Cemetery (IV.A.1).

(Panel 109) Pte. 2184, Frederic Bartle, 1/4th Bn. The King's Own (Yorkshire Light Infantry), (T.F.): *s.* of Francis Ernest Bartle, of 12, Burke Street, Bilton, Harrogate, by his wife Laura, *dau.* of Edward Cooke, of Gloucester: *b.* Harrogate, co. York, 25 January 1898: *educ.* Grove Road School: Occupation – Painter's Apprentice: joined King's Own (Yorkshire Light Infantry), 8 October 1915: served with the Expeditionary Force in France and Flanders from October 1917, and was killed in action at Mount Kemmel, 29 April 1918. Buried where he fell. His Commanding Officer wrote: "He was a splendid soldier, and did his duty fearlessly and conscientiously, and was a man whom we could ill afford to lose.": Age 21. *unm.* (*IWGC record 1212184*)

(Panel 109) Pte. 242657, Herbert Butler, 10th (Service) Bn. The King's Own (Yorkshire Light Infantry): brother to Pte. 24612, E. Butler, Duke of Wellington's Regt., who fell 13 April 1918: enlisted Bradford, co. York. Killed in action 4 October 1917: Age 18. All correspondence should be addressed to his brother, Mr F. Butler, 55, Sydenham Place, Bradford.

His brother Edward also has no known grave; he is recorded on Panel 83.

(Panel 109) Pte. 47726, Ernest Albert Collinson, 2nd Bn. (105th Foot) The King's Own (Yorkshire Light Infantry): *s.* of Albert Abraham Collinson, of 26, Gordon Street, The Fall, East Ardsley, Wakefield, by his wife Mildred Mary: *b.* Ardsley, co. York: enlisted Wakefield. Killed in action 8 March 1918, during a counter-attack to retake some lost outposts: Age 19. See Canada Farm Cemetery (III.G.10-13).

PANEL 109 ENDS: PTE. C.J. EATON, KING'S OWN YORKSHIRE LIGHT INFANTRY.

PANEL 110 BEGINS: PTE. H.A. ECCLES, KING'S OWN YORKSHIRE LIGHT INFANTRY.

(Panel 110) Pte. 22091, Robert Fisher, 8th (Service) Bn. The King's Own Yorkshire Light Infantry: *b*. Ledstone: enlisted Normanton. Killed in action 29 September 1917. Remains 'Unknown British Soldier, 8 K.O.Y.L.I., 29.9.17' recovered unmarked collective grave (28.J.20.b.4.7), refers GRU Report – Elverdinghe 25/28E, identified – Clothing, Boots marked 22091; reinterred 26 January 1925. *Known to be buried in Hagle Dump Cemetery, Elverdinghe (IV.D.2).*

(Panel 110) Pte. 39752, Charles George Gellatly, 'A' Coy., 9th (Service) Bn. The King's Own (Yorkshire Light Infantry: *s*. of Isabella Gellatly (43, Allardice Street, Stonehaven, co. Kincardine): *b*. Fetteresso, Stonehaven, *c*.1887. Killed in action 4 November 1917: Age 30.

(Panel 110) Pte. 43899, Albert William Harrold, 8th (Service) Bn. The King's Own (Yorkshire Light Infantry): formerly no.183291, Royal Field Artillery: *s*. of Aldridge Harrold, of Ferry House, East Twerton, Bath, by his wife Lucy E.: *b*. Claverton, nr. Bath, *c*.1897. Killed in action 21 September 1917: Age 20. One of three members of the Bath City Divn. St. John's Ambulance Brigade who gave their lives, he is remembered on the memorial situated in Bath Abbey.

(Panel 110) Pte. 24570, Arthur Edwin Holwell, 8th (Service) Bn. The King's Own Yorkshire Light Infantry: *s*. of Emma Rebecca Holwell (18, Belton Street, Hyson Green, Nottingham): *b*. Nottingham: enlisted there. Killed in action 29 September 1917: Age 21. Remains 'E.M.H., 8 K.O.Y.L.I., 29.9.17' recovered unmarked collective grave (28.J.20.b.4.7), refers GRU Report – Elverdinghe 25/28E, identified – Provenance (believed to be) Shirt marked E.M.H., Numerals; reinterred 26 January 1925. *Known to be buried in Hagle Dump Cemetery (IV.D.3).*

(Panel 110) Pte. 27763, Charles Lapish, 10th (Service) Bn. The King's Own (Yorkshire Light Infantry): *yst. s*. of the late George Lapish, by his wife Mary Ann (36, Clarkson Street, Ravensthorpe, Dewsbury, co. York), *dau*. of J.S. Thompson: *b*. Asselby, co. York, 11 June 1888: *educ*. Mirfield and Heckmondwike: Occupation – Analytical Chemist: enlisted Dewsbury, 29 February 1916: served with the Expeditionary Force in France and Flanders from the following December; killed in action as he was going to the trenches near Polygon Wood 23 October 1917. Buried there. Pte. Lapish was a popular amateur actor: Age 29. *unm*.

(Panel 110) Pte. 35143, Donald MacIntyre, 7th (Service) Bn. The King's Own (Yorkshire Light Infantry): only *s*. of Detective Sergeant John MacIntyre, formerly of Police Buildings, Oban; resident Caledonian Mansions, George Street, Oban; by his wife Margaret Fletcher, *dau*. of John Ferguson: *b*. Kintyre, co. Argyle, 4 April 1894: *educ*. Grammar School, Campbeltown: Occupation – Clerk; Argyleshire Motor Company: enlisted Argyle Mounted Battery, Campbeltown, 20 December 1915: transf'd. Durham Light Infantry, no.5111: served with the Expeditionary Force in France from 2 September 1916, when he was transferred to the King's Own (Yorkshire Light Infantry). Reported missing after the fighting at Langemarck, 16 August 1917; now assumed to have been killed in action on that date. Reported buried near Langemarck Station: Age 23. *unm*.

PANEL 110 ENDS: PTE. T. ODDY, KING'S OWN YORKSHIRE LIGHT INFANTRY.

PANEL 111 BEGINS: PTE. G.H. OLDROYD, KING'S OWN YORKSHIRE LIGHT INFANTRY.

(Panel 111) Pte. 201088, Charles Edward Parrott, 1/4th Bn. The King's Own (Yorkshire Light Infantry), (T.F.): *s*. of Albert Parrott, of 10, John Street, Barnsley: *husb*. to Mary A. (81, Rothery's Yard, Batley Carr, Dewsbury, co. York). Killed in action 14 April 1918: Age 30. "*In Memory of my great-great uncle Charles Edward Parrott .. A dearly missed brave soldier. To live in the hearts of those we leave behind is not forgotten. Claire Hurst, great grand-niece. 16 November 2006.*"

(Panel 111) Pte. 235150, Ernest Sykes Pawson, 6th (Service) Bn. The King's Own (Yorkshire Light Infantry): formerly no.148966, Royal Field Artillery: *s*. of John William Pawson, of 6, Hirst's Yard, Thomas Street, Huddersfield, by his wife Mary: Occupation – Postman: *b*. St. Mark's, Huddersfield.

Killed in action 24 August 1917: Age 31. One of 224 members of Huddersfield & District Post Office Staff who served their country; 20 made the supreme sacrifice.

(Panel 111) Pte. 40328, Frank Cyril Saynor, 9th (Service) Bn. The King's Own (Yorkshire Light Infantry): *yst. s.* of John William Saynor, Silver Engraver; of 41, Cliffe Field Road, Meersbrook Park, Sheffield, by his wife Emma, *dau.* of the late William Cooper, Fork Manufacturer, of Sheffield: and *gdson.*, of the late John Saynor, Steel Merchant, of that place: *b.* Sheffield, co. York, 20 July 1892: *educ.* Duchess Road School: Occupation – Clerk; Messrs Cammell Laird Ltd., Sheffield: volunteered for Active Service, 1915, but owing to the application of his employers he was not immediately called up: enlisted York and Lancaster Regt. May 1916, being subsequently transf'd. Kings Own (Yorkshire Light Infantry): served with the Expeditionary Force in France and Flanders from August 1917, where he saw much fighting, taking part in the operations at Ypres and at Passchendaele, and, later, in the Cambrai offensive. Killed in action at Kemmel Hill 26 April 1918. Buried where he fell: Age 25. Actively interested in athletics, a member of the Duchess Road, and Western Road Gymnastic clubs, he was a member of the teams of eight winners of the National Physical Recreation (Yorkshire) Championships for 1909 and 1912, and Evening Schools Championship, 1911. He *m.* South Street Methodist Church, The Moor, Sheffield, 10 June 1916; Lily (29, Cemetery Avenue, Eccleshall Road, Sheffield), eldest *dau.* of Leopold Arthur Patrick Griffin: *s.p.*

(Panel 111) Pte. 41004, Clarence Sowden, 6th (Service) Bn. The King's (Own Yorkshire Light Infantry): *s.* of Arthur Sowden, of 7, Croft Terrace, Farnley, Leeds, and Phoebe Ann, his spouse: and brother to Gnr. 890, H. Sowden, Royal Field Artillery, died 11 June 1915: *b.* Farnley, afsd.: enlisted York. Killed in action 23 August 1917.

His brother Harold is buried in Ration Farm Military Cemetery, La Chapelle-D'Armentieres (V.C.21).

(Panel 111) Pte. 201962, Harry Wootton, 'W' Coy., 1/4th Bn. The King's Own (Yorkshire Light Infantry), (T.F.): *s.* of Alfred Wootton, of 80, Faith Street, South Kirkby, nr. Wakefield, co. York, by his wife Sarah: *b.* Sandal Magna, Wakefield, 16 January 1898: *educ.* South Kirkby Board School: Occupation – Pony Driver; South Kirkby Colliery: enlisted King's Own Yorkshire Light Infantry, Wakefield, 15 April 1915: served with the Expeditionary Force in France and Flanders, and was killed in action at Ypres, 14 April 1918. Buried where he fell: Age 20. *unm.*

PANEL 111 ENDS: PTE. G.H. YERWORTH, KING'S OWN YORKSHIRE LIGHT INFANTRY.

PANEL 112 BEGINS: CAPT. V.E. POWELL, KING'S SHROPSHIRE LIGHT INFANTRY.

(Panel 112) 2nd Lieut. Edward Meale Hannah, M.C., 1st (53rd Foot) attd. 6th (Service) Bn. The King's (Shropshire Light Infantry): formerly, Pte., Honourable Artillery Coy.: *s.* of Robert Hannah, of 115, Abbey Road, Barrow-in-Furness, by his wife Jessie: and yr. brother to 2nd Lieut. R. Hannah, 7th Royal Irish Rifles, reported missing, later killed in action, 16 August 1917. Died of wounds 16 August 1917. Awarded the Military Cross (1916) for conspicuous gallantry when, during an assault, all the officers had become casualties, he assumed command, consolidated the captured position, put out posts to protect his flank, and by his example was an inspiration to his men: Age 19.

His brother Robert also has no known grave, he is recorded on Panel 138.

(Panel 112) L/Corpl. 14287, John William Prunnell, 7th (Service) Bn. The King's (Shropshire Light Infantry): *s.* of William Prunnell, of 20, Knowsley Avenue, Eccles, Manchester, by his wife Mary Ann: and elder brother to Pte. 10666, H. Prunnell, 2nd Border Regt., killed in action, 26 October 1914; crossroads Zandvoorde, Kruiseecke – Wervicq roads: *b.* Eccles, co. Lancaster: enlisted Bishop's Castle, co. Salop. Killed in action 26 September 1917; Polygon Wood: Age 26. *unm.*

His brother Harry also has no known grave; he is commemorated on the Ypres (Menin Gate) Memorial (Panel 35).

(Panel 112) Pte. 11813, Edwin Austin, 6th (Service) Bn. The King's (Shropshire Light Infantry): *s.* of the late Robert Austin, of Oakengates, co. Salop, by his wife Ellen: and elder brother to Pte. 60573,

H. Austin, Royal Welch Fusiliers, who also fell: *b.* Oakengates, *c.*1889: enlisted Wellington. Killed in action 22 August 1917: Age 28.

His brother Harry also has no known grave; he is commemorated on the Ypres (Menin Gate) Memorial (Panel 22).

(Panel 112) Pte. 201861, William Wallace Bain, 1/4th Bn. The King's (Shropshire Light Infantry), (T.F.): *s.* of the late Pte. 18993, W. Bain, King's (Shropshire Light Infantry), died 2 May 1917, in England; by his wife Mary Jane (45, Coleham, Shrewsbury): *b.* Shrewsbury: enlisted there. Killed in action 19 April 1918: Age 20. *unm.* William and his father are commemorated on the Belle Vue (Holy Trinity) Church War Memorial.

His father Wallace is buried in Shrewsbury General Cemetery (198.4.F).

(Panel 112) Signlr. 200501 John Lilburne Davison, H.Q. Coy., 7th (Service) Bn. The King's (Shropshire Light Infantry): *s.* of the Rev. William Hope Davison, of 545, Chorley Old Road, Bolton, co. Lancaster, M.A., Congregational Minister, by his wife Jessie, *dau.* of James Weir, of Glasgow: and brother to 2nd Lieut. W.H. Davison, 2/32nd Sikh Pioneers, Indian Army, died of enteric fever, Military Hospital, Murree, Punjab, 6 September 1917: *b.* Portobello, Edinburgh, 28 August 1893: *educ.* George Watson's College, and Bolton School: Occupation – Chief Assistant; Astley Bridge Library; afterwards Assistant, Goldsmith's Library, London University: enlisted April 1916: served with the Expeditionary Force in France and Flanders, and was killed in action, 26 September 1917, by shrapnel near Polygon Wood. Buried in an open field near Zonnebeke. His Commanding Officer wrote, "I am grieved to have to tell you of the death of your son in action. It would be idle to attempt to tell you how highly esteemed he was. His noble character, unassuming bearing, intelligence and efficiency in his work soon came to my notice. He was a keen and untiring worker, and a man in the highest sense of the word. I can assure you that his loss is deeply mourned by his fellow-signallers and myself for he was respected and loved by us all. We know that quite recently he had lost a brother; both his comrades and myself tender to you our heartfelt sympathy in this second loss that you have been called upon to bear.": Age 24. *unm.*

The grave of Signaller Davison's brother, 2nd Lieut. William Hope Davison, was subsequently lost; he is commemorated on the Karachi Memorial, Pakistan

(Panel 112) Pte. 23709, Ernest Dyke, 5th (Service) Bn. The King's (Shropshire Light Infantry): *s.* of Sarah Dyke (60, High Street, Albrighton, Wolverhampton): and brother to Pte. 21223, A. Dyke, 1st K.S.L.I., killed in action 23 July 1918: *b.* Albrighton, co. Salop, 1881: enlisted Wolverhampton: served with the Expeditionary Force in France, and was killed in action nr. Inverness Copse, Veldhoek, 19 October 1917. Buried there: Age 36.

His brother Alfred is buried in Raperie British Cemetery, Villemontoire (IIA.E.4).

(Panel 112) Pte. 26542, Robert Jarman Edwards, 6th (Service) Bn. The King's (Shropshire Light Infantry): eldest *s.* of Charles Edwards, Farmer; of Widgeon Hill Farm, Leominster, by his wife Annie Eliza, *dau.* of the late John Jarman, of Rhayader, co. Radnor: *b.* Upper Hamnish, Leominster, 15 February 1893: *educ.* Queen Elizabeth's Grammar School, Bromyard: Occupation – Farmer: joined Shropshire Yeomanry, February 1915: served with the Expeditionary Force in France and Flanders from October 1916, transf'd. King's Shropshire Light Infantry, and was killed in action by Bird House, nr. Langemarck, north-east of Ypres, 20 September 1917. His Platoon Commander wrote, "He was shot by a German machine gun while advancing in the attack of 20 September. He was a very good fellow, and worked hard in his platoon.": Age 24. *unm.*

(Panel 112) Pte. 21623, Thomas Henry Farman, 5th (Service) Bn. The King's (Shropshire Light Infantry): *yst. s.* of Thomas Henry Farman, of 10, Middle Craig, Stirling, School Janitor, by his wife Elizabeth, *dau.* of Leslie Neilson, of Stirling: *b.* Stirling, 3 September 1896: *educ.* Craigs Public School: Occupation – Despatch Clerk: joined A.S.C., Bandsman, 14 August 1915: transf'd. South Wales Borderers, May 1917; served with the Expeditionary Force in France transf'd. King's Shropshire Light Infantry from August 1917, and was killed in action, nr. Ypres, 19 October following. Buried nr. Inverness Copse, Veldhoek, east-south-east of Ypres: Age 21. *unm.*

At zero hour, 22 August 1917, after advancing in small sections through Inverness Copse, and successfully reaching all their objectives, with the exception of their right flank, 'A' and 'B' Coys., 5th Shropshire Light Infantry, were denied further progress in order to connect with 43rd Brigade who were held up by machine gun fire from 'L'Farm. Within five minutes all the officers of the right company had become casualties, and only one junior officer remained with the left company. By the time this information reached the Commanding Officer at Battalion H.Q. 'D' and 'C' Coys. had begun their advance and before further orders could be issued the battalion effectiveness had been reduced by over 25 percent casualties, due to considerable opposition being encountered from machine gun fire. With an enemy counter-attack anticipated, the Shropshires were ordered to dig in and hold their positions and, at 4.30am. the following morning, a heavy enemy attack was launched against 43rd Brigade. Only on the extreme right were the Shropshires able to take any part in repelling it; 'considerable execution in the enemy ranks being done by our Lewis Gunners.' The casualty report stated – 1 officer, and 19 other ranks killed, 4 officers and 107 other ranks wounded, 12 other ranks missing. Among the missing:

(Panel 112) Pte. 26156, William Monnery, 5th (Service) Bn. The King's (Shropshire Light Infanry): 3rd *s.* of William Monnery, of Pullenburry Cottages, Grinstead Lane, Lancing, Market Gardener, by his wife Mary: and brother to Pte. 18431, H. Monnery, 3rd Coldstream Guards, killed in action nr. Poelcapelle, 9 October 1917: *b.* Sompting, co. Sussex, November 1891: previously served with Sherwood Foresters (no.5160): on the outbreak of war, in August 1914, was on the Reserve, in the employ of Messrs H. and A. Pullen-Burry: reported to his old regiment on mobilisation: subsequently went to France, transf'd. King's Shropshire Light Infantry, August 1916; reported missing, believed killed in action after the fighting nr. Hooge, 22 August 1917. Age 25. *unm.*

His brother Harry also has no known grave; he is recorded on Panel 10.

(Panel 112) Pte. 26454, Samuel Thelwall, 5th (Service) Bn. The King's (Shropshire Light Infantry): formerly no.4662, Cheshire Regt. (T.F.): *s.* of Charles Thelwall, of 29, St. James Terrace, Hollins Lane, Marple, Stockport, co. Chester, by his wife Hannah Maria: and yr. brother to Pte. 34742, F.J. Thelwall, 10th Cheshire Regt., died 28 July 1916, of wounds: *b.* Marple: enlisted Cheshire T.F., Hyde, 1916: proceeded to France with a draft of reinforcements, transf'd. King's Shropshire L.I. Reported missing 25 October 1917, following the battalion's relief from the front line on the night of the 24th: Age 20. *unm.*

His brother Frederick is buried in Gezaincourt Communal Cemetery Extension (II.B.3).

PANEL 112 ENDS: PTE. B. TIPTON, KING'S SHROPSHIRE LIGHT INFANTRY.

PANEL 113 BEGINS: PTE. R. TONG, KING'S SHROPSHIRE LIGHT INFANTRY.

(Panel 113) Major Stanley Preston, 1st Bn. (57th Foot) The Duke of Cambridge's Own (Middlesex Regt.): *yr. s.* of Lieut.Col. Alfred Charles Preston, of 8, Milverton Road, Brondesbury Park, V.D., by his wife Clara, *dau.* of Lieut.Col. John Holt: *b.* Hampstead, London, N.W., 7 June 1882: *educ.* Aldenham School: gazetted 2nd Lieut. 5th Bn. (Tower Hamlets Militia) Rifle Brigade (Prince Consort's Own) 20 May 1905: exchanged into 3rd (Militia) Bn. East Yorkshire Regt.: received his commission Regular Army, gazetted 2nd Lieut., 4th Middlesex Regt., 17 May 1906: went to India; transf'd. 1st Battn. there: was on the Embarkation Staff for the Abor Expedition; also during H.M. King George's visit to India in 1912 (Durbar Coronation Medal) seconded, 7 March 1913, apptd. Adjt., 1st Calcutta Volunteer Rifles: promoted Capt. September 1914: on the outbreak of war he raised two extra European Volunteer Battns., returned to England, July 1915: served with the Expeditionary Force in France and Flanders, being placed on the Staff, 5 August: apptd. D.A.A. and Q.M.G., 32nd Divn., 6 December 1916: rejoined his battalion 17 February following; gazetted Acting Major the following month, and was killed in action near Polygon Wood, Ypres, 25 September 1917. Buried where he fell: Age 35. His Commanding Officer wrote, "…was respected and esteemed by all ranks, and died fighting for his country." Mentioned in Despatches by his Staff Colonel. He *m.* Aden, 27 January 1913; Amy ('Beachy,' Darley Road, Eastbourne), *dau.* of the late Rev. Henry Sells, and had a son Hugh de Grave Westbury, *b.* 26 August 1916. (*IWGC record 12th Bn.*)

(Panel 113) 2nd Lieut. George William Graham, M.M., 6th (Reserve) Bn. The Duke of Cambridge's Own (Middlesex Regt.) attd. 2/5th (Territorial) Bn. The Lancashire Fusiliers: *s.* of the late Thomas Graham, of Whitefield: *b.* Whitefield, co. Lancaster, 31 July 1887: *educ.* All Saint's School: enlisted Middlesex Regt., 8 September 1914: served with the Expeditionary Force in France and Flanders, taking part in many engagements: gassed and invalided home, April 1916: received a commission, gazetted 2nd Lieut., 6th Middlesex Regt., July 1917: joined his battalion in France, August following, attd. Lancashire Fusiliers, and was killed in action east of Ypres 20 September 1917. Buried at Langemarck: Age 30. His Commanding Officer, Col. G. Brighton, wrote, "He faced death as a true soldier, and was a very gallant and just officer, most courteous and ready to assist in every way. He will be missed much by one and all, and his battalion greatly deplores his death, for he was very popular with all ranks." Mentioned in Despatches (and commended for good work on the Somme), and awarded the Military Medal for 'gallant and distinguished service in the field.' He *m.* St. Andrew's Church, Catford, London, S.E., 26 June 1915; Winnifred (29, Portland Road, Hove, co. Sussex), 3rd *dau.* of Willian Huntley Hughes: *s.p.*

(Panel 113) 2nd Lieut. Gordon Mackay, 24th (Reserve) Bn. The Duke of Cambridge's Own (Middlesex Regt.) attd 44th Coy., Machine Gun Corps (Inf.): *s.* of the late Eric Mackay, by his wife Mary (47, Schubert Road, Putney, London, S.W.), *dau.* of the late James Gordon, of Edinburgh: *b.* 13 March 1894: *educ.* Moyle's School, Putney Hill, London, S.W., and King's College School, Wimbledon, London, S.W.: was on the staff of the British Linen Bank: joined Artists' Cadet Corps, November 1915, and excelled as a Musketry Instructor: obtained a commission Middlesex Regt., July 1916; transf'd. Machine Gun Corps, January 1917: served with the Expeditionary Force in France and Flanders from 31 March following, and was killed in action 16 August 1917. Buried there. His Colonel wrote, "He was very keen on his work, and was an excellent young officer. Young soldiers who went through their musketry courses with him were perfectly devoted to him.": Age 23. *unm.*

(Panel 113) Corpl. TF/200402, Samuel Gant, 1/7th Bn. The Duke of Cambridge's Own (Middlesex Regt.), (T.F.): 3rd *s.* of James Frederick Gant, of 72, Percival Road, Bush Hill Park, Enfield, by his wife Emily Ann, *dau.* of Ann Jenkins, of London: *b.* Enfield, co. Middlesex, 22 August 1896: *educ.* there: volunteered for Active Service on the outbreak of war, joined Middlesex Regt., August 1914: served in Gibraltar, also with the Expeditionary Force in France and Flanders from 28 July 1915; killed in action at Ypres 16 August 1917. Buried where he fell. His Commanding Officer wrote, "…Corpl. Gant. was one of my best N.C.O.'s, and his loss is keenly felt by officers and men. He was a splendid fellow, always ready, willing and cheerful.": Age 20. *unm.*

(Panel 113) Pte. TF/242337, Francis Charles Brown, 1/8th Bn. The Duke of Cambridge's Own (Middlesex Regt.), (T.F.): *s.* of James Brown, of Black Hall, Berkeley, co. Gloucester, by his wife Elizabeth: *husb.* to Georgina Eleanor Brown (Parsonage Street, Dursley), brother-in-law to Margaret E. Brown (Severn House Cottages, Clapton, Berkeley), and brother to Pte. 23018, A.E. Brown, 1st Gloucestershire Regt., killed in action 24 August 1916, aged 26 years: *b.* Berkeley: enlisted Bristol. Killed in action, 16 August 1917: Age 30. Dedicated 'Greater Love Hath No Man Than This That A Man Lay Down His Life For His Friends,' the brothers Brown are remembered on the Berkeley (St. Mary's) Church War Memorial.

His brother Albert also has no known grave; he is commemorated on the Thiepval Memorial, Somme.

PANEL 113 ENDS: PTE. W. BUTTON, MIDDLESEX REGT.

PANEL 114 BEGINS: PTE. G. BYRNE, MIDDLESEX REGT.

(Panel 114) Pte. TF/292437, Reginald Thomas Draper, Trench Mortar Bty., attd. 3/10th Bn. The Duke of Cambridge's Own (Middlesex Regt.), (T.F.): eldest *s.* of Thomas Draper, of 4, Park View, Ringwood, Railway Porter, by his wife Ada, *dau.* of Alfred James Upward: *b.* Ringwood, co. Hants, 9 April 1897: *educ.* National School, Ringwood: Occupation – Tailor: enlisted 26 April 1916: served with the Expeditionary

Force in France from May 1917, and was killed in action 5 October following. Buried in Eagle Trench, between Langemarck and Poelcappelle.: Age 20. *unm.*

(Panel 114) Pte. G/11473, Ernest William Godwin, 16th (Service) Bn. The Duke of Cambridge's Own (Middlesex Regt.): *s.* of the late Benjamin Godwin, by his wife Annie (64, North Grove, St. Ann's Road, Tottenham, London, N.), *dau.* of John Burt: *b.* Tottenham, 23 December 1896: *educ.* Seven Sisters Road County School: volunteered for Active Service, and enlisted Middlesex Regt., 14 December 1915: served with the Expeditionary Force in France and Flanders from May 1916, and was killed in action at Langemarck, 1 October 1917. Buried where he fell: Age 20. *unm.*

(Panel 114) Pte. G/71207, Robert James, 16th (Service) Bn. The Duke of Cambridge's Own (Middlesex Regt.): *s.* of John James: *b.* Sevenoaks, co. Kent, 1894: enlisted Royal West Surrey Regt. (no.G/32179), Kingston-on-Thames: served with the Expeditionary Force in France and Flanders from 1916; killed in action 5 October 1917: Age 23. At the beginning of October 1917, during the Third Battle of Ypres, 16th Middlesex were in the front line at Langemarck. On 3 – 4 October, part of the battalion was attached to 1st Battn. Royal Dublin Fusiliers for an offensive operation, which jointly suffered 35 killed (33, Royal Dublin Fusiliers), mostly from enemy shellfire. He leaves a widow Rose (27, Queen's Road, Mitcham, co. Surrey). See also L/Corpl. E.H. Hodges, Bedford House Cemetery (VIII.B.25/Enc.No.4)

(Panel 114) Pte. TF/293037, Alfred 'Alf' Payne, 3/10th Bn. The Duke of Cambridge's Own (Middlesex Regt.), (T.F.): late of Manor Park, co. Essex: *s.* of F. (& Mrs) Payne, of Haverhill, co. Suffolk: and brother to Pte. 242031, C.A. Payne, Northumberland Fusiliers, killed in action 26 October 1917; and Pte. 33394, F. Payne, Yorkshire Regt., killed in action, 27 September 1917: enlisted Stratford, co. Essex. Killed in action 4 October 1917.

His brothers Charlie and Fred also have no known grave; they are commemorated on Panels 22 and 53 respectively.

PANEL 114 ENDS: PTE. J.H. PINK, MIDDLESEX REGT.

PANEL 115 BEGINS: PTE. J. PIVODA, MIDDLESEX REGT.

(Panel 115) Pte. TF/202055, Ralph Leonard Saunders, 'D' Coy., 1/7th Bn. The Duke of Cambridge's Own (Middlesex Regt.), (T.F.): only *s.* of John Saunders, of 45, Maldon Road, Lower Edmonton, by his wife Mary Jane, *dau.* of John Smith, of Gobsor Farm, Honiton, co. Devon: *b.* Stoke Newington, London, N., 5 October 1892: *educ.* Lower Edmonton Latymer School, there: joined Middlesex Regt., 24 January 1916: served with the Expeditionary Force in France and Flanders from 29 November following: took part in the fierce fighting around Arras, and was killed in action at Polygon Wood 16 August 1917. His Platoon Commander wrote, "We moved forward under terrific artillery fire, and your son was struck by a piece of shell, and died instantaneously. He was both a good and brave soldier, and much missed by us all," and another officer, "He was a good soldier and a very brave one too, and we can ill afford to lose such a man.": Age 24. *unm.*

(Panel 115) 2nd Lieut. Ebeneezer Charleston, 11th (Service) Bn. The King's Royal Rifle Corps: *s.* of William John Charleston, of 8, May Terrace, Plymouth, by his wife Elizabeth Eva: and nephew of the Hon. D.M. Charleston, Senator of the Australian Parliament: *b.* Plymouth, 26 June 1881: *educ.* Plympton Grammar School: was a Teacher, Camel's Head Boys' School, Devonport: enlisted 3 June 1916; joined O.T.C., Christ's College, Cambridge, October following: obtained a commission, March 1917: served with the Expeditionary Force in France and Flanders from 5 April, and was killed in action at Langemarck 20 September 1917. Buried there: Age 36. His Commanding Officer wrote, "On 20 September the battalion took part in a big attack. Your husband was leading his platoon on the right of the front line. Shortly after the start we came up against a very strong German position, which was undamaged by our artillery, and which was held by six machine guns. Your husband most gallantly led two attacks against the position. In the first attack he was hit on the body, but his steel plate saved him. In the second attack he was hit by a bullet in the head and killed instantly. His conduct was most gallant and he died like a real rifleman, doing his utmost in a most difficult and trying position. Your husband's splendid conduct will always be remembered by me, and it certainly greatly assisted." He *m*. Plymouth, 26 December 1911; Ernestine ('Greenbank,'Saltash), *dau*. of Charles Limpenny, and had two sons; Edmund Vivian, *b*. 7 November 1912 and Eustace David, *b*. 1 March 1916.

(Panel 115) 2nd Lieut. John Low, 13th (Service) Bn. The King's Royal Rifle Corps: *s*. of William Low, of Balquhindochy, Turriff, co. Aberdeen, Farmer, by his wife Jane, *dau*. of Andrew Gammie: *b*. Balquhindochy, *afsd*., 1 November 1894: *educ*. Turriff Higher Grade School, and Gordons College, Aberdeen: joined 4th (Territorial) Battn. Gordon Highlanders, 19 October 1914: served with the Expeditionary Force in France and Flanders, from February 1915: returned home January 1917, and after a period of training at Aldershot gazetted 2nd Lieut., King's Royal Rifle Corps, 30 August 1917: returned to France, October following, and was killed in action at Circus Point, nr. Ypres, 10 January 1918. Brigadier-General S.G. Francis wrote, "I had frequently noticed the splendid work he had been doing. He seems to have been absolutely fearless, and the reports sent in by him were always accurate and reliable. He set a splendid example to his men, and they would have followed him anywhere. His reputation here is one that you may be proud of. He will be greatly missed in his battalion and in the brigade;" and his Commanding Officer, "My admiration for your boy was intense. I was devoted to him, and so were all those who had the privilege of knowing him well, and it is with grief, only surpassed by your own, that I can tell you the story of how he fell. He had not long joined my battalion before I realised his capability, and, as is always the case, the best are always selected for the undertakings which demand resource, determination and courage, all of which attributes he possessed in a very high degree. He was put in command of a raiding party, which was to operate against a strong enemy position; the enterprise had every aspect of complete success, mainly due to the valuable information he had brought back after having, on three separate occasions, patrolled right up to and into the enemy's wire under the nose of a German sentry. On the night of the raid he led his party up to the German wire, a distance of over five hundred yards from our outposts; there, owing to casualties, he had to reorganise the party, which had previously each been allocated definite tasks; this he did without attracting the attention of the enemy. On the prearranged signal he led the assault on the main pill-box. Unfortunately some of the shells fired by the artillery, which was co-operating in the enterprise, fell short, and some of the groups of the party were temporarily disorganised. He, however, led on, and when within close range of the pill-box, his way was barred by a German, who was firing a machine gun from his hip without pause, your son, smashing a bomb into his face, and following it with a revolver bullet, reached the entrance to the pill-box, and called on the garrison to surrender. He got no answer, so he threw a bomb in. Then, acting on his instructions to obtain prisoners, though he still got no assurance that they were ready to surrender, he plunged into the pill-box. Most were prepared to yield, but the leader, treacherously hiding behind a man who had his hands up, diverted his attention by a trick; this man shouted out in excellent English, "Look out, Sir, there is another behind you!" Your boy turned round and he shot him; I believe, through the neck. He fell and those in the pill-box with him say he was dead. In the excitement of the moment they could not tell absolutely definitely, as their examination of him could not be thorough. But, he appeared lifeless, and I am afraid the shock of a revolver bullet at point-blank range in a vital spot must have proved fatal. His courage was magnificent, and ranks with any which has been displayed in this war. I have furnished the General with a full report of this," and the Second in Command: "We had no such officer. His utter fearlessness, his great skill in scouting, his power with his men who almost worshipped him, were all enhanced and set off by his gentleness." Mentioned in Despatches by F.M. Sir Douglas Haig (*London Gazette*, 24 May 1918) for 'gallant and distinguished services in the field.' Age 23. *unm*.

(Panel 115) Coy.Q.M.Sergt. A/509, Sidney Ellis, M.M., 7th (Service) Bn. The King's Royal Rifle Corps: *b*. St. Saviour's, York: enlisted Marylebone, London. Killed in action by the bursting of a shell 15 October 1917. See Coy.Q.M.Sergt. E.R. Johnson, Lijssenthoek Military Cemetery (XXI.H.6).

(Panel 115) Coy.Q.M.Sergt. A/1259, William Herbert Stannard, 7th (Service) Bn. The King's Royal Rifle Corps: late of Tooting, London, S.W.: enlisted there. Killed in action by the bursting of a shell 15 October 1917. See Coy.Q.M.Sergt. E.R. Johnson, Lijssenthoek Military Cemetery (XXI.H.6).

(Panel 115) Sergt. A/3723, Walter Clapham, 10th (Service) Bn. The King's Royal Rifle Corps: s. of Walter Clapham, of 20, Suffolk Road, Sheffield, co. York, by his wife Sarah: *b.* St. Mary's, Sheffield, *c.* 1888: enlisted Sheffield. Killed on the evening of 19 September 1917, by a shell which landed on the Battalion Headquarters dugout east of Langemarck: Age 29. Lieut.Col. Rixon, Comd'g. 10th Battn., Capt. Wallington (Adjt), and seven other men were also killed. Sergt. Clapham leaves a widow, Annie (191, Granville Street, Park, Sheffield).

Lieut.Col. T.M. Rixon, M.C., is buried in Poelcapelle British Cemetery (XLVII.F.17). Capt. G.S. Wallington is also commemorated there (Sp.Mem.7).

PANEL 115 ENDS: SERGT. J.C. THORNE, KING'S ROYAL RIFLE CORPS.

PANEL 116 BEGINS: SERGT. G.H. WOOLBARD, KING'S ROYAL RIFLE CORPS.

(Panel 116) Rfn. R/23175, Edgar James Harold Allen, 10th (Service) Bn. The King's Royal Rifle Corps: *s.* of Maria Allen (44, Richford Road, Portway, West Ham): *b.* Bow, London, E.: enlisted Stratford. Killed in action 19 September 1917, east of Langemarck; his Commanding Officer, the Adjutant and seven other men were also killed: Age 21. (*SDGW record R/24175*)

(Panel 116) Rfn. R/10794, Alfred Bourton, 10th (Service) Bn. The King's Royal Rifle Corps: *s.* of Edward Bourton, of Limehouse, London, E.: enlisted St. Paul's Churchyard. Killed in action 19 September 1917, 10th Battn. H.Qdrs., east of Langemarck: Age 39. He leaves a widow, Marguerite (16, Queen's Street, Leytonstone, London), and family.

(Panel 116) Rfn. R/31797, Horace Charles Brazie, 8th (Service) Bn. The King's Royal Rifle Corps: *s.* of the late James Brazie, by his wife Alice Mary: *b.* Hackney, London, E., 23 August 1881: *educ.* Stockwell, London, S.W.: enlisted 8 August 1916: served with the Expeditionary Force in France and died at Passchendaele, 26 December 1917, of wounds received in action there: Age 36. The Chaplain wrote, "I knew your husband personally, and had an admiration for his thoughtful openness; he was one of the happiest of the company." He *m.* Marylebone, 8 June 1908; Lois (63, Algernon Road, Lewisham, London), *dau.* of George Irons, and had two daughters, Olive Lois, *b.* 31 December 1910 and Gertrude, *b.* 10 June 1915. (*IWGC record Brazil*)

PANEL 116 ENDS: RFN. W.H. CAMPBELL, KING'S ROYAL RIFLE CORPS.

PANEL 117 BEGINS: RFN. R.M. CANHAM, KING'S ROYAL RIFLE CORPS.

(Panel 117) Rfn. R/21620, Walter James Castro, 9th (Service) Bn. The King's Royal Rifle Corps: *s.* of Henry Castro, of Homerton, London, by his wife Laura Sophie: and brother to Rfn. R/21621, W.F. Castro, K.R.R.C., who fell the same day: *b.* Shoreditch, 1882: enlisted Hackney Baths. Killed in action 23 August 1917: Age 35.

His brother William also has no known grave; he is recorded below.

(Panel 117) Rfn. R/21621, William Frederick Castro, 9th (Service) Bn. The King's Royal Rifle Corps: *s.* of Henry Castro, of Homerton, London, by his wife Laura Sophie: and brother to Rfn. R/21620, W.J. Castro, K.R.R.C., who fell the same day: *b.* Hackney: enlisted Hackney Baths. Killed in action 23 August 1917.

His brother Walter also has no known grave; he is recorded above.

(Panel 117) Rfn. A/202949, Frederick Thomas John Cattle, 17th (Service) Bn. (British Empire League) The King's Royal Rifle Corps: formerly T/492, Royal Army Service Corps: late of Taunton St. James: *s.* of Edward Cattle, of 6, All Saints Terrace, Bridgwater, co. Somerset, by his wife Sarah: and yr. brother to A/B. J24374, W.E. Cattle, HMS 'Acasta,' R.N., died 22 December 1917 when that ship, operating as escort in the Norwegian Sea, was sunk by the German 'Scharnhorst' and 'Gniesenau': enlisted Bridgwater. Killed in action 18 November 1917: Age 19.

With no known grave but the sea, his brother Wyndham is commemorated on the Plymouth Naval Memorial (21).

(Panel 117) Rfn. 13060, Christopher Denham Cobbett, 13th (Service) Bn. The King's Royal Rifle Corps: *s.* of William Cobbett, of 66, Market Place, Henley-on-Thames, by his wife Susan: and yr. brother to Pte. 201735, F.T. Cobbett, 1/4th Oxford & Bucks Light Infantry, killed in action, 13 August 1916, aged 21: *b.* Henley, afsd.: enlisted Aldershot. Killed in action 1 October 1917: Age 19.

His brother Frank also has no known grave; he is commemorated on the Thiepval Memorial.

(Panel 117) Rfn. A/200533, Charles Henry Cocker, 11th (Service) Bn. The King's Royal Rifle Corps: formerly no.5587, 3rd London Regt.: *b.* Huddersfield, co. York: Occupation – Postman: enlisted London. Killed in action 20 September 1917. One of 224 members of Huddersfield and District Post Office Staff who served their country; 20 made the supreme sacrifice.

(Panel 117) Rfn. R/2676, Enoch Cowell, 10th (Service) Bn. The King's Royal Rifle Corps: *s.* of Ishmael Cowell, of 40, Cliff Street, Rishton, Blackburn, co. Lancaster, and Selina, his spouse: *b.* Rishton, afsd.: enlisted Blackburn. Killed in action 19 September 1917, in company with his commanding officer, the adjutant, and seven other men, by a shell which landed on the Battalion Headquarters dugout: Age 21.

(Panel 117) Rfn. 5/5016, George Albert Fowler, 11th (Service) Bn. The King's Royal Rifle Corps: *s.* of George Fowler, of 130, Elsley Road, Battersea, London, by his marriage to the late Regenda Fowler: and elder brother to Pte. 9106, C.W. Fowler, Coldstream Guards, who fell 21 October 1914, at St. Julien: enlisted Battersea, September 1914: served with the Expeditionary Force, and was killed in action 20 September 1917: Age 19.

His brother Charles also has no known grave; he is commemorated on the Ypres (Menin Gate) Memorial (Panel 11).

(Panel 117) Rfn. R/33827, George Edward Ford, 17th (Service) Bn. The King's Royal Rifle Corps: *s.* of the late Henry Ford, Clerk, by his wife Mary Anne, *dau.* of the late William Hawkes, of Dover: *b.* Hounslow, co. Middlesex, 2 August 1887: *educ.* Cambridge Schools, Twickenham: was employed by Mr A.L. Graham, Dairyman, of Belvedere: enlisted King's Royal Rifle Corps, 29 May 1916: served with the Expeditionary Force in France and Flanders from 24 October following; killed in action nr. Ypres 18 April 1918. Buried on the crest of the Wytschaete Ridge: Age 30. He *m.* Christ Church, Deptford, London, S.E., 29 June 1913; Alice Elizabeth (1, Standard Road, Belvedere, co. Kent), *dau.* of the late John Hurley, and had two children, John Henry, *b.* 26 May 1914 and Joan Ellen, *b.* 28 February 1916.

(Panel 117) Rfn. A/201577, Robert Harold Fretwell, 20th (Service) Bn. The King's Royal Rifle Corps: *s.* of Robert John Fretwell, of 24, Queen's Gate Street, Hull, Elementary School Teacher, by his wife Agnes Ann, *dau.* of Samuel Decent: *b.* Hull, co. York, 22 October 1882: *educ.* St. George's R.C. School, there: Occupation – London Newsagent: joined K.R.R.C., February 1917: served with the Expeditionary Force in France from May, and was killed in action near St. Julien 16 October following. Buried in the German Cemetery nr. Langemarck: Age 34. Rifleman Fretwell was an enthusiastic worker in the North London Branch of the London and Provincial Newsagents' Association. He *m.* in London, 12 June 1909, Mary Lillian (370, Essex Road, Islington, London, N.), *dau.* of William Ridley, and had three sons, Ernest, *b.* 19 May 1910, Stanley, *b.* 12 January 1913, and Sydney, *b.* 27 September 1916.

(Panel 117) Rfn. A/201848, Henry Greaves, 18th (Service) Bn. The King's Royal Rifle Corps: *s.* of the late Henry Greaves, by his wife Maria: *b.* Sheffield, co. York, 16 January 1886: *educ.* there: Occupation – Checker; Vinegar Works: twice rejected for Active Service as medically unfit, eventually passed, and enlisted King's Royal Rifle Corps, 1 March 1917: served with the Expeditionary Force in France and Flanders, and was killed in action 19 September 1917: Age 31. His Commanding Officer, 2nd Lieut. E.G. Math, wrote, "He was a thorough and competent soldier, and did his duty well." He *m.* St. Paul's Church, Birmingham, 16 April 1906; Edith (52, Alpha Square, Walworth, London, S.E.), *dau.* of Alfred Turner, and fathered three children.

(Panel 117) Rfn. R/13892, Alfred Helme, 10th (Service) Bn. The King's Royal Rifle Corps: *s.* of James Helme, of 17, Worcester Street, Barrow-in-Furness, by his wife Sarah: *b.* Barrow, co. Lancaster: enlisted there: killed in action 19 September 1917; Battalion Hqdrs., east of Langemarck: Age 22. *unm*. Lieut.Col. T.M. Rixon, M.C., and Capt. (Adjt) G.S. Wallington were also killed.

Lieut.Col. Rixon is buried in Poelcapelle British Cemetery (XLVII.F.17); Capt. Wallington, commemorated therein (Sp.Mem.7).

(Panel 117) Rfn. Y/548, Walter Frederick John Hill, 7th (Service) Bn. The King's Royal Rifle Corps: *s*. of John Hill, of 191, Cattell Road, Small Heath, Birmingham, by his wife Rose Helena, *dau*. of William Wilson: *b*. Birmingham, 28 October 1892: *educ*. Tilton Road County Council Schools: enlisted 31 August 1914: served with the Expeditionary Force in France and Flanders from 13 October 1915: wounded at Loos, 5 March 1916, and invalided home: returned to France on recovery October following, and was killed in action at Ypres 27 August 1917. Buried there. His Commanding Officer wrote, "He was always bright and willing, and a very good soldier," and a comrade, "He was so brave and fearless, doing several brave deeds, but was never noticed, and everyone saying they could not speak too highly of him.": Age 24. *unm*.

PANEL 117 ENDS: RFN. C.H. JOHNSON, KING'S ROYAL RIFLE CORPS.

PANEL 118 BEGINS: RFN. F.W. JOHNSON, KING'S ROYAL RIFLE CORPS.

(Panel 118) Rfn. R/34343, James Lindop, 11th (Service) Bn. The King's Royal Rifle Corps: formerly no.TR/13/38875, and S/24722, Rifle Brigade: *s*. of S.V. (& F.L.) Lindop, of 68, Poole's Park, Finsbury Park, London: and brother to Pte. S/1757, W.J.A. Lindop, 2nd Royal Fusiliers, who fell 20 April 1917: *b*. Holloway, *c*.1897: enlisted there. Killed in action 20 September 1917: Age 20. *unm*.

His brother William also has no known grave, he is commemorated on the Arras Memorial (Bay 3).

(Panel 118) Rfn. R/14127, Wilfred Henry Moore, 12th (Service) Bn. The King's Royal Rifle Corps: *s*. of John William Moore, of 8, Jackson Street, Baldock, co. Hertford, by his wife Grace Mary: and brother to Pte. 43177, S.W. Moore, 6th Northamptonshire Regt., killed in action, 3 May 1917, at Arras: *b*. Chatteris, co. Cambridge: enlisted Hitchin. Killed in action 16 August 1917: Age 20. *unm*.

His brother Sidney also has no known grave, he is commemorated on the Arras Memorial (Bay 7).

(Panel 118) Rfn. R/6890, Charles Henry Newbon, 7th (Service) Bn. The King's Royal Rifle Corps: *s*. of James Newbon, of 60, Wise Street, Dresden, by his wife Hannah: Occupation – Coal Miner; Florence Colliery: enlisted October 1914. Killed in action 22 December 1917. In a letter to Rfn. Newbon's mother his Captain said, "He was acting as my servant at the time, and we were going up to the trenches when a shell fell very near to us and your son was killed instantly. I have known him for over a year now and he was one of the best men and soldiers in the Battalion. It is all the sadder as he would have been going home on leave about this time had he lived. Mr MacGregor to whom he was previously servant will be very much grieved I am sure when he learns of your sons death. All the officers and men are very sorry to lose him.": Age 27. *unm*.

(Panel 118) Rfn. R/32282, James Orams, 21st (Service) Bn. (Yeoman Rifles) The King's Royal Rifle Corps: *s*. of Arthur Robert Orams, of 34, Hubbard Street, West Ham, London, by his wife Sarah Ann: and brother to Gnr. 53008, C.W. Orams, 80th Bde. Royal Field Artillery, killed in action 8 December 1915; and Pte. 17537, S.F. Orams, 2nd Grenadier Guards, died of wounds, 10 November 1916: *b*. Stratford, London, E.: enlisted there. Died of wounds 20 September 1917: Age 19.

His brother Charles is buried in Divisional Cemetery (J.9). Samuel is buried in Etaples Military Cemetery (VII.A.3).

(Panel 118) Rfn. 12833, Frank Page, 7th (Service) Bn. The King's Royal Rifle Corps: *s*. of Frederick Page, of 6, Prospect Terrace, Baldock, co. Hertford, by his wife Annie Isaline: and yr. brother to Sergt. 3/6527, A.E. Page, 1st Bedfordshire Regt., died 18 June 1918, of wounds: *b*. Clothal, co. Hertford, *c*.1898: enlisted Luton, co. Bedford. Killed in action 9 December, 1917: Age 19.

His brother Alfred is buried in Aire Communal Cemetery (III.C.26).

(Panel 118) Rfn. R/31615, Pte. G/9746, John Robert Perry, 12th (Service) Bn. The King's Royal Rifle Corps: *s.* of the late William Perry, by his wife Sarah (110, Bridge Road West, Battersea, London): and twin brother to Pte. G/9746, G.E. Perry, 10th Queen's (Royal West Surrey Regt.), killed one month later (22 September): *b.* 1881: enlisted Battersea. Killed in action 16 August 1917: Age 36. Rfn. Perry's widow, Ellen Catherine, is currently resident with the deceased's parents at the family home Battersea.

His brother George also has no known grave; he is recorded on Panel 16.

(Panel 118) Rfn. R/25402, Henry Piller, 'A' Coy., 10th (Service) Bn. The King's Royal Rifle Corps: *s.* of George Piller, and Hannah Maria, his wife: *b.* Shadwell, London: enlisted Stepney. Killed in action east of Langemarck on the evening of 19 September 1917, by a shell which landed on the Battalion Headquarters dug-out: Age 33. He was married to Ellen Mary Sinclair, *née* Piller (32, Commodore Street, Stepney Green, London, E.1). Lieut. Col. T.M. Rixon, M.C., Officer Comdg'g. 10th Battn., his Adjutant, Capt. G.S. Wallington, Sergt. W. Clapham, Rfn. E.J. Allen, A. Bourton, E. Cowell, A. Helme, J. Razzall, and R/2637, J. Smith were also killed.

Lieut. Col. Rixon is buried in Poelcapelle British Cemetery (LXVII.F.17), Capt. Wallington commemorated therein. The eight other ranks killed all have no known grave, Sergt. W. Clapham, Rfn. E.J. Allen, A. Bourton, E. Cowell, A. Helme, are commemorated above, Rfn.J. Razzall and R/2637, J. Smith, below.

(Panel 118) Rfn. R/17162, John Razzall, 10th (Service) Bn. The King's Royal Rifle Corps: formerly no.S/22876, The Rifle Brigade: *s.* of William Razzall, of 83, Rosslyn Crescent, Wealdstone, and Jane Razzall, his spouse: *b.* Brighton, co. Sussex: enlisted Harrow. Killed in action 19 September 1917: Age 22. *unm.* See Rfn. H. Piller, above.

PANEL 118 ENDS: RFN. C.W. SHEERER, KING'S ROYAL RIFLE CORPS.

PANEL 119 BEGINS: RFN. H.E. SHELBROOKE, KING'S ROYAL RIFLE CORPS.

(Panel 119) Rfn. R/2637, James Smith, 10th (Service) Bn. The King's Royal Rifle Corps: late of Margate, co. Kent: *husb.* to Ellen Mary Smith (106, Clayton Grove, Margravine Road, Hammersmith, London, W.6): *b.* Higham, co. Kent: enlisted Fulham. Killed in action 19 September 1917: Age 33. See Rfn. H. Piller (Panel 118).

(Panel 119) Rfn. 33601, William Smith, 17th (Service) Bn. The King's Royal Rifle Corps: *s.* of Richard Smith, of 4, Batchelor's Hall Place, Peckham, London, S.E., Builder, by his wife Margaret: *b.* Peckham, 25 October 1888: enlisted King's Royal Rifle Corps, 6 March 1916: served with the Expeditionary Force in France and Flanders from the following September, and was killed in action 20 September 1917. Buried where he fell: Age 28. He *m.* Peckham, 25 December 1907; Kate, *dau.* of Robert Lynn, and leaves five children.

(Panel 119) Pte. 10435, Arthur Victor Somerset, (Bglr.) 12th (Service) Bn. The King's Royal Rifle Corps: late of Harringay, co. Middlesex: *s.* of the late Alfred Somerset (late Bugle Maj. 2nd K.R.R.C.), by his wife Alice Emma: and yr. brother to rfn. 6500, G.W., Somerset, 1st K.R.R.C., died 14 September 1914, of wounds: *b.* Leicester: enlisted Dover. Killed in action 16 August 1917: Age 21. *unm.*

His brother George also has no known grave; he is commemorated on the La Ferte-Sous-Jouarre Memorial.

(Panel 119) Rfn. R/10835, William Wildsmith, 13th (Service) Bn. The King's Royal Rifle Corps: *s.* of the late Charles Wildsmith, Bricklayer's Labourer; by his wife Mary Ann, *née* Renshaw (31, Park Street, Sutton-in-Ashfield): and brother to Pte. 23598, W.A. Wildsmith, 15th Sherwood Foresters, who fell 28 March 1918; and Pte. 306454, G. Wildsmith, M.M., 8th Sherwood Foresters, killed in action, 17 October 1918: *b. c.*1894: enlisted Sutton-in-Ashfield. Killed in action 30 September 1917: Age 23. *unm.*

His brother Wilfrid also has no known grave; he is commemorated on the Pozieres Memorial, Somme; Gershom lies in Vaux-Andigny British Cemetery (A.16).

PANEL 119 ENDS: PTE. G. FIFER, WILTSHIRE REGT.

PANEL 120 BEGINS: PTE. J.H. FLETCHER, WILTSHIRE REGT.

(Panel 120) Pte. 27244, Edward Hick, 1st Bn. (62nd Foot) The Duke of Edinburgh's (Wiltshire Regt.): formerly no.012610, Royal Army Ordnance Corps: *s.* of John Thomas Hick, of 2, Groves Lane, York, by his wife Jane: and brother to Pte. PO/17960, H. Hick, R.M.L.I., who was lost at sea when H.M.S. 'Hampshire' was sunk off Marwick Head, 5 June 1916, with the loss of 643 lives, among them Secretary of State for War, Lord Kitchener of Khartoum: *b.* York, about 1893: *educ.* Shipton Street School: enlisted York. Killed in action 1 September 1917, at Inverness Copse: Age 24. *unm.*

His brother Harold has no known grave; he is commemorated on the Portsmouth Naval Memorial (22).

(Panel 120) 2nd Lieut. William Oliver Lancaster, 21st (Service) Bn. The Manchester Regt.: *s.* of William Lancaster, of 'Morningside,' Carlton Road, Burnley, co. Lancaster, by his wife Mary Eliza: kinsman (mother's cousin) to 2nd Lieut. A. Bellingham, 4th Loyal North Lancashire Regt., killed in action the same day (26 October 1917): *educ.* Burnley Grammar School, and Rydal Mount School, Colwyn Bay: joined Royal Fusiliers (Public Schools Battn.) as Pte., April 1916: gazetted 2nd Lieut., Manchester Regt., May 1917: served with the Expeditionary Force in France from 21 June: missing/confirmed killed in action, 26 October 1917: Age 26. Lieut.Col. Lomax wrote, "It is with the very greatest regret that I have to write and tell you that your husband was killed in action on 26th October. Your husband was commanding an assaulting company and was killed instantaneously as he led them into battle. There could have been no pain. Your husband was an exceedingly promising officer and I had already earmarked him for the permanent command of the company. May I offer to you the heartfelt sympathy of the officers and men of our battalion in your great loss, especially the sympathy of the men of his company, who were devoted to him in every way." He *m.* Sion Baptist Chapel, 2 June 1915; Bessie J. Walton (Willow Bank, Burnley), *yst. dau.* of Robert Walton: *s.p.* One of four brothers who served.

2nd Lieut. Alan Bellingham also has no known grave; he is recorded on Panel 102.

(Panel 120) 2nd Lieut. Leslie Duncan Young, 2/7th Bn. The Manchester Regt. (T.F.): *yr. s.* of the late Alexander Stuart Young, Grey Cloth Agent; by his wife Helen ('Birnam,' Wilbraham Road, Chorlton-cum-Hardy, Manchester), *dau.* of the late Edward Ashworth; Shipping Merchant: *b.* Withington, Manchester, 16 April 1893: *educ.* Loretto School, Musselburgh: entered the firm of his uncle, Messrs Edward Ashworth & Co., Manchester; went to Rio de Janeiro (1913): consequent to the outbreak of war, returned to England, joined Artists' Rifles O.T.C., 7 August 1916: gazetted 2nd Lieut., Lancashire Fusiliers, 15 January 1917: served with the Expeditionary Force in France from the following February: transf'd. Manchester Regt., May 1917; killed in action nr. the Zonnebeke Railway, 7 October following. Buried nr. Ypres. His Commanding Officer wrote, "Your son transferred to my battalion at his own wish, and I am proud to think he was really happy with us. I saw a great deal of him, and the more I saw of him the more I liked him. Though I may consider, I hope, all my officers as my personal friends, yet your son was particularly so, and I feel his loss most keenly. He was a splendid worker, and what was given to him to do, one knew would be well and efficiently carried out. He was always most solicitous for his men's safety, and his care was repaid by the affection they all had for him. Finding that his platoon's position was under very heavy fire, he went forward to select a safer one, and to ask permission to move. He had obtained the authority from his company officer when he met his death instantaneously;" and another officer, "I was more upset at losing your son than anything else that has happened. He had been with me, practically since he joined this battalion. I could never have a more willing, loyal and conscientious officer, and I know I am voicing the opinion of my other officers and also of the men in this.": Age 24. *unm.*

(Panel 120) Sergt. 25531, Stanley Francis Carrington, 22nd (Service) Bn. The Manchester Regt.: *s.* of Arthur William Carrington, of 11, Shrewsbury Street, Old Trafford, Manchester, by his wife Sarah Ann, *dau.* of the late James Cooper: *b.* Hulme, Manchester, 24 February 1894: *educ.* St. Mary's Higher Grade School: employee Manchester Ship Canal Company: enlisted 21 June 1915, and while training won the distinction of being the best shot in his company: served with the Expeditionary Force in France and Flanders from June 1916: took part in the operations on the Somme and at Bullecourt, where he was awarded the Military Medal, March 1917, for conspicuous bravery in leading his platoon out of an almost impossible position: wounded May 1917, but remained in France, and was killed in action 4 October following, by a sniper, while leading his platoon at Passchendaele. Buried there. A comrade wrote, "He died as he had lived, a brave, God-fearing lad, a gentleman in the best sense;" and another, "The Army could not spoil him. His men looked upon him more as a friend than as a Sergt. He never bullied or threatened, but a request from him brought a readier response than an order from most other sergeants would." His Platoon Officer also wrote, "As one who was closely associated with him, who can honestly say, loved him, I must offer you, his parents, my humble congratulations on having such a brave son; he died doing his duty.": Age 23. *unm.*

(Panel 120) L/Sergt. 352161, Walter George Salter, 2/9th Bn. The Manchester Regt. (T.F.): *s.* of William Salter, of 115, Old Street, Ashton-under-Lyne: *husb.* to Ethel Salter, *née* Greenwood (6, Egerton Street, Ashton): and brother to Pte. 266321, E. Salter, 6th Cheshire Regt., killed in action 31 July 1917: *b.* Blackburn, *c.*1893: enlisted Ashton, afsd.: killed in action, 9 October 1917: Age 24. In a letter to his widow, a comrade said Sergt. Salter always had a cheery word and a smile for all, and if there was anything he could do for anyone it needed only to be asked of him and it was done. At the time of his death he was where he always felt it his place to be – at the front – ever doing his duty.

His brother Ernest also has no known grave; he is commemorated on the Ypres (Menin Gate) Memorial (Panel 22).

(Panel 120) Corpl. 352651, William Bardsley, 2/9th Bn. The Manchester Regt. (T.F.): *s.* of George (& Mrs) Bardsley, of 14, Ladbrooke Grove, Hurst: prior to enlistment, Ashton-under-Lyne, December 1915, was a Wages Clerk: served with the Expeditionary Force in France and Flanders from March 1917, and was killed in action 9 October following: Age 25. Numerous letters of condolence have been received by his widow, Emma Bardsley, *née* Marsh (11, Uxbridge Street, Ashton-under-Lyne); Sergt. Dickinson wrote, "It is with deep regret that I write to inform you of the death of your husband. He was killed in action by an enemy sniper and died instantly, but perhaps it may be some consolation to you to know that he suffered no pain. I can assure you that you have the deep sympathy of everyone who remains in the Company. He was one of the most promising N.C.O.'s, and will be missed by all." And Pte. Haigh, "We were advancing at Ypres, on the 10th inst. Corpl. Bardsley received a wound, and was making his way to the impromptu dressing station on the field, when he was shot through the head by a sniper."

(Panel 120) Corpl. 353181, John William Gudgeon, 2/9th Bn. The Manchester Regt. (T.F.): formerly no.10166, Lancashire Fusiliers: *s.* of Joseph W. Gudgeon, of 29, Walton Fold, Mildwood, Todmorden, co. Lancaster, by his wife Mary: *b.* Manchester: enlisted Todmorden. One of 12 other ranks of his battalion killed in action on the morning of 28 November 1917; shellfire: Age 19. See Pte. J.F. Cheeswright, Lijssenthoek Military Cemetery (XVI.A.20A).

PANEL 120 ENDS: CORPL. A. WINTERBOTTOM, MANCHESTER REGT.

PANEL 121 BEGINS: L/CORPL. P.H. ARDEN, MANCHESTER REGT.

(Panel 121) L/Corpl. 350900, Edward Margerison, 'A' Coy., 2/9th Bn. The Manchester Regt. (T.F.): *s.* of John Henry (& Mrs) Margerison, of 17, Jermyn Street, Ashton-under-Lyne, co. Lancaster: enlisted there. Killed in action 28 November 1917; nr. the Chateau, Zonnebeke: Age 24. He leaves a wife, Pollie Margerison (21, Booth Street, Denton, Manchester). See Pte. J.F. Cheesewright, Lijssenthoek Military Cemetery (XVI.A.20A).

(Panel 121) Pte. 40478, William Henry Beeley, 23rd (Service) Bn. The Manchester Regt.: formerly no.2092, Cheshire Yeomanry: *s.* of Joseph Henry Beeley, of 41, Cross Leach Street, Stalybridge, by his wife Clara: and brother to Pte. 22588, J. Beeley, 1st King's Own, killed in action, 9 October 1917, aged 21 years: *b.* Stalybridge, co. Chester: enlisted there. Killed in action 22 October 1917: Age 24. *unm.*

His brother Joseph is buried in Cement House Cemetery (III.D.6).

(Panel 121) Pte. 352875, Richard Henry Brookes, 2/9th Bn. The Manchester Regt. (T.F.): enlisted Salford, Manchester. One of twelve other ranks killed by an early morning strafe 28 November 1917; near the Chateau, Zonnebeke. See Pte. J.F. Cheeswright, Lijssenthoek Military Cemetery (XVI.A.20A).

PANEL 121 ENDS: PTE. F. CROPPER, MANCHESTER REGT.

PANEL 122 BEGINS: PTE. J. CROPPER, MANCHESTER REGT.

(Panel 122) Pte. 270090, George Harry Game, 2/6th Bn. The Manchester Regt. (T.F.): *s.* of Harry Game, of Alwood Green, Rickinghall, Diss, co. Norfolk, by his wife Jane: and brother to Pte. 23839, W. Game, 2nd Suffolk Regt., who fell, 13 November 1916: enlisted Rickinghall: proceeded to France, February 1917; killed in action 10 October 1917: Age 28. *unm.*

His brother Walter also has no known grave, he is commemorated on the Thiepval Memorial, Somme.

(Panel 122) Pte. 377356, Clarence Hebblethwaite Holt, 2/10th Bn. Manchester Regt. (T.F.): late of 2, Blakey Street, Longsight, Manchester (formerly of Carr Villa, Luddenden): enlisted July 1916: went to France, March 1917, where he served as a Stretcher Bearer. Killed 9 October 1917: Age 35.

PANEL 122 ENDS: PTE. L.D. KIRBY. MANCHESTER REGT.

PANEL 123 BEGINS: PTE. C. KNIGHT, MANCHESTER REGT.

(Panel 123) Pte. 352070, James Moss Lee, 2/8th Bn. The Manchester Regt. (T.F.): s. of Mr (& Mrs) Lee; Confectioners, of Stamford Square, Cockbrook, Ashton-under-Lyne: *b.* Ashton, 28 October 1895: enlisted there, 1915: proceeded to France with a draft of reinforcements, July 1917, trained six weeks at Etaples, moved up to the Ypres front, 22 September and was killed in action 6 October 1917. In a letter to his parents, a comrade Pte. J. Fleming, wrote, "Your son was one of my very best chums, and we promised each other that should anything befall either of us we would let their parents know. I feel his loss very much, and it will be a very hard blow to bear, so please accept my greatest sympathy in the loss of such a good son and good soldier.": Age 21. *unm.*

(Panel 123) Pte. 351369, John Richard Lloyd, 2/9th Bn. The Manchester Regt. (T.F.): *s.* of John (& Mrs) Lloyd, of 14, Norbury Street, Hyde, co. Chester: enlisted Ashton-under-Lyne, co. Lancaster. One of 12 other ranks killed in action on the early morning of 28 November 1917, by shellfire; Zonnebeke sector: Age 21. *unm.* See Pte. J.F. Cheeswright, Lijssenthoek Military Cemetery (XVI.A.20A).

(Panel 123) Pte. 352672, Harry Lunn, 9th Bn. The Manchester Regt. (T.F.): late of Curzon Road, Hurst, Manchester: Occupation – Contractor's Clerk Messrs Marshall; Cockbrook: enlisted Ashton-under-Lyne, co. Lancaster, August 1916: sent to Egypt; he was aboard the S.S. 'Arcadian' when that ship was torpedoed and sunk by German submarine UC74, off the coast of Greece, 17 April 1917, with the loss of 279 lives: subsequently sent to France; killed in action 2 September 1917: Age 29. In a letter to his widow, Sarah Jane Lunn (10, Hope Street, South Shore, Blackpool), Lieut. Greenwood wrote, "By the time you receive this letter you will no doubt have had official word of the death of your husband in action yesterday, September 2nd. It is impossible for me to express in this letter the feeling of regret and sympathy which I have experienced. He was in my platoon, and by his death I feel that I have lost one of my best men. He was a good soldier in every way. In your great loss may you find all possible consolation in the fact that he gave his life whilst fighting for his King and country."

(Panel 123) Pte. 14521, Thomas Marshall, 21st (Service) Bn. The Manchester Regt.: *s.* of John William Marshall, of 64, Whiteley Street, Oldham, by his wife Fanny, *dau.* of John William Marshall: *b.* Oldham, co. Lancaster, 4 July 1891: *educ.* Oldham Parish Church School: Occupation – File Cutter; Messrs Platt's, Oldham: enlisted 24th Manchester Regt., 9 November 1914: served with the Expeditionary Force in France and Flanders from 24 November 1915: subsequently transf'd. 21st Battn. Reported wounded and missing after the fighting at Passchendaele 24 October 1917; no further word being heard of him, he is now (1918) assumed killed in action on or about that date: Age 26. *unm.*

(Panel 123) Pte. 40320, Albert Page, 20th (Service) Bn. The Manchester Regt.: formerly No.5562, Lancashire Fusiliers: *s.* of the late William Page, of Heywood, co. Lancaster, by his wife Sally: *b. c.*1883: He leaves a wife Patience Page (101, Peel Lane, Heywood, co. Lancaster), to whom – on the eve of his death – he wrote, "30 September 1917. Sorry, I will not be able to come to England as we go into the trenches tomorrow.". Killed in action 1 October 1917: Age 34.

(Panel 123) Pte. 350907, Harold Perks, 2/9th Bn. The Manchester Regt. (T.F.): *s.* of the late William E. Perks, by his wife Mary E. Perks (299, Astley Street, Dukinfield, co. Chester): *b.* Dukinfield: enlisted Ashton-under-Lyne. Killed in action, 28 November 1917, when the battalion's trenches near Zonnebeke Chateau were subjected to an early morning strafe. 12 men were killed, and one – Pte. 53310, J.F. Cheeswright – died of wounds the following day.

Pte. J.F. Cheesewright is buried in Lijssenthoek Military Cemetery (XVI.A.20A).

(Panel 123) Pte. 277243, Herbert William Reeves, 2/7th Bn. Manchester Regt. (T.F.): eldest *s.* of Charles Reeves, of 28, Lark Hill Road, Stockport, Railway Wagon Examiner, by his wife Fanny, *dau.* of Edwin Knight: and brother to L/Corpl. 52478, C.H. Reeves, Cheshire Regt., who was killed in action at Messines: *b.* Manchester, co. Lancaster, 25 May 1896: *educ.* St. Matthew's School, Stockport: employee Messrs W.A. Shaw, Princes Street, Stockport: joined Manchester Regt., 5 August 1916: served with the Expeditionary Force in France and Flanders from 4 March 1917, and was killed in action near Ypres 7 October following: Age 20. *unm.*

His brother Charles also has no known grave; he is commemorated on the Ypres (Menin Gate) Memorial (Panel 19).

(Panel 123) Pte. 53334, Percy Rushton, 2/9th Bn. The Manchester Regt. (T.F.): formerly no.38504, North Staffordshire Regt.: late of Uttoxeter: *b.* Lichfield, co. Stafford. Killed in action 28 November 1917. See Pte. J.F. Cheesewright, Lijssenthoek Military Cemetery (XVI.A.20A).

(Panel 123) Pte. 376767, Charles Ellis Smethurst, 2/10th Bn. The Manchester Regt. (T.F.): *s.* of the late James Smethurst, by his wife Kate Helena (Oldham, co. Lancaster): *b.* 20 October 1896: served with the Expeditionary Force in France and Flanders, and was killed in action at Passchendaele 9 October 1917: Age 20. *unm.*

(Panel 123) Pte. 42837, Cyril Joseph Smith, 2/7th Bn. The Manchester Regt. (T.F.): *s.* of Daniel Burling Smith, of Common Lane, Royston, co. York, Gardener, by his wife Annie, *dau.* of George Raynor: *b.* Cagthorpe, Horncastle, co. Lincoln: *educ.* Royston: employee Messrs Pickles; Clothiers, Wakefield: enlisted 22 December 1916: served with the Expeditionary Force in France and Flanders from 5 June 1917, and was killed in action at Passchendaele Ridge 8 October following. Buried north of Zonnebeke, north-east of Ypres. An officer wrote, "I was on leave at the time, or I should have written to you before to express not only my sympathy to you, but the respect and admiration I felt for your son. He has won the respect of us all, and we have lost a gallant soldier. My brother was killed two days ago. This will tell you that my sympathy is real, however much my words fail to express it. I feel proud of every man of my company, and your son was worthy of it;" and another, "Your son had not been with us a long time, but I soon realized what a sound and reliable soldier he was, and made him my platoon runner and had marked him for promotion.": *unm.*

PANEL 123 ENDS PTE. J. SOLLERY, MANCHESTER REGT.

PANEL 124 BEGINS: PTE. E. SOUTHALL, MANCHESTER REGT.

(Panel 124) Pte. 14883, Thomas Wolstencroft, 22nd (Service) Bn. The Manchester Regt.: *s.* of the late Samuel (& Mary) Wolstencroft: *b.* Oldham, co. Lancaster, about 1878: *educ.* Coldhurst School, there: was a Minder in the employ of the Werneth Spinning Co.: enlisted 2 January 1915: served with the Expeditionary Force in France and Flanders from 7 November following, and was killed in action at

Passchendaele 26 October 1917. Buried at Ypres: Age 39. He *m.* at Hyside Parish Church, co. Lancaster, 28 May 1902, Annie (10, Bottomley Street, Werneth, co. Lancaster), *dau.* of Henry (& Emma) Bridgehouse, and had six children;Thomas, *b.* 20 May 1906, Samuel, *b.* 8 August 1907, John, *b.* 29 March 1909, Mary, *b.* 25 February 1911, William, *b.* 8 November 1912, and Edward, *b.* 29 June 1915.

(Panel 124) Pte. 40929, Harry Henry Anderson, 8th (Service) Bn. The Prince of Wales's (North Staffordshire Regt.): *s.* of John Anderson, of 10, Albert Street, Clifton, co. York, by his wife Anne Elizabeth: Occupation – Porter; Brighouse Railway Station: enlisted Lincolnshire Regt. (no.38183), April 1917: proceeded to France and was killed in action at Passchendaele 4 October following. Age 20.

PANEL 124 ENDS: PTE. R.A. FORSTER, NORTH STAFFORDSHIRE REGT.

PANEL 125 BEGINS: PTE. C.O. FOX, NORTH STAFFORDSHIRE REGT.

(Panel 125) Pte. 45785, Frederick Minor, 4th (Extra Reserve) Bn. The Prince of Wales's (North Staffordshire Regt.): *s.* of the late Henry (& Charity) Minor, of 26, Festing Street, Hanley, Stoke-on-Trent: and yr. brother to Sergt. 2521, M. Minor, 7th Royal Fusiliers, killed in action 30 October 1917: *b.* Hanley, co. Stafford, *c.*1885: enlisted Hanley. Killed in action 6 February 1918: Age 32. *unm.*

His brother Moses also has no known grave; he is recorded on Panel 28.

(Panel 125) Pte. 48795, Reginald Newing, 8th (Service) Bn. The Prince of Wales's (North Staffordshire Regt.): formerly no.921, Army Service Corps (Kent Bde.): *s.* of Edward Thomas (& Emmeline) Newing, of 14, Hedley Street, Maidstone, co. Kent: and brother to Pte. 204398, E.T. Newing, 2/6th South Staffordshire Regt., killed in action, 21 March 1918, aged 26 years: *b.* Maidstone: enlisted there. Killed in action 10 April 1918: Age 21.

His brother Edward also has no known grave; he is commemorated on the Arras Memorial (Bay 6).

(Panel 125) Capt. Stanley Gummer, 5th Bn. The York & Lancaster Regt. (T.F.): elder *s.* of William Guest Gummer, of Totley Rise, Sheffield, by his wife Gertrude, *dau.* of Jonathan Hemingway: *b.* Rotherham, co. York, 14 February 1890: *educ.* Leys School, Cambridge: Occupation – Partner; Messrs Gichard and Gummer, Solicitors, of Rotherham: volunteered for Active Service on the outbreak of war: gazetted 2nd Lieut., York and Lancaster Regt., 9 February 1915: promoted Lieut., 1 June 1916; Capt., 8 July following: served with the Expeditionary Force in France and Flanders from 19 September 1915, taking part in many engagements, and was killed in action at Passchendaele 9 October 1917. Buried there: Age 27. A good all-round cricketer, he played with the Rotherham Town Team and Yorkshire County Reserves, and was also a keen Rugby footballer. He *m.* Rotherham Town Church, 24 September 1913; Vera (Broom Lane, Rotherham) *dau.* of William Michael Gichard, and had two children – Dinah Gichard, *b.* 12 June 1914, Michael Gichard, *b.* 7 July 1917.

(Panel 125) Capt. Arthur Francis Kingdon, 6th (Service) Bn. The York & Lancaster Regt.: 5th *survg. s.* of William Edward Kingdon, of Bemerton, Buxton, co. Derby, by his wife Annie, *dau.* of James Lock: *b.* Sheffield, 28 March 1896: *educ.* Trent College, co. Derby: joined Public Schools Camp, Epsom, September 1914: transf'd. Inns of Court O.T.C., November: gazetted 2nd Lieut., York and Lancaster Regt., 15 January 1915: promoted Capt. December 1916: served with the Egyptian Expeditionary Force, Egypt (from January 1916), where he took part in actions against the Turks on the Suez Canal: proceeded to France the following July: took part in the fighting on the Somme, September 1916, being then given command of his company: wounded January 1917 and invalided home: returned to France, August: took part in the fighting for the ridges east of Ypres, and was killed in action at the Third Battle of Ypres 9 October 1917, while leading his company. Buried where he fell. His Commanding Officer wrote, "He was always the life and soul of the mess, loved and respected by his men, and one of the most valiant and efficient officers in the regiment;" and one of his subalterns, "I thought a great deal of him, and had a truly happy time under his command. An excellent soldier, always cheery and most unselfish, he was loved by both his fellow-officers and men.": Age 21. *unm.*

(Panel 125) Capt. Stanley Fenton Smith, 5th Bn. The York & Lancaster Regt. (T.F.): *s.* of the late Harry Fenton Smith, of 35, Eccleshall Road, Sheffield, by his wife Mary (33, Woodholm Road, Eccleshall, Sheffield, co. York), *dau.* of Joseph Bransall: *b.* 3 November 1894: *educ.* Milton Abbas Grammar School, Blandford, co. Dorset: Occupation – Clerk; Alliance Insurance Co.: joined Honourable Artillery Company, January 1915: after training with them was given a commission and gazetted 2nd Lieut. York and Lancaster Regt., November following: promoted Capt., July 1917: served with the Expeditionary Force in France and Flanders from December 1916: took part in the fighting on the Somme; wounded there. Killed in action at Passchendaele Ridge 9 October 1917. Buried where he fell. His Commanding Officer wrote, "A most splendid fellow, resolute and cool at all times, full of courage, and loved by all ranks;" and a brother officer "Of his conduct that day the greatest praise is given by those who were with him. Despite severe conditions, Capt. Smith's company took all its objectives and having consolidated them, he seized the opportunity and took the remainder of his men to take further ground, and whilst attacking a system of very strong enemy posts, he was wounded and afterwards killed outright.": Age 22. *unm.*

(Panel 125) Lieut. Thomas Alexander Greenwood Mashiter, 10th (Service) Bn. The York & Lancaster Regt. attd. 1/5th Bn. Lancashire Fusiliers (T.F.): *s.* of Thomas Edward Mashiter, of 68, Rosendale Road, West Dulwich, London: killed in action on the night of 31 August/1 September 1917, by the direct hit of a shell: Age 26. *unm.* See account re. Capt. A.P. Hudson, Lancashire Fusiliers (Panel 54).

(Panel 125) Lieut. William John Roland Ernest Poole, 'C'Coy., 4th (Hallamshire) Bn. The York & Lancaster Regt. (T.F.): only *s.* of the late William Poole, of Masham, by his wife May (53, St. George's Road, Harrogate), *dau.* of the Rev. W.J. Slacke: *b.* Masham, co. York, 1 March 1895: *educ.* Clifton College, Harrogate, and Aldenham School, co. Hertford: Occupation – Articled Clerk; J.W. Render, J.P., Solicitor: enlisted 2 September 1914, after the outbreak of war: gazetted 2nd Lieut., July 1915; promoted Lieut., October 1917: served with the Expeditionary Force in France and Flanders from November 1915, and was killed in action 9 October 1917, south-west of Passchendaele: Age 22. *unm.*

(Panel 125) 2nd Lieut. Raymund Wilfrid Jackson, Intelligence Officer, 4th (Hallamshire) Bn. The York & Lancaster Regt. (T.F.): *s.* of Edmund Jackson, of Sheffield, by his wife Olive M., *dau.* of the Rev. H.M. Wellington, of Athelhampton Rectory, Dorchester, co. Dorset. Killed in action, south-west of Passchendaele, 9 October 1917: Age 19.

(Panel 125) 2nd Lieut. Bernard Oates Robinson, 'D' Coy., 4th (Hallamshire) Bn. The York & Lancaster Regt. (T.F.): *s.* of Ernest Bernard Robinson, of 'Barn Close,' Curbar, Sheffield, co. York, by his wife Harriet E. Reported missing following the attack south-west of Passchendaele 9 October 1917: Age 20. *unm.*

PANEL 125 ENDS: L/CORPL. R. ASHTON, YORK & LANCASTER REGT.

PANEL 126 BEGINS: L/CORPL. J. BRADY, YORK & LANCASTER REGT.

PANEL 126 ENDS: PTE. S. HAYTHORNE, YORK & LANCASTER REGT.

PANEL 127 BEGINS: PTE. H. HEATON, YORK & LANCASTER REGT.

(Panel 127) Pte. 39043, John William Huscroft, 9th (Service) Bn. The York & Lancaster Regt.: *s.* of John Huscroft, of Kellingley, Knottingley, co. York: and yr. brother to Pte. 47537, E. Huscroft, 26th Bn. Northumberland Fusiliers, killed in action, 9 April 1917: *b.* Kellingley, *c.*1898: enlisted Pontefract. Killed in action 10 October 1917: Age 19. Unveiled by Col. C.C. Moxton, 25 September 1921, the Knottingley War Memorial records the names of 202 local men who made the supreme sacrifice in the Great War; the brothers Huscroft are but two of them.

His brother Edward is buried in Orchard Dump Cemetery, Arleux-en-Gohelle (V.G.19).

(Panel 127) Pte. 242401, William Henry Knowles, 1/5th Bn. York & Lancaster Regt. (T.F.): only *s.* of John William Knowles, of West Lawn, Tewit Well Road, Harrogate, by his wife Emily: *b.* Harrogate, co. York, 3 September 1892: *educ.* Western, and Horst Colleges, there: assisted his father in business: joined Yorkshire Dragoons (Yeomanry) 1 November 1915, subsequently transf'd. York and Lancaster Regt.: served with the Expeditionary Foce in France and Flanders from December 1916; killed in action at Passchendaele 9 October 1917. Buried where he fell. His Platoon Commander wrote, "… I should like to add that I found in him a stout and willing soldier, and at the time of his death he was in charge of his platoon.": Age 25. *unm.*

(Panel 127) Pte. 33195, Ernest Redfearn, 1/5th Bn. The York & Lancaster Regt (T.F.): formerly no.30719, Duke of Wellington's Regt.: *s.* of William Redfearn, of 7, Mount Pleasant, Rastrick, Brighouse, Yorkshire, by his wife Elizabeth: attended New Road Sunday School: a member of Rastrick Conservative Club: Occupation – Twister; Messrs T. Helm and Sons: enlisted March 1917, proceeded to France June following; last seen alive 9 October 1917 – since reported / recorded missing – during the fighting at the 3rd Battle of Ypres. Despite extensive enquiries no further information has to date been received and it is now (March 1918) assumed Pte. Redfearn was killed in action on the aforementioned date: Age 20. *unm.*

(Panel 127) Pte. 18597, Ralph Senior, 6th (Service) Bn. The York & Lancaster Regt.: *s.* of the late Joseph D. Senior, of 33, Bridge Street, Swinton, by his marriage to Eliza Ann Wright, *née* Senior (238, Roman Terrace, Wath Road, Mexborough, Rotherham): and brother to Pte. 18596, J. Senior, 6th York and Lancaster Regt., fell 7 August 1915, at Gallipoli; and Pte. 43339, M. Senior, 1/5th York and Lancaster Regt., fell 13 October 1918, during the severe fighting for the village of Haspres: *b.* Swinton, 1889: enlisted Mexborough, co. York. Killed in action 19 October, 1917: Age 28.

His brother Jesse also has no known grave, he is commemorated on the Helles Memorial; Matthew is buried in York Cemetery, Haspres (B.3).

4th York and Lancaster Regt.: 18 March 1918: "Moved forward to our old sector in the front line. Instructed that the enemy were to annoyed as much as possible, efforts were to be made to secure identifications. A raid was promptly arranged, Lieut. S.E. Warburton, M.M., selected to lead. The raiding party, according to usual custom, sent down to train and rest behind front-line area. Scouts reconnoitred positions to be raided and reported information obtained."

'On March 25th, our last night in the line, our raid took place. The Scout Officer laid tapes from the front line up to within a few yards of the enemy post, and led various detachments of the raiders into their positions….The night was almost perilously moon-lit, but the enemy was taken completely by surprise, and in a very few minutes our men had returned with four live Boche and two machine-guns. They had also killed several Huns and damaged his machine-gun position considerably. Our total casualties for the raid were 2nd Lieut. S.E. Warburton and seven men wounded. Not until the Battalion was out of the line next day did we learn that Lieut. Warburton's servant (Pte. Stocks), who had been watching the raid from the crater, was missing. It transpired that he had attempted to follow Warburton, and had doubtless got lost and killed."

For gallantry in connection with the raid 2nd Lieut Warburton was awarded with the Military Cross, Sergt. C. Firth, the D.C.M.; Corpl. F. Lupton, Ptes. Barron, Day, Adey, Peart and Hopkinson the M.M. Archie Stocks received no award, no commendation; simply missing 'no known burial.'

(Panel 127) Pte. 201189, Archie Stocks, Officer's Servant, 1/4th (Hallamshire) Bn. The York & Lancaster Regt. (T.F.): enlisted Sheffield. Missing / believed killed, night of 25-26 March 1918; Judge Cross Roads sector, Polygon Wood.

We were together since the war began,
He was my servant – And the better man.
Rudyard Kipling.

Killed in action one week later, Sergt. C. Firth, D.C.M., M.S.M., is buried in Hooge Crater Cemetery (XIV.J.11). Pte. H. Peart, subsequently promoted Corpl. was killed in action near Cambrai, 13 October 1918; he is buried in York Cemetery, Haspres (D.24).

PANEL 127 ENDS: PTE. R.E. TODD, YORK & LANCASTER REGT.

PANEL 128 BEGINS: PTE. A. TOWNSEND, YORK & LANCASTER REGT.

(Panel 128) Pte. 31374, James Henry Webster, 'D'Coy., 6th (Service) Bn. The York & Lancaster Regt.: eldest *s.* of William Henry Webster, of 3, Bramber Place, Pitsmoor, Sheffield, by his wife Theodosia, *dau.* of Henry W. Moore: *b.* Sheffield, co. York, 27 November 1895: *educ.* Pye Bank, there: Occupation – Apprentice; Yorkshire Motor Co., Darnhall: enlisted 9 January 1915: served with the Expeditionary Force in France and Flanders from October 1915, and was killed in action near Bullieu Farm, Ypres, 26 September 1917. Buried there: Age 21. *unm.*

(Panel 128) Capt. Arnold Pumphrey, D.S.O., 'A' Coy., 20th (Service) Bn. The Durham Light Infantry: *yst. s.* of Thomas Edwin Pumphrey, of Mayfield, Sunderland, co. Durham, J.P., by his wife Mary Anna, *dau.* of the late Joshua Wilson: and *yr.* brother to 2nd Lieut. H. Pumphrey, Cheshire Regt., who was killed in action at Kemmel Hill: *b.* Sunderland, 25 July 1891: *educ.* Strainongate School, Kendal, and Quaker School, Bootham, York: Occupation – Solicitor: joined London Rifle Brigade, 1 September 1914: gazetted 2nd Lieut., 20th Durham Light Infantry, 7 October 1915: promoted Lieut. 15 January 1916; Capt., 1 April 1916: served with the Expeditionary Force in France and Flanders from 5 November 1914: wounded at Ploegsteert Wood, 2 December following: gassed at Ypres, May 1915: invalided home later in the year, and after a period of training at Bedford and Strensall, was gazetted and promoted as mentioned: returned to France, May 1916, and was killed in action at Tower Hamlets, 21 September 1917, while leading his men after nearly three years' service in France and Flanders. He was devoted to the regiment, and very keen on his own men, who in their own words "worshipped the Captain;": while one under whom he had served wrote of him and one of his friends who was killed about the same time, "They in many ways were so much alike; never failed to do the right thing under the most trying conditions; brave as lions, with always the first thought for others; very gallant English gentlemen both." Mentioned in Despatches by F.M. Sir Douglas Haig (*London Gazette*, 25 May 1917), for 'gallant and distinguished service in the field,' and awarded the D.S.O. (*London Gazette*, 2 June 1917), for 'conspicuous bravery and devotion to duty in the field.' Captain Pumphrey was a descendant of a long line of Quaker ancestry, one of his soldier ancestors having laid down his sword and turned Quaker in Oliver Cromwell's time. He was a keen sportsman, yachting, fishing and riding being his chief pastimes: Age 26. *unm.*

His brother Hubert also has no known grave, he is recorded on Panel 61.

(Panel 128) 2nd Lieut. Nigel Walter Cartwright, 20th (Service) Bn. The Durham Light Infantry: 2nd *survg. s.* of the Rev. William Digby Cartwright, Rector of Aynhoe, Banbury, co. Northampton, by his wife Lucy Harriette Maud, *dau.* of Edward Bury, of 26, Westbourne Square, London, W.: *b.* Aynhoe Rectory, 25 August 1897: *educ.* Durnford Private School; Wellington College; Royal Military College, Sandhurst: gazetted 2nd Lieut., Durham Light Infantry, 7 April 1916: served with the Expeditionary Force in France and Flanders from December following, and was killed in action in the Ypres salient 21 September 1917. Buried where he fell: Age 20. *unm.*

(Panel 128) 2nd Lieut. Bernard Grime Lodge, 4th (Extra Reserve) attd. 10th (Service) Bn. The Durham Light Infantry: *s.* of John James Grime Lodge, of Yorebridge, Askrigg, co. York, by his wife Sarah Ann: and nephew of Mrs W. Balderston, of Yorebridge House, Askrigg: *b.* Dent, co. York, 23 March 1894: *educ.* Minster Yard School, York; Yorebridge Grammar School, and Giggleswick School, Settle, co. York (member of the O.T.C.); thereafter entered the employ of Messrs Barclay and Co., Bankers: enlisted 19th (Universities and Public Schools) Battn. Royal Fusiliers, December 1914: served with the Expeditionary Force in France and Flanders from November 1915: returned to England and joined an Officers' Cadet Corps: obtained a commission, Special Reserve of Officers, 10 August 1916: returned to France, attd. 10th Durham Light Infantry; apptd. Battn. Bombing Officer and Intelligence Officer (after acting as Company Bombing Officer). Killed in action 24 September 1917, at Inverness Copse. His Colonel wrote, "It is with the deepest sympathy that I write to tell you of the death in action of your charming boy, who was my Intelligence Officer. A braver, cooler and more reliable officer could not be found. He had done wonderfully gallant work on patrol on numerous occasions, and whatever the job he had to do, I could absolutely rely on him doing it thoroughly. I know no officer in the battalion I could have spared less than he. He was brave as a lion. We were counter-attacked at 4.30 a.m. on the 24th, and I turned out all the men at H.Q. He, without any orders, dashed off with the leading men up to the front where danger threatened. I don't know how I shall replace him, as not only was he valuable as an officer, but I was very fond of him, as were all of us." His Adjutant wrote, "We shall never get another Bombing Officer up to his standard." Another officer wrote, "I cannot tell you how we miss your lad. He was one of the most capable, and certainly the most popular and coolest officer that has served with us since the formation of the battalion. It will be some time before we can get used to the loss of his charming personality. From my own point, I simply loved him; we were very much together. Even now I cannot realise he has gone from us." Mentioned in Despatches (*London Gazette*, 21 December 1917) by F.M. Sir Douglas Haig, for 'gallant and distinguished service in the field.': Age 23. *unm.*

(Panel 128) 2nd Lieut. William Patrick McGibbon, 4th (Extra Reserve) attd. 28th (Service) Bn. Durham Light Infantry: *yst. s.* of the late John McGibbon, of the Royal Bank of Scotland, by his wife Margaret (Cathcart, Glasgow), *dau.* of James Morrison: *b.* 7 December 1883: *educ.* John Street Elementary School, and High School, Glasgow: Occupation – Clerk; London Office, Royal Bank of Canada: joined Artists' Rifles, February 1916, and after a period of training at Romford, co. Essex, gazetted 2nd Lieut., Durham Light Infantry: served with the Expeditionary Force in France and Flanders from 6 February 1917, and was killed in action at Tower Hamlets 23 September following: Age 33. His Commanding Officer, after referring to the high opinion he had of him, wrote, "This opinion was substantiated to the full by his gallant conduct on 21 September, when the battalion attacked the enemy position under great difficulties. He was a splendid man, and I can assure you his loss is very sincerely felt throughout the whole battalion;" and another officer, "He had done so much to make our share of the offensive of 20 September a success, that his death, when the battalion were being relieved, came as a blow to everyone. You may find some consolation in the knowledge that he died at the post of duty, and in the very front of the newly acquired ground." He *m.* Eltham, 6 November 1915; Millie Beatrice (42, Gourock Road, Eltham), *dau.* of Alfred Gardner, of Eltham (formerly of Lee): *s.p.*

(Panel 128) Sergt. 320008, Waddington Mais, 19th (Service) Bn. (2nd County) The Durham Light Infantry: *s.* of Thomas Mais, of 158, Park Lane, Darlington (late of 16, Clifton Road), by his wife Sarah: and elder brother to Pte. 79731, A. Mais, 13th Royal Fusiliers, killed in action 8 October 1918: *b.* Darlington: enlisted there. Killed in action 20 October 1917: Age 31. He leaves a wife, Francis Georgina Mais (85, Pensbury Street, Darlington).

His brother Alfred also has no known grave; he is commemorated on the Vis-En-Artois Memorial.

(Panel 128) Pte. 200266, William Bamlett, 20th (Service) Bn. (Wearside) The Durham Light Infantry: *s.* of the late James Bamlett, by his wife Elizabeth ('The Poplars,' Haughton-le-Skerne, Darlington): and elder brother to Corpl. 43155, R. Bamlett, 2nd Durham Light Infantry, killed in action 6 March 1917: *b.* Spennymoor: enlisted Durham. Killed in action 21 September 1917: Age 22. *unm.* Two of eighteen local men recorded on Haughton-le-Skerne War Memorial, Darlington; 'Their bodies are buried in peace, but their name liveth for evermore.'

His brother Robert is buried in Philosophe British Cemetery, Mazingarbe (I.M.35).

PANEL 128 ENDS: PTE. W. BAMLETT, DURHAM LIGHT INFANTRY.

PANEL 129 BEGINS: PTE. H. BARKER, DURHAM LIGHT INFANTRY.

(Panel 129) Pte. 15340, Henderson Brankston, M.M., 13th (Service) Bn. The Durham Light Infantry: *s.* of George Brankston, of 'Oyster Shell Cottage,' Lanchester, Co. Durham, by his wife Mary: and brother to L/Cotrpl. 22431, A. Brankston, 13th Durham Light Infantry, killed in action, 11 October 1918; and Pte. 21034, J. Brankston, 2nd Northumberland Fusiliers, killed in action, 1 October 1915: *b.* Lanchester: enlisted Durham. Killed in action, 18 October 1917: Age 22. *unm.* The three brothers are remembered on Malton (Yorkshire) War Memorial.

His brother Alexander is buried in Quietiste Military Cemetery, Le Cateau (B.7); James has no known grave, he is commemorated on the Loos Memorial.

(Panel 129) Pte. 82436, Albert Edward Fuller, 20th (Service) Bn. (Wearside) The Durham Light Infantry: late of 67, Robert Street, West Gorton, nr. Longsight, Manchester: *s.* of the late William James Fuller, and his wife Agnes (Beaconsfield Place, Oliver Lane, Marsden, Huddersfield): and brother to L/Bmdr. 97743, T. Fuller, Royal Field Artillery, killed in action, 19 July 1918: *b.* Greenfield, co. York: enlisted Manchester, May 1917; served with the Expeditionary Force in France from September following, and was killed in action 14 October 1918. In Remembrance: "*His Memory Is Cherished With Pride*"

His brother Thomas also has no known grave; he is recorded on Panel 6.

(Panel 129) Pte. 201231, Arthur Ingham, 15th (Service) Bn. The Durham Light Infantry: formerly no.29/778, Northumberland Fusiliers: *s.* of Mason (& Mrs) Ingham, of 30, Devonshire Street, Skipton, co. York: formerly employed by Messrs Smith Hartley, Union Mills: enlisted Northumberland Fusiliers, Skipton, 1914; discharged 'unfit' during training: recalled to the Colours 1916, posted Durham Light Infantry, and proceeded to France, October of that year, where he was wounded 5 November following and evacuated to England: returned to France, March 1917, and was killed in action 3 November following, at Passchendaele: Age 29.

PANEL 129 ENDS: PTE. H. JACKSON, DURHAM LIGHT INFANTRY.

PANEL 130 BEGINS: PTE. T.A. JACKSON, DURHAM LIGHT INFANTRY.

(Panel 130) Pte. 92051, Charles Lazenby, 2nd Bn. (106th Foot) The Durham Light Infantry: *s.* of Thomas Wilson (& Annie Eliza) Lazenby, of 11, Church Road, North Ferriby, co. York: and yr. brother to Pte. 242296, F. Lazenby, 1st Sherwood Foresters, killed in action 26 March 1918, aged 30 yrs: *b.* Hull: enlisted there. Killed in action 9 August 1918: Age 18.

His brother Fred also has no known grave, he is commemorated on the Pozieres Memorial.

(Panel 130) Pte. 245332, Edward Sidney Such, 10th (Service) Bn. The Durham Light Infantry: *s.* of Henry Edward Such, of 50, Hamilton Road, Heath Park, Romford, co. Essex, by his wife Charlotte: and yr. brother to Rfn. C/6847, J.H. Such, M.M., 18th King's Royal Rifle Corps, killed in action, 21 September 1917: enlisted Romford. Killed in action 17 October 1917: Age 19.

His brother John is buried in Hooge Crater Cemetery (XVIII.E.8).

(Panel 130) Pte. 200390, Lawrence Unitt, 1/5th Bn. The Durham Light Infantry (T.F.): late of Blackhall Colliery, Castle Eden: *s.* of the late A.E. Unitt, by his wife Margaret (4, Fairfield Street, Darlington): and brother to Pte. 2316, D. Unitt, Durham Light Infantry, killed in action, 23 June 1915: enlisted Stockton-on-Tees. Killed in action 28 October 1917: Age 20.

His brother Dennis, commemorated on the Ypres (Menin Gate) Memorial (Panel 38), is buried in Sanctuary Wood Cemetery (IV.U.3).

PANEL 130 ENDS: PTE. J.H. WARDELL, DURHAM LIGHT INFANTRY.

PANEL 131 BEGINS: PTE. C. WATERS, DURHAM LIGHT INFANTRY.

(Panel 131) Pte. 21335, Albert Hewitson Whaley, 13th (Service) Bn. The Durham Light Infantry: *s.* of Thomas Whaley, of 5, Siemen's Street, Blackhill, Co. Durham, by his wife Isabella: and *yr.* brother to Pte. 17/388, R.A. Whaley, 10th Northumberland Fusiliers, died 1 October 1916, of wounds; and Pte. 18948, T.W. Whaley, 12th Durham Light Infantry, killed in action, 8 December 1915: *b.* Blackhill: enlisted Consett. Killed in action 22 September 1917: Age 30.

His brother Richard is buried in Dernancourt Communal Cemetery Extension (III.D.47), Thomas lies in X Farm Cemetery, La Chapelle-d'Armentieres (B.17).

(Panel 131) L/Corpl. 3456, Hector Sutherland Cormack, 'A' Coy., No.2 Platoon, 17th (Service) Bn. (3rd Glasgow) The Highland Light Infantry: 2nd *s.* of the late Alexander Cormack, Accountant, by his wife Catherine (3616, 11th Avenue West, Vancouver, British Columbia, formerly of 377, Bath Street, Glasgow), *dau.* of George Sutherland: *b.* Wick, Caithness, 8 April 1885: *educ.* there, and Pollokshields, Glasgow: Occupation – Electrician: enlisted 25 March 1915: served with the Expeditionary Force in France and Flanders from 22 November following, and was killed in action at Passchendaele 2 December 1917. An officer wrote, "He was a fine soldier, and the best N.C.O. of my platoon, loved by all his comrades both in his platoon and company.": Age 33. *unm.*

(Panel 131) L/Corpl. 38513, Arthur Wright, 8th (T.F.) attd. 17th (Service) Bn. (3rd Glasgow) The Highland Light Infantry: *s.* of the late John Wright, by his wife Jane ('Cranswick,' Beverley, co. York): *b.* Cauldon: *educ.* North Burton, co. Stafford: Occupation – Farm Labourer: enlisted Rudston, Driffield, 6 August 1914: served with the Expeditionary Force in France and Flanders from 1915, and was killed in action 2 December 1917. An officer wrote, "He was a fine soldier and we all miss him greatly. He was ever ready to make light of the most adverse circumstances, always cheerful and happy, and his chums greatly respected him." *unm.*

(Panel 131) Pte. 27631, John Barrie, 16th (Service) Bn. The Highland Light Infantry: *s.* of the late John Barrie, of Dundee, Grocer, by his wife Mary (1, Blackfriars Avenue, Dundee): *b.* Dundee, co. Forfar, 7 February 1889: *educ.* Blackness School: enlisted Highland Light Infantry, 15 February 1915: served with the Expeditionary Force in France and Flanders. Reported wounded and missing after the fighting at Passchendaele 2 December 1917; now assumed to have been killed in action on or about that date: Age 27. *unm.* (*IWGC record age 29*)

PANEL 131 ENDS: PTE. G. DONALDSON, HIGHLAND LIGHT INFANTRY.

PANEL 132 BEGINS: PTE. W.M. DOUGLAS, HIGHLAND LIGHT INFANTRY.

(Panel 132) Pte. 42447, Harry Gardiner, 16th (Service) Bn. (2nd Glasgow) The Highland Light Infantry: formerly no.27261, Royal Scots Fusiliers: *s.* of Harry Gardiner, of 54, Dalziel Street, Hamilton, co. Lanark, by his wife Jeannie: and *yr.* brother to Sergt. 202134, W. Gardiner, M.M., 5/6th Cameronians (Sco.Rif.), who fell, 8 May 1918: enlisted Hamilton. Killed in action 28 November 1917: Age 20. *unm.*

His brother William also has no known grave; he is recorded on Panel 68.

(Panel 132) Pte. 241625, Edward Rayner Midgley, 9th (Glasgow Highlanders) Bn. The Highland Light Infantry (T.F.): *s.* of the late John Midgley, of 2, Woodbine Place, Hebden Bridge, co. York, and his wife, the late Elizabeth Anwell Midgley: and *yr.* brother to Pte. 205307, J.T. Midgley, 1/6th West Yorkshire Regt., who fell, 3 May 1918: *b.* Hebden Bridge: enlisted Halifax. Killed in action 27 September 1917: Age 24. *unm.*

His brother John also has no known grave; he is recorded on Panel 46.

(Panel 132) Capt. George Muir Thornton, 8th (Service) Bn. The Seaforth Highlanders (Ross-shire Buffs, The Duke of Albany's): *s.* of the late George Boyd Thornton, of Feddal, Braco, co. Perth, and Grange Park, Edinburgh, by his wife Elizabeth King Galbraith: *b.* Edinburgh, 7 February 1882: *educ.* Merchiston Castle School, Edinburgh; Trinity College, Oxford; Edinburgh University – graduated LL.B.

(admitted Faculty of Advocates, March 1910): obtained a commission, Seaforth Highlanders, November 1914: promoted Capt. December 1915: served with the Expeditionary Force in France and Flanders, and was killed in action at Iberian Farm, about three miles east of Ypres, 22 August 1917: Age 35. *unm.* (*IWGC record age 36*)

(Panel 132) Lieut. Horace Macaulay, 3rd (Reserve) attd. 7th (Service) Bn. The Seaforth Highlanders (Ross-shire Buffs, The Duke of Albany's): *s.* of John Macaulay, of Clunie, Eskbank, co. Midlothian, J.P., by his wife Janet, *dau.* of Thomas Richardson: and brother to 2nd Lieut. B.W. Macaulay, Seaforth Highlanders, reported missing after the fighting at Arras, 3 May 1917, now assumed to have been killed in action on or about that date: *b.* Liverpool, co. Lancaster, 4 May 1894: *educ.* Christ College, Brecon, and Shrewsbury School: joined Honourable Artillery Company, 8 September 1914: received a commission, gazetted 2nd Lieut., 3rd Seaforth Highlanders, September 1915: promoted Lieut., November 1917: attd. 7th Battn., July 1916; served with the Expeditionary Force in France and Flanders from the 16th of that month: took part in several engagements: returned to England for home service, October 1917: rejoined his regiment in France 24 April 1918, and was killed in action the following day at Wytschaete, while ordering the retirement of his men. His Commanding Officer wrote, "We were all so pleased to see your son back from his six months at home. He was most popular with everyone, and will be greatly missed;" and his Captain, "Your son was, I think, one of the best-known and most popular officers in the battalion, always cheerful and willing to help a fellow in any circumstances. He was very considerate of his men, and one of the straightest fellows I've met.": 25 April 1918: Age 23. *unm.*

His brother Bruce also has no known grave; he is commemorated on the Arras (Faubourg d'Amiens) Memorial.

PANEL 132 ENDS: LIEUT. R. NICHOL, SEAFORTH HIGHLANDERS.

PANEL 133 BEGINS: LIEUT. A.D. STUART, M.C., SEAFORTH HIGHLANDERS.

(Panel 133) 2nd Lieut. William Grant Murray, 7th (Service) Bn. The Seaforth Highlanders (Ross-shire Buffs, The Duke of Albany's): only *survg. s.* of the late Donald Murray, by his wife Isabella ('The Poles,' Dornoch, co. Sutherland), *dau.* of Mr (& Mrs) Grant: *b.* Benarmin, co. Sutherland, 17 July 1889: *educ.* Dornoch Academy: went to the Argentine, 1911; settled there as Major Domo on an Estancia: returned to England, April 1915; joined 5th (Territorial) Bn. Seaforth Highlanders the following month: rose to the rank of Coy.Quartermaster Sergt. served with the Expeditionary Force in France and Flanders from 1 November 1917: gazetted 2nd Lieut., 13 April 1918, and was killed in action north of Wytschaete on the 16th of that month. Buried there. An officer wrote, "Your son was given a commission in the field, and was leading his men very gallantly," and another: "There was no man more deeply respected or admired in the battalion, both by officers and men alike; one of the most capable and straightforward men I have ever had the privilege to meet.": 16 April 1918: Age 28. *unm.*

(Panel 133) Sergt. 200962, William Sutherland, 4th Bn. The Seaforth Highlanders (Ross-shire Buffs, The Duke of Albany's), (T.F.): only *survg. s.* of the late William Sutherland, Farmer; of The Slaggan, Strathpeffer, by his wife Sarah Lullah, *dau.* of William MacDonald, of The Baileehaul, Dingwall: *b.* Strathpeffer, co. Ross, 9 January 1878: *educ.* Fodderty School: was for 21 years with the firm of Mackintosh and Co. Ltd., Auctioneers and Livestock Salesmen: rejoined Territorial Force (to which he had formerly belonged) early April 1915: served with the Expeditionary Force in France and Flanders from June 1916: took part in most of the fighting from a very short time after going out, and was killed in action at Poelcapelle, 20 September 1917. Buried in the British Military Cemetery there. His officer wrote, "He was killed on the morning of the 20 September. The fighting was of the fiercest, and he was advancing with his platoon towards his objective when part of a bomb hit him in the forehead, killing him instantaneously. Many a brave man fell around that spot, where the heaviest fighting on the whole front took place, and it was only by the fine example and bravery of men like your son that the stubborn resistance of the enemy was overcome. He was buried in a little British cemetery within the ground he helped to win and paid so dearly for…He was not only one of the mainstays of my company, but also the most popular N.C.O. in the whole battalion;" and a friend, "He was the staunchest friend a man ever had, true as steel, and one who never went back on his word; of whom it might be said 'he never turned his back, but marched breast forward,' and in many a home in Easter and Wester Ross his memory will be sacred as one who made them richer by his passing by." An athlete of distinction, he was a genuine sportsman, and a great organizer and trainer of battalion sports behind the lines: Age 39. *unm.* (*IWGC record 19-21 September 1917*)

(Panel 133) Sergt. S/41561, Matthew Henderson Webb, 7th (Service) Bn. The Seaforth Highlandes (Ross-shire Buffs, The Duke of Albany's): 2nd *s.* of James Webb, of 13, Trinity Street, Hawick, co. Roxburgh: *b.* Edinburgh, 13 December 1887: *educ.* Teviot Grove Academy, Hawick: enlisted Argyll & Sutherland Highlanders, 19 March 1916: served with the Expeditionary Force in France and Flanders from 8 February 1918: transf'd. Seaforth Highlanders on arrival in France: killed in action at Bailleul, 16 April following. Buried where he fell: Age 30. He *m.* Hawick, 22 January 1918; Helen French (4, Wilton Place, Hawick), *dau.* of Thomas Jardine, of Wilton Hill. (*IWGC record Corpl., age 31*)

(Panel 133) L/Corpl. 265772, Alexander 'Alick' Simpson, 4th Bn. The Seaforth Highlanders (Ross-shire Buffs, The Duke of Albany's), (T.F.): *s.* of Alexander Simpson, of Beaufort Home Farm, Beauly, co. Inverness, by his wife Mary Cumming: *b.* Burghead, nr. Elgin, 26 June 1897: *educ.* Milne's Institution: Occupation – Farm Servant: enlisted Lossiemouth, co. Moray, 4 September 1914: served with the Expeditionary Force in France and Flanders from 3 December 1915, and was killed in action 20 September 1917: Age 20. *unm.* (*IWGC record 19 September, age 18*)

Written by Scottish poet W.D. Cocker in 1917 '*The Sniper*' relates not only to the effect the sniper has had on the soldier he has killed, but also the impact his death has on the family he leaves behind. It illustrates the disgust Cocker felt regarding the anonymous cold-blooded killing of men from varying distances (200 yards in the poem) in relation to the days of warfare before the age of industrialisation, when men fought each other face to face, the stronger individual invariably emerging the victor.

> Two hundred yards away he saw his head;
> He raised his rifle, took quick aim and shot him.
> Two hundred yards way the man dropped dead;
> With bright exulting eye he turned and said,
> "By Jove, I got him!"
> And he was jubilant, had he not won
> The meed of praise his comrades took to pay?
> He smiled; he could not see what he had done,
> The dead man lay two hundred yards away.
> He could not see the dead, reproachful eyes,
> The youthful face which Death had not defiled,
> But had transfigured when he claimed his prize.
> Had he seen this perhaps he had not smiled.
> He could not see the woman as she wept
> To the news two hundred miles away,
> Or through his very dream she would have crept.
> And into all his thoughts by night and day.
> Two hundred yards away, and bending o'er
> A body in a trench, rough men proclaim
> Sadly that Fritz, the merry is no more.
> (Or shall we call him Jack? It's all the same!)

Fritz? Jack? Johan? John? – They were all the same!

(Panel 133) L/Corpl. S/25114, John Allan Stuart, 7th (Service) Bn. The Seaforth Highlanders (Ross-shire Buffs, The Duke of Albany's): *yr. s.* of Walter Stuart, of 34, Balhousie Street, Perth, Director of

Messrs C.C. Stuart Ltd., Wholesale Whisky Merchants, by his wife Mary Ann Umpleby: *b*. Perth, 7 July 1899: *educ*. Perth Academy: Occupation – Clerk in his father's office: enlisted 9 July 1917: served with the Expeditionary Force in France and Flanders from 30 March 1918; killed in action eleven days later on 10 April, being shot by a sniper and killed in the trenches, at Dammstrasse, nr. St. Eloi. Buried there: Age 18.

(Panel 133) Pte. 202248, Percy Grace Charlesworth, 5th Bn. (Sutherland & Caithness) The Seaforth Highlanders (Ross-shire Buffs, The Duke of Albany's), (T.F.): *s*. of Rev. J. (& Mrs) Charlesworth: *b*. Padiham, co. Lancaster: enlisted Harrogate, co. York. Killed in action 6 September 1917: Age 35. A stained glass window in Tadcaster Church is dedicated to the memory of Pte. Charlesworth and Lieut. F.W. Sykes, Royal Field Artillery (La Clytte Military Cemetery, IV.B.5).

(Panel 133) Pte. S/25784, Robert Gibson, 'C' Coy., 7th (Service) Bn. The Seaforth Highlanders (Ross-shire Buffs, The Duke of Albany's): *s*. of John Love Gibson, of Riversdale, Millikenpark, Johnstone, co. Renfrew, Partner in Messrs Gibson Brothers, of the Cortbank Laundry, by his wife Margaret Craig, *dau*. of Matthew Kerr, of Beith: *b*. Kilbarchan, co. Renfrew, 8 November 1898: *educ*. Public School, there; Johnstone Higher Grade School, and Technical College, Paisley: was associated in business with his father: enlisted Queen's Own (Cameron Highlanders), 26 February 1917: transf'd. Seaforth Highlanders, and served with the Expeditionary Force in France and Flanders from January 1918, where he was employed as a Lewis Gunner, and was killed in action at Wytschaete 16 April 1918. Buried where he fell. His Commanding Officer wrote, "He was a particularly good and willing lad, and we were very fond of him in the company. He was killed by a machine gun bullet in a counter-attack at Wytschaete;" and a comrade, "He is sadly missed by us and all who knew him. All the time he has been on the gun team he has never grumbled at what he had to do, and he always faced danger with a smile." He was a keen athlete, and a member of the School football team and represented the district schools against the Glasgow schools: Age 19.

PANEL 133 ENDS: PTE. D.M. GOODFELLOW, SEAFORTH HIGHLANDERS.

PANEL 134 BEGINS: PTE. K.J.MCD. GORDON, SEAFORTH HIGHLANDERS.

(Panel 134) Pte. (Signlr.) 202382, Robert Hughson, 2/4th (T.F.) attd. 8th (Service) Bn. The Seaforth Highlanders (Ross-shire Buffs, The Duke of Albany's): eldest *s*. of the late Robert Hughson, Painter and Decorator, by his wife Elizabeth (101, Ferry Road, Leith, Scotland): *b*. Leith, 6 September 1886: *educ*. Leith Academy: enlisted Cameronians (Sco.Rif.) 1 July 1916, afterwards transf'd. Seaforth Highlanders: trained Kelling Camp, Holt, co. Norfolk, England – gained First-class Certificate, Brigade Signalling School: served with the Expeditionary Force in France and Flanders from 5 July 1917, and was killed in action 26 August following, by a shell whilst in the trenches at Ypres. Buried at Square Farm, east of Ypres: Age 30. *unm*.

(Panel 134) Pte. 265352, Robert Melvin James, 7th (Service) Bn. The Seaforth Highlanders (Ross-shire Buffs, The Duke of Albany's): eldest *s*. of Alexander James, of The Cottage, Birnie, Longmorn, co. Elgin, Road Foreman, by his wife Jessie, *dau*. of George Ellis: *b*. Lhanbryde, St. Andrew's, co. Moray, 17 November 1897: *educ*. Birnie Public School: Occupation – Cycle Assistant: joined 6th Seaforth Highlanders, 1 May 1914; called up on mobilisation, 5 August following: served with the Expeditionary Force in France and Flanders from October 1916: transf'd. 7th Battn., November 1917. Killed in action at Kemmel Hill 11 April 1918. Buried at St. Eloi: Age 20. *unm*.

(Panel 134) Pte. S/17441, Gwillim Jenkin Jones, M.M., 8th (Service) Bn. The Seaforth Highlanders (Ross-shire Buffs, The Duke of Albany's): only *s*. of Sylvan Justin Jones, of Sunnyside, Caerphilly, Decorator and Hardware Merchant, by his wife Mary Jane Gwillim, 2nd *dau*. of Joseph Price, of Tygwyn, co. Brecon: *b*. Caerphilly, Cardiff, 14 July 1895: *educ*. there: subsequently assisted his father in business: joined Army Service Corps, 8 September 1914: went to Marseilles on the 17th., where he was attached to the Indian Expeditionary Force: proceeded to the firing line, 1 January 1915: voluntarily transf'd.

Seaforth Highlanders, November 1916, coming home to train, January 1917: returned to France, April, and was killed in action at the Third Battle of Ypres 22 August following. The Chaplain wrote, "The Seaforths went into action on 22 August last, and early in the action he was killed when taking a party of bombers to a forward position... His loss is one which we very deeply regret. Though he had been here but some three months, he had given great evidence of extraordinary bravery and coolness, and was respected for the high and unblemished character that he bore before others. Yesterday we received news that he had been awarded the Military Medal for his gallant conduct in the previous action. The Commanding Officer recommended its award in the following words, 'Throughout the operations north-east of Ypres, from 30 July to 3 August 1917, Private Jones displayed the greatest bravery as a Company Runner and on forward patrol work. His energy was inexhaustible, and his coolness under fire was an example to his comrades.' And a comrade, "He was with us roughly about four months, yet in that time he became one of our most popular boys... He was known as one of the pluckiest men, and already we miss him greatly... Your son, who had charge of the bombers, called on the rest to follow him, and had only proceeded a few yards when he got a bullet through the head." Awarded the Military Medal for 'gallant and distinguished service in the field.': Age 22. *unm.*

(Panel 134) Pte. S/12652, John MacLeod, 7th (Service) Bn. The Seaforth Highlanders (Ross-shire Buffs, The Duke of Albany's): eldest *s.* of the late Norman MacLeod, by his wife Margaret (Inverkirkaig Hill, Lochinver), *dau.* of Hugh McLeod: and brother to Pte. A. MacLeod, 16th Canadian Infantry, died at Ypres, 6 June 1915: *b.* Lochinver, co. Sutherland, 22 April 1882: *educ.* Public School: Occupation – Marine Engineer: enlisted Seaforth Highlanders, April 1916: served with the Expeditionary Force in France and Flanders from the following September, and was killed in action at Kemmel Ridge 16 April 1918. Buried where he fell: Age 35. *unm.* (*IWGC record McLeod*)

His brother Angus is commemorated by a Special Memorial (H.12) in Railway Dugouts Burial Ground (Transport Farm).

(Panel 134) Pte. 204959, John Martin, 7th (Service) Bn. The Seaforth Highlanders (Ross-shire Buffs, The Duke of Albany's): *s.* of George Martin, of 22, Grieve Street, Dunfermline, by his wife Margaret: enlisted Black Watch, no.4519, Dunfermline: subsequently transf'd. Seaforth Highlanders: served with the Expeditionary Force in France and Flanders, and was killed in action, 15 April 1918, by enemy shell fire whilst in a camp near Kemmel: Age 18. See also Ptes. C. Reid (below) and A. Watt (Panel 135).

(Panel 134) Pte. S/25074, Charles Dickson Reid, 7th (Service) Bn. The Seaforth Highlanders (Ross-shire Buffs, The Duke of Albany's): *s.* of Charles Stuart Ross, D.C.M., of 2, East Links Place, Broughty Ferry, co. Forfar: enlisted Dundee, co. Forfar: formerly no. TR/1/14010, T.R. Battn.: served with the Expeditionary Force in France and Flanders, and was killed in action 15 April 1918, by the explosion of an enemy shell whilst in a hutted camp near Kemmel: Age 18. See also Ptes. J. Martin and A.Watt.

(Panel 134) Pte. 285345, John Ian Rose, 6th Bn. (Morayshire) The Seaforth Highlanders (Ross-shire Buffs, The Duke of Albany's), (T.F.): *s.* of John Hector Rose, of 'Dunchurch,' Tobermory, Isle of Mull, Postmaster of Bridge of Allan, by his wife Janet Stewart, *dau.* of William Montgomery, J.P., of co. Ayr: *b.* Inverary, 24 May 1898: *educ.* Grammar School, there: Occupation – Clerk; North of Scotland Town and County Bank Ltd.: enlisted 8th Argyll & Sutherland Highlanders, 23 January 1917: served with the Expeditionary Force in France and Flanders from June 1917, transf'd. Seaforth Highlanders the following month, and was killed in action at Poelcapelle 30 August of the same year, being hit by a shell while on outpost duty. His Commanding Officer wrote, "His death was deeply lamented throughout 'A' Coy., and the sympathy of all is extended to you. He had not been long with us, but it was long enough for him to become a popular and esteemed comrade." He was a member of the local golf club, and treasurer of the Y.M.C.A.: Age 19.

PANEL 134 ENDS: PTE. D. STEWART, SEAFORTH HIGHLANDERS.

PANEL 135 BEGINS: PTE. P. STEWART, SEAFORTH HIGHLANDERS.

(Panel 135) Pte. S/25490, Archibald Watt, Princess Louise's (Argyll & Sutherland Highlanders) attd. 7th (Service) Bn. Seaforth Highlanders (Ross-shire Buffs, The Duke of Albany's): 5th *s.* of Robert Andrew Watt, Schoolmaster; of Tyninghame, Prestonkirk, East Lothian, J.P., by his wife Margaret, *dau.* of the late Capt. Peter Lawson: and brother to 2nd Lieut. J. Watt, Royal Flying Corps, killed in aerial action at Salonika, 2 May 1917: *b.* School House. Tyninghame, 17 April 1899: *educ.* Tyninghame Public School, and Dunbar Higher Grade School: Occupation – Apprentice Clerk; Commercial Bank of Scotland, Dunbar: enlisted Argyll & Sutherland Highlanders, Territorials (no.TR/1/12/02), Edinburgh 18 December 1916: served with the Expeditionary Force in France and Flanders attd. 7th Battn. Seaforth Highlanders, and was killed in action near Kemmel 15 April 1918. Pte. 24769, R. McFadyean wrote, "He was killed by an enemy shell...Your son was well liked by everyone with whom he came in contact and was always one of the best. We came out of the line on 13 April, and had been resting in huts a few miles back. Early on the morning of the 15th the enemy shelled our camp and got a direct hit on the hut in which Archie was. It killed Archie and two other men, and wounded several others. Archie was buried the same afternoon in a Military Cemetery near by.": Age 18 years, 363 days.

His brother James is buried in Sarigol Military Cemetery, Kriston (D.594). The two other men killed with Pte. Watt – Ptes. J. Martin and C. Reid, also have no known grave; they are recorded on Panel 134. Pte. McFadyean (promoted L/Corpl.) was killed in action three months later; he too has no known grave and is commemorated on the Ploegsteert Memorial (Panel 9).

(Panel 135) Pte. 265480, George Williamson, 2nd Bn. (78th Foot) The Seaforth Highlanders (Ross-shire Buffs, The Duke of Albany's).: *s.* of George Williamson, of Rosehill, Urquhart, co. Elgin, by his wife Jane, *dau.* of James Mitchell: *b.* Urquhart, aforesaid, 24 June 1896: *educ.* there: Occupation – Gardener: enlisted 2 September 1914: served with the Expeditionary Force in France and Flanders from May 1915. Reported wounded and missing after the fighting at Poelcapelle 4 October 1917; now assumed killed in action on that date: Age 21. *unm.*

(Panel 135) Capt. John Shedden Dobbie, 'C'Coy., 2nd Bn. (75th Foot) The Gordon Highlanders: *s.* of Col. Herbert H. Dobbie, Indian Army, of St. Erin's, Tarbert, Loch Fyneside, co. Argyll, by his wife Margaret, *dau.* of the late T. Forlong-Gordon: and brother to 2nd Lieut. H.W. Dobbie, Royal Berkshire Regt., killed in action 14 November 1916, at the Somme: *b.* Landour, India, 1894: *educ.* Tyttenhanger Lodge, St. Albans, and Weymouth College, co. Dorset: removed to Canada, 1911, where, after a brief period of farming, he entered Highfield College, Hamilton, from which he passed the entrance examinations to the Royal Military College: entered the service of the Bank of Montreal, 1913: proceeded overseas 1914; Sergt., no.430433, 15th (48th Highlanders of Canada) Battn.: received his commission in England, 2nd Gordon Highlanders, and went to France, July 1916: severely wounded 6 September following; rejoined his battalion, April 1917; was again wounded May (slightly); killed by shellfire, 5 October 1917, while making the rounds of his front line at Broodseinde: Age 23.

His brother Herbert also has no known grave; he is commemorated on the Thiepval Memorial (Pier & Face 11D).

(Panel 135) 2nd Lieut. George Bernard Locking Price, 8/10th (Service) Bn. The Gordon Highlanders: *s.* of the late Lieut.Col. William Locking Price, I.M.S., by his wife Minnie Mary (7, Duncan Street, Newington, Edinburgh), *dau.* of James Morrow: *b.* Pachmari, India, 4 August 1896: *educ.* Daniel Stewart's College, Edinburgh, where he was a member of the College Cadet Corps, and played for the First XI: thereafter entered University of Edinburgh as Medical Student: enlisted Royal Scots, 1915: served with the Expeditionary Force in France and Flanders from June 1916, wounded at the Battle of the Somme the following month, and invalided home: joined Officers' Training Battn., Gailes on recovery: obtained a commission, 27 March 1917; returned to France, May following. Killed in action at Ypres 22 August 1917. Buried in the captured territory there. His Colonel wrote, "He was killed while leading his men forward in the most gallant manner. He was a keen and fearless leader, and a big loss to us as well as to you." His Medical Officer wrote, "He was so full of spirit and anxiety to go up, and he knew his men so well... I admired him greatly, and his spirit permeated his platoon.": Age 21. *unm.* (*IWGC record 3rd attd. 8th Bn.*)

(Panel 135) Coy.Sergt.Maj. 1417, Charles O'Brien, 2nd Bn. (75th Foot) The Gordon Highlanders: *s.* of John O'Brien, of Uppermill, Asloun, Alford, Aberdeen, by his wife Christina, *dau.* of George McKay: *b.* West Balnakellie, 26 April 1896: *educ.* Gallowhill Public School, Alford: enlisted June 1914: served with the Expeditionary Force in France and Flanders from November 1915, and was killed at Ypres, on the Menin Road, 5 October 1917. His Chaplain wrote, "He was with the battalion in the recent successful advance. All objectives had been taken, and the positions consolidated, but the enemy continued to shell heavily. A big shell came right through, killing all the officers. Your son proved himself a good soldier, and his going is a severe loss to the company, and battalion.": Age 21. *unm.*

(Panel 135) Sergt. 6705, Charles Baillie, M.M., 8/10th (Service) Bn. The Gordon Highlanders: *s.* of the late William Baillie, by his wife Margaret Dodds (formerly Baillie, 181, Galapark Road, Galashiels), *dau.* of William Johnstone: *b.* Galashiels, 3 October 1894: *educ.* Burgh School, there: Occupation – Mill Worker: enlisted September 1914: served with the Expeditionary Force in France and Flanders from April 1915, and was killed in action at Square Farm 22 August 1917. A comrade wrote, "He was so well liked by the whole battalion." Awarded the Military Medal for 'gallant and distinguished service in the field.': Age 22. *unm.*

(Panel 135) Sergt. 200728, William Brodie, 4th Bn. The Gordon Highlanders (T.F.): *s.* of Isabella Ferrier (10, St. Mary's Place, Aberdeen): *b.* Miltonduff, 24 September 1896: *educ.* Grantown-on-Spey: was an Ironmonger: joined Gordon Highlanders, 4 November 1914: served with the Expeditionary Force in France from February 1915, and was killed in action north of Ypres 20 September 1917: Age 20. *unm.*

(Panel 135) Corpl. 240878, John Stuart Baird, 2nd Bn. (75th Foot) The Gordon Highlanders: *s.* of the late William Baird, by his wife Isabella Davidson Baird (11, Port Henry Road, Peterhead, co. Aberdeen): and yr. brother to Sergt. 240761, G. Baird, 1st Gordon Highlanders, died of wounds, 11 May 1918: *b.* Peterhead: enlisted there. Killed in action 26 October 1917: Age 20.

His brother George is buried in Etaples Military Cemetery (LXV.B.15).

(Panel 135) Corpl. 866, William Campbell, 6th Bn. The Gordon Highlanders (T.F.): *yst. s.* of Alexander Campbell, of Woodside, Tullynessie, Alford, co. Aberdeen, by his wife Elizabeth, *dau.* of Robert Stuart: *b.* Tullynessie, 29 January 1894: *educ.* there: Occupation – Mason: joined Gordon Highlanders, 1912: volunteered for Foreign Service on the outbreak of war, August 1914: served with the Expeditionary Force in France and Flanders, from November following: invalided home, September 1915: returned to France, January 1916: wounded at Vimy Ridge, June, after which he was in hospital for 11 months, only rejoining the regiment in June of the following year, and died at Zonnebeke, 26 September 1917, from wounds received in action there a few hours previously. Buried 50 yards behind the line at Zonnebeke: Age 23. *unm.* (*IWGC record 265080*)

(Panel 135) L/Corpl. 200063, William Greig Lawrie, 'C' Coy., 4th Bn. The Gordon Highlanders (T.F.): *yr. s.* of the late Hugh Hutcheson Lawrie, of the Aberdeen Northern Friendly Society, and Grand Treasurer of the Caledonian Order of United Oddfellows, by his wife Isabella (5A, Loanhead Place, Aberdeen), *dau.* of the late John Thain: *b.* Aberdeen, 21 March 1896: *educ.* Sunnybank, and Kittybrewster Public Schools, co. Aberdeen: employee Speyside Boot Works: joined 4th Gordon Highlanders, June 1910; mobilised on the outbreak of war, August 1914: served with the Expeditionary Force in France and Flanders from January 1915: previously wounded on two occasions; L/Corpl. Lawrie was killed in action nr. Passchendaele, 20 September 1917, while dressing the arm of a wounded comrade. His Officer wrote, "If it could be said of anyone that he had done his bit, surely it could be said of your son, who not only 'did his bit,' but 'did his all.' Over two and a half years' service in France is truly a record to be proud of. He had been my Lewis Gun Corpl., and did splendidly. His share in this war has been a glorious one, and to fall after so long and so faithful service seems very hard indeed, but no death could have been nobler.": Age 21. *unm.*

(Panel 135) L/Corpl. 202023, Robert McConnachie, 4th Bn. The Gordon Highlanders (T.F.): elder *s.* of Alexander McConnachie, of Pattiesmill, Keith-hall, Inverurie, Farmer, by his wife Margaret

'Maggie,' *dau*. of William Walker: *b*. Kinmuck, Inverurie, co. Aberdeen, 13 January 1898: *educ*. Keith-Hall Public School, and Inverurie Academy, where he gained the full leaving certificate entitling him to enter Aberdeen University: volunteered for Foreign Service, and joined Gordon Highlanders, 24 July 1916: served with the Expeditionary Force in France from 8 February 1917, and was killed in action at The Battle of the Menin Road, south-east of Ypres, 20 September following. Buried where he fell. The Chaplain wrote: "He was a very good N.C.O., and his place will be hard to fill," and his Classical Teacher: "He will live for ever in the memory of his teachers and schoolmates, and our heartfelt sympathy goes out to you in the loss of an excellent young man of great promise.": Age 19.

(Panel 135) L/Corpl. 265045, John Reid, 1/4th Bn. The Gordon Highlanders (T.F.): *s*. of Mrs E. Moir (Bridgefoot Cottage, Oyne, co. Aberdeen): *b*. Rhyhill, Oyne, 3 January 1892: *educ*. Public School, Oyne: joined Territorial Force, 1911: called up on the outbreak of war, undertook Active Service obligations and served with the Expeditionary Force in France and Flanders from November 1914. Killed in action by a sniper 20 September 1917. Age 25. *unm*.

(Panel 135) Pte. S/3395, John Gray Connor, 9th (Service) Bn. The Gordon Highlanders: brother to L/Corpl. S/4773, D. Connor, 10th Gordon Highlanders, killed in action 25 September 1915, at the Battle of Loos; and Pte. S/5959, D. Connor, 1st Gordon Highlanders, killed in action 25 September 1915, at Hooge: *b*. Paisley, co. Renfrew: enlisted there: served with the Expeditionary Force in France and Flanders from July 1915; killed in action 25 August 1917. (*SWM records Conner*)

His brother Daniel also has no known grave, he is commemorated on the Loos (Dud Corner) Memorial; David is buried in Bedford House Cemetery (X.H.8/Enc.No.4).

(Panel 135) Pte. 13671, Albert Coutts, 'B' Coy., 5th Platoon, 1st Bn. (75th Foot) The Gordon Highlanders: *s*. of George Coutts, of Duddington, Alford, co. Aberdeen, by his wife Mary, *dau*. of the late John O'Brien: *b*. Leochel, Cushnie, co. Aberdeen, 18 May 1893: *educ*. Cushnie: Occupation – Farm Labourer; Breda Home Farm: joined 6th (Territorial) Bn. Gordon Highlanders, August 1915: served with the Expeditionary Force in France and Flanders from April 1916; wounded June following and invalided home: returned to France, January 1917, there transf'd. 1st Battn. Reported wounded and missing, 26 September 1917, now assumed killed in action on or about that date: Age 24. *unm*.

PANEL 135 ENDS: PTE. A.P. DONALD, GORDON HIGHLANDERS.

PANEL 136 BEGINS: PTE. R.D. DONALD, GORDON HIGHLANDERS.

(Panel 136) Pte. 17567, James Cruickshank Downie, 2nd Bn. (92nd Foot) The Gordon Highlanders: *s*. of Alexander Downie, Shoemaker; of 23, Albyn Grove, Aberdeen, by his wife Jane, *dau*. of Alexander Cruickshank: *b*. Arbroath, co. Forfar, 31 January 1898: *educ*. Gordon's School, Huntly, co. Aberdeen: Occupation – Law Apprentice; Messrs A. & W. Robertson, Solicitors, Aberdeen: enlisted Seaforth Highlanders, 26 September 1916; trained Fort George: transf'd. Gordon Highlanders, March 1917: served with the Expeditionary Force in France and Flanders, and was killed in action 4 October 1917: Age 19.

(Panel 136) Pte. 266653, Frank Etwell, 2nd Bn. (92nd Foot) The Gordon Highlanders: *s*. of William Etwell, by his wife Elizabeth: and brother to Wheeler Corpl. 118972, W.H. Etwell, Royal Garrison Artillery, who also fell: *b*. Bawtry, co. York, 1894: employee Messrs Vickers Ltd., Sheffield: enlisted Sheffield: served with the Expeditionary Force in France and Flanders, and was killed in action at Passchendaele 4 October 1917: Age 23. *unm*.

His brother William is buried in Talana Farm Cemetery (III.J.8).

(Panel 136) Pte. 20457, Andrew Coutts Findlay Harper, 1/4th Bn. The Gordon Highlanders (T.F.): 3rd *s*. of George Hall Harper, of Tillyoch Cottage, Peterculter, co. Aberdeen, by his wife Elizabeth, *dau*. of the late George Findlay: *b*. Kenellar, co. Aberdeen, 16 March 1897: *educ*. Central School, Skene: Occupation – Farm Servant: joined Gordon Highlanders, 24 July 1915: served with the Expeditionary Force in France and Flanders, and was killed in action south-west of Poelcapelle 20 September 1917: Age 20. *unm*.

(Panel 136) Pte. S/41603, David Murray Henderson, 2nd Bn. (92nd Foot) The Gordon Highlanders: *s.* of the late George Henderson, by his wife Mary Ann. Killed in action 26 October 1917 at Passchendaele: Age 19.

(Panel 136) Pte. S/15802, James Leiper, 2nd Bn. (92nd Foot) The Gordon Highlanders: *s.* of Spr. John Leiper, Royal Engineers, by his wife Maria (11, Crimon Place, Aberdeen), *dau.* of the late Robert Courage, of Aberdeen: *b.* Aberdeen, 29 October 1899: *educ.* Middle Public School: employee Messrs Henderson, Aberdeen: enlisted Gordon Highlanders, 6 November 1916: served with the Expeditionary Force in France from 8 October 1917, and was killed in action on the 26th of that month; eighteen days after arriving in France; three days before his eighteenth birthday: Age 17.

(Panel 136) Pte. S/17275, John MacCaskill, 9th (Service) Bn. The Gordon Highlanders: *s.* of Alexander MacCaskill, of 34, Shiprow, Aberdeen, by his wife Margaret, *dau.* of Richard Jones: *b.* Aberdeen, 3 May 1898: *educ.* Frederick Street School: Occupation – Assistant Ship's Surveyor: enlisted Gordon Highlanders, 12 March 1917: served with the Expeditionary Force in France and Flanders from 6 July; killed in action nr. Ypres on the 26 August of the same year. Buried at Frezenberg, north-east of Ypres: 26 August 1917: Age 19. (*IWGC record McCaskill*)

(Panel 136) Pte. S/40486, Donald McIntyre, 8/10th (Service) Bn. The Gordon Highlanders: *s.* of James McIntyre, of Home Farm, Craigends, Johnstone, co. Renfrew, by his wife Agnes, *dau.* of John Moffat: *b.* Home Farm, Castle Toward, co. Argyle, 14 June 1888: *educ.* Bishopton, co. Renfrew; Holmscroft Higher Grade School, Greenock, and Glasgow Agricultural College: Occupation – Farm Servant: joined 1st Lovat's Scouts (T.F.), no.3685, 7 December 1915: served with the Expeditionary Force in France and Flanders with that unit from the following December; transf'd. Cameron Highlanders, January 1917: transf'd. Gordon Highlanders, and was killed in action near Ypres 26 August following: Age 29. An officer wrote, "He died doing his duty and death was instantaneous." He *m.* Bensley, Montgreenan, co. Ayr, 1906; Agnes, *dau.* of John McCulloch, and had a son James, *b.* 2 February 1907.

(Panel 136) Pte. 291084, Stuart Morrison, 4th Bn. The Gordon Highlanders (T.F.): eldest *s.* of John Wilson Morrison, of Hopewell Place, Mount Street, Banchory, by his wife Margaret, *dau.* of Stuart Russell: *b.* Midtown, Strachan, co. Kincardine, 8 July 1899: *educ.* Central Higher Grade School, Banchory: employee Messrs A & G Patterson Ltd., Sawmills, Banchory: joined Gordon Highlanders, 1 September 1915: served with the Expeditionary Force in France and Flanders from June 1916, wounded 22 September following, reported wounded and missing after the fighting at Poelcapelle 20 September 1917; now assumed killed in action on or about that date: Age 18. (*IWGC record 20 September 1917*)

(Panel 136) Pte. 292654, Edward Stevenson Pitblado, 7th Bn. The Gordon Highlanders: late of Isbister, North Roe, Shetland: late *husb.* to Mary Jane Sandison Pitblado (45, Sandport Street, Leith): *b.* Fortingal, co. Perth: enlisted Fort George: Reported missing 26 August 1917, since which date no further word has been received: Age 39.

(Panel 136) Pte. 266124, Gordon Robertson, 2nd Bn. (92nd Foot) The Gordon Highlanders: *s.* of William Robertson, of 6, Chapel Street, Portsoy, co. Banff, Shepherd, by his wife Margaret, *dau.* of James Webster: *b.* Portsoy, 15 February 1896: *educ.* Public School, Portsoy: Occupation – Farm Servant: enlisted 20 March 1915: served with the Expeditionary Force in France and Flanders from April to July 1916, and again from June 1917, until he was killed in action on the Menin Road, nr. Passchendaele, 26 October following. Buried where he fell: Age 21. *unm.*

(Panel 136) Pte. 202161, Joseph Skene, 1/4th Bn. The Gordon Highlanders (T.F.): *s.* of William Skene, of Mid Angustown, Peterculter, co. Aberdeen, Crofter, by his wife Annie, *dau.* of S. Beattie: *b.* Mureskie, Maryculter, co. Aberdeen, 20 May 1898: *educ.* West School, Maryculter: Occupation – Farm Servant: enlisted Aberdeen, 15 January 1916: served with the Expeditionary Force in France and Flanders from June following. Reported missing after the fighting at Ypres, 20 September 1917; now assumed killed in action on that date: Age 19.

(Panel 136) Pte. S/15566, Albert Thomson, 2nd Bn. (92nd Foot) The Gordon Highlanders: *s.* of Alexander Thomson, of 10, Richmond Terrace, Aberdeen, by his wife Mary. Killed in action 4 October 1917: Age 19.

Time and time again the fate of individual soldiers was decided purely by random; odd coincidences became so numerous as to be commonplace. One such incidence occurred on 4 October 1917 at the Battle of Broodseinde. 2nd Gordon Highlanders in continuing the attack from 8th Devons, who had successfully reached their objective with little opposition, strayed over to the left in tandem with the Australians sector of attack near Molenaarelsthoek. Despite 2nd Borderers having to spread themselves out to cover the gap the Gordons also attained their objective and consolidated the position. During the course of the advance the Gordons lost 65 men killed, of which fate decreed that three, although totally unrelated, should be named Thomson: Albert, John R. and John S. Coincidence enough in itself but for one of them the story did not end there.

In the early morning of Tuesday, 4 October 1917, John Robertson Thomson did not have long to live. By the end of the day he would become just another statistic, one of an eventual 270,000 British casualties of the Third Battle of Ypres. Like so many of those killed in this battle and others before it, his body simply disappeared into the quagmire of shell-blasted mud; seemingly fated to be one of the thousands who would have no known grave remembered only by name on a memorial to the missing.

In August 1998 a gardener at Molenaarelsthoek, near Zonnebeke, discovered three sets of human remains which, after initial examination and investigation by the Belgian Police who, by virtue of regimental insignias discovered with the remains (vital clues as to their possible identification), handed them over to the Commonwealth War Graves Commission. Each set of remains bore the badge of the Gordon Highlanders, one had a knife with his initials on and, following DNA tests, was positively identified as John R. Thomson. Six years later, on 21 October 2004, his remains and those of the other two Gordons (who could not be identified) were laid to rest in Polygon Wood Cemetery.

(Panel 136) Pte. 235495, John Robertson Thomson, 2nd Bn. (92nd Foot) The Gordon Highlanders: *b.* Cowdenbeath, co. Fife: enlisted Milnathort, nr. Loch Leven. Reported wounded and missing nr. Molenaarelsthoek, 4 October 1917, since confirmed killed. He was married to Annie Thomson (13, Auchterderran Road, Lochgelly, co. Fife). *Buried Polygon Wood Cemetery (Coll.Grave D.2A).*

Fare Thee Well Our Scottish Soldier
Rest In Peace Your Battles 'Oer

(Panel 136) Pte. 203025, John S. Thomson, 2nd Bn. (92nd Foot) The Gordon Highlanders: *s.* of Andrew S. Thomson, of 'Deolali,' Kulaisbrae, Alloa, by his wife Agnes B.: *b.* Alloa, co. Clackmannan: enlisted Aberdeen. Killed in action 4 October 1917: Age 26. *unm.* Assistant Classical Master, Mackie Academy, Stonehaven; Pte. Thomson was one of three Masters of the Academy to fall in the Great War: Capt. A.B. Burton, M.C., Highland Light Infantry, and L/Corpl. T. Wilkinson, Cameron Highlanders, being the other two.

Capt. Burton is commemorated on the Ploegsteert Memorial (Panel 9), Pte. Wilkinson on the Thiepval Memorial (Pier & Face 15B).

(Panel 136) Pte. 202897, Alexander Watt, 1/4th Bn. The Gordon Highlanders (T.F.): eldest *s.* of Alexander Watt, of Sheilbog, Keithall, Inverurie, co. Aberdeen, Farmer, by his wife Annie, *dau.* of Nathaniel Rennie: *b.* Aberdeen, 8 September 1896: *educ.* Keithall Public School: Occupation – Farm Servant: joined Gordon Highlanders, 27 March 1917: served with the Expeditionary Force in France and Flanders from 26 June following, and was killed in action at Menin Road 20 September of the same year. Buried where he fell. The Chaplain, Rev. Alexander Macleod, wrote, "We miss your son very much indeed, for he was a great favourite in the battalion. He was always a soldier, and he did his duty faithfully, and never better than on the last day of all.": Age 21. *unm.*

Cha Till Maccruimein

(Departure of the 4th Cameron Highlanders)

The pipes in the street were playing bravely,
The marching lads went by,
With Merry hearts and voices singing
My friends marched out to die;
But I was hearing a lonely pibroch
Out of an older war,
"Farewell, farewell, farewell, MacCrimmon,
MacCrimmon comes no more."

And every lad in his heart was dreaming
Of honour and wealth to come,
And honour and noble pride were calling
To the tune of the pipes and drum;
But I was hearing a woman singing
On dark Dunvegan shore,
"In battle or peace, with wealth or honour,
MacCrimmon comes no more."

And there in front of the men were marching,
With feet that made no mark,
The grey old ghosts of the ancient fighters
Come back again from the dark;
And in front of them all MacCrimmon piping
A weary tune and sore,
"On the gathering day, for ever and ever,
MacCrimmon comes no more."

E.A. Mackintosh

PANEL 136 ENDS: SERGT. D. DOIG, CAMERON HIGHLANDERS.

PANEL 137 BEGINS: SERGT. H. LAWSON, CAMERON HIGHLANDERS.

(Panel 137) Sergt. 200044, Robert John Macgregor, 4th (T.F.) attd. 5th (Service) Bn. The Queen's Own (Cameron Highlanders): eldest *s.* of the late Robert Macgregor, of Duror, School Master, by his wife Christina 'Tina' ('Craigroyston,' Tightehan, Duror), *dau.* of the late John Menzies: *b.* Duror, co. Argyll, 22 August 1893: *educ.* Duror and Appin Public Schools; Kingussie High School (Bursary Scholar), and Skerry's College, Edinburgh (Bronze and Silver Medals): was an Excise Officer, taking First Place for the United Kingdom in the Custom and Excise Examination, November 1913: joined 4th (Schoolboys') Battn. Cameron Highlanders 1909, while at Kingussie High School: called up on mobilisation, 4 August 1914: served with the Expeditionary Force in France and Flanders from February 1915, taking part in many engagements there, including the Battle of Loos, 25 September following: subsequently offered a commission – declined it, preferring to stay in the ranks: apptd. Drill Instructor at the Base; subsequently attd. 5th Battn. Cameron Highlanders, and was killed in action at Poelcapelle 12 October 1917. Buried in the Military Cemetery, near Burn's House Farm, there. His Commanding Officer wrote, "Your son was a brave man, and a good comrade, cool and collected under fire; beloved and trusted by his officers and men, and one who will be sorely missed in the regiment;" and a comrade, "We have indeed lost a true friend and gallant comrade.": Age 24. *unm.*

(Panel 137) Corpl. 202981, William Dott, 4th (T.F.) attd. 5th (Service) Bn. The Queen's Own (Cameron Highlanders): *s.* of Mrs H. Dott (Spey Street, Kingussie, co. Inverness): and brother to Pte. 3003, A.C. Dott, 4th Cameron Highlanders, who fell, 18 May 1915, at Festubert. Killed in action 12 October 1917: Age 25. *unm.*

His brother Alexander also has no known grave; he is commemorated on the Le Touret Memorial.

(Panel 137) Corpl. 200346, Alexander Peter Ewen, 5th (Service) Bn. The Queen's Own (Cameron Highlanders): *s.* of the late Alexander Ewen, by his wife Annie (9, Land Street, Keith), *dau.* of Alexander Pirie: *b.* Keith, co. Banff, 7 November 1893: *educ.* Grammar School: Occupation – Grocer: joined 4th Cameron Highlanders, 9 September 1914: served with the Expeditionary Force in France and Flanders from 19 February 1915: transf'd. 5th Battn., 9 October 1917; reported missing after the fighting on the 12th of that month, and is now assumed to have been killed in action on that date, 12 October 1917: Age 23. *unm.*

(Panel 137) L/Corpl. 15676, William Fernie, 5th (Service) Bn. The Queen's Own (Cameron Highlanders): 2nd *s.* of William Fernie, of 'Dungoyne,' Sandy Road, Renfrew, by his wife Margaret, *dau.* of Donald McLean: *b.* Maryhill, Glasgow, co. Lanark, 9 September 1893: *educ.* Eastpark Public School, there, and Moorpark School, Renfrew: Occupation – Apprenticed Draughtsman: volunteered for Active Service, enlisted Cameron Highlanders, November 1914: served with the Expeditionary Force in France and Flanders from August 1915 until October 1916, when he was wounded in the head: hospitalised England, and then in Ireland till March 1918, when he was sent back to France. Killed in action at Kemmel Hill, 25 April 1918. Buried nr. Damstrasse: Age 24. *unm.*

(Panel 137) L/Corpl. S/22886, Hugh McLean, 1st Bn. (79th Foot) The Queen's Own (Cameron Highlanders): *yr. s.* of the late Robert McLean, of St. Ninian's, Stirling: *b.* Kilbrandon, co. Argyle, 7 September 1885: *educ.* Connell Ferry, Oban: Occupation – Upholsterer: enlisted 2 June 1916: served with the Expeditionary Force in France and Flanders, and was killed in action at Passchendaele Ridge 15 November 1917: Age 32. He *m.* Stirling, 11 September 1914; Margaret Mitchel (18, Bruce Street, Stirling), *dau.* of the late James Page, and had a son Robert, *b.* 4 July 1915.

(Panel 137) Pte. S/18269, Charles Stanley Dann, 5th (Service) Bn. The Queen's Own (Cameron Highlanders): *s.* of Albert Thomas Dann, of Criers Cottage, Five Ashes, Mayfield, co. Sussex, and Fanny Dann, his spouse: and brother to Gnr.103660, H. Dann, 56th Bde., Royal Field Artillery, died of wounds, 26 August 1918: *b.* Mayfield: enlisted London. Killed in action 18 April 1918: Age 21.

His brother Herbert is buried in Bac-sur-Sud British Cemetery, Bailleulval (III.E.16).

(Panel 137) Pte. S/27545, Alexander Downie, 5th (Service) Bn. The Queen's Own (Cameron Highlanders): *s.* of McEwan Downie, of Sunnyside Cottage, Kilwinning, and Isabella, his wife: *husb.* to Annie (5, Newhunterfield, Gorebridge, Midlothian): and brother to A/Bmdr. 655224, D. Downie, Royal Field Artillery, died of wounds, 10 November 1917: *b.* Straiton, co. Ayr, 1888: enlisted Bathgate, 1915. Killed in action 12 October 1917: Age 29. At 5.25 a.m., 12 October 1917, 9th Division attacked towards Wallemolen; 5th Cameron Highlanders and 7th Seaforths were in support. The attack went well at first but after encountering strong enemy resistance from the vicinity of Wallemolen, Beek and Meunier Houses, the brigade was forced back. After a day of hard fighting and heavy casualties the Brigade advance had ground to a halt 100 yards from its start; among the casualties was 29 year old Alexander Downie, killed between Inch House and the Cemetery. Within a month his brother David would join him, another casualty of the war.

His brother David is buried in Wimereux Communal Cemetery (VI.G.20A).

(Panel 137) Pte. S/22238, Peter Lugton, 7th (Service) Bn. The Queen's Own (Cameron Highlanders): *s.* of the late John Lugton, by his wife Susan (School Road, Gifford, Edinburgh, co. Midlothian): *b.* West Bearford, Haddington, co. East Lothian, 1886: prior to enlistment was 3 yrs. Telegraph Messenger; 12 yrs. Postman. Missing / believed killed in action, 21 – 24 August 1917; vicinity Pommern Castle – Hill 35: Age 31.

(Panel 137) Pte. 220076, James Middleton, 6th (Service) Bn. The Queen's Own (Cameron Highlanders): formerly no.202828, Argyll & Sutherland Highlanders: late of Alloa: enlisted Stirling. Killed in action 28 August 1917.

(Panel 137) Pte. 203391, David Skelly, 5th (Service) Bn. The Queen's Own (Cameron Highlanders): *s.* of Eliza Skelly (South Ailey Cottage, Cove, co. Dumbarton): and brother to Pte. S/16894, A. Skelly, M.M., 7th Cameron Highlanders, killed in action, 25 September 1915, at Loos: *b.* Cove, 1898: enlisted Dumbarton. Killed in action 3 October 1918: Age 20. *unm.*

His brother Archibald also has no known grave; he is commemorated on the Loos Memorial.

(Panel 137) Pte. S/27530, David Smith, 5th (Service) Bn. The Queen's Own (Cameron Highlanders): *s.* of the late Hugh Smith, by his wife Margaret ('Meadowside,' Dunachton, Kingussie, co. Inverness), *dau.* of David Reid: and brother to Pte. S/40962, H. Smith, Cameron Highlanders, killed south-east of Ypres 23 August 1917: *b.* Kincraig, co. Inverness, 31 January 1892: *educ.* Alvie Public School: Occupation – Farm Servant; Croftcarnoch and Kincraig Farm: enlisted Cameron Highlanders, 29 May 1916: served with the Expeditionary Force in France and Flanders from January 1917, and was killed in action at Zonnebeke, north-east of Ypres, 23 September following. Buried there. Lieut. Charlton wrote, "He carried on bravely till his hour came, and I only hope a justifiable pride may temper your grief.": Age 25. *unm.*

His brother Hugh also has no known grave; his name is recorded below.

(Panel 136) Pte. S/40962, Hugh Smith, 6th (Service) Bn. The Queen's Own (Cameron Highlanders): *s.* of the late Hugh Smith, by his wife Margaret ('Meadowside,' Dunachton, Kingussie, co. Inverness), *dau.* of David Reid: and brother to Pte. S/27530, D. Smith, Cameron Highlanders, who fell north-east of Ypres, 23 September 1917: *b.* Kincraig, co. Inverness, 28 September 1893: *educ.* Alvie Public School: Occupation – Farm Servant: joined Cameron Highlanders (Territorials) 18 March 1910: called up on mobilisation, August 1914, transf'd. 6th (Service) Bn.: served with the Expeditionary Force in France and Flanders from February 1915, and was killed in action south-east of Ypres 23 August 1917. Sergt. Major D.P. Fraser wrote, "There are many sad homes caused by the war, but you have the consolation that your son came to France voluntarily early in the war when men were badly needed; he did his bit and died a soldier's death advancing to attack the enemy under heavy machine-gun fire.": Age 23. *unm.* (*IWGC record 24 August*)

His brother David also has no known grave; his name is recorded above.

PANEL 137 ENDS: PTE. J. SMITH, CAMERON HIGHLANDERS.

PANEL 138 BEGINS: PTE. G. SMITH, M.M., CAMERON HIGHLANDERS.

(Panel 138) Capt. Arthur John Ross, 5th (Extra Reserve) attd 1st Bn. (83rd Foot) The Royal Irish Rifles: *s.* of Charles John Ross, of Oaken Holt, co. Oxford, by his wife Clarissa Findlay, 3rd *dau.* of I. Wyllie Guild, of Park Terrace, Glasgow: *b.* Busby House, co. Renfrew, 22 May 1876 *educ.* Britannia: served in the Merchant Service, 1892-1899: joined Paget's Horse, 1899: served in the South African War 1899-1902 (Queen's Medal with clasps): gazetted 2nd Lieut., Royal Irish Rifles, 1909: served with the Expeditionary Force in France and Flanders from 1 May 1915: wounded nr. Ovillers, La Boiselle, 31 July 1916, and invalided home; returned to his unit in Flanders on recovery the following May. Reported wounded and missing after the fighting at Westhoek, Ypres Sector, 16 August 1917; now assumed to have been killed in action on that date: Age 41. He *m.* St. Stephen's Church, Kensington, London, W., 30 July 1904; Una Mary, now Lady Ross (Old Court, Strangford, co. Down), *dau.* of the Hon. Anthony Lucius Dawson and the Baroness de Ros, and had two sons, Peter, *b.* 8 August 1906 and Charles Dudley Anthony, *b.* 5 October 1907.

(Panel 138) 2nd Lieut. Robert Hannah, 7th (Service) Bn. The Royal Irish Rifles: formerly Tpr. Westmorland and Cumberland Yeomanry: *s.* of Robert Hannah, of 115, Abbey Road, Barrow-in-Furness, by his wife Jessie: and elder brother to 2nd Lieut. E.M.. Hannah, M.C., 1st attd. 6th King's Shropshire Light Infantry, killed the same day. Reported missing, later killed in action, 16 August 1917: Age 22.

His brother Edward also has no known grave; he is recorded on Panel 112.

(Panel 138) 2nd Lieut. John Alexander Patterson Bill, 18th (Reserve) attd. 12th (Service) Bn. The Royal Irish Rifles: *s.* of Samuel Alexander Bill, of Mission House, Qua Iboe, Southern Nigeria, by his wife Grace: *b.* Edinburgh, 8 July 1895: educ. Royal Belfast Academic Institution (entered 1907), and Queen's University (awarded Drennan Exhibition) from whence – had the outbreak of war not intervened – it was his intent to follow in his father's footsteps as a missionary: enlisted Royal Army Medical Corps, subsequently obtaining a commission and transferring Royal Irish Rifles, 1915: served with the Expeditionary Force in France, and was killed, 16 August 1917, in the vicinity of Gallipoli Farm, at the Battle of Langemarck. A fellow officer, 2nd Lieut. Stokes wrote, "This officer was last seen about map ref. D 19 b 10 90. He was lying on the ground apparently wounded in the groin or lower abdomen. Rfn Matthews went out to dress him but was himself killed in the act of doing so, and it is supposed that the same bullet also hit Mr Bill. The men had by this time started coming back and Mr Bill was left behind apparently very seriously wounded.": Age 22. *unm.*

Rfn. Matthews also has no known grave (recorded as 15 August 1917), he is commemorated on the Ypres (Menin Gate) Memorial (Panel 40).

(Panel 138) Sergt. 6142, Arthur Bagnall Henry, 7th (Service) Bn. The Royal Irish Rifles: *s.* of the late William Henry, Farmer, by his wife Charlotte (Ballinafad, co. Roscommon), *dau.* of John Bagnall: *b.* Ballinafad, 17 July 1886: *educ.* National School, there: Occupation – Shop Assistant: enlisted 27 April 1915: served with the Expeditionary Force in France and Flanders from the following December, and was killed in action at Ypres 17 August 1917. Age 31. He *m.* Thomastown Parish Church, co. Kilkenny, 30 November 1916; Lillian E. Rumball, *née* Henry (since remarried: resident – Ashley House, Glastonbury, co. Somerset), *dau.* of William Lecky, of Mallow, co. Cork: *s.p.* (*IWGC record age 36*)

(Panel 138) L/Corpl. 40839, William John Robinson, D.C.M., 1st Bn. (83rd Foot) The Royal Irish Rifles: 2nd *s.* of Joseph Robinson, of Rathkeel, Broughshane, Ballymena, Co. Antrim, Farmer, by his wife Agnes, *dau.* of the late James Gordon, of Craigywarren, Ballymena: *b.* Rathkeel *afsd.*, 19 February 1897: *educ.* Lisnamurrican National School: joined North Irish Horse (Special Reserve), November 1915: volunteered for Foreign Service; transf'd. 1st Royal Irish Rifles, December 1915; served with the Expeditionary Force in France and Flanders from that month, taking part in the Somme offensive, also in the Ypres operations (31 July 1917), and was killed in action nr. Ypres 16 August 1917. Buried at Westhoek. Awarded the D.C.M. (*London Gazette*, 26 February 1918), "For conspicuous gallantry and devotion to duty. When all his company runners had become casualties he acted as Runner all day, taking messages under severe conditions, to advanced posts, or shell holes. His successful efforts in performing this extremely dangerous and most important work, contributed very greatly to the repulse of two subsequent counter-attacks.": Age 20. *unm.*

(Panel 138) Rfn. 1420, John Biggart, 14th (Service) Bn. (Young Citizens) The Royal Irish Rifles: *s.* of John Biggart, of Bendooragh, Ballymoney, Co. Antrim, by his wife Mary Ann, *née* McNeill: and brother to Pte. 41388, W. Biggart, 9th Royal Irish Fusiliers, died of wounds, 3 April 1918, aged 23 years: *b.* Bendooragh, 1898: enlisted Ballymoney, 1914. Killed in action 16 August 1917: Age 19.

His brother William also has no known grave; he is commemorated on the Pozieres Memorial.

PANEL 138 ENDS: RFN. J. CLARKE, ROYAL IRISH RIFLES.

PANEL 139 BEGINS: RFN. L. CLAY, ROYAL IRISH RIFLES.

(Panel 139) Rfn. 52438, Alfred James Evans, 12th (Service) Bn. The Royal Irish Rifles: formerly no.38482, Royal Warwickshire Regt.: *s.* of Joseph George (& Minnie) Evans, of Chapel Street, Borough Green, Sevenoaks, co. Kent: *b.* Sevenoaks: enlisted Maidstone: transf'd. Royal Irish Rifles late May 1918 (shortly after his 19th birthday) and was killed on the afternoon of 6 June 1918, when, while at duty on a working party (Kemmel – Vierstraat sector), a shell burst close by, killing nine men; a further three (Rfn. T.A. Evered, G. Quinlan, W.L. Mills) died of wounds shortly afterwards: Age 19.

The other eight killed are buried in Klein-Vierstraat British Cemetery (V.A.17); Rfn. Evered, Hagle Dump Cemetery (I.A.3); Rfn. G. Quinlan and W.L. Mills, Lijssenthoek Military Cemetery (XXVIII.F.1/1A).

(Panel 139) Ptc. 41478, Frederick Harold Goodship, 12th (Service) Bn. The Royal Irish Rifles: formerly no.3824, 1/5th Bedfordshire Regt.: *husb.* to Dorothy Goodship (169, High Town Road, Luton, co. Bedford): and brother to Pte. 3840, H. Goodship, 5th Bedfordshire Regt., killed in action, 16 August 1915, at Gallipoli: enlisted Luton. Killed in action 15 April 1918: Age 30. Remembered on Stopsley (St. Thomas') Church War Memorial.

His brother Horace also has no known grave; he is commemorated on the Helles Memorial.

(Panel 139) Rfn. 43688, Frederick Manktelow, 13th (Service) Bn. The Royal Irish Rifles: *s.* of William (& Ann) Manktelow, of Riverside House, Lamberhurst, Tunbridge Wells, co. Kent: and yr. brother to Pte. 1702, A. Manktelow, 56th Australian Infantry, killed in action 1 November 1916: *b.* Lamberhurst: enlisted Woolwich. Killed in action 16 August 1917: Age 33. He was married to Matilda Scott Manktelow (113, Queen's Road, Tunbridge Wells).

His brother Albert also has no known grave; he is commemorated on the Villers-Bretonneux Memorial (Panel 26).

PANEL 139 ENDS: RFN. H. PARKER, ROYAL IRISH RIFLES.

PANEL 140 BEGINS: RFN. R.W. PARRY, ROYAL IRISH RIFLES.

(Panel 140) Rfn. 18648, Alexander Quinn, 12th (Service) Bn. (Central Antrim) The Royal Irish Rifles: *s.* of Davidson Quinn, of 582, Cottage, Ballylough, Annsborough, Co. Down, by his wife Susan: and elder brother to Rfn. 18649, T. Quinn, 13th Bn. Royal Irish Rifles, died 3 June 1917, of wounds: *b.* Kilwinning, co. Ayr: enlisted Downpatrick, Co. Down. Killed in action 13 April 1918: Age 25. *unm.*

His brother Thomas is buried in Bailleul Communal Cemetery Extension (III.B.225).

(Panel 140) Rfn. 4935, Scott Thompson, 12th (Service) Bn. (Central Antrim) The Royal Irish Rifles: *s.* of James Thompson, of Lisnafillin, Gracehill, Co. Antrim, by his wife Mary Jane: and brother to Carpenter's Crewman M/16988, C.M. Thompson, H.M.S. Vanguard, who was one of 843 members of that ships' company killed when she sank, 9 July 1917, following an explosion caused by a stoke-hold fire overheating cordite stored against the bulkhead in an adjacent magazine amidship: enlisted Ballymena: served with the Expeditionary Force in France and Flanders from October 1915, and was killed in the vicinity of Somme Farm at the Battle of Langemarck, 16 August 1917: Age 35. Both brothers are commemorated on a memorial in Gracehill Moravian Cemetery, Ballymena.

His brother Charles also has no known grave; he is commemorated on the Chatham Naval Memorial (Panel 24).

(Panel 140) Rfn. 7281, Samuel Topping, 'A' Coy., 11th (Service) Bn. (South Antrim) The Royal Irish Rifles: *b.* Blaris, Co. Antrim: resided Lisburn: volunteered and enlisted in Royal Irish Rifles, Lisburn, with his nephew Corpl. 11/18838, H. Topping: trained Bordon Camp: served with the Expeditionary Force in France and Flanders from October 1915: reported missing in action on the Somme, 16 July 1916, and wounded September following. '*The Lisburn Standard*,' 31 August 1917, recorded – '...it is unofficially reported that he was seen to fall in the attack at Langemarck.': subsequently reported killed in action, 16 August 1917, the same day as his nephew: Age 45. Rfn. Topping leaves a wife, Annie (27, Millbrook Road, Lisburn).

His nephew Henry is recorded on the Addenda Panel.

(Panel 140) Capt. Charles Beauclerk Despard, D.S.O., M.C., 9th (Service) Bn. (Co. Armagh) The Princess Victoria's (Royal Irish Fusiliers): *yst. s.* of the late William Francis Despard, of 'Sheelagh,' Malone Park, Belfast, by his wife Mary, *dau.* of Col. Arthur Hunt, R.A.: *b.* Cultra, Co. Down, 31 December 1880: *educ.*

Royal Academical Institution, Belfast: served with the Imperial Yeomanry as 2nd Lieut. in the South African War 1899-1902 (Mentioned in Despatches by Col. Parris; Queen's and King's Medal): went to Canada, 1909; settled Lloydminster, Saskatchewan: Occupation – Rancher: returned to England on the outbreak of war, August 1914, volunteered for Active Service: gazetted Lieut., 6th Inniskilling Dragoons, October 1914; Capt. November 1915: transf'd. Royal Irish Fusiliers, October 1917: took part in the fighting nr. Cambrai, November 1917; the retreat from St. Quentin, 21-29 March 1918, and was killed in action at Kemmel Hill, 18 April following. Buried in Kemmel Cemetery: Age 37. Awarded the D.S.O. and the M.C. for 'gallantry and distinguished services in the field.' He *m.* at Leixlip, Co. Kildare, 20 February 1915, Josephine ('The Acacias', Portarlington, Queen's Co.), elder *dau.* of the Rev. R. Madden: *s.p.*

(Panel 140) 2nd Lieut. Harry Albert Mostyn Hoops, 4th (Extra Reserve) Bn. The Princess Victoria's (Royal Irish Fusiliers) attd. 7th (Service) Bn. Royal Irish Rifles: *s.* of Dr. Harry Lysaght Hoops, L.R.C.S., L.R.C.P., of 119, Albany Road, Cardiff, Physician & Surgeon; by his wife Frances Elizabeth, *dau.* of William D. Nisbet, of London: and *gdson.* of the Very Rev. Samuel E. Hoops, D.D., Dean of Armagh, of Fenagh Rectory, co. Leitrim: *b.* Eccles, nr. Manchester, co. Lancaster, 10 February 1897: *educ.* Cardiff High School: Occupation – Articled Clerk; Richard Leyshon, Chartered Accountant, Cardiff Docks: joined Inns of Court O.T.C., 8 August 1915: gazetted 2nd Lieut., Royal Irish Fusiliers, 26 October 1916: served with the Expeditionary Force in France and Flanders from 9 January 1917, attd. 7th Royal Irish Rifles, and was killed in action by a sniper on the Ypres – Menin Railway, 16 August following, while leading his men into action. Buried where he fell. His Commanding Officer wrote, "He was a splendid officer, and most popular with his men;" and an N.C.O., "Lieut. Hoops fell cheering his men onward, and he died with his face to the enemy.": Age 20. *unm.*

(Panel 140) Corpl. 49875, James Walter Fowler, 1st Bn. (87th Foot) The Princess Victoria's (Royal Irish Fusiliers): formerly no.8040, 9th Bn. (Queen Victoria's Rifles) London Regt.: *s.* of James (& Mrs) Fowler, of Lambeth, London, S.E. Killed in action 22 October 1918: Age 21. He leaves a widow, Alice (90, Tyers Street, Vauxhall, London). *Known to be buried in Harlebeke New British Cemetery (VIII.C.18).*

PANEL 140 ENDS: PTE. H. DALZELL, ROYAL IRISH FUSILIERS.

PANEL 141 BEGINS: PTE. A. DAVEY, ROYAL IRISH FUSILIERS.

(Panel 141) Pte. 43215, James William Herring, 9th (Service) Bn. (Co. Armagh) The Princess Victoria's (Royal Irish Fusiliers): formerly no.40325, Sherwood Foresters: *s.* of the late John James Herring, of Mason Street, Sutton-in-Ashfield, Miner, by his wife Mary Ann, *née* Rhodes (48, St. Michael Street, Sutton-in-Ashfield): and brother to Pte. 41856, F. Herring, Northamptonshire Regt., died of wounds, 3 September 1918, at Rouen; and brother-in-law to Pte. 50006, S. Sills, Lincolnshire Regt., who also fell: *b.* Mansfield, *c.*1889: Occupation – Miner, New Hucknall Colliery: enlisted Mansfield, Nottingham, November 1914: subsequently went with a draft to the Dardanelles where he was wounded and following a period of convalescence, was thereafter transf'd, Royal Irish Fusiliers, with which regiment he went to France, and was reported missing believed killed in action 16 August 1917: Age 28. He was married to Sarah Ann Smith, *née* Herring (186, New Buildings, Doe Lea, Chesterfield, co. Derby), late of New Houghton, and had three children. *The Notts Free Press*, 16 August 1918, carried the following 'In Memoriam' notices:

> *Under the shade of the dear old flag, Out in a strange lone land,*
> *Lies one of the best and bravest lads, Slain by the enemy's hand.*
> *So sad and sudden was the call, His sudden death surprised us all;*
> *Our trial is hard we will not complain, But trust in God to meet again.*

Loving Wife and Children.

> *Dear is the grave where my brother is laid, Sweet is the memory that never will fade;*
> *'Tis sad, but 'tis true, and we cannot tell, why the best are the first who are called to die.*

Sister, Frances and Children.

His brother Fred is buried in St. Sever Cemetery Extension, Rouen (R.II.J.21); Samuel Sills has no known grave he is commemorated on the Arras Memorial, Faubourg d'Amiens.

(Panel 141) Pte. 41762, Edward McKenna, 1st Bn. (87th Foot) The Princess Victoria's (Royal Irish Fusiliers): formerly no.S/4/094647, Royal Army Service Corps: *s.* of Edward McKenna, of 49, Tallow Street, Carlow, by his wife Minnie: and brother to Pte. 9508, J. McKenna, 2nd Leinster Regt., killed in action, 10 November 1914, aged 21 years: *b.* Omagh, Co. Tyrone: enlisted Carlow. Killed in action 14 April 1918: Age 24.

His brother James is buried in Canadian Cemetery No.2, Neuville-St. Vaast (II.E.2).

(Panel 141) Lieut. James Emil Burleigh, M.C., 12th (Service) Bn. The Princess Louise's (Argyll & Sutherland Highlanders): 3rd *s.* of the late Bennet Burleigh (former *Daily Telegraph* War Correspondent; *d.* 17 June 1914), by his wife Bertha Bennet (19, Glyn Mansions, West Kensington, London): and brother to Lieut. B. Burleigh, 7th Lancashire Fusiliers, died of wounds, 15 July 1915, received at Krithia, Gallipoli; and Lieut. R. Burleigh, 15th Sqdn. Royal Air Force and Royal Engineers, killed in action, 29 August 1916, at the Somme: *b.* Clapham, London, 1897. Killed in action 12 October 1917. He was awarded the Military Cross (*Edinburgh Gazette*, 10 January 1918), "For conspicuous gallantry and devotion to duty during a raid on the enemy's lines. He led his party with great determination, bombed a strong point which was holding him up, and caused considerable casualties, and when the signal to withdraw was given, carried back a badly wounded man himself and afterwards returned twice in search of others. It was entirely owing to his personal reconnaissance on the previous night that the enemy were located so that the raid could be planned.": Age 21. *unm.*

His brother Bennet is buried in Lancashire Landing Cemetery (A.50); Robert, Knightsbridge Cemetery, Mesnil-Martinsart (C.9).

(Panel 141) Lieut. Charles William Hewer, 9th (Dumbartonshire) Bn. (T.F.) attd. 11th (Service) Bn. The Princess Louise's (Argyll & Sutherland Highlanders): *s.* of the late Capt. William Chibbet Hewer, Mercantile Marine, by his wife Jessie Mair, *dau.* of the late Charles Freebairn: *b.* Bowling, co. Dumbarton, 19 September 1894: *educ.* Larchfield; Helensburgh, and Merchiston Castle, Edinburgh: formerly Staff Member, General Assurance Corporation Ltd., Glasgow: enlisted 9th (Dumbarton) Battn. Argyll & Sutherland Highlanders, 12 September 1914: gazetted 2nd Lieut., 23 April 1915; promoted Lieut. 1 July 1917: served with the Expeditionary Force in France and Flanders from July 1915. Reported missing after the fighting nr. Ypres, 22 August 1917; now assumed killed in action on that date: Age 22. *unm.*

(Panel 141) 2nd Lieut. William 'Willie' Boyd Whyte, 9th (Dumbartonshire) Bn. (T.F.) attd. 8th (Argyllshire) Bn. The Princess Louise's (Argyll & Sutherland Highlanders), (T.F.): eldest *s.* of James Boyd Whyte, of 9, Greenvale Terrace, Dumbarton, Pattern Maker; by his wife Abbie, *dau.* of John Robinson: *b.* Dumbarton, 25 December 1891: *educ.* College Street Public School; Dumbarton Academy, and Glasgow University: Occupation – Solicitor: joined 6th (Territorial) Battn. Highland Light Infantry, 2 March 1916: obtained a commission; gazetted 2nd Lieut. 9th (Dumbarton) Battn. Argyll & Sutherland Highlanders, 8 February 1917: subsequently transf'd./attd. 5th (Renfrew) Battn. as Anti-Gas Officer: served with the Expeditionary Force in France and Flanders from 2 August 1917, being attd. 8th (Argyll) Battn., and was killed in action, north of the Lekkerboterbeek, 20 September following; his battalion's only officer fatality that day. Buried where he fell: Age 25. *unm.* (*IWGC record age 26*)

(Panel 141) Sergt. 350789, Donald McIvor, 1/7th Bn. The Princess Louise's (Argyll & Sutherland Highlanders), (T.F): *s.* of the late John McIvor, by his wife Jane (35, Greenfield Street, Alloa), *dau.* of William Sharp, of Clackmannan: *b.* Alloa, 30 July 1892: *educ.* there: Occupation – Cooper: joined 7th Battn. Argyll & Sutherland Highlanders, 11 January 1906: volunteered for Foreign Service on the outbreak of war, August 1914: served with the Expeditionary Force in France and Flanders from December following: slightly gassed – Hill 60, 25 April 1915 – invalided home, January 1916: returned to the Front, May 1917, and was killed in action at Ypres, 20 September following. Buried in a British Cemetery, north-east of Ypres: Age 25. *unm.*

(Panel 141) Sergt. S/5034, William McQuarrie, M.M., 11th (Service) Bn. The Princess Louise's (Argyll & Sutherland Highlanders): *s.* of John McQuarrie, by his first wife Rebecca, *née* McSherry: step-son of Mary

McQuarrie (Hillhead, Gatehouse of Fleet, co. Kirkcudbright): and yr. brother to Pte. 8574, L. McQuarrie, 6th King's Own Scottish Borderers, killed in action, 25 September 1915: enlisted September 1914: served with the Expeditionary Force in France and Flanders from July 1915; missing, presumed killed in action, 22 August 1917: Age 29. He *m.* Gatehouse, 1915; Agnes Jane McQuarrie (Twynholm, co. Kirkcudbright).

His brother Lauchlin also has no known grave; he is commemorated on the Loos Memorial.

PANEL 141 ENDS: SERGT. W. MCQUARRIE, M.M., ARGYLL & SUTHERLAND HIGHLANDERS.

PANEL 142 BEGINS: SERGT. H.J. RAE, ARGYLL & SUTHERLAND HIGHLANDERS.

(Panel 142) Pte. 301053, Christian Taylor Bryan, 'A' Coy., 1/8th (Argyllshire) Bn. The Princess Louise's (Argyll & Sutherland Highlanders) (T.F.): *s.* of John Taylor Bryan, of 24, Darnley Street, Old Trafford, Manchester, by his wife Sarah: and yr. brother to Pte. 250842, C.T. Bryan, Manchester Regt., who fell, 2 September 1918, aged 26 years: enlisted Manchester, May 1915. Killed in action 20 September 1917: Age 21. *unm.*

His brother Charles is buried in Bancourt British Cemetery (II.J.11).

(Panel 142) Pte. S/10206, David Morton Cameron, 10th (Service) Bn. The Princess Louise's (Argyll & Sutherland Highlanders): *s.* of the late Allan Cameron, by his wife Mary Morton, *dau.* of David Morton, of Paisley: *b.* Glasgow, 26 September 1888: *educ.* Overnewton Public School, there: employee to a firm of Sanitary Engineers: enlisted February 1916: served with the Expeditionary Force in France and Flanders from that month, and was killed in action nr. Ypres 12 October 1917: Age 29. *unm.*

(Panel 142) Pte. S/14253, Henry Davidson, 10th (Service) Bn. The Princess Louise's (Argyll & Sutherland Highlanders): *yst. s.* of the late William Davidson, of Savoch, Longside, co. Aberdeen, Crofter, by his wife Ann (Nether Kinmundy, Longside), *dau.* of William Mitchell: *b.* Savoch, 10 January 1890: *educ.* Kinmundy School, Longside: Occupation – Drayman and Salesman; Great Canal Brewery: enlisted 27 October 1915: served with the Expeditionary Force in France and Flanders from June following, and was killed in action 12 October 1917: Age 27. *unm.*

(Panel 142) Pte. 301376, Duncan Leitch, 'A' Coy., 1/8th (Argyllshire) Bn. The Princess Louise's (Argyll & Sutherland Highlanders) (T.F.): *s.* of Alexander Leitch, of 45, Union Street, Lochgilphead, co. Argyll, by his wife Margaret McArthur: and yr. brother to Corpl. 301439, N. Leitch, 1/8th Argyll & Sutherland Highlanders, 7 September 1917: *b.* Kilmichael: enlisted Lochgilphead. Killed in action 20 September 1917: Age 20. *unm.*

His brother Neil is buried in Gwalia Cemetery (II.B.7).

PANEL 142 ENDS: PTE. T. MAJOR, ARGYLL & SUTHERLAND HIGHLANDERS.

PANEL 143 BEGINS: PTE. A. MALLINSON, ARGYLL & SUTHERLAND HIGHLANDERS.

(Panel 143) Pte. S/7116, John McLauchlan, 11th (Service) Bn. The (Princess Louise's) Argyll & Sutherland Highlanders: late of 147, Kinloch Street, Carnoustie: served with the Expeditionary Force in France and Flanders: three times previously wounded; treated for shell-shock and trench fever. Reported missing, 22 August 1917; assumed to have died on that date. (*IWGC record McLachlan*)

(Panel 143) Pte. S/12188, David Alexander Ogilvie, 10th (Service) Bn. The (Princess Louise's) Argyll & Sutherland Highlanders: *s.* of Alexander (& Margaret Orrock) Ogilvie, of 14, Taymouth Terrace, Carnoustie, co. Forfar: Occupation – Police Constable, Perth: enlisted July 1915: served in France and Flanders from June 1916 (wounded late same month), and was killed in action in the advance toward Passchendaele 12 October 1917: Age 24. The Q.M. Sergt. wrote, "He was very popular with both officers and men, who held him in high esteem, as he was such a cheerful and willing lad, never grudging to do his duty, no matter how dangerous." Two brothers also served; John, in the Australian Infantry, Ormiston, in the Reserve Cavalry.

(Panel 143) Pte. S/11755, Jean Ulysse Robert-Tissot, 11th (Service) Bn. The Princess Louise's (Argyll & Sutherland Highlanders): elder *s.* of the late Ernest Lucien Robert-Tissot, French Professor and Lecturer, Athenaeum, Glasgow; by his wife Rose (7, Rupert Street, Glasgow), *dau.* of Richard Sharland, of Bristol: and brother to Pte. 202440, E.L. Robert-Tissot, Argyll & Sutherland Highlanders, who died at No.23 C.C.S, 12 April 1918, from wounds received in action at Locon: *b.* Glasgow, 16 March 1897: *educ.* Hillhead High School, there: Occupation – Clerk; Messrs Spencer, Moulton and Co., Motor Tyre Manufacturers, Glasgow: enlisted 9 May 1916: served with the Expeditionary Force in France and Flanders from the following August, and was killed in action at Ypres, 21 August 1917, being hit by a sniper while being carried to the dressing station, after having been wounded by shrapnel in the leg. Buried in the British Cemetery, Frezenberg. An officer wrote, "I needn't tell his mother what a good soldier he was, a gallant gentleman, and withal so kind, sympathetic and generous towards others. He will be greatly missed by the men.": Age 20. *unm.*

His brother Emile is buried in Lapugnoy Military Cemetery (VIII.C.12).

Leinster Regt.

Royal Munster Fusiliers.

(Panel 143) Pte. 5942, Robert Sydney Harman, 'D' Coy., 2nd Bn. (104th Foot) The Royal Munster Fusiliers: *yr. s.* of the late Edward Harman, of Borrisokane, co. Tipperary, by his wife Mary (St. David's, Naas, co. Kildare), *dau.* of the late Francis Peyton: *b.* Ballineen, Co. Cork, 17 December 1890: *educ.* St. Michael's College, Listowel: was qualifying as a Pharmaceutical Chemist when the war broke out: immediately volunteered for military service, and joined the Royal Army Medical Corps in August 1914: trained at Aldershot and Farnham and, on the Colonel's asking for volunteers for a combatant regiment, he offered at once, being transferred to the Munster Fusiliers in April 1915: served with the Mediterranean Expeditionary Force at Gallipoli and was present at the evacuation of Suvla Bay in January 1916: contracted enteric, and was invalided home: on recovery he volunteered for France and served with the Expeditionary Force there from November 1916, and was killed in action at Passchendaele 10 November 1917. Buried where he fell. His Captain wrote, "He was one of my company, and fell while gallantly taking part in an attack on an enemy position. He was a good and gallant soldier, and he and several of his comrades who also fell will be hard to replace.": Age 27. *unm.*

(Panel 143) Pte. 6320, Thomas McAvoy, 2nd Bn. (104th Foot) The Royal Munster Fusiliers: yr. brother to Pte. 25/1135, J. McAvoy, 8th Northumberland Fusiliers, who also fell: *b.* Dipton, *c.*1883: enlisted Sunderland: served with the Expeditionary Force in France and Flanders, and was killed in action, 10 November 1917, at Passchendaele: Age 34. All correspondence should be addressed c/o J. McAvoy, Esq., 13, South View, Chester-le-Street, Co. Durham.

His brother John also has no known grave; he is recorded on Panel 22.

PANEL 143 ENDS: PTE. D.W. MULLAN, ROYAL MUNSTER FUSILIERS.

PANEL 144 BEGINS: PTE. J. MURPHY, ROYAL MUNSTER FUSILIERS.

(Panel 144) Capt. James Owen William Shine, 2nd Bn. (103rd Foot) The Royal Dublin Fusiliers: eldest *survg. s.* of Col. J.M.F. Shine, C.B., Army Medical Services, of Abbeyside, Dungarvan, Co. Waterford, by his marriage to the late, Kathleen Mary: and brother to 2nd Lieut. J.D. Shine, Royal Irish Regt., who was killed at the Battle of Mons, 25 August 1914, and 2nd Lieut. H.P. Shine, Royal Irish Fusiliers, killed at the Second Battle of Ypres, 25 May 1915: *b.* 1891: religion – Roman Catholic: *educ.* Downside School, and Royal Military College, Sandhurst: served with the Expeditionary Force in France and Flanders, and was killed in action 16 August 1917: Age 26. *unm.*

His brother John is buried in Mons Communal Cemetery (IV.B.18). Hugh has no known grave; he is commemorated on the Ypres (Menin Gate) Memorial (Panel 42).

(Panel 144) 2nd Lieut. William Roche Brereton-Barry, 9th (Service) Bn. The Royal Dublin Fusiliers: 2nd *s.* of His Honour Judge Ralph Brereton-Barry, K.C., of Langara, Glenageary, Co. Dublin, by his wife Claire, *dau.* of William Roche, late Crown Solicitor, Co. Limerick: *b.* Dublin, 11 January 1899: *educ.* The Oratory School, Birmingham; Trinity College, Dublin, where, on the outbreak of war, he was an undergraduate and O.T.C. member: gazetted 2nd. Lieut., 10th Royal Dublin Fusiliers, February 1916: served through the Irish Rebellion, April 1916: proceeded to France, March 1917, served with the Expeditionary Force there. In the advance of the 16th Division at Frezenberg, 16 August 1917, he was severely wounded in the arm, but refused to go to the Dressing Station, and went forward with his men, leading an advance on an enemy strong point near Vampir Farm, in the course of which his right leg was shattered by a shell. On the morning of 17 August he sent a note by a runner to the Adjutant of his battalion, saying that he was in a shell-hole within the German lines; search parties were sent out that night, but failed to find him, and he is now assumed to have been killed in action, 17 August 1917. An officer wrote, "He was a splendid fellow; whenever I mentioned his name, both officers and men speak of him as one who was respected by all, because he knew his job, and did it with pluck and cheerfulness. The Army could do with hundreds like him." He was awarded a Parchment Certificate, signed by General Hickie, for 'gallant conduct and devotion to duty on 16 April 1917.': Age 18.

(Panel 144) 2nd Lieut. George Stride Falkiner, 2nd Bn. (103rd Foot) The Royal Dublin Fusiliers: *s.* of the late Henry Baldwin Falkiner, Solicitor; by his wife Euphemia ('Greenoge,' Terenure Road, Dublin), *dau.* of Thomas McEwen: and brother to 2nd Lieut. F.E.B. Falkiner, M.C., R.F.C. and Royal Irish Rifles, killed in aerial action over the enemy's lines at Ypres, 21 August 1917: *b.* Dublin, 6 September 1897: *educ.* St. Stephen's Green School; Oxford Preparatory School, and Blundell's, Tiverton: entered the Royal Military College, Sandhurst, with a prize cadetship: gazetted 2nd Lieut., October 1916: served with the Expeditionary Force in France and Flanders from 25 December following: took part in the operations at Wytschaete, where he was awarded the Parchment Certificate, 27 May 1917, for gallant conduct in a raid, and was killed in action at Frezenberg, near Ypres, 16 August following, while leading his platoon up through a heavy barrage to support troops in front. His Commanding Officer wrote, "All we know is that he led his men forward in a very gallant manner, after his Company Commander had been badly wounded. If he had only been spared, he had a great career before him.": Age 19.

His brother Frederick is buried in Tyne Cot Cemetery (I.AA.20).

(Panel 144) Sergt. 10347, Ralph Prestage, M.M. & Bar, 1st Bn. (102nd Foot) The Royal Dublin Fusiliers: eldest *s.* of Ralph Prestage, of 'Belmont,' Brookfield Road, Kilmainham, employee at Messrs Guinness Brewery, by his late wife Annie, *dau.* of James Moody: *b.* Dublin, 22 December 1891: *educ.* St. James's School, there: enlisted Royal Dublin Fusiliers, 31 December 1907: served with his regiment in India from March 1909: returned to England, January 1915: proceeded to France the following February, and served with the Expeditionary Force there, taking part in every big offensive, including the Battle of the Somme: was wounded at Ypres and at St. Quentin, and was killed in action at the Battle of Langemarck, 4 October 1917. Buried there. His Captain wrote, "He was one of the best N.C.O.'s I ever had, and will be greatly missed by all, but by none more so than myself." Five times Mentioned in Despatches for 'gallant and distinguished service in the field;' awarded the M.M. and Bar for 'bravery in the field.': Age 25. *unm.*

(Panel 144) Pte. 40916, Joseph Corry, 1st Bn. (102nd Foot) The Royal Dublin Fusiliers: *s.* of Bridget Corry (Braffa, Milltown Malbay, Co. Clare): and brother to Pte. 850463, T. Corry, 75th Canadian Infantry, died of wounds, 30 September 1918, aged 26 years: *b.* Milltown Malbay, *c.*1898: enlisted Limerick. Killed in action 5 October 1917: Age 19.

His brother Thomas is buried in Cantimpre Canadian Cemetery, Sailly (F.32).

(Panel 144) Pte. 18626, William McCann, 1st Bn. (102nd Foot) The Royal Dublin Fusiliers: *s.* of Patrick McCann, of 21, Kenmore Street, Shettleston, Glasgow, by his wife Catherine: and brother to Pte. 34278, P. McCann, 2nd Royal Scots, killed in action, 3 May 1917, at the Battle of Arras: *b.* Baillieston, co. Lanark: enlisted Glasgow. Killed in action 21 October 1918: Age 22. *unm.*

His brother Patrick also has no known grave, he is commemorated on the Arras Memorial.

PANEL 144 ENDS: PTE. J.C. PALLIN, ROYAL DUBLIN FUSILIERS.

PANEL 145 BEGINS: PTE. G.T.R. PREVETT, ROYAL DUBLIN FUSILIERS.

(Panel 145) 2nd Lieut. Clement Ayres, 12th (Service) Bn. The Prince Consort's Own (The Rifle Brigade): eldest *s.* of Joseph Ayres, of 8, Romer Place, Lewisham, London, S.E., Fishmonger, by his wife, Florence, *dau.* of Jason Forbes: *b.* Lee, co. Kent, 19 June 1892. *educ.* Lewisham Bridge School: Occupation – Chauffeur: joined Royal Berkshire Regt., 20 October 1914: served with the Expeditionary Force in France from April 1916, attaining the rank of Sergt.: returned to England, 27 December following, and after a period of training was gazetted 2nd Lieut., Rifle Brigade, 29 May 1917: went back to France, 18 July, and was killed in action on the Menin Road, 20 September 1917. One of his senior officers wrote, "He had not been very long with the battalion, but had become very popular with the officers and men, and had proved himself a most excellent officer.": Age 25. *unm.*

(Panel 145) 2nd Lieut. William Macpherson Gardiner, 2nd Bn. The Prince Consort's Own (The Rifle Brigade): *husb.* to Annie Gardiner (59, Land Street, Keith, co. Banff). After one week employed on working parties in the Wieltje – St. Jean area followed by a brief spell at Bellevue, behind Passchendaele, 2nd Rifle Brigade returned (16 January 1918) to the front line – left sub-sector, Passchendaele – where it found the posts allotted to the battalion in extremely bad condition. Relieved on 18 January, the battalion were moved back by stages to Wieltje, Abeele and into billets at Steenvoorde. On their first day in the Passchendaele sector, the battalion lost Lieut. Gardiner, killed by British artillery fire, he had only joined the battalion four days previously: 16 January 1918: Age 24.

(Panel 145) 2nd Lieut. John Bertram Greenup, 5th (T.F) attd 1st Bn. The Prince Consort's Own (The Rifle Brigade): elder *s.* of the Rev. Albert William Greenup, D.D., Litt.D, of St. John's Hall, Highbury, London, N., Heath End, Basingstoke, and Great Oakley Rectory, Harwich, co. Essex, Principal of the London College of Divinity, by his wife Evelyn Helen, *dau.* of A.P. Heron, of Oxford: *b.* Aldburgh, co. Norfolk, 10 March 1898: *educ.* Merchant Taylors' School, and Wadham College, Oxford (Hebrew Scholar); passed Responsions (June 1916): gazetted 2nd Lieut., Rifle Brigade, 4 August 1916: served with the Expeditionary Force in France and Flanders from June 1917; killed in action nr. Poelcapelle 13 October following: Age 19.

(Panel 145) 2nd Lieut. Arthur George Tyndall, 'A' Coy., 2nd Bn. The Prince Consort's Own (The Rifle Brigade): only child of George Herbert Tyndall, Bookseller; of Minster Cottage, Ely, by his wife Annie, *dau.* of George (& Rosina) Wemling, of Harston: *b.* Ely, co. Cambridge, 16 May 1898: *educ.* Ely High School; Lynfield, Hunstanton, and Fitzwilliam Hall, Cambridge (member O.T.C.): prior to enlistment was a pupil of the County Surveyor: received a commission, gazetted 2nd Lieut., Rifle Brigade, 18 September 1917: served with the Expeditionary Force in France and Flanders from 18 October following, and was killed in action at Passchendaele 18 November. of the same year. His Commanding Officer, Lieut.Col. Brand wrote, "He had only been with us a short time, but had shown promise of doing excellent work...I am very sorry that such a promising young officer's life should have been cut short.": Age 19.

(Panel 145) Sergt. 1538, Francis 'Frank' John Gosling, 12th (Service) Bn. The Prince Consort's Own (The Rifle Brigade): formerly 4th Battn: late of Plaistow, London, E.13: *s.* of John Francis Gosling, of 35, Edward Street, Barking Road, Canning Town, London, E.16, by his wife Annie: *b.* West Ham, *c.*1888: enlisted Stratford, co. Essex: served with the Expeditionary Force in France and Flanders from July 1915; killed in action 20 September 1917: Age 29. A Masonic Brother, Adams Lodge, No.158; all correspondence should be addressed c/o his widow, Florence Elizabeth Gosling (81, Lindsey Road, Chadwell Heath, co. Essex).

(Panel 145) L/Corpl. S/14758, George Edgar Fuller, 'A' Coy., 16th (Service) Bn. The Prince Consort's Own (The Rifle Brigade): *s.* of Mountjoy Stephen James Fuller, of 25, Montem Road, Forest Hill, London, by his wife Hannah Sophia: and yr. brother to Bty.Sergt.Major, 940279, S. Fuller, Royal Field Artillery, died 29 August 1918, of wounds: *b.* Lewisham, London, S.E: *educ.* Brockley School there: enlisted Lewisham: served with the Expeditionary Force in France, and was killed in action 27 September 1917: Age 23. *unm.* L/Corpl. Fuller is remembered on the War Memorial, Brockley School, and Trinity Congregational Church, Catford, London, S.E.6.

His brother Stephen is buried in Terlincthun British Cemetery (II.F.15).

PANEL 145 ENDS: RFN. S. BERNSTEIN, THE RIFLE BRIGADE

PANEL 146 BEGINS: RFN. H.A. BETTS, THE RIFLE BRIGADE

(Panel 146) Rfn. B/203695, Frederick Thomas Eales, 7th (Service) Bn. The Prince Consort's Own (The Rifle Brigade): 2nd *s.* of William Eales, of 22, Stephen Street, Consett, Journalist, by his wife Isabella, *dau.* of John (& Sarah) Henderson: and brother to 2nd Lieut. F. Eales, Rifle Brigade, who after demobilisation in February 1918, died at Consett, 2 March 1919, of pneumonia, following influenza, contracted while returning home from France: *b.* Consett, co. Durham, 28 January 1893: *educ.* National and Secondary Schools: Occupation – Clerk: enlisted King's Royal Rifle Corps, 31 March 1916, subsequently transf'd. Rifle Brigade; served with the Expeditionary Force in France and Flanders from the following July: reported wounded and missing after the fighting at Passchendaele, 26 December 1917, and is now known to have been killed in action by machine gun fire while attempting to rescue a wounded comrade. Rifleman F. Eales was a cricket player, and connected with the Consett Corps of the Church Lads' Brigade: Age 24. *unm.* (*IWGC record age 25*)

His brother Frank is buried in Consett (Benfieldside) Cemetery (IV.C.108).

(Panel 146) Rfn. S/23369, John Charles Hayhoe, 'A' Coy., 1st Bn. The Prince Consort's Own (The Rifle Brigade): *s.* of the late John (& Ann) Hayhoe: *b.* Soham, co. Cambridge, 20 December 1879: *educ.* there: employee Borough of Southwark: enlisted, 21 June 1916; served with the Expeditionary Force in France and Flanders from 14 November following, and died at Langemarck, 13 October 1917, from wounds received in action there the same day: Age 37. He *m.* St. Mary's Church, Lambeth, London, S.E.; Ada Sarah (4, Heiron Street, Walworth, London, S.E.), *dau.* of Charles Munnings, of Soham: *s.p.*

PANEL 146 ENDS: RFN. R. KILGOUR, THE RIFLE BRIGADE.

PANEL 147 BEGINS: RFN. S. KING, THE RIFLE BRIGADE.

(Panel 147) Rfn. S/15065, Thomas Edward Muckle, 8th (Service) Bn. The Prince Consort's Own (The Rifle Brigade): eldest *s.* of Thomas Edward Muckle, of 55, Lucas Street, St. John's, London, S.E., Mechanical Engineer, by his wife Jane Maria, *dau.* of Thomas Hollidge: *b.* Greenwich, London, S.E., 8 April 1893: *educ.* Central School, there: was on the Staff; Prudential Assurance Company: enlisted Rifle Brigade, 15 November 1915: served with the Expeditionary Force in France and Flanders from 22 May 1917, being a Lewis Gunner, and was killed in action at Glencorse Wood, nr. Ypres, 24 August following. Buried where he fell. He was secretary and player of St. John's United Football Club, and was one of their best forwards: Age 24. *unm.*

(Panel 147) Rfn. B/200086, Berry William Newton, 11th (Service) Bn. The Prince Consort's Own (The Rifle Brigade): 3rd *s.* of James Newton, Farm Labourer; of Great Snoring, Fakenham, co. Norfolk, by his wife Harriet, *dau.* of John Burton Wright: *b.* Great Walsingham, co. Norfolk, 17 March 1896: *educ.* there: Occupation – Farm Labourer: served with the Expeditionary Force in France and Flanders from 12 September 1916; invalided home December following: returned to France, 16 August 1917; reported missing after the fighting at Langemarck, 20 September following; now assumed killed in action on that date: Age 21. *unm.*

(Panel 147) Rfn. S/23401, William Ewart Scott, 1st Bn. The Prince Consort's Own (The Rifle Brigade): 2nd *s.* of the late James Scott, of Edinburgh, General Draper, by his wife Julia Ann: *b.* Edinburgh, 17 April 1880: *educ.* there: Occupation – Post Office Sorter: enlisted Rifle Brigade, 21 June 1916: served with the Expeditionary Force in France and Flanders from November following; reported wounded and missing after the fighting in the Ypres sector, 13 October 1917; now assumed to have been killed in action on or about that date: Age 37. He *m.* Walworth, London, S.E.; Harriet (64, Hayles Street, Southwark, London, S.E.), *dau.* of Thomas Hudson, and leaves three children.

(Panel 147) Rfn. S/28946, George Speight, 10th (Service) Bn. The Prince Consort's Own (The Rifle Brigade): formerly no. C/7688, Norfolk Regt.: *s.* of Joseph Edward Speight, of 2, Oddfellows Street, Brighouse, by his wife Laura: employee Messrs G.W. Armitage and Co., Worsted Spinners:

enlisted November 1915: served with the Expeditionary Force in France and Flanders, and was killed at the Third Battle of Ypres, whilst attacking a German strong-point at Eagle Trench, 23 September 1917: Age 19.

(Panel 147) Rfn. S/13704, Thomas George Towersey, 7th (Service) Bn. The Prince Consort's Own (The Rifle Brigade): *s*. of Thomas Zachariah Towersey, Book Binder; of 19, St. John's Road, Aylesbury, co. Buckingham, by his wife Mary Jane: and elder brother to Gnr. 47068, A.L. Towersey, Royal Field Artillery, killed in action 6 July 1916: *b*. 1 July 1891. Killed in action 15 October 1917: Age 26. *unm*.

His brother Alfred also has no known grave; he is commemorated on the Thiepval Memorial, Somme.

(Panel 147) Rfn. S/21505, Frank Charles Roberts Yeats, 16th (Service) Bn. The Prince Consort's Own (The Rifle Brigade): *s*. of Frank Charles Yeats, of 167, Clarence Road, Lower Clapton, London, E: *b*. Clapton, 1886: *educ*. Rushmore Road County Council School: enlisted Rifle Brigade, Hackney, 10 June 1916: served with the Expeditionary Force in France and Flanders, and was killed in action 20 September 1917. Buried where he fell: Age 31. His Major wrote, "Your husband has made the supreme sacrifice, and laid down his life on the altar of patriotism, while fighting for freedom and justice... You may receive some little consolation in the knowledge that he has surrendered his life in order that others may live; such examples of abnegation leave behind them something more than cherished memories;" his Commanding Officer also wrote: "...Your son was a good soldier, and is greatly missed by all his officers and comrades." He *m*. 1905; Susan (29, Highwick Road, South Tottenham, London, N.), and had a *dau*. Susan Grace.

PANEL 147 ENDS: PTE. T. THOMPSON, MONMOUTHSHIRE REGT.

PANEL 148 BEGINS: CAPT. F.W. FORD, M.C., CAMBRIDGESHIRE REGT.

(Panel 148) Capt. Francis William Ford, M.C., 1st Bn. The Cambridgeshire Regt. (T.F.): only *s*. of the Rev. John Thomas Ford, of 'Thor's Dune,' Churchdown, co. Gloucester, formerly Rector of Rede, Bury St. Edmunds, by his late wife Gertrude Lucy Ann, *dau*. of the late W. Leggott: *b*. Ipswich, 10 June 1893: *educ*. Grammar School, March, co. Cambridge, and entered Selwyn College, Cambridge, 1912: passed both parts of the History Tripos, and took his B.A. degree 1915, being a member of the University O.T.C.: joined Honourable Artillery Company, June 1915; served with the Expeditionary Force in France and Flanders from the following October: entered a Cadet School (France); obtained a commission, November 1916: took part in the operations at St. Julien, and was killed in action on the Menin Road, near Gheluvelt, 26 September 1917: Age 24. *unm*. His Commanding Officer wrote, "He did very gallant work on 31 July, and his M.C. was a quite inadequate recognition of his gallantry on that occasion. He showed the greatest disregard of personal danger, and was loved by his men in a way that few officers are fortunate enough to be loved." Brigadier-General Riddell wrote, "Your brave son died at the head of his men – a position he always held in times of danger. He was one of the bravest men I have ever known and he was beloved by all ranks. I cannot speak too highly of his qualities as a soldier. He was always cheerful, always working – an ideal leader of men." Mentioned in Despatches (*London Gazette*, February 1918) by F.M. Sir Douglas Haig, for 'gallant and distinguished service in the field;' awarded the Military Cross (*London Gazette*, 18 October 1917), the official record stating, "In an action he took command of his company, when the company commander had been wounded, and held a very important position against four hostile counter-attacks, holding on with only a few men until ordered to withdraw. His courage and leadership inspired all ranks."

(Panel 148) L/Corpl. 326290, Joseph Stanley Claydon, M.M., Lewis Gun Section 1st Bn. The Cambridgeshire Regt. (T.F.): *s*. of the late W. Claydon, of 17, Hamlet Road, Haverhill, co. Suffolk, by his wife Alma ('Endway', Steeple Bumpstead, co. Essex): *b*. Haverhill, 29 March 1897: *educ*. Board School, there: joined 1st Cambridgeshire Regt., 2 April 1915: served with the Expeditionary Force in France and Flanders, and was killed in action 15 November 1917. His Commanding Officer wrote, "He was a good soldier, and would no doubt very shortly have risen in the ranks but for this misfortune. Greatly liked and respected by both officers and men of his company, his loss is most deeply felt and mourned. He died a soldier's death, bravely sticking to the post of duty regardless of danger." Awarded the Military Medal for gallant and distinguished service in the field: Age 20. *unm.* (*IWGC record Pte.*)

(Panel 148) Pte. 41404, Arthur Ashley, 1st Bn. The Cambridgeshire Regt. (T.F.): formerly no.203913, Bedfordshire Regt.: *s.* of Thomas Arch Ashley, of Bell Yard, Lavendon, co.Bedford, formerly of Yardley Hastings, co. Northampton, by his wife Hannah: and brother to Pte. 43373, F. Ashley, 2nd Bedfordshire Regt., killed in action, 12 October 1916, at Flers; and Corpl (A/Sergt.) 147142, T. Ashley, 'K' (Special) Coy. (Gas) Royal Engineers, died 23 May 1918, of wounds: *b.* Yardley Hastings: enlisted Denton, co. Northampton. Killed in action 26 September 1917. Sometime, also served in a Territorial battalion of the Northamptonshire Regt.

His brother Fred also has no known grave; he is commemorated on the Thiepval Memorial, Somme. Timothy is buried in Pernes British Cemetery (II.C.14).

(Panel 148) Pte. 41409, George James Thomas Dawkes, 1st Bn. The Cambridgeshire Regt. (T.F.): formerly no.203907, Bedfordshire Regt.: *s.* of John George Dawkes, of Ramsey St. Mary's, co. Cambridge, by his wife Sarah Elizabeth: and elder brother to Pte. 9664, F.E. Dawkes, 2nd Bedfordshire Regt., killed in action, 30 July 1916, at the Somme: *b.* Ramsey St. Mary's, *c.*1889: enlisted Bedford. Killed in action 26 September 1917: Age 28. (*IWGC record Dawks*)

His brother Francis also has no known grave; he is commemorated on the Thiepval Memorial, Somme.

(Panel 148) Pte. 328053, Percy John Garwood, 1st Bn. The Cambridgeshire Regt. (T.F.): *s.* of Eliza Oakley, *née* Garwood (Pond Hall, Stanstead, co. Suffolk), and the late James Garwood: and brother to Pte. 40032, R. Garwood, 7th Leicestershire Regt., died of wounds, 2 May 1917; and *husb.* to Laura Ethel Garwood, *née* Smith (14, Upper Street, Stanstead), whose brother Pte. 40392, J.P. Smith, 2nd Lincolnshire Regt., also fell: *b.* Stanstead: enlisted Bury St. Edmunds. Killed in action 26 September 1917: Age 37.

His brother Robert and brother-in-law John also have no known grave; they are commemorated on the Arras Memorial (Bay 5) and the Thiepval Memorial (Pier & Face 1C), respectively.

(Panel 148) Pte. 201599, Thomas William Geer, 1st Bn. The Cambridgeshire Regt. (T.F.): formerly no.31292, Suffolk Regt.: *s.* of F. (& Mrs) Geer, of 39, Terminus Road, Eastbourne: and brother to L/Corpl. G/3747, F. Geer, 7th Royal Sussex Regt., killed in action, 30 June 1918, aged 21 years: enlisted Eastbourne: served with the Expeditionary Force in France, and was killed in action 26 September 1917: Age 32. He was married to Grace Geer, since remarried (Lynden Farm, Stonegate); late of 50, Latimer Road, Eastbourne.

His brother Frederick is buried in Harponville Communal Cemetery Extension (E.6).

(Panel 148) Pte. 325406, Charles Wilfred Sturman, 1st Bn. The Cambridgeshire Regt. (T.F.): formerly no.1875, Cambridgeshire Regt.: *s.* of Charles (& A.) Sturman, of 29,Wisbech Road, March, co. Cambridge: and brother to Pte. 1888, A.G. Sturman, Cambridgeshire Regt., who fell during the closing stages of the Somme Offensive 1916: enlisted March, *afsd.* Killed in action 26 September 1917: Age 19. (*IWGC record age 39*)

His brother Albert also has no known grave; he is commemorated on the Thiepval Memorial, Somme.

1st London Regt. Royal Fusiliers

(Panel 148) Pte. 228160, Frederick Gibbs, 1st (City of London) Bn. (Royal Fusiliers) The London Regt. (T.F.) attd. 13th (Service) Bn. Royal Fusiliers: formerly no.4487, Royal Sussex Regt.: *s.* of Henry George Gibbs, of 91, Longstone Road, Eastbourne, by his wife Alice: and brother to Pte. L/8653, H. Gibbs, 1st Royal Fusiliers, died 17 December 1914, of sickness; and Dvr. 10369, T.E. Gibbs, 117th Bde., Royal Field Artillery, died of wounds, 9 September 1918: Occupation – Greenkeeper; Willingdon Golf Course: enlisted Eastbourne. Killed in action 30 September 1917: Age 22. He was married to Fanny Emma Blake, *née* Gibbs (1, Clay Hill Cottages, Pevensey Road, Westham, co. Sussex).

His brother Harry, buried Peshawar (Right, B.C.XXI.280), is commemorated on the Delhi (India Gate) Memorial; Thomas is buried in Peronne Communal Cemetery Extension (IV.D.13).

PANEL 148 ENDS: PTE. H.W.N. BARNETT, 2ND LONDON REGT. ROYAL FUSILIERS.

PANEL 149 BEGINS: PTE. S.E. BARRY, 2ND LONDON REGT. ROYAL FUSILIERS.

(Panel 149) Pte. 248039, Robert Edward Coutts, 2/2nd (City of London) Bn. The London Regt. (Royal Fusiliers): formerly no.2064, 3/1st Highland Field Ambulance, R.A.M.C. (T.F.): *s.* of Edward Coutts, of Glengirnaig Post Office, Ballater, co. Aberdeen, by his wife Jessie: and brother to Pte. 267978, J. Coutts, 8th Black Watch, killed in action, 19 July 1918; and Pte. 41688, H. Coutts, 8th Black Watch, killed in action, 1 October 1918, aged 26 years: *b.* Braemar: enlisted Aberdeen. Killed in action 26 October 1917: Age 28.

His brother John also has no known grave; he is commemorated on the Ploegsteert Memorial (Panel 7), Harry is buried in Dadizeele New British Cemetery (VI.B.14).

3rd London Regt. Royal Fusiliers

(Panel 149) 2nd Lieut. William Edward Moorey, 3rd Bn. The London Regt. (Royal Fusiliers): eldest *s.* of William Edward Moorey, Auctioneer and Surveyor; of 15, Castle Street, Christchurch, co. Hants, and Mary Jane Moorey (264, Kensington Park Road, London), his wife: and brother to Pte. 1714, F.L. Moorey, 13th (Kensington) Bn. London Regt., died 19 February 1915: *b.* 1892: *educ.* Bournemouth School; member of the O.T.C.: Occupation – Surveyor's Clerk: enlisted Pte. no.767, 10th (Service) Battn. Royal Fusiliers, London, August 1914: proceeded to France July 1916: obtained his commission 2nd Lieut., 3rd London Regt., mid.-1917, and was killed in action 26 October 1917: Age 25.

His brother Frank is buried in Kensington (Hanwell) Cemetery (170.5).

(Panel 149) Corpl. 252195, William John Doney, M.M., 2/3rd Bn. (Royal Fusiliers) The London Regt. (T.F.): *s.* of Frederick William Doney, of Trenchley's Farm, Limpsfield, co. Surrey: *b.* St. Pennick, co. Cornwall: enlisted Harrow Road, Warlingham, 1915. Killed in action 26 October 1917, nr. Poelcapelle: Age 28.

(Panel 149) Pte. 253940, Albert Kohle, 3rd attd. 2/4th Bn. (Royal Fusiliers) The London Regt. (T.F.): *s.* of Mr (& Mrs) Kohle, of 1, Challis Court, Cannon Street, Commercial Road, London: neighbour to Pte. 202755, H. Filar, 10th Royal West Kent Regt., killed in action, 29 September 1918; and brother to Pte. 92323, W. Kohle, 3rd London Regt. (Royal Fusiliers), who died 11 September 1918, of wounds: *b.* St. George in the East, London, E.1, 1898: enlisted Stratford. Killed in action 26 October 1917, nr. Cameron House: Age 19. He was married for but a short time to Catherine Keller, *née* Kohle (118, Pennington Street, St. George in the East, London, E.1).

His neighbour Harris Filar also has no known grave, he is commemorated on Panel 107; William Kohle is buried in St. Sever Cemetery Extension, Rouen (R.III.H.7).

In their futile attack toward Passchendaele, 26 October 1917, the Second Line London Regiments suffered extremely heavy casualties. Most of them were due to the state of the ground across which their objectives lay; the men being shot down as they struggled to advance through mud which was, in some places, up to their waists. 2/4th Londons incurred losses of 11 officers, 368 non-commissioned officers and other ranks killed, missing and wounded, many of whom drowned in water filled shell holes. Four days before the attack the somewhat ironically named Jack Mudd had written home to his wife:

> "Out here we're all pals. What one hasn't got, the other has. We try to share each other's troubles, get each other out of danger. You wouldn't believe the Humanity between men out here. Poor little Shorty, (Pte. 295027, W.W. Short) that's one of the fellows that came out with me, he used to tell me about his Hilda – that was his young lady's name – about his home he had already bought and when he got home he would get married and come over to see me and introduce her to you. He used to make me laugh with his talk, how he loved his Hilda. But, unfortunately he will never see her again, poor fellow. He would give me half of anything he had. I often think of him. Yet, poor fellow, I don't think he even had a grave but still lies there in the open. Still, dear, I don't want to make you sad but it just shows you how we seem to stick together in trouble. It's a lovely thing is friendship out here."

Jack Mudd, poor fellow, would never see his beloved Elizabeth again either; four days later he was reunited with his pal Shorty in eternity.

(Panel 149) Pte. 295024, John William 'Jack' Mudd, 2/4th Bn. (Royal Fusiliers) The London Regt. (T.F.): *s.* of Rachel Mudd (22, Whitchurch Street, Bow, London, E.3): *b.* Stepney, 1886: enlisted Stepney, 7th (Territorial) Battn. London Regt. (no.9065): served with the Expeditionary Force. Reported missing in action after the fighting before Westroosebeke, 26 October 1917; no remains found – now assumed killed on or about that date: Age 31. Pte. Mudd leaves a widow, Elizabeth (49, Knapp Road, Bow, London, E.3).

William Short also has no known grave, he is commemorated on the Ypres (Menin Gate) Memorial (Panel 52).

PANEL 149 ENDS: PTE. P.H. NORTH, 4TH LONDON REGT. ROYAL FUSILIERS.

PANEL 150 BEGINS: PTE. W.A. PETRIE, 4TH LONDON REGT. ROYAL FUSILIERS
*   LONDON RIFLE BRIGADE*
*   CITY OF LONDON RIFLES*

(Panel 150) Rfn. 323098, Charles William Costin, 2/6th (City of London) Bn. (Rifles) The London Regt. (T.F.): *s.* of Arthur Samuel Costin, of 59, Chesterfield Gardens, Harringay, London, by his wife Elizabeth: *husb.* to Alice Eliza Costin (57, Digby Road, Green Lanes, Stoke Newington, London): and brother to Pte. 353599, A.J. Costin, 7th London Regt., killed in action, 12 July 1918, aged 42 years; and Corpl. 282556, E.T. Costin, 1/2nd London Regt. (Royal Fusiliers), killed in action, 20 May 1918, aged 29 years: previously served King's Royal Rifle Corps (60th Foot), South African Campaign: *b.* Stoke Newington: enlisted there. Killed in action 30 October 1917: Age 39.

His brother Arthur is buried in Contay British Cemetery (IX.A.29); Edward, in Dainville British Cemetery (I.C.8).

7th Bn. London Regt.

(Panel 150) L/Corpl. 35560, Horace Torbit Peskett, 2/8th (City of London) Bn. (Post Office Rifles) The London Regt. (T.F.): *s.* of the late George Peskett, of Leiston, co. Suffolk, by his wife Sarah: and elder brother to Drmr. 10926, F. Peskett, South Wales Borderers, killed in action 4 November 1914: *b.* Leiston, *c.*1877: enlisted Leyton, London. Killed in action 30 October 1917: Age 40. He leaves a wife, Alice Peskett (66, Hainault Road, Leytonstone, London).

His brother Frank also has no known grave, he is commemorated on the Ypres (Menin Gate) Memorial (Panel 22).

PANEL 150 ENDS: RFN. G.A. MEYER, POST OFFICE RIFLES.

PANEL 151 BEGINS: RFN. J. MILLINGTON, POST OFFICE RIFLES.

(Panel 151) Rfn. 372861, Ernest John Pigg, 2/8th (City of London) Bn. (Post Office Rifles) The London Regt. (T.F.): *s.* of John Pigg, of 1, Gower Road, Royston, co. Hertford: and brother to Pte. 206172, A.G. Pigg, Machine Gun Corps (Heavy), killed in action, 7 June 1917: *b.* Royston: enlisted London. Killed in action 30 October 1917: Age 30.

His brother Arthur also has no known grave, he is commemorated on the Ypres (Menin Gate) Memorial (Panel 56).

(Panel 151) 2nd Lieut. Reginald Browett, 2/9th (County of London) Bn. (Queen Victoria's Rifles) The London Regt. (T.F.): *s.* of Henry Leonard Browett, of Tedburn St. Mary, Exeter, by his wife Annie

(Lower Kingwell, Longdown, Exeter): and elder brother to 2nd Lieut. A. Browett, 37th Coy. Machine Gun Corps (Inf.), killed in action, 20 November 1917. Killed in action 26 September 1917: Age 28.

His brother Archibald also has no known grave; he is commemorated on the Cambrai Memorial.

(Panel 151) Rfn. 390710, Henry J. Cattell, 2/9th (County of London) Bn. (Queen Victoria's Rifles) The London Regt. (T.F.): *husb.* to Sarah Cattell (20, Bristow Road, Hounslow, co. Middlesex); and father to Pte. 1449, R.G. Cattell, 13th London Regt. (T.F.), killed in action, 11 March 1915, at Aubers Ridge: enlisted London. Killed in action 27 September 1917.

His son Richard, whose grave was lost in later fighting, is commemorated in Neuve-Chapelle Farm Cemetery (Sp.Mem.B.6).

(Panel 151) Rfn. 392019, Leonard Harry Hudson Clark, 2/9th (County of London) Bn. (Queen Victoria's Rifles) The London Regt. (T.F.): *s.* of Harry Elias Clark, of 22, Tivoli Place, Cheltenham, by his wife Emily Jane, *dau.* of the late James Watts, of London: *b.* London, 22 February 1896: *educ.* Naunton Park Council School, where he won a scholarship for Cheltenham Grammar School, and St. John's Training College, Battersea, London, S.W.: Occupation – Student Teacher: enlisted, 10 July 1915: served with the Expeditionary Force in France and Flanders, and was killed in action at Passchendaele, 26 September 1917. His Commanding Officer wrote, "He was in the front line with the Lewis gun, his lieutenant, and the rest of the gun team, and rather than retire they fought their gun most gallantly to the end, when they were laid out by much greater numbers in the counter-attack, after having gained their objective. Only one of the gun team came back, and he was dreadfully wounded." He was a keen sportsman, Captain and Hon. Secretary of his battalion's Rugby football team, and prominently connected with the B.P. Scouts: Age 21. *unm.* (*IWGC record 27 September*)

(Panel 151) Rfn. 392020, Frank Woodhead Pogson, 2/9th (County of London) Bn. (Queen Victoria's Rifles) The London Regt. (T.F.): *s.* of Louis Pogson, of 23, New Queen Street, Chesterfield, co. Derby; late of 40, Newbold Road, by his wife Emma: and elder brother to Pte. 515645, A.L. Pogson, 14th London Regt., killed in action, 31 March 1918, aged 19: *b.* Loughborough, co. Leicester: enlisted London, July 1915. Killed in action 27 September 1917; Passchendaele: Age 22.

His brother Arthur is buried in Aubigny Communal Cemetery Extension (III.D.38).

10TH BN. LONDON REGT.
11TH BN. LONDON REGT.

PANEL 151 ENDS: RFN. J.W. BUSHNELL, 12TH BN. LONDON REGT. (THE RANGERS).

PANEL 152 BEGINS: RFN. R.H.CHALK, 12TH BN. LONDON REGT. (THE RANGERS)
    13TH (KENSINGTON) BN. LONDON REGT.
    LONDON SCOTTISH

(Panel 152) Rfn. 474403, Victor George Tremlett, 2/12th (County of London) Bn. (The Rangers) The London Regt. (T.F.): eldest *s.* of James Tremlett, of Appledore, Burliscombe, Wellington, co. Somerset, by his wife Annie, *dau.* of John Osmon: *b.* Culmstock, co. Devon, 5 February 1895: *educ.* Uffculme Council School: Occupation – Baker's Assistant: enlisted Army Service Corps, 11 June 1915, thereafter employed as Cook, South Western Mounted Brigade, A.S.C.: served with the Expeditionary Force in France and Flanders from 2 July 1917, transf'd. 13th Battn. King's Royal Rifle Corps; subsequently 12th London Regt., and was killed in action at Ypres 26 September 1917. Buried where he fell. His Commanding Officer wrote, "He will be a great loss to me, and to the company, although he had not been with us long he was already very popular with his comrades. As regards his qualifications as a soldier, I am unable to speak too highly. It may be some satisfaction to you to know he did not died in vain, as the attack was completely successful.": Age 22. *unm.*

(Panel 152) Pte. 517023, William George Herbert Newell, 14th (County of London) Bn. (London Scottish) The London Regt. (T.F.): posted 2nd Bn. Gordon Highlanders: *s.* of William Robert Newell, of 21, Ferme Park Road, Stroud Green, London, N., by his wife Elizabeth: *b.* Finsbury Park, London, N., 8 March 1893: *educ.* London College School: Occupation – Registered Chemist: joined London Scottish, 26 May 1917: served with the Expeditionary Force in France and Flanders from 10 October. Reported missing after the fighting at Gheluvelt (Passchendaele), 26 October 1917, and is now assumed to have been killed in action on that date: Age 24. He *m.* Edmonton Old Church, London, N., 31 October 1915; Ivy Frances Selina Tott (13, Arthur Road, Church Street, Edmonton, London, N.), and had a *dau.* Dorothy Elizabeth Mary, *b.* 7 October 1916.

PRINCE OF WALES'S OWN CIVIL SERVICE RIFLES
16TH (QUEEN'S WESTMINSTER RIFLES) BN. LONDON REGT.
17TH BN. LONDON REGT.
LONDON IRISH
19TH BN. LONDON REGT.
20TH BN. LONDON REGT.

(Panel 152) Rfn. 653674, Donald William Buck, 1/21st (County of London) Bn. (First Surrey Rifles) The London Regt. (T.F.) attd. 8th (Service) Bn. The East Surrey Regt.: *s.* of Herbert Buck, G.E.R. Railway Stationmaster; Clare, co. Suffolk, by his wife Ellen Mary, eldest *dau.* of William (& Mary) Webb, of 'The Elms,' Walpole: *b.* Kirby Cross, co. Essex, 23 November 1897: *educ.* Village School, Wrabness, co. Essex, and Beccles College, co. Suffolk, where he took several distinctions: Occupation – Bank Clerk; Messrs Cook and Sons, Ludgate Circus, London, E.C.: enlisted Camberwell, 9 September 1914: served with the Expeditionary Force in France and Flanders from 25 May 1917; attd. 8th East Surrey Regt., as First Class Signaller, and was killed in action nr. Passchendaele, 12 October following, while laying a wire under heavy fire. Buried nr. Gloucester Farm, between Passchendaele Ridge and the Poelcappelle Road. His Commanding Officer wrote: "He was a fine lad, and had he lived, would have been recommended for a decoration 'for bravery.'": Age 19.

PANEL 152 ENDS: PTE. C.W.C. SLY, 23RD BN. LONDON REGT.

PANEL 153 BEGINS L/CORPL. C.C. JEAL. LONDON CYCLISTS BN.
28TH BN. ARTIST'S RIFLES

In October 1917, after a period of relative quiet in the Oppy – Gavrelle sector, Artists' Rifles (28th London Regt.) journeyed to the Ypres Salient and, on the 28th, left their camp at Reigersburg to take part in their first major action. Informed by the C.O., Major Edlmann, that owing to the impossible state of the ground the Divisional front had not been advanced so far as had been expected, what was to have been the Artists jumping off line was now their objective. Sir Phillip Gibbs wrote, "...to describe the ground over which the London men and the Artists had to attack. Nothing...will convey remotely the look of such ground and the horror of it. Unless one has seen vast fields of barren earth, blasted for miles by shell-fire, pitted by deep craters so close they are like holes in a sieve, and so deep the tallest men can drown in them when they are filled with water, as they are now filled. Imagination cannot conceive the picture of this slough of despond. The London men had to wade and haul out one leg after another from deep sucking bog as though in glue, and sank above their waists. A rescue-party led by a Sergt.Major could not haul out men, breast high in the bog, until they had surrounded them with duck-boards and fastened ropes to them. Our barrage went ahead, the enemy's barrage came down, and from the German blockhouses came a chattering fire of machine-guns, and in the great stretch of swamp they struggled.

And not far away from them, but invisible in their own trouble among the pits, the Artists' Rifles, Bedfords, and Shropshires were trying to get forward to other blockhouses on the way to the rising ground beyond the Paddebeeke...severely tried by shell-fire...No doubt the enemy had been standing at his guns through the night ready to fire at the first streak of dawn, which might bring an English attack. A light went up and instantly there roared a great sweep of fire from heavy batteries and field guns; 4.2's and 5.9's fell densely and in depth, and this bombardment did not slacken for hours. It was a tragic time for our men, struggling in the slime with their feet dragged down. They suffered but did not retreat: no man turned back but either fell under the shell-fire or went on...the dear old Artists,' who, in the old volunteer days looked so dandy in their grey and silver across the lawns of Wimbledon...suffered in hellish fire and made heavy sacrifices to prove their quality..."

On 30 October 1917, the Artists' Rifles went into the line 500 strong; they suffered 350 casualties. Among those killed, Capts, Bare, Chetwood, Gordon Williams, Lieut. Haslam, 2nd Lieut. Howe "... and our splendid Padre, Capt. Harry Dickinson. The toll of deaths would have been still higher but for the untiring efforts of our dear M.O. Capt. Matthew who, for 72 hours, hardly rested from the work of collecting and dressing the wounded..."

The Tyne Cot Memorial records the names of 116 members of Artists' Rifles killed / died of wounds, 28 – 30 October 1917; a further six are buried in Tyne Cot Cemetery.

(Panel 153) Capt. Arnold Edwin Bare, M.V.O., 1/28th (County of London) Bn. (Artists' Rifles) The London Regt. (T.F.): *s.* of Thomas Edwin (& Blanche) Bare: *husb.* to Janie H. Bare ('Rokra,' Bushey Grove Road, Watford, co. Hertford): joined Artists' Rifles, 1897: awarded Territorial Force Efficiency Medal, gazetted Lieut. 7 January 1911; promoted Capt.: volunteered for Foreign Service, August 1914: served with the battalion in France and Flanders from October following. Killed in action at Passchendaele 30 October 1917: Age 36. He was made a companion M.V.O. in recognition of his duties as Officer Commanding His Majesty's Honour Guard, 1916.

(Panel 153) Capt. Ernest Stanley Chetwood, 1/28th (County of London) Bn. (Artists' Rifles) The London Regt. (T.F.): *s.* of Stephen Chetwood, of Waltham Abbey, co. Essex, and Mary, his wife: joined Artists' Rifles, 1908; Pte. 505: volunteered on the outbreak of war, promoted Corpl., gazetted 2nd Lieut. 17 October 1914; proceeded to France. Killed in action 30 October 1917: Age 28. Mentioned in Despatches by Field Marshal Sir Douglas Haig for 'gallant and distinguished service in the field.'

(Panel 153) Capt. Gordon Williams, 'F' Coy., 1/28th (County of London) Bn. (Artists' Rifles) The London Regt. (T.F.): *s.* of Howard (& Lilian) Williams, of 'Ardna,' Bickley, co. Kent: joined Artists' Rifles, 1909; Pte. 799; promoted Sergt.: awarded Royal Victorian Medal: promoted Capt. 12 March 1916. Killed in action 30 October 1917: Age 26. (*IWGC record Lieut.*)

(Panel 153) Lieut. James Haslam, 1/28th (County of London) Bn. (Artists' Rifles) The London Regt. (T.F.): *s.* of Dryland Haslam, of Warren House, Caversham, Reading, by his wife Alice: and late husb. to Florence Mary Haslam (2, The Park, Ealing, London): *educ.* Bradfield College, co. Berks: Occupation – Architect: served in the South African Campaign (Paget's Horse): joined Artists' Rifles, Pte. 367; October 1914, after the outbreak of war: proceeded to France, promoted Q.M.Sergt.: applied for and obtained a commission; gazetted Lieut. 12 March 1916. Killed in action 30 October 1917.

2nd Lieut. A.E. Howe is buried in Poelcapelle British Cemetery (XVIII.A.17); Chaplain Rev. H. Dickinson is commemorated in Passchendaele New British Cemetery (Sp.Mem.5).

(Panel 153) Sergt. 760085, Allan Lionel Freaker, 1/28th (County of London) Bn. (Artists' Rifles) The London Regt. (T.F.): elder *s.* of Charlton Henry Freaker, of 12, Culmstock Road, Clapham Common, London, S.W., by his wife Emily Lavinia: *b.* London, 4 February 1891: *educ.* Christ's Hospital, Horsham, co. Sussex: Occupation – Architect: joined Artists' Rifles, late 1913: volunteered for Active Service – Regimental Headquarters, Dukes Road – after the outbreak of war, August 1914: served with the Expeditionary Force in France and Flanders, from 21 October following, and was killed in action, at a point south-east of Poelcapelle and north of Ypres 30 October 1917. His Captain wrote, "I am sure your son died a gallant death, and I am certain he is amongst the most regretted of our losses, as he was also one of the most popular of my sergeants. I had a great personal liking and admiration for him, as he was not only a good soldier, but a fine gentleman.": Age 26. *unm.*

(Panel 153) Corpl. 760448, Harry Dean Maudsley, 1/28th (County of London) Bn. (Artists' Rifles) The London Regt. (T.F.): *s.* of James Pearson Maudsley, of 18, Hartington Road, Bolton, Leather Merchant; by his wife Kate E., *dau.* of Henry W. Dean: *b.* Cherry Tree, nr. Blackburn, co. Lancaster, 4 July 1890: *educ.* High School, and Grammar School, Blackburn: Occupation – Leather Manufacturer: joined Artists' Rifles, 1 February 1915: served with the Expeditionary Force in France and Flanders, and was killed in action at Passchendaele 29 October 1917. Buried where he fell. One of his officers wrote, "He was in my recruit squadron when he first joined, and in my company out here, and I knew him very well. He was an excellent soldier, and a straight and honest man, and we all miss him badly. I am glad to think he was a friend of mine. You will be proud to know that he did good work before he was hit. He more than justified in action the position which he held.": Age 27. *unm.*

(Panel 153) L/Corpl. 760993, Percy William Kennett, 1/28th (County of London) Bn. (Artists' Rifles) The London Regt. (T.F.): *s.* of Richard William Kennett, of 126, Wellmeadow Road, Catford, London, S.E., by his wife Florence Emily, *dau.* of Eugene Charles Mascot: *b.* Hornsey, London, N., 1 February 1897: *educ.* St. Dunstan's College, Catford, London, S.E.: Occupation – Staff Member; Standard Bank of South Africa: joined Artists' Rifles, November 1915: served with the Expeditionary Force in France from 2 March 1916. Reported wounded and missing after the fighting at Passchendaele, 30 October 1917; later found and buried, 18 March 1918: Age 20. *unm.*

(Panel 153) Pte. 764756, Robert Ashley Crowder, 'C' Coy., 1/28th (County of London) Bn. (Artists' Rifles) The London Regt. (T.F.): 2nd *s.* of the late William Ashley Crowder, of Thimbleby, Horncastle, co. Lincoln, by his wife Ann (Hillside, Thimbleby), 3rd *dau.* of the late Richard Harrison, of Thimbleby House: *b.* Thimbleby, 24 April 1896: *educ.* Grammar School, Horncastle: joined Artists' Rifles, 7 January 1917: served with the Expeditionary Force in France and Flanders from 15 February following, and was killed in action on the Passchendaele Ridge 30 October 1917. F.M. Beddow, who brought out the few survivors of 'C' Coy. wrote, "Our opening barrage was terrific, and opened on the tape line along which, we in our turn, were aligned....When I saw your son last, he, with one or two companions, was still advancing, and had neared his platoon's objective, but was being subjected to a merciless machine gun fire from an adjacent pill-box which was still held by the enemy....It was my privilege to know Robert, and I may say that he was most certainly on good terms with all the N.C.O.'s. We were simply a great family in the Artists', and everybody was a friend to everybody....But I admired him, not the least because he was a man, straight and true and good...Robert has left behind him a legacy of very pleasant memories, and you will be proud to know that we who are left behind cannot fail to be inspired by our knowledge of him," and L/Corpl. E.W. Carter, "I knew your boy very well, and was in the same tent with him for some time while out of the line resting. He was always a great favourite. It is small consolation to you, I know, but I think you will be pleased to hear how wonderfully the boys went over the top that morning, and personally I feel that it was a great honour to have gone into action with such splendid pals as your son." Private Crowder was an excellent musician, and gave his services as organist at St. Margaret's Church, Thimbleby, for more than two years prior to his enlistment, in which church a memorial service was held on 2 December 1917: Age 21. *unm.*

(Panel 153) Pte. 762365, Harold Henry Dawes, 'C' Coy., 1/28th (County of London) Bn. (Artists' Rifles) The London Regt., (T.F.): *s.* of Ralph Jones Dawes, of Meyrick Mansion, Bournemouth, co. Dorset, by his wife Annie, *dau.* of John Chappell: *b.* Chiswick, London, W., 8 May 1888: *educ.* Magdalen College School, Oxford: employee Bank of England Head Office from 1906: joined Artists' Rifles, September 1916: served with the Expeditionary Force in France and Flanders from the end of October following, and was killed in action at Passchendaele 30 October 1917. Buried at Poelcapelle. His Commanding Officer wrote: "He was most popular with his comrades, always ready to use his talents for their amusement." He was a talented musician and a fine cricketer: Age 29. *unm.*

(Panel 153) Pte. 761023, William Cecil Hartley, 1/28th (County of London) Bn. (Artists' Rifles) The London Regt. (T.F.): eldest *s.* of James Henry Hartley, of 'Belgravia,' Skipton, co. York, by his wife Mary Hannah, *dau.* of William Dale Barrett, of Skipton: *b.* 12 August 1890: *educ.* Skipton Grammar School, and Newcastle High School: Occupation – Partner; Messrs Tee Bros & Co., Manufacturers & Merchants, Bradford: joined Artists' Rifles, June 1915: served with the Expeditionary Force in France and Flanders from August 1916, and was killed in action 30 October 1917: Age 27. (*IWGC record L/Corpl.*)

(Panel 153) Pte. 76467, Victor Hampden Heron, 'C' Coy., 1/28th (County of London) Bn. (Artists' Rifles) The London Regt. (T.F.): *s.* of J.H. (& Mrs) Heron, of 146, Leander Road, Brixton Hill, London: *b.* Great Hampden, co. Buckingham: *educ.* Alleyn's School, Dulwich (Roper's House; Prefect), won the Athletic Championship; matriculated London University: Occupation – Assistant; Wellcome Research Laboratories, Euston Road, London, in the manufacture of anti-tetanus serum for the troops: a pre-war member of Artists' Rifles, rejoined Brixton, January 1916. Killed at Passchendaele Ridge 30 October 1917: Age 22. Roper's House Book recorded, " He was a fine manly boy of powerful and most attractive personality, willing at all times to give of his best for the honour and good name of House and School. As honest as the day, thoroughly trustworthy, and dependable. It is with the greatest regret and sorrow that we receive the news of his death." In a letter to his brother he said, "Above all things be cheerful. The most cheerful man is the most happy. You cannot go far wrong if you do everything cheerfully and willingly. I am just realising too the value of games, and am now only too thankful that I spent more than a share of my time at School at games. There is no doubt out here that the man who has kept himself fit by playing games sticks it the best..." '*The Daily Chronicle*,' quoting from a letter from his friend L/Corpl. E.A. Cook, recorded, "He fell bravely facing a murderous fire neither faltering nor wavering, but indeed as the open, kind-hearted, unselfish Englishman that he was."

(Panel 153) Pte. 764435, Duncan Clark Bain Johnston, 'C' Coy., 1/28th (County of London) Bn. (Artists' Rifles) The London Regt. (T.F.): *s.* of Andrew Johnston, by his wife Marion Walker Bain Johnston ('Glenacre,' 10, St. John's Road, Pollokshields, Glasgow): and elder brother to 2nd Lieut. T.McK. Johnston, 3rd attd. 1st Royal Scots Fusiliers, killed in action, 13 November 1916, aged 18 years: *b.* Basonby, co. Lanark: joined Artists' Rifles, 8 January 1917; killed in action 30 October following: Age 24.

His brother Thomas is buried in Serre Road Cemetery No.1 (I.B.55).

(Panel 153) Pte. 764609, Andrew Charles McLaren, 'A' Coy., 1/28th (County of London) Bn. (Artists' Rifles) The London Regt. (T.F.): *s.* of W.F. (& Mrs) McLaren, of 'Dunollie,' Osbaldwick, York: and elder brother to 2nd Lieut. E. McLaren, York & Lancaster Regt., who fell, 22 November 1917, at Cambrai: *b.* York: enlisted 12 January 1917: Killed in action 30 October 1917: Age 27. He leaves a widow, Louisa A. McLaren (75, Lindley Street, Acomb Road, York), to whom all correspondence regarding her late husband should be forwarded.

His brother Eustace also has no known grave; he is commemorated on the Cambrai Memorial, Louverval.

(Panel 153) Pte. 764847, Eric Glyn-Renshaw, 1/28th (County of London) Bn. (Artists' Rifles) The London Regt. (T.F): *s.* of the late James Renshaw, by his wife Eva Glyn-Renshaw (15, Winslade Road, Brixton Hill, London): enlisted Lambeth, 14 January 1917. Killed in action 30 October 1917: Age 34.

(Panel 153) Pte. 760676, Harold Penry Garnons-Williams, 1/28th (County of London) Bn. (Artists' Rifles) The London Regt. (T.F.): *s.* of the Rev. Arthur Garnons-Williams, of Abercamlais, co. Brecon, by his wife Anna Jane, *dau.* of William Rickards Glennie: *b.* New Radnor, co. Hertford, 26 November 1897: *educ.* Shrewsbury School; member of the O.T.C.: joined Artists' Rifles, October 1916: served with the Expeditionary Force in France and Flanders from February 1917, and was killed in action at Passchendaele, 30 October following: Age 19.

29TH CITY OF LONDON BN.
33RD BN. LONDON REGT.

(Panel 153) Pte. 266763, Joseph Ambrose, 1st Bn. The Hertfordshire Regt. (T.F.): *s.* of John (& Mrs) Ambrose, of 16, Austin Place, Hemel Hempstead, co. Hertford: and elder brother to Pte. 266041, R.W. Ambrose, Hertfordshire Regt., who fell on the first day of the Third Battle of Ypres: prior to enlistment, was an employee of Messrs John Dickinson and Co., Paper Manufacturers, Apsley Mill: enlisted Hemel Hempstead. Died of wounds, 1 November 1917, at Passchendaele: Age 27. *unm.*

His brother Reginald also has no known grave; he is commemorated on the Ypres (Menin Gate) Memorial (Panel 56).

(Panel 153) Pte. 270933, Harris Arthur William Gray, 1st Bn. The Hertfordshire Regt. (T.F.): *s.* of Frederick Gray, of 61, Knox Road, Wellingborough, co. Northampton, by his wife Katherine, *dau.* of Henry Harris of Hardingstone, co. Northampton: *b.* Wellingborough, 14 May 1888: *educ.* All Saints School there: Occupation – Grocers Assistant: joined Hertfordshire Yeomanry, May 1915; transf'd. Hertfordshire Regt., December 1916: served with the Expeditionary Force in France and Flanders from the 24th of that month, and was killed in action 21 September 1917. Buried where he fell: Age 29. *unm.* His Commanding Officer wrote, "He was instantaneously killed by a shell whilst doing his duty, and made one supreme sacrifice for his King and Country. He was a brave man, and will be missed very much by all that knew him." (*IWGC record Harry*)

(Panel 153) Pte. 270220, George Rayner, 1st Bn. The Hertfordshire Regt. (T.F.): 3rd *s.* of Thomas Rayner, of Beauchamp Farm, Shopland, Southchurch, co. Essex, by his wife Amelia: *b.* Great Wakering, 9 July 1893: Occupation – Farmer: enlisted Warley, October 1916. Killed instantaneously by a shell, 21 September 1917, during a heavy bombardment of the battalion's trenches: Age 27. (*IWGC record age 24*)

PANEL 153 ENDS: PTE. W.R. YOUNG, HERTFORDSHIRE REGT.

PANEL 154 BEGINS: SERGT. A.J. BRATT, HEREFORDSHIRE REGT.
   ARMY CYCLISTS CORPS

(Panel 154) Pte. 20971, Ernest Leonard Gays, 'X' Corps Cyclist Bn., Army Cyclist Corps: formerly no2747, Northern Cyclist Corps (T.F.): *s.* of S.E. (& Mrs E.) Gays, of 44, Milligan Road, Leicester: *b.* Leicester, *c.*1898: enlisted there. Killed in action 18 August 1917: Age 19.

Northern Cyclist Bn.

Hunts Cyclist Bn.

(Panel 154) Capt. George Howard Bickley, 237th Bn. Machine Gun Corps (Inf.): *yst. s.* of Henry Octavius Bickley, of Holm Lea, Lyme Regis, J.P., by his wife Jane Mary Ashford, *dau.* of the late William Archer Ellis, of Woodbury, co. Devon: *b.* Lyme Regis, co. Dorset, 6 September 1892: *educ.* St. Edward's School, Oxford, where he was Senior Prefect, and Pembroke College, Cambridge, where he was studying for the Medical Profession when war broke out: obtained a commission 2nd Lieut. Devonshire Regt., 28 October 1914: promoted Lieut. October 1915; Capt. 237th Machine Gun Corps, September 1917: served with the Expeditionary Force in France and Flanders from October 1915: invalided home, May 1916, and on recovery transf'd. Machine Gun Corps (Inf.): returned to France as Second in Command, 203rd Machine Gun Corps, February 1917; transf'd. 237th M.G.C. September following, and was killed in action nr. Ypres, 4 October 1917, while carrying out control duties in an advanced position. He was in the act of taking a message from an orderly when a large shell burst, killing Capt. Bickley and two or three others standing with him. Buried where he fell. His Commanding Officer wrote, "The officers, N.C.O.'s and men of this company wish to convey to you their deep lament at losing your son as their commanding officer." He was a fine Rugby player, having played at different times for Cambridge University, the Harlequins, Devon County and the Exeter Football Clubs: Age 25. *unm.*

(Panel 154) Lieut. John Taylor, M.C., 35th Bn. Machine Gun Corps: *s.* of Samuel Edward Taylor, Coal & Builders' Merchant; of 22, London Road, Oldham, late of Acre House, Acre Lane, by his wife Jane Helena, *dau.* of Joseph Hague: *b.* Oldham, co. Lancaster, 30 July 1897: *educ.* Municipal Secondary School, Oldham: enlisted 24th Manchester Regt. (Oldham Pals) as Private, November 1915: served with the

Expeditionary Force in France and Flanders from March 1916; wounded in the hip during the Battle of the Somme, 16 July following, and sent to hospital at Exeter; returned to his battn. August, being then offered a commission: gazetted 2nd Lieut., Machine Gun Corps, 26 January 1917, after a period of training at Bisley; promoted Lieut., 26 July 1917; went back to France, December 1917, and was killed in action during General Plumer's advance south-east of Ypres, 29 September 1918: Buried at Pan Cottages, Zandvoorde. His Colonel wrote, "I cannot tell how sorry I am that we have lost him. He was such a good fellow, a very good officer and always cheery, and in the attack when he was killed he did magnificently. He will be a very great loss to us, both as a friend and as an excellent officer." And a brother Officer, "Throughout the period I have had his friendship, he has always displayed a spirit of unselfishness and a consideration for others to a degree seldom found in men. In all his bearings he has been most gentlemanly and Christianlike, and it was plain to see he came from a Christian home, and to which he was a credit." Another officer also wrote, "He was one of the finest and bravest fellows I have ever met, and all the officers and men feel his loss keenly. He was the one we could least afford to lose." Awarded the Military Cross (*London Gazette*, 30 November 1918). "For conspicuous gallantry and devotion to duty when in command of four machine guns on 28 September 1918. He got his guns forward with the infantry, advancing under very heavy fire, engaged a machine gun nest with one gun (which he personally fired), and effectively silenced the hostile guns, at the same time allowing the remaining three guns of his section to get into action, and the infantry to continue their advance. He rendered valuable assistance.": Age 21. *unm.* (*IWGC record M.M. also*)

(Panel 154) 2nd Lieut. Peter McKinnie, 10th Coy., Machine Gun Corps (Inf.): *s.* of Peter McKinnie, of 16, Bruce Street, Bannockburn, by his wife Margaret, *dau.* of James Johnstone: and brother to Pte. 42734, J. McKinnie, 8th Cameronians (Sco.Rif.); died 3 August 1918: *b.* Longriggend, co. Lanark, 12 October 1894: *educ.* Airdrie Academy: joined 2/2nd Lovat's Scouts Yeomanry (T.F) 26 November 1914; qualified as Instructor, Bayonet Fighting: recommended for a commission; gazetted 2nd Lieut., 3rd (Reserve) Battn. Highland Light Infantry, 26 September 1916: transf'd. Machine Gun Corps, 20 November following: served with the Expeditionary Force in France from 28 February 1917; killed in action at Passchendaele 4 October following. Buried where he fell. His Commanding Officer, Major P.G. Pettle, wrote, "He was killed instantaneously by a shell, and died doing his duty. We miss him tremendously, as he was a splendid officer and a very good friend." Twice Mentioned in Despatches for 'gallant and distinguished service in the field.': Age 22. He *m.* Parish Church, Great Stukeley, 23 December 1916; Gladys Mary (12, Ermine Street, Huntingdon), only *dau.* of Charles Hibbins, of Great Stukeley, co. Huntingdon.

His brother James has no known grave; he is commemorated on the Hollybrook Memorial, Southampton.

(Panel 154) 2nd Lieut. Lionel Henry Mulkern, 123rd Coy., Machine Gun Corps (Inf.): *s.* of the late Henry Charles Mulkern, and Fanny J. Mulkern (123, Kingston Road, Staines, co. Middlesex); his spouse: *husb.* to Mary Louise Mulkern (19, The Crossways, Onslow Village, Guildford, co. Surrey); and *gdson.* to the late Edmund Cowell Mulkern (*d.*1897): *b.* 1 September 1884. Killed in action on the morning of 26 September 1917, when an attack on Shrewsbury Forest 'caused the enemy to retaliate heavily, the right battery suffered particularly severely; 2nd Lieut. Mulkern, 6 O.R. killed; 2 O.R. wounded, 2 guns blown up.': Age 33. At the time of his death, 123rd Coy. were temporarily attached to 39th Divn.; they were relieved from the line the following day. 2nd Lieut. Mulkern held the Territorial Efficiency Medal. Remembered on Croydon Roll of Honour, 1914-1918.

The 6 O.R. – L/Corpl. R.C. Hall, M.M.; Ptes. T.F. Eyles, A. Morris, H.O. Dudderidge, H.A. Neville and C. Arliss – are buried in Hooge Crater Cemetery (VII.K.9-14).

(Panel 154) 2nd Lieut. William John Watts, 49th Bn. Machine Gun Corps (Inf.): elder *s.* of the late Robert John Watts, of 213, Marylebone Road, London, N.W., by his wife Eliza Mary (15, Lyncroft Gardens, Ealing, London, W.), *dau.* of William Murray, of Leyton, co. Essex: *b.* London, W., 28 May 1882: *educ.* Hampden Gurney School: Occupation – Accountant; Railway Clearing House: joined London Irish Rifles, 4 September 1914: served with the Expeditionary Force in France and Flanders from March 1915: transf'd. Machine Gun Corps the following July: returned home to train for a commission, gazetted 2nd

Lieut., Machine Gun Corps, 23 July 1917: joined 49th Battn. (Infantry) in France, January 1918, and was killed in action between Neuve Eglise and Wuverghem six weeks before his thirty-sixth birthday, 12 April following. Buried north of Armentieres. His Commanding Officer wrote, "He was one of my best officers, and I felt his loss very much. May it be of comfort to you to know that he gave his life for his country, and died a soldier's death in action against the enemy.": Age 35. *unm.* (*IWGC record age 36*)

(Panel 154) Coy.QM.Sergt. 6188, Ernest Winfield, 34th Coy., Machine Gun Corps (Inf.): formerly no.9099, King's Shropshire Light Infantry: *s.* of Clr.Sergt., Joseph Winfield, of 'The Hen & Chickens,' 37, Longden, Coleham, Shrewsbury, by his wife Florence: and elder brother to Bglr. 200504, L.F. Winfield, King's Shropshire Light Infantry, who died 19 November 1918, at Rouen; and Corpl. 18902, A.V. Winfield, Royal Engineers, died 27 January 1919: *b.* Cork, Ireland: enlisted Shrewsbury. Died 16 April 1918, of wounds: Age 27. *unm.* One of three brothers who fell.

His brother Leslie is buried in St. Sever Cemetery Extension (S.III.W.18); Alfred, Shrewsbury General Cemetery (204.2.D).

(Panel 154) Corpl. 64984, Harold Montague Baillie, 175th Coy., Machine Gun Corps (Inf.): formerly no.S/17163, Argyll & Sutherland Highlanders: late of 12, Wilson Street, Hillhead, Glasgow: *yst. s.* of James Baillie, of 12, Oakfield Avenue, Glasgow: *b.* Barony, 1897: *educ.* Hillhead High School: Occupation – Clerk; Messrs Burrell & Sons, Ship-owners: enlisted A. & S. Hdrs., Glasgow, 1915; transf'd. M.G.C., 1916; proceeded to France, March 1917 (promoted Corpl.). Killed on the morning of 26 September 1917, being struck by a piece of shrapnel while advancing into action in the neighbourhood of Polygon Wood. Death was instantaneous. His Lieut. said, "Corpl. Baillie's death is most deeply felt throughout the company. He was a gallant gentleman who fought and died for the land we love so well.": Age 20. Of a refined and sensitive nature, Harold's tastes did not lie toward sports and athletics, but rather towards books and music of which he was passionately fond; for two years previous to his enlistment he had acted as pianist at the Kelvin Street Mission Sabbath School. Corpl. Baillie had a high sense of duty and was a staunch and faithful soldier. He was a loving and devoted son and brother, and a faithful and loyal friend.

PANEL 154 ENDS: CORPL. A. KNOX, MACHINE GUN CORPS (INF.).

PANEL 155 BEGINS: CORPL. J. LEVER, MACHINE GUN CORPS (INF.).

(Panel 155) Corpl. 58099, George Ennis Livesey, 173rd Coy., Machine Gun Corps (Inf.): *s.* of the late Henry Livesey, by his wife Lucy (30, Lynwood Avenue, Darwen), *dau.* of the late William Clothier: *b.* Darwen, co. Lancaster, 3 April 1887: *educ.* there: Occupation – Under Grinder; Hollins Paper Mill, Darwen: enlisted Machine Gun Corps, 1 March 1916: served with the Expeditionary Force in France and Flanders from 15 February 1917, and was killed in action near Ypres 29 October following. Buried there. Lieut. C.H. Brock wrote: "It was a great blow to me when I heard that he had been killed: Age 30." He *m.* at Lynwood United Methodist Chapel, Darwen, 4 November 1915, Annie Jane (20, Queen Street, late of 30, Lynwood Avenue, Darwen), *dau.* of the late Ralph Pomfret: *s.p.*

(Panel 155) L/Corpl. 22783, William Elliott, 47th Coy., Machine Gun Corps (Inf.): formerly no.2801, Royal Irish Regt.: *s.* of Francis Elliott, of 49, Main Street, Sion Mills, Co. Tyrone, by his wife Catherine: *b.* Ballyfattro, Co. Tyrone, about 1897: enlisted Royal Irish Regt., Omagh: subsequently transf'd. Machine Gun Corps, and was killed in action 16 August 1917: Age 21. *unm. Known to be buried in Sanctuary Wood Cemetery (IV.C.1).*

(Panel 155) L/Corpl. 66042, William Charles Washer, 206th Coy., Machine Gun Corps (Inf.): formerly no. 6894, Middlesex Regt.: *s.* of William Washer, of 26, Cowper Street, Hove, co. Sussex, by his wife Elizabeth: and elder brother to L/Corpl. 3720, G. Washer, 7th Royal Sussex Regt., who also fell: *b.* Hove, 1886: enlisted Brighton. Killed in action 20 September 1917: Age 31. He was married to Edith Dando, *née* Washer (47, Old Shoreham Road, Southern Cross, Portslade, co. Sussex).

His brother George is buried in Harponville Communal Cemetery Extension (C.12).

(Panel 155) Pte. 42698, Philip Henry Airey, 198th Coy., Machine Gun Corps (Inf.): formerly no.27098, King's (Liverpool) Regt.: *s.* of Richard K. Airey, of 52, Belvedere Road, Burnley, co. Lancaster, by his wife

Ellen: Occupation – Book-keeper; Messrs Browning's, Spring Garden Mills: enlisted Nelson, March 1915: served with the Expeditionary Force in France from December 1916, and was killed in action 20 September 1917. Capt. R.S. Mayne conveyed the circumstances of his death in a letter to his mother: "I am most awfully sorry to have to tell you that your son, Pte. P.H. Airey, was killed in action on September 20th. He was hit in the head by a German machine gun bullet, by the same burst which wounded his officer. I saw him that morning, and he must have died instantaneously and could have suffered no pain at all. He was one of my very best men, and will be missed by the whole company. His officer (Lieut. Pucker) asked me to write to you, as he himself is hit in the arm and cannot write.": Age 20. *unm.*

(Panel 155) Pte. 46423, Austin Charles Axell, 146th Coy., Machine Gun Corps (Inf.): formerly no.G/8978, The Buffs: *s.* of Aaron (& Mrs) Axell, of Valenciennes Road, Sittingbourne: *b.* Tunstall, co. Kent: Occupation – Grocer's Assistant: enlisted Sittingbourne. Killed by a shell, 23 February 1918, in company with Pte. 60609, J. McKenna, whilst asleep in a dugout.

Pte. McKenna also has no known grave, he is recorded on Panel 158.

PANEL 155 ENDS: PTE. J. BLACK, MACHINE GUN CORPS (INF.).

PANEL 156 BEGINS: PTE. J. BLAIR, MACHINE GUN CORPS (INF.).

(Panel 156) Pte. 63526, Robert Brockbank, 198th Coy., Machine Gun Corps (Inf.): *s.* of the late Henry Moore Brockbank, by his wife Mary (Bankrigg Cottage, Bay Horse, nr. Lancaster): *b.* Forten, nr. Lancaster, 14 April 1887: *educ.* Ripley Hospital, Lancaster: enlisted 10 August 1916: served with the Expeditionary Force in France and Flanders from 15 December following, and was killed in action at Ypres, 28 September 1917, while in a Tank: Age 30. His Commanding Officer wrote, "He was very plucky, and I have never known him to turn a hair even when in very tight corners." He *m.* Blackpool; 9 September 1911; Elizabeth Alice ('The White House,' Marton Moss, Blackpool), *dau.* of Thomas Webster, and had a son, Robert Reginald, *b.* 7 February 1917. (*IWGC record age 29*)

(Panel 156) Pte. 66870, Edmund Percival Barrett Davies, 75th Coy., Machine Gun Corps (Inf.): 3rd *s.* of James Henry Davies, Nurseryman – Gardener; of Seaton Cottage, Camp Road, Ross, by his wife Mary Maria, *dau.* of Edmund Barrett: *b.* Ross, co. Hereford, 13 December 1897: *educ.* Council School, there: Occupation – Clerk: joined Ross Volunteers on the outbreak of war, August 1914: enlisted King's Own Shropshire Light Infantry, 16 September 1916; six weeks later, transf'd. Machine Gun Corps, Grantham, co. Lincoln: finished training course, Clipstone Camp, co. Nottingham: served with 104th Machine Gun Corps, Expeditionary Force, France and Flanders, from 6 January 1917: took part in the fighting around St. Quentin until his health broke down and he was sent to hospital, where he remained for nine weeks: subsequently joined 75th Machine Gun Corps, Ypres-Menin sector, and was killed in action near the Chateau Wood, north of the Menin Road, 9 September 1917. Buried thirty yards north-east of Chateau Wood. Letters from his Commanding Officer, the Chaplain, and his comrades all spoke of his gallant conduct and his good comradeship: Age 19. (*IWGC record 5th Coy.*)

(Panel 156) Pte. 34840, John Dudley, 143rd Coy., Machine Gun Corps (Inf.): *s.* of John Dudley, of 121, Phoenix Street, Sutton-in-Ashfield, Miner, by his wife Martha: *b.* Bulwell, co. Nottingham, c.1893. Killed in action 22 August 1917: Age 24. *unm.* In response to enquiries made via the British Red Cross his parents received the following, "Ever since you requested us to do so we have been making enquiries for you, and a report has reached us which we send you although it is possible you may have already received it from 2nd Lieut. Brown, as suggested by our informant, Pte. V. Carey, R25168, at present abroad, who reports as follows: 'The action was at Ypres on or about the 22nd August last. The attack started at 6 a.m. I was in the reserve and therefore did not go over with the first lot, when Dudley did, and I did not hear what became of him until at the request of 2nd Lieut. Brown (143 MGC), who had had a letter from his people. I made enquiries all round, and got the information that Dudley had been badly wounded and had died while being taken to the Dressing Station by the stretcher bearers. I cannot now remember the name of the stretcher bearer who gave me the information, but I feel sure that 2nd Lieut. Brown passed the particulars on to Dudley's people. Dudley was a dark chap, about 5ft. 4in., aged about 20 to 23."

PANEL 156 ENDS: PTE. J.L. GARNER, MACHINE GUN CORPS (INF.).

PANEL 157 BEGINS: PTE. R.W. GASH, MACHINE GUN CORPS (INF.).

(Panel 157) Pte. 8693, George Hall, 91st Machine Gun Corps: *s.* of James Hall, of 2, New Road, Tintwistle, co. Chester, by his wife Esther Lily, *dau.* of George Hayward: *b.* Tintwistle, *afsd.*, 7 August 1895: *educ.* Wesleyan School, Rishton, nr. Blackburn: Occupation – Baker: enlisted Royal Scots, 11 September 1915; transf'd. Machine Gun Corps, December following: served with the Expeditionary Force in France and Flanders from March 1916, and was killed in action during the advance north of Ypres, 26 October 1917. Buried there. Pte. Hall was a good sportsman; he showed promise of becoming a good musician, and played the violin in the Etherow Orchestra: Age 22. *unm.*

(Panel 157) Pte. 102677, Albert Henry Houghton, 154th Coy., Machine Gun Corps: eldest *s.* of Albert Edward Houghton, of New Road, Netley, co. Hants, Ostler, by his wife Rose, *dau.* of Henry (& Susan) Harvey: *b.* Bitterne, nr. Southampton, 12 October 1889: *educ.* Boys' School, there: Occupation – Baker and Confectioner: joined Hampshire Regt. 28 February 1917: transf'd. Machine Gun Corps abt. 14 April: served with the Expeditionary Force in France and Flanders from 8 August, and was killed in action 22 September following: Age 27. His Commanding Officer wrote, "Your husband was a very good soldier, and is sadly missed by the company." He *m.* Sholing Church, Southampton, 28 December 1912; Daisy Ethel (Church Road, Sholing), *dau.* of William (& Emily) Young, of Sholing, and had three children, Ronald Albert, *b.* 19 October 1913, Doris Margery, *b.* 17 April 1915 and Sydney Francis William, *b.* 2 January 1917. (*IWGC record 20 September*)

(Panel 157) Pte. 99356, Samuel Edward James, 249th Coy., Machine Gun Corps (Inf.): formerly no.M2/265688, Army Service Corps: *s.* of Samuel (& Mrs) James, of Pwyllrarian, co. Pembroke: *b.* Clynderwen, nr. Swansea, abt. 1893: enlisted Army Service Corps, Carmarthen: transf'd. Machine Gun Corps (Inf.) attd. 14th (Light) Divn., serving with that unit in the Passchendaele Offensive, and was killed in action near Langemarck 23 August 1917: Age 24. *unm.* At the time of his death Pte. James had been just seven weeks on Active Service.

(Panel 157) Pte. 37458, John Hugh Joel, 47th Coy., Machine Gun Corps: only *s.* of the late Abraham Joel, by his wife Margaret (9, Green Gardens, Trefechan, Aberystwyth), *dau.* of the late Evan Morgan, of Trefechan: *b.* Trefechan, 5 January 1883: *educ.* Alexandra Road Council School; on leaving was apprenticed as a Carpenter: enlisted 22nd Royal Welsh Fusiliers, 29 February 1916; volunteered for Machine Gun Corps two months later: served with the Expeditionary Force in France and Flanders from 13 July following, and was killed in action at Ypres 16 August 1917. Buried in a cemetery on the Ypres-Menin Road. His Commanding Officer wrote, "Joel was one of the cheeriest men I had, and I could never want a better soldier with me in a fight.": Age 34. *unm.*

(Panel 157) Pte. 33120, Richard Kay, 112th Coy., Machine Gun Corps (Inf.): *s.* of W.H. (& Mrs) Kay, of 13, Turf Street, Radcliffe, Manchester: and brother to Sergt. R/2984, P. Kay, M.M., 1st King's Royal Rifle Corps, killed in action, 17 February 1917: *b.* Radcliffe, 1891: enlisted there. Killed in action 8 October 1917: Age 26. *unm.*

His brother Peter is buried in Regina Trench Cemetery (VII.B.8).

(Panel 157) Pte. 64293, Walter Layfield, 214th Coy., Machine Gun Corps (Inf.): formerly no.37543, Durham Light Infantry: *s.* of James Layfield, of Willow Hill Farm, Denton, Ben Rhydding, Leeds, by his wife Frances: and yr. brother to Pte. 37277, C.E. Layfield, 11th West Yorkshire Regt., killed in action, 7 June 1917: *b.* Denton: enlisted Keighley. Killed in action 20 September 1917: Age 20. *unm.*

His brother Charles also has no known grave; he is commemorated on the Ypres (Menin Gate) Memorial (Panel 21).

PANEL 157 ENDS: PTE. T.W. MARSH, MACHINE GUN CORPS (INF.).

PANEL 158 BEGINS: PTE. F. MARSHALL, MACHINE GUN CORPS (INF.).

(Panel 158) Pte. 60609, James McKenna, 146th Coy., Machine Gun Corps (Inf.): formerly no.5604, Royal Fusiliers: *b.* Manchester. Killed in company with Pte. 46423, A.C. Axell, by a shell, 23 February 1918, whilst asleep in a dug-out.

Pte. Axell also has no known grave, he is recorded on Panel 155.

(Panel 158) Pte. 68536, John Middleton, 28th Coy., Machine Gun Corps (Inf.): formerly no.2692, The Royal Scots: *s.* of Allan (& Jessie Weir) Middleton: *b.* Granton, co. Midlothian: enlisted Bo'ness. Killed in action 20 September 1917.

(Panel 158) Pte. 87443, Henry John Paddington, 8th Coy., Machine Gun Corps (Inf.): formerly no.36099, King's Royal Rifle Corps: *s.* of Henry Whitehorne Paddington, of 37, Handforth Road, Clapham, London, S.W., and Isabella, his spouse: and brother to Pte. G/11382, L. Paddington, 23rd Middlesex Regt., died of wounds, 18 September 1916, at Abbeville: *b.* Bermondsey, 1888: joined Army Reserve; New Court, St. Swithin's Lane, London, E.C., 9 December 1915; posted K.R.R.C., 28 December 1916, transf'd. M.G.C. (Inf.) 3 March 1917: served with the Expeditionary Force in France from 15 May following; missing / believed killed in action 26 September 1917: Age 29. He *m.* St. Mary Magdalene, Southwark, 25 December 1911; Alice Paddington, *née* Taylor (15, Marcia Road, Old Kent Road, London), and had a *dau.* Isabella Alice, *b.* 23 November 1913.

His brother Leonard is buried in Abbeville Communal Cemetery Extension (I.A.21).

(Panel 158) Pte. 39021, Fred Patchett, 32nd Coy., Machine Gun Corps (Inf.): formerly no.10884, Duke of Wellington's Regt.: *s.* of Albert Patchett, of 41, Institute Road, Eccleshill, Bradford, co. York, by his wife Alice: and yr. brother to Pte. 4858, J. Patchett, Gordon Highlanders, killed in action, 13 November 1916, at Beaumont Hamel, Somme: *b.* Eccleshill, afsd.: enlisted Halifax. Killed in action 27 August 1917: Age 21.*unm.*

His brother John is buried in Y Ravine Cemetery (B.55).

(Panel 158) Pte. 131564, Shaw Stewart Picken, 25th Bn. Machine Gun Corps (Inf.): *s.* of S.S. Picken, Esq., of 44, Kelvingrove Street, Glasgow: *educ.* Hillhead High School: on leaving school (1914), entered into business with his father: enlisted 1917: proceeded to France, early 1918, and was killed in action, 18 April 1918, at Neuve Eglise, serving his gun, endeavouring to stem the German advance: Age 19. 'Bright and cheery, a great favourite with his comrades; he carried into young manhood the simple truthful heart of his early years, played a man's part and fell gloriously on the field of fame.'

(Panel 158) Pte. 90058, Fred Price, 171st Coy., Machine Gun Corps (Inf.): eldest *s.* of Robert Price, Foreman Moulder; of 34, Hatherley Road, Tinsley, Sheffield, by his wife Lorinder, *dau.* of Thomas (& Hannah) Percival: *b.* Chapeltown, co. York, 26 March 1897: *educ.* Tinsley County Council School, Sheffield: Occupation – Cost Clerk; Messrs Edgar Allen & Co. Ltd.: enlisted Machine Gun Corps, 22 January 1917: served with the Expeditionary Force in France and Flanders from 16 June, and was killed in action at Poelcapelle 31 October 1917. Buried where he fell: Age 20. *unm.*

(Panel 158) Pte. 132227, Frederick George Tapp, 19th Bn. Machine Gun Corps (Inf.): *s.* of Albert (& Prudence A.) Tapp, of Little Harrowden, Wellingborough: and yr. brother to Pte. 18984, W.A. Tapp, 5th Northamptonshire Regt., who also fell: enlisted Kettering, co. Northampton. Died 29 April 1918: Age 19.

His brother William is buried in Duisans British Cemetery, Etrun (III.K.53).

(Panel 158) Pte. 103244, Harry William Reeve, 149th Coy., Machine Gun Corps (Inf.): formerly no.24176, Royal Warwickshire Regt.: *s.* of William Reeve, of High Street, Barford, by his wife Rebecca Jane: *b.* Warwick: enlisted Birmingham: served with the Expeditionary Force in France and Flanders from January 1916; killed in action, 25 October 1917: Age 31.

(Panel 158) Pte. 99369, Thomas Robinson, 249th Coy., Machine Gun Corps (Inf.): *s.* of William Robinson, of Pincock Street, Euxton, nr. Chorley, by his wife Mary, *dau.* of Thomas Bennett: *b.* Euxton, *afsd.*, 22 March 1898: *educ.* St. Mary's School: employee Leyland Rubber Works: enlisted, 27 November 1916: served with the Expeditionary Force in France and Flanders from 15 July following, and was killed in action at Zillebeke, 23 August 1917. An officer wrote, "He was one of my best men. He was always very cheerful, and did his work exceedingly well, and I'm sure that the gap he left won't be so ably filled;" and another, "His example of courage and devotion to duty will live in the memory of the company." Age 19.

(Panel 158) Pte. 64537, David Sievwright, 76th Coy., Machine Gun Corps (Inf.): formerly no.3727, 5th Black Watch: *s.* of John Sievwright, of Bonnington, Arbirlot, Arbroath, co. Forfar, and Ella, his wife: *b.* Arbirlot: Occupation – Shepherd; T. Mitchell, Shielgreen, Memus, Kirriemuir: attested December 1915; joined 5th Black Watch, Arbroath, June 1916: trained Ripon, co. York, transf'd. Machine Gun Corps; proceeded to France, January 1917. Killed in action at Hansbeek Wood, nr. Ypres, 26 September 1917; buried by his comrades close to where he fell: Age 20. His Commanding Officer wrote, "He was fixing his gun during an intense bombardment when a piece of shell struck him in the head, and he died shortly afterwards without regaining consciousness. He was an excellent soldier, always attending his duties with utter disregard for his personal safety. He was a great favourite."

(Panel 158) Pte. 34288, John Silcock, 10th Coy., Machine Gun Corps (Inf.): formerly no.3654, Argyll & Sutherland Highlanders: *s.* of John Silcock, of Falkirk, co. Stirling, by his wife Janet, *née* Wright: and brother to L/Corpl. S/13307, R.M. Silcock, 1st Seaforth Highlanders, killed in action, 21 April 1917; Mesopotamia: enlisted Falkirk. Killed in action 14 October 1917; Passchendaele.

His brother Robert has no known grave; he is commemorated on the Basra Memorial.

PANEL 158 ENDS: PTE. F. STAGG, MACHINE GUN CORPS (INF.).

PANEL 159 BEGINS: PTE. G.H. STANDBRIDGE, MACHINE GUN CORPS (INF.).
    MACHINE GUN CORPS (CAVALRY)

PANEL 159 ENDS: PTE. T.A. RICHARDS, TANK CORPS

PANEL 160 BEGINS: PTE. H.J. ROWLANDS, TANK CORPS
    LABOUR CORPS
    ROYAL ARMY SERVICE CORPS
    ROYAL ARMY MEDICAL CORPS

(Panel 160) Pte. 405490, Ernest Gunn, 1/3rd (West Riding) Field Ambulance, Royal Army Medical Corps: *s.* of John Gunn, of 38, Rosehill, Rawcliffe Bridge, co. York, by his wife Sarah Ann: and brother to Pte. 405491, J. Gunn, R.A.M.C., killed by the same shell: Occupation – Paper Mill worker: enlisted 10 December 1915: proceeded to France late Spring 1916. Killed in action 9 October 1917. The Officer Comdg., in a letter to the parents, wrote: "Dear Mr Gunn, I am writing to tell you some very sad news. It is not easy to convey such news and give proper expression to our feelings. Your two lads were killed in action on the 9th inst. During active operations they were working as bearers to casualties. While engaged in bringing a stretcher case down to the dressing station they were killed by a shell. My information is that death was instantaneous and there was no suffering. They were a splendid pair of brothers. Devoted to each other, earnest and conscientious to their work, they died as they had lived, doing their duty together. This is terrible news to you, for I feel that their home life must have been happy. There is some consolation in the knowledge of the good lives they had lived, and their sacrifice was indeed in a righteous course for the protection of their home and those they loved. I would wish to express my deepest sympathy with you in the sad loss that has come to you, and pray that you may be given strength in your hour of trial."

(Panel 160) Pte. 405491, John Gunn, 1/3rd (West Riding) Field Ambulance, Royal Army Medical Corps: *s.* of John Gunn, of 38, Rosehill, Rawcliffe Bridge, co. York, by his wife Sarah Ann: and brother to Pte. 405490, E. Gunn, killed by the same shell: Occupation – Paper Mill Worker: enlisted 10 December 1915: proceeded to France late Spring 1916. Killed in action 9 October 1917.

Royal Army Chaplain's Dept.

The chaplains of the various denominations and the representatives of the great religious bodies played an important part not only in the spiritual but in the material life of the troops. The army chaplains were not only comrades sharing the common dangers, leaders in the outward observances, and comforters in sickness and death, called affectionately by the name "padre," but they seemed to be the indiscernible link with those at home, that other life of peace, once known but perhaps never to be recovered. For most troops, nothing could be truer than the chaplain; he was someone on whom they could rely, someone to look up to and they took comfort from having chaplains with them.

At the outbreak of war the Army Chaplains department was small, containing only 117 commissioned chaplains, of whom 89 were Church of England, 11 Presbyterian and 17 Roman Catholic, many of them serving in foreign stations. There were also a small number of temporary acting chaplains, including Wesleyan, Baptist and Congregationalist, whose names were shown in the Army List; and, similarly, there were the chaplains to the Territorial Force. On mobilisation, providing the 65 chaplains required for the British Expeditionary Force wasn't difficult; indeed, there were more volunteers than available appointments. And, during the early retirement from Mons and Le Cateau, it was considered the chaplains might best be of service assisting the field ambulances; a consideration that, after removing most of them to these units, proved absolutely correct.

Besides performing spiritual duties, conducting services and comforting the sick and dying, much welfare work was done by the chaplains. They organised some of the earlier entertainments, and one of them introduced the first cinema; they turned their hands to any service required and they were a potent influence in the domain of morale. They were often a useful link between the man in the ranks and his officer and they were the first to keep records of burials.

It should be noted that many Regimental chaplains spent much time in the front line positions with the troops, and on many occasions tended to the wounded in no man's land or after an attack had moved the positions forward. Their official place was at Battalion HQ, usually in a building, dug-out or trench close behind the front line, where they would be in close contact with the officers of the unit.

By the end of the war, 878 Church of England chaplains and 820 of other denominations had been sent to the theatre of war. Of these, 176 had given their lives.

(Panel 160) Chaplain 4th Class William Lorraine Seymour Dallas, Army Chaplain's Dept. attd. 5th Bn. King's (Liverpool) Regt. (T.F.): formerly of Burgess Hill, co. Sussex: *s.* of Charles Dallas, of Shanghai, China, by his wife Emily: *educ.* Oxford University, and Wells Theological College: ordained Curate, St, Mary Abbotts, Kensington, under the late Prebendary Pennefather: went to Canada, 1911, joining the Prairie Brotherhood, Edmonton, Alberta, where 'he worked with great self-sacrifice and earnestness': returned to England, 1915, and offered his services as Chaplain to the Forces: accepted and apptd. King's Liverpool Regt.: subsequently went to France and was killed instantaneously by a shell, 20 September 1917, whilst administering in the front line: Age 33.

(Panel 160) Chaplain William Joseph Gabriel Doyle, M.C., Army Chaplain's Dept. attd 8th (Service) Bn. Royal Dublin Fusiliers: *yst. s.* of Hugh Doyle, of Melrose, Dalkey, co. Dublin: *b.* Dalkey *afsd.*, 3 March 1873: *educ.* Ratcliffe College, Leicester: became a member of the Society of Jesus, 1891; ordained by the Archbishop of Dublin, 1907: volunteered his services after the outbreak of war, being gazetted in November 1915: served with the Expeditionary Force in France and Flanders from the following February, and was killed in action at Ypres, 17 August 1917: Buried on the Frezenberg Ridge. General Hickie wrote, "He was loved and reverenced by us all. His gallantry, self-sacrifice and devotion to duty were all so well-known and recognized. I think that his was the most wonderful character that I have ever known." Father Doyle was awarded the Military Cross (*London Gazette*, 1 January 1917), for gallant service, and also a Parchment Certificate, given to him by the Commander of 16th Irish Division, which states, "I have read with much pleasure the reports of your Regimental commander and Brigade commander regarding your gallant conduct and devotion to duty in the field on 27 and 29 April, and have ordered your name and deed to be entered in the Record of the Irish Division.": Age 44. *unm.*

(Panel 160) Capt. Chaplain Wilfrid John Harding, M.A. Cantab., M.C., attd. Drake Battn. Royal Naval Volunteer Reserve: *s*. of Richmond Arthur Harding, of Cranmore, Osterley Road, Isleworth, co. Middlesex, by his wife Alice Emily (*née* Tucker): *b*. Battersea, London, SW., 2 December 1885: *educ*. St. Paul's Preparatory School, Colet Court, Hammersmith, W., St. John's, Leatherhead, and Christ's College, Cambridge: Occupation – Curate; Luddenden, co. York, 1912-14: enlisted Royal Army Medical Corps, 17 October 1914, serving two years as Private: gazetted Chaplain to H.M. Forces 29 May 1917: served with the Expeditionary Force in France and Flanders, and was killed in action at Passchendaele, 30 October 1917, while stretcher-bearing during the heavy fighting. Buried there. The Lieut-Commander, Drake Battn. wrote, "The work for which your husband was awarded the M.C. was as follows: Stretcher-bearers had each case to carry over two miles over the most impossible ground before reaching a road or ambulance. Your husband insisted on going out into 'No Man's Land' with the stretcher-bearers in search of wounded men under the most intense fire and in broad daylight, when he was exposed without any cover of any kind, regardless of his own safety so long as he could be a comfort or of use to any of the wounded. Everyone was loud in his praises. It was just behind the line, while returning, that he was killed. No man could have done his duty more nobly than he has done since joining this battalion. He was always with the men, early and late, and in front of the forward posts. He was a great favourite among all ranks, always cheerful and self-denying under all conditions, and his devotion to duty was an example to us all. No M.C. was ever more thoroughly earned." And another Officer: "Where the fight was thickest, there he was, and when he was with us we knew no fear." The Senior Chaplain of the Division wrote, "For over two years Capt. Harding had been a private in the Royal Army Medical Corps at the base, but his heart was at the front, for he followed the Drake Battn., to which he was attached, all through their wanderings into the trenches and back again. On his own initiative, he got a little 'dug-out' made in the 'Red Line' and set it apart as a church and a reading room, in memory of gallant comrades. When the Brigade moved, and sections of the men were set apart as stretcher-bearers, during a 'push' he immediately joined one of the squads, and whilst engaged in this work a shell pitched among his squad and killed him. He was a general favourite and a splendid example. Such a capable, brave and experienced Chaplain is hard to replace. All who knew him found in him the man and padre. His body is buried near the spot where he laid down his life whilst serving his comrades." Awarded the M.C. (*London Gazette*, 18 January 1918), "For conspicuous gallantry and devotion to duty; continually tending the wounded during four days' operations and repeatedly crossing 'No Man's Land' under heavy fire to carry them in to the front line.": Age 31. He *m*. St. Thomas' Church, St. Anne's-on-Sea, co. Lancaster, 11 May 1917; Mary, (5, Osborne Rd., St. Anne's-on-Sea), *dau*. of the late Robert Thomas Riley, of Luddenden, co. York.

PANEL 160 ENDS: W.J. HARDING, M.C., ROYAL ARMY CHAPLAIN'S DEPT.

PANEL 161 BEGINS: S/SERGT. F.L. DAVIES, ROYAL ARMY ORDNANCE CORPS
CORPS OF MILITARY POLICE
GENERAL LIST

(Panel 161) Capt. Charles John Constable La Coste, M.C., General List attd. 1/8th Bn. (Leeds Rifles) The Prince of Wales's Own (West Yorkshire Regt.), (T.F.): *s*. of Col. Charles Frederick La Coste, Royal Marine Light Infantry, by his wife Margaret Mary Ann, *née* Banks: b. 1881: *educ*. Wellington College; Royal Military College, Sandhurst, from whence he was gazetted 2nd Lieut. Royal Warwickshire Regt. (ret'd. 1905): thereafter went to South America: returned to England and rejoined, September 1914: appointed Staff Capt., 57th Bde., 1915: Bde. Major, Chisledon, co. Wilts, November 1916: returned to France, June 1917, and was killed nr. Battn. H.Q., Kronprinz Farm, 9 October following: Age 36. He was married to Grace La Coste, of Philadelphia, United States of America (Manor House, Shottermill, Haslemere, co. Surrey).

Channel Islands Militia

(Panel 161) Pte. 704, Adolphus Gallienne, 1st (Service) Bn. The Royal Guernsey Light Infantry: *s.* of Thomas Gallienne, of Les Issues, St. Peter's, Guernsey, by his wife Eliza De Carteret: and twin brother to Pte. 1665, A. Gallienne, 1st Royal Guernsey Light Infantry, who fell two days previously, and yr. brother to Pte. 1097, T.J. Gallienne, Royal Guernsey Light Infantry, who fell 30 November 1917, aged 35 years: *b.* Guernsey, Channel Islands, *c.*1894: enlisted there: served with the Expeditionary Force in France and Flanders from 27 September 1917, and was killed in action 23 March 1918; Passchendaele: Age 24. *unm.*

His twin brother Archibald is recorded below; Thomas also has no known grave, he is commemorated on the Cambrai Memorial, Louverval (Panel 13).

(Panel 161) Pte. 1665, Archibald Gallienne, 1st (Service) Bn. The Royal Guernsey Light Infantry: *s.* of Thomas Gallienne, of Les Issues, St. Peter's, Guernsey, by his wife Eliza De Carteret: and twin brother to Pte. 704, A. Gallienne, 1st Royal Guernsey Light Infantry, who fell two days later, and yr. brother to Pte. 1097, T.J. Gallienne, Royal Guernsey Light Infantry, who fell at the Battle of Cambrai 30 November 1917, aged 35 years: *b.* Guernsey, Channel Islands, *c.*1894: enlisted there: served with the Expeditionary Force in France and Flanders from 27 September 1917, and was killed in action, 21 March 1918, at Passchendaele: Age 24. *unm.*

His twin brother Adolphus is recorded above; Thomas also has no known grave, he is commemorated on the Cambrai Memorial, Louverval (Panel 13).

(Panel 161) 2nd Lieut. Harold George Barrett, M.M., 1st Bn. Newfoundland Regt.: *s.* of H.G. Barrett, of 50, Freshwater Road, St. John's, Newfoundland: 16 August 1917. *Recorded on the Newfoundland Regt. Memorial, Beaumont Hamel.*

In July 1921, Lieut. Col. Rendell, Chief Staff Officer (Minister of Militia, St. John's, Newfoundland) wrote, in response to enquiries made, to the Director of Graves Registration, London, "The father of the above mentioned deceased officer has made enquiries as to whether any trace has been found of his grave. Since his decease, all the ground around Steenbeke has, of course, been fought over, and it is most likely that any marks would have been destroyed. However, I should be glad to know if any trace has been found."

In reply, the Director of Graves Registration wrote, "11 August 1921. Telegram sent to you on 8th August in reply to enquiry is confirmed as follows. With reference to your letter of July 12th, Barrett, Artillery Wood Cemetery. We have found the body of Lieut. H.G. Barrett, N.F. and had it re-interred in Artillery Wood Cemetery, near Ypres. Would you kindly make enquiries as to whether any other Newfoundlanders are buried with Barrett, please."

There is no headstone recording Lieut. Barrett in Artillery Wood Cemetery.

PANEL 161 ENDS: 2ND LIEUT. H.G. BARRETT, M.M., ROYAL NEWFOUNDLAND REGT.

(Addenda) Lieut. (Temp) Francis Cedric Balcombe, 1st Bn. Royal Marine Light Infantry, R.N.V.R., 63rd (Royal Naval) Divn.: *yst. s.* of Edward L. Balcombe, of 48, Bassett Road, Kensington, London, and Fittleworth, co. West Sussex, Member of the London Stock Exchange: *b.* Redhill, 8 October 1893: religion – Presbyterian: *educ.* Tonbridge School: Occupation – Seaman: 5'11" tall, dark complexion, grey eyes, black hair: previously served 2 years, O.T.C.; volunteered and enlisted Valcartier, Canada, 11 November 1914: posted 29th Battn. C.E.F., no.75266: served with the Canadian Contingent in France and Flanders. After obtaining a commission, Temp. 2nd Lieut., Royal Marines, 25 October 1916, transf'd. Royal Marines, 9 December following, serving with that unit from 14 December 1916 to 7 February 1917, on which latter date he was invalided out – Venereal Disease (Syphilis): rejoined 11 April 1917, serving until 26 June when he was again invalided out – Neurasthenia: rejoined 27 August following: promoted Temp. Lieut. 25 October 1917, and was killed in action the following day (26 October 1917): Age 24. *unm.*

(Addenda) Capt. Hugh Vyvyan Edward Byrne, M.C., 8th attd. 9th (Service) Bn. The Norfolk Regt.: 4th *s.* of the late Patrick James Byrne, A.R.I.B.A., Architect and Surveyor, of Windsor and London, by his wife Barbara (2, Grove Road, Brislington, Bristol), *dau.* of the late Capt. Samuel Scoltock, 46th Foot, Military Knight of Windsor: *b.* Windsor, co. Berks, 16 September 1884: *educ.* Privately, and at Clondalkin, co. Dublin: joined 10th Royal Fusiliers, August 1914: served with the Expeditionary Force in France and Flanders from 1915: recommended for a commission for service in the field; returned to England, and after a period of training at Chatham and Colchester, was gazetted 2nd Lieut., Norfolk Regt., being promoted Lieut., and Capt. August 1917: returned to France, where he took an active part in all the Battles of Montauban, Delville Wood, Thiepval, Schwaben Redoubt, Regina Trench, Irles, the Third Battle of Ypres, the Battles of Poelcappelle, and the Somme, and was killed in action at Dranoutre, nr. Mount Kemmel, 15 April 1918. A fellow officer wrote, "We were all fond of Harry, as we called him, he was one of the best soldiers and comrades I ever knew; the country has lost a splendid man...I am sure his death was a glorious one." Awarded the Military Cross (*London Gazette*, 22 October 1917), for 'gallant and distinguished service in the field.": Age 33. *unm.*

(Addenda) Capt. Gerard Leader Hill, 2/5th Bn. The Lincolnshire Regt. (T.F.): *s.* of the late Lieut. Col. Herbert Francis Hill, 1st Essex Regt., by his wife Mary (Morningside, Newby, Scarborough), *dau.* of John Leader, of Keale, J.P.: and *gdson.* of the late Rev. Henry Thomas Hill, Prebendary of Hereford Cathedral: *b.* Warley, Brentwood, co. Essex, 16 June 1882: *educ.* Felsted's: subsequently entered Mr John Browne's works as Naval Architect; sent by him on business to Turkey, later to Petrograd, where he was British Naval Representative to the Russian Admiralty engaged on important shipbuilding operations: on the outbreak of war, applied to rejoin his battalion of the Cameronians, with whom he had served ten years previously, but was not released from his work until April 1915: obtained a commission as Lieut. the same month, being promoted Capt. in July 1915: underwent a staff course at Camberley, and a bombing course in London, after which he became Commandant of the Essex School of Bombing: transf'd. to Lincoln Regt., January 1917: served with the Expeditionary Force in France and Flanders from February: took part in several engagements, and was killed in action at the Third Battle of Ypres, 26 September 1917. Mentioned in Despatches (*London Gazette*, 18 December 1917) by F.M. Sir Douglas Haig, for 'gallant and distinguished service in the field.': Age 35. *unm.*

(Addenda) Sergt. 132223, Charles Kenny, 74th Chinese Labour Coy., Labour Corps: Killed 10 June 1919, whilst clearing the battlefields he was blown to atoms by the detonation of a quantity of munitions.

In the attack toward Poelcapelle, Robert Quinn and his pal Morris Jenkinson were both wounded by the explosion of a shell which struck the lip of a shell hole in which they were taking shelter. Quinn had one of his legs blown off and Jenkinson, although badly wounded himself, struggled back toward the battalion lines to find help. Forty-eight hours later stretcher-bearers found Quinn but, just as they were lifting him onto a stretcher, a shell pitched nearby killing him and his rescuers.

(Addenda) Pte. 35277, Robert Quinn, 24/27th (Service) Bn. The Northumberland Fusiliers: *s.* of Thomas Quinn, of Church Road, Norham-on-Tweed, co. Northumberland, and Annie Quinn, his spouse: and elder brother to Pte. 291016, T. Quinn, 4th Northumberland Fusiliers, died 23 November 1918, of pneumonia. Died of wounds / killed in action 23 October 1917: Age 21.

His brother Thomas is buried in Norham (St. Cuthbert) Churchyard.

(Addenda) Pte. 19864, George Henry Pratt, 12th (Service) Bn. (2nd South Down) The Royal Sussex Regt.: *s.* of John Pratt, of 4, Denison Road, Merton, co. Surrey, by his wife Eliza, *dau.* of Thomas Young: *b.* London, 20 March 1881: *educ.* Harrow Road Council School: enlisted 14 July 1916: served with the Expeditionary Force in France and Flanders from the following November, and was killed in action 24 September 1917: Age 36. He *m.* London, 18 August 1906; Ellen Margueritta (83, Hatfield Road, Ipswich), *dau.* of Alfred Barney, and had a son, George Leslie Richard, *b.* 24 October 1908. (*IWGC record 25 September*)

(Addenda) Corpl. 11/18838, Henry Topping, 'A' Coy., 11th (Service) Bn (South Antrim) The Royal Irish Rifles: *s.* of Henry Topping, of 124, Longstone Street, Lisburn, co. Antrim, by his wife Mary: resided Lisburn: prior to the outbreak of war was sometimes employed in the Engine Shop, Great Northern

Railway, Windsor: volunteered and enlisted Royal Irish Rifles with his uncle Rfn. 7281, S. Topping: trained as a rifleman at Bordon Camp: subsequently promoted Corpl.: served with the Expeditionary Force in France from October 1915. A notice in *The Lisburn Standard*, 24 August 1917, stated there was '..much anxiety concerning him following an attack at Langemarck.' He was subsequently reported killed in action, 16 August 1917, the same day as his uncle. A letter to Corpl. Topping's parents from Capt. Ellis described how he 'was killed by a fragment from a shell which burst close to his section during the first ten minutes of our advance on the 16th. Everything possible was done for him at the time, but he passed away a few minutes afterwards, apparently suffering no pain. It will comfort you in your sad hour of bereavement to know that he died doing his duty nobly and faithfully to the end.' A Death Notice, *Lisburn Standard*, 31 August 1917, included a poem with a line from a poem by Laurence Housman to the effect that battles and peace 'are won by the men that fell.' He is commemorated on the Lisburn War Memorial as H. Lovie, his mother's maiden name: Age 20.

> Oh lads, dear lads, who were loyal and true,
> The worst of the fight was borne by you;
> So the word shall go to the cottage and hall,
> Our battles are won by the men that fall.
>
> When peace dawns over the countryside
> Our thanks shall be to the lads that died,
> Oh quiet hearts; can you hear us tell
> How peace was won by the men that fell.

His uncle Samuel is recorded on Panel 140.

Tyne Cot New Zealand Memorial

Inscription: *Here Are Recorded The Names Of Officers And Men Of NEW ZEALAND Who Fell In The Battle Of Broodseinde And The First Battle Of Passchendaele October 1917 And Whose Graves Are Known Only To God.*

(Panel 1) Spr. 4/1736, Edgar Woodward Boucher, Signal Co., New Zealand Engineers, N.Z.E.F.: late of Remuera: *s.* of Edward Woodward Boucher, of Tarewa, Rotorua, by his wife Anna A.: *educ.* Pah College, Auckland, and King's College: Occupation – Surveyor; Messrs T. MacFarlane, C.E.: went with the Advance Party to Samoa (15 August 1914), where he joined the Civil Service; apptd. Assistant Surveyor to Mr McDonald: subsequently re-enlisted; departed Wellington, HMNZT 37 'Maunganui,' 8 January 1916; 9th Rfts. N.Z. Engineers: served in Egypt, and with the Expeditionary Force in France (slightly wounded, Pozieres) and Flanders, and reported missing, 12 October 1917, since confirmed killed in action by a shell when returning from carrying out a telephone wire repair: Age 24. *unm.*

(Panel 1) Capt. 14347, Arthur Charles Hubbard, M.C., 16th (Waikato) Coy., 2nd Bn. Auckland Regt., N.Z.E.F.: *s.* of John Charles Hubbard, of Paeroa, Thames, by his wife Elizabeth Anne: *b.* 2 January 1872: religion – Anglican: Occupation – Farmer: 6' tall, medium complexion, blue eyes, light brown hair: enlisted 11 January 1916: served with the Expeditionary Force in France and Flanders from 14 September 1916, and was reported missing / believed killed in action 4 October 1917; since confirmed killed. He was awarded the Military Cross (*London Gazette*, 17 April 1917), 'For conspicuous gallantry and devotion to duty. He displayed great courage and initiative in leading his company in the assault on the enemy front line. Later, he was largely instrumental in rescuing several wounded men.': Age 45. *unm.*

(Panel 1) Sergt. 36771, Ernest George Campbell, 1st Bn. Auckland Regt., N.Z.E.F.: *s.* of the late Robert Campbell, of Taupiri, Waikato, by his wife Clara (Edendale Road, Kingsland): and brother to Pte. 12/1581, S.R. Campbell, Auckland Regt., missing believed killed in action, 25 April 1915, at Gallipoli: was Sergt. Instructor: departed Wellington, HMNZT 81 'Devon,' 5 April 1917: arrived Devonport

10 June following; proceeded to France shortly thereafter and was killed in action 4 October 1917: Age 25. *unm.*

His brother Sidney has no known grave, he is commemorated on the Lone Pine Memorial (72).

(Panel 1) Sergt. 12/3920, Edwin Mitchelson Clark, 'A'Coy., 2nd Bn. Auckland Regt., N.Z.E.F.: *yst. s.* of the late George Clark, by his wife Harriet (20, Herbert Road, Mount Eden, Auckland): and brother to Corpl. 4/1905, H.G. Clark, M.M., N.Z. Field Artillery, died 23 August 1918, of wounds: *b.* Whakahara, Northern Wairoa, *c.*1896: Occupation – Carpenter: departed New Zealand, 4 March 1916: served in Egypt with the Expeditionary Force in France and Flanders, and died 4 October 1917 of wounds: Age 21. *unm.*

His brother Henry is buried in Bagneux British Cemetery, Gezaincourt (VI.A.2).

(Panel 1) Corpl. 21216, David Coates Cole, 2nd (Waikato) Coy., 2nd Bn. Auckland Regt., N.Z.E.F.: 2nd *s.* of David Graeme Cole, of 'Clontivern,' Trafalgar Street, Onehunga, Auckland, by his wife Minnie: *b.* 1896: *educ.* Auckland Grammar School: Occupation – Clerk: embarked Wellington, HMNZT 61 'Aparima,' 19 August 1916; Sergt., 16th Rfts., 'A' Coy., Auckland Regt. Killed in action 4 October 1917: Age 21. *unm. The Auckland Weekly News,* 2 May 1918:-

Brave soldier come home, for the victory is won.

(Panel 1) Corpl. 31758, George William Worner, 2nd Bn. Auckland Regt., N.Z.E.F.: *s.* of Mrs F.M.C. Smith, *née* Worner (123, Ilam Road, Fendalton, Christchurch): and brother to Sergt. 14725, A. Worner, 2nd Canterbury Regt., who fell, 12 October 1917, in the attack at Bellevue; and Rfn. 14727, A.W. Helem (*a.k.a.* Worner), N.Z. Rifle Brigade, who also fell: *b.* Geraldine, Christchurch: was a Blacksmith, and member of Auckland City Fire Brigade: departed New Zealand, 15 November 1916, with 19th Rfts., 'A' Coy., Auckland Regt.: served with the Expeditionary Force in France and Flanders, and was killed in action 4 October 1917: Age 30. Well known as a footballer, prior to enlistment Corpl. Worner had played for City Rovers and Grafton Athletic Club, and had previously been a member of Waitemata Boating Club. All correspondence regarding the deceased should be addressed to his friend, Miss L. Priest (4, Surrey Street, Grey Lynn, Auckland).

His brothers Alexander and Alfred also have no known grave; they are recorded on Panel 2, and the Messines Ridge (New Zealand) Memorial respectively.

(Panel 1) Pte. 24/1589, Linton Ball, 2nd Bn. Auckland Regt., N.Z.E.F.: *s.* of E.W. (& Mrs) Ball, of Matakohe, Kaipara, Auckland: Occupation – Labourer: enlisted Wellington, 1915: departed New Zealand, 8 January 1916; 3rd Rfts., 2nd Bn. 'F' Coy. N.Z. Rifle Brigade: served with the Expeditionary Force in Egypt (from February) and in France and Flanders, and was killed in action, 4 October 1917, at Broodseinde Ridge. *The Auckland Weekly News,* 3 October 1918:

He left his home in perfect health, so cheery and bright was he.
He bade farewell to all his friends and sailed far o'er the sea.
Nobly he did his duty and answered his country's call,
Somewhere on the battlefield he gave his life, his all.

Father, mother, brothers and sisters

(Panel 1) Pte. 25671, Archibald Donald Campbell, 3rd (Auckland) Coy., 1st Bn. Auckland Regt., N.Z.E.F.: *s.* of the late Angus Campbell, by his wife Sarah Eliza (17, Collingwod Street, Ponsonby, Auckland): and yr. brother to Spr. 25258, A.J. Campbell, N.Z. Engineers, died (and buried) at sea, 18 July 1916, en-route to New Zealand: Occupation – Sail Maker: departed Wellington, 25 September 1916: served with the Expeditionary Force in France and was killed in action, 4 October 1917, nr. Ypres: Age 31.

With no known grave but the sea, his brother Angus is commemorated on the Auckland Provincial Memorial.

(Panel 1) Pte. 33693, John Chisnall, 3rd Bn. Auckland Regt., N.Z.E.F.: *s.* of the late W.H. Chisnall, by his wife Mary (21, Melrose Street, Christchurch): and brother to Pte. 6/3652, C. Chisnall, 2nd

Canterbury Regt., killed in action, 16 September 1916: Occupation – Shepherd: departed New Zealand, 19 January 1917. Killed in action 4 October 1917. *unm.*

His brother Charles also has no known grave; he is commemorated on the Caterpillar Valley (New Zealand) Memorial.

(Panel 1) Pte. 28331, John Lawrence Finlayson, 'J' Coy., 1st Bn. Auckland Regt., N.Z.E.F.: *s.* of William Finlayson, of Petane, Hawke's Bay, Napier, by his wife Martha: and *yr.* brother to Pte. 10/2602, R.L. Finlayson, N.Z. Light Trench Mortar Bty., died, 30 August 1918, of wounds: *b.* 5 September 1895: Occupation – Shepherd: enlisted 27 June 1916: embarked Wellington; 18th Rfts, HMNZT 67, 'Tofua,' 11 October following: served with the Expeditionary Force in France and Flanders from 28 February 1917: joined his battn. In the field, 31 March; reported missing after the fighting, 4 October 1917; subsequently confirmed (April 1918) by a Court of Enquiry as having been killed in action on that date: Age 22. *unm. (IWGC record age 19)*

His brother Robert is buried in Bagneux British Cemetery (VI.B.32).

(Panel 1) Pte. 20998, Percy Hamilton, 3rd Bn. Auckland Regt., N.Z.E.F.: *s.* of the late John Kennedy Hamilton, by his wife Mary Honor (21, Gordon Road, Mount Eden): and *yr.* brother to L/Corpl. 20999, R. Hamilton, 3rd N.Z. Rifle Bde., accidentally killed, 24 January 1918: *b.* Whitianga, 1895. Killed in action 15 October 1917: Age 22. *unm.*

His brother Raymond is buried in Menin Road South Military Cemetery (III.O.38).

(Panel 1) Pte. 40335, Lionel Gregory Kemp, 1st Bn. Auckland Regt., N.Z.E.F.: *husb.* to Alice Hildagarde Kemp (32, Pine Street, Dominion Road, Auckland): *b.* 25 July 1888: religion – Presbyterian: Occupation – Engine Driver, Talisman Gold Mine, Karangahake: 6' tall, fair complexion, blue eyes, brown hair: enlisted Trentham Camp, 2 November 1916; posted 'E' Coy. 23rd Rfts: embarked Wellington, HMNZT 80, S.S. 'Corinthic,' 2 April 1917: arrived Plymouth via Cape Horn and Cape Town, 10 June: underwent further training, Sling Camp: served with the Expeditionary Force in France and Flanders from 9 July 1917, joining 1st Auckland in the field (5 August), and was killed in action 4 October following. In a letter to his sister, 'Gerty' (23 September) he wrote, "It is a rather dull day, but I don't think it will rain, I hope not anyway, there is enough mud and slush around now without any more rain…" Eleven days later, 4 October 1917, the weather had worsened, a light but steady rainfall and a cold westerly wind added further discomfort to the soldiers waiting in the mud filled trenches for the order to go over the top. At exactly what point Pte. Kemp was killed is unknown, immediately the battalion left their trenches, heavy machine-gun fire swept through their ranks, killing and wounding scores of them. One of his obituary notices contained the line, "One of nature's gentlemen, who died fighting for King, Country and Liberty."

(Panel 1) Pte. 12/2011, James Leatt, 1st Bn. Auckland Regt., N.Z.E.F.: *s.* of the late George Gore Leatt, by his wife Sarah Ellen (43, Pendle Street, Broughton, Skipton, co. York): and brother to L/Corpl. 17932, T. Leatt, 8th Royal Berkshire Regt., died 1 May 1916, of wounds (G.S. chest); Pte. 7573, G. Leatt, 9th Regt. South African Infantry, died in German East Africa 25 April 1916, of fever; and Pte. H. Leatt, Royal Navy (surv'd.): *b.* 1884: enlisted Auckland, 1914: departed Wellington, 17 April 1915: served in Egypt, and with the Expeditionary Force in France, and was killed in action, 4 October 1917, at Gravenstafel: Age 33. Capt. G. Coates, in a letter to Mrs Leatt, wrote, "With great regret I write to condole with you in the loss of your brave son. He was killed during our advance on the 4th inst., and it was a great pity that he was not spared to enjoy the fruits of the success to which he probably contributed. It is a time of self-sacrifice, and right nobly did your son respond to the call. He died as you could wish him to die – like a soldier and a man; and you have reason to be proud of him. I just wish to extend to you the sympathy of myself and of your son's comrades in the Company in your time of sorrow." Comrades Ptes. E. W. Johnstone and H. Waldron also wrote, "Jim was a pal of ours. We went into the trenches on the night of the 2nd, and we went over the top on the morning of the 4th. At six o'clock we went forward. Well, this was where your son died for his country, and we must say that he suffered no pain. Shortly after we reached our objective we came back to find him, but evidently another enemy shell must have struck him. Jim was well known throughout his Battalion as a good soldier, and his 'gap' will be felt by all. It is very hard for us to sit down and write of our mates who have gone before."

His brother Tom is buried in Le Treport Military Cemetery (II.L.8); George is buried in Dar Es Salaam War Cemetery (V.G.19).

From a 1914 population of little more than one million, approximately 100,000 New Zealanders (predominantly between the ages of 20 and 45) volunteered and went to war. Of this number almost 60% became casualties; more than 18,000 died of wounds and disease – 12,483 in France and Belgium alone. The impact of the war reached far beyond the direct involvement of the men at the front; back home in New Zealand hardly a family, community, workplace, school or club was unaffected by the war and the huge sacrifices it demanded. For one family, the Newloves of Takaka, the sacrifice was perhaps greater than most; out of eight sons, three of them – Edwin, Leonard and Leslie – were killed at Passchendaele within a week of each other. For their mother the three weeks following the battle must have been both agonisingly anxious and heartbreaking. The death notifications for each of her son's arrived individually.

(Panel 1) Pte. 33755, Leonard Charles Newlove, 3rd Bn. Auckland Regt., N.Z.E.F.: *s.* of Mary Ann Newlove (Takaka, Nelson): and brother to Pte. 40234, E. Newlove and Pte. 31530, L.M. Newlove, 2nd Canterbury Regt., who both fell in the second attack at Bellevue Spur eight days later: Occupation – Farmer: enlisted 1916: departed New Zealand, 19 January 1917: served with the Expeditionary Force in France from July following, and was reported missing following the attack at Gravenstafel, 4 October 1917, later confirmed killed in action: Age 41. *unm.*

His brothers Edwin and Leslie also have no known grave; both are recorded on Panel 2.

(Panel 1) Pte. 26966, John William Orr, 2nd (Waikato) Coy., 2nd Bn. Auckland Regt., N.Z.E.F.: *s.* of the late John Orr, by his wife Matilda (Main Road, Maheno, Oamaru, Otago): and brother to Pte. 26967, R.C. Orr, Auckland Regt., killed in action, 21 February 1917: Occupation – Ploughman: departed Wellington, HMNZT 77 'Mokoia,' 25 September 1916. Killed in action 4 October 1917: Age 30.

His brother Robert is buried in Pont-du-Hem Military Cemetery (IV.F.25).

(Panel 1) Pte. 38740, William Parker, 6th (Hauraki) Coy., 2nd Bn. Auckland Regt., N.Z.E.F.: *s.* of John Parker, of 1, Waterview Road, Devonport, Auckland, by his wife Marian: and brother to Corpl. 2/2896, E.J. Parker, N.Z. Field Artillery, 26 September 1918: Occupation – Mill-Hand: departed Wellington, 13 February 1917. Killed in action 4 October 1917: Age 24. *unm.*

His brother Edward is buried in Lebucquiere Communal Cemetery Extension (IV.B.12).

(Panel 1) Pte. 24063, William Sanderson, 15th (North Auckland) Coy., 2nd Bn. Auckland Regt., N.Z.E.F.: *s.* of the late Benjamin Sanderson, by his wife Eliza (8, Kelly Street, Mount Eden, Auckland): and brother to Pte. 24064, R. Sanderson, 2nd Auckland Regt., killed in action, 30 March 1918, and Spr. 40643, J. Sanderson, N.Z. Tunnelling Coy. (surv'd.): *b.* Okupu, Great Barrier Island, *c.*1885: Occupation – Labourer: departed Wellington, 27 May 1916. Killed in action 4 October 1917: Age 32.

His brother Robert is buried in Euston Road Cemetery, Colincamps (IV.B.2).

(Panel 1) Pte. 40395, Henry George Tavinor, 'E' Coy., 1st Bn. Auckland Regt., N.Z.E.F.: *s.* of the late Albert Tavinor, by his wife Hannah (Puwera, Whangerai): killed in action, 4 October 1917: Age 28. Dedicated – "The Fittest Place That Man Can Die Is Where He Died A Man" – the Maungakaramea War Memorial, the first such monument to be commissioned (and erected) by a northern New Zealand district, was constructed by E.C. Kerr (Whangerai) and described by a local newspaper article as "a massive Coromandel Granite obelisk, measuring 15 feet by 4 feet at the base." The memorial records the names of twelve local men who gave their lives in the Great War (later amended to include three who fell in World War II). Six of the Great War casualties – Ptes. D. Hannam, E.C. Cook, L.B. Hayward, H.G. Tavinor, and Gnr. W.J. Gunson – died within three months of each other; all are to be found within the Ypres salient.

Pte. Hannam has no known grave, he is commemorated on the Buttes New British Cemetery (New Zealand) Memorial; Pte. Cook is buried in The Huts Cemetery (XV.A.18), Pte. Hayward, Lijssenthoek Military Cemetery (XX.I.16A); and Gnr. Gunson, Menin Road South Military Cemetery (III.O.23).

(Panel 2) Regtl.Sergt.-Major, 6/244, Albert Hector Guy, M.S.M., 1st Bn. Canterbury Regt., N.Z.E.F.: 2nd *s.* of John Arliss Guy, of Ngatimoti, Nelson, by his wife Elizabeth Mouter: and brother to Pte. 25996, W.A.C. Guy, 1st Canterbury Regt., killed in action, 27 March 1918; and Pte. 11652, Arthur L.

Guy, Cyclists Corps (surv'd.): Occupation – Farmer: enlisted Ngatimoti, following the outbreak of war: departed Lyttleton, 16 October 1914. Killed in action 12 October 1917. He was awarded the Meritorious Service Medal (*London Gazette*, 1 January 1918), "For conspicuous gallantry and devotion to duty. On the 7, 8 and 9 June 1917, Sergt.-Major Guy was in command of the Regimental carrying party taking S.A.A., food and water to the Companies in the front line, and although the overland tracks were under continuous heavy shellfire, he never failed to get his partics through. His personal bravery and disregard for safety inspired his men to carry through an extremely dangerous and difficult task. Again at the capture of the Au Chasseuk Cabaret on the 15 June, and until the 19 June, Sergeant-Major Guy was in command of the ration and water party carrying forward to shell-hole positions; and through his personal efforts, gallantry, and devotion to duty, the men in the line were well and regularly fed in spite of intense enemy bombardment." And Mentioned in Despatches (*London Gazette*, 28 December 1917), "For conspicuous gallantry and devotion to duty. On the night of the 1/2 October on Zonnebeke-Kanas Cross Road, an evening attack was expected and Sergt.-Major Guy was sent up to the forward posts with a supply of S.O.S. flares which had just been received – the signal having been altered. Although a very heavy H.E. barrage had been put down on the support line, S.M. Guy worked his way through with his party in spite of great personal risk. His fine personal example inspired his men in their task and they delivered the flares without casualties. The signal was used about four hours later and the forward posts near Otto Farm would have been in great danger if the flares had failed to arrive.": Age 27. *unm.*

His brother Walter also has no known grave; he is commemorated on the Grevillers (New Zealand) Memorial.

(Panel 2) Sergt. 14725, Alexander Worner, 12th (Nelson) Coy., 2nd Bn. Canterbury Regt., N.Z.E.F.: late of Charles Street, Blenheim: *s.* of Mrs F.M.C. Smith, *née* Worner (123, Ilam Road, Fendalton, Christchurch): and brother to Corpl. 31758, G.W. Worner, 2nd Auckland Regt., who fell, 4 October 1917, in the attack at Broodseinde; and Rfn. 14727, A.W. Helem (*a.k.a.* Worner), N.Z. Rifle Brigade, who also fell: Occupation – Butcher: departed Wellington, 26 June 1916; 5th Rfts., 4th Battn. N.Z. Rifle Brigade. Killed in action 12 October 1917: Age 27. Mentioned in Despatches. Sergt. Worner leaves a wife, Elizabeth Jane Worner (Dunbeath Street, Blenheim).

His brothers George and Alfred also have no known grave; they are recorded on Panel 1, and the Messines Ridge (New Zealand) Memorial respectively.

(Panel 2) Pte. 29203, Robert Breachin Allan, 3rd Bn. Canterbury Regt., N.Z.E.F.: *s.* of John (& Mrs) Allan, of 237, Papanui Road, St. Albans, Christchurch: and brother to L/Corpl. 26/382, J. Allan, No.3 Coy., New Zealand Machine Gun Corps, killed in action, 7 June 1917. Died of wounds 17 October 1917.

His brother John is buried in Wulverghem-Lindenhoek Road Military Cemetery (III.C.14).

(Panel 2) Pte. 24138, Isaac Edward Claridge, 1st Bn. Canterbury Regt., N.Z.E.F.: *s.* of Thomas (& Mrs) Claridge, of 25, Chapel Street, Harewood Road, Papanui, Christchurch: and brother to Pte. 51338, C.R. Claridge, Canterbury Regt. (surv'd); Pte. 15500, B.S. Claridge, 2nd Canterbury Regt., died of wounds, 9 June 1917, aged 22 years; Pte. 25/2962, T.G. Claridge, N.Z. Rifle Brigade, died of sickness, 7 June 1918, aged 35 years; and cousin to Pte. 23/2553, S.T. Claridge, 2nd Auckland Regt., died of wounds, 16 November 1918, aged 25 years: *b.* 1895: *educ.* Harewood School: Occupation – Labourer; Watson's Farm, McSaveney's Road: served with the Expeditionary Force in France and Flanders from September 1916, and was reported missing presumed killed in action, 12 October 1917; verified by a Court of Enquiry, 22 April 1918: Age 24. *unm.*

His brother Benjamin is buried in Bailleul Communal Cemetery Extension (II.C.203); Thomas lies in Christchurch (Papanui) St. Paul's Anglican Church Cemetery (Section A, Plot 588); cousin Sydney is buried in St. Sever Communal Cemetery Extension (S.III.V.11).

(Panel 2) Pte. 29230, Henry Edward Debenham, 13th Coy., 1st Bn. Canterbury Regt., N.Z.E.F.: late of Jackson, Westland: *s.* of A.G. Debenham, of Bright Street, Cobden, Greymouth, by his wife Mary E.: and elder brother to Pte. 38266, C. Debenham, 3rd Canterbury Regt., died of peritonitis, 17 June 1917: *b.* Kumara, 31 January 1888: Occupation – Labourer: enlisted 27 June 1916: departed Wellington, HMNZT 67 'Tofua,' 11 October following: served with the Expeditionary Force in France from

28 March 1917, joining his battn. in the field 3 June, and was killed in action 12 October 1917. Buried at Passchendaele: Age 28. *unm.* His brothers George and James also served; both survived. *(Archives New Zealand record his father's initials as both H. and A.G., address Jackson's, Westland)*

His brother Charles is buried in Trois Arbres Cemetery (I.S.32).

(Panel 2) Pte. 46565, Thomas Dennehy, 1st Bn. Canterbury Regt., N.Z.E.F.: *s.* of the late Michael Frederick Dennehy, by his wife Margaret Josephine (North Street, Timaru): and brother to Rfn. 26/990, F.M. Dennehy, N.Z. Rifle Brigade (surv'd); and Gnr. 2817/A, E.J. Dennehy, who fell, 6 August 1915, at Gallipoli: *b.* 21 October 1892: religion – Roman Catholic: Occupation – Clerk: 5'7" tall, dark complexion, dark hair, brown eyes: enlisted 22 January 1917: embarked Wellington, HMNZT 84 'Turakina,' 26 April 1917: disembarked Devonport, 20 July following: proceeded to France 5 September 1917, joining his battn. in the field on the 16th of that month, and was killed in action 12 October 1917: Age 24 years, 11 months. *unm.*

His brother Edward also has no known grave; he is commemorated on the Chunuk Bair (New Zealand) Memorial (8).

(Panel 2) Pte. 27252, Herbert Horace Ellis, 1st Bn. Canterbury Regt., N.Z.E.F.: *s.* of William Ellis, of 79, Ollivier's Road, Linwood, Christchurch, by his wife Susan Cecilia: and brother to Pte. 6/1524, R.W. Ellis, Canterbury, who died, 21 July 1915, of disease contracted at Gallipoli: Occupation – Farm-Hand: departed Wellington, 25 September 1916: arrived Devonport via Cape of Good Hope, 21 November following. Killed in action at Bellevue 12 October 1917: Age 26. *unm.*

His brother Reuben is buried in East Mudros Military Cemetery (II.B.22).

(Panel 2) Pte. 27906, William Frederick Jensen (*a.k.a.* Jenson), 2nd Bn. Canterbury Regt., N.Z.E.F.: *s.* of Edward Jensen, of Whakatu, Hawkes Bay, by his wife Ada Mary: and brother to Rfn. 24/809, E.M. Jenson, N.Z. Rifle Brigade, killed in action, 30 December 1916: *b.* Woodville, Wellington, 1897: Occupation – Labourer: departed Wellington, 13 February 1917, HMNZT 77 'Mokoia;' 22nd Rfts., 'F' Coy., N.Z.E.F.: arrived Plymouth via Cape of Good Hope, 2 May following: proceeded to France and was killed in action there 12 October 1917: Age 20. *unm.*

His brother Edward is buried in Y Farm Military Cemetery, Bois Grenier (K.10).

(Panel 2) Pte. 51223, Alexander McNicol, 2nd Bn. Canterbury Regt., N.Z.E.F.: *s.* of Margaret McNicol (Ross, Westland, Greymouth): and brother to Pte. 69964, D.W. McNicol, 43rd Rfts. (surv'd): Occupation – Gold Miner: departed Wellington, 9 June 1917, HMNZT 85 'Willochra,' 26th Rfts., 'C' Coy., Canterbury Regt.: arrived Devonport via Cape of Good Hope, 16 August following: proceeded to France and was killed in action 12 October 1917.

(Panel 2) Pte. 6/1621, Owen Mellon, 1st Bn. Canterbury Regt., N.Z.E.F.: late of Millerton, South Island: *s.* of John Mellon, of 53, Auchinstarey, Ross, Croy, Glasgow: and brother to Gnr. 2/1183, J. Mellon, N.Z. Field Artillery (surv'd.): enlisted Canterbury: departed Wellington, 14 February 1915. Killed in action 2 October 1917

(Panel 2) Pte. 47679, Michael Moriarty, 'C' Coy., 2nd Bn. Canterbury Regt., N.Z.E.F.: *s.* of Timothy Moriarty, of Stillwater, Westland, Greymouth, by his wife Johanna: and elder brother to Pte. 6/678, T. Moriarty, Canterbury Regt., killed in action, 3 May 1915, at Gallipoli: Occupation – Storeman: departed Wellington, 12 June 1917, Rfn. N.Z. Rifle Brigade: subsequently transf'd. Canterbury Regt., and was killed in action 12 October 1917, at Bellevue: Age 26. *unm.* He leaves a wife, Mrs M. Moriarty (3, Austin Street, Wellington).

His brother Timothy also has no known grave; he is commemorated on the Lone Pine Memorial (75).

(Panel 2) Pte. 40234, Edwin Newlove, 2nd Bn. Canterbury Regt., N.Z.E.F.: s. of Mary Ann Newlove (Takaka, Nelson): his brothers – Pte. 33755, L.C. Newlove, 3rd Auckland Regt., and Pte. 31530, L.M. Newlove, 2nd Canterbury Regt. – also fell: Occupation – Farmer: enlisted 1916: departed New Zealand, 2 April 1917: served with the Expeditionary Force in France from July following, and was killed in action at the second attack at Bellevue Spur 12 October 1917. Buried behind the jumping off line: Age 32. unm.

His brothers Leonard and Leslie also have no known grave; they are recorded on Panels 1 and 2 (below) respectively.

(Panel 2) Pte. 31530, Leslie Malcolm Newlove, 2nd Bn. Canterbury Regt., N.Z.E.F.: s. of Mary Ann Newlove (Takaka, Nelson): his brothers – Pte. 40234, E. Newlove, Canterbury Regt., and Pte. 33755, L.C. Newlove, Auckland Regt. – also fell: Occupation – Farmer: enlisted 1916: departed New Zealand, 15 November of that year: served with the Expeditionary Force in France from July 1917, and was killed in action at the second attack at Bellevue Spur 12 October 1917, approximately 45 yards from the battalion jumping off line: Age 22. He leaves a wife, Maude Newlove (Takaka, Nelson), to whom he was married for but a short while.

His brothers Leonard and Edwin also have no known grave; they are recorded on Panels 1 and 2 (above) respectively.

(Panel 2) Pte. 6/3114, Nelson Newport, 2nd Bn. Canterbury Regt., N.Z.E.F.: s. of George Newport, of Haven Road, Nelson: and brother to Pte. 13463, A. Newport, 2nd Wellington Regt., killed in action, 23 August 1916, at the Somme: departed Wellington, 9 October 1915. Killed in action 12 October 1917: unm.

His brother Allan also has no known grave; he is commemorated on the Caterpillar Valley (New Zealand) Memorial. (IWGC record 1 October 1916)

(Panel 2) Pte. 24214, Alfred William Nordstrom, 1st Bn. Canterbury Regt., N.Z.E.F.: s. of Alfred Hermann Nordstrom, of Wheatstone, South Canterbury, by his wife Annie: and elder brother to Pte. 6/3118, H.A Nordstrom, Canterbury Regt., killed in action, 7 June 1917, at Messines: Occupation – Farm-Hand: departed Wellington, 27 May 1916. Killed in action, 12 October 1917, at Bellevue: Age 34. unm. Correspondence regarding the deceased should be forwarded c/o his brother Milo R. Nordstrom, Esq., Tinwald, South Canterbury.

His brother Hermann also has no known grave; he is commemorated on the Messines Ridge (New Zealand) Memorial.

(Panel 2) Pte. 16786, Daniel O'Donoghue, 3rd Bn. Canterbury Regt., N.Z.E.F.: s. of Mary Ann O'Donoghue (103, Shakespeare Road, Napier): and brother to Dvr. 13/2468, W.J. O'Donoghue, N.Z. Field Artillery, died 31 May 1918, of disease, aged 29 years: departed Wellington, HMNZT 72 'Athenic,' 30 December 1916. Killed in action, 4 October 1917.

His brother William is buried in Bagneux British Cemetery, Gezaincourt (II.D.14).

(Panel 2) Pte. 34143, Percy Noel Radcliffe, 2nd Bn. Canterbury Regt., N.Z.E.F.: late of Pikowai: s. of the late James Radcliffe, by his wife Frances Emily Rosa (Ngaio, Wellington): and brother to Sergt. 25/44, J.V. Radcliffe, N.Z. Rifle Brigade, killed in action, 25 May 1916: Occupation – Farmer: departed Wellington, HMNZT 75 'Waitemata,' 19 January 1917. Killed in action 12 October 1917: Age 32.

His brother Julian is buried in Cité Bonjean Military Cemetery, Armentieres (I.B.34).

(Panel 2) Pte. 32472, George James Schumacher, 1st Bn. Canterbury Regt., N.Z.E.F.: s. of the late Philip Clement Schumacher, by his wife Emily Kezia (54, Blenheim Road, Riccarton, Christchurch): and brother to Pte. 12/2835, E.N.R. Schumacher, Auckland Regt., killed in action, 3 July 1916, and Pte. 55550, F.W. Schumacher, Canterbury Regt., died, 14 April 1918, of wounds: b. 14 March 1890: Occupation – Law Clerk: enlisted 26 July 1916: served with the Expeditionary Force in France and Flanders from 25 May 1917, and was killed in action 12 October 1917. Buried at Passchendaele; vicinity of Bellevue: Age 26. unm.

His brother Edward is buried in Cite Bonjean Military Cemetery (II.C.7), Frederick in Doullens Communal Cemetery Extension No.1 (VI.B.29).

(Panel 2) Pte. 34754, John Christopher Tulloch, 1st (Canterbury) Coy., 3rd Bn. Canterbury Regt., N.Z.E.F.: late of Collafirth, by Olaberry, Shetland Islands, Scotland: s. of the late John Tulloch, of 76, Barbour Street, Linwood, Christchurch, New Zealand, by his wife Agnes (459, Papanui Road, Papanui): Religion – Presbyterian: Occupation – Tram Conductor; Christchurch Tramways Board: proceeded overseas 20th Rfts., Canterbury Regt., 7 December 1916; hospitalised (gonorrhoea) aboard ship, 23 – 27 December: trained Slingsby Camp, England (from 18 February 1917); proceeded to France 25 May; killed in action in France, 4 October 1917: Age 31.

In the attack on the Bellevue Spur, 12 October 1917, after scrambling from crater to crater, splashed by shell-bursts and floundering over the slippery and treacherous semi-liquid mud of their allotted sector, 2nd New Zealand Brigade were brought to a virtual standstill astride the Gravenstafel Road, in Marsh Bottom. Quickly realising the enemy was holding his front in considerable strength, 2nd Otago, the leading battalion, under a torrent of machine gun fire, pressed on to the wire entanglements only to find them between 25 and 50 yards deep and completely unbroken. The only way forward was a lane where the sunken Gravenstafel Road ran uphill. It proved a veritable lane of death. The men, on seeing their comrades foiled by the wire, made for this passage only to be cut down by cunningly-sited machine guns in shellholes and blockhouses which commanded this trap from either side. Rifle grenades and Lewis guns were used with effect on the machine guns in the shellholes, and under this covering protection 2nd Otago fought desperately to break through the wire and reach the blockhouses. Among those cut down, Major W.W. Turner showed unsurpassable bravery. He cut his way through the first belt of wire before being riddled with bullets.

(Panel 3) Major 23469, William Wilson Turner, 2nd Bn. Otago Regt., N.Z.E.F.: late of Balclutha: Occupation – School Teacher: departed Wellington with 13th Refts., 'D'Coy., Otago Regt., 27 May 1916. Killed in action 12 October 1917. He leaves a wife, Ann Turner (Leamington, Cambridge, Waikato, Hamilton). Major Turner was Mentioned in the Honours Despatch covering the period 22 September 1917 – 24 February 1918 (London Gazette, 28 May 1918).

1st Otago, following up behind 2nd Otago, were not destined to reach their objective in the attack, the Blue Line. Pushing on into the gap left by the heavy casualties and with what remained of their sister battalion, the officers and men tried to crawl beneath the wire. Several actually managed to cut a passage through the first band of entanglements, and a few through the second, just beyond which lay the pillboxes almost completely surrounded by an interior ring of wire. In the left company of 1st Otago, every officer was killed or wounded; 2nd Lieuts. J.J. Bishop and N.F. Watson actually reached the aperture of one pillbox only to be killed whilst in the act of throwing a bomb into it.

(Panel 3) 2nd Lieut. 23294, John Joseph Bishop, 4th Coy., 1st Bn. Otago Regt., N.Z.E.F.: *s.* of John Joseph Bishop, of 'Dunvegan,' Titirangi, Auckland, by his wife Emily: and brother to Pte. 54813, W.N.C. Bishop, Auckland Regt., who also fell: *b.* 7 July 1893: Occupation – School Teacher: enlisted 15 December 1915: served with the Expeditionary Force in France and Flanders from 5 September 1916, joining his battn. In the Field, 3 October following: underwent officer training in England, 19 April – 20 June 1917 (commissioned 2nd Lieut. 24 May): returned to France, 22 June, rejoining his battn. on the 30th of that month, and was killed in action 12 October 1917. 2nd Lieut. Bishop was Specially Mentioned in Despatches by F.M. Sir Douglas Haig, 7 April 1918, for 'distinguished and gallant services': Age 24. *unm.*

His brother William is buried in Euston Road Cemetery, Colincamps (I.J.6).

(Panel 3) 2nd Lieut. 12/2495, Norman Tompsett, 2nd Bn. Otago Regt., N.Z.E.F.: *s.* of Benjamin Tompsett, of "Castlemaine," Hollington Park, St. Leonards-on-Sea, England: Occupation – Architect: enlisted 15 February 1915, address c/o L. Nooderton, Te Kuiti: departed Wellington, 13 June 1915, as Pte., 5th Rfts., Auckland Regt.: served with the Expeditionary Force in Egypt and at Gallipoli from whence, after contracting enteric fever, he was invalided to England: after prolonged convalescence at Hornchurch, proceeded to France, transf'd. Otago Regt.: selected for officer training in the field, went to England where, after qualifying, he received his commission, 2nd Lieut., 2 June 1917: returned to France shortly thereafter and was killed in action in the attack at Passchendaele 12 October 1917: Age 23. *unm.*

(Panel 3) 2nd Lieut. 9/96, Norman Forrester Watson, 1st Bn. Otago Regt., N.Z.E.F.: *s.* of John Watson, of 'Bellevue,' Port Chalmers, Dunedin, by his wife Helen: *b.* 1 September 1888: religion – Presbyterian: Occupation – Clerk: 5'5½" tall, sallow complexion, blue eyes, brown hair: enlisted, 12 August 1914:

departed Port Chalmers, as Tpr., Otago Mounted Rifles, 16 October 1914: promoted L/Corpl. 13 November following; Corpl. 4 March 1916 (Ismailia); apptd. Coy. Bomber, 30 July (France); promoted Sergt. 11 November following: served with the Expeditionary Force in Egypt from 3 December 1914, and at Gallipoli from May 1915: wounded in action at Anzac, 20 August following, subsequently evacuated to Mudros (23 August) thence to England (September): returned to Egypt, joining his unit at Zeitoun, 3 January 1916: proceeded to France, 9 April 1916: selected for a commission in the field, 13 April 1917, and proceeded to England for training on the 18th of that month: apptd. 2nd Lieut. (Supernumerary), posted Pioneer Battn., 2 June 1917 (Sling Camp), joining 4th Otago, 18 June: returned to France, 16 July 1917, joining 1st Otago in the field, 10 August following; killed in action, 12 October 1917, in the attack at Bellevue: Age 29. *unm.*

(Panel 3) Coy.Sergt.Major 8/738, William Thomas Carruthers, 1st Bn. Otago Regt., N.Z.E.F.: *s.* of Mrs M. Carruthers (33, Brunswick Street, Dunedin): enlisted Otago, August 1914: departed Port Chalmers, Pte., Otago Infantry, 16 October 1914: served at Gallipoli, Egypt, and in France and Flanders, and was killed in action 12 October 1917.

(Panel 3) Sergt. 24331, James McKenzie Boyle, M.M., 10th Coy., 2nd Bn. Otago Regt., N.Z.E.F.: *s.* of James Boyle, by his wife Mary Stuart: *b.* New South Wales: served in the South African Campaign, 1900–02: Occupation – Electrician: departed Wellington, 17th Rfts., Otago Infantry; HMNZT 65 'Pakeha,' 23 September 1916: served with the Expeditionary Force in France, and was killed in action 12 October 1917: Age 34. He was awarded the Military Medal (*London Gazette*, 16 August 1917), for his actions when: 'During the attack on the Messines Ridge on the 7th June 1917, seeing some of the enemy in a trench to the right of the position of his company occupied, he rushed into the trench, and as they refused to surrender, he cleared the trench with his bayonet. Later when both his platoon Officer and Sergeant were wounded he assumed command and by his gallant conduct under heavy shellfire set a fine example of cheerfulness to his men.' Sergt. Boyle was married to Frances Arbon, *née* Boyle (164, Jackson Street, Petone), formerly of 53, Wellington Road, Kilbirnie.

(Panel 3) Sergt. 23/1646, William Elliot Gordon, M.M., 2nd Bn. Otago Regt., N.Z.E.F.: *s.* of Douglas Gordon, of 28, Abbotts Road, Mount Eden, Auckland, by his wife Susannah: and brother to Pte. 12/2303, R.H. Gordon, Auckland Regt., killed in action, 27 September 1916, at the Somme. Killed in action 12 October 1917; Bellevue, Passchendaele. Awarded the Military Medal (*London Gazette*, 11 May 1917), for his actions on the – 'British front Neuve Eglise sector opposite Messines – 24 March 1917. Under cover of an intense artillery and Minnenwerfer bombardment, lasting from 4am till 5.10am on the above date, the enemy raided a portion of our front line, about the Wulverghem – Wytschaete Road. Out of a raiding party estimated about 90. Six of the enemy managed to make an entrance, the remainder of them being driven back by Lewis Gun, fire and bombs. The men of the 2nd Otago Battallion holding the line displayed the greatest gallantry, endurance and devotion to duty in sticking in their posts under the severest bombardment and driving the enemy back. Corpl. W.E. Gordon, a Lewis Machine Gunner, was the first to observe the enemy coming across "No Man's Land". He immediately gave the alarm and turned his gun on the enemy. Throughout the whole bombardment he displayed the greatest coolness, self composure and bravery, he set a splendid example to his men, showing great initiative and devotion to duty.': Age 31.

His brother Robert also has no known grave; he is commemorated on the Caterpillar Valley (New Zealand) Memorial.

(Panel 3) Sergt. 24368, Herbert Ingram, 'D' Coy., 2nd Bn. Otago Regt., N.Z.E.F.: Occupation – Ironmonger: enlisted 1916: departed Wellington, Sergt., 17th Rfts., Otago Infantry, HMNZT 65 'Pakeha,' 23 September 1916: disembarked Devonport (via Cape of Good Hope), 19 November following: trained England, thereafter proceeded to France, and was killed in action, 12 October 1917, at Ypres, Belgium. He was married to Ellen Ingram (95, Ritchie Street, Invercargill), late of Lune Street, Oamaru.

(Panel 3) Sergt. 29696, John McCorley, 1st Bn. Otago Regt., N.Z.E.F.: late of Balclutha, New Zealand: a pre-war Regular: departed Wellington, Coy.Sergt.Major, 20th Rfts., 'D' Coy., Otago Infantry, HMNZT

72 'Athenic,' 30 December 1916: trained England, thereafter joined the Expeditionary Force in France, and was killed in action 12 October 1917. All correspondence should be addressed c/o his sister, Miss Margaret McCorley (245, Cashel Street, Christchurch, New Zealand).

(Panel 3) Sergt. 8/443, William Millar, 1st Otago Regt., N.Z.E.F.: late of Tuatapere, New Zealand: *s.* of Alex (& Mrs) Millar, of Puketiro, Catlins Branch, Otago: enlisted Waimotu, Otago on the outbreak of war: departed Port Chalmers, 16 October 1914: served in Egypt, Gallipoli, and with the Expeditionary Force in France and Flanders, and was killed in action, 12 October 1917, in the attack at Bellevue. *unm.*

(Panel 3) Sergt. 8/2134, Walter Graham Sinclair, M.M., 1st Otago Regt., N.Z.E.F.: *s.* of Robert Paterson (& Mrs) Sinclair, of Browns, Southland, Invercargill: departed Wellington, Pte., 5th Rfts., Otago Infantry, 13 June 1915: served in Egypt, and with the Expeditionary Force in France and Flanders, and was killed in action 12 October 1917. Awarded the Military Medal (*London Gazette*, 16 August 1917), for his actions when – 'During the attack on Messines 7th June 1917, this Battalion suffered heavily as regards Officers. Sergt. Sinclair, when his Officer had been killed in the advance, immediately took command of the Platoon, carried them on to their objective with complete success, and handled them with marked ability. As there was only one Officer left unwounded in this Company, Sergt. Sinclair was indefatigable in supervising the consolidation under heavy enfilade shellfire, and throughout set a fine example of bravery and determination.': Age 26. *unm.*

(Panel 3) Sergt. 8/3108, George Wallace, 1st Bn. Otago Regt., N.Z.E.F.: late of Gore Road, Mataura: *s.* of the late William Wallace, by his wife Jane (Selbourne Street, Mataura, Southland, Invercargill): departed Wellington, Pte., 7th Rfts., Otago Infantry, 9 October 1915: served in Egypt and with the Expeditionary Force in France, and was killed in action 12 October 1917: Age 28. *unm.* Commemorated on Akaroa War Memorial.

(Panel 3) L/Sergt. 11283, Thomas Hodgson, 'D' Coy., 2nd Bn. Otago Regt., N.Z.E.F.: late of Motukaraka: *s.* of the late Thomas Hodgson, by his marriage to Jane Reid Crow, *née* Hodgson (14, Helens Street, Dunedin), late of 173, King Edward Road: Occupation – Moulder: enlisted 1916: departed Wellington, Pte., 12th Rfts., Otago Infantry, HMNZT 51 'Ulimaroa,' 1 May 1916: served in Egypt, and with the Expeditionary Force in France and Flanders. Reported wounded and missing, 12 October 1917, at Bellevue; confirmed killed: Age 30. *unm.*

(Panel 3) L/Sergt. 8/1776, Hugh William McCall, 1st Bn. Otago Regt.: late of Wallacetown, Otago: *s.* of John McCall, of Scandrett Street, Invercargill, by his wife Marion: *b.* Eastern Bush, Otautau, 1891: enlisted Otago: proceeded overseas, Pte. 4th Rfts., Otago Infantry, 17 April 1915: served with the Expeditionary Force at Gallipoli, and in France and Flanders, and was killed in action 12 October 1917: Age 26. *unm.*

(Panel 3) Corpl. 22211, Alex Stronach Hewat, 1st Bn. Otago Regt., N.Z.E.F.: *s.* of E.C. (& J.W.) Hewat, Rector of District High School, Havelock Street, Riverton, Invercargill: and *yr.* brother to Capt. 6/2485, J.P. Hewat, 1st Otago Regt., killed in action, 8 October 1918: Occupation – Clerk: enlisted 4 May 1916: served with the Expeditionary Force in France and Flanders from 13 February 1917: promoted Corpl. 7 July following, and was killed in action 3 October 1917. Buried in a shell-hole in the front line. Memorial cross erected at Dochy Farm New British Cemetery, Langemarck, 4 miles E.N.E. of Ypres: Age 22. *unm.*

His brother John is buried in Marcoing British Cemetery (II.E.6).

(Panel 3) L/Corpl. 8/3517, Angus Cameron, 2nd Bn. Otago Regt., N.Z.E.F.: *s.* of the late Angus Cameron, by his wife Mary Frances (Woodend, Awarua Plains, Southland, Invercargill): and brother to L/Corpl. 8/805, J. Cameron, 2nd Bn. Otago Regt., died 24 September 1916, of wounds: *b.* Edendale, Southland: Occupation – Farmer: departed New Zealand, 8 January 1916. Killed in action 12 October 1917: Age 26. *unm.*

His brother John is buried in St. Sever Cemetery (B.18.65).

(Panel 3) L/Corpl. 8/1958, Alexander Dempster Craig, 1st Bn. Otago Regt., N.Z.E.F.: late of Palmerston South: brother to Rfn. 23/715, A.C. Craig, N.Z. Rifle Brigade, who fell, 12 August 1917, at Messines: embarked Wellington, 13 June 1915. Killed in action 12 October 1917. *unm.* All correspondence should be addressed c/o his brother William E. Craig, Esq., Puketapu, Palmerston South, New Zealand.

His brother Andrew also has no known grave; he is commemorated on the Messines Ridge (New Zealand) Memorial.

(Panel 3) L/Corpl. 8/3618, Cyril Hartnett, 2nd Bn. Otago Regt., N.Z.E.F.: c/o Mrs M. Hanseg (Waratah, Tasmania, Australia): *s.* of Patrick Hartnett, of Deloraine, Tasmania, by his wife Mary: and brother to Pte. 24/1996, J. Hartnett, 2nd Canterbury Regt., died of wounds, 23 September 1916, at Rouen; Rfn. 24/2216, D. Hartnett, 2/3rd N.Z. Rifle Brigade, killed in action at the Somme, 5 October 1916; and L/Corpl. 8/2601, P.J. Hartnett, Canterbury Regt., lost at sea when returning to New Zealand, 17 March 1919: Occupation – Labourer: departed Wellington, HMNZT 37 'Maunganui,' 8 January 1916; 9th Rfts., 'D' Coy., Otago Regt. Killed in action 12 October 1917.

His brother John is buried in St. Sever Cemetery (B.18.63), Dennis and Philip have no known grave, they are commemorated on the Caterpillar Valley (New Zealand) Memorial and Otago Provincial Memorial respectively.

(Panel 3) L/Corpl. 24/1071, Edmund John Heald, 2nd Bn. Otago Regt., N.Z.E.F.: *s.* of Edmund John Heald, of Wreys Bush, Invercargill, by his wife Ellen: and brother to Pte. 24/464, T.J. Heald, killed in action, 15 September 1916, at the Somme. Killed in action, 12 October 1917, in the attack at Bellevue Spur.

His brother Thomas also has no known grave; he is commemorated on the Caterpillar Valley (New Zealand) Memorial.

(Panel 3) Pte. 9/2045, Theophilus Barber, 2nd Bn. Otago Regt., N.Z.E.F.: *s.* of Stephen Barber, of 42, Richmond Street, South Dunedin, New Zealand, by his wife Margaret Alice: and elder brother to Pte. 41067, E.A.B. Barber, 1st Bn. Canterbury Regt., died of wounds, 22 January 1918, aged 21. Killed in action 12 October 1917: Age 22. *unm.*

His brother Edward is buried in Lijssenthoek Military Cemetery (XXVII.F.3).

(Panel 3) Pte. 26/535, John Scott Cook, 3rd Bn. Otago Regt., N.Z.E.F.: late of Awamangu, via Balclutha, New Zealand: *s.* of David Cook, of Hilderthorpe, Oamaru, by his wife Elizabeth: and *yr.* brother to Pte. 39171, G.S. Cook, 1st Otago Regt., killed in action, 12 October 1917, aged 27 years: *b.* 24 May 1894: Occupation – Labourer: enlisted 11 October 1915: departed Wellington, 5 February 1916, 'D' Coy, 4th N.Z. Rifle Brigade: disembarked Suez, Egypt, 15 March: served with the Expeditionary Force in France from 7 April 1916: wounded and evacuated to England, September following: transf'd 3rd Battn. Otago Regt. after convalescence and treatment for mumps, and returned to France, March 1917, and was killed in action 4 October following. Buried near Fokker Farm: Age 23. *unm.*

His brother George is buried nearby in Tyne Cot Cemetery (XXXVI.F.10).

(Panel 3) Pte. 22309, Bertie Coulson, 2nd Bn. Otago Regt., N.Z.E.F.: *s.* of John Watson Coulson, of Alexandra South, Central Otago, by his wife Louisa Sarah: and brother to Pte. R.W. Coulson, Otago Regt. (surv'd), and Pte. 8/2882, J.W. Coulson, who fell, 7 June 1917, at the Battle of Messines. Killed in action 12 October 1917: Age 22. *unm.*

His brother John also has no known grave; he is commemorated on the Messines Ridge (New Zealand) Memorial.

(Panel 3) Pte. 8/3224, James Crabbe, 2nd Bn. Otago Regt., N.Z.E.F.: *s.* of James (& Mrs) Crabbe, of Bannockburn, Otago: and brother to Pte. 8/130, T.A. Crabbe, Otago Regt. (surv'd): enlisted Bannockburn: departed Wellington, 13 November 1915, 8th Rfts.: trained in Egypt, thereafter proceeded to France and was killed in action, Ypres, Belgium, 12 October 1917. *unm.* (*IWGC record 813224*)

(Panel 3) Pte. 40891, James Cree, 10th Coy, 1st Bn. Otago Regt., N.Z.E.F.: *s.* of James Cree, of Otekaike, Oamaru, North Otago, by his wife Margaret: and elder brother to Pte. 40890, H.S. Cree, 1st Otago Regt., who fell 3 December 1917: *b.* Dunedin, 9 November 1879: Occupation – Farm Labourer: enlisted 4 November 1916: embarked Wellington aboard HMNZT 79 'Ruapehu,' 14 March 1917: arrived Devonport, 21 May following: served with the Expeditionary Force in France and Flanders from 23 June, and was killed in action, 12 October 1917, at Bellevue, Passchendaele. Buried Anzac Cemetery, Waterloo Farm, by Rev. C. Pringle attd. 43rd Bn. Canadian Infantry: Age 37. *unm.*

His brother Herbert also has no known grave; he is commemorated on the Buttes New British Cemetery (New Zealand) Memorial.

(Panel 3) Pte. 33036, Leslie Hastie Dewar, 1st Bn. Otago Regt., N.Z.E.F.: late of Queenstown, Lake Wakatipu, Invercargill: *s.* of the late Stewart Dewar, by his wife Margaret (12, Bellevue Street, Roslyn, Dunedin): and yr. brother to L/Corpl. 9/31, S.G. Dewar, 1st Otago Regt., who fell, 3 December 1917, aged 32 years. Killed in action 12 October 1917: Age 19.

His brother Stewart also has no known grave; he is commemorated on the Buttes New British Cemetery (New Zealand) Memorial, Polygon Wood.

(Panel 3) Pte. 24/417, William Thomas Faull, 3rd Bn. Otago Regt., N.Z.E.F.: *s.* of the late William Faull, by his marriage to Elizabeth Ann Foreman, *née* Faull (Ward Street, Dannevirke, Hawkes Bay, Napier): and elder brother to Pte. 10/2797, H.J. Faull, No.1 Coy., New Zealand Machine Gun Corps, killed in action, 26 September 1916: *b.* Kaponga, Taranaki, 28 February 1893: Occupation – Cheesemaker: enlisted Kaponga, 28 May 1915, posted 'B' Coy., N.Z. Rifle Brigade: departed Wellington, 9 October 1915: disembarked Egypt, 18 November following: proceeded to France, 6 April 1916; transf'd. 'C' Coy., Lewis gun section, 8 July: wounded (G.S.W. rt. shoulder) 15 September, and evacuated to No.3 General Hospital, Brockenhurst: on recovery transf'd. 3rd Otago Regt., 2 May 1917: returned to France on the 25th of that month and was killed in action 17 October 1917: Age 24.

His brother Henry is buried in A.I.F. Burial Ground (I.E.5).

(Panel 3) Pte. 9/1170, George William Funnell, 2nd Bn. Otago Regt., N.Z.E.F.: late of 408, Cumberland Street, Dunedin: *s.* of William F. (& Mrs) Funnell, of South Street, St. Andrews, Blenheim, New Zealand: *b.* 14 August 1886: Occupation – Shearer: enlisted 17 April 1915: departed New Zealand, 14 August 1915: served at Gallipoli until 23 December following, thereafter in Egypt before proceeding to France, April 1916: awarded 14 days F.P. No.2, and forfeiture of pay, 29 May following for (1) Being absent from billet from 8.30 p.m till 9.25 p.m when apprehended in the town (2) Giving wrong name and number, and (3) Refusing to show pay book or disc. Killed in action 12 October 1917. A comrade, Pte. 10095, F.C. Jones, wrote, "We went over at Belle-Vue Spur, Passchendaele. We had gone about 300 yards when Funnell was hit in the leg by a bullet and almost immediately was struck in the head and killed. I was about 15 yards away and saw the body afterwards; he must have been killed instantly. I cannot say anything of his burial…He was in the Lewis Gun section with me.": Age 31.

(Panel 3) Pte. 32842, Guy Genge, 3rd Bn. Otago Regt., N.Z.E.F.: *s.* of Thomas Genge, of Wyndham, Southland, Invercargill, by his wife Jane: and *yr.* brother to Pte. 11453, B. Genge, Auckland Regt., killed in action, 26 September 1916. Killed in action 4 October 1917: Age 21. *unm.*

His brother Ben also has no known grave; he is commemorated on the Caterpillar Valley (New Zealand) Memorial.

(Panel 3) Pte. 29779, John Joseph Hartstonge, 8th Coy., 2nd Otago Regt., N.Z.E.F.: *s.* of Patrick Hartstonge, of 349, York Place, Dunedin, by his wife Margaret: and *yr.* brother to Pte. 63151, J. Hartstonge, Wellington Regt., fell 1 October 1918. Killed in action 12 October 1917: Age 22. *unm.*

His brother Jeremiah is buried in Flesquieres Hill British Cemetery (VI.C.17).

(Panel 3) Pte. 23557, Thomas Jenkins, 4th Coy. 1st Bn. Otago Regt., N.Z.E.F.: *s.* of the late William Jenkins, by his wife Mary Ann: *b.* Arrowtown, Invercargill, 1882: and yr. brother to Pte. 56931, J. Jenkins, 2nd Otago Regt., who died 1 April 1918, of wounds: Occupation – Grocer: departed Wellington, 27 May 1916, 13th Rfts., 'D' Coy., Otago Regt. Died of wounds 16 October 1917: Age 35. All correspondence should be addressed c/o his sister Miss E. Jenkins (32, Fitzroy Street, Caversham, Dunedin).

His brother James is buried in Doullens Communal Cemetery Extension No.1 (VI.F.38).

(Panel 3) Pte. 23145, Karl Kjoss (served as Curtiss, K.), 'H' Coy., 2nd Bn. Otago Regt., N.Z.E.F.: *s.* of Oluf Emil Kjoss, of Kristiansand, Norway, by his wife Jorgine Kathrine: Occupation – Seaman: departed Wellington, 27 May 1916, 4th Rfts., 'H'.Coy., 4th N.Z.Rifle Brigade: subsequently proceeded to France, transf'd. 2nd Otago Regt. and was killed in action 12 October 1917: Age 30. All correspondence should be addressed c/o his brother-in-law, F. Kjoss, 13, Romilly Street, Westport, New Zealand.

(Panel 3) Pte. 37934, Raymond Shirley McHardie, 1st Bn. Otago Regt., N.Z.E.F.: *s.* of James McHardie, of People's Palace Hotel, Wellington (formerly L/Corpl. 18692, N.Z. Rifle Brigade), by his wife Florence Grace (23, Heads Road, Wanganui), late of Railway Tearooms, Otaki: and brother to Pte. 10/1895, C.V. McHardie, Wellington Regt. (surv'd.); and 2nd Lieut. 3/700, C.J. McHardie, Wellington Regt., killed in action, 22 May 1918: Occupation – Cadet: departed Wellington, HMNZT 80 'Corinthic,' 2 April 1917, 23rd Rfs., Specialist Coy. Signal Section. Killed in action 12 October 1917. Dedicated Anzac Day, 25 April 1932 – 'To The Glory Of God And To The Memory Of The New Zealanders That Died In The Great War' – Pte. McHardie and his brothers are commemorated on one of the bells (donated by his father) of the Wellington War Memorial Carillon. The pamphlet published for the dedication of the bells records "…The main ideas governing the gift and installation of the Wellington War Memorial carillon are that it shall be regarded essentially as a memorial to the New Zealanders who gave their lives in the Great War, that it shall commemorate their deeds by the giving of special recitals on the anniversaries of the principal engagements in which they fell, and, the carillon being the greatest instrument in existence for the cultivation of the folksong and national and religious airs, it shall help to rekindle among New Zealanders the love of old England, Scotland, Ireland and Wales and of their own land, and the ideals for which so many New Zealanders died – the triumph of right over wrong, and the establishment of peace and goodwill amongst men."

His brother Cyril also has no known grave; he is commemorated on the Grevillers (New Zealand) Memorial.

(Panel 3) Pte. 42552, Patrick McKone, 3rd Bn. Otago Regt., N.Z.E.F.: *s.* of Michael McKone, of Torridge Street, Oamaru: and brother to L/Corpl. 25/665, J. McKone, N.Z. Rifle Brigade, died 1 October 1916, of wounds: Occupation – Labourer: proceeded overseas, 5 April 1917. Killed in action 4 October 1917

His brother John is buried in Heilly Station Cemetery, Mericourt-L'Abbé (V.B.22).

(Panel 3) Pte. 39300, John O'Brien, 'D' Coy., 2nd Bn. Otago Regt., N.Z.E.F.: *s.* of the late John O'Brien, by his wife Norah (359, Cargill Road, South Dunedin): and yr. brother to Pte. 8/136, T. O'Brien, Otago Regt., killed in action, 9 August 1915, at Gallipoli: Occupation – Labourer: departed Wellington, HMNZT 76 'Aparima,' 16 February 1917. Killed in action 12 October 1917: Age 22.

His brother Thomas also has no known grave; he is commemorated on the Chunuk Bair (New Zealand) Memorial (16).

(Panel 3) Pte. 29832, John Buchan Moir, 2nd Bn. Otago Regt., N.Z.E.F.: *s.* of the late John Moir, of Wickliff Terrace, Port Chalmers, by his wife Margaret (20, Mary Street, Port Chalmers, Dunedin): and brother to Gnr. 74638, W.A. Moir, N.Z.Field Artillery (surv'd.); Corpl. 78801, E. Moir, 40th Rfts. (surv'd.); and Gnr. 43518, W. Moir, N.Z. Field Artillery, killed in action, 11 September 1918, at Havrincourt: Occupation – Shipwright: departed Wellington, 16 October 1916. Killed in action 12 October 1917: Age 22. *unm.*

His brother Walton is buried in Lebucquiere Communal Cemetery Extension (II.E.21).

(Panel 3) Pte. 24274, John O'Gorman, 1st Bn. Otago Regt., N.Z.E.F.: *s.* of the late Thomas O'Gorman, of 12, Lewisville Terrace, Tinakori Road, Wellington, by his wife Bridget (2, Upton Terrace, Wellington): and brother to Rfn. 37008, J.T. O'Gorman, N.Z. Rifle Brigade (surv'd); Pte. 30396, T. O'Gorman, Wellington Regt., killed in action, 4-6 October 1917; Rfn. 62706, C. O'Gorman, N.Z. Rifle Brigade, died 28 August 1918, of wounds; and Pte. 24273, T. O'Gorman, Otago Regt., killed in action, 23 October 1918. Killed in action 12 October 1917, at Passchendaele.

His brother Thomas also has no known grave, he is recorded on Panel 6; Cornelius and Timothy are buried in Bagneux British Cemetery, Gezaincourt (V.B.32) and Romeries Communal Cemetery Extension (III.E.8), respectively.

(Panel 3) Pte. 9/1343, Stephen William O'Rourke, 1st Bn. Otago Regt., N.Z.E.F.: late of Tuturau, Mataura: *s.* of Michael O'Rourke, of Gore, Southland, Invercargill: and brother to Pte. 46776, P. O'Rourke, Otago Regt., died 6 December 1917, of wounds: departed Wellington, 14 August 1915. Killed in action 12 October 1917. *unm.*

His brother Patrick is buried in Lijssenthoek Military Cemetery (XXVI.BB.8).

(Panel 3) Pte. 32781, Ernest Perfect, 2nd Bn. Otago Regt., N.Z.E.F.: *s.* of the late George J. Perfect, of Woodville, Wellington, by his wife Jane (c/o C.W. Perfect, Cross Creek): and brother to Rfn. 23/1151, S. Perfect, N.Z. Rifle Brigade, killed in action, 15 September 1916: Occupation – Mill-Hand: departed Wellington, HMNZT 68 'Manganui,' 15 November 1916. Killed in action 12 October 1917: Age 25. *unm.*

His brother Stanley also has no known grave; he is commemorated on the Caterpillar Valley (New Zealand) Memorial.

(Panel 3) Pte. 8/1314, Michael Piper, 4th Coy., 1st Bn. Otago Regt., N.Z.E.F.: *s.* of the late George Piper, of Rotherham, North Canterbury, by his marriage to Alice Gillespie, *née* Piper (Culverden, North Canterbury): and brother to Pte. 6/1377, G. Piper, Canterbury Regt., died of wounds, 10 May 1915, at Gallipoli: departed Wellington, 14 December 1914: served with the Expeditionary Force in the Dardanelles (wounded there), and in France and Flanders, and was killed in action, 12 October 1917, at Gravenstafel: Age 25. *unm.*

His brother George is buried in Lancashire Landing Cemetery (E.49).

(Panel 3) Pte. 39308, Edward Arthur Poole, 2nd Bn. Otago Regt., N.Z.E.F.: *s.* of the late Edward Samuel Poole, by his wife Margaret (Isla Bank, Southland): and brother to Pte. 8/2098, A.P. Poole, Otago Regt., killed in action, 4 December 1917; and Pte. 9/1091, T.H. Poole, N.Z. Pioneer Battn., killed in action, 15 September 1916: Occupation – Farmer: departed Wellington, HMNZT 76 'Aparima,' 16 February 1917. Killed in action 12 October 1917: Age 23. *unm.*

His brothers Albert and Thomas also have no known grave, they are commemorated on the Buttes New British Cemetery (New Zealand) Memorial (Polygon Wood), and Caterpillar Valley (New Zealand) Memorial respectively.

(Panel 3) Pte. 40076, Henry Wilson Smith, 'F'Coy., 2nd Bn. Otago Regt., N.Z.E.F.: *s.* of William Wilson Smith, of Clareville, Carterton, Wellington, by his wife Eliza: and elder brother to Pte. 10/1342, W.R. Smith, Wellington Regt., killed in action, 8 May 1915, at Gallipoli: Occupation – Farm-Hand: departed Wellington, HMNZT 79 'Ruapehu,' 14 March 1917. Killed in action, 12 October 1917, at Gravenstafel: Age 31. There is a distinct possibility that Pte. Smith may be the man referred to in the account by Pte. W. Smith as Sergt. Smith.

His brother Walter also has no known grave; he is commemorated on the Twelve Tree Copse (New Zealand) Memorial, Gallipoli.

(Panel 3) Pte. 27614, Henry Spratt, 4th Coy., 2nd Bn. Otago Regt., N.Z.E.F.: *s.* of Patrick Spratt, of Sutton, Central Otago: and brother to Pte. 27615, J.A. Spratt, Otago Regt. (surv'd.), Pte. 8/112, J.R. Spratt, Otago Regt. (surv'd.), and Rfn. 72429, T.A. Spratt, N.Z. Rifle Brigade, killed in action, 28 October 1918: Occupation – Farmer: departed Wellington, 23 September 1916. Killed in action 12 October 1917: Age 24. *unm.*

His brother Thomas is buried in Cross Roads Cemetery, Fontaine-au-Bois (II.F.20).

Lyn Macdonald, author of *They Called It Passchendaele*, wrote, "At 5.25 a.m. 12 October 1917, 1st and 2nd Otago, attacking left of Passchendaele Ridge toward the Gravenstafel Road encountered uncut barbed wire some 25 to 50 yards deep in places, and fierce opposition from heavily defended concrete pillboxes. Pte. W. Smith described the scene, "We made a bad 'blue' in sticking to that main Passchendaele Road. It certainly looked the best part to get a footing on – covered with inches of mud, of course, but with a fairly firm footing underneath. I suppose Fritz had anticipated this. As we started up the road we were being caught in enfilade fire from the big pillboxes in the low ground on our right. People were dropping all the way. Then, as we turned the corner on top of the rise, we saw this big bank of wire ahead, maybe a hundred yards way. A rat couldn't have got through that. The bombardment should have cut the wire but it hadn't even dented it. Not that we could get near it anyway, for it was positively spitting fire. The hail of lead we tried to go through was simply incredible. More than half of us fell. We hadn't gone far when our oldest surviving sergeant, Jock Stewart, dropped alongside me. I just had time to see that he had fallen on his back, with a bullet-hole in his chest in the vicinity of his heart. We went a few yards more and then pulled into the right for a breather...We were down to a dozen or so men. Young Harold Stewart was with us, Jock's younger brother *(q.v)*. He hadn't seen Jock go down. He didn't realise it until we stopped, and when he did we couldn't hold him. He crawled back on his stomach to where Jock was lying, and got hold of his body and dragged him back along the road to where we were sheltering. The machine-gun bullets were splashing up the mud all around them. Harold got right through them all. Then, just as he reached us he eased himself up slightly to pull Jock down below the road surface, and a German sniper put a bullet through his throat. I practically saw the bullet that hit him. It must have got him in the jugular vein. His blood gushed out all over me...Now we were down to one N.C.O. When we had finished laying out young Stewart to die, this N.C.O., a Sergeant Smith, suddenly issued the order, "Prepare to advance." Now this was just sheer suicide. Whatever was left of the N. Zedders round about us was just a disorganised rabble, so much so that the Germans had become very cheeky. They weren't bothering to take cover, they had come out and were perched on top of their concrete forts, picking off any fool who showed his nose. I thought to myself, "Well, Sergeant Smith, if we're going, you'll go first!" Sure enough, up he stepped. As he showed his nose the sniper fired. He came crashing back on top of me with his face twisted in a look I'll never forget. He was killed outright."

(Panel 3) Pte. 41421, James Roy Campbell Stewart, 'F' Coy., 3rd Bn. Otago Regt., N.Z.E.F.: *s.* of Dugald Stewart, by his wife Jemima Flora (Aokautere, Palmerston North): Occupation – Farmer: departed Wellington aboard HMNZT 79 'Ruapehu,' 14 March 1917, 23rd Rfts., 'F' Coy.: arrived Devonport via Cape Horn and Cape Town, 21 May following: subsequently proceeded to France and was killed in action 12 October 1917: Age 19. Referred to in the account by Pte. W. Smith as Sergt. Stewart, Harold Stewart's elder brother, existing evidence contradicts.

(Panel 3) Pte. 37886, Harold Stephen Douglas Stewart, 'F' Coy., 2nd Bn. Otago Regt., N.Z.E.F.: *s.* of the late John Stephen Stewart, by his wife Jane Elizabeth Rhoda Maud Shalders, *née* Stewart (Ridgelands, Feilding, Wellington): Occupation – Farm-Hand: departed Wellington, HMNZT 77 'Mokoia,' 13 February 1917, 22nd Rfts., 'F' Coy.: arrived Plymouth via Cape of Good Hope, 2 May following: trained at Sling Camp: served with the Expeditionary Force in France, and was killed in action at Bellevue 12 October 1917: Age 21. *unm.* Referred to in the account by Pte. W. Smith as Jock Stewart's younger brother, existing evidence contradicts.

Archives in New Zealand and at the Commonwealth War Graves Commission record 12 Otago Regt. sergeants killed in action on 12 October 1917. Ten are recorded on Panel 3 and the other two are buried in Tyne Cot Cemetery and Passchendaele New British Cemetery. None are named Smith; similarly, no brothers who served in the regt. are recorded as having died that day.

(Panel 3) Pte. 24/301, George Taylor, 3rd Bn. Otago Regt., N.Z.E.F.: late of Tarata: *s.* of John Taylor, c/o Post Office, Fitzroy, New Plymouth, by his wife Margaret: and brother to Sergt. 23/295, A. Taylor, M.M., N.Z. Rifle Brigade, died 23 June 1917, of wounds: enlisted Wellington: proceeded overseas, 9 October 1915: served in Egypt; France and Flanders, and was killed in action 16 October 1917: Age 28. He leaves a wife, Louisa M. Taylor (Richmond Street, Fitzroy).

His brother Andrew is buried in Trois Arbres Cemetery (I.S.41).

(Panel 3) Pte. 39368, Robert Wards, 2nd Bn. Otago Regt., N.Z.E.F.: *s.* of David Fubister Wards, of Tuturau, Mataura, Invercargill, by his wife Catherine: and brother to Pte. 22295, H. Wards, Canterbury Regt. (surv'd.); Rfn. 29954, F.M. Wards, N.Z. Rifle Brigade (surv'd.); and Pte. 3/740, J. Wards, killed in action, 2 September 1915, at Gallipoli: Occupation – Labourer: proceeded overseas, 16 February 1917. Killed in action 12 October 1917: Age 30.

His brother James also has no known grave; he is commemorated on the Lone Pine Memorial (76).

(Panel 6) Sergt. 10/3966, Francis McLaughlan, 3rd Bn. Wellington Regt., N.Z.E.F.: *s.* of Patrick McLaughlan, of Main Street, Taihape, Wanganui, Wellington, by his late wife Jane: and brother to Pte. 10/3016, M.N. McLaughlan, Wellington Regt. (surv'd.); Pte.10/2692, J. McLaughlan, 2nd Wellington Regt., killed in action, 15 September 1916, at the Somme; and Pte. 10/1591, J.P. McLaughlan, Wellington Regt., killed in action, 8 August 1915, at Gallipoli: Occupation – Storekeeper: departed New Zealand, 4 March 1916: served in Egypt, France and Flanders, and was killed in action 4 October 1917.

His brother John is buried in Flatiron Copse Cemetery (II.E.2). James has no known grave; he is commemorated on the Chunuk Bair (New Zealand) Memorial (21).

(Panel 6) Corpl. 10/12953, Carl Walter Hansen, M.M., 1st Bn. Wellington Regt., N.Z.E.F.: s. of J. Hansen, of 10, Domain Street, Palmerston North, Wellington: and brother to Gnr. 2/1166, J.S. Hansen, N.Z.F.A., died 27 October 1915: b. Waitara, New Plymouth, 22 August 1893: Occupation – Labourer: enlisted 14 June 1915. Killed in action 4 October 1917. Awarded the Military Medal (*London Gazette*, 16 August 1917), 'For gallantry in the field. At Messines on 7th June 1917, this N.C.O. was one of the 12 left in a platoon advancing against a large number of the enemy who had taken cover in shell holes. When his platoon Commander was wounded, this N.C.O. covered him and then rushed up and shot a party of 3 of the enemy. Later he gave his platoon Sergeant valuable help in organising the work of killing and driving the enemy from cover. He has done excellent work previously. He was wounded on 8th June 1917.': Age 24. *unm.*

His brother Johannes also has no known grave; he is commemorated on the Chunuk Bair (New Zealand) Memorial, Gallipoli (8).

(Panel 6) Corpl. 7/2323, Ronald Burnsall Twisleton, 3rd Bn. Wellington Regt., N.Z.E.F.: s. of Frederick Fiennes Twisleton, of Ashurst, Wellington, by his wife Rachel: and yr. brother to Tpr. 11/158, F.D. Twisleton, Wellington Mounted Rifles, who fell, 9 August 1915, at Gallipoli: Occupation – Farmer: departed New Zealand, 4 March 1916, as Tpr., 10th Rfts., 'C' Sqdn., Canterbury Mounted Rifles: served in Egypt (from 8 April): subsequently went to France, transf'd. Wellington Regt., and was killed in action, 4 October 1917, at Passchendaele: Age 22. *unm.*

His brother Francis also has no known grave; he is commemorated on the Chunuk Bair (New Zealand) Memorial (6).

(Panel 6) L/Corpl. 30593, Ernest Reuben Jacobson, 'B' Coy., 3rd Bn. Wellington Regt., N.Z.E.F.: s. of s. of the late John Alfred Jacobson, and his wife Caroline Charlotte Jacobson (43, Stanley Street, Berhampore, Wellington, New Zealand); and elder brother to Pte. 2926, E.A. Jacobson, 59th Australian Infantry, killed in action 14/15 October 1917: b. Wellington, 1884: Occupation – Builder: departed Wellington, HMNZT 71 'Port Lyttleton,' 20th Rfts., Wellington Regt., 7 December 1916; killed in action 4 October 1917: Age 33.

> *Mothers hearts every where is breaking for loving sons and comforters gone.*
> C.C. Jacobson, Nov. 1917.

His brother Enoch, buried in Sanctuary Wood Cemetery (III.C.39), is also recorded on the Ypres (Menin Gate) Memorial (Panel 31).

(Panel 6) L/Corpl. 10/4487, Walter Blaymires Penny, 2nd Bn. Wellington Regt., N.Z.E.F.: s. of Edward Henry (& Mrs) Penny, c/o P.O. Box 80, Blenheim: and brother to Pte. 6/323, S.M. Penny, Canterbury Regt., killed in action, 7 August 1915, at Gallipoli: Occupation – Bank Clerk: departed Wellington, 1 April 1916. Killed in action 4 October 1917.

His brother Samuel also has no known grave; he is commemorated on the Chunuk Bair (New Zealand) Memorial (13).

(Panel 6) L/Corpl. 10/523, Neil Souness, 1st Bn. Wellington Regt., N.Z.E.F.: s. of the late Richard Thomas Souness, of Kaponga, Cardiff (Taranaki), and Mrs Souness (South Norsewood, Hawke's Bay): and brother to Tpr. 11/1859, C.J. Souness, Wellington Mounted Rifles (surv'd.), and Gnr. 15788, C.J. Souness, N.Z. Field Artillery, died 4 July 1917, of accidental wounds (bursting of a bomb): Occupation – Rail Worker; Otaki: enlisted Otaki, Wellington: proceeded overseas, 16 October 1914: served Egypt (from 3 December 1914), Gallipoli (25 April-18 December 1915), France and Flanders, from April 1916, and was killed in action, 4 October 1917, at Gravenstafel.

His brother Cecil is buried in Longuenesse (St. Omer) Souvenir Cemetery (IV.C.44).

(Panel 6) Pte. 30500, Henry Jocelyn Allardice, 3rd Bn. Wellington Regt., N.Z.E.F.: s. of James Allardice, of Burns Street, Dannevirke, Napier, by his wife Agnes: and brother to Tpr. 11/679, D.N. Allardice, Wellington Mounted Rifles (surv'd.), Gnr. 2/2570, P.E. Allardice, N.Z. Field Artillery (surv'd.), and

Pte. 69180, J.S. Allardice, Auckland Regt. (surv'd.): Occupation – Clerk: departed Wellington, HMNZT 71 'Port Lyttleton,' 7 December 1916: trained England (from 29 January 1917). Killed in action at Gravenstafel Ridge 4 October 1917: Age 20.*unm*.

(Panel 6) Pte. 10/2083, David Burton Brown, 1st Bn. Wellington Regt., N.Z.E.F.: s. of John Brown, of Burton, Vogeltown, New Plymouth, by his wife Jessie: and yr. brother to Corpl. 8/648, M.C. Brown, Otago Regt., killed in action, 2 May 1915: b. Upper Mangorei, Taranaki, 1895: educ. New Plymouth Boy's High School: departed Wellington, 13 June 1915: served in Egypt, and with the Expeditionary Force in France, and was killed in action 4 October 1917: Age 22. unm.

His brother Morris also has no known grave; he is commemorated on the Lone Pine Memorial (75).

(Panel 6) Pte. 33110, James Carmody, 1st Bn. Wellington Regt., N.Z.E.F.: s. of John Carmody, of 14, North Street, Palmerston North, Wellington: and brother to Rfn. 35158, W. Carmody, 3rd N.Z. Rifle Brigade, killed in action, 12 October 1917: educ. St. Patrick's College, Wellington: prior to the outbreak of war, was 1st Assistant Master, Huntly School, for five years: departed Wellington, HMNZT 80 'Corinthic,' as Sergt. Major, 23rd Rfts., 'E' Coy., 2 April 1917: arrived Plymouth via Cape Horn, 10 June following: reverted to Pte. that he might rapidly proceed to France, and was killed in action 4 October 1917. A keen bowler, he was a prominent member of the Gisborne Lawn Bowls Club.

His brother William also has no known grave; he is recorded on Panel 7.

(Panel 6) Pte. 29360, Alfred Henry Connell, 1st Bn. Wellington Regt., N.Z.E.F.: 4th s. of the late R. Connell, of the Mata Mata Hotel, and Mrs M. Connell (Mata Mata): b. 4 July 1876: was a Storeman, Farmer's Auctioneering Co.: enlisted 27 June 1916: departed Wellington, HMNZT 67 'Tofua,' 12th Rfts., 1st Bn. N.Z. Rifle Brigade (E.Coy), 11 October following: trained at Sling Camp, England, 29 December 1916 – 1 February 1917: served with the Expeditionary Force in France and Flanders from 5 February 1917: joined his battn. In the Field, 1 March: took part in the Battle of Messines; reported missing after the fighting, 4 October following, confirmed (13 October) as having been killed in action on that date. A keen footballer, cricketer and tennis player Pte. Connell had represented Mata Mata in each sport for several seasons: Age 41.

(Panel 6) Pte. 45859, Lawrence Hackett, 3rd Bn. Wellington Regt., N.Z.E.F.: s. of the late Edward Hackett, of Bull Street, Aramoho, by his wife Elizabeth (Gibson Street, Town Belt, Wanganui): and brother to Spr. 4/1161, C. Hackett, N.Z. Engineers (surv'd.), and Dvr. 55846, G.S. Hackett, N.Z. Army Service Corps, died of disease (influenza), 11 February 1919: Occupation – Farmer: departed Wellington, HMNZT 84 'Turakina,' 26 April 1917: disembarked Plymouth, 20 July following: proceeded to France and was killed in action 4 October 1917.

His brother George is buried in Cologne Southern Cemetery (II.C.1).

(Panel 6) Signlr. 23832, James Henry Heys, 3rd Bn. Wellington Infantry Regt., 4th Bde., N.Z.E.F: yst. s. of Richard Heys, of 410, Colne Road, Burnley, co. Lancaster, by his wife Mary: b. Padiham, nr. Burnley, co. Lancaster, 30 April 1884: educ. Fulledge, Burnley: Occupation – Confectioner; Burnley, prior to emigrating to New Zealand, April 1909; settled at Wellington, finding employ as a Salesman: enlisted 7 February 1916: embarked Wellington, 31 May following: served with the Expeditionary Force in France from 27 May 1917: wounded at Messines, 4 June, but remained at duty: detached to School of Instruction (Signals), 13 August for one week: reported wounded in action, 4 October following, confirmed the following day as being killed in the attack at Broodseinde, Passchendaele. Buried D.14.B. Central, Frezenberg. An officer wrote, "Signaller Heys was a very conscientious worker and a very good man, and I am very sorry to have lost him;" and a comrade, "Jim was absolutely game all through, and we always shared the same billets, dug-outs and shell-holes, being all the time together in the New Zealand and English camps. He was one of the best, and a better chum I never wish to have.": Age 33. unm.

(Panel 6) Pte. 12240, John McPhee, M.M., 1st Bn. Wellington Regt., N.Z.E.F.: s. of James McPhee, of Rakauroa, Poverty Bay, Gisborne, by his wife Ellen: and brother to Pte. 59137, W. McPhee, 36th Rfts. (surv'd.); and Rfn. 24/1441, J. McPhee, N.Z. Rifle Brigade, killed in action, 25 June 1916: Occupation –

Fencer: proceeded overseas, 3rd Rfts., 3rd N.Z. Rifle Brigade, 6 May 1916: served in Egypt, France and Flanders (transf'd. Wellington Regt.), and was killed in action 9 October 1917. Awarded the Military Medal (London Gazette, 28 September 1917), "For gallantry and devotion to duty. Near La Bassée Ville on 1st August this man, being a Platoon Runner, displayed great bravery and devotion to duty on three separate occasions in carrying out urgent messages from the advanced post of his platoon to Company Headquarters. On each occasion he had to pass over open ground which was being swept at the time by enemy machine guns and heavy shellfire. When stretcher bearers were required he made the journey again under similar conditions. Throughout the engagement he displayed the utmost devotion to duty.": Age 21. unm.

His brother James is buried in Cité Bonjean Military Cemetery, Armentieres (II.B.11).

(Panel 6) Pte. 30396, Thomas O'Gorman, 3rd Bn. Wellington Regt., N.Z.E.F.: s. of the late Thomas O'Gorman, of 12, Lewisville Terrace, Tinakori Road, Wellington, by his wife Bridget (2, Upton Terrace, Wellington): and brother to Rfn. 37008, J.T. O'Gorman, N.Z. Rifle Brigade (surv'd); Pte. 24274, J. O'Gorman, Otago Regt., killed in action, 12 October 1917; Rfn. 62706, C. O'Gorman, N.Z. Rifle Brigade, died 28 August 1918, of wounds; and Pte. 24273, T. O'Gorman, Otago Regt., killed in action, 23 October 1918: killed in action, 4 – 6 October 1917, at Passchendaele.

His brother John also has no known grave, he is recorded on Panel 3. Cornelius and Timothy are buried in Bagneux British Cemetery, Gezaincourt (V.B.32) and Romeries Communal Cemetery Extension (III.E.8), respectively.

(Panel 6) Pte. 10/3694, Samuel Francis Paget, 2nd Bn. Wellington Regt., N.Z.E.F.: s. of Samuel Francis Thomas Paget, of 'Ferndale,' Takapau Road, Waipukurau, Hawke's Bay, by his wife Nielsine: and brother to Rfn. 23/1462, R.G. Paget, N.Z. Rifle Brigade (surv'd); Pte. 10/3693, G.E. Paget, Wellington Regt. (surv'd); and Pte. 10/3049, B.L. Paget, Wellington Regt. (surv'd): Occupation – Farmer: departed Wellington, HMNZT 37 'Maunganui,' 8 January 1916. Killed in action 4 October 1917: Age 24. unm.

(Panel 6) Pte. 38750, George Henry Rogers, 1st Bn. Wellington Regt., N.Z.E.F.: eldest s. of the late Samuel Rogers, by his wife Martha (Leigh, North Auckland): killed somewhere in France, 3 October 1917: Age 34. Auckland Weekly News, 1 November 1917: -

> *Grieve Not For Him, If From The Fire Emerges Again Love Stronger, Wider Higher,*
> *Compassion Deep And Strength To Fight For Right, Then Does Our Trial Lead Us To The Light*

(Panel 6) Pte. 45918, William Charles Rowe, 3rd Bn. Wellington Regt., N.Z.E.F.: s. of Charles William Rowe, of Lower Matakana, Auckland: and brother to Sergt. 12/2559, H.J. Rowe, 1st Auckland Regt., who fell 7 June 1917, at Messines: Occupation – Labourer: departed Wellington, HMNZT 84 'Turakina,' 26 April 1917: arrived Plymouth via Cape of Good Hope, 20 July following; thereafter proceeded to France; killed in action, 4 October 1917, at Passchendaele. Unveiled 12 January 1919, William and his brother Henry are two of thirteen local men recorded on the Matakana War Memorial.

His brother Henry also has no known grave; he is commemorated on the Messines Ridge (New Zealand) Memorial.

(Panel 6) Pte. 39920, Thomas Charles Webb, 3rd Bn. Wellington Regt., N.Z.E.F.: s. of Thomas Charles (& Mrs) Webb, of 276, Cuba Street, Wellington, late of 38, Albert Street, Masterton: departed Wellington, HMNZT 79 'Ruapehu,' 14 March 1917, L/Sergt., 23rd Rfts., 'B' Coy., Wellington Regt.: arrived Devonport via Cape Horn and Cape Town, 21 May following. Killed in action 4 October 1917. The *Auckland Weekly News*, 8 November 1917, reported, "The fruit growing community in particular has sustained a severe loss in the death of the late Sergt. T. C. Webb (*q.v.*), who has recently been reported killed in action in France. Before he enlisted, he was an officer of the Orchards Division of the Department of Agriculture. He carried out the arduous duties of secretary of the National Apple Show held in Wellington in 1916, and his work in this connection had much to do with the successful inauguration of the New Zealand Fruitgrower's Federation. The Department devoted Mr. Webb's services to this work alone for some considerable time, and he generously spent the greater part of his own leisure time on it for many weeks, and was untiring in his efforts to make it a success."

(Panel 7) Lieut.Col. 26/11, Alfred Winter-Evans, D.S.O., 3rd Bn. 3rd New Zealand Rifle Brigade, N.Z.E.F.: Occupation – Mining Engineer; Manager; Consolidated Goldfields, Reefton: previously held commission Motor Service Corps: apptd. Major, 1 February 1916: departed Wellington, Comdg. 'C' Coy., 4th Battn. N.Z.R.B., 5 February: promoted Lieut.Col. 20 November 1916. Killed in action on the early morning of 12 October 1917. The Official Historian recorded, 'Lieut.Col. Winter-Evans had come with the unit from New Zealand, and had led his men in all the main engagements in which the Brigade as a whole had taken part. His remarkable genius for organization was only equalled by his extraordinary gallantry under fire. In connection with the Battle of Messines, his plans for training, assembly and attack were not less notable for their minute attention to detail than for the remarkable precision which characterized their execution. When his battalion's objective had been taken on that day he was amongst his men as they laboured at the task of consolidation, and heedless of the bombardment he moved along the parapet of the trench directing and cheering them on. In like manner, at Passchendaele, as soon as it appeared that the check was more than temporary he had gone ahead to endeavour by direct personal efforts to get his troops forward, but moving from shell-hole to shell-hole amongst the scattered groups, he drew upon himself the inevitable bursts of machine-gun fire, under which, fearlessly persisting, he at last fell mortally wounded.' Twice Mentioned in Despatches (*London Gazette*, 1 June 1917, 28 December 1917); awarded Distinguished Conduct Medal (*London Gazette*, 14 August 1917), 'For conspicuous gallantry and devotion to duty. During an attack and the subsequent consolidation of the captured position he showed the greatest coolness and energy, inspiring all ranks by his magnificent personal example and never sparing himself to make the operation of his battalion the success which it was. His work at all times has been of the same high standard.' He leaves a widow, Mrs A. Winter-Evans (Reefton, New Zealand).

(Panel 7) Capt. 14025, Daniel Cornelius Bowler, M.C., 2nd Bn. 3rd New Zealand Rifle Brigade, N.Z.E.F.: late of 15, Buller Street, Wellington: Occupation – School Teacher: departed Wellington, 25 June 1916, 5th Rfts., 'G' Coy., 3rd N.Z. Rifle Brigade: served with the Expeditionary Force in France and Flanders, and was killed in action, 12 October 1917, at Ypres. Awarded the Military Cross for 'showing great gallantry in leading a successful raid against the enemy, capturing a large number of prisoners, and effecting his withdrawal at a critical time with great ability.' He leaves a wife, Alice Bowler (Davis Street, Hastings, Napier).

(Panel 7) Lieut. 24311, George Thomas McIlroy, 'G' Coy., 1st Bn. 3rd New Zealand Rifle Brigade, N.Z.E.F.: s. of William John McIlroy, of 108, Rossall Street, Christchurch, by his wife Mary Ann Laura: and yr. brother to Corpl. A.H. McIlroy, 3rd N.Z. Rifle Brigade, who fell the same day: b. Kumara, Greymouth, c.1895. Killed in action 12 October 1917: Age 22. *unm.*

His brother Arthur also has no known grave; he is recorded below.

(Panel 7) 2nd Lieut. 5/166, Arthur Grattan Guinness, 2nd Bn. 3rd New Zealand Rifle Brigade, N.Z.E.F.: s. of Edwin Roland Guinness, c/o Guinness & Le Cren, Timaru, by his wife Florence Annie: and elder brother to 2nd Lieut. 7/921, F.B.H. Guinness, who died of wounds, 25 August 1915, received at Gallipoli, and was buried at sea: b. 29 August 1890: enlisted 23 December 1914: departed Wellington, 17 April 1915: served with the Expeditionary Force in France from 29 June 1917, and was killed in action, 12 October 1917, in the attack at Bellevue Spur. Buried at Passchendaele, by 2nd Anzac Corps Burial Officer: Age 27. *unm.* Two other brothers 2nd Lieut. 53845, Edwin R. Guinness and Spr. 4/367, John C. Guinness, also served; both survived.

His brother Francis has no known grave but the sea; he is commemorated on the Lone Pine Memorial (71).

(Panel 7) Sergt. 24/355, Arthur Alexander Boyd, 'B' Coy., 2nd Bn. 3rd New Zealand Rifle Brigade, N.Z.E.F.: late of 25, Edward Street, Rangiora: s. of Alexander Boyd, of Rosedale, Kaikoura, Christchurch, by his wife Lucy Jane: and brother to Pte. 12/4139, H.R. Boyd, 2nd Auckland Regt., killed in action, 15 September 1916, at the Somme: enlisted Canterbury: departed Wellington, 9 October 1915. Killed in action 12 October 1917: Age 23. *unm.*

His brother Henry also has no known grave; he is commemorated on the Caterpillar Valley (New Zealand) Memorial.

(Panel 7) L/Sergt. 18508, Frederick Charles Urwin, 3rd Bn. 3rd New Zealand Rifle Brigade, N.Z.E.F.: *s.* of Frank Victor Urwin, of Houhora, North Auckland, by his wife Emma (123, Carlton Gore Road, Newmarket): and brother to Pte. 12/3176, W.E. Urwin, Auckland Regt., killed in action, 3 July 1916: Occupation – Butcher: departed New Zealand, 26 July 1916; Rfn., 6th Rfts., 3rd Battn. Killed in action 12 October 1917.

His brother William is buried in Cité Bonjean Military Cemetery, Armentieres (II.C.19).

(Panel 7) Corpl. 17807, Arthur Harold McIlroy, 'H' Coy., 4th Bn. 3rd New Zealand Rifle Brigade, N.Z.E.F.: *s.* of William John McIlroy, of 108, Rossall Street, Christchurch, by his wife Mary Ann Laura: and elder brother to Lieut. G.T. McIlroy, 3rd N.Z. Rifle Brigade, who fell the same day: *b.* Kumara, Greymouth, *c.*1893. Killed in action 12 October 1917: Age 24. *unm.*

His brother George also has no known grave; he is recorded above.

(Panel 7) Rfn. 30340, Leonard French Broadmore, 1st Bn. 3rd New Zealand Rifle Brigade, N.Z.E.F.: *s.* of Frederick Arnold Broadmore, of Ngatoro, Inglewood, Taranaki, by his wife Sarah: and brother to L/Corpl. 47849, U. Broadmore, 2nd Otago Regt., killed in action 29 September 1918: *b.* 1884: Occupation – Farmer: departed Wellington, HMNZT 71 'Port Lyttleton,' 7 December 1916. Killed in action 12 October 1917: Age 33. He leaves a wife, Emmalene Broadmore, c/o. W. Gribble, 27, Williamson's Avenue, Grey Lynn, Auckland. Four other brothers – Harold, Cyril George, Ernest and Harry William – also served.

His brother Urban is buried in Fifteen Ravine British Cemetery (IV.H.8).

(Panel 7) Rfn. 44251, Thomas Butler, 4th Bn. 3rd New Zealand Rifle Brigade, N.Z.E.F.: *s.* of James Butler, of Settlement Road, Papakura, Auckland, by his wife Annie: and elder brother to Pte. 10/1429, R.P. Butler, Wellington Regt., killed in action, 1 October 1916, at the Somme: departed Wellington, 24th Rfts. N.Z.E.F. ('H' Coy., N.Z.R.B.), HMNZT 82 'Pakeha,' 26 April 1917: arrived Plymouth, England, 28 July following from whence, after training, he went to France and was killed in action near Wolf Copse, Ypres, 12 October 1917: Age 41.

His brother Richard also has no known grave; he is commemorated on the Caterpillar Valley (New Zealand) Memorial.

(Panel 7) Rfn. 35158, William Carmody, 3rd Bn. 3rd New Zealand Rifle Brigade, N.Z.E.F.: *s.* of John Carmody, of 14, North Street, Palmerston North, Wellington: and brother to Pte. 33110, J. Carmody, 1st Wellington Regt., killed in action, 4 October 1917: Occupation – Barman: departed Wellington, HMNZT 71 'Port Lyttelton,' 7 December 1916. Killed in action 12 October 1917. Correspondence and effects should be addressed c/o his sister, Mrs. L. Hutton (Raurimu, New Zealand).

His brother James also has no known grave; he is recorded on Panel 6.

(Panel 7) Rfn. 31401, Henry Archibald Basil 'Boy' Cruller, 2nd Bn. 3rd New Zealand Rifle Brigade, N.Z.E.F.: only *s.* of William Rufus Cruller, of Keri Keri, by his wife Annie Kathrine: *b.* Kaeo, North Auckland, 1895: Occupation – Bushman: departed Wellington, 15 November 1916: trained Sling Camp (from February 1917), thereafter proceeded to France, and was reported missing / believed killed in action 12 October 1917: Age 22. *unm. (IWGC record A.H.B.)* The *Auckland Weekly News,* 6 June 1918, carried the following verse from his mother, father and sisters Lovey and Willa:

> *On the 12th October oh! That dreary morning, after the battle was done*
> *They called the roll, you answered it not, they knew not where you had gone.*
> *You were not on that blood-stained battlefield, you were not among the slain,*
> *You were numbered with the missing, that is how the message came.*
> *In silence we mourn for you, dearest Boy, as you bid us not to complain,*
> *In a far distant land you are sleeping dear, that is how the last message came.*
> *All hopes now are gone, our only boy too, We pray God in his mercy, will guide us to you.*

In the 31 October edition of the same newspaper his family inserted a second verse:

Somewhere in France, dear Basil, under the bright starry sky.
Our brave young lad is sleeping with his comrades by his side.
All our bravest, thousands like him, died that we might live,
Freely for their country all that might have been they give.
Trembling lips are asking sadly, why this mystery of pain?
And our cry goes up to heaven "Lord, will we meet him again?"

(Panel 7) Rfn. 42633, John Henry Dawson, 'D' Coy., 3rd Bn. 3rd New Zealand Rifle Brigade, N.Z.E.F.: *s.* of the late Herbert Henry Dawson, of Kennington, Invercargill, by his marriage to Margaret A. Dawson (Post Office, Kennington, Southland): *b.* Brunswick, 26 December 1893: Occupation – Farmer: enlisted 6 December 1916: embarked Wellington, 2 April 1917, HMNZT 'Corinthic': served with the Expeditionary Force in France from 6 July following: joined his unit in the Field, 9 August; reported missing, wounded, believed killed in action, 12 October 1917: Age 23. *unm.*

(Panel 7) Rn. 31403, George Irvin Delaney, 'A' Coy., 3rd Bn. 3rd New Zealand Rifle Brigade, N.Z.E.F.: *s.* of Thomas Delaney, of Tapuhi, via Hukerenui, Northland, by his wife Emily: and yr. brother to Gnr. 13/2754, A.A. Delaney, N.Z. Field Artillery, who died of wounds, 9 May 1918, in the Base Hospital, Etaples: *b.* 4 November 1894: religion – Church of England: Occupation – Bushman: 5'9¼" tall, medium complexion, light brown hair and eyes: enlisted 26 July 1916: departed New Zealand, as L/Corpl., 15 November following: arrived Devonport, 29 January 1917: reverted to Rfn. (Temp.), posted 5th (Reserve) Bn., the following day: served with the Expeditionary Force in France from 2 March 1917: posted 'A' Coy., 3rd Bn., 25 May: detached to Brigade School, 28 September – 5 October, and was killed in action at Passchendaele one week later, 12 October 1917: Age 22 years, 11 months. *unm.*

His brother Albert is buried in Etaples Military Cemetery (LXVII.B.2).

(Panel 7) Rfn. 36430, Walter Downes, 'B' Coy., 2nd Bn. 3rd New Zealand Rifle Brigade, N.Z.E.F.: *s.* of Thomas Downes, of Waitati, Otago, by his wife Grace: and brother to Pte. 34825, J.M. Downes, Otago Regt. (surv'd); and Pte. 8/149, T.S. Downes, Otago Regt., who fell 26 – 30 April 1915, at Gallipoli, aged 31 years: *b.* 15 March 1896: religion – Presbyterian: Occupation – Labourer: 5'11" tall, dark complexion and hair, brown eyes: enlisted 20 September 1916: served with the Expeditionary Force in France from 10 July 1917: joined his battn. in the Field, 9 August following; reported missing after the fighting 12 October 1917. A Court of Enquiry, 27 April 1918, found him killed in action on that date: Age 19.

His brother Thomas also has no known grave; he is recorded on the Lone Pine Memorial (71).

(Panel 7) Rfn. 45200, Peter Flannery, 2nd Bn. 3rd New Zealand Rifle Brigade, N.Z.E.F.: *s.* of Thomas Flannery, of Poolburn, Dunedin, by his wife Ann: and brother to Pte. 63324, M. Flannery, Otago Regt., died 23 February 1918. Killed in action 12 October 1917.

His brother Michael is buried in Tidworth Military Cemetery (C.357).

(Panel 7) Rfn. 44637, James Chris Galbraith, 1st Bn. 3rd New Zealand Rifle Brigade, N.Z.E.F.: *s.* of Christopher Galbraith, of King Edward Street, Dominion Road, Auckland, by his wife Flora: and brother to Pte. 89429, F.W. Galbraith, N.Z. Training Unit, died 12 November 1918, aged 27. Killed in action 12 October 1917.

His brother Frederick is buried in Featherston Cemetery (653).

(Panel 7) Rfn. 22378, Albert Smith, 3rd Bn. 3rd New Zealand Rifle Brigade, N.Z.E.F.: late of Waitaki, North Otago: *s.* of Edward Smith, of 26, Hawke Street, New Brighton, Christchurch, by his wife Emma: and brother to Sergt. 22377, C. Smith, N.Z. Rifle Brigade, died of wounds 6 April 1918: Occupation – Ploughman: departed Wellington 25 September 1916. Killed in action 12 October 1917.

His brother Charles is buried in Gezaincourt Communal Cemetery Extension (II.J.27).

(Panel 7) Rfn. 45688, Frederick Harold 'Tod' Gleeson, 1st Bn. 3rd New Zealand Rifle Brigade, N.Z.E.F.: *s.* of Frederick J. Gleeson, of Havelock North, Hawkes Bay, Napier, by his wife Emily: Occupation – Plasterer: departed Wellington, HMNZT 84 'Turakina,' 26 April 1917: arrived Plymouth via Cape of Good Hope, 20 July following: proceeded to France and was killed in action, 12 October 1917, near Ypres, Belgium: Age 24. *unm. Auckland Weekly News*, 10 October 1918:-

In a hero's grave he is lying, somewhere in France he fell,
Little we thought when we parted it would be our last farewell.

Parents, sisters, brother-in-law

(Panel 7) Rfn. 45334, Walter John Green, 2nd Bn. 3rd New Zealand Rifle Brigade, N.Z.E.F.: *s.* of John Green, of Tokomaru Bay, Gisborne, by his wife Margaret, *dau.* of the late Daniel (& Mrs) Lorrigan, of Auckland. Killed in action 12 October 1917: Age 24. *Auckland Weekly News*, 6 December 1917:-

In the prime of early manhood like the dawn of a beautiful day
He fought with the bravest of the brave in the thickest of the fray
What could we have more glorious, who paid a greater toll
Than he who fought through Western France, and gave his life and soul.

R.I.P.

(Panel 7) Rfn. 15901, Cecil Morland Hight, 3rd Bn. 3rd New Zealand Rifle Brigade, N.Z.E.F.: *s.* of Albert Hight, of 27, High Street, Timaru, by his wife Mary: and yr. brother to Rfn. 15902, L.H.D. Hight, N.Z. Rifle Brigade, who fell the same day. Killed in action 12 October 1917: Age 22. *unm.*

His brother Leonard also has no known grave; he is recorded below.

(Panel 7) Rfn. 15902, Leonard Henry Dixon Hight, 3rd Bn. 3rd New Zealand Rifle Brigade, N.Z.E.F.: *s.* of Albert Hight, of 27, High Street, Timaru, by his wife Mary: and elder brother to Rfn. 15901, C.M. Hight, N.Z. Rifle Brigade, who fell the same day. Killed in action 12 October 1917: Age 27. *unm.*

His brother Cecil also has no known grave; he is recorded above.

(Panel 7) Rfn. 44645, James Francis Leslie, 'J' Coy., 2nd Bn. 3rd New Zealand Rifle Brigade, N.Z.E.F.: *s.* of William Day Leslie, of Kaeo, North Auckland, by his wife Cecelia: and yr. brother to Pte. 44646, J.G. Leslie, 3rd N.Z. Rifle Brigade, who fell the same day: *b.* Kaeo, 1887. Killed in action 12 October 1917: Age 30.

His brother John also has no known grave; he is recorded below.

(Panel 7) Rfn. 44646, John George Leslie, 2nd Bn. 3rd New Zealand Rifle Brigade, N.Z.E.F.: *s.* of William Day Leslie, of Kaeo, North Auckland, by his wife Cecelia: and elder brother to Pte. 44645, J.F. Leslie, 3rd N.Z. Rifle Brigade, who fell the same day: *b.* Kaeo, 1870. Killed in action 12 October 1917: Age 47. He was married to Olive Leslie (84, Nelson Street, Auckland).

His brother James also has no known grave; he is recorded above.

(Panel 7) Rfn. 26/193, John McNeil, 4th Bn. 3rd New Zealand Rifle Brigade, N.Z.E.F.: *s.* of Archibald McNeil, of Benhar, Dunedin, Otago, by his wife Grace: and brother to Pte. 8/2088, D. McNeil, Otago Regt. (surv'd.); and Pte. 39293, A. McNeil, Otago Regt., died of wounds, 5 October 1917, at Remy Siding: Occupation – Labourer: proceeded overseas, 5 February 1916; 1st Rfts., 4th N.Z. Rifle Brigade: served in Egypt; France and Flanders, and was killed in action, 12 October 1917, nr. Wolf Copse.

His brother Archibald is buried in Lijssenthoek Military Cemetery (XX.F.8).

(Panel 7) Rfn. 33913, Thomas Henry Mettam, 2nd Bn. 3rd New Zealand Rifle Brigade, N.Z.E.F.: *s.* of John Tunnard Mettam, of Swanson, Auckland, by his wife Lavinia: and brother to Staff Nurse 22/532, L. Mettam, N.Z. Army Nursing Service (surv'd.); Rfn. 11071, A.E. Mettam, N.Z. Rifle Brigade (surv'd.); and Corpl. 12/3421, F.J. Mettam, 2nd Auckland Regt., died 6 April 1918, of wounds: Occupation – Driver: departed Wellington, HMNZT 75 'Waitemata,' 19 January 1917; arrived Plymouth 27 March, and was killed in action, 12 October 1917, at Passchendaele: Age 31.

His brother Frederick is buried in Etaples Military Cemetery (XXXIII.D.5).

(Panel 7) Rfn. 22348, John Edward Morgan, 1st Bn. 3rd New Zealand Rifle Brigade, N.Z.E.F.: *s.* of John Gavin Morgan, of 211, Main Road, North East Valley, Dunedin; late of Granville Place, Ranfurly, by his wife Mary Jane: and brother to Pte. 8/982, R. Morgan, Otago Regt., killed in action, 2 May 1915, at Gallipoli: *b.* Ranfurly, *c.*1895: Occupation – Labourer: departed Wellington, HMNZT 64 'Devon,' 25 September 1916. Killed in action 12 October 1917: Age 22. *unm.* (*Archives N.Z. record Corpl.*)

His brother Richard is buried in Quinn's Post Cemetery, Anzac (B.10).

(Panel 7) Rfn. 44005, Henry Edwin Mumford, 4th Bn. 3rd New Zealand Rifle Brigade, N.Z.E.F.: *s.* of the late William Robert Mumford, and Mary, his wife: and brother to Pte. 54067, A. Mumford, 27th Reinforcements (surv'd.); and Rfn. 44004, A. Mumford, N.Z. Rifle Brigade, died of wounds, 14 October 1917: Occupation – Labourer: proceeded overseas 26 April 1917: arrived Plymouth, England via Cape of Good Hope, 28 July following. Killed in action 12 October 1917. Correspondence regarding the deceased should be addressed c/o his brother Robert Samuel Mumford, Esq., 35, Lytton Street, Sydenham; or Mrs. Hill (14, Scott Street, Sydenham), his sister.

His brother Alfred is buried in Lijssenthoek Military Cemetery (XXI.A.21A).

(Panel 7) Rfn. 25/1198, William Charles Patton, 3rd Bn. 3rd New Zealand Rifle Brigade, N.Z.E.F.: late of Tairua, Thames: *s.* of John Patton, of Piopio, Te Kuiti, Hamilton, by his marriage to the late Annie Jane Patton. Killed in action 12 October 1917: Age 29. *unm. Auckland Weekly News*, 8 November 1917: -

He Did His Level Best

(Panel 7) Rfn. 12/1815, Alexander McNaught Tyrie, 2nd Bn. 3rd New Zealand Rifle Brigade, N.Z.E.F.: *s.* of William Campbell Tyrie, of Kayle, Ayr, Scotland, by his wife Mabel Ann, *née* McNaught: and brother to Pte. 12/1816, S. Tyrie, N.Z. Machine Gun Corps, killed in action 26 September 1916, at the Somme: Occupation – Cook; Commercial Hotel, Hamilton: enlisted Auckland: proceeded overseas, 14 February 1915; 3rd Rfts., N.Z. Rifle Brigade: served at Gallipoli from whence, after being wounded, he was removed firstly to Egypt, thereafter returned to New Zealand: after recovery and convalescence, departed Wellington, HMNZT 79 'Ruapehu,' 14 March 1917; 23rd Rfts.: disembarked Devonport, 21 May following: subsequently proceeded to France, and was killed in action, 12 October 1917, at Passchendaele: Age 29. *unm.* Correspondence regarding the deceased Rfn. Tyrie should be addressed c/o his brother James Tyrie Esq., 178, High Street, Ayr; for Pte. S. Tyrie, c/o Thomas Tyrie Esq., 298, Whitehall Road, Gateshead-on-Tyne.

His brother Stuart also has no known grave; he is commemorated on the Caterpillar Valley (New Zealand) Memorial.

(Panel 9) Capt. 41286, Guy Spencer Bryan-Brown; Chaplain (IV Class), New Zealand Chaplain's Force, N.Z.E.F.: 2nd *s.* of the late Rev. Willoughby Bryan-Brown, of 33, Vicarage Drive, Eastbourne, M.A., by his wife Grace Margaret ('Lydgate,' Boar's Hill, Oxford, England), *dau.* of Charles Nash, of Bristol: *b.* Stroud, co. Gloucester, 3 July 1885: *educ.* St. Andrew's, Southborough; Tonbridge School; Downing College, and Ridley Hall, Cambridge (Exhibitioner, Classics, 1904), graduated D.D. (Hon.; Theological Tripos): Occupation – Master at Glenalmond, co. Perth; thereafter Chaplain to Christ's College, Christchurch, New Zealand, and the O.T.C. there: departed Wellington, 21 January 1917, HMNZT 74 'Ulimaroa,' as Temp. Chaplain, 21st Rfts.: arrived Plymouth, 27 March: served with the Expeditionary Force in France and Flanders from 29 May following, and was killed in action at an advanced aid post, near Ypres, 4 October 1917: Age 32. *unm.* Buried Otto Farm, near Passchendaele. In a report (5 October 1917) describing the New Zealanders advance upon Gravenstafel and Abraham Heights, the New Zealand War Correspondent said that during the battle a padre who had been helping the wounded at an advanced dressing station had come out to get a breath of fresh air when a shell burst beside him and killed him. And a Staff Capt. wrote, "The doctors who were with him say that he rendered invaluable assistance during the day in bringing in and dressing the wounded, and I am sure, from what I know of him, that he never spared himself or thought for one moment of the risk he was running, so long as he could help those who were in need," and a fellow Chaplain, "He was busy blocking up the window of a dressing station from the outside, when three shells came in quick succession; I saw him fall staggering sideways, and I rushed to him at once, but he was dead...If ever a man gave away his life for others, that man was G. Bryan-Brown." House Preposter, Tonbridge School, September 1902; Captain of the School House (1903), and member of the Cricket XI (1903 – 04); and at Downing College, Cambridge (1904), Captain of the Cricket XI, Hockey XI and Tennis Club; represented his College in Rugby and

Association Football; and gained his Blue for Hockey (1908). Correspondence regarding the late Chaplain Bryan-Brown should be forwarded c/o G.E. Blanch, Esq., Headmaster, Christ's College, Christchurch.

(Panel 9) Sergt. 25/1818, Thomas Smith, No.2 Coy., New Zealand Machine Gun Corps, N.Z.E.F.: *s.* of the late John Smith, of 6, Havant Street, Portsea, Plymouth, co. Devon, by his wife Catherine (64, Abingdon Road, Southsea, co. Hants): Occupation – Seaman: embarked Wellington as Corpl., 2nd Rfts., 'G' Coy., 3rd N.Z. Rifle Brigade, 1 April 1916: arrived Suez, Egypt, 3 May following: subsequently proceeded to France, transf'd N.Z. Machine Gun Corps, and was killed in action, Peter Pan sector, 12 October 1917: Age 31.

(Panel 9) Pte. 31010, Philip Leslie Alfred Bolton, No.2 Coy., New Zealand Machine Gun Corps, N.Z.E.F.: *s.* of Granville Edward William Bolton, of 9, Seddon Road, Hamilton West, Waikato, by his wife Georgina, *née* Curgenven: *b.* Addlestone, co. Surrey, about 1896: emigrated to New Zealand with his family, 1914; found employ as Motor Mechanic: joined New Zealand Force, Machine Gun Corps, 23 August 1916: embarked for the European War aboard HMNZT 'Ulimaroa,' 19 January 1917, 21st Rfts. Specialist Coy., Machine Gun Section,: arrived Plymouth, co. Devon, 27 March following: underwent further training before departing for France, where he was killed in the fighting on the Gravenstafel Ridge, before Passchendaele, 4 October 1917. Buried where he fell: Age 21. *unm.*

(Panel 9) Pte. 18219, 22662, Michael John Harold, No.5 Coy., New Zealand Machine Gun Corps, N.Z.E.F.: *s.* of David Henry Harold, of Waimaro, Dannevirke, Napier, by his wife Emily: and yr. brother to Pte. 22662, W.E. Harold, N.Z. Machine Gun Corps, killed in action, 7 June 1917, at Messines. Killed in action, 11 October 1917, before Passchendaele: Age 21. *unm.* Both are commemorated on the Akitio R.S.A. Roll of Honour, Pongaroa War Memorial, Wellington.

His brother William also has no known grave; he is commemorated on the Messines Ridge (New Zealand) Memorial.

(Panel 9) Pte. 41118, Clair Nelson Sutherland, No.1 Coy., New Zealand Machine Gun Corps, N.Z.E.F.: *s.* of Rev'd. Robert Rose McKay Sutherland, of 21, Sheen Street, Dunedin, by his wife Elizabeth Juliet: and twin brother to Pte. 25123, J.F. Sutherland, N.Z. Machine Gun Corps, killed in action, 8 June 1917, at Messines: *educ.* Kaikorai School, Dunedin. Killed in action 12 October 1917; Passchendaele: Age 21. *unm.*

His brother James also has no known grave; he is commemorated on the Messines Ridge (New Zealand) Memorial.

(Panel 9) Pte. 22134, Edgar Taylor, No.5 Coy., New Zealand Machine Gun Corps, N.Z.E.F.: *s.* of William Taylor, of Otara, Invercargill, Southland, by his wife Rachel: and yr. brother to Pte. 8/3417, G.F. Taylor, 1st Otago Regt., died 25 September 1916, of wounds: Occupation – Labourer: departed Wellington HMNZT 63 'Navua,' 20 August 1916. Killed in action 12 October 1917. Buried at Waterloo Farm: Age 21. *unm.*

His brother George is buried in Heilly Station Cemetery, Mericourt-l'Abbé (IV.H.43).

(Panel 9) Pte. 13131, James Thompson, No.2 Coy., New Zealand Machine Gun Corps, N.Z.E.F.: late of 106, North Street, Invercargill, New Zealand: *s.* of James (& Catherine) Thompson, of Brakes, Haroldswick, Unst, Shetland, Scotland: late *husb.* (*m.*29 March 1916) to Lulu Thompson (34, Helen Street, South Dunedin): *b.* 8 March 1893: religion – Presbyterian: occupation – Farm Labourer; Grenville Farm, Kanana: enlisted Trentham, 14 January 1916; proceeded overseas Rfn., 3rd Rfts., 3rd N.Z. Rifle Brigade, 6 May following; trained Egypt (from 21 June); joined the Expeditionary Force in France transf'd. 2nd Otago Regt., 26 August 1916: Awarded (23 December 1916) 14 Days Field Punishment No.2; 'Insolence to an N.C.O.': transf'd. N.Z. Machine Gun Corps, 3 March 1917: Awarded (16 April) 4 Days Field Punishment No.2; 'Hesitating to obey an order given by an N.C.O.'. Killed in action 12 October 1917, being shot by a sniper while assisting a wounded comrade at Passchendaele: Age 24. (*IWGC record age 25*)